BOOKS BY OTTO J. SCOTT

THE PROFESSIONAL

J B S A U N D E R S

Portrait by Robert Joy

THE
PROFESSIONAL

A BIOGRAPHY OF
JB SAUNDERS

by Otto J. Scott

New York Atheneum 1976

Library of Congress Cataloging in Publication Data
  Scott, Otto J
    The Professional.
    Includes index.
    1. Saunders, Joseph Benjamin, 1901-
  2. Petroleum industry and trade—United States—
  History.   I. Title.
  HD9570.S28S37 1976   338.2'7'2820924 B 76-11779
  ISBN 0-689-10726-9

All greatness is unconscious, or it is little and naught.

Carlyle

ACKNOWLEDGMENTS

This biography is an outgrowth of a program created by Stanley Draper, head of the Oklahoma Heritage Foundation. At a time when antiheroes appear to enjoy the limelight, Mr. Draper was anxious that young people, and students in particular, should learn about men and women whose lives and efforts helped strengthen, rather than weaken, our society and this civilization. His original idea was to honor Oklahomans in a series of books. Mr. Saunders's activities, however, influenced a larger region. It was at that stage of the discussion that I met both Mr. Saunders and Stanley Draper; this book is the result. Mr. Draper followed its preparation with keen interest and great enthusiasm. It is a matter of considerable regret to me that he died in early January, 1976, only a few weeks before the completion of the work. He was eighty-eight.

I have others to thank as well. These include M. J. Rathbone; J. Howard Marshall II; Dean McGee; F. C. Love; J. J. Kelly; Tom Seale; Claude Huffman; W. H. McLean; William T. Carthaus; Earl Sneed; Harvey Everest; John Kirkpatrick; Dolphus Whitten, Jr.; Robert Aycock; Celeste Rockenback; J. Forsyth; J. Wightman, Sr.; Philip Siteman; H. D. Moore; George Brown; Foster Parker; Robert Cresap; Hugh Q. Buck; Dean Krakel; Kurt Schroeter; Ralph A. Worley, Jr.; Suzanne Saunders Inkley; J. R. Butler; Robert Moore; C. D. Tinsley; John Atkins, Jr.; Raoul Allstetter; Philip Hamilton; David Smitherman; Pete Weil; Charles M. Bliss; Kenneth B. Zwiener; Raymond D. Young; Paul Strasbaugh; W. W. Horadam; C. Ross Anthony; Max Lents; J. B. Saunders III; Esther Gutknecht; Nelle Latimer Gallagher; Georgia Jungerman Saunders—and, of course, JB himself—for their patience, courtesy, and cooperation.

All the quoted remarks in this book are from the interviewer's notes unless otherwise attributed.

OTTO J. SCOTT

CONTENTS

ILLUSTRATIONS

An album of photographs will be found

following page 242

THE PROFESSIONAL

CHAPTER ONE

The Man in the Suite

THE MAN in the corner office of a modest suite in the Bank of the Southwest Building in downtown Houston appeared to be in his middle sixties. He was dressed in what is known as "a business suit," and his desk was clear. In the outer office three people—two women and a man—worked quietly. The atmosphere was one of solid comfort, but not opulence.

Outside a number of people—men, women, and children—rode horses or drove wagons and buckboards: part of a gathering of almost a thousand to share in the Annual Rodeo and Stock Show. The event was preceded by several weeks on the trail; some of the people who took part in the revival of former times were professionals, others were amateurs.

Around them rose huge structures which represent, in the main, the large petroleum firms of the nation. Houston is, after all, the center of the petroleum industry of the United States. Yet the riders, despite their gaudy costumes, were saved from incongruity by the huge expanse of sky above, streets dappled by a midwinter sun, and the western atmosphere that pervades in the city.

The man in the corner suite stood at the window watching with a quiet smile. "I love Texas," he said, "but the state is changing."

It was indeed. Crime soared in Houston, and the fact belied many sociological contemporary myths about the causes, for it was a high-employment city, teeming with enterprises, bulging with the signs of prosperity. That seemed odd in midyear 1975, when the national telecasts were heavy with gloomy statistics regarding inflation and job losses, and when the proud financial capital of the nation—New York—teetered on the edge of unbelievable bankruptcy.

The fact was that a great reversal had taken place in the regions of the United States—a shift immense in scope and greatly misunderstood, because it had taken place while the nation's media had diverted attention into other directions. Student unrest, the Viet Nam war, activities in Washington, the Middle East—a host of issues had dominated the headlines for over a decade, while millions of people had, virtually unnoticed, silently shifted their residences and their businesses. The stream had more than one direction: blacks had left the South, and whites had left the North.

Only the Census figures later revealed the extent of these changes, but such statistics are not everyday reading. Business magazines and trade journals had covered, in highly specialized articles, segmented specifics of this great movement, but these were mainly read by men in special occupations. The people, on the move, remained largely unaware of how great a move was involved.

None of this was news to the man in the suite. He had been watching the flow of population, the rise and fall of real estate values, the movement of goods, for most of his life. His interests had carried him deep into the commercial life of the nation, and in mid-1975 he remained keenly interested as ever. Such observations were, after all, part of his profession.

There is a myth—one of many that cloud the minds of modern men—that schooling determines ability. But there are signs that this assumption is now creaking toward collapse under the weight of millions of academic degrees. The lessons of life, after all, cannot be forever ignored by boards and committees. Some of these lessons were coming home to the United States in 1975.

Some lessons, however, remain unplumbed. The man in the suite was greatly concerned over these, and his comments were realistic. "I was young during the last Depression," he said. "I reduced my standard of living and worked harder, and knew I could wait it out. This time I am older; I may not see the end."

Early in 1972 he took some protective steps. He invested in gold coins, which was legal at the time—and in gold-mining stocks in South African and Canadian firms. He advised his friends to do the same. In these investments he realized a profit of approximately $600,000. He took the profit and gave most of it to charity. Then he reinvested.

He did not regard this as a coup. He had, to his thinking, merely made a series of sensible steps. In a way it was like the action of a trained physician who orders his household to boil its water and to have the house fumigated, and warns his friends to take similar steps, when he sees the signs of plague.

The analogy may sound stretched but is actually precise. The man in the suite is a professional, though his calling is seldom so regarded, and even more rarely so described. He is a businessman.

As such he has hired the talents of attorneys and accountants, engineers and salesmen, writers and musicians. He learned his profession in the classic way: through apprenticeship and as an assistant, serving under older and more experienced practitioners. He did not launch into his own venture until he was a middle-aged thirty-six. His training, therefore, was long and arduous.

He moved forward, however, with patience and skill, climbing higher with the years. These brought him into competition with huge corporations whose executives—envious of his independence—sometimes sought to impede his progress, and sometimes cooperated. In time he became wealthy and turned toward philanthropy. But he could not retire, any more than any other professional can retire. The life of the mind is fascinating, as every intellectual knows. But the life of the mind applied to living situations is probably the most fascinating of all.

Few individuals except its practitioners seem to realize that business is, in all its reaches, a life of the mind. That perception is hidden from many who are dazzled by the tools of business: by its goods, machines, and money. They seem to assume that these instruments operate outside, and beyond the control, of human beings. They confuse, in other words, the caretakers and landlords of business—its rank-and-file managers, so to speak—with its leaders, prime movers, and innovators.

That confusion is assisted, in part, by the misleading similarity of the surface of business everywhere in the world. There are bankers in the Soviet Union, managers of grim factories in Socialist Britain, and automobile salesmen in the heart of tribal Africa. All nations, no matter how ruled, produce goods to sustain life and use money as a medium of exchange.

In most of the world, however, business has remained a subprofession: a collection of traders, loan sharks, and landlords, hindered and dominated by a restricting élite. It was only in western Europe and the United States that business was freed from the grip of the state and the privileges of ruling groups. Any intelligent, practical, and energetic person could enter—and can still enter—the ranks of business in the United States. And it is mainly in the United States that business grew so intertwined in the nation's life, and so relatively unfettered, that it could develop into a creative, highly skilled profession.

In the process American business created huge fortunes and complex enterprises, ushered a wave of innovations into everyday life, catapulted diverse personalities into prominence—and made many errors. One was to ignore the intellectuals of the nation too long, and to arouse their seething resentment. Widespread misunderstanding led to restrictive regulations that checked much of the momentum of business. Politicians worked for years to curb its ebullience. The fact that businessmen gradually evolved better controls and higher skills, and improved industrial output, was overshadowed by societal programs in which business was only a component. Large antibusiness pressures emerged, and individual ventures began to decline. Whether business creativity will outlast this trend, or ever return to a full flowering, is highly problematical. By 1975 the signs of an authoritarian drift in the American government and a demand for protection from the rigors of freedom on the part of the people were far too numerous to nourish optimism.

The American business phenomenon was visibly fading as the final quarter of the twentieth century dawned. Proponents of a planned and controlled economy were in the ascendancy. Before the memory of economic freedom fades entirely, therefore, it might be salutary to review the record of one of its real professionals: the man in the suite.

Many factors combine to make his life worth special examination. One is that he was born with the century. That means he has, in one yet-unfinished life, lived through changes that will probably never be repeated. He can be compared to a man who was born in ancient Rome when the early kings had been overcome and the Senate ruled the nation, and who worked and prospered through to the time of the Caesars and even lived to see the signs of decay appear.

It takes no great powers of imagination to realize how avidly historians would examine such a life, to trace how complex and immense events impinged upon the career of a single intelligent individual. Yet such a life would have been incredible—possible only in fantasy. The ancient world was physically active, but it resisted quick and easy change. The sequence from the strong Republic to the troubled Empire took centuries to be enacted.

It is our time that has compacted the changes of centuries into decades. These changes have come, tumbling upon one another, so rapidly we can hardly keep them in view. We are inundated with change; Toffler's *Future Shock* described sensations that many share.

Yet there are people—who are now elder citizens—who not only lived through these changes, but prospered and thrived in their excitement. Their enthusiasm was not shattered nor their courage shaken. Like the man in the suite, some are still keen and alert, and as capable of mastering the problems of today as they were those of yesterday. Time, with its inexorable impatience, has thrust most of them off the center of the stage. That alone is no great change; every generation must give up its place in the center.

But there is a disturbing possibility that in our national rush toward new solutions we may forget answers discovered in the past. We may even forget, amid clouds of propaganda, what that past contained.

6

Before the man in the suite vanishes, therefore, we should look over his shoulder at the events he surmounted. His comments are the comments of a trained professional; they shed light on what was cloudy. His experiences are worth review.

That would be true if he acted as an individual; it is even more true because he did not, as a businessman, work alone. His career was in the matrix of commerce, and brought him into contact with people on all levels, of every sort.

Some of these friends and contacts are still active and important. They include the leaders in Oklahoma City as well as Houston. In personal terms they range from men like C. R. Anthony, in his nineties and still a great businessman; to George Brown, who recently purchased thirty-three square blocks of downtown Houston to build his own version of an Inner City; to people in other lands in all walks. Some are in business, others are employees, still others too young or too old to take part in the worries of the world.

The Old and New jostle together against one another in every life. The Old fades in time, and all that is left is the New and the New. Before that time arrives, we should consider what it meant to be a professional businessman during the greatest days of American business so far—when its accomplishments and methods dazzled not only this nation, but all the world—and what it means today.

CHAPTER TWO

Background

HIS LIFE BEGAN as a footnote to that of his parents. His father, Joseph Benjamin Saunders, was born in Tennessee, in 1857, and matured during the bleak days of the Reconstruction, in the Occupied South.[1] He was, therefore, a member of the only truly lost generation in the nation's history.

Much has been written about the tribulations of those who came to the United States as emigrants or refugees. Relatively little has been said about the Southerners dispossessed and dispersed by defeat in war. Yet these were the only Americans to have suffered such a defeat in this land, and they were largely descendants of the original colonists. In the 1870s and 1880s they streamed west; huge numbers of them poured into Texas.

Most of them never looked back. Joseph Benjamin Saunders was one of these. JB does not recall his father reminiscing. He became aware of him, at first, as a huge figure almost six feet tall, with a bulky, wedge-shaped torso and lean legs, whose face was hardened by time and weather—taciturn and aloof.

Joseph Benjamin Saunders had an uncle, Boot Saunders, who had gone to Texas and had been killed by Indians. Nevertheless, the lure of the frontier was strong, and he determined to test the West for him-

1. *Saunders* is a Scots name. The family is a sept—shares a common ancestry—with the Clan MacDonell of Glengarry, a northwest Highland region that looms above the Isle of Skye. Like most other Scots-Irish settlers in colonial America, the Saunders family lost sight of its origins as its members scattered. *Saunders* remains, however, a familiar name in Tennessee and is now widespread in the United States.

self. It was a time when childhood was short, and adolescence was a word—and a concept—that had not yet been coined. It is unlikely, therefore, that he was more than twenty. That would place his arrival in Texas in the year 1876.

He took the trains as far west as possible, and did not stop till he had reached Sherman, Texas—the last outpost. From there, there was nothing but "vast plains and plateaus, and a handful of nomadic Stone Age savages."[2] He traveled a few miles southward, and stopped at Palmer, Texas, a tiny dot. Two years later he sent for an older brother: Andrew Jackson Saunders. And a little later Joseph Benjamin proceeded a few more miles, to Waxahachie. Both locations were very near the end of the green belt on the map. From there the cartographers use a light tan, to indicate the end of farming lands, and beginning of vast, semiarid, trackless, and seemingly endless wastelands.

According to legend, an ox train was caught in a snowstorm on the plains and abandoned. The driver returned to the scene later and was astonished to discover the oxen alive and well. The answer was in the formerly unknown qualities of mesquite grass, also known as *grama grass* and *buffalo grass*. Unlike that in the East and Europe, where special grains had to be grown, harvested, and stored to feed kine, mesquite grass dried where it grew. It spread under the hoofs of cattle and provided shrubs that could be cropped even in snows.

That magic grass is what enabled the longhorn cattle to survive in a wild state, and to increase until they numbered thousands upon thousands. It earlier—and later, after 1876—supported the buffalo. The longhorns, however, were smarter than buffalo; they learned more quickly. The longhorns could track down water, traveled in small groups, and could protect themselves against wolves. Horsemen to round them up, to brand these fierce creatures, to drive them to railroads, appeared as miraculously from the western soil as the mesquite itself.

By the time Joseph Benjamin Saunders appeared in Waxahachie, the cattle business had flared aloft as swiftly as wildfire. The great drives were underway in which steers "bought for $3 or $4 a head in Texas and sold for $35 or $40 a head up North."[3]

No young man as tall and husky as Joseph Benjamin could resist the allure of being one of those men on horseback called *cowboys*. He

2. T. R. Fehrenbach, *Lone Star: A History of Texas and Texans* (New York: Macmillan, 1968), p. 536.
3. Daniel J. Boorstin, *The Americans: The Democratic Experience* (New York: Random House, 1973), pp. 5-9.

9

sought and found a ranch near Waxahachie and was hired at once. It was not a time when men were afraid to hire and test for themselves; those who were too weak would soon be driven out or fall away.

Much has been written about that time and place, but except for the songs created by the cowboys themselves, far too little has centered around the work and its meaning. The living herds the cowboys from the Waxahachie region drove northward along the Chisholm Trail through Oklahoma and Wichita to Kansas City, or from the Brazos to Dodge City, or farther west along the Goodnight Trail to Pueblo, were far from the placid creatures beloved by eastern painters of the period. They were sharp-horned and fearsomely strong; bunched together in a thin file that could stretch a mile or more, they sent out an almost overwhelming stench. "The heat," recalled the famous cattleman Charles Goodnight, ". . . was surprising. . . . Animal heat seems to attract electricity, especially when the cattle are wet, and after a storm I have seen the faces of the men riding with a herd scorched as if some furnace blast had blazed against them. . . ."[4]

Two men rode at the front to navigate the herd, three men rode at the end to gather the strays, and others rode along the sides to keep the ranks closed and steady. At night the herd was serenaded to keep the beasts secure and away from stampedes, and safe from interlopers. These could range from Indians to wolves to range thieves, whose characteristics combined the worst features of the first two.

Joseph Benjamin Saunders became a part of this life, and learned its work, from the spring roundups and the intricate vocabulary of brands, which in their symbolic intricacy resembled, in abstract, the heraldic devices his distant forebears had used to mark their lands, their men, and their clans. His training extended from the hot, stinking, and brutal work of branding, to the complex tasks of the drive itself.

It was a life made for men, for it contained hard work, companionship, danger, and the possibilities of sudden terror, interspersed with periods of orgiastic celebration. It was these end of the trail experiences that gave rise to a worldwide legend of lawlessness and violence, but the other parts also contained unforgettable images: nights under the stars, Homeric encounters, and a sense of limitless space.

It could not last, of course, and it did not. As long as the land was open and the branding iron was near, men could build herds by stealth at first and by more honorable methods later. However, the idea that the vast plains could be held in common was contrary not only to the

4. Ibid., p. 11.

English common law—the only one known in the East—but also to common sense. Barbed wire came first, in 1876, when it was patented by Joseph F. Glidden, and with it came portable windmills that could make water available for private use.

Land wars erupted—water wars. Those private collisions carried some badmen from the periphery of the industry into places nearer the center, and later provided the basis for endless plays and movies. Owen Wister, the novelist, went west and met some of these men; his descriptions provided material for hundreds of dime novels and cheap magazines that flooded, thrilled, and horrified the East.

The larger ranchers began to enclose huge acreage behind barbed wire. The cattle were unused to it and at first mangled themselves on the cruel wired knots. But surprisingly enough they learned—by ancestral means that science has not yet recognized—so that in a few generations the steers understood the meaning of a wire fence.[5]

Other factors, other changes arrived. The railroads created more miles of track that reduced the long and dangerous trail drives. Joseph Benjamin Saunders had succeeded, by the time these changes came, in becoming a trail boss. That was success, of a sort, but it was time to look in new directions. By the time he married Irene McQuarters in the mid-1880s, he had decided to move to town and go into business for himself.

He chose Hillsboro, Texas, a division point on the Houston & Texas Central Railroad. That was shrewd: a division point is where the trains are broken up and remade, where railroad crews rest and are replaced. It held a roundhouse, restaurants for the railroaders, hotels, a great many saloons, and—in Texas—churches. Those considerations had grown important to Joseph Benjamin. He was twenty-eight—an age no longer considered young at time when most men died before fifty.

He opened a butcher shop. In those days steers were driven to the butcher, who would emerge to estimate them and name his price. If a deal was concluded, the butcher did his own slaughtering and dressed his own meat. In a land where a knowledge of livestock was widespread, the butcher had to be an expert among experts.

According to JB, who heard the story when he was young, another man came to Hillsboro and decided to open a competitive shop. Joseph Benjamin Saunders went to see him. He was blunt. "The town isn't large enough for two shops," he said. "Either you buy me out, or I'll buy you out." The newcomer decided to sell and left town. Not too long afterward another arrived and the same sequence took place. Joseph Benjamin Saunders then had three butcher shops in Hillsboro,

5. *Lone Star*, p. 607.

and that was too many for any newcomer, no matter how optimistic, to compete against.

Every man's life is shaped by the forces of his times. Joseph Benjamin Saunders was driven from his native state by such forces, and they overshadowed his efforts all his days. His eldest son, George, was born in 1886. In that winter, and the following winter as well, unprecedented blizzards covered the plains and created an awesome and immense catastrophe by killing uncounted thousands of steers.

The catastrophe was compounded when General Ulysses S. Grant, bumbling in the Presidency, ordered branded cattle removed from Indian reservations and other public lands. This collision between the cattlemen's concept of unrestricted grazing rights and eastern legal codes provided a paradise for the lawyers, but hell for the West.

In Texas an added tribulation also appeared: a seemingly mysterious, far-reaching change in the weather. Immigrants from Tennessee, Georgia, Mississippi, Alabama, and Missouri had rushed to Texas to obtain free land and to recreate an agricultural economy. During the early 1880s their eyes had been dazzled by miles of waving buffalo grass and beautiful spring wildflowers. "But there existed," says T. R. Fehrenbach, "another phenomenon not experienced by Anglo water and woodlanders: the Pleistocene-like, cyclical climate. There might be seven good years, but inevitably, despite protests and prayers, good years were followed by the dry and lean. People pushed into these expanses, [but] . . . they did not understand that the grass was a cover of eons, or understand the full horror of the brassy sun of summer, sucking moisture from plowed earth, or the wild winds that warred from north to south and soon began to carry aloft tons of earth."[6]

The 1880s started off with wet years, and the settlers poured into the very edge of the High Plains, an edge in which Hillsboro was located. Then the dry years started, and "millions of dollars were lost and thousands of lives blasted. Men sweated themselves to death, anguished as their plants withered; their sunblackened women grew gaunt and died." He cites an old description: "the tracks west, littered by tin cans; the tracks east, marked only by lark feathers and jackrabbitt bones."[7]

Yet as one wave of emigrants retreated, broken in health and hope, another wave came surging west. The cattlemen raged against the plows that were tearing grazing lands to useless dust storms and fought

6. Ibid., p. 606.
7. Ibid., p. 610.

one another in and out of the courts for acreage. As the farmers retreated the stockmen bought their lands, and a process of human waste, of useless effort and hopeless struggle, continued and was "accelerated by every recurrent, hideous drought from 1887 to 1917."[8]

A situation that bore some distant but discernible resemblance to feudalism arose; a great divide separated the operators of vast cattle empires and the strugglers on the land. The masses of people were pressed down not only by the ferocity of the soil and the climate, but also by the steady depreciation of the dollar. Hooked to the gold standard, currency grew scarcer every year. A loan of five hundred dollars took six hundred dollars' worth of harvested crops to repay a year later. In this vise, which narrowed year by year, many Texans declined from men of property to tenants chained to their plots, peons in all but name—and spirit.

At such a time, exacerbated by the aftermath of a great war, many lost their self-control. In 1876, the year Joseph Benjamin Saunders arrived in Texas, there were three thousand listed fugitives in the state. In 1879, the governor said crime in the region was "unprecedented" in the United States.

Yet struggles, dangers, a sense of living evils, and inscrutable changes also foster, in some people, a sense of Providence. The growth of churches in Texas was a phenomenon. These structures were far different from the chaste white steeples of New England, with their "transcendental" thoughts, their melting sympathy for aborigines in other regions, and their lofty intellectualism. The Methodists, Baptists, and Presbyterians of Texas produced a religious amalgam of their own: fundamental, evangelical, earthy, and punitive at the same time. The question of hard liquor aroused more opposition than did that of sex, for it created more immediate and more terrible problems.

"Can anyone remember when the times were not hard and money not scarce?" asked Ralph Waldo Emerson. It was, as the nineteenth century drew toward its closing decade, an obvious observation, but anything Mr. Emerson said in the height of his fame was hailed and repeated. Certainly the times in Texas were hard, and money was scarce. That Joseph Benjamin Saunders and his quiet but capable wife prospered in such times is remarkable.

8. Ibid., p. 611.

In the manner of the day they had a large family. George arrived first, in 1886, then Fay, then Beulah, then another boy, Earl. They were not the last; those were the beginning years of the family.

They were spent on a house on Rose Hill which Joseph Benjamin Saunders owned, and from its environ JB would later recall the earliest recollections of his earliest childhood, when he would wave at the engineers and the brakemen of the Houston & Texas Central Railroad as the trains trundled past.

Those were also years in which the Saunders family established those inner rules and patterns by which all families govern themselves. They had weekly Bible readings, and cards and liquor were not allowed and not missed.

What was missed, obviously, was land. Joseph Benjamin Saunders had loved the trail and the cowboy days of his youth; he gave them up willingly enough but, like all men, continued to look back upon them. His butcher shops were prospering, but that was not enough. In the East new forms of property had risen: stocks and bonds bewildering in their complexity, abstractions that meant the difference between millions and ruin. Other forms of wealth were also common: paintings and jewels, rents and factories; the churnings of commerce and the goods of trade. But in Texas a man was measured by his land.

Joseph Benjamin Saunders was not alone in his longing. The pressures upon Washington to allow more emigration to the Indian Territory in the North,[9] to be known as Oklahoma, were irresistible. In 1889 Washington acceded to political reality, and a great new land rush developed.[10] Joseph Benjamin Saunders knew that area: he had traveled it on the Chisholm Trail and camped—as had hundreds of others—with herds on Persimmon Hill.

But he did not join the land rush of 1889, nor the one in 1891, nor even the one in 1893. A prosperous merchant, he had passed the stage where he wanted to engage in a horse-and-buggy race to stake the first open land he reached. Merchandising makes a man more cautious than that; by subtle stages it makes a man practical and measured. But he began to make trips to the Indian Territory and to carefully survey its possibilities.

9. The Indian Territory harbored over thirty tribes, of which the Five Civilized Tribes—Cherokee, Choctaw, Chickasaw, Seminole, and Creek—were the most advanced. The Civil War disrupted the Territory; divided allegiances combined with uprisings to provide a basis for new governmental controls later. In 1872 railroad penetration of the Territory presaged its later economic development.

10. In 1889 "unassigned" lands in the eastern region of the Indian Territory were opened to homesteaders. At the same time, and equally important, whites were given the right to purchase land from Indians. By 1890 the homestead area was reorganized as the Oklahoma Territory, and the process of settling and organizing toward a new state was well underway by the turn of the century.

In the end, when he finally decided to move, he had evolved a plan that neatly combined experience and desire. He would be a rancher. He would raise his own cattle behind his own barbed wire, and have his own horses to ride, and have his own cowboys to round up, brand, and drive to market his own herds.

It was a good plan, but it was a plan formed, unconsciously, on the past—on the pattern of success that Joseph Benjamin Saunders saw in Texas. It also combined all the elements of his own past—and that was probably inescapable, for by the time he found the property he liked and could obtain, he was forty-three years old, and the nineteenth century was in its last year.

It was a century that had seen enormous changes—changes so sweeping that any man could have been forgiven for believing that novelties were drawing to a close. Yet when the worldly and experienced Mark Sullivan sat down years later to describe the year 1900, he said in part, "Only the Eastern seaboard had the appearance of civilization. . . . From the Alleghenies to the Pacific Coast the picture was mainly of a country still frontier and of a people still in flux; the Allegheny mountainsides scarred by the axe, cluttered with the rubbish of improvident lumbering, blackened with fire; mountain valleys disfigured with ugly coal-breakers; western Pennsylvania and eastern Ohio an eruption of ungainly wooden oil derricks; rivers muddied by the erosion from lands cleared of trees but not yet brought to grass, soiled with the sewage of raw new towns and factories; prairies furrowed with the first breaking of sod. . . . On the prairie farms sod houses were not unusual . . . villages were just past the early picturesqueness of two lines of saloons and stores. . . . At the gates of the country great masses of human raw material were being dumped from immigrant ships. . . . One whole quarter . . . the South, presented chiefly the impression of the weedy ruins of thirty-five years after the Civil War and comparatively few years after Reconstruction—ironic word."[11]

It was, in other words, like every other time—one in which old and new were jumbled together in such disorderly fashion that the average man could not foretell which would prevail.

In such a time the men who could best foresee the shape of the future were those in the great commercial centers, where plans were unrolled, presentations made, and decisions taken that would develop a region, a market sector, an industry, or an invention. Such centers had

11. Mark Sullivan, *Our Times,* 6 vols. (New York: Charles Scribner's Sons, 1926–1935), 1: 28–30.

arisen in New York and Chicago and other points, where such initial determinations could set off armies of running feet in one direction or another, that in some places resembled herds.

Several such herds roamed the landscape of the nation searching for oil. Some oil had been found in Kansas. Each strike had resulted in a forest of derricks and drilling efforts, and in the creation of an oil-boom town very similar—in raucous misbehavior, swindles, strangers, and sudden fortunes—to the cow-boom towns of an earlier generation.

Joseph Benjamin Saunders, however, was not interested in oil booms or oil towns. He was a product of the cattle booms and the cow towns. As such, his trips to the Indian Territory carried him over familiar trails, and well-remembered landsites. The town of Tulsa, which had for years been a harbor for many of the outlaws who hid in the Territory, was familiar to him. It was a cattle terminus with both a railroad and the Arkansas River, to which surrounding ranchers and trail drivers brought their steers to market for final transport.

In all likelihood Mr. Saunders either had friends in Tulsa or was able to make some easily, for in his search for property he was unusually lucky. He found a site not far from Tulsa at a place called Fisher Switch, near a location on the Arkansas River called Sand Springs. It was in a part of the Territory granted to the Creek Indians, one of the Five Civilized Tribes, and had formerly been owned by an Indian named Sodie Fife. Fife was in the territorial prison for killing a white man and was due to be released at some not-too-distant date. Mr. Saunders was not made nervous by that eventuality, but he was pleased to have found property he wanted that was near both water and the point of final sale.

He set about his preparations, which were complicated. It was necessary to build a house, and to fence the land, and to put up stables for horses and quarters for the ranch crew. At a time when money was scarce this was a large undertaking: a ranch, then and now, is a form of big business.

Had Mr. Saunders launched his ranch some years earlier, his efforts would have been more physically dangerous. The West in the 1870s was the scene of many brutalities. Even in the 1880s massacres of individual wagon trains and isolated ranches by the Plains Indians were not uncommon; they were marked by nauseating tortures of the men, and permanent captivity of the women and children. Outlaws were also dangerous. They were not inclined toward torture, but sudden death is no reward for hard work and honest ambition. The Dalton Gang, the Youngers, the Doolin and Cook gangs, Cherokee Bill, and others were not company that sensible people made efforts to find, and all these and more had hidden in the Indian Territory.

But by 1900 the times had settled, and the gangs had dwindled, though the habit of harboring fugitives in the Oklahoma Territory would persist for years to come. Indians had become objects of pity, like caged tigers; sentiment was swinging toward them as their menace faded. By the time Joseph Benjamin Saunders bought his Fisher Switch property, the region was being rapidly settled and appeared permanently cast in a cattleman's mold.

Saunders must have read, like everyone else, the newspaper accounts of a fabulous gusher discovered in southeastern Texas, on the rim of the Gulf of Mexico, called Spindletop. But that news would not have meant much to a man in Oklahoma starting a new venture.

His work went slowly, for it had to be interrupted for trips back to Texas to insure that his butcher shops were being properly managed, and to see his family. On July 25, 1901, Joseph Benjamin Saunders had the pleasure of smiling down at a new son. He was named Joseph Benjamin Saunders, Jr.—JB.

There was, at the time, some argument over whether the new century properly began in 1900 or 1901. Dr. Albert Shaw, the famous editor of the *Review of Reviews*, settled the matter for purists. No creditor, argued Dr. Shaw, would accept a payment of $1,899 for a debt of $1,900. Therefore the twentieth century began with it own first year: 1901. JB had arrived with the century.[12]

Unfortunately his father knew that another novelty had also arrived, only a month earlier, in Tulsa. Dr. Fred Clinton and Dr. J. C. W. Bland had persuaded some oilmen to drill on property owned by Mrs. Bland in Red Ford, Oklahoma. They made the effort and struck oil in June, 1901. Overnight the region around Tulsa seethed with promoters, real estate lawyers, lease hounds, drillers, equipment men, major company scouts, and all their camp followers.

The cattlelands that Joseph Benjamin Saunders had so arduously attained were engulfed by men from the industry that would, above all others, arouse, fuel, and epitomize the new century.

12. Ibid., pp. 12–13.

CHAPTER THREE

Early Days

IT TOOK JOSEPH BENJAMIN SAUNDERS from 1901 to early 1904 to build his ranch house, corral, barn, and bunkhouse; string his fences; buy his horses, stud bulls, steers, and cows; and assure himself that his new Bar S was a functioning and profitable venture. His efforts were interspersed with trips back to Texas, where he gradually sold his three butcher shops and his house in Hillsboro. A shift from one state to another, and from one sector of the meat industry to another, was complicated; it was a speculative shift in his own life, and in the lives of his wife and children. But the changes that took place around and beyond him were infinitely larger. Their impact upon his efforts were inescapable, and not all were foreseeable.

There is a lingering legend about a young man who talked to an elderly financier at the time, regarding the expert's opinion of the future of the horseless carriage. The financier began with the examination of the limitations of these new, uncertain vehicles, in the context of general conditions.

"In order for them to travel," he said, "they need a special track, for they get stuck in mud and snow and cannot operate over rough terrain. Therefore new roads would have to built everywhere.

"At the same time," he continued, "they can operate only a limited distance before their fuel is exhausted. Therefore, these new roads would also have to have fueling stations built every so many miles, to meet that need. And, since the horseless carriage is subject to frequent breakdowns, such fueling stations would also have to employ special crews to make repairs. In order to make the repairs, the crews would have to stock spare parts, and in order to have spare parts, special factories would have to be constructed, with all their attendant equipment, personnel, and expense."

The financier leaned back. "Young man," he concluded, "when I consider all the factors that have to be put into place before the horseless carriage could become a common vehicle, it would seem the world itself would have to be changed to meet the needs of such machines. I wonder that you bother to inquire about their long-range possibilities."

But even as the financier spoke, changes were underway beyond the grasp or the concept of any individual, or even of any boards or groups of experts.

Mr. Saunders had learned the details of the stockman's trade, but it had proceeded, by 1904, far beyond the ability of a single individual to follow. Swift, Armour, and Wilson had changed the meat industry from one whose consumers were dependent on fresh meat to one in which meat was available all the year round. Swift introduced refrigerated railroad cars; cattle was quartered and transported in frozen sections and then further reduced by assembly-line methods in packing houses. Wilson's cans made it possible to sell meat that could be kept ready for the table indefinitely and shipped around the world.[1] Those innovations alone changed the industry, but it was altered even more by an additional abstract but significant dimension more difficult to grasp: new work methods. Pioneered by John D. Rockefeller and improved by later innovators, these systems enabled businessmen to integrate all the previously scattered steps of an entire industry into a single continuous flow that stretched from raw material to the sale of the final product.

In the spring of 1904, therefore, when the Saunders children were gathered together by Mrs. Saunders and taken on a long, tiring train trip to the ranch their father had created in Oklahoma, they traveled in a changing world. In his own way, Mr. Saunders had recreated the frontier experience. Certainly many signs of frontier life remained in the Indian Territory where his Bar S Ranch was situated. Young JB was fortunate that his earliest years of awakening to the larger world around him were to be in such a place and circumstances. But, despite surface appearances, these circumstances were not destined to last much longer.

One proof of that was provided by clusters of wooden oil derricks that sprouted on the plains of western Kansas and the eastern Indian Territory like strange new leafless trees. The smell of oil had brought

1. Daniel J. Boorstin, *The Americans: The Democratic Experience* (New York: Random House, 1973), pp. 317–322.

men running from all over the country, from Pennsylvania and Ohio and the offices of Standard Oil in New York City. Many of the newcomers, however, were from Texas and the western Louisiana regions, where great oil discoveries had been made in the wake of the Lucas gusher at Spindletop.[2]

There were multiple ironies involved in the appearance of these oilmen from Texas and Louisiana. They were, in the main, descendants of the same Southerners the Yankees had driven from their ancestral homes in Tennessee, Alabama, Georgia, and other strongholds of the eastern Confederacy. They were also, by a strange coincidence of history, descendants of the settlers who had originally driven the Indian tribes from the East into the Indian Territory.

The oil properties in Texas and Louisiana enabled these men to create Texas Oil, Humble Oil, Sun Oil, and other firms that, for the first time, could pose a competitive challenge to the Rockefeller interests. Oklahoma oil discoveries, therefore, became the scene of a great struggle that drew the attention of men in far places. That attention was drawn not because so many firms were directly involved, but because oil—as a commodity—was expanding and drew increasing sectors of the nation's economy into its vortex.

All this, however, was far beyond life on Bar S Ranch. The memories of childhood are whimsical and uncertain; they expand, generally speaking, into regular patterns only after schooling begins. The Bar S region had no school; the Territory had not yet reached that stage of development.

Mr. Saunders joined with neighboring ranchers Jim Russell and Jim Evans to share the expense and effort in building a one-room schoolhouse, designed to serve on Sundays as a church for visiting preachers. The three families also agreed that each would board a schoolteacher for a third of the year, pay her salary, and provide a horse.

The one-room schoolhouse was regarded by later generations with some disdain. But it is interesting to note that educators in the last quarter of the century rediscovered its values, and again began to mix grades together, to the accompaniment of soaring polysyllabic educational theories. JB recalls the virtues of the originals succinctly.

"I sat on the front benches with the other beginners," he says, "and the ranks rose with the benches in the back. I learned to concentrate on my own work while other conversations were being held on

2. Carl Coke Rister, *Oil! Titan of the Southwest* (Norman: University of Oklahoma Press, 1957), pp. 80–94.

other topics around me. But I would listen while waiting for our turn to come back, and between hearing the other grades and the help I received at home from my older brothers and sisters, I was able to learn quickly."

Some of the lessons were unspoken: there were grown men sitting on the back benches. JB noticed that they learned very quickly, and did not have to remain long. The lesson struck home: intelligence precedes—and extends beyond—schooling.

There were other observations, more complex and subject to subtle arguments, that involved both the similarities and the differences of racial groups. The Saunderses had a black cook named Sherman who had been raised among the Indians and whose personality, therefore, showed a striking individuality. There were many Indians all around the ranch area, but their lives were apart. JB noticed that the Creeks, who were numerous, had black families among them, and that they wore the same clothes as white people, but that the Osage would appear in braids and blankets, their faces closed.[3]

These observations are made in childhood without inhibition; neither JB nor his family, nor Americans in general in those days, were afraid to observe or to comment upon the infinite variety of mankind as it appeared around them. In later years that early knowledge of the racial amalgam of the Indian Territory would be an advantage for JB: he was to mature into a calm acceptance of human diversity; it was never to become a matter of worry or irritation to him.

In part this clear-eyed acceptance of the world might well have been due to subconscious impressions. "The open spaces provided," he says, "an enduring sense of God." His parents deepened that impression by surrounding him with a stable Christian atmosphere. On Sundays—whether a preacher appeared at the schoolhouse or not—the entire family dressed formally in honor of the Sabbath and held its own private Bible reading.

The sense of family was deeply rooted. Everyone was present at three full meals, each of which was needed because of the physical nature of their chores. Grace was said before each meal, and cowboys ate with the family. They were a different breed, however, than those with whom Mr. Saunders had ridden the trail drives years before.

3. Before the Civil War the Creeks owned black slaves. After the Civil War the Indian Bureau census, ignoring that former relationship, counted the blacks among the Creeks as full members of the tribe and treated them as such. In the long, poverty-stricken period of their residence in the Indian Territory, the Creeks and the blacks lived together harmoniously, though actual integration seems to have been slight. Later some all-black communities were established.

The railroads, the barbed wire fences, and the packing-house companies had reduced the cowboy to the status of hired hand. JB recalls that their wages in those days before World War I were eight dollars a month, their meals, a horse, and a plug of chewing tobacco that Mr. Saunders would cut and distribute each morning. That final detail provides a telling glimpse into the extent of their decline.

Yet the West was far from tame. There were drifters who would appear out of the prairie haze in time for breakfast. Their horses would be watered and fed, and the travelers would sleep in the barn all day, emerging in time for the last meal. At dusk they would ride away; they traveled at night. JB learned, and learned so early he does not recall when and from whom he learned, that it was best to give these wanderers "from noplace to nowhere" hospitality—and to keep their passage a secret. Otherwise they might unexpectedly return to set fire to the ranch—or worse.

The knowledge that this world contains bad people as well as good, therefore, was one that came so soon to the boy that it became a bedrock part of a lifetime's knowledge.

Around them the region burgeoned with the oil boom. In the winter of 1905–1906 when the weather was chill and sharp, Bob Galbreath hit three producing wells in a row on a farm ten miles south of Tulsa. Other drillers came running, and the Glenn Pool development began. Rockefeller men, calling themselves the Prairie Oil & Gas Company, were on the scene early and achieved a beachhead. But fierce competitors to the Rockefellers appeared, and the turbulence of the scene left enduring images.

By 1907 the town of Sapulpa—only twelve miles from the Bar S—as well as Red Fork, Tulsa, and a little place called Kiefer, "known as a hellhole," were crowded with newcomers. The whole hubbub of an oil boom surged into life. Wooden banks appeared, as did hastily erected office buildings with legal offices. Newspapers, barber shops, and groceries blossomed, as did the darker sides of commerce as represented by pool halls, gambling rooms, saloons, and whorehouses. All these ventures and people rolled together in a heady and headstrong mixture of money, opportunity, vice, and virtue scrambled together.

Mr. Saunders and his wife must have wondered how they could hold their lives orderly in this mixture of old and new, which brought both perils and opportunities to their doors. The Territory had filled with people more rapidly than any other in the history of the expanding nation; it applied for statehood and its entrance into the Union was set for November 15, 1907. That was only eighteen years since the pistol shot that launched the first land rush—little more than half a generation.

The change in status from an Indian Territory to a state did not sit well with some of the younger Indians. Several hundred gathered under a self-appointed leader named Crazy Snake, who threatened an uprising. Mr. Saunders was among the ranchers enlisted against this threat. On the evening of November 16, 1907, he and his men collected their guns and rode away toward Bald Hill, where Crazy Snake and his force had gathered, built huge fires, put on warpaint, and were dancing into the proper frenzy for an attack.

The Saunders ranch was without men, therefore, when Mrs. Saunders, sitting up in wait, heard the sound of horses' hoofs striking "the hard limestone rocks at the creek crossing." At first she thought it was her husband and his men returning. Then she and the children heard what sounded "like a turkey gobble—only louder. It was," says JB, "a chilling sound, especially when punctuated by a sudden scream."

Mrs. Saunders, who could easily recall when such a sound had presaged a frightful massacre, gathered what guns and ammunition she and her children could carry, and hastily hid the rest. Then, with her brood, she slipped out the back door and, instructing the children in fierce whispers, distributed them—flat on their stomachs and silent as shadows—among the corn rows.

The Indians—dark evening riders—came through the front gate and circled around the ranch house for several minutes, gobbling and making war cries. JB, clutching a .22 rifle, worried over two puppies, aroused by the excitement, that scrambled clumsily in their path. The house, however, remained blind and silent; the woman and the children held their breaths. After a time the Indians rode out the gate and away, but JB recalls the moment vividly. It seared him, as well it might.

Later they learned that Mr. Saunders and his fellow ranchers had quietly surrounded Bald Hill, and charged Crazy Snake and his braves at dawn, firing their guns in the air and whooping. The Indians, caught by surprise, surrendered without incident. They were convoyed back to the ballpark at Muskogee and held there while the rest of the new state celebrated its admission into the Union.

Later, comparing notes, the family learned that the Indians who frightened them had repeated that demonstration, with all its sinister undertones, at several other ranches in the vicinity. That reduced its importance, but JB never forgot. It did more than mark Statehood Day

23

in his memory: it provided him with a glimpse into a dark and bloody past that most Americans, by 1907, had relegated to myth.

No circumstances could better illustrate the collision of old and new in the region than the fact that Bob Galbreath, discoverer of the Glenn Pool and tireless driller, found oil on Bald Hill only weeks after Crazy Snake and his braves had danced on its slopes.[4]

Land was the original lure that drew settlers to Oklahoma, but oil drew people whose talents extended far beyond frontier needs: lawyers, businessmen of every sort, entrepreneurs, and adventurers of both sexes. As a commodity oil had growing importance. In the nineteenth century it had replaced whale oil as an illuminant, with natural gas playing a subsidiary role. Its use spread as distilling progressed to kerosene, but it became important industrially when refineries made special lubricants that, in turn, made large-scale steam and electrical machinery practical. Oil products were increased by the refiners to the creation of special greases that made many new engines functional, and assisted in the spread of electrical power.[5] Heavy oils came into use as fuels and were used to replace wood-burning and coal-burning locomotives and ships.

Yet all these uses, huge in the aggregate, could not supply a market for all the oil that was being discovered, had it not been for the great automobile race, now virtually forgotten in history, in which the steam and electrical engines were produced, tested, and marketed against the gasoline engine. Gasoline was, for a long time, considered a dangerous and useless by-product of kerosene. Huge quantities were taken out to sea and dumped. The first engines used to create a horseless carriage were, in keeping with the traditions of the Industrial Revolution, powered by steam. The Stanley Steamer was only one such product. Others, inspired by Edison and others, were built by men who believed the future of the horseless carriage was in an electric car.

In Germany, however, Nikolaus Otto, a former salesman, improved on previous efforts to develop a four-stroke engine powered by gasoline. His discoveries were in turn improved by Gottlieb Daimler and Karl Benz, both of whom also produced gasoline-powered vehicles. In the United States imitative experiments were inspired, though they were retarded when an attorney, George Selden, jealously guarded his patents on many of the principles of gasoline engines.[6]

4. Rister, *Oil! Titan*, p. 94.
5. Leonard M. Fanning, *The Rise of American Oil*, rev. ed. (New York: Harper and Brothers, 1948), pp. 35–43.
6. Boorstin, *Americans*, pp. 58–61.

It remained for the oilmen, for whom gasoline had been a waste product, to push the gasoline-powered internal combustion engine. The Duryea brothers tried it with outstanding success, and others rushed to follow their example—including Henry Ford.

The names of most of these pioneers have faded from all but the most highly specialized histories, and even their recital rings strangely on the ears. "Pope, Winton, White, Whitney, Prescott, Gaeth, Lane, Farmer, Wilkinson, Moon, Pierce, Packard, Marmon," are some of them.[7] They worked so well, and promoted races and their vehicles so assiduously, that by the beginning of the century more than $338 million in capital was devoted to the manufacture of automobiles. By 1905 almost 80,000 had been built and were in use; in 1907 more than 43,000 cars and 1,000 trucks were manufactured, and the Ford Motor Company alone made $1 million in profits.[8]

By then huge quantities of gasoline were being refined, transported, and sold; the sequence the elderly financier at the turn of the century considered too improbable for serious consideration began, illogically, to appear. Wealthy motorists complained about roads; "fueling stations" started to rise; oil industry promoters worked with car manufacturers to create contests, races, and exhibitions; Tin Pan Alley was inspired to song—*In My Merry Oldsmobile*[9]—and the *automobile*, a name that came from the air, began to capture the mind of America.

That was, however, only the spectacular end-product of a chain of effort complex when it began, that soon grew mind-boggling. Oils had to be developed for the transmission and the differential, lubricating oils created for the cylinders, special oils produced that could resist extremes of temperature, and so on. No group was more intimately involved with the development of the gasoline-powered automobile than the oil industry. An entire symbiosis of mutual effort came into being: the automobile industry began to expand and the oil industry took on added impetus, size, and importance.[10]

The area around the Bar S Ranch began to assume the appearance of a semi-industrialized region. Tulsa, competing fiercely against Oklahoma City and all the globe as well, proudly termed itself the Oil Center of the World. Big-company scouts toured the environs of dozens of towns in the vicinity, and farmers entertained new visions of sudden wealth.

7. Mark Sullivan, *Our Times*, 1: 494.
8. Bellamy Partridge, *Fill 'Er Up! The Story of Fifty Years of Motoring* (New York: McGraw-Hill, 1952), p. 221.
9. Frank Donovan, in his *Wheels for a Nation* (New York: Thomas Y. Crowell, 1965), pp. 14–15, cites a number of others: *Love in an Automobile, The Automobile Honeymoon, The Automobile Kiss*, and so on.
10. Fanning, *American Oil*, pp. 52–54.

Beyond the oil regions of Oklahoma and Texas and others being scouted, the world began to adjust, subconsciously, to a New Age. It was to prove even more innovative in its impact than the Age of Steam introduced by Fulton, or the electrical discoveries of Michael Faraday. It was rushed, invented, and promoted into life by relatively unschooled men who worked with incredible energy and largely unrecognized genius to change the world.

The world does not upend, however; it turns slowly and its days pass with deceptive monotony. On the Bar S, where life was arduous, dreams of sudden wealth seemed as distant as the stars. Mr. Saunders was dressed, had his breakfast, and was out the door every morning at 6:00 A.M., ready to order his ranch into its rounds. On many mornings he was confronted by poverty-stricken families waiting in their buckboards, to whom he would distribute sacks of flour, sugar, potatoes, and other necessities. It was a period when men automatically assumed that the revenues obtained from all by taxes were not to be used for the benefit of some—even the needy. Yet charity, as a Christian duty and as a national custom, was deeply imbedded throughout the land; foreign visitors marveled at its extent.

It was a period when hard work was normal and extraordinary efforts taken for granted. Huge disparities in the human condition were accepted by most people as being as permanent and unremarkable as time itself. Mr. Saunders was no longer a young man, and had a family of eight children—for Luther had followed JB, then Izora and then Florence had arrived, and finally a last boy: Newell. (One infant died early.) But the ranch was doing well—very well. Mr. Saunders was able to board a series of schoolteachers, feed wayfarers, and assist his neighbors without stinting his family.

The years had taught the head of the family patience. Told that Sodie Fife was out of the territorial prison and vowing vengeance on a number of whites, and that his own name was at the head of the list, he only laughed. "He's drinking," he guessed, "and maybe doesn't realize what he's saying."

That was close to the truth. Fife was, indeed, drinking heavily— but he did ride toward the Bar S. On his way, in one of those inexplicable acts that leave no true explanation behind, he fell off his horse and lay down on the railroad tracks. In due course a train came by, and the ranch learned that Sodie Fife was dead. Mr. Saunders, who had a keen appreciation of what the loss of land could mean, paid to have Fife buried in an old Indian graveyard near the Saunders home. That was a curious gesture, which gave rise to some jokes. Some of the

Indians were reputed to have said that the rancher wanted to have Sodie's ghost located where he could keep it in sight. But there was a better reason, which Mr. Saunders did not voice aloud: sympathy.

Life was simpler for the children, as always. Young JB had chores, as did everyone in the family. One was to ride to Sapulpa, eight miles away, to pick up the mail once a week, and to do some minor shopping. Because the store held the delights of a candy counter he was also given ten cents, to buy whatever he chose for himself. Town was interesting; it held strange sights. One piqued the boy's curiosity: he saw men going up and down a flight of wooden steps outside the saloon, and decided to investigate. He climbed the stairs and knocked. "A pretty lady opened the door," he told his mother later, "and asked me what I wanted. I said I just wondered what was happening, and she laughed and invited me inside. There were a whole lot of pretty ladies sitting around all dressed up. They talked to me, and held me on their laps, and ate my candy. Then they gave me a whole dollar, and told me it was time to go home."

Mrs. Saunders coughed into her handkerchief but accepted some of the candy he held out; he still had ninety cents left. But the following week, his mother decided it was Earl's turn to pick up the mail.

Life near an oil-boom town presented some problems, but not all that appeared in urban areas in later times. Sapulpa was rough and raw, but respectable women and young girls were physically safe. It would have been unthinkable to do them harm; that, at least, was a certainty. The land was boisterous, but not evil.

Mr. Saunders sent his daughters away, therefore, not to keep them safe, but to insure that they would mature into proper young ladies. His choice was a private school in Whitewright, Texas. JB, with a boy's lack of sympathy, was scornful to see his older sister Fay, on her visits back home, riding—"very prim and proper"—on a sidesaddle. Beulah, on the other hand, rode astride like a man; she was a notable tomboy.

The boy found his father a figure of awe, worthy of emulation. He recalls riding with his father, who was carrying a jar of acid and some cotton. Spotting a steer with sores—a sign of worms—the rancher cut the steer from the herd. Then he chased it and, in the manner made familiar in hundreds of rodeos later, threw himself from his horse onto the fleeing animal. The difference was that Mr. Saunders's landing thrust the steer's horn into the ground, so it could not rise. Then he applied his remedies, ending with smearing some ointment on the steer. His son watched, absorbed, until Mr. Saunders told him to ride off. "He won't be happy when he gets up," he said.

JB rode off a distance, then turned to watch as his father kicked the horn loose and ran to his horse with the angry steer behind. Mr. Saunders swung into his saddle with practiced ease and galloped away.

It was neatly done. "He was a big man, but awfully fast," his son recalls.

Other events were less pleasant. George Saunders, the eldest, was engaged to marry Miss Goldene Finley, who taught school at Glenn Pool. George made a trip to Mexico in 1909 and there contracted what the puzzled doctors called "a fever," and died. It was the family's first death in many years[11] and left Miss Finley bereft. She had grown to know, and to grow fond of Mrs. Saunders. The year after George's death, 1910, she came to teach at Fisher Switch, and to live in the Saunders home. She taught JB in the one-room schoolhouse.

JB and his brothers grew in a highly masculine environment where the lines between home, church, school, and the outdoors were very clearly drawn. A ranch, in the first decade of this century, had achieved a special position in the mind of the world. Much of that was due to literature, and to the spreading magazines and newspapers that began to cover this nation and Europe. Theodore Roosevelt helped this image immensely. He had popularized a myth around his Oklahoma Rough Riders in the Spanish-American War; his later trips west were followed by hordes of big-city newspapermen who filed dispatches glowing with color, accompanied by photographs of the hero himself, grinning under a huge western hat. People began to believe Roosevelt was a Westerner—almost a cowboy. Some never learned otherwise.

Millions of people, trapped in the teeming cities of the American East and in Europe, turned longing eyes toward the regions of the Great Plains, the vast expanses of Oklahoma, Texas, New Mexico, and the rest of the seventeen western states. Movies, which attained an almost instant popularity, helped to spread this appeal in images that retained their allure for generations.[12] Frederic Remington, four years younger than Mr. Saunders, made the West and its people artistically

11. A twin died in 1898, in infancy.
12. Neville Williams, *Chronology of the Modern World: 1763 to the Present Time* (New York: David McKay, 1967), p. 441, sets the American movie attendance by 1912 at five million a day.

28

immortal with his sketches, painting, and sculpture. Many other artists preceded and followed him in these efforts, but Remington was uniquely able to capture and convey the sense of its last untrammeled period. Yet when Remington died, in 1909, the West he portrayed was being uprooted. The region and its people were caught in a great series of changes that swept across the entire nation, and whose effects were felt in Europe and all the rest of the world as well.

Some trace these changes in the first decade of the century to the great mail-order houses and the ubiquitous Sears, Roebuck and Montgomery Ward catalogues. Much has since been made of their contents. They do provide a sort of peek into the past, in which the styles of clothing, furniture, popular books and patent medicines, musical instruments and everyday articles, are jumbled together, as in a family attic.

But to assume that the merchants alone changed the country is to mistake the fish for the water. The unprecedented freedoms of the Americans and the relatively minor role its government played in the lives of the people provided the climate in which nothing was—or seemed to be—impossible to attain. Inventions poured from the most unlikely and diverse individuals, and they were not always physical.

Businessmen and lawyers combined to devise new ways to raise money, to launch enterprises, and to market inventions. Their new instruments, abstract and dazzling in their variety, included stocks and bonds with special, interchangeable, and convertible characteristics, patent agreements, partnerships that comprised interlocking directorships, holding companies, and subsidiaries, ventures pyramided atop one another. These inventions, as arcane, esoteric, and closed to outsiders as the formulae of physics or the nuances of theology, created enterprises and personal fortunes for their inventors that dazzled and attracted the envy of all the world.

A great gulf of misunderstanding arose. The vast majority of people could appreciate their latest purchase of the latest marvel—a telephone or electric lights inside the house, a typewriter or a new harvester—but they could not grasp how these marvels had been placed within reach. They could not discern and therefore could not realize that without the connecting links of business, these and virtually all the other novelties that were lightening their burdens and changing their lives, would have remained—like the steam- and water-powered machines of ancient Athens—useless and forgotten toys.

In 1902 *McClure's* magazine, in an effort to increase its circulation and raise its advertising rates, ran a series of articles by Ida M. Tarbell entitled *The History of the Sandard Oil Company*. They created a sensation by their candor, in which John D. Rockefeller was etched in acid. Unfortunately Miss Tarbell did not seem to realize that not only did Standard Oil compete against firms as avid as the winner, but Standard's success in integration virtually created a huge industry where none had existed before. To the surprise of the publisher, however, the series zoomed the circulation of *McClure's*.

Both newspapers and magazines turned toward this new avenue of exposure, and jeremiads appeared on a bewildering number of subjects. Ray Stannard Baker put *The Railroads on Trial*. Charles Edward Russell attacked the meat-packers in *The Greatest Trust in the World*, Burton K. Kendrick wrote *The Story of Life Insurance*, and a onetime loser on Wall Street, Thomas Lawson, wrote *Frenzied Finance*.[13]

It was clear the newspapers and magazines were on a popular track; book publishers soon followed. But there were some ironic aspects to their disclosures that the average reader did not seem to grasp. All these publications were products of the technology they derided: the linotype, the color printing plate, the camera, the telephone, the electrical telegraph, the typewriter were all instruments placed before them by the industrial enterprises whose methods they deplored. Their great circulation owed much to Rural Free Delivery, which extended their distribution at the expense of the taxpayer, and their ability to pay writers large sums was based on the growth of advertisements by the huge department stores, manufacturers and, especially, the new automobile business.

There is little doubt that both the reporters and their readers often shared a common indignation, but it seemed embarrassingly overdone. After all, the nation was moving forward at a pace that outstripped all the world. Its industries were able to accept and find places for a huge wave of immigrants from eastern Europe and the Mediterranean countries—and entire cities were being created at headlong speed. Most Americans were able to buy goods and live in a style far better than their forebears; virtually everyone was convinced their children would live in an even more bountiful land. To mount an antibusiness campaign in the midst of such accomplishments did not betray a tender conscience so much as an abiding envy searching for a cause. That envy was an unremarked element of the open society itself. In the unfettered climate of the day, most persons fell short of their goals, and few of those could accept that their inability to outshine their fellows in open competition was due to their own medi-

13. Foster Rhea Dulles, *The United States Since 1865* (Ann Arbor: University of Michigan Press, 1959), p. 184.

ocrity; they preferred to believe that they were being cheated out of success by someone else—or by the shape of the world itself. The antibusiness writers, therefore, had a ready, eager, and even avid audience at hand.

There were other reasons, of course, for the popularity of critical literature. The composition of the nation was being changed by its latest wave of immigrants. Many of these were individuals of outstanding ability, able to make their talents felt with amazing rapidity. But many brought the fevers and prejudices of Europe in their luggage. New attitudes gave rise to shifting values. A Socialist movement, long minor and ineffectual, swelled with new members and energy. The older traditions of English liberalism, Irish independence, and Anglo-Scot puritanism that had so long dominated the nation's intellectual life were confronted by new arguments. Wild Bill Haywood and others led the Industrial Workers of the World into violent action; the national dialogue was punctuated by new outcries, and a new and strident tone appeared.

Theodore Roosevelt, who had established a reputation as a "trust-buster," was alarmed at the rise of radicalism. "Muckrakers," he said, were injuring the nation.[14] The description, taken from Bunyan's *Pilgrim's Progress*, was instantly recognizable to an older generation. But Roosevelt left office in 1909, and once out of office, his influence declined.

A new generation, with different manners, had appeared. The immense popularity of the new automobiles led to shorter skirts, so women could drive themselves. A new suggestiveness entered the lyrics of popular songs. Church groups were alarmed not only at the kissing scenes, but at the inherent vulgarity of the movies, which attracted millions to their showings every day.

On May 15, 1911, the Supreme Court ruled that the Standard Oil Company had been guilty of "unreasonable" restraint of trade, and ordered the firm to break itself up into eleven separate firms.[15] The decision was hailed by some as a great triumph for democracy, but that was an exaggeration. The firm was in decline; its top men were rich and old, and newer competitors were in the process of reducing its dominion without the help of the elderly Justices.

The Supreme Court had merely, as so often before, made a popu-

14. The Pilgrim meets a man intent upon raking dung, who refuses to look up and see a celestial crown suspended above—his for the taking.
15. Gorton Garruth and Associates, *The Encyclopedia of American Facts and Dates,* 4th ed. (New York: Thomas Y. Crowell, 1966), p. 423.

lar decision that created more problems than it solved. In effect, it had ruled Standard Oil was too large to be allowed to exist. Instead of enlarging the rights of citizens, however, by setting limits on "reasonable restraints" or on size, or an any other factor that could guide businessmen, the Court had declared—and enlarged—its own authority to rule against any enterprise, if such enterprises became unpopular. The precedent was ominous, and it was one reason Roosevelt decided to run again for the Presidency.

He included in his platform a Right of Judicial Recall, in which a national referendum would be held to determine whether or not a "constitutional" ruling by the Supreme Court would, in its turn, be upheld or rejected by the people. Otherwise, he said, the Court would be a supreme arbiter beyond the nation's ability to control.[16]

Early the following year a new oil strike was made near Cushing, a town southwest of Sapulpa, well within riding distance. The strike was not an isolated one; Tom Slick and others began to hit oil almost anywhere they drilled in an area "six miles north and south and five miles east and west" of the first. "News of Cushing's prolific production and its great fortunes brought prospectors and speculators from every direction," wrote Carl Rister later. "They came from Pennsylvania, Ohio, Indiana, West Virginia, Illinois, Texas, California and Wyoming. The sole topic of conversation on Oklahoma railroad trains and in stations was Cushing oil and the lucky strikes men had made. The ragged, unkempt little town of Cushing was presently overwhelmed by a noisy excited army of men—millionaires, laborers, hoboes, gamblers, prostitutes and men of small means—all hopeful that fortune would smile on them. Men with surface-pipe boots and swedge-nipple pants, red eyed and keen eyed, close mouthed—prospectors, promoters, pimps, scouts, scalpers and scavengers—were everywhere, overflowing the hotels, boardinghouses, shanties and tents.

"Cushing pool halls closed at midnight, so that men could sleep on the tables, under the tables and in chairs, at from fifty cents to one dollar a head. At dawn the 'crum bosses' cleaned out the places."[17]

The rush included far more than the men in the hotels, shanties, pool halls, and offices; it drew wagonloads of materials from the entire region, to supply the instruments and tools, provisions and supplies to

16. The decision provoked many conservatives because its grounds were held to be vague, and not to establish any clear guides for business, leaving the Court free to rule any way it chose, from case to case. Roosevelt's proposal, however, was misunderstood by the public and misrepresented by his political opponents. It died in the Bull Moose campaign of 1912.

17. Rister, Oil! Titan, p. 120.

feed the toilers of the new fields. "One who made the journey heard the rattle and clang of the heavily loaded freight wagons and the shouting of the drivers. Here he passed a six-horse wagon laden with a steam boiler with its smokestack and other equipment. Next came a wagon creaking and straining under a mass of wire cable." These streams and loads passed, day and night, toward the fields; "on one trip to Cushing a traveler counted 276 outfits, all outward bound."[18]

The giant new field around Cushing pushed Oklahoma into the lead among oil producing states. Tulsa's brag became true: the city was the Oil Capital of the World in all reality. Tulsa, Sapulpa, Red Fork, Oklahoma City, and other towns served as so many magnets imbedded in a region that sparkled with the lures of opportunity. All this was too much to resist, and finally drew, among others, the owner of the Bar S.

There remains a photograph of what appears to be a sale at the ranch. Taken by a view camera, it shows a huge area, fenced with barbed wire, with a dark herd of cattle in the center that straggles toward the edges. In the foreground are the figures of men in business suits and derbies, standing on what appear to be loading platforms. To one side, seated on a large white horse, and also in a dark suit but wearing a rancher's large Stetson, is Mr. Saunders himself. The specific occasion remains unknown, but it appears to be a stock sale. It will serve, in terms of illustration, for the final one—in which not only the stock, but all the Bar S, was sold—in 1912.

18. Ibid., p. 121.

CHAPTER FOUR

Sapulpa

I N 1912 the prairie town of Sapulpa, about fifteen miles from Tulsa, was raw and had an unfinished look. It had been born only fourteen years earlier, largely because the Frisco Railroad ended its tracks at that point. The railroad yards and repair shops had enabled the creation of a hotel, a restaurant, and some fledging enterprises, including a brick factory.

It was oil that lifted Sapulpa. The town fathers would recall, for many years afterward, the fact that the Sapulpa oil boom was among the first, and that Tulsa began to burgeon by harboring the Sapulpa overflow of oilmen.

The town had a banner that indicated its sentiments. It read: Oil City of the Southwest. The Tulsans went them one better. Their banner read: Oil Capital of the World.

By 1912 even the most stubborn Sapulpan could admit that Tulsa's banner carried more credibility. That city had received over 65,000 people, while Sapulpa barely exceeded 10,000. But if the leaders of Sapulpa had to look up, in one sense, to the Tulsans, they could look down, in another, on the city fathers of Kiefer, a few miles to the southwest. Kiefer was also benefiting from the Glenn Pool, but it was behaving in a profligate and disgraceful way. Its "Madhouse," a combination gambling hall and brothel, which featured live entertainments of both a planned and an impromptu nature, was only one of scores of sinful spots toward which its city fathers turned a benign eye.

Situated between a city determined to become a metropolis and a town cheerfully headed toward extinction, Sapulpa had eight churches, four banks, several newspapers, scores of stores, and a trolley-car line. It was connected to both Tulsa and Kiefer by an electric Interurban.

The Frisco Railroad, by 1912, had a Sapulpa payroll of six hundred, and brought twenty passenger trains a day to the city. No record remains of the freight traffic, but the strenuously industrial nature of the town leaves little doubt that it was heavy.[1]

For all its rawness, therefore, Sapulpa had its attractions. The oil boom that soared with the first discoveries of the Cushing field in early 1912 was only a beginning. Every passing week brought news of new wells, new fortunes, and new ventures. It is little wonder that Mr. Saunders, making his last career turn at the age of fifty-five, chose Sapulpa instead of its neighboring extremes.

The Saunderses moved into a comfortable house that had five bedrooms upstairs, and a dining room, living rooms, and kitchen downstairs. No American needs to be told what a well-to-do family home of 1912 was like: those rambling structures with their multiple rooms, their surrounding porches, gabled roofs, and variegated windows are familiar across the country.

Mr. Saunders's new career was in real estate. That was a business that required capital, a knowledge of the community and the region, a good reputation, and a keen awareness of the values of the land—and of men. It rewards those best who enter it early in a rising community. It was a careful choice; it was clear his pursuit was not toward speculative fortune but toward stability.

In this, his last move, the head of the family achieved a new and final status. His ranch mustache vanished; the new styles called for men to be clean-shaven. He wore a business suit and left for the office every day, and the entire family settled into small-city life. All that remained of the ranch were some mementoes, guns for hunting, and several favorite saddle horses quartered in stables behind the house.

The Jefferson School in Sapulpa was only four years old when young JB entered it in 1912, but it looked as old, firm, and immovable as a fortress. It was a period when architects built institutions that left no doubt of their character. Made of red brick, three stories high, it squatted grimly in the midst of raw land at Mound and Cleveland streets.

Inside, each of the eight elementary grades had its own classroom, with the boys seated on one side and the girls on the other; it was a time when the division between the sexes was as clear as sunlight. Each

1. Sapulpa (Okla.) *Herald*, July 1, 1973, Seventy-fifth Anniversary Issue.

school day began with the Lord's Prayer and the Pledge of Allegiance. JB soon learned his classwork was much easier than in his old, one-room schoolhouse. But his teachers were quick to make the same observation; he found himself skipped from the fifth to the seventh grade. It was a time when educators believed in pushing the bright ahead, and letting the dullards remain at the level of their incompetence until they improved.

JB found himself in a new environment, in every sense. He did not mind the jeers that rose when it was learned he was known only by his initials; the names that floated after him were clues to attitudes. At first he was called John the Baptist—probably because he had brought to his new, citified situation, some caution of early behavior. As time passed and he and the other boys became better acquainted, the nicknames began to alter: Jail Bird, Jugabug.

A new boy in school is a classic situation often described in terms of the crowded cities of the American East; the southwestern version was, if anything, rougher. It was a time when a boy who could not or would not fight was apt to be beaten until he turned. JB was not the sort to accept that humiliation; his ranch upbringing had made him muscular, and he was a chunky handful. But when he was transferred to the Woodlawn School, noted for its roughness, he encountered some remarkably mean boys, some of whom later had serious troubles in life. The time came when JB found himself in the basement of Woodlawn, surrounded by a ring of young toughs determined to break him down.

Bodie Warren, a classmate noted for his athletic ability and popular with most factions, intervened. He said, "I won't let you all jump him. Let him fight one at a time."

The ring snarled, but the compromise, with its inherent challenge to their mettle, could hardly be denied. That was a mistake: JB fought the first boy down, and when the next came forward his blood was up and he was moving fast. In the end his stamina proved the point. He ended bloodied and bruised, but established. After that, the Woodlawn School held no problems.

There were other lessons. "Sapulpa was a wild town then," recalls an early settler. "The worst, as well as the best, elements of society tried their fortunes in oil and made their headquarters in the town. If the oil scalpers didn't get them, the thugs and highwaymen did. But, my goodness, how money was made! Everybody in Sapulpa in those days either had money or was preparing to make it; the sky was the limit for almost any kind of enterprise that had attached for it the magic word 'oil.' "[2]

To an extent, that viewpoint accounted for the stream of newcomers who arrived in town on the Frisco Railroad and the emergence of downtown hotels: the Frisco, the St. Charles, the Gilstrap, the Dewey House, the St. James, the Loraine, and the inevitable Harvey House. Young JB found it easy to get a newspaper route in a town where several papers competed for attention, and on his round began to discover the bold face of the world at the time.

There were four whorehouses on the boy's route; a stop at each meant a tip of from fifty cents to a dollar. Despite the fact that Oklahoma was one of the first states to pass a Prohibition law, saloons were wide open and "anyone who was big enough to walk in and hand over the money could get a drink." Pool halls were numerous; there was an Air Dome theater, and the town fathers were intent upon the creation of an opera house and other places of decent entertainment. But, as the early settler and the Sheriff's Office could attest, the town was far from tame and the frontier was far from dead.

Indians in their braids still walked quietly among the newcomers, and J. M. Sapulpa, son of the Creek chief whose name the town bore, occupied one of its larger homes.[3]

In early 1912 the territories of New Mexico and Arizona were admitted to the Union, and the flag was changed to carry forty-eight stars. A sequence started over three hundred years earlier, when the first English settlers landed in Virginia, had finally reached a continental conclusion. But the victory was hardly noticed; the nation was embroiled in ugly, troubling political disputes, whose principles remain as yet unresolved.

To the newspapers, and to most Americans, the political arguments appeared rooted in the ambitious personalities inside the Republican and Democratic parties. The Republicans, although a majority party for generations, were divided between traditionalists and a group calling themselves Progressives, headed by Senator Robert M. La Follette of Wisconsin.

2. Ibid.

3. Born in Alabama, the Creek chief arrived in the Indian Territory in 1850, and established a farm and trading post where the town later emerged. During the Civil War he fought with the Confederates and was commissioned a lieutenant in the Confederate army. In 1875 he converted to Christianity with the Methodists, sent away one of his two wives, and became a rancher whose property was ten miles square. He took the name *Sapulpa* from the Creek word *sapulpakah*, or climbing vine. His son, J. M. Sapulpa, was a leading citizen; three grandsons are college-educated citizens of the region.

Deeper observers, however, were aware that large issues were at stake. One of these was the Senator from Massachusetts, Henry Cabot Lodge. A scholar of remarkable qualities and former editor of the prestigious *North American Review*, Lodge was an internationalist; a friend of both President Taft and former President Roosevelt; he was worried about their break with one another.

His worry went beyond which of the two competitors would gain control of the Republican party nomination. Unlike most Americans, Senator Lodge—a student of seapower and follower of the theories of Admiral Alfred Mahan—knew that the Great White Fleet sent around the world by Roosevelt when he was in office, had not so much proven U.S. power as exhibited its weakness. The American battleships could hardly have continued beyond the environs of their country had they not been accompanied by a flotilla of twenty-four escorting supply vessels that flew foreign flags. Furthermore, Britain commissioned the *Dreadnought* before the Great White Fleet returned home—and that new warship made every American ship of the line obsolete.[4]

At the same time a change had overtaken the political climate of the United States. The economic theories of socialism, which had captured the Germans and made large inroads in British intellectual circles, had grown prominent in America. Its argument that basic industries should be controlled by the state fit the antibusiness climate of much of academia and the literati. Arguments that the people should have more direct influence on the government also rose to shrill decibels. A clamor appeared for the direct election of U.S. Senators. That would alter the Constitution, whose authors had deliberately constructed an upper House unreachable by direct vote, whose members were to serve as a brake upon the Representatives, who were designed to be the people's tribunes.

The demand for the direct election of Senators was only one. Labor, whose tactics had grown increasingly violent since the 1880s, mounted a spectacular Pullman strike whose leader then became head of a newly formed Socialist party. Women known as *suffragettes*, notably unrestrained in their tactics, demanded the vote. Cries for a minimum wage law, restrictions on the hours of work, a graduated tax on personal incomes, and other features familiar to the world Socialist movement had achieved respectable status in many quarters of the land.

Most persons assumed that these demands, which emerged from widely separated groups and persons, stemmed from domestic causes. But to Senator Lodge, his friend Brooks Adams, and other conserva-

4. George C. Reinhardt and William R. Kintner, *The Haphazard Years* (New York: Doubleday, 1960), pp. 57–58.

38

tives, they added together to a movement to establish a direct democracy in the United States.

Lodge was particularly alarmed by a speech Roosevelt gave, in early 1912, at Columbus, Ohio, in which the former President called not only for the direct election of Senators, but for an *initiative* that would give the people the right to propose laws, a *referendum* that would force the government to accept such laws, and a *recall* that would remove all governmental officials—including judges—who lost popular support. To this, Roosevelt added his idea that the people should ratify—or negate—constitutional rulings by the U.S. Supreme Court.[5]

Lodge, thoroughly alarmed at the conversion of his old friend, rummaged through his library at Nahant, Massachusetts, and plucked illustrations "from the direct democracy of Athens, to the Italian city-states of the Middle Ages, to France of 1848" to prove the story "had not changed." The sequence was as clear to Lodge as it had been to John Adams, who had made a monumental study of the subject of democracies through the ages: first anarchy, and then tyranny. The "decline of the law-making body resulted ultimately in the rise of the executive . . . the plebiscite itself was the favorite tool of dictators, be he Caesar or Louis Napoleon."[6]

That was not a new subject to Lodge, who had written a biography of his great-grandfather George Cabot, a contemporary and friend of George Washington, who had seen the horrors of the Terror in the French Revolution at first hand. Lodge himself was not unacquainted with such events; he and his bride had visited Paris on their honeymoon only three months after the holocaust of the French Commune of 1871.

Roosevelt was not impressed. The Lodge parallels, he said, were "not exact"—as though any two historical events could fit one another precisely. Just because "a totally different people" had failed, he could see no reason why Americans would. In other words, Roosevelt shared the common belief of his countrymen that the United States was somehow outside the laws of history, that America was different—and so were its men.

Lodge and his friends were appalled. Brooks Adams said Roosevelt "is not big enough. He is like a man trying to solve problems in celestial mechanics without the calculus. . . . He does not appreciate his ignorance enough to have the instinct to learn."[7]

5. Alden Hatch, *The Lodges of Massachusetts* (New York: Hawthorn, 1973), p. 98.

6. John A. Garraty, *Henry Cabot Lodge: A Biography* (New York: Alfred A. Knopf, 1953), p. 285.

7. Ibid., p. 291.

To less erudite observers the situation was simpler. Roosevelt had adopted and even exceeded the program of La Follette's followers. At the Republican convention in June, 1912, where Taft forces dominated and renominated the President, Roosevelt proceeded to bolt the party and took all La Follette's Progressives with him. The Wisconsin Senator never forgave what he considered a betrayal, but Roosevelt was unheeding. He summoned his Bull Moosers to the strains of *Onward, Christian Soldiers,* and the gleeful Democrats saw their opponents split down the middle.

The Democratic convention was, however, almost equally agonizing. Champ Clark entered with a majority, and the Wilson followers, for all their rhetoric about the rights of the people, refused to accept that verdict. They held out for days, and after endless deals and compromises, promises and pledges, managed to swing the reluctant delegates behind Woodrow Wilson.

That left President Taft, an elephantine figure, to trumpet the conservative cause. He had Lodge and others to help him, but he lacked charisma—a word not then generally used—and his entire stance lacked intellectual support. Between them Wilson and Roosevelt seemed to attract everyone in favor of change, and to have in their hands virtually all those shining figures who—as distinct from scholars—are known as intellectuals.

In November, 1912, after a bruising campaign, the results proved that Roosevelt's vanity had helped to change the course of the nation. Wilson had a plurality of a little over 41 percent, with 6.2 million votes. Roosevelt trailed with 4.1 million. Taft bobbed behind with 3.4 million votes. Eugene Debs, who headed a Socialist party that outpromised everyone, achieved nearly 1 million votes. These results, putting personalities aside, meant that out of almost 15 million voters, over 11 million had voted against the traditional principles in which Lodge believed, and which had once dominated the nation. That was a turn in the road without mistake. It left, as the new captain of the American ship, a man in the Presidency whose entire life had, until only two years earlier, been spent in the cloistered halls of universities.[8]

Early in 1913 the Sixteenth Amendment to the Constitution was passed. It gave the federal government the authority to tax every citizen in the land, without sharing these revenues with the states. In May, shortly after President Wilson took office, the Seventeenth Amendment, allowing the direct election of U.S. Senators, also came into being. That eliminated one of the most important powers of the state

8. Wilson made only one venture into the larger world: he set up his shingle as an attorney in Atlanta, Georgia, for a little over a year, from 1882 to 1883. No record remains of any clients and the experience, which he abandoned to attend Johns Hopkins University in Baltimore, left him with an abiding contempt for "pettifogging lawyers."

legislatures. Both Amendments greatly reduced the influence of the states in the nation's capital, and enlarged those of the federal government.

Another innovation, complex in the making, was inaugurated under President Wilson, and was called the Federal Reserve Act. The title was a triumph of propaganda; in reality it was the creation of a central bank that was placed in charge of the nation's currency and given power enough to effectively dominate the banking industry. Although it was designed to avert the peaks and valleys of recurring booms and panics in the economic life of the nation, its record since 1913 indicates it has never succeeded in either goal, but its admirers remain as fervent today as when it was first proposed.

All change was not political, however. The momentum achieved by American business, which alarmed its critics and cheered its members, continued to be impressive. Henry Ford, during the election year 1912, had produced his 500,000th Model T. As 1913 started he adapted the overhead trolleys and assembly-line methods of the meat-packers to produce Model Ts at the rate of 1,000 a day. He accompanied this achievement in production by so reducing the price of his cars that their sales soared. At the same time a promoter named William Durant, who put together a corporation he called General Motors, was producing motor trucks designed to carry freight and tractors—designed to replace the horse on farms. These machines were changing the landscape as much as the Model T and its competitors, and in as important ways.

The movies added their part. "Little Mary" films made Mary Pickford the nation's sweetheart; John Bunny convulsed millions. Westerns were exciting enough, but to make them even more attractive the movie-makers adopted a system used by popular magazines and introduced the serial, in which the heroine and the hero were left at the end of each episode in inextricable situations from which they, in one fortuitous manner or another, escaped at the beginning of the next.

In towns like Sapulpa all across the country, therefore, the entertainments and products of a new age were pouring forth to make abstruse political discussions and remote government appear almost unimportant. In eastern Oklahoma the attention was focused on the progress of the oil boom. In the first half of 1913 it appeared as though the Cushing field might be in decline, though in August a new field was discovered in Healdton, near Ardmore. On November 30, toward the very end of the year 1913, a new gusher was found in the Bartlesville sands of the Cushing field.[9] It sent hopes soaring; Oklahoma finally moved into the front rank. It became the largest oil-producing state in the Union, and famous around the world.

9. Rister, *Oil! Titan*, p. 122.

The town of Sapulpa grew under the impact of these developments; its streets were heavy with traffic and equipment headed for the oil fields; wells were drilled on Sugar Hill and their lights could be seen and the sounds of their rigs could be heard in the town.

Every town has a character, however, set by its leaders and their ideas of the relative importance of events. Years later Miss Pauline Jackson wrote a history of Sapulpa, in which she notes that "Sapulpans as a whole were very little touched by the oil development around them, and certainly very few of them made any amount of money from the oil business directly. . . . large numbers of citizens were interested in the fight with Bristow over the location of the county seat, and earnest efforts were made to get railroads in addition to the Frisco to enter Sapulpa. [But] Tulsans meantime through many years gave consistent emphasis to banking, free building sites, bonuses, better transportation and persuasive argument toward the one goal of becoming the Oil Capital of the World. . . ."[10]

Tulsa, therefore, was forging ahead of Sapulpa even during the boom days of 1913 and early 1914. Mr. Saunders, whose business was to deal in lands made promising by that boom, and in houses it made necessary, undoubtedly shared its benefits with other Sapulpans, despite Miss Jackson's surmise. But in common with his fellow citizens, he was not swept away by its speculative opportunities. That is not to say that he lacked force.

Young JB, thirteen years old in 1914 and big for his age, discovered that the hard way. Life in town had toughened the boy; he had seen sights and people who made the austere patterns of his parents appear old-fashioned amid a changing world. That led him, on some minor occasion, to openly defy his father. That stance was not so much a rejection as a reflection of the spirit of the times, which were rough, unruly, and challenging, as well as the inevitable urge of a boy reaching toward manhood, who must—to achieve it—stand up to his father.

Mr. Saunders was sufficiently taken aback to loom before his son in silence for a breathless moment. Then he rushed upon him with amazing swiftness, grabbed him and, *turning him upside down*, pinned him against the wall.

"It was an ego-shattering experience," says JB. As helpless as one of the unruly calves his father had handled on the ranch, the blood pounding in his ears, he heard his father's voice thundering a question regarding his future behavior, and demanding a Yes or No answer. The answer was Yes.

10. Sapulpa *Herald*, July 1, 1973.

That was unusual, and was never repeated in either actuality or essence. JB could only recall one whipping in his entire life, and that had been when he was very young. And after his one experience of openly defying his father, there were no further confrontations. These were, in any event, rare in the family. Its life in general was unremarkable.

A large family is apt to have many friends and acquaintances, visitors and activities. Miss Goldene Finley, who had once been engaged to the eldest son and who later married a young man with the imposing name of Lyman Hartwell Latimer, was a frequent visitor. JB recalls when the Latimers had difficulties, and their young daughter, Nelle, came to live at the Saunders home.

For the most part the days passed quietly. Young JB finished the eighth grade at the age of thirteen, and entered high school. It was located in The Castle, a forbidding, huge building capped by a cupola and bell, that harbored every grade from kindergarten to the twelfth. He entered the ninth early, but he had no way of knowing that he would graduate far later than most—or that the world he knew would be turned, as he had been so briefly turned by his father, upside down.

That turning began, as the world knows, with the assassination of the Austrian Archduke Ferdinand and his wife at Sarajevo. The double murder was reported in the press of the United States, but its significance was not understood nor made clear to the nation. The very surprise of Americans to the events that followed the strike at Sarajevo provides a yardstick of how poorly the American press reported the world to its countrymen.

It is remarkable that such a situation existed in a nation that, in the years from 1900 to 1914, accepted approximately one million immigrants a year.[11] The overwhelming majority of these immigrants came from the very centers of European unrest: from Russia, Hungary, Poland, Slovakia, Bohemia, and Italy. New York, Chicago, Boston, Baltimore, and other parts of the country seethed with these immigrants, many of whom launched foreign-language newspapers, formed political clubs, and maintained an extensive correspondence with their relatives and friends in Europe.

Much the same could be said about German-American and Irish-American groups, who maintained many ties with their homelands, or the homelands of their forebears. Theodore Roosevelt was only one of many older Americans who raged against this practice, and who spoke against "hyphenated Americans." Agitation and immigration was part of the Progressive party program. It led to demands for literacy tests—

11. Dulles, *United States Since 1865*, p. 224.

conducted, of course, in English—before immigrants could be accepted into the country. Taft vetoed that, but the sentiment continued to rise.

In such a polyglot land it was more than remarkable that American newspapers reported—and their cartoonists portrayed—Europe as a continent of stereotypes. The Kaiser was always shown as a be-medaled figure of fun; the Germans were either lovable professors or goose-steppers. The Englishman wore a monocle, the Italian a curling dark mustache, the Frenchman a top hat.

Little effort was made to follow or report European politics in any serious sense. The reasons Germany and Britain armed against one another for a generation were seldom analyzed. Instead, great peace movements arose throughout the land; pacifism was promoted. Part of the reason was that Americans saw no need on their part to fight for anything and, by a natural projection, believed others should be equally happy. A large part, however, was a simple ignorance of the rest of the world—an ignorance the literati shared.

For that reason the events of August, 1914, seemed as incredible to most Americans as a bulletin saying the moon had fallen from the sky. On August 1, 1914, Germany declared war on Russia, France mobilized, Italy announced neutrality, German troops occupied Luxembourg and issued an ultimatum to Belgium demanding access, and Russians invaded east Prussia. On August 3, Germany declared war and invaded Belgium. On August 4, England declared war on Germany. On August 5, Austria-Hungary declared war on Russia. On August 6, Serbia and Montenegro declared war on Germany. On August 8, British troops landed in France, and France occupied Togoland, in Africa. On August 10, France declared war on Austria and the Germans occupied Liège. On August 12, Britain declared war on Austria-Hungary. On August 15, Japan demanded that Germany evacuate Kiau-Chow, in China. On August 20, the Germans occupied Brussels. On August 22, the French and Germans clashed at Namur and Mons. On August 24, the French retreated at Mons. On August 26, the Germans crossed the Meuse River and occupied Lille. On August 28 the Germans defeated the Russians at Tannenberg, and Austria-Hungary declared war on Belgium. On August 30, 1914, the Germans took Amiens.[12]

These events astonished those who had been lulled into the belief that "progress"—a mysterious, disembodied spirit generally held to somehow direct human activity—had led the world beyond the need for war.[13] Germany's violation of Belgian neutrality created astonish-

---

12. Williams, *Chronology of the Modern World*, p. 448.
13. William E. Leuchtenburg, *The Perils of Prosperity, 1914–1932* (Chicago: University of Chicago Press, 1958), pp. 12–13, quotes Dr. David Starr Jordan, director of the World Peace Foundation, saying on the eve of the outbreak, "What

ment that deepened into indignation when the German Chancellor was quoted as calling the German-Belgian treaty "a scrap of paper."

That indignation was fanned when the British, who severed the transatlantic cable between Germany and the United States on August 15, 1914,[14] moved—with remarkable skill—to make the most of their propaganda monopoly by embroidering the genuine horrors of the war with lurid atrocity stories.

The immediate impact of the European war upon the United States was to disrupt its commerce with Europe. American exports, which had achieved impressive levels, were in effect cancelled. In turn this led to a wave of dislocations that rolled westward and severely affected agriculture and other industries, sending prices down and creating a depression.

Had all other factors remained the same, that alone would have hurt the oil-producing regions of Oklahoma, but this area had already achieved, in the last half of 1914, its own brand of economic trouble. The discovery of new wells and uncontrolled drilling and production combined to send crude oil prices plummeting down from over one dollar a barrel in the spring of 1914, to an official forty cents a barrel in the late autumn and early winter. Unofficially, oil sold at any price that found a buyer.[15]

No Sapulpa family could escape the effects of these worsened conditions, and the Saunderses were no exceptions. JB, who was active in sports and hopeful of becoming a member of the high school baseball and football teams, was told that he would have to go to work; the family was—like everyone else—cutting back on extras and seeking ways to earn more money.

After a brief stint at Plater's Clothing Store on Main Street, young JB went to work for Max Meyer, whose clothing store was at Park and Dewey in downtown Sapulpa. His store day began in time to watch Mr. Meyer, who would not trust him with a key, open in the morning

---

shall we say of the Great War of Europe, ever threatening, ever impending, and which never comes? We shall say that it will never come. Humanly speaking, it is impossible."

14. Charles Roetter, *The Art of Psychological Warfare, 1914–1945* (New York: Stein and Day, 1974), p. 38. The author explains that the Germans could not even send cables from The Hague or Amsterdam, because they too were controlled from London. By the time Berlin managed to establish a transatlantic wireless service, Germany had already fallen behind the tides of opinion in the United States.

15. Kendall Beaton, *Enterprise in Oil* (New York: Appleton-Century-Crofts, 1957), pp. 130–131.

at 7:00 A.M. Then JB would sweep the sidewalk, mop the floor inside, and help to ready the stock for the day's business. One morning he was five minutes late; Mr. Meyer had already opened.

"Good evening," said the proprietor when JB appeared. "It was a nice morning, wasn't it?"

JB would leave the store in time to attend his classes, but return to act as a clerk in the evening. That was more rewarding than sweeping and mopping; he enjoyed the efforts to jockey a customer into a series of purchases, and proved to have a flair for selling.

Mr. Meyer had flexible closing hours. On occasion there would be a sale, and the store would be kept open as long as either customers were present or potential customers going past. JB enjoyed these evenings: he was not a self-conscious youth, and the variations in customers and their attitudes were inherently interesting. On one occasion a drunken Indian woman, elderly but robust, wandered into the store and would neither buy nor leave. Mr. Meyer was finally driven by impatience to struggle with her. Before staggering out, she threw him to the floor, to JB's delight.[16]

On the surface, therefore, life in the United States appeared much the same, in the autumn of 1914, as before. "There were men still living," wrote one historian, "whose fathers had known Jefferson and John Adams. . . . There were thousands of men still alive who had fought under Stonewall Jackson, and . . . even a few veterans who had marched with Winfield Scott on the Halls of Montezuma. A small company who voted for Woodrow Wilson in 1912 had cast their first votes for Martin Van Buren or James K. Polk."[17]

Sapulpa, like hundreds of other towns and hamlets in the land, was packed with memories of that still-living past. Old Indian fighters intermingled with Indians on its streets; former Confederate and Union soldiers sunned themselves at midday. The church groups still met; listened, enthralled, to evangelists; held their socials; and warned the community leaders about strong liquor, from which, they held, all evils flowed. Throughout the West, as the trains ran past thousands of empty miles, Indian tribes still lived who rarely saw a white face; the plains were mostly empty; the immense forests of the Northwest remained virgin and remote, ruled by wind, rain, and sun, and harboring hundreds and even thousands of miles of nonhuman life.

Yet it was all on the verge of irrevocable change. That change

16. Mr. Meyer's son, Lewis Meyer, who abandoned law for literature and authored a number of books, wrote a biography of his father. Titled *Preposterous Papa*, and published by Hawthorn, it was translated into Spanish, German, and Hebrew. In it he mentions that his father paid for the construction of Sapulpa's first temple, situated at the corner of Park and Thompson, as well as a dance pavilion at his one thousand five hundred-acre ranch.

17. Leuchtenburg, *Perils of Prosperity*, p. 1.

would have occurred even had there been no war in Europe at all. Its causes were partly in the advances of technology inspired and organized by business and partly due to changes in the cultural mix of the nation.

The technological marvels were the easiest to see and to understand. There were 1.7 million cars on the road and over 100,000 trucks, and the automotive industry had reached a production of 500,000 vehicles a year. Henry Ford, who confounded Socialists everywhere by instituting a minimum wage of $5 for an eight-hour day, simultaneously reduced the price of his Model T, launched at $950, to $290. The movies began to produce feature-length films that were to become more than a pastime, and almost a passion, for millions. The Yale Bowl, seating eighty thousand, was inaugurated; baseball, pugilism, and other professional sports became immensely, hugely popular. So was dancing, and the new dances. These included the fox trot and the bunny hug, the one-step and the tango, to syncopated music. The results were described by one critic as "a substitute for the Turkish bath and the masseuse."[18]

Some of these were changes; some, symptoms of change. Added together, they constituted a great shaking of the traditional manners and customs of the country, and although none can trace all the strands of these changes, in the overall novelties owed much to the polyglot population that was rapidly outnumbering the older American families. By 1900, when the country had a population of 76 million, 26 million of these were the children of foreign parents and 10 million had been born in a foreign country. In the fourteen years between 1900 and 1914, the nation had received over 14 million more immigrants.[19] That meant that on the outbreak of World War I, a little over half of all Americans learned what they knew of American history from the schools, or the newspapers, or the movies, or books—but not from the recollections of their forebears. That had a subtle but real influence on the nation, and on the fact that its behavior was increasingly difficult to define.

Even so, the changes might have come more gradually and been less disruptive for the nation, had the European war ended as the Germans planned, after their lightning strokes. The von Schieffen Plan, drawn in 1905, was relatively simple. It called for a holding action on the Russian front and concentration upon France. The Germans were to attack in force through Belgium, whose borders with

18. Dulles, *United States Since 1865*, p. 221.
19. Ibid., p. 225.

France were relatively undefended, but whose borders with Germany held fortresses then considered impregnable. The Germans had monstrous new guns that reduced those fortresses to rubble.

By the end of August, 1914, two million Germans had marched through Belgium and were swinging south toward Paris: the heart, nerve center, and soul of France. At that point the relatively small German army on the Russian front, engaged at Tannenberg by a huge Russian force, appeared in danger. It was extricated from that peril by a double envelopment "worthy of Hannibal," and achieved victory. While that victory was in doubt, an impulsive staff officer in the West dispatched two German corps and sent them toward Tannenberg, weakening the immense right front of the German western army: the ones needed to swing around Paris. The Germans therefore shortened their swing. The British, who had troops with the French, nevertheless withdrew in the face of what appeared inevitable. The French government fled from its capital. The French forces remaining, however, detected an opening left by the German change of plan. General Ferdinand Foch, following the French army mania for attack, and the orders of Marshal Joseph Joffre, attacked. The battle of the Marne was the result. It was one of the bloodiest and most terrible battles ever fought in all the history of the world—and it halted the Germans.

In effect, the war in Europe, at the end of the first month, had reached a stalemate. Both the German and the French armies dug the strange network of ditches known as *trenches*, and the eerie barrier between them called *no man's land* came into being.[20]

The British decided to blockade central Europe. They mined the North Sea; forbade any vessels to carry goods either to the Germans or to neutral nations without British approval; and forced all merchant vessels, including American, to endure search or possible seizure.

At one time similar action by the British had provoked a war with the United States. In 1812 the Americans were not inclined to be forced to support any other nation's policies. But in 1914 the sympathy of the upper reaches of the American government, and that of many other Americans, was with Britain. France was a different matter; the French did not emigrate in any great numbers to the United States, their language was different, and their customs were viewed in a suspicious light. But their courage in battle evoked a new feeling of admiration for the French. In addition, the Belgians had the nation's

20. Robert Leckie, *The Wars of America*, 2 vols. (New York: Harper & Row, 1968), 2:76–85.

sympathy, and the Germans, who were now being accused by the British of bayoneting babies before their mothers' eyes, were rapidly becoming unrecognizable.

In addition to atrocity stories, however, the British and French sent a stream of war purchase orders to the United States. They needed supplies, food, trucks, goods, commodities, and products alike. These orders had the effect of lifting the depression and quickening the nation's economic activities.

No region remained outside this stream of revived prosperity. In Sapulpa, Cushing, Healdton, and other oil towns, the pace visibly quickened though the price of crude oil did not at first improve very rapidly. One firm that moved to buy leases, acreage, and wells, and to drill with noticeable expertise, was called Roxana. It was, though only the sophisticated knew it, an arm of the Royal Dutch Shell which—since the oil fields of the Nobel and Rothschild interests in Russia were now cut off from the world market—remained the greatest global competitor of Standard of New Jersey.[21]

The first and most important war commodity that began to flow toward the Allies was oil. Britain, which had the world's largest tanker fleet in 1914, was pleased when it was augmented by tankers owned by Standard of New Jersey, Atlantic Refining, Gulf, Sun, Texas, and Vacuum, the largest U.S. firms.[22]

The Allies needed all sorts of other commodities, weapons, goods, and products as well. But they learned, as did many alarmed Americans, that the immense and advanced industries of the United States had forged ahead while the military had remained rooted in concepts ancient a generation before. A good rifle, the Springfield, had been developed, but the country lagged behind the French in creating field artillery and had no standard machine gun. American factories grew heavy with orders from France and Britain for metal products, chemicals, and explosives, while its own military was caught, tied, and virtually helpless in the hands of Congress.

In Europe millions of men from France, Germany, and England were caught in a different sort of situation, similarly beyond their unaided powers to resolve. The machine gun froze the front. In effect, it would destroy attackers at a time when offensive weapons, except

21. The Royal Dutch Shell was the result of an international merger between Shell, founded by Marcus Samuels, and Royal Dutch, managed by Henri Deterding. It pioneered the production of toluene—TNT—from oil. In World War I, its fleet of seventy tankers was chartered by the British government, with which it worked very closely. Roxana's founding president on the scene was Marcus Abrahams, nephew of Samuels.

22. Harry F. Williamson, Ralph L. Andreano, Arnold R. Daum, and Gilbert C. Klose, *The American Petroleum Industry: the Age of Energy, 1899–1959* (Evanston, Ill.: Northwestern University Press, 1963), pp. 266–267.

for long-range cannons, had not been developed. The generals, spotless in their boots and medals, settled back in chateaus to study their maps and receive, impassively, dispatches describing the deaths of thousands who achieved only small advances in the trench war that developed.

Life in the United States might as well have been on a different planet, as far as the average citizen was concerned, in comparison to the European war. Billy Sunday, a former baseball player turned evangelist, attracted immense crowds who delighted in the colorful way he intermingled his efforts with traditional exhortations. "D'you know what a décolleté gown is?" he would ask, "It's a dress with a collar around your waist."

In the spring of 1915, in Havana, in a ring at a racetrack the world's heavyweight champion Jack Johnson lost his title to a giant former cowboy named Jess Willard. That exchange took place in the twenty-third round when Johnson slowly sank to the canvas. As the referee counted him out, he raised one huge arm to shield his eyes from the blazing overhead sun. That provoked a memorable series of disputes that lasted for months.

It was only one dispute; the nation seethed with others. D. W. Griffith enraged liberals in the North and delighted southern regions with his *The Birth of A Nation*, based on Thomas Dixon's novel, *The Clansman*. The movie evoked violent reactions and provided serious observers into a startled recognition of the power of the medium. That was not lost on propaganda groups; Hollywood began to burgeon with films in which goose-stepping invaders landed and took over the country.[23]

These images juxtaposed oddly against the popular comedies of Mack Sennett, who found a new star in Charlie Chaplin. Chaplin eclipsed all competitors. *Photoplay* magazine said, "He has become a national habit."

Yet the art—especially the popular art—of a nation is like its subconscious. The images it projects may be jumbled and incoherent, but they are reflections of a nation's thought.

On May 7, 1915, a German submarine torpedoed the well-known passenger liner *Lusitania*. It sank with 1,924 aboard, including over a hundred United States citizens and a number of infants. The event serves as a sort of milestone in American reaction to Germany's role in

23. Reinhardt and Kintner, *Haphazard Years*, p. 62. The authors also cite, in a footnote, two films of this sort that gained large audiences—*The Battle Cry of Peace* and *The Fall of a Nation*—and Hudson Maxwell's best-seller, *Defenseless America*.

the war. The Germans had specifically warned Americans not to travel on the *Lusitania*, which—although British—flew an American flag and was suspected of carrying munitions. That warning, however, paled beside the violence shown to unarmed civilians, which struck most Americans as an act of barbarism. Many observers believe American neutrality began to waver because of the sinking of the *Lusitania*.

In reality that neutrality had already been eroded. It was undermined, almost from the start of the European war, by American industry which moved to fill Allied orders. In order to fill these orders, which grew very large very quickly, it was necessary for industry to borrow money from the banks in order to pay for the expense of hiring people, adding new machinery, and filling the orders.

By the time the *Lusitania* was torpedoed, the nation had already become a silent, unofficial partner of the Allied war effort. Secretary of State William Jennings Bryan, whose hatred of liquor and whose pacifism had combined to make him unpopular with metropolitan groups although he retained his following in the hinterlands, was one of the few at the top to believe this trend was wrong. When the *Lusitania* was torpedoed, Bryan urged the President to blame the British blockade equally with the German submarine tactics. The President refused, and Bryan accused him, or at least some in the Cabinet, of taking sides. That led in short order to a parting between them and Bryan resigned. He launched a countrywide campaign for peace. It brought him derision from the press; some newspapers portrayed him as a coward—but he persisted.

By the autumn of 1915 the impasse that Bryan had foreseen developed. "Money," he had told President Wilson, "is the worst contraband of all because it commands everything else."[24] The French government needed money; the British government could not afford to support it. Both turned to the United States, and President Wilson, whose inner thoughts were shared only with his personal advisor, Colonel Edward M. House, gave his consent.

The British and French had asked for $1 billion, a sum that seemed nearly inconceivable at the time. The figure finally reached was $500 million. Final papers were signed in the offices of J. P. Morgan & Company, the American channel for investments to and from Britain. The money itself was provided by the American banks; repayment was guaranteed by the French and British governments. The sequence is interesting because it has often been repeated since. The money would be lent the two governments, who in turn would use it to pay for orders of war materiel purchased from individual American firms.

In effect it moved the United States government, as well as im-

24. Leuchtenburg, *Perils of Prosperity*, p. 17.

mense sectors of its private industry, into the position of partner and provider to the Allies. The nation therefore had an immense stake in an Allied victory.

By early 1916 the boom was widespread. More money was in circulation than at any time anyone could recall. Prices went up, wages went up, jobs opened on all sides. One result was that women began to go to work in industry, and to appear in business offices in larger numbers than ever before. Stores were crowded; firms reported record sales of virtually every article and commodity.

In Sapulpa, where the price of oil had soared because of its war-time usefulness, more oil was discovered as drilling continued. The Cushing field extended for over thirty miles, all productive. Its output was to amount, in a few years, to almost a fifth of all the oil of the United States.[25]

The region therefore was in a position to benefit from every aspect of its economy. In such a time real estate, which is always responsive to the economy, made a great leap forward. JB not only ended his job with Max Meyer but was able to take advantage of a special opportunity, which in itself showed how a shortage of labor had arisen, at a time when everyone seemed able to buy everything.

The Buick agency in Sapulpa had ordered forty cars from Flint, Michigan, and had no way to bring them to Sapulpa. The railroads were overloaded; there was a railroad car shortage. No men were interested. Customers in Sapulpa were waiting; the forty Buicks were sitting, all paid for, in Flint. The agency owner turned toward boys of JB's age, and the word went through the high school. JB was among those eager to travel; he had never been more than twenty miles away from home in his life.

The boys received a railroad ticket to get them to Flint. Once in that city, staring at all that appeared, they each got behind the wheel of a new Buick and headed, in a long caravan, for Sapulpa. The cars had two-wheel brakes and the roads were incredibly dusty. As the caravan proceeded the drivers in the rear learned, the hard way, the meaning of the phrase then popular: "Eat my dust."

Rains were worse. Then a car could sink down to the hubcaps, and great efforts were necessary—including the use of horses—to extricate it. The trip back to Sapulpa, therefore, was a test of endurance. The roads were so bad the cars could only go about twenty miles an hour, but to JB it was a great and glorious adventure. He was with

25. Rister, *Oil! Titan*, p. 124.

other boys. They received no pay, only expenses. They drove the cars for the joy of it. It was a time when driving was considered a sport.

As so often happens, that adventure whetted his appetite. He asked his father for permission, and then traveled to Palmer, Texas, to see his Uncle Bud.

Uncle Bud, whose proper name was Andrew Jackson Saunders, had left Tennessee with Joseph Benjamin Saunders in the 1870s. He had stopped at Palmer and remained there, and though letters had been exchanged for years, young JB had never actually seen his uncle.

JB arrived at Palmer late in the evening. It was a town of three or four thousand people, judging from its appearance. He asked directions and was immediately told where Mr. Saunders lived; everyone knew him. The boy rang the bell and it was opened by a man, neatly combed and polished, dressed in a dark suit, a white shirt, and a tie. Young JB was surprised; he had expected someone who looked more like a *Texan*.

He stayed a week and in that time learned his uncle was an original. He was the constable, and kept a sharp eye on law-breakers. He was a preacher, and would ascend the pulpit on Sundays. He was the postmaster, and kept track of outgoing and incoming mail. He was also a storekeeper. From these varied vantage points he knew the people of Palmer in terms of law, religion, their external connections, and their shopping habits. He had never married, and the usual legend of an early, unrequited, and unforgotten love affair clung to him, but he had made himself the father of the town.

JB returned to Sapulpa, his curiosity regarding his uncle Bud satisfied on the surface. Beyond that, he was to be forever puzzled by the vast difference between his father and his father's brother.

As young JB sat in the coach car of the train carrying him back to Oklahoma from Texas, retracing—in 1916—the journey his family had made years earlier, he felt the excitement of the times. The landscape through which he traveled was being transformed by the boom attendant on the war in Europe. The price of cotton and wheat—two commodities the farmers of Texas and Oklahoma excelled in producing—had soared to record levels. Every region was improving its roads, and there were 3.5 million cars in registration; a new one cost a little over seven hundred dollars.

Employment had surged remarkably; jobs were open on every

hand. The factories clamored for people; even children—child labor was then legal—flocked in response. Young JB could no longer endure the minor jobs he had held part-time; he determined to do a man's work, at least during the summer.

Lyman Latimer, who worked for the Prairie Oil & Gas Company in Sapulpa, arranged for young JB to be hired by the Gypsy Pipeline Company out of its Watkins Station. He began at the bottom, a starting place then traditional for all young men without exception, no matter what their background. He joined the ditch-digging crowd and worked through the balance of the summer. It was hard but also exhilarating; there is something in physical labor that pleases the soul. In September he returned to school reluctantly; the Gypsy then found extra-hours work for him, measuring the contents of gasoline tanks.

JB's world in 1916 was one of hard work and simple pleasures. His family was a large one; his older sisters had suitors and his brothers had friends. They kept the big house crowded with visitors and conversation; in the evenings the parlor, as it was called then, would ring to the music of the player piano and the sound of singing voices. It was a time when poetry could still stir the nation, when the names of Joyce Kilmer and Carl Sandburg and Edwin Arlington Robinson were as famous and could thrill people as much as the feats of athletes and great inventors.

Yet across the ocean the continent of Europe was blazing as though in a great furnace, in which the shapes of nations were being altered into strange forms. The heat from that process shimmered in the air above the United States. It affected—and changed—the country.

By 1916 the Great War had enlarged almost beyond description. Britain had attempted to take the Dardanelles and failed at the cost of almost a quarter of a million men. The débâcle darkened Churchill's career for almost a generation. Russia had lost an estimated 3 million men and a hundred miles of territory, and the Czar's throne was shaken. Italy, Portugal, and Rumania had entered the war on the side of the Allies. Turkey declared war against Russia, Bulgaria had joined Germany. Huge western battles at Verdun and the Somme had cost the Allies 1.2 million men killed, captured, or wounded, and Germany 800,000.

Yet it was not battles alone that made the war different from all other wars. That change was due to propaganda, whose extension was made possible by the high-speed presses, the radio and telegraph, the telephone, and the other advances of industry. That made it possible for arguments, persuasions, rumors, excuses, and exhortations to be carried in such volume so ubiquitously that none could escape intellectual involvement. People hundreds and even thousands of miles from the battles were as caught in spirit as the soldiers themselves—in some respects, even more so. Front-line troops on home leaves in every combatant country were to discover their families locked in armchair battles, to their universal astonishment.

These arguments were reflected inside the United States, though in muted form. No group openly emerged in favor of joining the war; the overwhelming majority of Americans believed their nation should stay out of Europe. But a "preparedness" campaign arose. Theodore Roosevelt and Taft, two former Presidents, as well as Senator Lodge and other Republican stalwarts, were its leading voices. William Jennings Bryan, whose speeches best summarized the pacifist and neutral viewpoint, believed that preparedness was simply a cloak for those who desired to intervene.

His stance attracted many. There were few, after all, who could define the peril against which the United States was urged to arm. Certainly Germany could not have mounted or carried out an invasion of the country. Neither France nor Britain could have afforded the men and ships, supplies and arms, for such an inconceivable venture, even had they toyed with the idea of destroying their only source of support and supplies. Japan was a remote Oriental power limited to a region most Americans ignored; Latin American countries were limited and divided.

Yet the European powers were exhibiting fearsome war machines, and any peaceful nation had reason to worry about its long-range security. The United States, in contrast, had an Army of only 133,000 men, a Navy one-third the size of Germany's, less than one hundred obsolete planes and pilots, and a military establishment woefully underpaid and underarmed.[26]

Obviously preparedness was a timely subject at a time when the rules of international relations had been virtually destroyed, and the rules of war—once agreed upon by all European powers—had been swept aside.

The country moved toward the Presidential elections of 1916, however, in some confusion. The Republicans, who had raised the issue of preparedness, raised a standard that aroused few emotions: "America first and America efficient." Its leaders nominated Charles Evans Hughes, who resigned from the Supreme Court to run, and whose style was lordly and erudite. Former Presidents Roosevelt and Taft, who had reconciled their differences, campaigned ardently, and so did Senator Cabot Lodge. But these were men whose most popular days were in the past. The party they represented seemed to mirror that past. It was an older, traditional, and conventional America.

In contrast, the White House was occupied by the greatest orator

26. Reinhardt and Kintner, *Haphazard Years*, pp. 66–79.

the United States ever produced: a man who could thrill, arouse, and enthuse audiences as could no other. He headed a Democratic party composed of Populist-minded farmers, labor union members, dissident intellectuals, teachers, a remarkable number of journalists and intellectuals, and big-city machines who had organized and represented the ethnic groups known as New Americans.

The President had puzzled and alienated many with his lofty notes to the combatants of Europe and his tendency to grow caustic whenever his desires were thwarted. But he campaigned on a platform of both peace and preparedness, and the slogan his managers created was an adroit blend of undeniable fact and an implied but unstated promise: He Kept Us Out of War.

The campaign was not easy for either side. The nation's mood was difficult to read, and polls had not yet been invented. In July, 1916, someone tossed a bomb into a Preparedness Day parade in San Francisco that killed ten and left forty people wounded. Two labor leaders were arrested and charged with the crime.[27] In August a nationwide railroad strike was threatened, and the President intervened to suggest that Congress mandate the eight-hour day into law to settle the issue. Both these events indicated that pressures for change were stronger than the Republicans realized and that the President's attitudes were closer to those of the people.

Yet in the end the vote was so close that on election night the New York *Times* hailed the election of Hughes, and Wilson went to bed believing he had lost. It was not until noon the following day that returns from the Far West began to shift the scales, and not until three days was the nation sure that President Wilson had been reelected. The margin was only 600,000 votes out of 17.6 million.

By 1917 the president of the First National Bank in Sapulpa wrote a letter in response to a query regarding the city's future. "Never forget," he said in part, "that it sits in the midst of an oil empire 300 miles long and 100 miles wide, scattered over which there were on January 1, 1917, over 37,622 oil wells in operation, 4,121 of which represented the increase for the year, and that from these wells 126 million barrels of oil were produced. . . ." He then went on to describe "the automobiles, the sky-scraper buildings erected and being

27. Tom Mooney and Warren K. Billings. Found guilty after a sensational trial, Mooney was sentenced to death and Billings to life in prison. President Wilson commuted Mooney's sentence to life imprisonment because some of the trial witnesses later confessed to perjury. Carruth and Associates, *American Facts and Dates*, p. 400.

erected, the enormous bank clearings and holdings, the restless energy of the people," and to predict a future population of thirty thousand for the town.[28]

A similar optimism and tone permeated Tulsa and Oklahoma City, whose statistics were even more impressive and, for that matter, the entire enormous span of the United States in the opening weeks of the new year. Yet Mr. Benson's excellent letter remains as evidence of the great disparity that existed, then and now, between the close and detailed concerns of business, industry, and the average citizen, and the distant but nevertheless enormously influential activities of government, which in 1917 seemed so remote but were actually on the verge of changing every life, in every town and city of the nation.

The decisions being made in Paris, Berlin, and Moscow were no different in that respect than the decisions being made in Washington, D.C. During the last month of the year 1916, the Germans made a public peace offer. Berlin said it had no desire "to annihilate" and wanted to discuss terms. For a brief period, lasting no more than a week or so, the Great War could have ended, and all the peaceful dreams of all the Mr. Bensons might well have been realized, had not the President of the United States intervened.

His intervention sent the Germans back to unlimited submarine warfare, encouraged the French and British to reject the peace overture, and carried the country into the most fateful change in its history as a republic. "The United States was not in April 1917 swept into war," wrote the latest of the innumerable Wilson biographers. "She was not dragged into it by treaties. . . . She was not directly threatened. She made no calculation of probable gains or losses. Why then did she go to war? . . . I reach the conclusion that it was because Wilson so decided."[29]

Such a conclusion was, of course, beyond the nation to realize in the opening months of 1917; events crowded upon everyone, and all issues grew distorted, fevered, and irrational. Germany was portrayed not as a country at war for limited purposes, but as the enemy of all civilized values everywhere. The country was converted from neutrality and a desire to remain at peace into a patriotic fervor with astonishing speed. By the time the President spoke to Congress on April 2, 1917, arguments had virtually ended; all but irreconcilable minorities were united.

JB's older brother Earl enlisted, and so did all of his friends who could pass a physical. The recruiting stations were jammed; the United States entered the war—as had the Germans, British, and Russians

28. Sapulpa *Herald*, July 1, 1973.
29. Patrick Devlin, *Too Proud to Fight: Woodrow Wilson's Neutrality* (New York: Oxford University Press, 1975), p. vii.

almost three years before—with incredible enthusiasm. Young men marched to their train depots singing; older men took off their hats and stood at attention as they passed.

In such an atmosphere school paled into agony; jobs seemed unimportant. JB burned to enlist and said a dramatic good-by to his girl. She wept and went to Mrs. Saunders to commiserate with her, and JB learned that it was not always best to announce one's decisions. He arrived at the railroad station to find his sister Beulah, stern and cold, waiting for him.

"*You're* not going," she said, and led him ignominiously home.

Around them the country underwent a remarkable transformation. The President had determined on a conscript army two months before he requested Congress to declare war. The plan had been adroitly prepared. Instead of having men go from door to door to call those of draft age, the system employed was deliberately designed to appear "like going to the polls to vote."[30] All those of draft age, therefore, had to register, and local civilians would select those who would be called.

The machinery of this system was extensive and elaborate, and conducted with all the skills of advertising and persuasion formerly devoted to industry, by men who had rallied to Washington and were serving for one dollar a year.[31] It was set into motion on June 5, 1917, when every man between the ages of twenty-one and thirty registered. The day was made to seem a holiday for heroes; on June 20 numbers were drawn from a goldfish bowl by the Secretary of War in a vast lottery—a final step that was symbolically precise in reflecting the unpredictable fortunes of war.

By that time young JB was working off his inner excitement in a ditch, digging a trench with grown men as companions, for the Gypsy Pipeline Company. That summer work was hard and sweaty, but there was an exhilaration in it, as there is in all physical labor. He was barely sixteen and doing a man's work, but too young to register for the draft or to join an army being formed along principles that left volunteers far behind.

The draft was only one part of the overall effort, which flowed from the top down and was accepted with an enthusiasm remarkable in so diverse and unruly a nation. The President received sweeping powers, unprecedented in American history. In turn he placed Bernard

30. Sullivan, *Our Times,* 5:291.
31. It does not detract from their sacrifice, but recalls realities, to remark that their one dollar a year was augmented by fairly generous expense accounts.

Baruch over all industry, business, and commodities; Secretary of War Newton Baker over all American men; and George Creel over propaganda.

Creel was more than brilliant; in later years Creel's methods would serve as a guide for every propaganda ministry in the world. He sparked a wave of atrocity stories, exhortations, films, speeches, cartoons, and articles that created an atmosphere close to hysteria. "We hated with a common hate that was exhilarating," recalls military historian J. F. C. Fuller. "[I] remember attending a great meeting in New England, held under the auspices of a Christian Church—God save the mark! A speaker demanded that the Kaiser, when captured, be boiled in oil, and the entire audience stood on chairs to scream its hysterical approval."[32]

It was no wonder, in that atmosphere, that young JB felt unhappy because he could take no part in exciting events.

The United States was torn loose from its traditional moorings, but it was not alone. All the western world, with the exception of Latin America, seemed to go a little mad in 1917.

Madness was contagious, and not confined to any capital. In Berlin the response of President Wilson to peace overtures had altered the internal politics of Germany. The Chancellor and the Kaiser were, in effect, thrust aside by General Erich Ludendorff, who, acting behind the benign façade of Hindenburg, became the virtual dictator.

Unrestricted submarine warfare was one result of that change. Many observers put that decision among Germany's errors, for it provided the final provocation for the United States to enter the war, but that is a moot point. By the time the United States entered the war, Britain's losses to U-boats had grown critical. Admiral John Jellicoe believed, in fact, that Germany would win unless those losses were stopped.[33]

German diplomacy, although clumsy on the surface, also had a more skillful underside "for each of their enemies, France, Britain, Italy and Russia, the Germans had long since worked out a scheme for treason from within. The plans all bore a rough similarity; first, discord by means of parties of the far left; next, pacifist articles published by defeatists either paid or directly inspired by Germany; and, finally, the establishment of an understanding with a prominent political per-

32. Leckie, *The War of America*, vol. 2:119.
33. Walter Millis, *Arms and Men: A Study of American Military History* (New York: Putnam, 1956), p. 175.

sonality who would ultimately take over the weakened enemy government and sue for peace."[34]

Events in Russia made that country the first to provide an opportunity for such German selections to succeed. The government of the Czar had long been held in disdain abroad and at home, for both its denial of democratic rights and its disgusting persecution of the Jewish people.[35] Although Russia was allied with Britain and France, its government was not admired. In 1917 its numerous defeats in the field and disorder at home culminated, shortly after the United States entered the war, in the abdication of the Czar. The western nations hailed the creation of a Russian republic and a democratic Duma under Premier Aleksandr Kerenski.

Berlin, however, saw opportunity in this event. Ten thousand dollars of German money found its way to a longtime international Socialist left revolutionary called Leon Trotsky, who was in New York City.[36] More sums went to Zurich, Switzerland, where another international Socialist revolutionary born Vladimir Ilich Ulyanov and called Lenin was living with his wife and a small coterie.

Trotsky left New York for Petrograd. He was halted by Canadian authorities at Halifax, where his ship stopped, but at the intercession of the White House was allowed to proceed. His shipboard companions included muckraker Lincoln Steffens, financier Charles Crane, and a number of more obscure figures. All—including Trotsky—carried American passports.

Lenin left Zurich at about the same time, with thirty-odd companions, and traveled through Germany in a sealed train. He arrived at the Finland station—Finland was then a Grand Duchy of Russia—described himself as a Christian and a journalist,[37] and was allowed to enter his homeland.

By the summer of 1917, therefore, the elements that would, in unwitting concert, demolish the traditional world of Europe, with consequences as yet unknown and unfinished, were in place. They were President Wilson in Washington, and a cluster of revolutionaries in Russia. Between them, these two centers would send millions of people marching in new directions. They have not yet stopped.

34. Richard M. Watt, *Dare Call It Treason* (New York: Simon and Schuster, 1963), p. 138.
35. President Taft, while in office, had abrogated the United States–Russia Treaty of 1832 in part because of this persecution; in 1911 Woodrow Wilson denounced the Czar on this account at a rally in Madison Square Garden. Many other Americans shared his indignation.
36. Anthony C. Sutton, *Wall Street and the Bolshevik Revolution* (New York: Arlington House, 1974), p. 22.
37. Robert Payne, *The Life and Death of Lenin* (New York: Simon and Schuster, 1964), pp. 291–308.

None of this was within the province of people in Sapulpa, but like people everywhere else, they were to feel the effects. During the summer of 1917, therefore, the United States mobilized and every family changed its plans. If they had young men preparing to go to war, that was one change. Other changes were affecting business and industry and the rules of everyday life.

Great patriotic rallies were held, but the rules of patriotism were being changed as well as all the others. An Espionage Act was passed, and the offices of the Industrial Workers of the World were raided across the country. Liberty Loan Drives were launched; everyone was urged to do his bit.

On one level it sounded, and was, impressive. On another, it held a dark side seldom described in the newspapers. Young girls from good families in Sapulpa went down to the depot to see the troop trains and to hand out coffee and doughnuts; they were sometimes even more generous. The town was amazed to hear that some entertained the soldiers in the fields near the trains, and unmarried pregnancies—hitherto almost unknown—began to increase.

There was, in other words, a general loosening. Mencken, that great expert on the American language, made notes of new vulgarities that were beginning to appear in everyday speech.

In other words, it was wartime.

When the school semester opened in September, 1917, young JB had to go back to his classes. He went reluctantly, and he was not alone. School seemed very tame compared to the excitement coursing through the land. It permeated all levels, as one young teacher in the high school discovered.

She took her class swimming, and to her dismay they decided to shed their suits and go naked. She was unable to stop them; she sat on the bank and wept as they cavorted. When her superiors learned of the incident, she was dismissed for being unable to maintain discipline.

That created an opening, and Miss Leita Davis, who had a B.A. from the University of Michigan and an M.A. from the University of Pennsylvania, and who had cut short her work toward a doctorate to tend her dying father, was interviewed and accepted.

She had JB among her pupils, but only for a week. He told her he was quitting to go to work for the railroad. She and another young teacher with whom she had grown friendly, a Miss Nell Schultz, tried to talk him out of it.

61

He listened politely enough, but after a time asked, "How much are you getting?"

"One hundred a month for nine months," she said, and her heart sank. This was an argument she knew she would lose.

"I'll get one hundred forty-five dollars a month at the railroad," JB told her. "I don't think education pays as much as you think."

"Ordinarily I would have forgotten him," says Miss Davis, "but he would come by the school from time to time, and stop to chat with us. He liked Nell Schultz, I think—but he would talk to me as well."

Around them the town of Sapulpa was booming. Miss Davis thought "it was a very rough place," but her standards were fairly high. It was, mainly, raw.

Meanwhile the mobilization of men was in full swing, and a huge construction task confronted the authorities. "A regiment of infantry of 3,500 men required 22 barracks buildings—frame structures 43 feet wide, 140 feet long, two stories high—each accommodating 150 men; and 6 officers' quarters for the 200 officers, 2 store houses, an infirmary and 28 lavatories. . . ." wrote Mark Sullivan later.[38] He added that each cantonment held from 10 to 14 regiments, plus division headquarters, quartermaster depot, kitchens, laundry, recreation facilities, and a post exchange. Each cantonment held 1,200 buildings for 40,000 men plus rifle ranges, drill grounds, sewer, and water supplies.

"Sixteen such cantonments and sixteen camps of the same capacity using tents had to be built from scratch in two months' time."[39] These details were only the surface. Special schools, proving and testing grounds, embarkation points—all had to be constructed almost simultaneously with the mustering of a huge army with its attendant physical and mental tests, sorting, classification, assignment, and the like.

The Army then began to recruit workers as it had recruited soldiers. The thirty-two large camps, not counting lesser installations and offices, housing and surrounding facilities was a project, says Sullivan, "second only to the Panama Canal." It was to cost one million dollars an hour for more than three months, and labor was to continue—virtually without ceasing—for the duration of the war.

JB decided to join that work force. He had not met with any strong objections from his family for dropping out of school and going to work for the railroad. It was not a period when education, or at least schooling, had become an American religion. And since he had been blocked from enlisting in the Army, and his parents had informed all

38. Sullivan, *Our Times*, 5:309–310.
39. Ibid.

recruiting offices in the region of his proper name and the fact that he was too young, they probably felt that it was not wise to thwart him altogether.

When he signed up to work on the camp projects, however, in company with several friends about his own age, he was surprised to hear his name called out a little later.

"Who is JB Saunders?" the officer said loudly, looking around.

"Here."

"You can't go; you're too young."

"How do you know?"

"Your mother called."

"If I get permission?"

"If you get permission you can go."

JB went to the phone and called home. When his mother came on the line, he told her that if he could not go with the construction crew, he was going to leave home anyway. Her resistance collapsed; he received her permission. His name was put back on the list. He looked around, smiling. He was sixteen, and he had, at last, managed to join the war effort.

CHAPTER FIVE

Youth

THE DAY COACHES were crammed with men sprawled across the seats, their legs stuck out into the aisles, their heads propped on duffel bags or suitcases. A blue haze that seared the eyes rose from their pipes, cigarettes, and cigars; a stench of sweat and unwashed bodies, tobacco and cheap whisky, clung in the air as heavily as a curtain.

The fourteen-car train lurched and bumped; the nearly sixteen hundred miles from Tulsa, Oklahoma, to Camp Eustis, Virginia, coiled and twisted past scenes that soon merged into an unheeded blur. Men strolled along the aisles, sometimes stepping carefully but as often unheeding where they trod, looking for familiar faces or stupid ones, to inveigle into a poker or dice game. Some were selling articles: items of clothing, bottles of whisky, a watch. Others seemed to be merely searching—examining faces as though taking some secret census of their own.

Their ages varied. Some had heavy mustaches; others were clean-shaven. Some were strays from the oil fields; others were inveterate drifters who had developed nearly professional skills in the art of collecting money by ruse and subterfuge; others were honest workingmen attracted by the security of a year's contract with the Army.

The train did not stop; no Red Cross ladies and pretty girls were waiting at the stations they passed to give them doughnuts, coffee, and cigarettes; they were not heroes. Nevertheless, in the eyes of the Army they were part of an immense contingent essential to the war. On other parts of the landscape, trains of as many as fifty cars holding workingmen were rolling, at the rate of twelve a day, toward one or the other of the thirty-two Army installations where 1.4 million soldiers would be housed and trained. Each of these installations was constructed by civilian workers hired by private contractors held to a fixed cost and a 3 percent profit, who worked under the Quartermaster Corps.[1]

Young JB's traveling companion was Chester Macklin, a minister's son who seemed determined to break every rule of civilized conduct and to challenge any man who entered his force field. Short but immensely built, Macklin wore a bandana wrapped around his head and a fixed, belligerent expression. That façade reflected a genuine inner violence; Macklin had countless fights as the train proceeded—and won them all.

JB himself did not escape problems. The train was dense with quarrelsome and difficult personalities. But he did not have to do much; Macklin protected the space around them as though it were a private domain.

They arrived at Lee Hall, Virginia, and then traveled to an area that had been selected by the naval authorities at Fort Monroe as a firing range. The Navy thought was to test big guns whose range was so extended that it was necessary to move inland a few miles. The Army then decided the area had possibilities for the handling of overflow troops pouring in to the Newport News region as an important port of embarkation. Ships were already carrying an estimated fifty thousand soldiers a month to Europe; the American Expeditionary Force under General John J. (Black Jack) Pershing was in full swing.[2]

As a result, the Army moved into the area and began to prepare facilities for what would, in time, become the largest transportation and training installation in the Tidewater area, and named it after Brigadier General Abraham Eustis, the first to command the firing of batteries from that site against the warships of the British in the War of 1812.

The entire area, in fact, reeked with American history. It was not far from where the original Virginia Colony had settled, and had been the scene of many Civil War encounters. Not far away the *Monitor* and *Merrimac* had held their historic duel in Hampton Roads.

But in the chill, rainy winter of 1917–1918, it was far from inviting; the Virginia landscape has its dreary aspects. Shortly after he

---

1. Sullivan, *Our Times*, 5:309–311.
2. The nickname came from his having commanded a black regiment in Cuba, and was almost ludicrously inapt. In person he was gray, hard, and rock-like. He seemed born to command. "No American soldier since Washington so thoroughly dominated an American war," says military historian Robert Leckie in *Wars of America*, 2:111.

arrived, young JB was the victim of the sort of joke then considered, on lower levels, hilarious. Someone muttered something in the dark and handed him, carefully cupped so he could not guess, a lighted cigar.

That sent him to the infirmary with a badly burned hand for several days. When he emerged, he was assigned to a gang building a railroad spur line to the James River. When they completed that task, they had to build a pier on the river shore, and JB learned, as did his companions, the meaning of the name *Tidewater*. The river came up over their boots when the tide was in, and left them working in sticky, ankle-deep mud when it retreated.

His pay was one dollar a day. At the end of the month he could expect to receive one ten dollar and one twenty dollar gold piece.

They lived in wooden-floored tents raised two and a half feet from the ground by uprights; when they stepped out in the morning it often was into pools of water—Virginia is rainy. The camp water had a high mineral content that gave everybody the trots; lines of men making their way to and from the rows of outhouses was one of the first sights JB encountered.

There were many other novelties. The camp was the scene of feverish and inveterate gambling. Certain tents were devoted to this activity; JB learned that the man who owned the lantern that shed a light on the night games also cut the pot.

He joined the play; it was fast and rough. Kneeling in a dice game, he rolled a four—a hard point—and a man behind called, "I fade you." After he rolled the point and looked around, the shouter had himself faded into the night, leaving JB with only his own money left on the floor. After that he paid no attention to shouters; he waited until the money was placed within reach.

Town was another story. Newport News was a major embarkation point seething with soldiers, sailors, marines, and military and local police. Its raunchy Red Light district was heavy with venereal disease, the worst sorts of prostitutes and pimps, saloons reeking with violence, thieves, gamblers, and storekeepers whose shoddy goods were priced as high as possible.

Despite the fact that the manufacture of whisky was legally halted, there seemed enough to drink to float the nation from its moorings.[3] JB, inclined toward carefulness, did not drink much, but he became a popular companion on trips to town because he would help steer his buddies safely back to camp.

3. The government had decreed the end of whisky manufacture on September 8, 1917, as a wartime measure, to save grain.

Paydays were especially ebullient. Then the loan sharks would stand beside the paymaster and, as each man answered to his number, would extend their hands to their debtors. A railroad caboose would be converted into a gambling den; those who entered the play were winners of smaller games through the preceeding month. JB learned to become one of these—to estimate the odds on a number in dice in milliseconds, and to gauge the firmness of a man making a raise at a poker table without conscious thought. He had joined a rough world, but it was not too rough for him; its lessons were within his grasp.

On the other side of the world, in a nation so far removed as to be incomprehensible to those raised in the American experience, other people were learning far rougher lessons of a sort not seen since the French Revolution. Like its great prototype, the Bolshevik uprising in October was led by men unknown to most of their countrymen, whose lives had been spent in obscurity. They had returned to Russia after years of exile with German assistance; how much German assistance was responsible for their remarkable ability to launch newspapers, fund expensive propaganda efforts, and arm and support their followers, remains—and will probably always remain—unknown.

Germany's efforts to subvert the governments of its enemies in 1917 were, however, far-flung. One tentacle touched Sir Roger Casement, who was expected to lead an Irish uprising. Sir Roger was arrested and hanged, but the Uprising proceeded without him. Another tentacle reached deep into France, penetrated the Chamber of Deputies, was in part responsible for mutinies in 68 out of 112 French army divisions, was barely suppressed by Pétain and Clemenceau, and was hidden from the world only by wartime censorship.[4] But it was only in Russia—a nation whose armies the Germans could have defeated in any event—that the revolutionaries secretly aided by the German high command became successful.

It was difficult for most of the world to understand what happened. The Czar had abdicated, and the creation of a democratic Russian government had been hailed by President Wilson, much of the press of the western world, and intellectuals everywhere, especially since the Kerenski government pledged to continue the Russian war effort against Germany and Austria-Hungary. The Bolsheviks, however, promised to end that effort and, in fact, all alliances. In that, as in

4. Phillip Knightley, *The First Casualty: From Crimea to Vietnam, the War Correspondent as Hero, Propagandist, and Myth Maker* (New York: Harcourt Brace Jovanovich, 1975), p. 103.

The entire account is brilliantly described in Richard M. Watt's *Dare Call It Treason*.

other aspects, the new Bolshevik government revealed its leaders to be not only new men come to power, but men with new ideas. Rummaging through the files of their predecessors, the Bolsheviks exhumed, copied, translated, and distributed every secret treaty made between the Allies regarding their postwar expectations in terms of territorial advances and trade gains over the Germans and the Austro-Hungarians in the case of victory. These documents revealed the Allied propaganda, which had claimed a war in defense of liberty, to be deceptive and hollow, and injured the credibility of every Allied government except the United States.[5]

The effect was dramatic. Whatever the reasons that brought the powers of Europe to war—and there was little doubt that the Germans were after territory and trade advantage, as were the Allies—knowledge of these motives alone could not stop the war. Fighting continued but the purposes of the conflict were clouded. Statesmen everywhere were appalled at the Bolshevik action and wondered how relations could be established with men so indifferent to the traditions of diplomacy. Only one man in high position, however, took their evidence as proof of perfidy, instead of as disclosures that all the Allied leaders were attempting to tend to the interests of their countries. That man was Woodrow Wilson. The Bolsheviks knew that wars were fought for power, but the President of the United States believed they should be fought for ideals.

While the American President pondered these matters, the Bolsheviks promised the Russian masses peace, bread, and land of their own. Shrouded from the rest of the world by distance and wartime propaganda, they proceeded to issue deafening propaganda about democracy, but where persuasion failed they were quick to resort to methods as direct, brutal, and bloody as those of Robespierre and his Jacobins. Only the names of their committees differed. The Bolsheviks called their execution squads the *Cheka*.[6]

Such savage regressions could be expected in a land famous for its tyrants and lack of freedom, but it was surprising that echoes of a similar, though more muted, reversion appeared in the United States.

5. The disclosure came at the suggestion and with the help of Philips Price, correspondent for the Manchester *Guardian*. He translated and transmitted the information that Russia would have a free hand in Poland and France in the West; that Britain and France would divide the Arab world. The *Guardian* printed these details; the London *Times* refused to so embarrass its government at war. Later, Price worked in the Bolshevist Foreign Office. Knightley, *First Casualty*, pp. 149–150, 155.

6. Acronym for All-Russian Extraordinary Commission for the Struggle against Counterrevolution.

From the beginning of the war the moves of the Wilson Administration had persistently outpaced its critics by the speed of its decisions and its ability to rally support in the name of democracy and to suppress dissent as unpatriotic. But by early 1918 it was clear that the speed with which the Army had been trained, supplied with weapons, and sent overseas left much to be desired.

The fault was not in the caliber of American manhood, which was remarkable. "My brother Earl and all his friends from Sapulpa were marched out to the rifle range and tested," recalls JB, "and each one was graded as an expert marksman on the spot." That was not surprising in a land where many young men were raised in rural areas and were born with a gun in their hands.

What was surprising was the gap between American industrial efficiency and the condition of the American Army in terms of weapons and equipment in hand or available. The First Division sailed for France without steel helmets and had to be supplied by the British.[7] Shortages in the first year of the war scrambled the American effort; freight cars were jammed in knots that extended for miles outside Atlantic coast ports. That condition grew so serious the government officially took control of the nation's railroads for the duration.

The construction of Army camps, in which young JB took part in Camp Eustis, was one of the more impressive and outstanding successes of the moment. In early 1918 that huge undertaking was still underway but other problems escalated alarmingly. Almost 11 percent of the men drafted became deserters.[8] Army weapons were insufficient, and the AEF did not even have planes for its pilots to fly; it had to use European guns, planes, and field artillery, although by late 1917, fifty thousand American soldiers a month were landing in Europe.[9]

They proved a great surprise to the French and British, and even more to the Germans. Fresh, cheerful, remarkable riflemen, and unafraid of the enemy, they were like a tonic at the front. Yet the first Americans did not see action until November 3, 1917.[10]

By early 1918 complaints against the Administration began to mount. President Wilson had ignored the Republican party and all those for whom, for a variety of reasons, he had formed a dislike. These included former President Roosevelt, Senator Lodge, and many others. Demand rose that the White House form a coalition Cabinet

7. Reinhardt and Kintner, *Haphazard Years,* p. 87.
8. Sullivan, *Our Times,* 5:39. The figure cited was 337, 649.
9. Ibid., p. 348.
10. Dulles, *United States Since 1965,* p. 263.

and bring in all the top leaders of the land, and not simply his favored coterie.

In response the President appeared before Congress in January to discuss American war aims. He opened his remarks by saying, "The Russian representatives have insisted—very wisely and in the true spirit of modern democracy—that conferences be held in the open."

He then proceeded to go the Bolsheviks one step further by reading off Fourteen Points he said represented the war aims of the United States. They ranged from freedom of the seas to freedom of people everywhere, and in between left virtually no milestone of Utopia untouched.

That created immense publicity inside the United States and around the world. Lenin expressed himself as pleased, as well he might have been. Press reaction in Europe was less flattering. None of the war leaders wanted to be pinned to such remote destinations, but none could openly say so. Meanwhile, President Wilson asked George Creel, the head of the Committee for War Information, to summarize the Fourteen Points into words that could reach the average man. The result was Four Points. They were brief and simple, and proved to be like the fabled dragon seeds: they sprouted a zealot everywhere they landed. The first promised the destruction "of every autocratic Government in the world." The second promised "that every territorial question would be decided by the consent of the people concerned." The third declared all international relations would be on a civilized basis, and the fourth promised "an organization of peace . . . to check every invasion of right."

In the wake of this great propaganda coup, which resounded around the world, the President asked for virtual dictatorial powers in order to conduct the war. Some objections were raised, but the Wilson men said the powers were essential to check the inefficiencies that had given rise to complaints. They were passed by Congress, and the question of a coalition Cabinet and virtually all others sank beneath the surface, never to reappear.

President Wilson then formally appointed Bernard Baruch the financier in charge of all American industry; Secretary of War Newton D. Baker in charge of all American manhood, and George Creel—head of the Office of War Information—in charge of all communications. Between them this trio commanded the resources, the people, and the minds of the nation—in the name of the President.

In later years Mr. Baruch's efforts received much retroactive praise, and most of this was, then and later, deserved. Newton D. Baker also handled his huge authority with discretion and intelligence. George Creel has, unaccountably, faded from historical review, though he deserves a more considered look. Creel mobilized writers, illustrators, singers, actors, musicians—all the intellectuals and the artists—and turned them into propagandists as though by magic.

Creel's efforts sowed a war fervor unmatched in American history before that time and proved that President Wilson was an uncannily accurate prophet of his people. "Once lead these people into war," he said, "and they'll forget there was ever such a thing as tolerance. To fight, you must be brutal and ruthless, and the spirit of ruthless brutality will enter into every fiber of our national life, infecting Congress, the courts, the policeman on the beat, the man on the street."

The country was sent into hysteria by the high-powered methods of advertising, films, music, theater, and virtually every approach of mass merchandising. The product was hate, and it permeated the land, discoloring the minds of millions. Millions of German-American families were made to feel suspect and uneasy, their very names the targets of open attack. Schools banned the teaching of the German language; German music was considered "unpatriotic." Sauerkraut was renamed *Liberty Cabbage;* a Sedition Act was enacted that made it illegal to "talk against the American form of Government, the Constitution or the flag."[11]

In this atmosphere hundreds of persons were arrested; "more than forty were given sentences as high as twenty years on charges of obstructing the draft or otherwise interfering with the war effort. Eugene Debs, the Socialist Party leader, received a ten-year sentence for a speech in opposition to the war."[12]

In other words, America was altered. "The United States was transformed from a highly individualized system . . . into what was almost a great socialistic state in which the control of industry, life and purpose of the nation was directed from Washington. It was . . . amazing," wrote James Truslow Adams later in his *The Epic of America.*

Mark Sullivan, a newspaperman who had followed the careers of Presidents and whose acquaintance among the political leaders of the country was probably unequaled in his time, put the matter more bluntly. "It was an abrupt reversal," he wrote, "of the evolution that had been underway for centuries. Since Magna Carta, substantially all political change had been in the direction of the cumulative taking of power from the state for the benefit of the individual. Now, in . . . America, the state took back, the individual gave up, what had taken centuries of contest to win."[13]

11. Carruth and Associates, *American Facts and Dates,* p. 446.

12. Others who went to jail included the Socialist Congressman Victor Berger, anarchist Emma Goldman, and Alexander Berkman and Wild Bill Haywood of the IWW.

13. Sullivan, *Our Times,* 5:489–490.

Yet it was taking place in Germany as well. The most socialistic nation in Europe, the most advanced in terms of codified conditions for labor unions—many of whose leaders were in the Reichstag—the most progressive, the most welfare-minded of all the great powers, was under the dictatorship of Ludendorff in all but name, and none dared defy him. England was undergoing rationing and wartime regulations of great severity. The Bolsheviks were creating an autocracy more fearful than any ever known since the declining horrors of Rome. In effect, the United States was reflecting a wind that blew around the world, and, like the wind, none could trace its source.

It was, therefore, not the best of times in which to be young, but the young never know that; it always seems the best of times for those who are young. Young JB was, at Camp Eustis, in the process of learning the lessons of regimentation. Some were subliminal, some were a matter of observation, some were actually imposed upon him.

"I watched some recruits being lined up on the field," he recalls, "and one of them said something back to the sergeant. The sergeant knocked him down on the spot."

There were other sights. The infirmary was heavy with those who had enjoyed their trips to town too much; they returned from Newport News with gonorrhea and syphilis, both diseases whose treatments then were painful and uncertain. Others had gotten drunk and wandered down the wrong streets to wind up beaten and robbed; still others had become prey to semiprofessional gamblers and were in constant debt.

JB learned a number of lessons and applied them without conscious effort. On one occasion he went so far as to enter a tattoo parlor with some companions and even picked out his design: a spread American eagle to go across his chest. But by the time his turn came, a saving caution had returned to him, and oblivious to jeers, he changed his mind.

Much the same sort of sequence came over him gambling. He liked poker; it was a game that enabled a man, by skill and shrewd assessment of his competitors, to overcome the cards. Dice were unarguable: the numbers either fell or did not fall. But a picture card or two on top of a stud hand could overcome a deuce in the hole, if a player could keep his face still and his eyes bold. JB could do both.

He began to win, and was careful not to allow the fact of winning to lead him into carelessness. He began to accumulate some money; the wages at the camp were not high, but the aggregate amount of money that flowed was impressive. Young JB's store of cash began to grow.

He was mature enough to put it in the bank at Newport News, and to keep from bragging.

His brother Earl and others he knew from Oklahoma were shipped overseas, and the war in Europe became a matter of intense interest for JB and all other Americans.

In March, 1918, the Bolsheviks signed a treaty of peace with Germany. It yielded 34 percent of the Russian population, 32 percent of its farmlands, 50 percent of its industrial holdings, and 90 percent of its coal mines. Trotsky's reputation never really recovered from this ruinous peace,[14] but a civil war was underway, and the treaty of Brest Litovsk did not lack for apologists.

At the moment it enabled Germany to turn its full force toward the west. Its first blow fell against the British at Amiens. It started with a gun duel between 6,000 German field pieces and 2,500 British cannon. When it ended, the Germans charged and broke through. The British appealed to the French for help, but they conferred. General Pershing offered his four divisions—325,000 men—and that settled matter. The French and the Americans joined the British, and the Germans were halted.

A week later the Germans tried again at Ypres, and fell short. In May, 1918, the Germans tried north of the Aisne River above Paris and broke through, eighty miles from the city. By June they were at the Marne, fifty-six miles from the French capital, east of a town called Château-Thierry. The French government prepared to flee south.

At that juncture two American divisions stopped the Germans in a brief engagement at Château-Thierry and at Belleau Wood. Ordered to retreat by the French, they resisted at heavy losses, and checked the German advance.[15]

It was a turn of the wheel that many Americans and many Europeans never really understood. The great contribution of the United States in terms of money, provisions, machinery, commodities, and equipment had undoubtedly extended the length of the European war. Without that aid, neither France nor Britain could have held out against Germany.

But it was less understood that the poorly equipped and poorly provisioned American Army turned the tide of battle. The Americans did not accept trench warfare; they used the hunting and tracking abilities many of their soldiers possessed from childhood.

14. There remains a mystery regarding Trotsky's actual nationality. In his book *Wall Street*, p. 33, n. 22, Anthony C. Sutton says, "Trotsky's real name was Bronstein; he invented the name 'Trotsky' . . . Bronstein is German and Trotsky is Polish rather than Russian." His first name is usually given as *Leon*; however, Trotsky's first book, which was published in Geneva, has the initial *N*, not *L*. Trotsky spoke only two languages, German and Russian; his Russian was accented.

15. Leckie, *Wars of America*, 2:120–129.

"Sergeant York was not really unusual," says JB. "I knew a lot of men who could shoot just as well and were just as cool."

Ludendorff began to share that high opinion, but he did not stop his effort. In June, 1918, he launched a fourth offensive and the French responded with a mixed army of Moroccans, French, and Americans. The Americans broke the German drive and sent them back across the Marne. The German army began to retreat, and the British, with mixed forces including Americans, attacked the Germans at Amiens. The French joined, and the Germans were caught between shifts and were penetrated. Ludendorff had gambled everything; he had used his last reserves of fuel and all the force he could muster. Three days after Amiens, on August 11, he told the Kaiser it was all over.[16] He was wrong; there was worse to come.

A great chunk fell out of the fortress known as the Central Powers of Europe when Rumania sued for peace. Farther east another historic event of peculiarly sinister nature took place, and news of this occurrence reached the West tardily. The former Czar of Russia, Nicholas II, his Czarina, and their children were all murdered in a cellar by the Bolsheviks. This atrocity, which exceeded even the Jacobins in sadism, created horror among the discerning. The Bolsheviks, it was clear, were intent upon destroying not only the old order, but also the values that civilization attached to individual life.

By August and September, 1918, the Germans were in retreat, though an orderly one; it was in Berlin, Munich, Düsseldorf, and other cities that disorders were beginning to erupt. A revolutionary movement that called itself *Spartacus,* headed by a Deputy—Karl Liebknecht—and Rosa Luxemburg—Red Rosa—was spreading propaganda of the Bolshevik type. Red Rosa was, in fact, an old friend and comrade in the Socialist International of Lenin, Trotsky, and others.

In September an American army 665,000 strong attacked the Germans at Saint-Mihiel and the Argonne in a series of continuing engagements that were to cost the Americans 100,000 casualties. Another American army, far smaller, landed in Arkhangelsk, Russia, to fight the Bolsheviks away from huge supplies landed at that port to assist the vanished pro-Allied Kerenski government. Matters were growing scrambled.

In the changes that now began to pour forth, not even men at the heads of government could retain a clear view of events. The Germans sued for peace, but Wilson decided that before he would accept such an offer the Kaiser would have to abdicate, their wartime leaders resign, their armies retire, and all sorts of other conditions be met. The other Allies were aghast; the British—with a King and Queen of their

16. Ibid., p. 126.

own—had not fought to unseat either the German monarch or any others.

The American people, meanwhile, were in a confused condition. That was no wonder; one historian later wrote, "there was no more discreditable period in the history of journalism than the four years of the Great War."[17] Lies and truth had so intermingled that none could tell one from the other. The national lack of understanding of the pattern of immense, tangled events was overshadowed by a sudden and deathly disease that swept across the country. It had erupted, according to some medical authorities, among the 200,000 Chinese imported to France for war work and was a form of pneumonic plague that had raged in China since 1910. It swept through Germany to add its horrors to that nation's mounting difficulties. It appeared first in Boston, then in New York, and then almost everywhere.

Given the name *influenza*, which means "influence" in Italian and therefore was no name at all—it created "death lists three or four times as long as those of the Black Death in London, the terrible Plague of 1665."[18]

At Camp Eustis young JB watched some of his companions stricken in the morning and carried away, or helped into the infirmary. He recalls going to see them at night only to be told they were dead.

The tolls were, in all reality, frightful. Deaths rose to over two hundred a day in October, 1918. It raged through the Army camps and cantonments, and killed half as many soldiers as went overseas. A menace of more illnesses hung over these installations, where shortages of doctors, nurses, medicines, and coffins became acute.

Young JB had wanted to stay in the East; he knew the war was winding toward its conclusion and had learned that his brother Earl had already been signed for the Army of Occupation. He wanted to join that Army himself; the lure of Europe was as strong as ever.

The influenza changed matters somewhat; those who were able to travel could obtain a leave of absence. JB signed for his; his thought was that he would visit home and then return with the Army of Occupation.

He shopped for gifts for his family and all the friends he could remember; with $2,800 he felt fairly well-to-do. He recalls, among other purchases, some silk shirts at a haberdashery; it was not until after he reached home that he discovered the collars and cuffs and the fronts of the shirts were silk, but the rest were of cotton. He had been cheated; he was experienced enough to shrug.

17. Arthur Ponsonby, *Falsehood in Wartime* (London: George Allen and Unwin, 1928), p. 34.
18. By the time it ran its full course, the influenza carried away between 400,000 and 500,000 American lives—far more than the 81,000 who died on the field of battle. Sullivan, *Our Times*, 5:652–654.

He took the series of trains that were necessary to carry him from Lee Hall, Virginia, to Sapulpa, Oklahoma. It was a long ride, but a train was the fastest and surest method of travel at the time, and that made it endurable, even pleasant.

He landed, to the delight of his parents, sisters, and friends, at home on the evening of November 10. It was cold in Oklahoma, but it had been cold in Virginia, also. The next morning he decided to go downtown; his mother warned him to wrap up well. It was Armistice Day, November 11, and he wanted to share it with his friends. They were, as always, in the pool hall and the barbershop, where he got a haircut. He recalls having a sandwich and a malted milk, and playing a little pool for two bits a game. By three o'clock in the afternoon he was back home in bed, seriously ill. The influenza had caught up with him.

CHAPTER SIX

Back Home

ALTHOUGH DOCTORS attended the sick and nurses did their best, there was no specific treatment, no known cure, and no settled method for coping with influenza. Young JB huddled beneath blankets and felt his strength ebbing.

At a late hour a boyhood friend, Bodie Warren, came by to see him. Warren had a bottle of whisky. He pulled it out, uncorked it, and thrust it at the sufferer. JB took a long swallow and felt the impact. Warren grinned, drew his chair closer, and began to talk.

JB does not recall the balance of that night very clearly. He tossed in a fever sent soaring by whisky, and recalls breaking out in a heavy sweat. Warren kept talking and shoving the whisky at him; he recalls gulping it down repeatedly. Toward morning he fell asleep and Warren left. Dawn arrived and JB awoke to discover that he felt immeasurably better. He credits Warren with having saved his life, for he began to mend at once.

He may have been right about the whisky; it was a remedy used for centuries. But if so, it was ironic, for the Eighteenth Amendment, which did not actually forbid anyone to drink, but made the manufacture, sale, and transportation of liquor illegal as far as the people were concerned, was on the eve of becoming the law throughout the land.[1] It would not be the first time that a civilization had attempted to outlaw liquor; the Moslems had accomplished such a decree, but they

1. The Eighteenth Amendment was declared ratified on January 29, 1919, to become operative January 16, 1920.

had supplied an alternative solace in the form of religion. The Americans had no alternatives in mind, though church groups were in the forefront of the Prohibitionist movement.

Prohibition was only one of the changes rushing upon the world in the wake of the Great War. These changes affected every nation and every government. In Washington President Wilson learned, briefly, that his virtual dictatorship was at an end when, on the eve of the November elections, he asked the voters to return a Democratic majority to the Senate and House. "If you want me to be your unembarrassed spokesman abroad . . ."

The request outraged the Republicans, with good reason. No President—not even Washington—had received such overwhelming support from his political rivals as had Wilson during the war. Now it was clear he intended to resolve the peace alone. The Republicans trumpeted their indignation to good effect; the voters returned a Republican majority for the first time since 1912. It was not clear the President understood the import of that reaction; his mind was intent upon Paris, where he planned to negotiate in person. But Senator Cabot Lodge, who was once again head of the Foreign Relations Committee, was not a man it was wise to snub.

Unheeding, President Wilson selected his peace delegation without bothering to discuss the matter with the Senate. He chose his confidant Colonel House, General Tasker Bliss, Secretary of State Robert Lansing, and a diplomat rumored to have once voted Republican, named Henry White.

Will Rogers, the Oklahoman who had made himself nationally famous for his quips, summed up the reaction of many. "There was so much argument about who was to go," he said, "that Wilson says, 'I tell you what. We will split fifty–fifty. I will go and you fellows stay.' "[2]

Most Americans were only too happy to stay. Their war had lasted only nineteen months, but they were as weary of it as any people could become. Speeches, flags, marching drums, and rhetoric had drenched them day and night to a sickening extent; they wanted to be finished with it all. Only the young, who mourned vanished chances for glory, and those whose lives were spent in total drabness, mourned the passing of events whose significance seemed beyond comprehension.

2. Sullivan, *Our Times*, 5:533.

JB was young; he longed to see the places about which he had read, and still had some idea of joining the Army of Occupation. In that desire he was in a distinct minority; most young men could not wait to be rid of their khaki. But JB had money; the sum he had won at Camp Eustis was burning in his pockets. He had no sooner recovered from his influenza than he was off again, this time to see his brother Earl, who was in that Army and stationed at Koblenz, Germany.

JB took the long train ride east, and a ship from New York to Europe. He made the crossing while former passenger liners converted into troop carriers passed his vessel in the opposite direction, bearing the doughboys back home to Fifth Avenue parades and demobilization. Once in Europe, JB traveled past scenes of devastation to Koblenz, found his brother amid the jumble of Army installations, and waited until Earl jubilantly obtained a leave. Then the two of them made their own trip to Paris.

They could hardly have chosen a moment, in the incredibly long history of that city, when it attracted more attention or was as crowded with strangers. The ancient world of Europe, which had for centuries provided mankind with its most variegated, rich, diverse, and soaring civilization, had been cracked apart as though by an immense, tectonic earthquake. From its newly opened crevices, creatures long submerged appeared to claim a hearing.

Arabs in their robes, King's hussars, bemedaled soldiers, top-hatted dignitaries, beggars, whores, thieves, and clerics jostled in the streets. JB and his brother Earl went to Place Pigalle and watched women dancing naked, drank the cognac that was sold as a potable, and stared at the sights and the streets.

It was not as much fun as JB had expected. His brother Earl had altered. "We had the same upbringing," JB said later. "We were raised in a firm Christian home with our own Bible reading, where we dressed for Sunday and behaved as well as we could. Earl had always seemed all right, but when I was with him in Paris I discovered that the war had changed him."

The war, in fact, changed everyone—and everything. The Kaiser boarded his cream-and-gold imperial train for the last time and rode into exile in Holland. General Ludendorff cowered in a Berlin boarding house briefly and, when the city erupted, scuttled—in a false beard and dark glasses—all the way to Sweden.

Prince Max of Baden, a world-famous Progressive, struggled in vain to hold Germany together, and lost when the German Navy mutinied at Kiel. The trade-union Socialists in the German Reichstag formed a council to take charge and announced a People's Republic, but they were immediately beset from the left by the Spartacus movement, which was in touch with the Bolsheviks of Russia. On the right, demobilized groups of soldiers wandered in bands, constituting another menace.

Similar divisions arose in Munich, the capital of the kingdom of Bavaria. Sailors created a People's Naval Division; returning soldiers rebelled against their officers and collected in dangerous groups. Kurt Eisner, a part-time newspaper drama critic and lifelong Socialist, unworldly, voluble, burning with grievances, and distinguished by a long gray beard and tiny pince-nez, orated from a balcony and aroused huge throngs.[3] Later, in the Mathäser Brauhaus—Munich's largest beer hall—Kurt Eisner was declared the head of a Bavarian Republic by an impromptu gathering of soldiers and "workers." King Ludwig III, informed he must abdicate, dutifully signed the papers and left the city by automobile, and the Wittelsbach dynasty ignominiously vanished from history.

To the south even larger demolitions took place. The great Austro-Hungarian empire—with its world-famous capital at Vienna and its twin at Budapest, with its carefully balanced quotas to placate its numerous minorities—split into half, and the halves split in turn. Charles I abdicated, ending six hundred years of Hapsburg rule; the Austro-Hungarian Empire, three hundred years old, collapsed as though it had never existed.

In Budapest the reins of government were held, briefly, by Count Mihály Károlyi, the wealthiest citizen of the country. In March, 1919, that power was seized by Béla Kun,[4] an agent of the Bolsheviks. He instituted their tactics of deliberate murder and terror, thinly covered by a program of slogans.

The balance of Central Europe, ranging through the Baltic countries to Russia, presented an even more mixed, tangled, and disorderly

3. Kurt Eisner, a native Berliner, was arrested and served nine months for writing an article against the Kaiser in 1897. He later joined the Social Democrats, and knew and was disliked by Rosa Luxemburg. In 1907 he deserted his wife and their five children, landed in Munich in 1910, and lived on the outskirts with the daughter of an old Socialist. In 1918 he was conspicuous in food and peace demonstrations and was imprisoned. He was released in an amnesty granted by Prince Max, whose overthrow he demanded.

4. Béla Kun was born in Transylvania, Hungary. He was a college graduate who majored in law and switched to journalism—a Social Democrat who embezzled party funds, was drafted into the Austro-Hungarian army, was made a POW by the Russians, and was converted by the Bolsheviks. He trained in Moscow, was sent to Hungary disguised as a Red Cross doctor and funded by the Bolsheviks. He founded the Hungarian Communist party in November, 1918. In early 1919 he was in jail; when released, took over the nation. His bloody reign lasted 133 days and was marked by atrocities. When it ended he fled to Moscow and worked for many more years as a Comintern agent.

landscape. The Magyars, Czechs, Slovaks, Croats, and other minorities of the dissolved Austro-Hungarian Empire struggled among themselves while each sent agents to Paris; similar scenes occupied Lithuania, Latvia, Estonia, Finland, and Russia itself, with its polyglot Ukrainians, Armenians, Georgians, and others engrossed in a civil war so extensive that Lenin and Trotsky were convinced the world was on the edge of universal revolution.

JB returned to Sapulpa loaded with gifts for his friends and family, with most of his money spent. He did not regret that; he had seen the region of the holocaust and learned more of the world. He came home convinced the Great War had been a catastrophe, and he was not alone in that opinion.

The President of the United States had played a role in that catastrophe still largely misunderstood—and misrepresented. The war could have been settled, and might well have been, in 1916, had Wilson not intervened. The effect of his intervention was to extend the conflict until it undermined the foundations of the major powers of Europe.

In their collapse, President Wilson chose to abandon the principles he had proclaimed, and to share in secret negotiations that ignored the rights of minorities and inflicted a vindictive peace upon the vanquished. He returned to his Washington office in June, 1919, to demand that the American people accept his plan for a League of Nations.

The Secretary of State objected because an effective League, such as Wilson described, would place the United States in a minority position and diminish its sovereignty. Senator Lodge, however, penetrated the League rhetoric, studied its structure, and decided it was essentially propagandistic. If some changes were made, he thought it harmless, but he preferred the final plan to be bipartisan. The President, who seemed to believe the League would solve every problem of mankind forever, declared no changes would be permitted by lesser men, and went on a campaign through the country. In the course of this effort the President made countless speeches; in most of them he misrepresented both the details and the powers of the League of Nations and the position of his critics. The Republicans sent two speakers to follow him, to correct his charges.[5]

In September, 1919, the President suffered a stroke in his train, and his trip was curtailed. On October 2 he suffered another stroke, and his wife found him on the floor of his bathroom in the White House. From then until his term of office ended, Woodrow Wilson

5. Senator Hiram Johnson of California and Joseph Medill McCormick, publisher of the Chicago *Tribune*.

was too enfeebled to properly manage the duties of the Presidency. He revived, from time to time; on one such occasion he refused to accept minor changes in the League of Nations agreement, and forbade his supporters in Congress to vote for them when the issue was joined. In the end, he chose to scuttle, rather than alter by a single sentence, an agreement he insisted would insure universal peace.

By that time the country no longer cared. Wilson had exhausted the patience of the nation, and despite the efforts of an army of propagandists, his figure remains enigmatic to many. Yet he left a mark. His wartime powers; the fervor of marching feet, bands, and bugles; the ability to call multitudes together; the power to issue edicts and decrees and to make rules for millions—all sank deep into the mind of the nation. The return to private life was difficult for some who had functioned as wartime "czars" over entire sectors of the economy and the lives of millions of people. Young Franklin D. Roosevelt sank back to relative obscurity as an Assistant Secretary of the Navy for the balance of the Wilson term. Mr. Bernard Baruch returned to private life and finance; he continued to advise Presidents for the balance of his long life. The Democratic party, which had soared to heights of power unknown in the entire life of the Republic, began to decline in popularity in tandem with the President.

The country, however, was relieved when the League of Nations was no longer an issue. Americans wanted no more of the great world, with its impossible quarrels and divisions. Ordinary life began to resume, but millions of people had to find new places, since their old ones had been uprooted or irremediably altered by the interruptions of government.

Young JB applied for a job with the Frisco Railroad and was hired at once. There were many men looking for work. A depression was underway, with all its attendant discomforts and high unemployment. But JB was a known local boy, preferred over strangers. He soon learned why. Conditions in the railroad yard, as everywhere, had become strange.

The back alleys and streets of Sapulpa were heavy with the human flotsam of the war. JB, working on the night shift from 11:00 P.M. to 7:00 A.M., walking down the dark street, heard a voice from the shadows.

"Come over here with your hands up," it said.

He walked over and the figure, face hidden behind a handkerchief beneath a dirty cap, ran expert hands over his pockets and ordered him to hand over his money. He had a twenty-one-jewel Hamilton, a valuable railroad watch, but the night was dark.

"You don't want that old Ingersoll, do you?" he asked, and the robber cursed and handed it back. Nobody wanted an Ingersoll; everybody wanted a Hamilton.

Similar incidents were frequent. A young boy walking near the yards was hailed from a dark doorway and, frightened, ran. He fell, skinned his knees, stumbled frantically to his feet, ran some more, fell again, picked himself up, and didn't stop till he reached the railroad detective's office. JB, working in the yard, saw that and fell into helpless laughter.

He soon discovered matters were too serious for laughter, however, for himself. Checking cars in the yard early one evening, he suddenly felt cold metal against his neck, saw a huge form looming out of the corner of his eye, and heard a deep voice rumble, "Douse your glimmer; I'll knock your head off."

JB bolted, fell, but kept going. Heart pounding, he ran into a carman with a gun. Another joined them, and the three searched along the cars, and even into the repair shed, but found no one. JB retrieved his pencil, pad, and lantern where he had dropped them, and then became aware of the cuts and bruises he had sustained in his own stumbling flight. He had, he knew, come very close to serious injury.

It seemed as though the world had darkened. A series of strikes swept the country, affecting railroads and transportation lines. A general strike was called in Seattle, and commuter lines were paralyzed in Boston and Chicago. The city of Chicago erupted in a wild race riot, and in August, 1919, over 300,000 steelworkers walked out. The resulting strike, led by William Z. Foster, a leftwing Socialist who would later become leader of the American Communist party, was marked by shoot-outs, deaths, woundings, and wild rhetoric.

In September the police of Boston organized a union, encountered resistance from their commissioner, and went on strike. The entire city was left without official protection, and to the horror of the nation, criminals appeared to take advantage of a thieves' holiday. The Mayor called for help and Governor Calvin Coolidge responded; all the striking policemen were dismissed and the force recruited new men.

These and other troubles were caused, in part, by a continued inflation that led, for the first time in the nation's history, to a "buyer's strike." Prices were, in fact, far beyond the ability of the average citizen to meet: shoes that sold for three dollars before the war were displayed at ten and twelve dollars; food prices soared. The government attempted to control the problem by fixing prices for bread, coal, and milk, and released wartime stockpiles to break the market. By November, through the action of the marketplace and not in response to these spasmodic and economically limited expedients, prices began to fall; merchants had to accept their losses and move their goods.

Many persons, however, believed there was more to the turbulent labor unrest than economics. On the eve of May Day, 1919, sixteen packages loaded with bombs were discovered in the New York Post Office, addressed to various public officials, including judges; throughout the country a search disclosed more. In June, 1919, the home of Attorney General A. Mitchell Palmer was wrecked by a bomb whose tosser was killed in the explosion; homes of a judge in Massachusetts and the mayor of Cleveland were similarly bombed.

It was in that atmosphere of disorder, fear, terror, and distress that the arrest of two Italian workmen, Sacco and Vanzetti, took place. They were charged with the murders of the guard and paymaster of a shoe factory in South Braintree, Massachusetts. Both were anarchists; the entire forces of the left launched in a campaign to convince the world they were innocent.

Life in Sapulpa was rougher and meaner than ever, and had grown far more cynical. JB spent a great deal of time in the pool hall; he had developed the habit of gambling at Camp Eustis and it was hard to shake, though he did not try very hard to shake it.

"I would bet on one pocket pool," he recalls, "and would sometimes have as much as five dollars riding on the outcome." That was high; his bets usually ran from twenty-five cents to one dollar.

Yet his life was not completely revolutionized, or he would not have become involved in the de Molays. That movement was authored by Dad Land, a thirty-third-degree Mason in Kansas City, who had grown concerned over the numbers of rootless adolescent boys who appeared in the wake of the Great War.

Land organized the de Molays along Masonic lines, and his pioneering efforts were aided in Sapulpa by Fred Verdun, who had the Ford agency. Verdun, who knew JB, called him in to become a master councilor and to assist the effort. JB was interested at once; he had already concluded that boys younger than himself were growing up in a worse atmosphere than he had known. Given a group of youngsters Verdun had collected, JB talked to them about their mothers and the respect they owed. The talk evolved, and he suggested that each boy take a flower home to his mother as a gift. The reminder of the debt of life they owed their parent, and the culminating gesture, with its inherent reconciliation and promise, proved remarkably effective and became known as the Flower Talk. As such, it became one of the integral steps in the de Molay program, and constituted an original and effective contribution to the creation of the de Molay organization on JB's part.

By early 1920 JB accompanied his group of boys, together with other groups and master councilors, on a trip to Kansas City, where Dad Land had robes and a prepared ritual for their formal induction into the Order of de Molay.[6] They were not Masons, being too young. But the de Molay organization and rites held the same fascination; their doctrines emphasized the brotherhood of man and the need for a moral order.

There seems little doubt, in retrospect, that the suggestion that he involve himself with helping younger boys and youths came at a very opportune moment for JB. The pool hall was not enough to hold his attention; he was uneasily aware that he was drifting. It was not that he was having any difficulty in earning his living; he had been promoted to bill clerk by the railroad, which paid enough for his needs. It was more that his life had no special direction, a fact that came inescapably to his own attention when he had to talk to aimless youths about theirs.

In this vaguely discontented humor he drifted by the Sapulpa High to chat with Miss Leita Davis and Miss Nell Schultz, his old teachers. They were busy; freshman enrollment was underway. But they were delighted to see him. "Nell began to prod him to come back to school," Miss Davis remembers, "and I mainly agreed."

They knew such a decision would not be easy. The enrolling freshmen were little better than children, and JB had grown into a young man. To their surprise, he agreed. They were greatly cheered. Miss Schultz had been at the school eight years, Miss Davis through the war. They had seen many changes. "Teachers left in droves," says Miss Davis. "The Board had to keep raising salaries to retain a staff."

They had, in truth, seen a silent revolution. Wartime inflation had sunk the American middle class as abruptly as though it had been torpedoed. "The purchasing power of the dollar," wrote Mark Sullivan later, "sank from a normal 100 to 45. Those with fixed incomes, who lived upon the returns from bonds, mortgages and rents . . . had

---

6. Named after Jacques de Molay, the last Grand Master of the Order of Knights Templars, who was burned at the stake in Paris on March 18, 1314.

85

become the 'new poor.' Their fate was shared by those who lived on fixed salaries, government employees, school teachers, college professors. . . ."

In that crunch Miss Davis and Miss Schultz were lucky both had private incomes to supplement their salaries. But they were different in other ways as well. Neither had entered schoolteaching for any reasons except the highest. They believed teachers were needed not to maintain the mediocre, but to discover, and to inspire, the gifted. They were not sentimentalists. "All the students were eager to go to college," says Miss Davis, "but very few had the qualifications." It was those few who made teaching worthwhile, and they watched with shining eyes as JB, sternly mature, took his seat in the junior class.

The nation was caught, in 1920, in a curious time-warp. The world had changed more than the newspapers could describe, let alone explain. There was some reason for this: the maps of the world were still largely covered with the red blotches that signified the holdings of the vast British Empire. That empire, in fact, had enlarged. In 1920 it covered Palestine and Egypt, two areas once dominated by the Ottoman Turks. French possessions had also increased in North Africa. The Dutch hold in Malaysia appeared as strong as it had been for the preceding four hundred years. The map of Europe showed changes that seemed to fulfill at least many of the promises of the Great War; the world family of nations had been enlarged from seventeen to twenty-six. Poland was independent again; Czechoslovakia had emerged; Latvia, Estonia, and Finland had been freed; Austria-Hungary had divided.

All of these changes were not accomplished in 1920 alone; the reverberations of the Great War took a long time to subside. Early in the year the Germans were given a list of their wartime leaders whom the Allies, or at least some Allies, wanted to arrest and put on trial. The Germans rose, in a paroxysm of national fury, and threatened to go back to war. The western leaders and press alike, stunned, dropped the subject. In the newly created Union of Soviet Socialist Republics—a name that was eventually to ring like a tocsin in the minds of the world—unbelievable horrors were underway; official executions were at the rate of one thousand a month,[7] and uncounted casualties of the civil war had risen into the tens of thousands. The revolutionary regime, however, was winning its struggle, and its leaders took time out

7. Aleksandr I. Solzhenitsyn, *The Gulag Archipelego, 1918–1956: An Experiment in Literary Investigation* (New York: Harper & Row, 1973), pp. 28–33.

to establish a Third International. Its purpose was to create, in a weird distortion of Calvin's famed effort at Geneva, a series of schools to train revolutionaries, whose task would be to subvert governments around the world, and to assist in bringing about the New World Order.

These matters were somewhat indistinctly reported in the western press; they were subject to hyperbole in some dispatches and soothing deprecations in others. Their credibility was discounted as millions of people came to realize that the atrocity stories of the Great War had largely been the inventions of respected journalists and leaders. The world began to discount newspapers and their reporters.

All that seemed of interest was the fiscal instability that affected the West: the loss of values and the disruption of trade, the immense debts that hindered capital plans and disrupted international credits, and the huge, inconceivable losses that affected individuals. These costs, which the Carnegie Institute set at almost $338 billion and ten million lives, had almost shattered civilization.[8]

Yet the people of the United States wanted to believe that everything could be put back as it had been. Toward that end the American government and many relief agencies launched a tremendous drive to send food, clothing, and medicine to Europe, under the leadership of Herbert Hoover.

But on the larger issues that worried the Allies, the Americans not only remained mute, but seemed oddly indifferent. Great Britain, which was owed more money than it owed, had been changed from a creditor to a debtor nation. The United States had transformed its industries, its agricultural methods, and its attitudes, but seemed unaware that it was the only great power left—it had little interest in the subject.

As a result, the President was allowed to remain in his sickbed; no Congressional movement was launched to replace the fallen leader. The nation drifted, and most people struggled to put their lives together and forgot the rest of the world.

The two major political parties met in the summer of 1920; the Democrats nominated James M. Cox, the governor of Ohio, and Franklin D. Roosevelt to head their ticket. The Republicans nominated Warren G. Harding, Senator from Ohio, and Calvin Coolidge, the governor of Massachusetts. Other interesting political maneuvers occurred. The Socialist party nominated Eugene Debs, who was still in prison, for President,[9] but the Socialist movement in the United States in 1920 was split between traditionalists and those, inflamed by the astounding success of Lenin, who wanted to emulate his example.

8. Sullivan, *Our Times*, 6:9n.
9. President Harding later pardoned Debs.

They formed the Comunist Labor party, complete with hammer-and-sickle emblem and raised-fist salutes.

Despite that evidence of unrest on what Theodore Roosevelt once called "the lunatic fringe," the majority of Americans wanted no more vast projects or soaring international goals. The Republicans campaigned, therefore, on what Harding called "a return to normalcy." There were sneers at his grammar; purists pointed out that *normality* was the proper word for a condition of being normal, but they were wrong. Most Americans knew exactly what Harding meant, and agreed. He was elected in a landslide that washed the Democrats almost out of existence.

By that time JB was accustomed to his new routine of work and school. He had obtained a second, overlapping job. He became weighmaster for the Western Weighing and Inspection Bureau. The yardmaster, J. J. Daly, whose favorable attention he had attracted, arranged to have the cars spotted for weighing set aside so JB could weigh them before and after school hours. His hours were shifted from four in the afternoon till midnight. Theoretically this left plenty of time for sleep, school, and study. But the times were erratic. His replacements did not always appear. It was a period of "railroad bums" who drifted from one line, and one job, to another. As a result, JB would often work two straight shifts. But he managed to attend an 8:30 history class promptly, and also managed to keep abreast of his studies.

That regimen was more difficult than it sounds—not in a physical or mental sense, but in a psychological one. In 1920 the intellectuals of the United States, always a discontented and resentful class, began to turn on the American culture in an amazing manner. Sinclair Lewis, whose first three novels had disappointed the critics, emerged with *Main Street*, in which the American businessman, proud of being a Rotarian, and of his income and home, car and standard of living, was made to seem synonymous with triviality, drabness and hypocrisy.

The novel created a sensation. Like all great caricatures, it contained truly recognizable traits, so cruelly distorted that many, after *Main Street*, regarded the actual small-town businessman with a certain residue of contempt. It launched a wave of imitators and greatly damaged the prestige of business throughout the land. Another wave of imitators arose in the wake of F. Scott Fitzgerald's *This Side of Paradise*, a novel about young people living for the moment in a world where all tradition had been shattered and all values lost.[10]

10. Garruth and Associates, *American Facts and Dates*, p. 454.

These mocking and bitter voices had great influence among intellectuals in the academy and the great cities. Their influence seeped into the movies, magazines, and newspapers, to sow cynicism among those leading hard-scrabble lives on weekly wages. Those, for the first time, comprised the majority of the population, living in cities, towns, and suburbs; the farm population had dwindled to less than 30 percent of the whole.

In Sapulpa, Oklahoma, even more immediate distractions were at hand. The city fathers had converted their canvas sign into an electric one, in which the legend Oil Center of the Southwest was distinguished by a flow of blinking lights that emerged in a miniature fountain over the *i* in oil, to spurt upward and fall downward like a gusher.

Situated in the very heart of the oil region, where new strikes were continuing to be made and new millionaries emerging from the numerous ranks of the hopeful, Sapulpa's population had burgeoned to more than twenty thousand. Its downtown district was marked by a number of good hotels, though their structures only rose about four stories high. But the city fathers of Tulsa had worked more shrewdly. "I was later told," said JB, "that about a half-dozen far-sighted men bought much of the downtown land of Tulsa. To lure newcomers they offered some of these sites to commercial establishments and to banks—free. In that way many businesses began to center their headquarters or their branch offices in Tulsa." He paused, and then added with a laugh, "The man who told me summed it in one sentence. He said the Tulsans put up some of their land and made the rest of it immensely valuable; the Sapulpans put up a sign."

Nevertheless, the war had made oil a crucial commodity everywhere in the world. Oklahomans kept rejoicing in the numbers of new strikes and fields that kept it in the front rank of producing areas in the country. Its boom towns continued to spring up, as though from the soil itself, bringing in the hordes made familiar in earlier times. The growth of the industry was in tandem with the huge increase in motor vehicles, which had soared to over ten million in the United States in 1920. Roads were being extended; the transportation revolution was coursing at full throttle.

Mansions, constructed by new oil millionaires, appeared in Tulsa and Oklahoma City. Osage Indians, who had been converted by the discovery of the Burbank field into one of the richest groups, on a per capita basis, in the world, astounded the nation with their profligate use of their new wealth.[11] On every side the struggle for the new black gold of industry surrounded him; it was a difficult time, psychologically speaking, for a young man to return to high school, and to stay

11. Ritter, *Oil! Titan* p. 195.

there. Yet, curiously enough, JB had no fixed goal in mind; no single, burning ambition in which education was essential. It was as though, like the country, his experience in the war years had been so overwhelming that he was attempting to return to the more settled pattern he had earlier known, while going through the motions of preparing for the future.

The country listened to the inaugural address of the new President, Warren G. Harding, on March 4, 1921, and almost visibly relaxed. It was Harding's misfortune, among many, to be unable to compose a direct sentence. His words, said William G. McAdoo in a famous sarcasm, "leave the impression of an army of pompous phrases moving over the landscape in search of an idea; sometimes these meandering words would actually capture a struggling thought and bear it triumphantly, a prisoner in their midst, until it died of servitude and overwork."[12]

The voters felt otherwise. They heard a great droning noise emerge from the new President which made little sense, but which left them as comforted as an organ concert. They turned back to their regular affairs with a sense of relief; the high drama of the democratic Wilson and all his glittering entourage, his professors and journalists, speech-makers and shakers, were gone.

Unfortunately there had been too many changes among the people to allow the nation to settle. A considerable migration—the first, but not the last—of blacks from the South to northern cities had taken place in the war years. These newcomers were welcomed when their labor was needed during the war. After the war their factory jobs vanished, and in the interregnum before business completed its tranformation, serious difficulties arose.

The blacks had settled into their own districts but appeared in other parts of town during the day. In Tulsa, Oklahoma, on the last day of May, 1921, a young white girl operating an elevator in the Drexel Building at Third and Main streets flew out, followed by a young black man. The girl claimed he had taken her arm and made advances, and she had hit him over the head with her pocketbook.

The incident, otherwise minor, was like a lighted match in a powder keg. The young black was arrested, but rumors began to course through the city. The newspaper reported that a carload of blacks drove up to the courthouse and fired several shots. Whites broke into downtown sporting goods and hardware stores and stripped

12. Sullivan, *Our Times*, 6:31.

them of rifles, shotguns, and ammunition. A large number of these whites attacked the black district on the "southern fringe of north Tulsa," near the Frisco tracks and Greenwood Avenue, and exchanged shots with the district until midnight. While the mayor called for the governor to send in the National Guard, the mob set fires and fought off the firemen who came in response.

A battle raged through the balance of the night. By morning it became clear that thirty-five blocks of north Tulsa had been burned to the ground; the scene looked as satanic as any seen during the war. Blacks made a last stand at the foot of Standpipe Hill; the National Guard mounted machine guns and sprayed them into submission.

Young JB was among the many who traveled near enough to the city to see flames during the night, and to hear shooting. Several thousand persons fled, in their cars, or on the Interurban, or in carriages, from the scene of conflict. He noticed that the newspapers attempted to play down the seriousness of the event, and the casualties.

"They said that only three whites and six blacks were killed," he remarked later, "but it seemed to me, and to most of the rest of us, that a great many more died. I was told there were bodies lying on the streets every which way."

The event shocked all Oklahomans, but similar events had taken place throughout the country, and even in Washington, D.C., itself. These collisions had been gradually building and were accelerated by wartime shifts in population which brought many persons jostling against others in cities, who were unused to the situation. The Ku Klux Klan, re-created in Atlanta, Georgia, in 1915, began to gain adherents. The riot in Tulsa—if that is the proper term for a conflict that came close to a pogrom—spurred the Klan's growth in the state.

These disorders, coming on the heels of the great Red Scare and its bombings, together with scary dispatches regarding the general state of Europe and the growth of the USSR, led to the adoption of the nation's first exclusionary immigration law, at least on a large scale, in its history. Passed in the spring of 1921, it established a quota of not more than 3 percent for every national group reported in the Census of 1910, with an overall ceiling of 375,000.[13] Later that system was to undergo withering attack, but the aggregate number of newcomers allowed under it was larger than any other country of similar stature would allow, and certainly larger, in terms of applicants, than any other country was asked to accept.

The new immigration rules, however, were a rare exhibition of

13. Carruth and Associates, *American Facts and Dates*, p. 458.

rationality. There were more signs that the government itself did not appreciate the changes in the American situation. Prior to the war foreign capital had provided the funds for virtually all American expansions and industrial growth. The continental rail lines, the creation of huge ranches, the erection of factories, and the building of ships would not have taken place without a constant flow of capital from such centers of international finance as London, Berlin, and Paris.

These debts were repaid with inflated dollars, worth only 40 percent of their value when they were obtained. The disruption of international trade during the war had also enabled the Americans to enter and attain dominance in South America, large sectors of the Orient, and neutral areas, and to purchase European investments in mines, railroads, factories, and enterprises as well.

While enjoying those fruits, the United States government then proceeded to raise tariffs against foreign goods entering the country to compete with domestic manufacturers. The London *Daily Chronicle* was caustic about that. "America," the *Chronicle* said, "could not be a lending nation and at the same time, a high-tariff nation. It is only in goods that the foreigner can pay—and in proportion as you keep his goods out, you will make his payments impossible."[14]

At the same time Washington did little on the matter of Germany, which was first ordered to pay the Allies 269 billion gold marks, and then 132 billion. Berlin protested this was impossible, Britain lost interest, but France and Belgium were intent upon satisfaction. The United States remained, in effect, aloof from that subject, but was not content to stop there.

Instead, Washington insisted on receiving its war debts in gold. In all, it established a system whereby it shipped agricultural and industrial products to Europe and competed with its industries in their attempts to regain their footing; blocked European goods from entering the United States; and undermined the financial stability of European governments. It was little wonder that European newspapers began to depict the United States as a money-mad nation of immoral people; overnight Uncle Sam changed to Uncle Shylock.

Agitators arose. In Italy Mussolini put together an amalgam of leftwing ideas and rightwing personalities he called the Fascists, after the fasces symbol of ancient Rome. Calling himself the "Lenin of Italy," his movement began to attract great support.

In England the government of Lloyd George began to encounter difficulties. The fruits of victory had not appeared, and the Labour party—a creature of the leftwing leaders of the Liberals—began to gain support. In Berlin the veterans in the Freikorps battled against the

14. Sullivan, *Our Times*, 6:202.

Communists and General Ludendorff appeared on the scene again. He was searching for a leader to lead Germany in another effort; he found his man in an obscure figure named Adolf Hitler.

All that seemed as distant as the moon from Sapulpa, Oklahoma. The summer came and school ended. Miss Leita Davis and her friend Nell Schultz went east, to attend Columbia University Teachers College. They took a postgraduate summer course on standard testing, a novelty sweeping through the upper ranks of the educational establishment.

Young JB, tiring of the railroad, turned toward the oil fields. He began as a roustabout, a handyman. His duties were whatever the men in charge considered necessary. He kept the water tank filled, and helped to hook wells. He helped bail water from the wells and watched the mud that was maintained to assist drilling; sometimes he squeezed the mud to see if it was an oil sand.

It was hard work in the hot sun, but JB tanned easily and enjoyed it. The derricks of the day were rickety wooden structures; if a well blew, the danger of fire was very great. The rig was animated by a diesel engine which rotated a great wheel; the boilers were fired with wood and coal. Their water level had to be carefully watched.

The details of an oil well are, therefore, as numberless and minute as a ship, and equally important. There was no school that taught roustabouting, no course that explained the priorities or the meaning of the essential tasks. That was not the system then in vogue. One was hired, if he looked strong enough, and survived to learn what needed to be done, if he was quick and willing. The pay was good; he was making eight dollars a day, at a time when twenty-five dollars a week was considered a good wage.

By the end of the summer he had been promoted from a roustabout to a tool-dresser. That meant a raise in pay; it also meant harder and more important work. In effect, a tool-dresser is a driller's assistant. The "tool" is a bit on the end of the cable used for drilling; each tower used four or five, whose sizes ranged from five to six or eight inches. "Dressing" was an art similar to blacksmithing, in which a bit would be heated until it was white-hot and malleable. Then one man would hold it on the anvil while the driller and tool-dresser would alternate in hammering it with eight-pound sledges until it was "dressed," or resharpened, before dousing it in water. There was, JB learned, a trick to hammering, as there is a trick to everything. One had to strike and then pull as the sledge landed, in order to properly shape the metal.

It was hard work of the sort that makes chopping a tree with a single ax enjoyable, or any other kind of expert hammering with a heavy sledge. No man would keep it up forever, of course. But it was, like blacksmithing, absorbing. JB developed heavy arms and legs; his back grew stronger, and so did his self-confidence. By the end of summer he was earning ten dollars a day.

In the autumn, school opened again and JB left the oil fields to return to the Frisco Railroad, where the hours were regular and the pay, though far lower, was equally regular. Miss Davis and Miss Schultz had returned from Columbia Teachers College filled with enthusiasm over the new testing methods. They had been propounded for a generation but were given enormous impetus in the war, when they were introduced by the Army to quickly sort and classify recruits. The results were not actually revealed until the summer of 1921, and indicated that almost half the whites and nearly 90 percent of the blacks had mental ages of less than twelve years. Neither then nor later was it made clear to the public at large that the top of the scale only went to seventeen years and that therefore an average of twelve years was fairly high. Instead the country was alarmed over the presumed threat of being inundated by the feeble-minded, a term then in vogue.[15]

That alarm was exaggerated and soon faded, but the enthusiasm for testing did not. Educators, who by the complexities of their profession are always seeking ways to measure their own efficiency and the true level of their pupils, were particularly caught.

Miss Davis and Miss Schultz returned from Columbia exuding enthusiasm, and convinced their principal and board that all the pupils of Sapulpa High should be tested along the lines they had learned. The undertaking was a fairly large one, since it involved many classes and all grades, and interfered with the regular schedules. Miss Davis and Miss Scultz had no idea, as they happily supervised this project, of the resentments they aroused among their fellow teachers.

They learned that, however, when all the tests had been completed, and the teachers announced they had no intention of sharing the grading. That could be done by Miss Davis and Miss Schultz, who stared with dismay at the mounds deposited on their desks.

JB heard about this, and appeared to help. Both the teachers were

15. Boorstin, *Americans*, pp. 222–225. It has since been pointed out that such tests can only estimate schooling and not intelligence; some critics believe they do not make sufficient allowances for differences in class and culture, in which the language and attitudes of minorities is neither directly faced nor accurately graded.

immensely pleased. The three of them toiled late, night after night, and finished the job.

"I had to be diplomatic about it," Miss Davis says, "but it was obvious we had to do something for JB in return. Nell and I would go to Tulsa fairly often to the theater, and it was very easy to tell JB that we had an extra ticket for a friend who could not attend. Would he like to come with us?"

"I had not realized there was much difference in our lives," she said later. "I remember his mother. She was a very quiet but firm and composed woman. Her youngest daughter had entered the school as a freshman when JB was in his senior year. And I knew that the Saunders family was in fairly comfortable circumstances.

"But when we went together to the theater in Tulsa, JB commented on the well-dressed and genteel people in attendance, and he compared their applause with that of those in Sapulpa at shows he had attended, who stamped their feet."

Afterward it was obvious he had enjoyed himself. "We had to keep thinking up reasonable excuses," says Miss Davis, "but we did, that year, attend a number of events. We saw Pavlova in the ballet and a number of plays and concerts. JB did not care too much for the concerts, and after a while we fell into a routine. On nights he did not attend, he would come down to meet us at the station when we returned, to see that we were safely home."

Life, in other words, was beginning to take on normal tones. In the greater world there were even hopeful events. A disarmament conference was held in which Britain, the United States, and Japan agreed to limit their naval power. Despite the growing evils of Prohibition, life in the United States began to take on the more pleasant colors of peace and security. JB's ideas about his future seemed to grow more coherent. He and another senior, Clifford Bassett, had decided they would become physicians. They even selected the school: Washington University, in St. Louis.

He graduated at the end of the spring semester, in 1922. The class picture taken at the time shows him, looking about the same as the rest of the students, in a cap and gown. Miss Davis and Miss Schultz were also graduating, in a way: they were leaving Sapulpa High to teach at Central State College in Edmond, Oklahoma.[16]

Miss Davis was aware that she was moving up, but she was, nevertheless, a little sad about leaving the high school. "High school students," she says, "are really the most interesting of all. They are half

16. Now Central State University.

children and half adults; one never knows which will appear. It is intensely interesting to watch the adult emerging from the child. By the time they reach college, the adult predominates, and much of their mystery is lost."

At the graduation ceremonies she and Miss Schultz congratulated JB. They were very pleased with him; it is a rare student who becomes a friend while he is still in school. The teachers were leaving, and they knew his plans to go to medical school; they teased him a little, and hoped he would not change his mind again.

In response, he pulled out a clipping, taken from the program of a play they had seen together, *The Masquerader*. Guy Bates Post, famous in his time, had played the lead. It read:

> To every man there openeth
> A way, a way and a way.
> The high mind climbs the high way,
> The low mind gropes the low,
> And in between on the misty flats
> The rest drift to and fro.
> But to every man there openeth
> A high way and a low.
> And every man decideth
> Which way his soul shall go.

He could still recite it from memory, fifty years later.

CHAPTER SEVEN

The Sunset Decade

IN LATER YEARS the twenties were described as trivial. Flappers, jazz, feverish speculation, parties, and the novelties of Freud have been pasted together to make a foolish montage. But in reality the decade was far different—so different it is almost as though a deliberate effort was made to blur its essence. For the decade of the twenties was the last truly free period in American life. The government, except for its inept efforts to enforce Prohibition, had receded into the background. The people were intent upon their individual lives.

It was not that life was particularly comfortable or easy. In 1922 the matter of earning a living, except for those with an inherited income, was harsh and inescapable. There was no alternative to poverty but to go to work in private industry, or mount a venture of one's own. The climate was competitive, teeming with unnoticed inequities but vibrant with opportunity. There was—and this is what is best remembered—a sense that life is as boundless as the skies, and no fear of the future.

JB was twenty-one in the summer of 1922, a time when that age was considered adult. He and his sister Fay attended the state convention of the Democratic party in Oklahoma City. Fay was an ardent Democrat who, with her friends, rejoiced in the ratification of the Nineteenth Amendment that spring, which gave women the vote. She was sure that would change the world, and the convention was a big event in her life. JB regarded it with far more coolness; his interest in politics was tepid. To him, as to many others at the time, politics seemed to resemble sports more than anything else. He would take sides, as did virtually everyone, and indulge in arguments that held sound but no fury; he often goaded his father, a lifelong Democrat, in this manner. But all issues were settled on Election Day; politics were mock-serious.

Matters were different in Europe, where politics had led to the Great War and where shocks were continuing. In the USSR the leader, Lenin, had recovered from being shot by a woman[1] but had suffered a stroke. His powers were in the process of being gathered in the hands of a more personally violent revolutionist, who called himself Stalin.[2]

The Soviets had seemed to have failed, although they attained control of a truncated nation. The Baltic countries were free and independent; the brief reign of Béla Kun and his Communists in Hungary had been overthrown and traditional factions restored to authority. Poland was on its own. Austria, greatly reduced, was a republic. The condition of Germany was mixed; great Communist efforts had been made to prepare an uprising that failed. The new Weimar Republic, which was assured of army backing, seemed able to control the situation. In Italy there were continuing disorders between Communists, who continued to call themselves Socialists, and Mussolini's Fascist party for dominance; the Crown was shaky but still seated.

The situation, in other words, was beginning to settle, but several conditions rose from the wreckage of the Russian and Austro-Hungarian empires. One was the emergence, over most of eastern Europe, of anti-Semitism on a scale not seen for centuries, if ever.[3] Another was the decision of the commissars to create a double-sided foreign policy. The surface would operate as did other chancellories, with the usual diplomatic agents, approaches, treaties, and assurances. The underside would consist of a Comintern—in which agents would be organized and sent abroad, and recruits from abroad brought to Moscow for training—which would extend tentacles of revolution through the world.

1. Lenin was shot twice at close range by a young woman named Doris Kaplan, whose parents lived in the United States of America. Her motives were political: she believed he had betrayed the Russian revolution by driving the Kerenski government out by force, and by unleashing terror. The Cheka, after questioning her, shot her in the back of the head. There was no trial.

2. His name at birth was Joseph Djugashvili; he had numerous aliases, served time in prison, lived underground, been to Vienna, known Lenin, and been no stranger to Siberia, the police, or violence.

3. No single explanation will cover this phenomenon. Raymond J. Sontag, in *A Broken World, 1919–1939*, (New York: Harper & Row, 1971), cites the most often used rationales. Two he omits may add to the list: the anti-Semitic propaganda used by counterrevolutionary groups, and the fact that the Jewish population of eastern and central Europe constituted its largest and most visibly different minority.

The Comintern's beginnings were modest and shadowy, however, and the foreign policy of the Kremlin, which was more visible, seemed more important. With the collapse of most of the revolutionary uprisings in eastern Europe other countries ceased to fear Communism as such. The USSR was recognized, by 1922, by most of the world, with the official exception of the United States. At Rapallo, Italy, the Germans and the Soviets signed a treaty of friendship and mutual assistance. One result was that the German Army was able to secretly send technicians into the USSR to assist in building arms factories, whose products benefited both nations, and evaded the Versailles Treaty.[4]

But in the autumn of 1922 the phantoms and new governments, the treaties—open and secret—and the maneuvers of eastern and central Europe seemed unimportant to the United States. Even the experiment of the new German government, recklessly expanding its currency and thereby launching inflation, was of only minor interest.

That is not to say that the United States was entirely healthy. The New York *World* discussed how Broadway had been converted, by Prohibition, into "a mere Main Street of motion-picture emporiums and synthetic orange juice booths," while a new phenomenon, masquerading as "clubs," had abruptly blossomed in cellars and basements, and behind a number of grillwork façades.[5] There a mixture of people, in once-unthinkable combinations, respectable citizens mingling with the fringes and sometimes even the underworld of society, began to break the laws against liquor.

In Tulsa, only a few miles from JB's home, an eerie demonstration was mounted when, according to the *Tribune*, "One thousand and twenty men pledged allegiance to the Ku Klux Klan at a giant ceremonial . . . near Broken Arrow Road. . . . More than 30,000 motorists from Tulsa and surrounding towns tried to reach the scene, but only a few succeeded. . . ."[6]

Those were also results of the Great War, but in relatively minor form compared to the events overseas. None of them, however, far or near, could reach a young man just out of high school at the belated

4. Technically these understandings included "Military bases in Russia put at the disposal of the Reichswehr for trying out the advanced techniques and weapons prohibited by the Versailles Treaty." German industry erected armaments factories in the Soviet Union the output of which was shared by the two countries. Finally, the two countries were to exchange technical military plans and instructors. Adam Ulman, *Expansion and Coexistence: The History of Soviet Foreign Policy 1917–1967* (New York: Frederick A. Praeger, 1968), p. 152.

5. Sullivan, *Our Times*, 6:568–569.

6. Ibid., pp. 573–574.

age of twenty-one, waiting to go to Washington University in St. Louis. JB had been accepted; he had already paid his fees.

The world of medicine, however, is aloof and distant. Its idea attracts many; Clifford Bassett, JB's good friend and son of a railroad man, was caught and would stay fixed in that goal. But with only a few days left of his summer vacation, JB's resolve weakened. He was not entirely aware of that; it seemed fortuitous that a driller searched him out at the pool hall and asked, "Are you working?"

"No," JB said, "I'm going to school in a few days."

"If you're going to school you'll need money. Now listen. My tool-dresser got drunk, got in a fight, got arrested and is in jail. I need a man tonight."

JB hesitated, and the driller added quickly, "I'll pay you twelve dollars." That was over the average ten dollars; they both knew it.

"I'll go for a day or two," JB said. After all, school was ten days off.

He worked the morning tower, which ran from midnight till noon the following day; there were only two shifts a day at the well in those days.

Later the driller talked to him again. "If you'll stay," he said, "I'll pay you fourteen dollars a day—and board. There's a cabin on the lease where you can live." Then he added, "But you'll have to keep your damn mouth shut."

Fourteen dollars a day. That was eighty-four dollars a week, practically all clear, with his board and room included. The driller added, "It's good for three months at least."

"It will only mean a delay," JB thought. "Instead of entering now, I can enter in midyear." Later he could not recall whether he himself believed that, but he does remember that was how he persuaded himself.

JB worked at his tower, swung his sixteen-pound sledge, and shaped the bits of a tool-dresser's trade through the autumn of 1922. His three months stretched into another three months, and then into an extra month. Around him vibrated all the sounds, sights, and smells of the oil fields. "At night," wrote Lewis Meyer later, "the yellowish uneven lights lent an incandescent dustiness to the air, matching the choking dustiness of the day.

"Each well was its own noise factory, the standard drilling tools clanged against hundreds of feet of pipe as they bit their way downward . . . at night these oilfield sounds became a kind of frenzy. . . ."[7]

7. Sapulpa *Herald*, July 1, 1973.

He was, at the age of twenty-one, in the middle of a scene that inspired Max Bentley, a brilliant writer, into a sort of perplexed eloquence. In a book published in 1923, Bentley asked, "What is it that made a quarter of a million men in dozens of oil fields forsake the comforts of home life last year and drill 17,338 producing wells and nobody knows how many dusters . . . ?"[8]

It was, of course, the search for riches for some, wages for others, hope for all. The oil business had flourished—had sent out as many branches and as many thousands of leaves as a great tree. Each of those represented an achievement or an effort to become an achievement. The names of men made wealthy within the memory of virtually everyone were on nearly everyone's lips. No series of discoveries since gold itself had opened so many gates of opportunity for so many men, in which the primary talents needed to succeed were still a matter of gifts from God, rather than Academe.

Yet JB was not enthralled. It may have been too familiar to be exciting. He had, after all, seen these sights almost all through his childhood, and some aspects of the industry did not charm. He recalls watching the special trains arrive in Tulsa for the Oil Congress, right after the Great War.

"The men would pile out in derbies, carrying canes," he says. He watched as they lined up in twos, and marched, sweating, down the street while their self-appointed commanders bellowed, "Fall in"; saw them arrive panting at their hall, and heard the shout, "Fall out," while they dissolved in sentimental laughter for their army days. He wondered at that; he was to always wonder at herds, and at men who enjoyed being inside them.

But it is a rare man who can mature inside any industry—whether it be shipping, soldiering, or the oil fields—who can break away.

In the spring of 1923 JB made an effort. He told himself he was still going to Washington University to proceed through to a medical career. This time no unforeseen situation arose to deflect him from that goal, so he devised his own evasion.

"I decided that I would be surrounded by younger students fresh from their studies, while the memory of mine had already grown dim," he says. "I decided I would have to take notes better than anyone—lots of them. Therefore, I thought I would need shorthand."

The proper place, if not the only place, to acquire shorthand in the conventional manner was in a business school. JB made some inquiries. His friends at the Frisco Railroad advised him to go to the Chillicothe Business College, in Chillicothe, Missouri, an establishment well known for its telegraphy courses. It was a period when telegraphy was used extensively by the railroads and the communications indus-

8. Ritter, *Oil! Titan*, p. 208.

tries; the railroads employed many graduates of the Chillicothe Business College.

None of that added up to a very clear-cut program, since JB was not intent on becoming a telegrapher; presumably Washington University was still waiting for its tardy enrolee. But Chillicothe was at least partway between Sapulpa and St. Louis; it was out of town, a change of scene, and connected—though thinly—with his presumed goal.

JB entered the business college and soon attracted the attention of its proprietor, President Allen Moore. Moore, whose students were largely farm boys seeking to escape their plows and barnyards, was impressed when he learned that JB attended the Presbyterian Church in Chillicothe and had become the assistant teacher of the men's Bible class. The "men" were only eight or nine years old. JB herded about thirty-five or forty of these not only on Sundays, but also on occasional weekday wienie roasts and picnics.

That activity was, in part, the result of Dad Land's de Molay organization, in which JB received the order's Legion of Honor, as one of the founding participants. When he reached twenty-one he joined the Masons, a step that seemed as natural as rain. It was equally natural for him to continue its practice of good works and to resume working with young boys in Chillicothe.

But he was more worldly than the farm youths who crowded into President Moore's classes; he had no compunction against a few drinks and a game of poker; he had girlfriends, though their individual importance was fleeting. As always, his energy seemed inexhaustible. The school faculty was impressed by the ease with which he grasped double-entry bookkeeping and put him to work part-time, on the school's own books. His facility in mathematics led President Moore to assign him some classes to teach. Meanwhile he mastered Gregg and learned to type at the rate of seventy words a minute. The school had a high-powered course to make court reporters; JB graduated as one. He had, all told, made enough of an impression at the Chillicothe Business College to be offered a permanent post as secretary. It was the highest compliment President Moore could offer; he was disappointed when JB turned it down.

It was difficult, in the summer of 1923, to say what aroused his interest. In theory Washington University was still available, by autumn, to enroll its tardy applicant a full year late. But JB took no steps in that direction. Instead he accepted some assignments as a reporter in the District Court of Chillicothe.

He soon discovered that a courtroom is a depressing arena. The cases were sordid, the defendants alternately cringing or overbold, the lawyers wolf-like. One would remain in his memory forever. Himself a sharp younger man, he seemed to form an instant and contemptuous distrust of JB, and would call, time and again, for an "echo" of the proceedings. The attention of the court would turn toward the young man, seated at his small table, who would read aloud from his notes to prove his efficiency. He was never found wanting, but the lawyer remained skeptical.

By midsummer the suffocating pettiness, endless bickering, and sheer dreariness of the court was too much for him. JB packed his bags and returned to Sapulpa. He had learned some more about the world and acquired new skills, and he had no further excuse to delay going to the university in the fall. But that desire, like the desire to become a physician, had finally died of neglect.

He was twenty-two years old and, in terms of his generation, well-educated. He was bursting with health and had several possible occupations. But he had no particular desire to repeat any of them, no special goals or purpose, and no idea of what to do next.

Listening to a man discuss the beauties of the state of Washington, far out in the West, he felt keen desire stir within him. The thought of virgin forests, blue skies, and an absence of civilization made him think of his earliest days on the ranch. That was the life; Washington was the place to go. The name *Walla Walla* sounded strange and interesting.

Yet he did not go. Instead, to fill in his time he appeared at the offices of the Frisco Railroad in Sapulpa, where he was warmly greeted. He was offered, and accepted, a job in which he used his new skills, taking dictation over the phone from eleven in the morning until three in the afternoon, and then typing letters, billing instructions, verifications of rates, and other clerical duties.

He had a made a transition that the farm boys and many tool-dressers dreamed of making—he had moved from the oil fields into the office. Yet he was still restless, still vaguely unsettled. He began to read the employment ads, and one finally caught his eye. The Imperial Refining Company wanted a shipping clerk in its Ardmore, Oklahoma, branch. The starting salary was $250 a month. At a time when laborers were receiving $.30 an hour, that was handsome. He decided, on the spur of the moment, to apply. Without knowing it, he was finally turning toward his true path.

By then the world was taking on a distorted shape. The Great War had shattered not only the international system of finance and law, but also the common understanding that had buttressed the western world in its dealings with Asia, Africa, and Islam. The wartime alliance against Germany and Austria-Hungary had lost its purpose and found no new goal. The British were painfully learning the extent of the changes coursing through a world they once dominated. The United States—itself the result, in large measure, of English culture and capital—insisted on British war-debt payments so strenuously that London declared it would only collect, on its own account, war debts equal to those demanded from it by Washington. That shift of onus did not improve relations between the two countries.

The British also had complex problems with the USSR. The Comintern, pursuing its goal of international subversion, held a huge conference at Baku attended by restless Indians and other colonials, and were encouraged to mount resistance to British rule. London protested, but the USSR blandly declared the Comintern was not part of its government, and therefore outside the context of treaties or control. In a short time much of the western press began to feature articles about agitation against the British in various parts of the globe.

Meanwhile matters in central Europe reflected more immediate problems. The core of central Europe was Germany, and by 1923 it became clear the German government had devised a passive resistance campaign against the payment of reparations. It took several forms and led France and Belgium to reoccupy the Ruhr, the rich mining district that sustained much of Germany's heavy industry. Meanwhile the German government, with chilling indifference to the impact on its own citizens, swung open the gates of inflation. Printing presses rolled out paper currency at such a rate that, by 1923, the people finally realized they were deliberately being made bankrupt. What Ludwig von Mises, the economist, later termed the "rush to real goods," took place. Individuals scrambled to obtain any sort of barter articles: art objects, clothing, land, houses, cars, jewelry, or junk. An eerie and frightening scene took place in which grocers changed their prices constantly, as relayed by observers stationed in banks. Citizens struggled to exchange old money for new; denominations on bank notes rose to figures once restricted to mathematicians. By October, 1923, one English pound was worth ten billion marks. Carloads of worthless paper were shipped to France as payment for the German war debts. The Weimar Republic then made plans to restore stability. But in the interim the entire savings of the German middle class, long noted for its hard work and docility, were consumed. From that time onward a change began to seep through the German nation, compounded of anger, suspicion, and cynicism.

It is surprising that such little attention was paid in the United States to the nightmarish inflation of Germany. Prior to 1914 promising young American theologians, engineers, scientists, musicians, and intellectuals had gone to Germany to complete their higher education. Americans of German descent were more numerous in the United

States than persons from any other region except the British Isles. But the Great War seemed to have created a permanent dislike of the Germans through the United States, even after the realization that many of the wartime atrocity stories had been deliberate inventions.

Instead, Paris had become the new Mecca. Several reasons flowed into that change. One was the impact of Prohibition; another was the legend of sexual promiscuity the doughboys had brought back from France. For centuries Paris's Left Bank had been a favorite of young Europeans. In 1923 few of these had either the money or the chance to go to Paris; the Americans were the only numerous group left with money.

American tourists flocked; so did a small but significant trickle of writers, artists, and bohemians. A remarkable colony began to collect, distinguished in terms of talent, not so distinguished in terms of ideas. It was a diverse set, or series of interlocking sets, their only common bond being a disdain—new among Americans—for their native land, a general agreement that the world was lost and that they were members of a Lost Generation.

To most Americans in 1923 such attitudes appeared lunatic, but few would have argued that the country was not having trouble. Prohibition would have been difficult to enforce in the best of times. Coming on the heels of a disruptive war, which had left many scars on the mind of the nation, it was a near disaster. The Eighteenth Amendment had its supporters in that vast stretch of the United States in the South and West where religion had diminished into morality, and liquor had replaced Antichrist as the font of all evil. But even those areas were conspicuous for a heavy consumption of liquor; even after Prohibition there were outlaw towns and sections in Oklahoma and Texas, Missouri and Kansas, and other midwestern and southwestern states, where saloons ran wide open. In the cities, where liquor was socially more accepted by the middle class, the speakeasy was accompanied by the *gangster*—a new word in the American language.

The effort to outlaw an entire industry, whose activities had ranged from agriculture through a host of other suppliers to manufacture and distribution, led to the creation of a black-market liquor industry. Its leaders were unscrupulous men who worked in concert with others more respectably placed. The black market led to the extension of an entire illegal underground system equipped with huge sums of money that coursed outside the tax structure and spread a network of bribes, corruption, and crime throughout the country. Those outrages inevitably expanded into robberies, murders, and outrages against the entire community. Few highly placed officials dared oppose Prohibition as such; it would have been too much like speaking against Goodness. Only New York State, under the leadership of Alfred E. Smith, dared to buck conventional wisdom and passed a law revoking its ratification of the Eighteenth Amendment. The gesture—it was no more than that—evoked, predictably, pious expressions of indignation from most official quarters.

President Warren G. Harding, meanwhile had more personal concerns. An amiable man, fond of his liquor—which he kept in his bedroom[9]—and foolish enough to sneak a mistress into the austere precincts of the White House, he learned that summer that some of his oldest and closest associates had taken bribes.

In an effort to improve his standing in the country in advance of the coming storm, the distraught President went on a speaking tour. Taken ill, he died with surprising suddenness in San Francisco on August 2, 1923, at the age of fifty-eight. His death was mourned; people instinctively knew that though he was not a great man, he was an amiable one. Calvin Coolidge, a tightly buttoned, dour individual whose rectitude was unquestionable, was sworn in at his family's farm in Plymouth, Vermont, by his farmer-father, who was also a notary public.

The transition was fortunate for the Republican party; Democratic zealots were preparing to break the scandals of the Harding Administration. They would blaze new political trails in the effort, but the man whose indolence was responsible had gone beyond reach.

Despite the pomp attending the funeral of the first President to die in office in twenty years, the event was to most people somewhat remote.[10] The Presidency under Harding was not the intrusion into the mind and life of the nation that it had been under Wilson; it was possible to deplore the death of the occupant without exaggerating his importance. In Oklahoma particularly there were more immediate problems. Random crime, exacerbated by racial strife, had soared; so had the Ku Klux Klan. The combination so alarmed Governor J. C. Walton that he placed the state under martial law.[11]

Those events made little impression on JB. He was not unique in that. It was a time when politics operated in restricted sectors; most

9. Mark Sullivan records being invited by President and Mrs. Harding into their bedroom for a drink and being told that they believed they should not drink in the ordinary rooms of the White House, but could maintain their personal standards in their private quarters. *Our Times*, 6:244.

10. Harding was the fifth President to die in office by 1923; McKinley, the previous occupant to die in the Presidency, was assassinated in 1903.

11. Carruth and Associates, *American Facts and Dates*, p. 464.

people were indifferent to the politicians and intent on their own activities. Youth was especially apolitical, and the politicians, aware of that indifference, were equally disinterested in the young.

It was an individual's era. When JB appeared at the offices of the Imperial Refining Company in the Kennedy Building in Tulsa in the fall of 1923, there was no outside agency or group concerned in his transaction. There was only J. R. Trisler, a vice president, waiting to interview applicants. Trisler was looking for someone with a background in freight rates and codes, able to take orders over the phone and type them rapidly and accurately later, and to keep the refinery abreast of incoming and outgoing traffic without the need for personal supervision. JB could have been created for the post; Trisler, who had once been an agent for the Rock Island Railroad, was delighted to find a young man who spoke the languages of both the railroad and the oil fields.

Trislar turned JB over to Carl Mayhall, who—after some further conversation—agreed the young man was well qualified for the job. A letter was prepared for Jack Reardon, the Imperial refinery superintendent at Ardmore, Oklahoma, and was handed to JB to deliver himself. Hands were shaken all around, and that was that.

No forms to fill out; no personnel specialists. Social security was unknown as a concept; it was a period when the citizens planned for their own futures. Therefore there was no identity number to send to the government. The idea that the government might someday become a third party to such transactions between citizens would have drawn astonished stares.

Ardmore, situated in the rolling hills of southeastern Oklahoma, almost precisely halfway between Oklahoma City and Dallas, Texas, is colored tan on the maps. That did not bode too well for the farmers in the region, but it proved exciting for geologists and oilmen. Once Indian Territory, the town proved a springboard for important oil discoveries. The largest of these was the Healdton field, discovered by Ardmore residents.[12] But a speckled geological map of the oil fields surrounding Ardmore shows others located in the west at Burkburnett, Electra, Petrolia, and Wichita Falls; in the northwest at Cement; and in many unnamed stretches to the south.

12. Although there were earlier efforts, the real boom at Healdton was not underway until 1913. It brought the Sun Oil Company (through its subsidiary, Twin State Oil), William G. Skelly, Robert Hefner, and others into the play. It was at Healdton that Hefner is credited with having introduced the idea of "royalty payments," in which purchasers bought a specified number of barrels out of production for the productive life of a lease.

By the time JB arrived, the boom of 1913 had passed its first heady stage and the town of Ardmore had settled into a headquarters for the oil regions that surrounded it. Its population was around sixteen thousand, which made it a little larger than Sapulpa. But it was far more important than Sapulpa, for it was not flanked by a Tulsa; no other terminus existed for southeastern Oklahoma.

John Ringling North, the circus magnate, had built a special railroad line from the Healdton fields to Ardmore; Magnolia Petroleum had invested heavily in the area and had an important pipeline, and so had Gulf. The railroads running into town included the Oklahoma, the New Mexico & Pacific, and the Santa Fe. Famous names had taken part in the Healdton play, which affected Ardmore; they included Bill Skelly and Robert A. Hefner, who was credited with inventing the royalty-purchase form, guaranteeing so many barrels for the life of a lease.

The town was the site of other innovations as well. When Magnolia, dominating the scene briefly with its eight-inch pipeline, decided to arbitrarily lower the price of crude, the independents at Ardmore combined to create an Oil Producers' Association which appealed to Congress. After many hearings and arguments the issues were finally decided by the U.S. Supreme Court, which ruled that all pipelines except those that ran directly into private refineries should operate as common carriers under the Interstate Commerce Commission.

Ardmore, therefore, was a site not only where all the tangible factors of the industry came together, but also where the interests of the men inside the industry collided and were coordinated. It would not have been possible to have landed in a more concentrated arena, where a young man could see both the high and mighty and the everyday, and learn the details of their common interests.

He entered the Imperial refinery office in Ardmore and handed his letter of introduction to Jack Reardon. The older man, after shaking hands, read it carefully. He was a big man; he had been a professional baseball player. He was Irish by descent, and looked it.

"What church d'you go to?" he asked abruptly.

JB was astonished.

"I was raised as a Presbyterian, but I'm not going to any church right now," he said.

"I'm a Catholic, but I know Dr. Wyeth, the Presbyterian minister. We play golf, together with Father Ryan. On Sundays I'll come here at eight-thirty; you'll take my car and go to church and Sunday School, and return the car at noon." His tone brooked no demurral.

Then he showed him where he would work, and introduced him to his new associates.

JB found a boarding house, operated by a widow, who placed him in a large room off the big dining room. Boarding houses were still in vogue in 1923, as they had been for many generations. They provided advantages a later generation might well envy. A young bachelor did not have to worry about his room or his linen; housekeeping was done around him. Meals were usually simple but ample, and there was always conversation.

His work in the refinery office was well within his capacity; his day was a straight eight hours but passed quickly. As he had promised, Reardon lent JB his car to drive to the Presbyterian church on Sundays. JB began to learn something about the firm that employed him and its refinery superintendent.

Imperial was owned and operated by W. B. Hassett, a veteran oilman from Pennsylvania who, like Reardon, had once been a professional baseball player. Baseball was not, when Hassett and Reardon played, a very mild game. When Joe McGinnity, one of its stars, was expelled from the National League for stepping on the toes of umpire Tom Connolly, spitting in his face, and punching him, fans believed that that penalty was extreme, and he was recalled.[13] Some measure of W. B. Hassett's temper is provided by the fact that he *was* expelled—and it stuck.

Hassett, however, was a native of Warren, Pennsylvania, and had grown up in the oil fields. So had Reardon, who came from Lock Haven, Pennsylvania, but Reardon lacked Hassett's remarkable business abilities. Those were sufficient to send him to Oklahoma, where he looked at a number of possibilities in a number of towns. Hassett's cover, while looking around, was virtually unexcelled. He would join local teams and pitch on Sundays—he was, of course, of major league ability—and would bet huge sums on the teams he joined. By the time he reached Chelsea, Oklahoma, and realized the extent of its producing field, he decided to build a small refinery.

His backer was a Colonel Armstrong, a wealthy banker in Lock Haven, Pennsylvania, who was a large shareholder in the Rock Island Railroad. Armstrong backed Hassett, and Hassett built the Chelsea Refining Company. That effort prospered, and Hassett was able to repay his backer; when the fields near Ardmore became highly productive, Hassett transferred operations to that town, built a refinery, and called it the Imperial Refining Company.

13. Carruth and Associates, *American Facts and Dates*, p. 391.

By that time Mr. Hassett, as he was known, had become a high flyer. He belonged, says JB, to clubs all over the country. When the owners of the Great Southern Refining Company in Lexington, Kentucky, grew dissatisfied with its progress in 1923, they asked Hassett to become its president. His terms, he told JB later, included a salary of fifty thousand dollars a year and 10 percent of the net profits. The directors laughed; they did not expect profits—they hoped to avert bankruptcy. The firm was, in effect, being managed by two very bright but not overly experienced young men named Eric Shatford and Paul G. Blazer.

The Great Southern operated boats on the Ohio. Hassett discovered that the captains and mates wore company uniforms and that shipboard parties were held. Shatford and Blazer explained that these were ongoing sales efforts, but Hassett came from a rougher school. He decided that both Shatford and Blazer were extravagant, and fired them after six months.[14] Then he sold what he called the "pleasure boats," and bought "working boats" and some barges. Carl Mayhall, a vice president of Imperial Refining Company, who handled that firm's efforts while Hassett was busy in Kentucky, was equally brisk. Mayhall organized the Imperial Oil Marketing Company, which handled product sales for Imperial and also for other firms. But Mr. Hassett, imperial in life as well as title, returned, surveyed Mayhall's efforts, canceled them, and launched changes of his own.

JB, who received this story partly as it developed, and partly in snatches from Jack Reardon and others, began to develop a sense of admiration for the head of the firm. His feelings toward Reardon, however, were warmer. Hassett was a remote figure who appeared only occasionally—a big, belligerent Irishman who bustled in and out. Reardon was another story. He took JB out to a driving range and began to teach him how to hold a golf club, how to drive, how to putt, how to get out of a trap.

When the weather permitted, JB found himself included as a fourth with a rare trio consisting of Reardon, Father Ryan and Dr. Wyeth, the Presbyterian minister. If it was not usual for clergymen of two different churches to play golf together, it was even rarer for refinery superintendents to include their office managers. But Reardon, who had a son and daughter of his own, was a fatherly man; he had taken an interest in JB, whom he watched, in all reality, much as a father might.

14. There are some who may dispute this, but this is Mr. Hassett's version, as told to JB Saunders. Paul G. Blazer, one of the two young men Hassett fired, was then hired by the Swiss Oil Company and placed in charge of a small refinery at Catlettsburg, Kentucky, which he remarkably built to such an extent that it in time overtook its own parent and became the huge Ashland Oil Company. See Otto J. Scott, *The Exception: The History of Ashland Oil* (New York: McGraw-Hill, 1968).

JB was aware of that, and it made his anger rise quickly when another young man at the boarding house leaned across the table at dinner one night and said, "You're working for a redneck Catholic."

"He's one of the finest men I know," JB said hotly. "Don't ever make any remarks to me against Reardon."

That undercurrent of ill will and prejudice, which reflected Klan influence, was very strong in Oklahoma that winter. On several occasions JB was asked if he knew "Mr. Cyclops," but only once was he asked openly if he belonged to the Klan.

"No," he said, shortly.

"Why not?"

"Because I don't believe in putting a sheet over my head to beat someone up."

"Forget it," said his questioner, and turned away.

But Oklahoma was far from the worst region during the end of 1923 and the beginning of 1924; the entire nation—and beyond the nation, the world itself—seemed suffused with angers, resentments, and violence.

The state of Oregon passed a law forbidding grammar school children to attend any but public schools;[15] a gang battle in downtown Washington, D.C., resulted in the accidental wounding of a United States Senator,[16] and the residents of a small town—Lilly, Pennsylvania—fought a pitched, hours-long gun battle with five hundred hooded members of the KKK.[17]

These violent episodes, however, did not entirely reflect the national humor. In an intellectual sense, the nation—with growing prosperity—turned somewhat silly. Popular songs reflected a carefree attitude: *Yes, Sir, That's My Baby* and *Sweet Georgia Brown* intermingled a new and more sophisticated jazz with such traditionally melodic offerings as *Indian Love Call*.

Politics reflected the same disparate mixture of dissension and triviality. Sinister events were underway in Europe, where virtually every government was abandoning democratic procedures. The USSR, conducting a covert war around the world, officially mourned the

15. The law, adopted by a state initiative, was challenged by a broad coalition of religious groups and was ruled unconstitutional by the U.S. Supreme Court in 1925.

16. Frank L. Greene of Vermont.

17. Sullivan, *Our Times*, 6:613.

death of Lenin and was consolidated into the hands of Stalin. The Baltic states resorted to strongman rule, as did Spain under Primo de Rivera. In Italy the Fascists boasted of their conquests over the Communists, but their methods were alike. In Germany the government was confronted with strikes, riots, and rebellions as a result of its inflationary policies. Only the support of the Army enabled the leaders of the Weimar Republic to overcome the situation. Among their successes was the suppression of illegal army reserves, who mounted an uprising, and subjugation of the charismatic Hitler, who marched in Munich beside Ludendorff. In England the Conservatives were defeated, and the Liberal party joined with Labour to form the first Socialist government. Yet the United States paid little attention to these events which, in their aggregate, boded no good for democracy. Instead, the headlines were heavy with shouts over Teapot Dome.

Not since the Dreyfus case in France had any issue been so distorted by propaganda. Simple in essence, it was quickly made complex by a tangle of descriptions, articles, charges, denunciations, and even books.[18]

Its origins were in a naval decision to have crude oil extracted from federal leases in Wyoming and California, in order to stockpile petroleum products at Pearl Harbor, a base that needed to be enlarged to meet the nation's new Pacific responsibilities.

The Secretary of the Navy, informed that private drillers operating on the edges of these leases were suspected of draining the naval reserves, asked the Secretary of the Interior—whose department knew more about the petroleum industry—to handle the arrangements to obtain lease reserves for the Navy. Interior, headed by former Senator Albert B. Fall, negotiated a contract with Harry Sinclair's Mammoth Oil Company and with Edward L. Doheny's Pan American Oil Company. The terms were not mild. Sinclair agreed to a royalty of up to half of all the oil produced and to build a $22 million pipeline. Doheny, who agreed to pay the same royalty, also agreed to build 1.5 million barrels of storage capacity for the Navy at Pearl Harbor. Both men believed the lease reserves of oil were large enough to be worth such huge premiums.

Under Democratic Senator Thomas J. Walsh, hearings were held to determine whether, and why, Fall had broken the law in concluding an agreement with the two firms rather than conducting open bids. It soon turned into an investigation of whether Fall had been bribed. Had President Harding been alive and in office, that Democratic inquiry into his Administration might well have hurt the Republican party.

18. The best, clearest, and most succinct description among all the sources to which I referred is to be found in Ruth Sheldon Knowles's excellent book *The Greatest Gamblers* (New York: McGraw-Hill, 1959), pp. 204–219.

But Harding was dead, and Coolidge had replaced Fall before the hearings started. The political impact on the Republicans was not as great as the headlines indicated.

But as the Teapot Dome hearings dragged on, month after month, their influence slowly, subtly, and steadily seeped into the mind of the nation. Images of wealthy oilmen corrupting relatively poor public servants merged into earlier agitations against John D. Rockefeller and the industry as a whole, strengthening an old legend in which oil and corruption were inextricably entwined.

Such a connection appeared so lunatic to men in the oil industry that it was not given the attention it deserved. The products of oil had become the indispensable links of technology. That technology, by 1924, was in the full of an immense sweep, in which Detroit was both laboratory and consumer, customer and seller. Experiments to develop tires had converted carbon black from a waste to an industry; the giant tire firms in Akron became satellites of the automobile, and by 1924 there was one automobile in circulation for every seven Americans.[19]

The men who dominated the petroleum industry were engrossed in change, and remarkably different from the men in the cities of the East. These differences in styles of speech, clothing, leisure, and business went deeper than the surface. The citizens of what had become Oil Country—a region that stretched from Kansas through Oklahoma, Arkansas, Louisiana, and Texas—were descendants of frontier fathers who carried their habits into the modern stream. To such men the idea that Doheny could lend Albert Fall $100,000 and consider it separate from a huge oil-lease proposition was nothing out of the ordinary: men in the industry often did one another personal favors that did not impede fierce competition during business hours.

As technological demands grew sharper, and the details of oil production, refining, and transportation grew more complex, whole series of changes coursed through the petroleum industry. At Imperial, a decision was made to acquire a Dubbs cracking unit in the Ardmore refinery.[20]

19. Partridge, *Fill 'Er Up!*, p. 224.
20. Created by Jesse Dubbs and his son Carbon Petroleum Dubbs, the unit combined a number of discoveries, involved the owners—Universal Oil Products—in complex litigation, converted many relatively worthless refinery stocks into valuable commercial products and greatly increased the refinery yield of gasoline. It was marketed on a license basis.

Universal Oil Products, which licensed and installed the Dubbs unit, placed one of its experts in charge of the installation, but Imperial had to hire men and—since the effort was inside its own refinery— place someone in charge to cooperate and to supervise the project on its own behalf. Jack Reardon turned to JB and told him he had been selected as the construction engineer on the project. JB was surprised, and protested that he was not an *engineer*—the term was beginning to acquire status.

"You can read a blueprint," Reardon said.

There was more, of course, to his decision than that. JB was too bright and ambitious a young man to remain long at an office desk, doing a clerk's work. Reardon, who had grown to know his protégé better than the younger man realized, was setting him onto a path to become more valuable, and had devised a shrewd way of using and educating him at the same time.

A construction engineer was really only in charge of maintenance projects and expansions inside the refinery. The crews had their own foremen, and consisted of skilled workmen. But Reardon made sure that JB began to learn how the refinery as a whole operated. JB spent some time in the laoratory and learned how to test products, how to gauge tank contents daily and run a percentage, and how to fill in all the crevices of the all-important yield report, by which the refinery flow was measured.

The lessons extended beyond the physical, and included that area so signally neglected in most management schools then and now, and so important: the relationships between the managers and the men in blue collars. JB, who had worked as a tool-dresser, and to whom physical tasks had been a part of life since childhood, was taken aback to discover the attitude of some of the workmen to the needs of the firm. The bricklayers astonished him.

It was a time when bricks were immensely important; brickyards were scattered all across the country and brick was the most important single building unit. JB, like most others, took this situation for granted; in Sapulpa the red Oklahoma clay had supplied the Brick & Tile Company since the inception of the town. Houses, streets, sheds— virtually every structure was made of brick.

But JB discovered at Ardmore that the bricklayers not only had a strong union, but that its members were a hereditary élite who set their own indolent pace and refused to be hurried.

"One day a bricklayer came down off the scaffold because there was no ice in the drinking water," he recalls. JB came along and discovered them sitting together, chuckling at jokes. He learned the problem and called the the iceman. The man reported he had broken a car axle on the way out. JB, glaring through the window at the expensive crew resting outside, told him to make a special trip in another car.

"When the iceman arrived and put ice into the drinking barrel, they sauntered over casually, and—one by one—took a sip from the cup, and then threw the rest on the ground."

He learned that if a brickwork extended more than fifty yards, a foreman, as well as a layer, had to be hired, and that each job had to have at least two bricklayers. Each layer received $1.87½ an hour, and the foreman $2.25 an hour. Watching and—involuntarily—timing their labors, he discovered a job estimated at a half day could take as long as three.

One experience was unforgettable. The refinery needed a new boilerhouse; plans were made and the bricklayers called in to do their part. They were not faceless to JB; he knew them by name and watched their performances closely. One, known as Ku Klux Klan Kelly—not from any affiliation but from a similarity in his initials—was outstanding for reporting to work still drunk every Monday from the strenuous celebrations that followed payday Saturdays.

JB, seeing Kelly stagger in, busy distributing the dogtags, would say, "Kelly, you're too drunk."

Kelly would stagger out through the gate and not reappear until Wednesday. On Wednesdays, Thursdays, Fridays, and Saturday mornings, Kelly would be as sober and work as well as the rest. He could not be fired; his foreman—a fellow union member—saw to that.

The days passed, as far as JB was concerned, with agonizing slowness, and so did the construction of the boilerhouse. Time and again he emerged with his blueprint and a yardstick to measure this snail-like progress or its lack, and earned sullen, resentful looks. There were seven bricklayers working on the project, and they usually passed a bottle around to sustain themselves in their labors.

Eventually, however, the boilerhouse was completed and steam was started. After three days, the east wall collapsed. The rubble brought men running, and the boilers were shut down, at some risk to everyone in the refinery. Because the lack of steam threatened to halt all operations, an emergency call was placed to the El Dorado & Wesson Railroad. Superintendent Reynolds, anxious to keep the flow of freight uninterrupted, sent in seven special locomotives. Steam from these engines kept the plant in operation while JB, with Reardon beside him, examined the remnants of the wall. The bricklayers had mixed their cement with too much sand; it could not possibly have held.

The sheer irresponsibility of this and similar efforts imbued JB with a feeling of deep contempt, not so much for the men—he was too worldly for that—but for the organization to which they belonged that sustained them in behavior that enabled their worst aspects to emerge with impunity: their union.

Other men in other parts were learning similar lessons. In England the Labour government recognized the USSR and negotiations began with the commissars. The British Liberals and, of course, the scattering of admitted British Communists, were optimistic; it was believed the USSR would settle the old Czarist debts and that trade between the nations would be instituted. Instead a letter purporting to be from Grigori Zinoviev, head of the Comintern, to the British Communist newspaper was unveiled, in which various subversive efforts—including penetration of the armed forces—was ordered. The disclosure created a furor, and resulted in the fall of the Labour government and a call for new elections.[21]

In the United States, however, as in Britain and other countries, it was not official communism that presented the most problem to industry, but the idea that the increasing numbers of products and quantities of goods being made available came not through the efforts of entrepreneurs but from a mystical figure known as Progress.[22]

With that fiction established, the disparity of incomes, and the differences of station and contributions of individuals, could all be ascribed to injustice of one sort or another. That Socialist doctrine, which demanded a broad spectrum of leveling programs as a means of improving society, fell on fertile ground. The newspapers did not improve the dialogue, for their explanations, upon which the average man relied, seldom gave a rounded account of the situation.

In 1924 banker Charles G. Dawes of Chicago invented a plan whereby the German government would obtain money from its industries, and receive loans of $200 million from the Allies and the United States. In other words, it was finally recognized that the destruction of the center of European heavy industry would inevitably injure the entire West.

That settlement led to others. British and French war debts were put on a reasonable basis, and the international financial world began to stabilize for the first time since the Great War. A flow of investment capital began to stream from the United States to Germany, the wheels of industry began to turn on the Continent, and imports began to enter the United States. These American purchases financed purchases of

21. The Zinoviev Letter, as it became known, has been described as a forgery. But Adam Ulam, in his book *Expansion and Coexistence*, p. 116n, does not see that as important, since the Comintern's standing instruction was to subvert all non-Soviet governments.
22. A rounded description of this attitude is provided by Ludwig von Mises in *The Anti-Capitalist Mentality* (South Holland, Ill.: Libertarian Press, 1972).

American goods abroad, and the economy of the world began to improve.[23] It did not improve as much as it should, because the high American tariffs kept these imports from reaching figures commensurate with the American position as creditor nation of the world. But it improved.

The reasons for that improvement, and for the remarkable stream of inventions, improvements, and financial activities that sent the stock exchanges soaring and ushered new enterprises into birth at an unprecedented rate, were not understood—among either the Socialists, the trade movement, or the general public.

As a result, the nation moved into its autumnal elections in 1924 with strange figures appearing on platforms across the land, making even stranger pronouncements. The list of parties and conventions alone is crowded. The Socialist Labor party ran candidates for president and vice-president; so did the Prohibition party, the Progressives, and the Farmer-Labor party. The last of these merged itself into the Workers party, which nominated Communists William Z. Foster and Benjamin Gitlow. The Republican party, upon which more attention was fastened, renominated President Coolidge and nominated Dawes for vice president.[24] The Democrats, after a bruising and protracted struggle in New York City, nominated—on the 103rd ballot—John W. Davis of West Virginia for President and Charles Bryan, brother of the orator, for vice president.

In all, the scene was not one to imbue any observers with the idea that the country was united. Yet burgeoning prosperity covered a host of differences. In every region people were doing better than ever before, and certainly far better than their fathers.

JB bought his first automobile that year. It was a brand new 1924 Ford touring car. It had side curtains and a half windshield, and cost $465.

Sunset, according to the astronomers, is the moment when the upper limb of the sun disappears toward the sensible horizon. It is the time when colors replace glare and soften the sky in a dazzling series of reflections—entrancing and hypnotic.

The year 1925 was, in that sense, the beginning of sunset for the old order of the western world. Spots of color began to appear. In the United States a whole group of young, talented poets made their names known: MacLeish, Benét, T. S. Eliot, Conrad Aiken, Frost, and others; the theater glowed with the productions of Eugene O'Neill, Maxwell

23. George Soule, *Prosperity Decade: From War to Depression, 1917–1929*, (New York: Harper & Row), 8:264–268.
24. Author of the Dawes Plan.

Anderson, Philip Barry, and Sholem Asch; the music of George Gershwin and Aaron Copland; the books of Theodore Dreiser, Sinclair Lewis, John Erskine, Willa Cather, and F. Scott Fitzgerald, whose masterwork was *The Great Gatsby*.

On every side the nation seemed bursting with energy. The Charleston, a dance described as "featuring exuberant side kicks," swept the land. Children performed it for pennies in front of theaters during intermission; contests arose.

A similar mood swept across Europe. Paris and Berlin blossomed with visitors, cabarets, and entertainments unprecedented in luxury and license. Pornography emerged from the alleys of Europe to seep into films, art, and drama. Tourists flocked; the shipping companies produced giant liners whose furnishings and services resembled great floating hotels; Monte Carlo boomed, and speculation began to soar—as in the United States.

The new Conservative government of Britain introduced, at the urgings of its Chancellor of the Exchequer, Winston Churchill, a sweeping series of changes, including a return to the gold standard. Even the USSR seemed influenced by the softening tides; the commissars relaxed their fierce campaign against private property and individual initiative, and continued their New Economic Policy, which allowed small businesses and trades to function, and some weak labor unions to emerge.

Sunsets, after all, look much like sunrises—for a time. The difference is one of direction. To JB Saunders—twenty-four years old and owner of his first car, holding a position as construction engineer and supervising a crew of two hundred men, well-paid and healthy, ambitious and hopeful—the world seemed as young and promising as he was himself. He had, it seemed, no problems beyond his capacity.

When W. B. Hassett, busy and bustling as ever, arrived at the Ardmore refinery and stalked into the office to ask, "Why is there no water in the Number Two condenser box?" JB was cocky enough to say quickly, "Perhaps you had an optical illusion."

The older man turned an alarming red. "My eyes are excellent," he snarled, *"and they see lots of things."*

By then JB realized he had answered hastily. Alarmed, he ran into the yard and checked. To his horror, he discovered someone had left a valve open and the condenser box was as dry as the boss's tone.

It took more than a minor contretemps, however, to dampen his mood in early 1925; he had met a girl. She worked as a student nurse, assisting in the emergency room of the Hardy Sanitarium in Ardmore—a place JB learned well. Part of his responsibility was to watch injuries on the job. To keep track of the insurance problems that so often arose as a result of these accidents, he would drive the injured man to the Sanitarium himself.

Gladys Edmondson, a tiny brunette whose nerves seemed equal to any sight, grew to know him on these visits; their attraction was quick to grow. "Eddy" was a bright presence in a grim setting.

He learned she came from Texas and was intensely ambitious, determined on finishing her training and becoming a full-fledged nurse before she made any other plans in life. JB liked that; he liked independence and firmness; he liked her more the more often they met. They began to date and, for the first time, JB grew seriously interested.

As so often happens when one's life becomes more serious, his challenges grew sharper. Mr. Hassett was not an easy man; he expected all he received, and was accustomed to ask for more. There were numerous gathering lines in the Ardmore region, which was studded with refineries and petroleum firms. Walking with JB on an inspection trip, Hassett saw a network of these pipelines, all going in different directions; each belonged to a different firm. Hassett pointed to one of them and asked JB, "Whose line is this?"

JB said he didn't know, and Hassett glared at him.

"In your position, *I would know*," he said, and walked away.

Hassett was irascible, but he was also a man with considerable presence who lived in a style that caught JB's imagination. The head of the Imperial Refining Company had homes in Tulsa; Lexington, Kentucky; and Florida. He belonged to clubs all across the country; it seemed to JB that Hassett was a member of some organization or another "everywhere."

"He would take large groups of men on hunting trips," JB recalled, "for as long as ten days at a time. He would fly them to Canada, with all expenses paid." He was, in other words, the very image and pattern of a successful oilman who knew how to deal effectively with other men on many levels. He golfed, fished, hunted, played poker, drank—but not to excess—and, in effect, promoted his firm not only through the usual channels of business, but also in the more subtle avenues of personal influence.

Inevitably JB was drawn toward such a pattern, and his knowledge of his Big Boss grew deeper when young Bill Hassett appeared at Ardmore. Bill, a student at Culver Military Academy, was caught smoking against the rules and disciplined. The punishment was the latest of a long stream of difficulties as a result of an even longer list of infractions, but was apparently more than young Bill could tolerate. He and a fellow cadet ran away.

They ran out of money in Kansas, and young Bill's buddy wired his mother. In turn, she appealed to Mr. Hassett, who was—at the moment—at his Lexington residence. He wired his eldest son—he had a younger named Bob—one hundred dollars. The boys received the money and continued on to California. From there they wired Mr. Hassett for more money. Infuriated, he growled, "Let them sell the car," and turned away.

That broke the partnership. Bill's buddy returned home to mother, but young Bill landed at Ardmore. He was driving a Ford coupe, had no money, and said he had not recently eaten.

Reardon came to JB's boardinghouse, described the situation, and turned young Bill over to JB. JB regarded his boss's heir. He saw a burly young man, sullen in temper, who regarded him with the coolly insolent eyes of one better placed by birth. JB talked to the widow, arranged for young Bill Hassett to be given a room, and suffered the embarrassment of sponsoring him at the boarding-house table.

In the morning the two of them left for the refinery together; Mr. Hassett had wired instructions that his son should be put to work digging ditches. Young Bill didn't seem to mind that. He joined the crew without demur. But JB was fascinated to note, a few days later, that his erstwhile charge went into downtown Ardmore to Max West-heimer's haberdashery and bought one pair of work pants, one blue shirt, a flashy leather jacket, underwear, socks, shoes, and a number of other items that caught his eye—including a tuxedo—and had the bill sent to his father.

About two weeks later Mr. Hassett arrived at the refinery. The weather was rainy, and young Bill was in the ditch, bedraggled and dirty, with the other men. He looked up as his father walked by, and said, "Hello, Dad."

"Hello, Bill," his father responded briefly—and kept walking.

In the refinery office, however, after discussing various business matters, Mr. Hassett turned to JB and said, "Tell young Bill I'll be at the hotel."

JB went out to the ditch at the end of the day and relayed the message, and young Bill, his face suddenly bright, climbed out. He almost ran to the car; they drove back to the boarding house together. At dinner he convinced his father he had learned his lesson, and talked himself into being allowed back to Lexington for a visit. His father, softened, gave him fifty dollars.

That night young Bill went out on the town, got drunk, and surged into JB's room in the boardinghouse at 3:00 A.M. to insist that he take a drink. JB groaned, rose, and struggled to keep young Bill on his feet until he could place him aboard an east-bound train at 7:00 A.M. He succeeded, and saw the train depart with a feeling of relief. He did not realize that that was far from the last of his encounters with young Bill Hassett.

The summer of 1925 was a full one. JB grew into his duties as a construction engineer and learned refinery processes. He was a member of the Sholem Aleichem International Lodge of the Oil Industry: his card read Derrick No. 1. He was Number 188.

Years later he learned that another Ardmore resident, who had a small ranch nearby and who trained horses, was also a lodge member, though he did not know it at the time. The horseman, however, was a familiar figure to JB, who was among those who would watch admiringly as the other young man displayed a trained animal to amuse local youngsters.

"Do you like sugar?" the trainer would ask, and the horse would nod its head. "If an Indian shoots, what will you do?" the trainer would persist, and the horse would lie down and roll over.

It was many years before JB would meet that trainer again, and realize he was—by then—the world-famous Gene Autry.

Life was, in other words, good. With a salary of $300 a month at a time when the national annual income was $750, JB was in comfortable circumstances. Around him the town of Ardmore reflected the raw behavior of the times, which he had known all his life and took for granted.

Driving in his Ford touring car with a friend from Ardmore to Tulsa, they came to a stretch in the road that had trees on both sides— and ran into a cable. They hit it hard before they saw it, driving too fast to stop. The wire grew taut and then slipped over the car. JB stepped on the gas; he and his friend looked back to see two men, one on each side of the road, staring after them. Robbers.

There were lots of robbers—American-style—in the region. They did not resemble city gangsters, who moved in groups and held secret executions, so much as the old-time badmen famous in the West. JB shared in boarding-house conversations about the crime in the region; some of the stories were tangled in fierce and unforgettable duplicities. One, which he never forgot, involved local lawmen and a quasi confederate who was arrested and taken near the train station, and told to run. "We'll shoot over your head, you swing aboard the train, and we'll forget about you."

The man ran as instructed, and was shot dead.

Such stories were too real to ignore. On more than one occasion he saw Bud Blue, an old-time badman as real as sin, walking close to the buildings, with an armed companion walking on his outside. Bud Blue had been ruthless as a deputy sheriff under the famed Garrett and could not abandon violence. He became a paid protector for still-operators and would shoot at lawmen who attempted a raid. In 1925 he was tracked down in Wichita Falls by a Texas Ranger, who found him in a saloon.

"Don't shoot," the Ranger warned as Blue turned, his arms half-raised. Blue glared at him and reached for his gun. The Ranger shot him dead. JB was among those who watched Blue's elaborate funeral cortège carried through the streets of Ardmore.

Yet, though the frontier was still near both in time and spirit, the nation in 1925 was changing fast. People in many regions thought it was changing too fast. Hollywood produced some epics under DeMille and others, but devoted more time to films of "flaming youth." The theories of Sigmund Freud, which had been introduced in the United States by the prophet himself, popularized in educational circles by G. Stanley Hall from 1909 onward, were received as indisputable revelations and gained the beginnings of what would be almost unanimous national acceptance during the twenties.

Religious leaders grew alarmed, especially in the areas outside the Northeast. A division opened between people in smaller towns and inland states, and those in such areas as New York, Boston, Chicago, San Francisco, and burgeoning Los Angeles, deeper and in many ways uglier than ever before.

Mencken, at the height of his powers, editing the popular *American Mercury*, a gifted satirist who spared neither people, places, traditions, nor taboos, became the virtual spokesman for all who were restless, discontented, impatient and scornful of what he dubbed the Bible Belt.

The people in that Belt, meanwhile, searched for some means of checking the tides that washed against virtually every institution. Their efforts were not marked by any great insight; to the astonishment of the intellectuals they took the form, in several states, of pressing laws against the teaching of evolution. In Tennessee, where one such law was passed, its opponents decided to press a test case through the courts and—with his consent—filed charges against a twenty-four-year-old high school biology teacher for its violation.

The press took up the issue, and prominent persons became engaged in the controversy. The teacher, John Scopes, found himself being defended by the famed Clarence Darrow, an agnostic whose sparkling performance in Chicago the year before had saved the sadistic homosexuals Leopold and Loeb from execution for the murder of a young boy. William Jennings Bryan, prematurely aged from years of fierce political struggles and noted for his evangelical Christianity, decided to assist the prosecution. The trial, held in sweltering heat, began on a courteous level; both Bryan and Darrow were old personal friends. Its final sessions, held on the lawn of the Dayton courthouse, with the participants in shirtsleeves, their collars removed, using palmetto fans, was more primitive and provided material for replays that will no doubt persist forever.

In the end Darrow, whose questions were savage, succeeded in making Bryan sound like a bigot and a fool. In the process he crossed the line between argument and injury. Bryan died five days later. Darrow remained famous, but his cynicism cast a permanent tarnish upon his fame.[25] The significance of the event was more than personal, however; it marked a semiofficial beginning of the decline of the clergy, in terms of public issues, in the United States.

That result was not clear at the time, perhaps because the Scopes trial was reported as farce. All that appeared on the surface were endless sarcasms at the expense of an older America. But it provides, in retrospect, both a striking contrast and a muted parallel to the infinitely more sweeping, murderous campaign being conducted, at the same time, in the Soviet Union against all religions, by the state and the GPU.[26]

Whether the Scopes trial—or indeed, any event—meant anything to JB Saunders that summer of 1925 is highly problematical. He was not a great reader; his interests were not in issues or politics. His life was an active one, and he had more than enough to keep busy. Both he

25. The critics of evangelical Christianity have celebrated Darrow's triumph almost continuously for fifty years afterward. In 1975 Henry Fonda was enthralling Londoners with his one-man imitation of Darrow, delivering his most brilliant lines and arguments in a theatrical pastiche.

26. The GPU had replaced the Cheka. The initials stand for State Political Administration.

and Jack Reardon luxuriated in the baseball season. The big refinery superintendent, who usually came to work at six thirty and was out of the office at seven and back only briefly at intervals through the day, would have his car at the door with the motor running at four o'clock. JB would run out and they would rush to the ball park to see the last half of a game, drink milk shakes, and make bets. A large bet was five dollars; Reardon was no great gambler. But JB loved to gamble; he spent many evenings playing poker and grew canny at that psychological game, which tests mettle perhaps better than any other ever devised.

No doubt Reardon also talked to Hassett, beyond JB's earshot or knowledge, for by the end of summer, with the Dubbs units in place and working, the younger man was told he was to be transferred back to Tulsa, to Imperial's head offices.

In later years such a transfer back to headquarters would be recognized as a sign of progress and also a portent of further grooming. But in the autumn of 1925 such decisions and maneuvers had not yet reached the cold state of formula; business—though it seems ruder and rougher to later generations—was then more subtly conducted. JB's transfer back to Tulsa was arranged so easily that he did not wonder at it.

He arrived when Tulsa's last livery stable was going out of business, when Will Rogers was entertaining large crowds at the Convention Hall, and when the city was preparing to welcome the American Petroleum Institution, as it was then known.[27]

The city was, in all truth, the petroleum industry's own creation. Many of the most famous oilmen had mansions inside its limits: Bill Skelly and Harry Sinclair—still struggling against politicians avid for his destruction—among others. Waite Phillips, who with his brother Frank were building their Phillips Oil Company into a formidable force, was building an Italian Renaissance home with formal gardens that would sprawl across twenty-three acres. Another oilman, F. B. Parriott, would build a home with an elevator and a ballroom to accommodate five hundred people.

Conspicuous consumption appeared on all sides. The twenties was not a time of inhibitions. It was taken for granted that the world was diverse and people eccentric, and that life was better enjoyed when it was lived to the full.

The population, which in JB's short life had once been less than

27. William Butler, *Tulsa 75* (Tulsa Chamber of Commerce, 1974), p. 158.

Sapulpa's, was moving in early 1926 toward the 100,000 figure. Tulsa, in other words, had ballooned into a city. Its leaders had raised large sums to pay for the construction of a seventy-mile-long flow of drinking water from Spavinaw Creek to the city; it had two radio stations and would soon have a third, had two small airports and was building a large, metropolitan stadium under the leadership of W. G. Skelly.

Yet, despite the civic activities, the mansions, the competition to see which magnate and his family could enter a winning horse in the Kentucky Derby—Harry Sinclair turned that corner in 1923—and all the other trappings of urban life, it was, at base, oil that built Tulsa, Ponca City, Ardmore, Enid, Duncan, Seminole, and Oklahoma City.

In moving back to easy driving distance from his parents' home in Sapulpa, JB was not so much transferring as consolidating his experience. To be a young veteran of the industry and situated at one of its core cities was a comfortable situation; everyone likes to be properly placed.

JB was in charge of Imperial's order department. That meant he received and expedited tank-car shipments. Technically he had two entities for which he operated: the Imperial Refining Company and the Imperial Oil Marketing Company. The job was more complex and involved larger sums of money, heavier traffic, and many more points of business contact than his initial post as a shipping clerk and office manager at Ardmore. The profits of the firm depended in part on his efficiency, and—since he was in headquarters—he grew to know more men of higher abilities than those at the refinery, with the exception of Reardon. His favorite, a man from whom he learned much, was Ralph Moon, the Imperial general sales manager.

For the rest, life was pleasant. He pursued some sports; hunting had been a passion since childhood. He liked to play golf; in the twenties, golf was popular with businessmen but had not yet become a mass passion. On weekends he played poker in the hotel downtown. The game was a one hundred dollar change in, the joker in aces, straights and flushes, with the only limit being the size of the pot.

It was the classic game. The players would usually play draw. Blind hands are the easiest with which to bluff. The deal circled the table. Neither JB nor the men he played with could afford huge sums; the stakes were relatively modest but the play was fast, hard, and skillful. That was what made it fascinating. JB formed the habit of coasting in the earlier part of the evening and making his big push late in the early morning hours. "The last pot of the game was always the largest; the winners would be reckless with their money and the losers would be desperate to recoup," he says. He played a hard game, but not a professional one. He liked to win but was not fond of seeing other men lose. The distinction is a fine one, but important.

Yet, though he was leading a bachelor's life, with all its easy pleasures, it had grown somewhat tiring. His letters to Eddy Edmondson, the little brunette student nurse, were frequent, and so were his trips to Oklahoma City to see her. They did not have too much time together; their lives were being lived in different cities. Miss Edmondson was adamant about earning her nurse's cap, and was studying at the University Hospital. As their plans took shape, JB, who had always put money aside, explored the possibility of buying some stock in Imperial.

He was not the only young man to consider the future brilliant and to think about stocks; the nation was experiencing a great boom. Its essence has since been described as speculative, but that was not true. Speculation was only the top of a great wave of progress that was based on inventions and a free marketplace.

The government had receded. The national debt was progressively reduced under Harding, and that reduction continued under Coolidge. Taxes were cut back; the distasteful clause publicizing income tax payments was canceled. Business taxes made up the slack, and business boomed as never before.

Mass production methods, breakthroughs in electronics, and expansions in electrical power and appliances poured across the nation. Despite the orations of labor leaders, who regarded their relatively low status and diminishing memberships as signs of bad times, the fact was that an immense transfer from steam to electricity lifted and eased, magnified and advanced the production of the nation in seemingly magic manner.

The change that overtook the nation was, moreover, not due to the fact that labor worked any harder; if anything, the American workingman worked less than any of his predecessors. Henry Ford introduced a five-day week, an unheard-of phenomenon, and his factories turned out cars at the rate of one every ten minutes.

Every industry appeared to take a giant leap forward. Telephones multiplied, steel and iron production increased by a factor of five, the rate of development of new petroleum products multiplied by sixteen, new metals, such as aluminum and magnesium, soared. A vast array of new products appeared in the marketplace—"cigarette lighters, oil furnaces, wrist watches, antifreeze products, reinforced concrete, paint sprayers, book matches, dry ice, radios"[28]—an endless list that grew as people watched.

As a result of the wartime disruption of the nation's long dependence on the German chemical industry, a new American chemical

28. Leuchtenburg, *Perils of Prosperity*, pp. 179–180.

industry arose behind a high-tariff wall that created a vast new sector in which new synthetic materials appeared: rayon, Bakelite, plastics, and lacquers altered other industries, such as clothing, manufacturing, and pharmaceuticals.

Visible signs of this boom were given dramatic emphasis by what appeared to be a nation in the process of rebuilding—or building—homes, plants, and even cities in new places. The boom in Miami was the largest ever seen in terms of real estate development; Los Angeles was growing like a mushroom, and skyscrapers were being sent straight toward the heavens in New York, Chicago, Detroit, Cleveland, and other cities.

States, encouraged by federal matching grants, laid highways across lands empty since the beginning of time—in Utah "over a sea of mud, in Florida through the swamps of the Everglade, in Arizona across the desert itself, west of Phoenix, in Massachusetts over the mountainous but beautiful Hoosac Trail."[29]

Of all decades, it was surely one of the greatest in the history of the world in which to be young and alive, and to be contemplating marriage—and to like one's job and company.

Young men in other parts were not so fortunate. Germany was experiencing a boom and had revitalized the Ruhr, which was back in its control. One result was to reduce British coal exports. The UK companies began to report losses and great political arguments arose. Churchill's decision to put the nation back on the gold standard, with its attendant deflation and unemployment, would have been bitter at the best of times; when times grew difficult, the taste was too bitter for the stomach of the British Labour party.

That party was permeated with disciples of the Fabian Socialists at the top and penetrated, some believed, by Communists at the bottom. Whatever the truth of these unprovable charges, the fact remains that strikes in the coal fields led by May, 1926, to a general strike.

Such a situation would have been inconceivable a century before—or in any century. A new weapon had appeared on a scale that could give any democratic government pause. The strike was not exactly a rebellion, but it was more than passive resistance. Churchill regarded it as a threat to constitutional government but neither he nor any other British leader could conceive of using naked force to coerce people into tasks for which they did not believe themselves sufficiently compensated. Only the commissars believed in that.

In the end the general strike was settled in the British fashion,

29. Ibid., p. 185.

with cajoling and compromise—and with none of its basic problems resolved.

In the United States the British problems appeared the result of poor management. The nation was experiencing a boom in the marketplace attended by inflation, and the belief began to take root that a magic system had somehow evolved that insured permanent prosperity. The Federal Reserve System was regarded as some sort of invisible guardian against any possible collapse. The stock exchanges began to lure first thousands and then hundreds of thousands of new investors, and any traveler could see enough pockets of poverty and enough opportunity for new ventures to become easily convinced of the brilliance of the future.

It did not dawn—and in most instances would never dawn—on the American experts that when the British Empire, whose Dominions literally spanned the globe, was tottering on the edge of unprecedented international crisis, and when sporadic crises were occurring in virtually every European nation, that the world was in patches rather than riches. The prosperity on every American side made such an observation almost beyond ordinary human comprehension.

W. B. Hassett also owned the Kettle Creek Refining Company in El Dorado, Arkansas. He operated that plant as part of Imperial Refineries, but its location made it one of his most profitable properties. In the fall of 1927 Hassett decided to have a Dubbs unit installed at Kettle Creek. Since JB had worked on the previous installation at Ardmore, he was the logical man to send to El Dorado to do the same.

That meant that he was no longer head of the order department in headquarters and was once again a construction engineer. JB didn't mind; El Dorado was a town whose boom was legendary.

It did not take place until 1921. Within months five thousand strangers were in town. Before that year was out, fields were discovered in Smackover, a short distance to the north, and El Dorado began to live up to its name.

By 1925, Carl Rister says, "El Dorado's dirt streets disappeared under concrete, the red brick courthouse was supplanted by one of stone and modern office buildings, stores, churches, schools and beautiful homes were built." There was little wonder: El Dorado was surrounded by productive fields, all within a few hours' drive. Meanwhile the town itself, surrounded by green, rolling hills, was small but prosperous and attractive.

It is probable, however, that JB would have been agreeable to almost any suggestion from Mr. Hassett at that point. JB had worked for Imperial for four years, was twenty-six years old, and doing well. Imperial was keeping him busy and he was satisfied.

"Get along with Red," Hasset had said. As instructions go, those were somewhat brief, but JB caught their significance at once. When he arrived at El Dorado and met Red Longino, the superintendent of the Kettle Creek Refinery, he knew what Hassett's warning meant. "Longino," says JB, "was dead set against any change of any kind."

Fortunately, he liked to play poker. Their games were held inside the projection booth of a local theater, a refuge made necessary by the nasty habit of raids formed by the El Dorado police force. It didn't take long for Red to learn that JB played well, and he suggested a sort of informal partnership. There was no need, he implied, for them to waste their efforts on one another. "If I bet heavy," he assured JB, "that means I'm really wired."

They played stud, and in one hand JB was dealt deuces back to back. Red stayed through all four draws and had no pair showing, but he did have an ace. He bet two hundred dollars—a respectable amount of money in even fancier places than a projection booth—and everyone dropped out except JB.

"Mr. Longino," he said, "I have a feeling you're not being honest. I'll call."

When Red saw that JB had been called with two deuces—the lowest possible pair—he was indignant. "You had no *business* calling," he said severely, and threw in his hand.

JB didn't smile, however, and that helped. He learned, in a little while, that "Red had a problem that came in bottles." Inevitably that habit led Longino into irregular absences and suspicious illnesses. JB covered for him; a man who drank too much was a familiar sight almost everywhere, especially during Prohibition. Once Red realized that JB would neither report him nor talk against him, he relaxed. Occasionally they attended cockfights together—spectacles that Longino liked.

One day JB asked the superintendent if the refinery lines crossed anywhere. Red looked at him as though he had lost his mind, but JB's figures showed two thousand barrels long on heavy fuel and two thousand barrels short on Number 2 burning oil. A crossed line and a valve error could send Number 2 into the heavy-fuel tank. Longino checked and found an open pump valve. Until then JB's yield report had seemed meaningless to him, but his attitude was transformed. "Any man who can spot an open valve while sitting in the office is worth listening to," he said, shaking his head in wonder. After that, Red and JB were a team.

Around them the bottom began to tremble. Car sales dropped 22 percent in 1927, and a slowdown appeared in construction and many other industries. JB and his associates, working as they were in the heart of the booming Oil Country, were probably not as aware of this decline as others in other regions. Certainly JB had little reason to think about it; his position, like that of most employed wage-earners, was that of a protected person; his firm was like a second home that cushioned him from cold winds and outside shocks.

Beyond that, he had other personal reasons to be unconcerned—to be happy. In the fall of 1927 Miss Gladys Edmondson, after working for three months as a graduate nurse, had agreed to become Mrs. JB Saunders. JB called her "Eddy," but she, with an odd but appealing formality that probably reflected her Texas background, called him "Mr. Saunders."

By itself the slowdown in the boom was not alarming; the production tempo of 1927 was far in advance of levels achieved only a few years earlier. Had the marketplace been allowed to make its own adjustments, there would have been a rise in interest rates, an increase in unemployement, the failure of some unsound enterprises, and the rigors of what was then called a *panic*. Like the depression of 1920, it would probably not have lasted long, had it not been for the Federal Reserve Board.

The Federal Reserve was created on the idea that the judicious use of governmental authority over the currency and banking policies of the nation could cool the economy when it grew too hot, and warm it when it grew too cold. Like most theories, that one had an inherent neatness that made it attractive to disorderly men. Its popularity, in 1927, was enormous.

The decline in the economy in 1927 alarmed the Federal Reserve Board to the extent that there was a split of opinion among its members. The chairmanship passed to Roy A. Young. Under Young the board proceeded to intervene in the situation. The nature of that intervention and its consequences proved, if any proof is necessary, that the board was staffed not by unearthly, omniscient beings, but by fallible men.

Armed with an authority the 1975 World Almanac & Book of

Facts describes as "to give the country an elastic currency" (a common error), the board decided, in late 1927, to lower the interest rates on rediscounted paper from 4 percent to 3.5 percent, to allow the purchases of stocks on the exchanges for a deposit of only 10 percent, and to encourage its member banks to expand credits and loans. These decisions amounted to inflation.[30]

Their results began to emerge in the spring of 1928. "On March 3, 1928, Radio sold at 94½. By the next Friday it had surged to 108. On the next day it had bounded to 120½. It seemed impossible, but when the market closed on Monday morning, Radio had gained another 18 points and was selling at 138½. The next morning Radio opened at 160, a gain of 21½ points overnight. And it did not stop. After a few days of relative quiet, Radio jumped 18 points on March 20. The Big Bull Market was underway."[31]

The landscape seemed to move, and everyone ran faster to keep up with it. The nation's leading economists assured the public that their "science," as they began to call it, had discovered the secret of permanent prosperity. A wave of optimism swept the land; virtually every firm made plans to expand eternally.[32]

Around them the tides of election swirled dizzily. The long Democratic hearings on Teapot Dome had subjected Doheny, Sinclair, and Fall to a protracted propaganda barrage that left permanent scars on all three men. Doheny, who broke down on the stand, was so disheartened he sold all his immense holdings including "rich Mexican properties, Venezuelan properties producing 45,000 barrels of oil a day, an interest in concessions in Iraq, one of the world's largest tanker fleets, refineries in Mexico, Venezuela and Louisiana and marketing facilities along the Atlantic seaboard and in Europe and South America"[33] to Standard of Indiana for $37.5 million. Although he was never to be convicted of any wrongdoing, the experience so embittered him that he spent much of the rest of his life outside the United States, and

---

30. "Between the middle and the end of 1927 rediscount rates were lowered from 4 to 3 1/2 percent and purchases of securities in the open market by the reserve banks totaled $435,000,000. . . . loans and investments of the member banks increased by $1,764,000,000 in the last six months of 1927, although only 7 percent of this increase consisted of commercial loans. . . . much of the credit flowed into stock market speculations, brokers' loans on the New York Exchange rising 24 percent." George Soule, *Prosperity Decade*, pp. 279–280.

31. Leuchtenburg, *Perils of Prosperity*, p. 243.

32. Ludwig von Mises, *Human Action* (Chicago: Henry Regnery, 1966), p. 853.

33. Knowles, *Greatest Gamblers*, p. 217.

his retirement from the industry removed one of its most creative and fertile contributors. It also made Standard of Indiana one of the most powerful petroleum firms in the world.

The scandal was still continuing during the election campaign, but so many other issues emerged that few could penetrate the barrage of rhetoric that veiled the true condition of the nation—and the world.

Peace, that eternal lure, was hoisted aloft once again. The American Secretary of State, Frank B. Kellogg, agreed with the French Foreign Minister, Aristide Briand, and a great conference was held in Paris to "outlaw" war. Signed by fifteen nations at first and sixty-two eventually, it represented a triumph of language over reality, for which Kellogg received the Nobel Peace Prize the following year.

The USSR and Germany were among the signers of that instrument; both were arming assiduously. The leaders of the Weimar Republic had secretly agreed to an off-budget series of military expenditures for years, which included experiments in rockets and many other long-range, ominous programs. In the Orient, Japan invaded and occupied Shantung, China; a military coup took place in Portugal; Mussolini restricted the number of voters in Italy from ten to three million; the President of Mexico was assassinated; and many other events occurred that made a mockery of the words *peace* and *democracy*. Yet the Kellogg-Briand treaty served to make the Republican Administration appear constructive in its foreign policy. And there was little doubt that the program of the Democratic party, in contrast, appeared mainly as a series of complaints mounted in a time of great prosperity.

The usual series of conventions were held: the Socialists nominated Norman Thomas, the Communists—calling themselves the Workers party—nominated William Z. Foster, the Republicans nominated Herbert Hoover, and the Democrats nominated Alfred E. Smith of New York.

Hoover was a famous internationalist, a mining engineer, and former administrator of the post–World War I effort to relieve the starving in Europe and Russia. He had served as Secretary of Commerce, and most businessmen considered him one of their own. His campaign was high-minded and somewhat unrealistic; it contained some curious undertones. Those mounted the curious charge that a defeat of the Republicans would lead to a depression; a phantom that hovered significantly over the incredible boom underway. Reelect a Republican, the sloganeers said, and there will be "two chickens in every pot; a car in every garage."

The Democratic campaign was even more interesting. Alfred E. Smith was the first Catholic to be nominated by one of the two major parties, but that advance in tolerance was presented almost as a challenge. Democratic propagandists came close to saying that those who opposed Smith would convict themselves of prejudice. The tactic aroused angry responses and, in fact, evoked much of the prejudice it sought to bully out of existence.

The actual issues would have been far more interesting and helpful to the nation, had they been discussed. The division was between the smaller cities and towns, the middle and business class, and the Populists in the countryside, on the one hand, and the avant-garde in the metropolis on the other. Smith was associated with virtually all that was novel, daring, and ethnic; Hoover was identified with the *Establishment*—a term then unknown.

Back in El Dorado, JB resumed his duties as the refinery construction engineer of the Kettle Creek refinery, and put his new knowledge to work by examining its processes and preparing yield reports that did more than simply record. He had learned that various approaches to blending could lift the output of the plant, and his grasp of operations impressed Ralph Moon, the Imperial general sales manager, who came down on a visit.

Moon's visit was, in part, a response to a problem that had arisen regarding Ed Praytor, the Kettle Creek sales manager. Praytor drove a big yellow Chrysler Imperial, obtained by a special deal with the El Dorado Chrysler agency, which bought so much gasoline from the refinery that Praytor could pay for the car out of these commissions alone. The arrangement was highly satisfactory to them, but left something of a bad taste to others. Praytor, however, was a man who believed in taking whatever advantages of his situation were possible, and he was a good salesman. His situation appeared secure until Mr. Hassett noted that Mrs. Praytor had acquired a mink coat.

Not long afterward Ralph Moon, the general sales manager of Imperial, paid another visit to the Kettle Creek refinery. He and several customers toured the plant. Moon listened carefully as JB described its equipment and the uses to which it was put. Later he spent some time in the office examining the yield reports and had JB come in and explain the systems of record-keeping he had installed.

Then he leaned back, regarded the younger man for a moment or so, and said, "You have no business being a refinery engineer."

Before JB could recover, the older man continued. "This country is going to do a dipsy-doodle. Building will stop. There won't be any new refineries. The push will be finding products markets. A young man with your intelligence should become a peddler. No matter how bad times get, a man can always sell."

JB wondered how he could switch from the skills he had mastered at such effort into a sector where he would become a raw newcomer all over again, and Moon made it, clear it would entail sacrifice. He would have to start at a smaller salary. Nobody likes to hear that. But Moon was a professional salesman and general sales manager of Imperial. He focused his powers on the younger man and made an impression JB never forgot.

Prosperity is one of the most difficult of all conditions to endure from a limited situation. The world in 1928 seemed bulging with novelties and luxuries on all sides, and on all sides there seemed crowds of people with money to burn. The newspapers were filled with tales of sudden success; barbershops were heavy with conversations about stocks and riches. There was a brokerage office in the smallest town, and stories of fabulous wealth gained in months, as easily as winning a lottery, were common.

The music of the moment reflected a frenetic gaiety: "Button Up Your Overcoat," "You're the Cream in My Coffee," "Makin' Whoopee." Radio sales soared, and new, invisible personalities, known only by their voices, became legends, stars, and famous entertainers. Animated electric signs, Mickey Mouse, transcontinental buses with sleeping quarters, Babe Ruth hitting sixty home runs, city streets jammed with cars, stores glittering with expensive and alluring items— all made it a difficult time to decide to start again at the bottom. Any bottom.

Yet, not long after Moon's conversation, Praytor came to JB and told him he was leaving. He asked JB to leave with him; he had another company lined up and they could use a skilled construction and refinery engineer. JB shook hands and wished him well, but said he would not go with him. In fact, he hoped to get the job Praytor was leaving.

Following that decision, he sent a wire to Mr. Hassett in Tulsa, saying, "I would appreciate your considering my qualifications for the sales position now open."

A few days later Hassett came to El Dorado, and JB met him as he was walking, with his usual rapid step, toward the office. "I think you're the man," Hassett said, "but we have to get Clive to think so too." Clive Alexander was the Kettle Creek superintendent; his cooperation was essential.

Later that day JB had to go into a side room and, by one of those coincidences that do occur but that are often difficult to explain, overheard part of a conversation about himself. Alexander was saying he thought Hardin, the bookkeeper, might be a better choice. "JB is just a roughneck," he concluded.

JB was frozen. He heard Mr. Hassett say, soothingly, "I've seen him with a collar and tie, and he doesn't look too bad." JB fled.

The year 1928 drew toward its end. Herbert Hoover was elected in a landslide, but the Democrats took defeat bitterly. The big cities now reflected an almost permanent disdain of the countryside. That phenomenon was not restricted to the United States; in Berlin the glittering intellectuals of the Weimar Republic made a fetish out of berating the German bourgeoisie, and Paris reflected the same dichotomy.

Yet the market continued to soar. Wages continued to rise, goods poured out in a glittering stream, and JB Saunders, twenty-eight years old, accepted a reduction in salary from $350 a month to $275 and was named sales manager for the Kettle Creek Refining Company.

In El Dorado, Arkansas—a town where lives were lived beyond the spotlights of notoriety, and where the oil business permeated the very air—business boomed amid brutal competition. JB put away his engineer's clothes, and bought some white shirts. He had moved—though at a sacrifice, as Moon had warned—into another rank.

Business is competitive and companies have hierarchies, but its essence is democratic. Men can move up the business ladder through ability rather than through being accredited by outside groups. JB was well known in El Dorado; it was a small town, and his new activities brought him instant attention from other firms. Salesmen, after all, are the shock troops of business. They made the first landings on beachheads, in those days. In fact, the twenties are still heralded, in many quarters, as the era of the salesman.

In a way, JB had repeated the experience of his father, who was in 1929 well established in the real estate business in Sapulpa. He had started in the field, worked his way through the various aspects of the industry that supplanted cattle—and emerged wearing a suit, engaged in its marketing sector. JB went through the chain of experience more rapidly, but that was due in large measure to the stepped-up pace of his times.

He had lots of competition, but on the other hand he had many more men, in close proximity, to observe and from whom to learn—and he had already proven that he could read men, and retain the lessons they taught.

His tasks involved setting a price based on the costs to the refinery and the freight rates, finding customers who could use a product, and closing the sale. In many ways these were functions that were later broken apart. In 1929 a salesman was able to commit his firm in terms that only an officer could do today. His skill could advance or retard his entire group.

JB had friends already, but he made more. One of them, Bob Aycock, had been in El Dorado since 1921, and worked for the Root Oil Company. Root, headed by the elegant Philip Hamilton, dealt mainly with majors. Hamilton liked to make long-term sales to well-heeled customers. Aycock functioned as his traffic manager and was superlative. A former railroader, his knowledge of freight rates and routes was encyclopedic. JB went to Aycock and asked him to draw up a master guide to these essential details, in which the Kettle Creek refinery would serve as a starting place, and the avenues of shipment from El Dorado everywhere could be graded, coded, and itemized. Aycock did it, for twenty-five dollars. JB paid him out of his own pocket; it was worth many thousands.

He was, in other words, in a situation he was now equipped to master. Ralph Moon's instincts were accurate; his protégé—and he was a protégé—plunged into customer contacts and made sales as though intuitively. But Moon and others knew better. Salesmen, like poker players, may appear to bet without thought, but those who survive do their studying in advance.

One other man took note of JB at that time: John B. Atkins.

Atkins was a Shreveport aristocrat, tall, athletic, and chilly. He was one of the owners of the Shreveport Producing & Refining Company, and a brother-in-law of Philip Hamilton, who years later said of him, "Atkins is the only man I ever knew who made money without working. He knew how to make other men work, to make money for him." But that was years later.

In 1929, Atkins looked at JB and unbent briefly. "If you are ever unhappy," he said, blunt as ever, "give me a ring."

Many businesses and industries boomed in early 1929, but oil captivated Oklahoma. In Oklahoma City itself a producing well was discovered in December, 1928. By early 1929 the ITIO-Foster interests had staked out a large city area, and Slick, Sinclair, Coline, Roxanna, and others came running. A great rush started. Shanty towns appeared on the city outskirts. Pipe, machinery, supplies, drillers, riggers, tool-dressers, and others rushed to the scene. As the year lengthened, it appeared Oklahoma City had been built atop a vast oil pool, and the city itself was in danger of being destroyed as a result of the discovery.

Seldom had a great discovery created so many arguments and problems, and the price of midcontinent crude oil began to drop as new floods of the black gold came rushing from dozens of wells.

Such abrupt changes could endanger many firms not engaged in production; backstage efforts to maintain prices that ensured profits on contracts made earlier were intense. JB, whose business education was now along these lines, was among the many who regularly received a bulletin—circulated in secret among refiners—listing the "price-cutters." These men were feared and almost hated; they could come into the marketplace and convert a good sale into a company loss, by flooding a region with cheaper products. JB had lots to learn; Mr. Hassett made more than the usual number of trips to El Dorado to talk to him, and to discuss customers, the industry, trends—and their meaning.

The significance of new developments was not always clear, and seldom for the naïve. The United States, in the first half of 1929, was almost the only modern nation that allowed its industries to operate with a minimal amount of interference from the government. In Britain the Conservative party had attempted to return to the gold standard, to issue a sound currency, and to allow the marketplace to operate on a realistic basis. That policy had led to widespread and apparently permanent unemployment, the creation of the dole, and bitter class struggle. In the British Isles themselves, that struggle revolved around a demand by the Socialists that the government retrench the empire and assist the people at home. It was exacerbated by intense propaganda from India and other colonies, which demanded more political rights and an end to the colonial system.

In Europe that same division appeared on many fronts. Spain was under a dictatorship, so was Portugal, so was Italy, and so was most of eastern Europe. Stalin was using the tools of western technology to create immense power plants and to build heavy industries, at the expense of virtually every life value of his people. The toll of murder, imprisonment, and terror in that vast land, however, was held secret from the knowledge of the world by a small coterie of western journalists anxious to keep their foreign posts, who relayed a stream of misleading dispatches to their papers back home.

Germany, the pivot of central Europe, was in the most peculiar position of all. Its leaders in the Weimar Republic were Socialists maintained only by the force of the Army, and the President, Hindenburg—a six-foot-five-inch giant symbol of the vanished empire—was nearing dotage. Most of German industry was operating under loans from private American investment sources. Its fabled recovery was based on quicksand, and its army was secretly rearming, while it even more secretly searched for new leadership.

In the summer of 1929 the inflation of credit loosened by the Federal Reserve Board alarmed even that august and remote body. A huge proportion of the nation was living on the installment plan. The number of people involved in selling stocks and working in banks and brokerage offices had increased enormously, and their aggregate wages equaled all those paid in mining and agriculture combined.[34] The nation's major exchanges listed over one billion shares, priced at over $87 billion—and these did not include those shares traded on the New York Curb, on the Consolidated Exchange, or over the counter.

Yet there were voices raised to describe that huge bubble as normal and good. Irving Bush, owner of the Bush Terminals in Brooklyn, said, "We are only at the beginning of a period that will go down in history as the golden age."[35]

The Federal Reserve Board, however, grew nervous. A welter of international factors, some of which had contributed to its previous decision to expand credit, were combining to bring the day of reckoning near. Both London and New York investment houses had turned from foreign loans to funding domestic speculators in New York. The Germans were having difficulties in borrowing money, and that threatened the stability of many long-standing arrangements. The board issued orders in April, 1929, to reduce credits for speculation.

In Britain the Conservative government was defeated, and the Liberals, as once before, joined Labour to introduce a Socialist government. That alarmed many British business interests, which sent large sums of capital to the United States. Those monies sent the stock exchanges even higher. Yet though paper continued to expand, cash was beginning to contract. The interest rates on call money rose from 7 percent at the end of 1928 to 13 percent in June, 1929. The tower began to tremble.

In late June, 1929, Ralph Moon announced he was leaving the Imperial Refining Company, to go into business for himself. He came to El Dorado and told JB his plan. His new firm would be known as the Moon Marketing Company and would sell gas furnaces, toasters, irons, and other appliances. He needed some backers. JB was one of ten friends who each put up two thousand dollars. With that twenty thousand dollars Moon formed a small loan company. In that manner he was able to sell appliances on the installment plan in his marketing

34. Soule, *Prosperity Decade*, pp. 288–289.
35. Ibid., p. 293.

company and then handle installment payments, hinged to salaries, through another. The combination was in perfect keeping with the spirit of the times.

The spirit of the times—in all and every time—is almost inescapable. JB himself, in the summer of 1929, had bought stock with his poker winnings and savings, and watched its value rise. Being inherently careful, he combined the hope of profit with proof of where he considered his interests to be placed, and held mostly stock in Imperial Refining. At the time Moon decided to strike out on his own, JB's stock was worth about twenty thousand dollars.

Mr. Hassett came to see him, and told JB he would replace Moon as general sales manager for all Imperial Refineries at a salary of $350 a month. He was pleased; he knew that was merely the starting point, and as general sales manager he was now on the top level of the firm.

He moved to Tulsa the day after Labor Day, 1929. His broker in El Dorado—"Just a country boy," says JB, "but smart"—told him not to transfer his account to Tulsa. "Sell everything," he advised. "This bubble will bust." JB's eyebrows rose; that sounded ominous.

He asked Harry Trower, head of marketing for huge Phillips Petroleum, whose stock was selling at a little over 30, whether he should follow that advice or not. Trower smiled. "I'll tell you how to make a million dollars," he said.

"How?"

"Buy Phillips."

JB was impressed, but moving from El Dorado to Tulsa, now that he was a married man, was not as simple as in his bachelor days. There was furniture and articles to pack, many arrangements to make. Shortly after he arrived, he learned that Mr. Hassett had decided to expand in Texas, and he was drawn into that effort to the virtual exclusion of other considerations.

Hassett, like all small, independent refiners at the time, had to work against handicaps imposed by the majors. Those included dominance of crude oil supplies. An independent was charged a premium when he purchased crude oil, which sent his refining costs soaring above those of the majors. Yet when he sold his refined products, he had to match or underprice his products against the majors' competition. That meant that independent profit margins were always thinner than those of their giant competitors, a situation that made the survival of independent firms somewhat remarkable at best, and difficult at all times.

Imperial was prospering, however, and Hassett—in common with most other firms—was optimistic enough in mid-1929 to consider expansion. As the result of a meeting in Dallas with a Mr. Wickett, owner of the Blue Bonnet Refining Company, he bought another small refinery in San Angelo, Texas, and made an unusual and promising deal regarding a small installation at a desolate watering stop along the Southern Pacific Railroad southeast of Pecos. For lack of a better name, the small refinery at that location had been named Wickett. It produced fuel oil for the Southern Pacific, but its operator had no special use for the lighter end of the barrel products, which JB called "toppings."

Hassett was offered those toppings on a long-range contract basis, at the posted price of fuel oil. That was a bargain. It meant he could create a small installation at Wickett and—assured of an economical and regular source of supply—could use those toppings as the basis from which to produce naphthas, kerosenes, and burning oils.

He sent for JB, who arrived at Wickett, looked around and said, "Sand, sage brush and cactus." He had, of course, more comments on the expansion and its possibilities. His years of experience with the firm had equipped him with a refinery engineer's knowledge of how a new installation at Wickett could be created. The task was not especially easy, but it was not complex either. Pipe had to be heated, bent, threaded, and cut at the site; a tower had to be created, and connections made with the original Wickett installation.

To that point the proceedings appeared almost unnaturally easy, but as usual, the initial advantage, which had lured Mr. Hassett into this expansion, was surrounded by a thicket of disadvantages which grew under closer examination. JB, who had matured beyond a refinery engineer into a sales manager, discovered these as the new installation was created, and initial production experiments conducted. One very large handicap was the fact that the Wickett and San Angelo plant production was based on high-sulphur crude oil. High-sulphur crude was widely unpopular because of its smell, which resembled concentrated rotten eggs. Its refinery products were similarly afflicted.

JB, like most of the refiners from Oklahoma and the midcontinent, was more accustomed to the products made from "sweet" crude oil, which had a low sulphur content and no obnoxious odor. At Wickett he had to conduct a series of experiments to discover the properties and possibilities of high-sulphur crude. The goal of these experiments was to produce a marketable gasoline for the automotive trade—the most important of all refinery products, commercially speaking. They culminated in the knowledge that the Wickett naphtha could be blended with casinghead gas to make a finished product. That was encouraging, but freight rates for natural gasoline into Wickett, so that blending could be done at the plant itself, were prohibitively high. That was discouraging and seemed to dash the project.

At that juncture JB switched from a refinery engineer into his larger role as sales manager. He had made a host of contacts throughout the central and eastern part of the country, and among his acquaintances was a jobber named Woffard in Birmingham, Alabama. Woffard, operating as the Woffard Oil Company, made a blend of gasoline and Benzoil, which competed with the ethyl gasoline being marketed, on a virtually monopolistic basis, by the majors.

JB went to Birmingham and taught Woffard that he could, by using perforated pipes, blend the Wickett naphtha, Benzoil, and natural gasoline during unloading, and have in hand an economical and excellent motor-car gasoline, marketable at excellent margins. Woffard was pleased. JB had, by establishing this initial and important customer, found a way for Wickett's production to enter the lucrative gasoline marketplace in a competitive, though novel, manner.

One handicap remained: the smell. That problem was solved when Woffard decided that a handicap that could not be eliminated could be overcome by describing it as an advantage. He called the smell of the Imperial gasoline "the odor of power"—a legend that carried the same sort of credibility as the old idea that a good medicine must have a bad taste.

The Pure Oil people were contacted and thought that approach had interesting possibilities. They not only purchased the high-sulphur fuel but carried the advertising claim into the marketplace. To the delight of Imperial, Woffard, and Pure itself, the product—and the crazy claim—were accepted. Some years later, in fact, Woffard sold out to Pure Oil for several million dollars.

JB, meanwhile, had established a marketing beachhead with Woffard that he proceeded to broaden through the rest of Imperial's marketing area. All his jobbers had to be taught how to blend at delivery. It was an ingenious route around the high freight rates that had threatened to defeat the entire Wickett expansion.

JB's problems did not end with the solution of the gasoline situation, however. Marketing burning oils for the factory or home, made from the same high-sulphur crude, did not present a freight-rate problem, but did present the odor problem. A spill in delivery could create a stench that lingered for weeks. "Like fried farts," JB said, in a memorable phrase.

The best solution he could suggest, then or later, was to sprinkle oil of mirbane around the spill, in an effort to mask an evil odor with one more pleasant. That helped. Shipping burning oils in open tank cars, JB taught jobbers to pour a gallon of oil of mirbane into the dome as soon as it was opened. In that manner customers could be assured that the odor was not really so bad.

He returned to Tulsa, where his bride waited in their new apartment, in a mood of exhilaration. By adding the San Angelo and

Wickett refineries to his responsibilities, he found his salary lifted from $350 a month to $750. That was a very large sum then, at a time when $10,000 a year was considered complete success. JB could see that goal virtually in hand; he looked around with sparkling eyes and was astonished to see that the world was falling apart.

The débâcle began in August, 1929, when a prominent British firm collapsed and created a panic in London financial centers that caused the Bank of England to raise its rates from 4.5 percent to 6.5 percent. That brought British money back from Wall Street to London, and the New York exchanges began to sag.

By early October there was a crack in the market, and some shares fell in price. That was to be expected in normal times, but in some subconscious way, everybody knew that the times were not normal. JB read the headlines, and looked for the Phillips Petroleum price. He was surprised to see it was 18.

Meanwhile, clouds of fear began to float through New York and the other exchanges. By the middle of October panic appeared, and Professor Irving Fisher of Yale spoke to say that stocks were on "what looks like a permanently high plateau." That chirp was almost like a signal; pieces began falling from the roof. On October 15 prices fell five or six points. On Saturday, October 19, a half day for trading, prices fell from five to twenty points. On October 21 over nine million shares were sold in one day, and on October 24 almost twenty million shares changed hands. Prices dropped like stones. That was known as Black Thursday.

The banks struggled to stop the slide, but they were beset from two sides. Many firms in industry knew the banks had been heavily engaged in the market, and withdrew their funds. That meant the bankers were in a terrifying vise that was closing on them fast. The ticker tapes ran hours behind transactions, and the lights of Wall Street and other financial canyons glowed through the dark as clerks struggled to keep up.

The Federal Reserve, that beneficent body, issued a report showing that although industrial production had been better than the year before, automotives, tires, steel, and construction had declined. On October 29, for the first time, selling began to affect the blue chip shares: General Electric, United States Steel, American Telephone, and others. On October 31, Professor Fisher said stocks were "absurdly low," and they fell apart.

The world had not seen such a phenomenon since the South Sea Bubble in the eighteenth century, and that had been limited to one financial center in one country. In the autumn of 1929 the Crash brought down projects, plans, people, and virtually what was left of the old order of the West. The sunset, with all its glowing and vivid colors, had proceeded below the horizon, and although it was still twilight, it was plain that the night was coming.

CHAPTER EIGHT

After Sundown

AT FIRST the landscape seemed unchanged. The crowds in Wall Street thinned, the headlines turned to other matters, and men seemed to recover their nerve. Cheerful statements were made from the top of the pyramid; newspapers began to discuss the new longer skirts for women introduced by the Paris couturiers, the crimes of gangsters, and the peculiarities of Prohibition, new books, movies and plays. In New York City construction began on the Empire State Building, and a new song appeared. It was titled *Happy Days Are Here Again.*[1]

In Oklahoma, where JB was busy as sales manager for the four Imperial refineries, the situation was more tangled. Imperial not only sold products from its own refineries, but also bought and resold surplus from about twenty-five or thirty smaller refiners throughout the country. JB had to visit some of these, which meant his travels were extensive. He would take trains to New York, then to Atlanta, then to Chicago, St. Louis, and other points. In most of these places he had salesmen who reported to him, or salesmen who regularly called on customers to whom he had them assigned. His field reports through November and December, 1929, showed a precipitous drop.

Similar drops appeared in other industries. They first affected luxury shops and then began to trickle downward. Although only 1 million out of the nation's 122 million people had actually owned any shares of stock, the large amount of credit these shares represented, in terms of both their purchase and their use as collateral for loans, amounted to huge sums that affected every sector. Yet no large firms collapsed; dividends remained high, and in the early months of 1930 the stock exchanges began to heat up again as though nothing had

1. Frederick Lewis Allen, *Since Yesterday: The Nineteen-Thirties in America, Sept. 3, 1929–Sept. 3, 1939* (New York: Harper & Row, 1940), p. 21.

happened. The volume of trading reached the peaks of the previous summer, and prices soared, but millions began to lose their jobs.

Very slowly at first, but with ever-quickening pace, the economy of the United States—and with it that of the entire western world— began to unravel. The country first and most directly affected was Germany. German industry had made what seemed a remarkable recovery, due largely to investments from the United States. As the twenties drew toward a close, these investments, short-range in nature, became more and more important. The Germans had, in early 1929, finally agreed to pay eighteen billion dollars over a thirty-seven-year period, and the Allies agreed to end the occupation of the Rhineland.

German ability to meet this promise depended, however, on continued foreign loans, mainly from the United States, which enabled its industries to function at capacity. These loans were, in the aftermath of the 1929 Crash, no longer renewable. A crisis arose in the Weimar Republic, and the army searched for a new German Chancellor. President Hindenburg, now in his eighties, obediently appointed a soldier *manqué* named Heinrich Brüning. He took office amid mounting unemployment, and rising shouts from both the German Communists and the National Socialists headed by Hitler.[2]

In Oklahoma a different situation prevailed. Oil discoveries in Oklahoma City threatened to engulf the market with cheap crude to such an extent it would inundate prices and drown profits. In late 1929 the entire field was closed for thirty days while the large firms that controlled its output struggled with the state commission to create controls and prorationing. In 1930, however, new discoveries threatened to blow their plans sky-high. The Mary Sudik well, in the south part of the field, was left without mud by a careless crew. On March 26 a gusher erupted, sending 200 million cubic feet of gas and 20,000 barrels of oil a day into the air, tossing the tower about like a toy.

"Men in slickers and steel helmets, wearing goggles, with cotton stuffed in their ears to keep out the deafening roar worked courageously. . . . Twice a day Floyd Gibbons, war correspondent and news commentator, broadcast 'Wild Mary's' antics to the radio-listening world. . . . A strong north wind caught the oil and blew it far southward, showering it on farms for five or six miles about, until they were covered by a black, oil coat. And oily globules, like soap bubbles, floated through the air to splatter homes in the university town of Norman, eighteen miles away."[3]

2. Golo Mann, *The History of Germany Since 1789* (New York: Praeger, 1968), p. 398.
3. Ritter, *Oil! Titan*, pp. 259–260.

Another huge oil-rush began in the region, which led, incredibly, to more oil discoveries than before. A tangled paradox emerged, in which crude oil was pouring out but being purchased mainly by the larger and richer firms. These kept the price of crude oil up, while the price of products in the marketplace dropped. Small refiners like Imperial were caught in the middle. JB watched the profits of Imperial melt as though in a fire, until the losses reached the rate of forty thousand dollars a month. For the first time, it began to appear that the firm itself might go under.

To a confused nation the news from the rest of the world appeared unimportant. It came, in any event, in such fragmentary and scattered form, so poorly reported, that most citizens found it difficult to track. Nothing could have seemed more remote than the bizarre behavior of Chinese warlords who disputed the control of various regions with Chiang Kai-shek, the collisions between Chinese and Soviet troops in Manchuria, or the fact that a new Emperor, Haile Selassie, had created himself by a coup in Ethiopia.

There was, however, a certain irony in dispatches from the Soviet Union, which announced a new Five-Year Plan. Walter Duranty, dean of American correspondents in that hidden part of the world, was ecstatic about Stalin who, Duranty said, "has behind him a young Russia which never knew Tsarist slavery and is free from the faults of servile psychology."[4] Later Duranty recanted, as well he should. The fact was that Stalin had launched a purge of old Bolsheviks capable of disputing his decisions, had instituted a reign of terror designed to fasten people in agriculture to the land and strip them of all possessions, and was being confronted with a peasant resistance that used "sawed off shotguns, the axe, the dagger, the knife. At the same time the peasants destroyed their livestock rather than let it fall into the hands of the State."[5]

For a time, in the first three months of 1930, it appeared as though the situation in the United States would soon recover. The stock market came to renewed life, and prices soared again to almost half what they had been the previous summer. The government stepped in to spend almost $500 million to buy farm commodities to keep their

4. *Time Capsule 1929* (New York: Time-Life, 1967), p. 101.
5. Robert Conquest, *The Great Terror: Stalin's Purge of the Thirties* (New York: Macmillan, 1968), p. 21.

prices from dropping too far. The large oil firms kept the price of crude oil up. Other, larger firms in other industries made similar efforts; many spent large sums to buy their own stock in the exchange.

Amos n' Andy and their Fresh Air Taxicab Company became a phenomenal success on radio; as the weeks passed increasing millions found the program addictive. Midget golf courses sprouted on previously vacant lots everywhere and became a fad as the weather grew warmer in the North, spreading from southern starting places in Florida.

As always, some individuals found fame and fortune. Hemingway's book *A Farewell to Arms* was an instant popular and critical success. People thronged the movies and thrilled to *All Quiet on the Western Front.* With jobs growing scarcer and money tight, many flocked to libraries and vocational schools and enrolled in correspondence courses.

Others found the new pressures more difficult to withstand. Robert Staughton and Helen Lynd, sociologists studying a town they dubbed "Middletown," were told "there seemed to be a collapse in public morals. I don't know whether it was the Depression, but . . . in 29–30 . . . things were roaring here. There was much drunkenness—people holding bathtub gin parties. There was a great increase in women's drinking. . . ."

Pressures, in other words, began to strip façades, and inner characters emerged. JB, in his thirty-first year and finding the post for which he struggled tottering beneath him, was not so much shaken as angered. "It seemed to me the majors were out to destroy all the smaller firms and independents," he said later. "They raised the prices of crude and lowered the prices of products, and had us in a bind."

He spent hours discussing this situation with Mr. Hassett, who had dropped his brusque and lordly manner. The climate for small, independent refiners grew chilly and harsh. The major firms were buying many independents as they fell into difficulties; each such sale included, as a matter of course, a circle of customers. That meant that JB's market was dwindling even faster than the wintry climate of the marketplace made necessary. It seemed to him, he said later, that "the majors were buying up the market."

His own salary remained high; most firms in the nation attempted, that season, to economize on blue-collar, rather than managerial, levels. Nevertheless, he knew that conditions would have to improve or his own would inevitably worsen. He also knew it was impossible for a firm to economize itself into prosperity. Only a way to improve profits could do that.

He was in his office in Tulsa one morning, turning those worn thoughts around in his mind, when his secretary brought in two business cards. The men were outside, waiting to see him. JB read the cards, and his memory, a remarkably retentive instrument, recognized them both immediately. He had seen those names six months earlier on a price-cutter's list—a blacklist—circulated by the state association to which Imperial belonged. When he had first read and memorized those names, JB believed there was nothing worse than a price-cutter: a man who made it impossible for others to earn a decent living. But as he turned the cards over in his hand, he made an equally quick shift in attitude. "Send them in," he said.

They appeared in the doorway and the larger of the two—Earl Paulson, president of the Trackage Oil Company of Milwaukee—asked abruptly, "Do you sell to a cut-price operator?"

"We haven't," said JB quickly, "but we'll have to start."

Only then did Paulson and his companion, Carl Wiedeman, president of the Tankar Gas Company of Minneapolis, enter and sit down.

JB leaned over his desk and said, "Please explain how you operate."

They did, and JB was fascinated. He glanced at the clock and suggested lunch; Paulson and Wiedeman were pleased. JB called Hassett, who came at once, bluffly cordial, and the four men went to the dining room of the Mayo Hotel.

It was almost two hours before they finished talking and parted company. JB and Hassett walked back to the office together; the older man was jubilant. The pair had agreed to buy a tank car of gasoline every day, indefinitely. In time their order would expand to sixty cars a day, but in early 1930 the initial order was worth jubilation.

"Get out that price-cutter's list," Hassett said when they entered JB's office. "We have to live."

JB agreed. He ran his hand down the association's listing. Imperial could no longer afford the luxury of turning away any customers. But as he did so, his mind kept circling about what Wiedeman and Paulson had told him of their operations. It was obvious that the Tankar Gas Company and the Trackage Oil Company had found a profitable way to operate; why couldn't Imperial do the same?

Paulson and Wiedeman had discovered the railroads had land, located on their rights of way, that they were willing to rent at nominal sums in return for receiving tank car traffic. Outlets located on these sites could be operated at rock-bottom costs, requiring only one attendant, and thereby enabling small operators to underprice even the ruinously low levels set by the market, to achieve a razor-thin but nevertheless real profit.

JB and Hassett not only sold to Paulson and Wiedeman, but also to all the other cut-rate operators on their list. When JB had scouted these operators as potential customers in the Oklahoma region, he repeated the performance in Missouri, Arkansas, Illinois, and other states. His activities did not go unnoticed.

"When are you going to get out of the basement and into the parlor?" asked a competitor one day. JB flushed, but did not reply. He knew he had broken the club rules in selling to cut-price operators; his questioner did not know that JB planned to join their ranks.

He began to search for suitable retail-outlet locations on his sales trips and found the first of these in Springfield, Missouri. The railroad was as interested as Paulson and Wiedeman had described, and a simple station was erected. Mr. Hassett believed in testing the water; JB agreed.

Meanwhile, general conditions continued to worsen. The farmers began to suffer a horrible drought that extended from Missouri and Arkansas to Virginia and Maryland on the eastern seaboard, in the entire Midwest up to the Dakotas. In the cities, one out of every two factory workers lost his job. Yet the unemployment did not hit executive levels, dividends remained high, and few persons believed the situation would last very long.

The newspapers reflected far more interest in the débâcle of Prohibition, and there were enough incidents of violent crime to convince most of the world that the United States was more dangerous than any other great power. In New York City, "Dutch" Schultz, Vincent Coll, and "Legs" Diamond fought a weird, gutter war; Al Capone—out after a year in prison—appeared untouchable in Chicago; Jack Lengle, a corrupt reporter on the Chicago *Tribune,* was found shot dead and at first believed to be a martyr.

All those were mere ephemera, however, compared to the soaring folly committed by the Congress of the United States. Elections were due in November, 1930, that would engage every Representative and a third of the Senate. Both houses were heavily packed with members of the Republican party, and all of them were woefully aware that the party that had claimed credit for the boom was getting the credit for the Crash.

Beset by businessmen worried about fading markets and anxious to be protected, Congress proceeded to put together a bill that raised the tariffs on 890 articles to prohibitive levels. In rare unanimity, over one thousand of the nation's top economists circulated and signed a petition of protest and sent it to the White House. President Hoover, however, bowed to pressures from his party and signed the Hawley-Smoot Act.

"It was," said D. F. Fleming, "virtually a declaration of economic war against the whole of the civilized world."[6] Actually, it was more like turning tail and scuttling from world responsibility. England could survive because it had its empire, though its troubles in India were growing serious. France was hoarding gold. But Germany was virtually doomed by the Congressional decision; its goods lost the American market as its industries lost American loans. Retaliation was swift from other countries; tariff walls were swiftly erected in all directions. For the first time the world headed not only toward depression, but back to retrograde trade rivalry reminiscent, in its nationalistic fear and economic illiteracy, of the seventeenth century.

In such a period it was better to be young and never have experienced much, than it was to be old and lose wealth. The newspapers were heavy with suicides—so heavy that suicide jokes became briefly popular. Unemployment soared. People delayed every venture that might cost money; every industrial indicator pointed down. The newspapers, traditionally Republican, turned against the Administration in a manner never before seen in the United States. JB began to learn business lessons of a new sort. Hardly a day passed without a man appearing—or several men—in search of a job. Imperial Refining fell behind in its office rent. Mr. Hassett, unwontedly subdued, helped make arrangements to have the rugs, office machines, and furniture removed and stored in a basement. JB and his dwindling staff moved to Ardmore, Oklahoma, and into more modest quarters.

There had been changes in Ardmore as well. Max Westheimer, who operated a prosperous haberdashery and whom JB knew well, had been hard hit. JB began to believe he was lucky; he and Eddy still had the expensive silver they had purchased when they married. Meanwhile, like everyone else, he had suffered a cut in salary.

It was a time of expedients, discoveries, and stratagems. Credit became an all-important aspect of operations. One day Floyd Rinehart, an executive in a firm in Kansas, called and ordered fifty carloads of gasoline. JB stalled, while a subordinate leafed through Dun's seeking to check the firm's credit rating. Rinehart, guessing, said it had Triple A credit. JB, finding the page, peered and saw that was true. But he also noticed the firm was listed as a refiner, and thought it odd that a refiner would order gasoline. Still, fifty carloads was a sizable order. He said he would ship it at once, providing a sight draft was prepared against delivery on the other end. "Draw it on a Kansas bank," he said,

6. Allen, *Since Yesterday*, p. 28.

wanting to shortcut delays in collection, and sought to cover his suspicion by adding quickly, "because we need the money."

That was agreed and JB sent the shipment on its way, but his qualms remained. He gave orders the shipment was not to be delivered if any delays, for any reason, resulted in the failure of a sight draft to be handed over. "Call me collect," he said, at the end of these instructions.

When the sight draft was prepared, JB checked with the Kansas Bank and learned it was not covered—insufficient funds. He immediately diverted all but four of the cars, but went to Kansas anyway. Arriving, he walked into the firm's offices and was told Rinehart was in the refinery. He went to the refinery and was told Rinehart was not in. "I'll wait," he said, and sat down in the refinery office. Then he said, "Will you announce me?" The secretary got up and went into an inner office. JB followed, and saw Rinehart rising from behind his desk.

"You put me in a helluva spot," JB said. "I need my money."

"I don't have it."

"You own pipelines and service stations," JB pointed out. "What happened?"

"We sold those, months ago," Rinehart answered, and sat down.

JB, staring, saw that he was a beaten man, and left. But the lesson burned. "Information has to be more current," he told Hassett. He was right, but collapses were taking place, toward the end of 1931, at a rate no service such as Dun's could possibly keep current. JB began to check the credit and standings of his customers personally. He soon learned to look for subtle signs seldom described in print, and his education expanded in proportion.

In October, 1930, the President announced official unemployment figures of almost five million, and asked Congress for an appropriation of between $100 million and $150 million for public works. The announcement was muffled; the press was engrossed in human-interest stories and the speeches of candidates running for office. In New York, which had become the nation's publicity capital, the International Apple Shippers Association, confronted with a surplus, had the helpful idea of selling these to unemployed men at wholesale prices so they could resell them at five cents each. One morning the metropolis was astonished to see apple salesmen "shivering on every corner," and soon photographs of the phenomenon conveyed an unforgettable, permanent image of the situation.

It was no wonder the Republicans were swept out of office that November as though by a tidal wave. The reaction of the voters was natural and no doubt inevitable. But it meant that in the spring of 1931 the President, at a time of deep national emergency, was pitted against

151

a hostile Congress. In view of the new ugliness that had now surfaced, that was virtually another disaster for the nation.

In Europe, meanwhile, other politicians were adding new difficulties to the troubles of their countrymen. Germany and Austria, balked from uniting in the wake of the Versailles Treaty, agreed to form a customs union, so goods could be exchanged as though within one country. The French bristled at once; the issue was brought before the World Court, which forbade the union. In that mood the Germans went to the polls, and the Nazis multiplied their seats in the Reichstag almost ninefold, soaring from 12 to 107. That put them behind the Social Democrats, with 143, and ahead of the Communists, who had 77. The mixture was explosive; German streets were filled with men in strange uniforms bearing arms and anxious to use them.

In the opening months of 1931, conditions in the petroleum industry in the United States became incoherent. The careful proration plan, with its controlled drilling and allocations, created by the Corporation Commission to control the rush in the Oklahoma City oil fields, was in collapse. Members of the commission, wrote Carl Rister later, "could watch from the capitol's windows and see the shambles. . . . both major and minor operators vied with each other in reckless drilling, and vented huge volumes of gas into the air. . . . it was estimated that 14 million barrels of oil were produced illegally." That meant that a black market was in existence.

There was nothing surprising about that; a black market had been created, as the result of Prohibition, which encompassed all the basic raw materials, manufacturing articles, and machinery of distilling, brewing, and wine-making, and extended into retail stores and underground speakeasies. Its extension, in time of economic distress, was facilitated by a nationwide intertwined network of open gangsters and secret allies easily able to expand their operations to include other industries. Tax evasion became the difference between profit and loss; firms that held to legal standards were placed at a disadvantage by remaining honest.

Imperial Refining continued to retrench and regroup. Mr. Hassett sold the San Angelo refinery he had bought and decided to close the largest of the firm's plants, at Ardmore. It had four Dubbs units, but their operation meant that Imperial had to pay a continuing royalty for every barrel cracked, to the UOP. Jack Reardon, whose salary—together with that of everyone else in the firm—had been reduced, was made caretaker of the industrial cadaver that resulted. Reardon kept himself busy and useful to the firm by constructing a bulk plant, useful for storage.

Mr. Hassett closed the Ardmore refinery in July, 1931, a fateful month in the history of the world, marked by closures abroad of global significance. In May the Credit-Anstalt of Vienna, a linch-pin in the banking structure of central Europe, had closed its doors, setting a series of bankruptcies and failures into motion. In June the newspapers discovered President Hoover was in the process of rounding up support for a suspension of the war debts, under the poorly understood name of a *moratorium*. The leak made it necessary to issue a premature announcement before the French were notified, and France erupted. The delays that caused prevented the rescue from being complete, though a brief market rally was staged and some signs of hope flickered briefly into life. But in July, 1931, the German Danatbank collapsed—and all the banks in Germany closed their doors.

By that time JB had decided that Mr. Hassett, who kept saying that business would improve when "the situation returns to normal," was in error. The situation, the younger man decided, might not be normal, but it appeared permanent. In his view, that meant that existing conditions would have to be accepted, and plans made on the basis not of hopes but of realities.

He reached that conclusion at a time when Mr. Hassett was beset by many problems, some of which involved his son and one of his daughters, both of whom were in school in Columbia, Missouri. The older man went there to attend to their problems, but before he left issued a bulletin advising his remaining employees that retrenchments were necessary and that they should seek other jobs. He also asked JB to pick up one of the Hassett automobiles, a Studebaker, in Tulsa, and to meet him at Columbia.

JB did, but took the precaution of putting his own suggestions for Imperial down on paper before he arrived. He knew their talk would be definitive and much would depend on whether he could convince Mr. Hassett that Imperial could survive. The two men sat together in the Tiger Inn in Columbia, and Hassett examined JB's plan.

It included a list of suppliers, consisting mainly of small refiners, whose output JB believed could be marketed from low-cost stations established on railroad rights of way, along the pattern described by the Milwaukee and Minneapolis price-cutting marketers. That meant that Imperial would maintain its plants in El Dorado and Wickett, but cut its overhead and administration costs to the bone.

JB's customer list indicated a cluster of possibilities in the St. Louis region. His survey indicated that relocating Imperial's headquarters in that city meant that many of these customers could be contacted by a local telephone call, rather than by long distance. The two refineries kept in operation, at Wickett and in El Dorado, could be kept in contact by teletype. Using St. Louis as a starting base, they could enter the cut-rate gasoline marketplace by erecting inexpensive stations while supplying cut-price operators already in business, and could create separate legal firms as they expanded, so that each new profit center could benefit by the legal tax limits on the first $25,000 in earnings. After that, tax rates rose sharply.

It was a careful, detailed, and comprehensive plan. In effect it would retain the remnants of Imperial's refining operations and customers, but shift the major emphasis of the firm to marketing on a competitive retail basis, and to living on the margins between buying and selling. In that manner it retained as much of the firm's traditional pattern as possible, while charting new paths for the future. Nor was that all. In conclusion JB said, "I've been drawing seven hundred and fifty dollars a month. But I believe Eddy and I can get along on three hundred and fifty dollars." In other words, his offer included not only a new plan, but a cut in his own salary while spearheading a pioneering effort.

Hassett looked at him and said heavily, "I think I can get by on five hundred dollars a month."

JB took a deep breath. He knew Mr. Hassett had been drawing $100,000 a year from Imperial. He knew that the older man's decision to take such an enormous step down from that eminence was painful, but also meant he was willing to follow JB's plan. The two men exchanged a long look; they were committed to mutual survival.

The city of St. Louis was one of the nation's three dominated, at that time, by descendants of German immigrants.[7] Situated at the confluence of great rivers, a railroad center, a transit point for heavy goods flowing in all four directions, it was hard hit by the Depression in 1931. A grimy industrial town in some sections but still notable for its Gashouse Gang, the St. Louis Cardinals, it was heavy with unemployment and distress. Prices had plummeted in the region, and it was thick with cut-rate gasoline station operations. "There must have been fifteen or twenty small cut-price firms," JB said later, "each owning anywhere from one to three to five service stations."

At first they planned to have a downtown office in a convenient location. But JB had rented some land from a lumber company in the suburbs, at the rock-bottom price of eighty-three dollars a month. He had a bulk plant built on the lot, which held about 200,000 gallons of gasoline, as a sales inventory and terminal. Then a service station was added, to pay for the location and earn some money. As the two men

7. The other two were Milwaukee and Cincinnati.

drove into St. Louis, a fog settled over the city from the river, and smoke from the industrial sections combined with that natural curtain to envelop the town in funereal gloom. They visited their prospective offices and drove toward the suburban bulk plant and service station in silence. Crossing Skinker Boulevard, they entered bright sunlight, which continued until they reached the station at 9500 Olive Street Road in St. Louis County. Both men got out of the car and looked around with a sense of relief. JB said, "Why not have an office here?"

In that fashion they fell, so to speak, into a remarkable economy. The service station and bulk plant had been organized as the Central States Oil Company. Four rooms were added to the rear of the station. In one sat the president, W. B. Hassett, when he was in town. In another JB and his salesmen, and one secretary, functioned. In the others were clerks and bookkeepers. The rent for those modest headquarters was eight dollars a month. The station paid the seventy-five dollars balance of the eighty-three-dollars-a-month rent the entire property returned to its lumber-company owners. Seldom was a cut-price operator's career more appropriately launched.

The times were never better for scrimping, doing without, cutting corners, and working feverishly. In the autumn of 1931 a new series of detonations erupted in the international financial marketplace. A run began on the English pound, and the bankers of London were told by the bankers of New York that British welfare would have to be cut before any loans would be granted. When the British attempted to meet these conditions, a mutiny was mounted by parts of the Navy, and riots occurred in other places. The government rescinded the efforts, changed hands, and England went off the gold standard.

That abrupt turn toward a managed currency was imitated by other nations, and the American bankers found their foreign bond holdings abruptly plummeting in value, their domestic bonds at new lows, and "mortgages frozen solid." In September, 1931, 305 American banks failed; in October, 522. People rushed to hoard gold and to withdraw their money while it was still available.

Large firms began to announce across-the-board salary cuts; smaller firms followed suit. By the end of the year the nation was filled with walking wounded. Unemployment figures were more than 1 million in New York City; 600,000 in Chicago; half of all workers in Cleveland; 80 percent in Toledo, Ohio; and almost 100 percent in Donora, Pennsylvania, where only 277 out of nearly 14,000 workers still held jobs at all. Every week that passed saw matters worsen; an average 100,000 a week were dismissed from their employment.[8]

8. Leuchtenburg, *Perils of Prosperity*, p. 247.

Those and even more complex problems bent the petroleum industry as well. JB and Hassett struggled in an industry that was being inundated by crude oil. The huge field in Oklahoma City was sending immense amounts of crude through every conceivable channel, and in late 1930, Dad Joiner, a wildcatter from Ardmore, had hit a heavy producing well at the Daisy Bradford farm in east Texas, and started the last, wildest, and most frantic of the American oil booms.

By 1931 the play in east Texas had sent the population of the tiny town of Kilgore from one thousand to ten times that number. Humble, Gulf, and Shell were at the scene in force, and a man whose name would later become famous—H. L. Hunt, whom JB knew well in Arkansas as a plantation owner and also a professional gambler—made his entry into the industry at the site.

As in Oklahoma, the problem of overproduction drew the attention of the government; the Texas Railroad Commission was given authority to set controls over drilling and prices. And as in Oklahoma, these efforts were in vain. Crude that had sold at $1.10 before Dad Joiner's strike fell to $.25 and even $.10 a barrel. Even that price was to fall.

Hassett and JB were, however, aware that if other cut-price operations could profit, they could profit by imitation. Mr. and Mrs. Hassett rented an apartment in St. Louis; JB and Eddy moved into an apartment in University City.

It did not take long to build the offices and install the modest equipment they needed for operations. JB's secretary had remained behind in Oklahoma, and he needed a replacement. Mrs. Hassett told her husband that one of their apartment neighbors was going through a divorce and needed a job. He sent her to JB.

Celeste Abbington took a cab to Olive Street Road and walked toward the rear of the service station, as she had been instructed. Entering, she looked about and was not at all impressed. "A hole in the wall," she said later. "It was obvious they had very little money."

JB Saunders rose to greet her, and asked some questions. Celeste said she was able to take orders on the phone, but "was not so good" on the typewriter. JB looked very young to her, as indeed he was. She thought he was the office manager; later she learned he was also the sales manager. She never quite understood that he was the heart of the company.

JB had to first make a sale and then collect the money. Mr. Pearson, of the Warson Petroleum Company, had paid with several checks so marred with erasures and changes that the bank had refused to honor them. JB visited Mr. Pearson, who showed some impatience. Scribbling quickly, like a man too busy to take time, he wrote another check, but made some erasures on that one also. At the bank JB was told it could not be processed. Too untidy. He went back to Mr. Pearson.

That gentleman listened with a sneer, then leaned back and said, "You're a country boy, and I'm a city man. It would have cleared." Then he started to write a new check, and, as before, made some erasures.

"I want a clean check, without erasures," JB said mildly.

"You'll break me!" Pearson shouted in sudden anger, and JB leaned over his desk. "I may have cockleburs on my clothes," he said, "but you'll pay."

Pearson changed his tone. "If you'll give me a little time," he said, "just a short delay, you'll get your money." His intention, clearly, was to get the shipment, to sell it, and then pay for it. JB wondered what customer was waiting; while he wondered he looked about.

"How did you get here?" he asked, and when Pearson looked surprised, added, "to your office."

"In my car."

"Where is it?"

"Up the road."

"What is it, a Cadillac?"

"No," Pearson answered, "A Pierce Arrow."

To JB, living in a modest apartment in University City with Eddy, that was enough. He now knew the man's character, and dismissed the idea of doing business with him. "I learned," he said later, "but I learned the hard way."

The petroleum marketplace was a quagmire; others a desert. The output of the nation's manufacturing industry fell to the levels of 1913. Detroit operated at one fifth of its 1929 level. Steel was at 12 percent of capacity, freight shipments cut in half. The Missouri Pacific, the Chicago & Northwestern, and the Wabash railroads were in receivership.

President Hoover called in the nation's bankers and asked the strongest to form a pool to assist the weaker. The suggestion was accepted, but the biggest bankers would not help anyone. No profession, in fact, behaved more ingloriously than bankers in the crisis.

They moved, blinded by self-interest, to exacerbate every situation. Finally Hoover pushed through the Reconstruction Finance Corporation, designed to lend money to starving companies. In later years, its activities would be counted among the jewels of his successor.

Mr. Hoover did not so regard it; he had taken a desperate step that was, as he knew, simply another intervention by the government into a situation brought about, in large measure, by previous interventions. Meanwhile, the run on gold continued, the dollar trembled, unemployment rose to almost fourteen million, and the destitute became so numerous they exhausted both the resources and the patience of private charities and communities.

The crisis—and it was that—was accompanied by a new chorus, unknown in the modern world, or, for that matter, at any time since the days of ancient Rome. Those voices thundered that it was the duty of the government to take care of the people. President Hoover, who heard the cries in many forms, answered them patiently. He was in favor of distributing corn and seed to farmers so they could grow crops, and of lending money at minimal interest to business firms so they could maintain or mount new ventures, but he was adamant in his belief that once the Treasury was opened on behalf of the mass of people, the fabled self-reliance of the Republic would be irretrievably dissipated.

No argument could possibly have been more unpopular. A wave of denunciation swept the nation. "Hoovervilles"—miserable shanties made of old license plates and driftwood, scraps and gatherings—appeared in clusters in all sorts of places. Veterans of the Great War, mostly representing drafted men, massed to march to Washington to demand a bonus in cash. Fanatics, orators, seers, fabulists, and demagogues arose on all sides.

Most of these were pitiful but some were effective. The Communist party, USA, which took orders from the Kremlin and masochistic pleasure at the opportunity,[9] could not attain more than a handful of official members, but around its twelve thousand members in 1932, it created an expanding interlocking series of front organizations that numbered in New York City alone more than "100 mass groups."[10] Later in the year, these expanded, under a dizzying number of names and purported purposes, into a national network that penetrated universities, political parties, labor, communications, the theater, arts in general, and even the government.

The most enticing of the many arguments mounted by this movement, which attracted large sectors of the population, was that depres-

9. Eugene Lyons, *The Red Decade* (New Rochelle: Arlington House, 1970), pp. 39–70, contains a graphic account of Stalin's personal direction of this group.
10. Ibid., p. 74.

sions would be unknown under a properly planned, managed economy. The argument was ironic, because at the very time it was being propagated, the USSR was enduring hideous agony, ushered into existence by Stalin's campaign to nationalize the peasants. Discovering that force was insufficient, and angered by the slaughter of the nation's livestock by individual, organized, but widespread rebellion, the dictator introduced a deliberate famine. Robert Conquest, who later put the dread story together in his book *The Great Terror*, says, "it was the only major famine whose very existence was ignored or denied . . . and even, to a large degree, successfully concealed from world opinion."[11] The number of deaths that took place in the Soviet Union in 1932 are estimated at six million human beings. A Soviet writer thirty years later described the process: "The men died first, then the children, and finally the women."[12]

Little of that trickled out, and what little did appear was rejected by the liberals and the vast majority of people in the western world. Such information seemed too incredible to be given a hearing; it evoked the atrocity legends of the Great War.

Instead the deepening Depression, the mounting evictions for nonpayment of rent, the loss of jobs, the loss of farms, the loss of businesses, seemed the worst of all possible catastrophes. President Hoover could say, and believe, that none were starving—that time would see a resurgence of the American spirit and ability, but that was cold comfort compared to strident demands that the wealthy American treasury be opened.

Much the same situation gripped the people of Germany, whose experiences in the twenties had been erratic, harsh, and spiritually degrading. Unemployment in Germany—a nation of sixty-five million people—rose to almost six million. The most advanced industrial power in Europe was dense with breadlines; its factories were silent and cold—and its streets echoed to the boots of the Nazis, who promised jobs, food, money and security. How this would be accomplished was never quite made clear, but the entire German nation, says Golo Mann, was—in 1932—suffused with hatred for "the System."[13] They were to learn there were worse.

JB, with seemingly inexhaustible energy, scoured the landscape for cut-price locations. He followed the outlines of the Paulson-Wiedeman approach, by renting railroad properties. He discovered

11. Conquest, *Great Terror*, pp. 22–23.
12. Ibid.
13. Mann, *History of Germany*, pp. 399–400.

some that rented for as little as twelve dollars a year. In return, the railroad was assured of the traffic the location would attract—not by agreement—but because JB located many small stations along spur tracks. The location spoke for itself.

JB contacted the Leader Iron Works of Decatur, Illinois, and the Graver Tank Corporation of East Chicago, Indiana. Both firms were avid for business; JB's concern was to put down as little money as possible, and spread his payments as long as he could—an approach common to everyone with cash problems. He gave the firms a plat of the lands he leased, and asked each for a turn-key bid on a complete service station. The easiest immediate cash terms received the contract. In that manner he obtained land and stations at immediate rock-bottom terms, and sold gasoline at two cents below the posted prices set by major firms. Profits were plowed into the next location.

In that bootstrap fashion he and Hassett created the Central States Oil Company, the Western Illinois Oil Company, the Consolidated Oil Company, the North Missouri Oil Company, the Imperial States Oil Company, and others.

In the dark year 1932, when the governor of Texas had troops in the fields to attempt to control the hot oil situation, and the governor of Oklahoma was doing the same, with prices falling like rain drops, the combination of Saunders and Hassett actually managed to earn money and to expand.

Around them the nation sank lower as the year 1932 lengthened. Bitterness arose in many quarters that was not assuaged by a newspaper campaign against the Administration that made it seem as though business, by collapsing, had somehow cheated the people. That impression was strengthened by a stream of revelations, in which genuine errors were linked to illegalities, so that few could untangle what had gone wrong, but many were convinced that it was due to sinister, rather than mistaken, behavior.

Yet, although arguments against the system began to rise, using many of the slogans heard in Europe and from the world Socialist movement, the American people did not turn against one another. If anything, there was a sense of drawing together, a belief that everybody—except the fat cats—was in the same, or a similar, boat. The onus fell on Hoover, and big business.

In that humor the nation went to the polls in November, 1932. The protagonists were President Hoover, whose decision to run seemed based more on a need to be vindicated than on any realistic assessment of his chances, and Franklin D. Roosevelt, whom Walter Lippmann, in an unforgettable moment of rare obtuseness, described as "a pleasant man who, without any important qualifications for the office, would like to be President."[14]

The outcome of the election was not surprising. Roosevelt won handily, carrying the Democratic party into the majority in both houses of Congress. What was surprising—and has drawn surprisingly little retroactive attention—was the fact that the President-elect refused, despite the distressed condition of the nation, to join in any action with the President still in the White House, whose term had almost four more months remaining. An eerie interregnum put the nation in a state of drift.

JB recalls driving downtown that winter with Eddy into the St. Louis theater district. They were on their way to the great all-American escape at the time: the movies. It was raining, the night was dark, and he slowed the car as it neared his favorite parking lot. Suddenly the figure of an old man loomed directly in front of his car. He braked hard, but the old man fell. His derby hat, JB noted as he stepped anxiously out of the car, rolled along for several feet before it toppled into the gutter. Mrs. Saunders stifled a scream.

"Are you hurt?" he asked anxiously, helping the old man up. "He was a pitiable sight," JB said later. "His dark clothes were all splattered with mud, and he was mumbling something about damages and 'a hundred dollars.' "

JB reached for his wallet when the parking-lot attendant rushed out.

"Not to my customers," the attendant shouted. "You've been pulling this trick up and down the block, but you won't get away with it this time."

The old man retrieved his derby, clapped it on his head, and stomped off, cursing into the night. JB stared after him, frozen with surprise, belatedly realizing that he had almost fallen for one of the Depression's endless ruses to get money: the fake automobile accident.

He thanked the attendant; he had nearly been swindled out of money he could not well spare. Nevertheless, as he thought of the mud-spattered, disappointed old man stomping angrily away, he could not feel angry. Instead a sense of great pity rose within him, pity and sorrow that they were all caught in a world where such desperate expedients were necessary.

14. Allen, *Since Yesterday*, p. 63.

The year 1933 dawned on a bleak landscape. The elections had resulted in 22.8 million votes for Roosevelt and 15.5 million votes for Hoover. The papers described that decision in terms that made it sound unanimous. That was an exaggeration; it was a mirror reversal of 1928. The majority had not voted for Roosevelt so much as for change; the minority had voted in favor of tradition. That conservatism was strengthened by the sheer volume of voices raised in outbursts against an older America and its ways, which seemed excessive even in a great Depression.

Such voices expanded the rift between the metropolis and the smaller towns, for by 1933 most of the country's people lived in urban or semiurban areas. The divide was reflected in the curious contrasts in popular literature and drama. Protest plays and proletarian novels emerged, but none achieved success. Instead, theater-goers thronged to watch the kindly and traditional wit of George S. Kaufman and Morris Ryskind's *Of Thee I Sing,* performed by George M. Cohan. The historical recreations of Kenneth Roberts and Hervey Allen outsold the bitter products of Socialist authors by hundreds of thousands of copies.

But theater-goers and book-buyers represented the more prosperous groups. On a national scale the intellectuals made a tremendous noise, and their ceaseless diatribes against business through the years appeared verified by events. Publishers' offices were inundated with amateur plans to solve the Depression; on the public stage a number of strange new figures arose with panaceas. One, Howard Scott, believed prices should be pegged to energy and that technocrats should run society. Another, gifted with insights but burdened by a lack of sophistication, was Huey Long, Senator from Louisiana and virtual dictator of that state. His program was as simple as a bullet and almost as irresistible to the descendants of Populists and working people in many regions: "Share the Wealth," he cried. "Every Man A King."

There was, in other words, a yearning for a man on horseback. In Germany that yearning turned into an obsession. The general staff of that nation watched the rise of Hitler with mixed emotions. Brüning was dismissed and the pliant diplomat Franz von Papen tried as Chancellor under the aged and senile Hindenburg. He proved too slight, and General Kurt von Schleicher himself took the post. That proved a mistake; generals are apt to be inept political leaders. Finally, on January 30, 1933—a date that will be rimmed in red as long as history is recorded—Hitler was called and made Chancellor. The man on horseback had arrived in Europe.

History, however, hangs on accidents. In Miami the United States almost gained John Nance Garner of Texas as its next president when

Giuseppe Zangara, an assassin, aimed a pistol at Roosevelt, fired, missed, and hit Chicago Mayor Anton Cermak.

The event was soon forgotten in the storm that had finally broken over the banks. On February 14, 1933, the Detroit banks were in such dire condition that the governor of Michigan ordered them closed in what was termed, with unconscious irony, a "bank holiday." Runs began on other banks throughout the country; the shipments of gold to other parts of the world by the wealthy increased. The Senate, holding another of its eternal second-guess hearings—this time on the bankers—forced Charles Mitchell, head of the huge First City Bank of New York, to admit he had paid no income taxes in boom years and sold his own bank's stock short for a profit in the Crash. Neither of these actions was illegal, though they left a bad taste; the hearings proceeded to uncover worse behavior, and could not have been worse timed as far as banking in general was concerned.

On February 24 the governor of Illinois closed the banks of that state. On March 1, two more states did the same. The next day—March 2, 1933—ten more states followed. On March 4, 1933, New York State and Illinois followed suit. President Hoover, dressing for the inaugural of his successor, was told the nation's banking system was in collapse. That was the moment he had sought to avert; it came precisely when Franklin D. Roosevelt took the stage.

CHAPTER NINE

Hassett & Sons

BUSINESS, in contrast to common myths, carries its practitioners into many strange and interesting corners of life. In Council Bluffs, Iowa, JB learned—chatting with customers—that land values in the region had fallen to new lows. Yet from the windows of his restaurant he could see a fairly heavy truck traffic passing through the town. Putting these observations together, he began to call on real estate people, saying he was thinking of starting a venture in truck farming.

At that period in the nation's history, no real estate expert expected a prospective farmer to have too much money, or even to have very much sense. Nevertheless, since business in real estate is nearly always in either a boom or a crisis, and in the thirties barely limped along at all, JB was shown a number of possible locations. The one he eventually chose was fairly large and consisted of seventeen lots.

On that location he had a truckers' station erected, using his usual competitive bid approach to the firms capable of such construction. Behind the station he supervised the creation of an apartment, equipped with a shower and with room for cots. Beside the station he built a restaurant. Inside the restaurant was a huge blackboard, showing the arrivals and departures of the rigs. The manager of the restaurant was given the numbers and in time grew to know the names and the locations, the voices and the needs, of the dispatchers of various trucking firms. Outside a sign was displayed, reading *Eats and Rooms for Truckers*. The oasis was an instant success, inspired many imitations, and marked JB's emergence as an innovator in the marketplace.

At the same time there were larger elements involved, as is true of all human activities. While most of the nation's industries had plummeted downward in the dark tunnel of the Depression, the petroleum industry was embroiled in a fierce internal competitive struggle.

164

That struggle was over the yields of two immense oil discoveries. One was in the Oklahoma City region. The other, in east Texas, was the largest oil pool ever discovered on the North American continent. Unlocked through the efforts of a seventy-one-year-old penniless wild-catter and a seventy-three-year-old self-taught geologist scorned by all the experts,[1] the east Texas field was shaped like a crooked leg with a thick thigh in the north and a pointed, irregular foot in the south. It stretched forty-five miles from top to toe, and from five to twelve miles from east to west.

Because the major companies were slow to reach the east Texas field after its initial discovery, its 140,000 acres had been occupied by hundreds of independent firms and thousands of individuals. They drilled and extracted crude oil in massive quantities which flowed to independent refineries all over the country by every conceivable means of transportation and sent the price of crude oil into new depths. Prices of gasoline, kerosene, and other petroleum products appeared on the market at such narrow margins that JB said later "the taxes were worth more than the products"—an only slight exaggeration.

The huge majors, which had operational and production control of fields in Venezuela and Asia, and were able to import this foreign crude oil, free of tariffs, into their giant refineries on the East and West Coasts, were in agony over the east Texas–Oklahoma situation. They not only grappled like dinosaurs with one another, but sought, through protests, lobbying, and persuasions, to stop the flood of cheap crude oil to the refineries and outlets of the independents.

Their arguments were persuasive, especially in terms of the con-servation of a valuable natural resource. The independents, however, were fighting for their very lives in an economic sense. Therefore, although both Oklahoma and Texas authorities moved to control drill-ing in the fields in their respective states, declared martial law and sent in troops, the struggle continued. Independents used every con-ceivable expedient and many that were so inventive they seemed in-credible to keep the flow of oil moving. Prices were cut; fines were levied. Prices were set and ignored. Legal and black-market operations intertwined in the marketplace.

It was this situation that enabled Hassett to continue his refineries, and provided JB with a constant source of low-priced crude. He re-

---

1. Columbus Marion (Dad) Joiner was born in 1860, three years after JB's father. He was seventy-one in 1931. A. D. Lloyd, born Joseph Idelbert Durham, was seventy-three in 1931, and is believed to have changed his name to avoid bigamy charges. Like John D. Rockefeller's father, Lloyd sold patent medicines based on crude oil, was a promoter of many shadowy ventures, and learned his geology by observation and studying the brochures of the U.S. Bureau of Mines. James A. Clark and Michel T. Halbouty, *The Last Boom* (New York: Random House, 1972).

calls one east Texas operator phoning in car numbers of a huge shipment of gasoline, who said, "My injunction is lifted over the weekend." A weekend was all he needed. On the other hand, other marketers received similar calls and shipments, which made marketplace competition as fierce as the struggle in the fields.

The independents in the petroleum industry were proceeding exactly as had their forebears and predecessors. Their struggle, their waste, their price-cutting, their rush for wells, and their competition in the marketplace were in the tradition of oil booms since the inception of the industry. There is no question that cheap gasoline and fuels, as well as the intense activities, the sales and use of equipment, the rise in real estate, the creation of new towns, the opportunities for labor and for new commercial establishments, and all the complex train of action that followed the work in the fields, provided the people of east Texas with the difference between near starvation and plenty during these Depression years, and that consumers for thousands of miles benefited from the price wars of the petroleum industry.

Cheap gasoline enabled small truckers to move goods at low cost; countless homes were kept warm in winter by low-priced fuels; many factories and stores, mills and shops alike were able to survive only by the competition of the east Texas and Oklahoma booms.

In the minds of some, however, these benefits were far overshadowed by the sheer crudity and excesses of the hot-oil operators. Derricks were erected with no regard for long-range considerations. Gas was flared to create Luciferian scenes at night. Hordes of gamblers, thieves, prostitutes, swindlers, and bootleggers created miles of raw and unbridled sin that horrified the upright.

There was nothing new in that reaction: it mirrored the shock created by boom towns in gold, coal, lumber, and oil in earlier rushes in American history. What was new was the sweeping changes in attitudes that had taken place at the top, where opinions had formed against such open, sweaty struggles.

The major oil companies had conducted a skillful legal and public relations campaign to convince the courts and the country that spaced wells and limited field production would simultaneously extend the extractive life of an oil pool and maintain an orderly market. Their geological proofs were overwhelming. They muted the fact, however, that such spacing and such limits to production would virtually eliminate the quick profits that marginal producers and independents needed for their survival, and would force these smaller entrepreneurs to sell out, at a bargain price, to the majors.

The independents, who knew that well, had in previous periods relied on court rulings that upheld the old English "right of capture," based on the observation that any man could entrap a wild beast that belonged to no man. The ruling was applicable because any well sunk into a pool can, by its extractions, diminish the holdings of the entire pool.[2] Those who waited, therefore, could have their chance to get oil diminished, or see it escape entirely. Their defiance of the new rules had many of the elements of the earlier struggles of small cattlemen, who had fought against the encroachments of the huge land-owners and their integrated industrial methods. Prorationing was the barbed wire of the oil industry. Once again, the people of Texas, Oklahoma, and the Oil Country in general were involved in a frontier struggle.

On March 4, 1933, the new President's inaugural address was delivered while much of the industry and the banks of the United States lay prostrate, as though in a coma. President Roosevelt's remarks, delivered over the radio in a voice ringing with self-confidence, contained a thrilling, remarkable passage assuring the nation it had nothing to fear but fear itself. But it also contained strange passages that had a punitive, slightly biblical ring. "The money-changers," Roosevelt said, "have fled from their high seats in the temples of our civilization." Then, after some encouraging remarks, he ended with a request never before made in peacetime and seldom even in war, for "great executive power . . . as great as if the nation were in fact, invaded by a foreign foe."[3]

Since the new President had been elected by an impressive margin and his party had a majority in both houses of Congress, his request—like some of the other elements in his inaugural speech—marked a distinct departure in the United States. The ringing tone, the biblical rhetoric, the lofty abstractions, and the appeal for support for programs that remained vague, resembled those of Roosevelt's old chief, Woodrow Wilson. But Mr. Roosevelt exceeded Wilson.

Within one hundred days—fabled and deplored ever since—the New Deal[4] passed measures so numerous, extensive, and influential that it was many months and even years before the nation and its courts could catch up with their details. By then they had been so embedded, altered, modified, and established that the nation was carried into a completely new terrain in terms of government. It was a revolution conducted during an emergency, at a time when its novelties were assumed, even by some of its authors, to be temporary. By the time it was realized that the nation had been altered beyond the point of reversal, the time for reversal was gone.

2. Clark and Halbouty, *Last Boom*, pp. 144–145.
3. Allen, *Since Yesterday*, p. 85.
4. Professor Raymond Moley of Columbia, an original advisor, read Stuart Chase's *A New Deal* and recommended the phrase to Roosevelt in a memo. He used it in his nomination acceptance speech, and it was picked up at once.

In that sense the United States appeared to be affected by winds blowing around the world. By a curious symmetry, Germany was undergoing a similar series of wrenching changes, accompanied by enormous popular enthusiasm on the part of a majority, and watched by a conservative minority with increasing disquietude.

Hitler's party, the Nazis, had similarly swept a national election and had attained a plurality that overshadowed the Social Democrat, Communist, Center, and Nationalist parties. With that victory the Chancellor asked for and received an "enabling law" that made his decisions final on all matters. His ascendancy was as legal as a courtroom brief; his supreme authority was to run until April, 1937.

There was, of course, a huge difference between the New Deal and the Nazi movement. The Nazis were political gangsters who had plotted to seize control of Germany for a decade, and whose methods included blackmail, murder, slander, and terror. In their years on the fringes of German society, they created a shadow government complete with secret police, armed forces, and subversive affiliates in all ranks of life; anti-Semitism was a basic ingredient in their campaign against both capitalism and democracy. On succeeding to power Hitler reversed the role of the German Army, and extracted an oath of personal loyalty from its general staff.

That distorted re-creation of Kaiserdom ushered into existence a wave of persecutions against the Jewish community, intellectuals in general, and all freedoms. An exodus, already started, was accelerated. Communists fled Germany in the direction of the Soviet Union; Social Democrats, who believed in Marxist principles but not in violence, fled to the West.

A numerically small but intellectually brilliant number of these refugees from the Nazis began to reach the shores of the United States in the early thirties and continued to arrive through the remainder of the decade. The contributions of those newcomers, most of whom had already achieved success or recognition in the Weimar Republic, began to emerge in an amazingly brief period of time. Not since the Puritans had any immigrants to American shores had such an impact.

That impact, however, was a tiny cloud on the horizon in 1933. That summer was the season of vast plans and huge programs whose details, implication, and sweep drew hordes of people to Washington, D.C., as to a great magnet of power. Men with briefcases from business and universities, people representing private and public agencies, states and cities and towns, farmers and industrialists, professional and business associations, individuals with solutions to problems and individuals with problems searching for solutions, all converged on the Capital.

It was the conventional wisdom of the New Deal economists that the nation had reached the limits of its industrial growth with the closing of the physical frontiers. Overall, therefore, the new Administration believed the nation's economy was in need of both regulations to end the excesses credited with the débâcle of the Depression, and also in need of measures to insure a more equitable distribution of the fruits of its industries. Those were assumptions widely shared which provided the rationale within which most of the early New Deal programs were created.

These were so numerous, covered so many sectors, so persuasively presented, and accompanied by so much generosity in meeting the immediate needs of the people, that virtually the entire nation felt lifted and carried along as in a strong, fresh breeze.

One of the President's first acts had been to bar the export of gold and to obtain sweeping authority to introduce inflation along several different or even simultaneous lines. The effect of that was to send prices up. His second most important measure was to raise farm prices by paying farmers not to plant all their land. After that startling innovation, known as the Agricultural Adjustment Administration, the New Deal received approval from Congress to spend $3.3 billion for public works, much of which instead went into direct relief, and to send a quarter of a million youths from impoverished families into Civilian Conservation Corps camps.

Most of those measures were shouted through Congress so rapidly that their substance, not to say their significance, was difficult to grasp. The Tennessee Valley Authority, which Hoover had rejected with a stinging message regarding a government that entered into competition with its own citizens, was passed handily. The utility companies of the United States, suffering from the aftermath of the collapse of Samuel Insull's pyramided firms, were staggered, but their protests could hardly be heard over other arguments, other issues, and other plans.

Most industries clamored for government help. The Chamber of Commerce of the United States had deplored "cut-throat competition" as piously as the major oil companies had deplored the actions of hot-oil operators. Many of these larger firms and associations came forward to join government attorneys and specialists in drawing up rules for various sectors of business and industry regulating wages, hours, working conditions, and prices. In their aggregate these rules comprised the National Industrial Recovery Act, soon known as the NRA, whose Blue Eagle emblem embellished shop windows and offices throughout the land. At the same time the government passed the National Labor Relations Act, which granted new privileges to labor unions and

169

created rules for employer-employee relationships, union proselytizing, and supervised union elections under the guidance of Government Labor Relations Boards.

Put together, those propositions, proposals, and programs added up to a stunning change in American life: a shift from the world's most open system into one that was guided and regulated by the government. A jumble of agencies, known by their letters, leaped into life. Their administrators, armed with sweeping authority and acting under the crackling pressures of emergency, soared to national prominence with a speed not seen in the nation since the time of the Great War and the heyday of Wilson's "czars."

New czars, in fact, appeared. One was a Secretary of the Interior, who was placed in authority not only over the nation's natural resource industries and territories, but also over the Public Works Administration. His name was Harold LeClair Ickes, and his activities impinged upon all the men in Oil Country, including JB.

The new, far-flung activities of the government impinged upon every life, however. In Sapulpa, Joseph Benjamin Saunders was drawn into new activities by the Farm Relief Administration, not by being a recipient but by being an expert. The government was granting farmers emergency loans, based on the value of their lands, livestock, and equipment.

The elder Saunders's experience, and his knowledge of the land and of livestock, brought him into some demand as an appraiser. In keeping with his lifelong practice of helping his neighbors he did not charge for this service. Many, however, sought his help, among them a farmer named Charley Brummet.

Brummet picked Mr. Saunders up in his car from his office and drove him out toward his farm. "But," JB said later, "Brummet was a clumsy driver.

"A car passed, going very fast, then suddenly cut between Brummet and some wagons and slowed down. Brummet, whose vision of the road ahead was cut off, was annoyed enough to swing out himself and saw, to his horror, why the other driver had cut in ahead of him. A heavy oil truck was coming, fast, from the opposite direction. Brummet tried to cross the road into the ditch on the other side but was too late: the truck hit his car broadside so hard that the wooden wheels were broken off his old Hudson and his vehicle was driven back two hundred and ninety-five feet."

The impact had landed precisely where Mr. Saunders was sitting, and broke both his arms and legs. Fortunately telephones were nearby and available. Calls were made to the police, who rushed to the scene with equipment. An ambulance was summoned and Mrs. Saunders notified. She made a number of calls, including one to JB in St. Louis. He called two of his brothers and picked them up, with their wives, and drove south—fast—toward the scene. Meanwhile, men with blowtorches worked to extricate Mr. Saunders. He was able to talk to them despite his immense shock and pain.

JB arrived at the hospital at two o'clock in the morning just as his mother emerged in tears. The sight brought him to a halt; his father had died a half hour before.

Joseph Benjamin Saunders was seventy-six years old, but he had seemed as large, strong, and indestructible as ever until the car crash. JB took his mother home and made all arrangements, handled all details. His father had left no will, and that made it necessary to go to court to get permission to pay various small debts and close the real estate office, and to distribute some small tokens among the family. JB himself inherited his father's old ranch hat, and a pair of spurs.

Those were enough. They brought a flood of memories of the Bar S and the days of childhood and youth, when his father had loomed so tall he seemed to dominate the landscape.

By the time JB returned to his duties in St. Louis, the Department of the Interior, whose experts had huddled with leaders in the petroleum industry and various concerned Congressmen, was on the verge of emerging with a master plan. One of the more interesting features of the New Deal was its use of a variety of euphemisms to maintain a façade of freedom to cover its mandatory regulations. Prices were not fixed, they were "fair traded." Industries were not regulated; they agreed to codes.

J. Howard Marshall, a luminary and assistant dean of the Yale School of Law at the tender age of twenty-eight, was one of two men who actually drew most of the details of the Petroleum Code together.[5] Both were members of Ickes's Brain Trust,[6] and Marshall's recollections of the Secretary are wry.

5. Marshall and Norman L. Meyers, while students at Yale Law, had visited the Oklahoma fields and wrote a paper on prorationing, followed up by a book titled *Two Years Later* in 1933. Searching for experts, Ickes called both men to the Department of the Interior—Marshall from Yale and Meyers from the Brookings Institution.

6. The first phrase was Roosevelt's *privy council*, which had English connotations that made it awkward. John Kieran, an ardent Roosevelt admirer who wrote for the *New York Times*, coined the more felicitous *Brain Trust*.

"The situation in the east Texas field was particularly chaotic," Marshall recalls. "One refinery bought 1 million barrels of crude oil for $25,000. And I remember driving through the area at a time when beer was 30 cents a bottle, and seeing a sign on an oil lease that read: *Three Barrels Best Crude Oil for a Bottle of Beer.*"

Since virtually everyone in the industry was clamoring for help, neither Marshall nor his associates considered that the government was involved in anything more than an emergency rescue. He was anxious to draw up the most practical and rapid plan, but Secretary Ickes alarmed him by an open desire to "fix the price of everything in the industry, down to the last pump."

"We can't do that," Marshall argued. "*We don't know enough.* We'll simply create a black market."

The fact was that a black market already existed, but both men ignored that reality—at first. The prestige of the federal government was so high in those days that legends about federal agents tracking men for years and spending enormous sums to capture and convict the theft of a postage stamp were widely believed. Secretary Ickes was one of the many who believed that order could be accomplished by setting rules. In the end Marshall succeeded in convincing Ickes that it was only necessary to "set an upward price on crude"—in other words, to fair trade crude oil. In effect, that would also transfer the problem of controlling the hot-oil operators from the states to the federal government. Ickes had no doubt that could be accomplished; Marshall was less sanguine. He regarded his boss as the soul of honesty, but also as somewhat unrealistic.

"Honest Harold," he called him later. "He wouldn't dream of taking a dime—*but he'd sell a man's soul for a headline.*" It was a judgment that could have been applied, with equal justice, to many other New Dealers.

The Petroleum Code, when finally released, contained elements that angered both the majors and the independents. An import tax was laid on foreign crude, which prevented the majors from undercutting the price of domestic oil, at least theoretically. At the same time prorationing and dollar crude oil was laid on the independents, which constituted a serious threat to small and marginal operators, no matter how much more orderly it might make the market.

In St. Louis JB found himself, as did other small marketers, confronting a very tangled situation. Mr. Hassett had provided the funds by which their operations had transferred from Oklahoma, and maintained his final word on all significant matters afterward. But JB's

efforts in finding new locations, supervising the construction of new
outlets, buying in quantity from other small refiners, and supervising
those stocks and products, as well as Imperial's own, had made him a
very important co-manager in the firm.

He and Hassett had together organized the Central States Oil
Company, which bought and sold petroleum products—including
those from Imperial's own refineries—and constructed service stations.
These in turn were organized in terms of separate firms operating
in five states: Missouri, Illinois, Minnesota, Wisconsin, and Arkansas.[7] The firms were all similar, but they constituted—for tax purposes—separate entities; each had its own records, invoices, and books.
The process of building that network, which was far-flung for the
times, was as arduous as any other pioneering effort. Each market
entity had its own regional, transportation, and pricing problems; JB
was kept busy supervising their sales, inventories, and personnel. Mr.
Hassett, meanwhile, began to take longer absences, as he had during
the twenties. He spent summers at his home in Lewiston, New York,
and his winters as before in Florida.

When Hassett was in St. Louis, however, his relationship with JB
was very close and cordial. They often played golf, a game at which
JB had grown to excel, with a handicap that ran between two and four
for many years. Their games, played on Tuesdays, Thursdays, and
Sundays, would stretch on the weekend to thirty-six holes. On week-
days, JB placed his business calls on the first, ninth, and eighteenth
holes. They were often joined by Jack Wightman, the insurance
broker. He recalls one game in particular.

"We were playing at the Meadowbrook Country Club," he said.
"JB hit a fine shot, straight down the fairway, but Mr. Hassett muffed
his. The caddy, a stripling, observed quietly that the old man had made
an error in his swing. Hassett's face turned red, and he swung around.

"'I've been playing for years,' he snapped, 'without being told
what to do.'"

On the next hole, the same sequence arose. JB hit a fine shot, and
Hassett muffed his. The caddy again remarked on his very poor form.
Hassett whirled around and bellowed, "One more remark out of you
and I'll wrap this club around your neck!"

On the third hole JB hit another fine drive, Hassett muffed his,
and the caddy spoke up again. To Wightman's alarm Hassett whirled
his club savagely in the air at the boy, who dropped flat on the ground.

7. Central States Oil Company, St. Joseph, Missouri; Western Illinois Oil
Company, Edwardsville, Illinois; Consolidated Oil Company, Quincy, Illinois;
North Missouri Oil Company, Macon, Missouri; Imperial Central Oil Company,
Chicago; Central States Oil Company of Wisconsin, Milwaukee; Wisconsin Central
States Oil of Minnesota, Minneapolis; Murphy Oil Company, Little Rock, Ar-
kansas.

Then Hassett, breathing heavily, said in a husky voice, "If you're so good, let's see what you can do."

The caddy stepped forward, took a club, and drove a fine shot, straight down the fairway. It landed on the green and bounced toward the pin. Hassett grunted. The game resumed, but Wightman noticed the caddy made no further comments.

The nation, in other words, was still largely unaware of the great and sweeping changes underway, in a societal sense. People took it for granted that the New Deal was simply another Wilsonian sort of Administration, whose rules and regulations would vanish as soon as the Depression lifted.[8] So far as JB, Hassett, and the firm were concerned, business was fairly good anyway; they had conquered the Depression in its opening years without outside help.

Nevertheless it was good to see people smiling and feeling optimistic again; there seemed little doubt that conditions would improve in general. Signs of life appeared on the stage and in music; O'Neill produced his happiest play of an earlier America in *Ah, Wilderness*, the music of Cole Porter set people humming, and the hated Prohibition laws were finally being erased from the books.

On that night, December 5, 1933, Jack Wightman, Forrest Moore, and JB sat up in a nightclub in St. Louis until one o'clock in the morning, to taste their first legal drink. It was only beer, but the fact that it was legal seemed worth the election.

The spring of 1934 was bitter and cold; the sales of fuel soared, and "cocktail lounges" began to appear in hotels, on corners, and in roadhouses. Prohibition was over, but every state and community, county and region, had emerged with its own versions of legalized liquors. Money-hungry tax departments, stripped to the bone by the Depression, hastily applied so many new taxes on legal spirits that bootlegging remained, in most localities, as entrenched as ever. Change of any sort is difficult to achieve.

The hot-oil situation in Texas and, presumably, Oklahoma, re-

8. Some statistics: Hoover in 1928 won by 6.3 million; Roosevelt in 1932 won by 7.1 million. The percentages were Hoover 39.7, and Roosevelt 57.4—certainly a resounding victory, but hardly one that deserved to be analyzed as a repudiation of American traditions.

In 1920 a far more lopsided verdict resulted in the highest percentage ever reached till that time—60.4—and the greatest defeat ever suffered till that time—28.8 percent. But in that instance the victor, Warren G. Harding, was mocked.

mained as turbulent as before, despite the Petroleum Code and the high hopes of Washington. There were more changes on the American surface in other areas than in the Oil Country.

Clothes had grown more formal. "Flaming youth" had vanished and serious, sweatered students in universities worked hard and kept their heads down. Nightclubs and floor shows appeared. The flood of New Deal measures continued, with farmers receiving more assistance in the form of a Mortgage Refinancing Act; the stock exchanges were organized and regulated by the Securities Exchange Act. Two thirds of the families on relief were at some sort of work under a huge Civil Works Administration funded by $400 million and directed by Harry Hopkins, a slight and relatively unknown figure, unusual among New Dealers in avoiding the limelight.

There were signs, not numerous, but sufficient, that the nation had regained its nerve. Life was less stark. The five-day week reduced the toils of city masses and factory workers, labor-union membership took a huge increase, there was a spurt forward in sports, and bridge became immensely popular. JB and his wife played with the Wightmans regularly; slot machines appeared.

Nevertheless, as the months began to pass and the weather warmed in 1934, the overall situation of the economy, far from improving, appeared to reflect mainly the huge amounts of money being poured in by the Administration, and the impact of inflation. Little seemed to stick in business, in the form of new ventures, expanded markets, or genuine increases. Unemployment remained huge, though diminished from former peaks. It was officially pegged at twelve million in January, 1934, and as the year extended did not make any significant change. Businessmen had been deeply shocked by the abrupt abandonment of the American gold standard, the tidal wave of regulations, and the rise of union power assisted by the Administration.

Those problems were, however, big-city problems. The problems that affected JB and his associates had their genesis in the fields of the Oil Country, where a struggle was underway to control production, shut down wasteful wells, and put a floor under prices. In their remarkable book on east Texas, James A. Clark and Michel Halbouty describe how J. Howard Marshall had traced a hot-oil shipment and brought the parties involved into court in Boise, Idaho, in the spring of 1934.[9] The decision in the case was blurry; the oil was sequestered so storage charges would destroy its potential for profit in the open market.

Marshall decided that a new system would have to be established, in which producers kept records of their oil and of their customers—as would refiners, who would have to cite sources and the disposition of

9. Clark and Halbouty, *Last Boom*, pp. 219–222.

their sales, and as would marketers and transporters. Each of those segments would be subject to fines by a failure to keep records and to produce them. Enforcement began; after a suitable interval records were examined and arrests were made.

By then, however, 1934 was fairly well advanced, and not only the men in the Oil Country, but also men throughout the United States, began to have second thoughts about the New Deal. Was it legal for the government to tell people how they should price their own goods?

Beyond the United States the world was taking on a darker cast. In Germany the Nazis had taken over the labor unions; suppressed the freedom of the press; persecuted Communists, Social Democrats, and Jews; and aroused the alarm of the Army. In midsummer, striking a double blow, Hitler suddenly ordered the massacre of his own lunatic fringe: the SA forces under Captain Ernst Röhm, and for good measure had General von Schleicher murdered as well. This move, like the leap of a wild beast, ended the vestiges of democracy in that land. When Hindenburg died in August, 1934, aged eighty-seven, the offices of President and Chancellor were combined in the person of the dictator.

The events in central Europe, were, in fact, stunning. At the same time that Hitler conducted his bloody purge, Nazis attempted a coup in Austria and murdered the Chancellor, Engelbert Dollfuss, in his own office. Photographs of these events and long accounts of Nazi atrocities appeared in the American press, creating more bewilderment than understanding.

On an international scale the only major powers whose leaders appeared aware of the significance of the new German government were Japan and the USSR. Japan took advantage of Europe's preoccupation and Soviet fears of German intentions to formalize its occupation of Manchuria, rename it Manchukuo, and to install a scion of the royal family of China as its puppet emperor.

In the Kremlin the Foreign Minister, Maksim Litvinov, spoke to the Central Committee and pointed out that the commissars were in danger of being confronted on two fronts: east and west. Describing events in Germany as "a revolution," Litvinov floated the idea, ever so carefully, that the USSR should in self-defense attempt to align itself with the western democracies—the capitalists.[10]

Not too long afterward the Soviets began to maneuver for American recognition, and leftists in the United States, France, and Britain—reacting to orders relayed through the Comintern—began to stress

10. Ulam, *Expansion and Coexistence*, pp. 203-219.

peace and world brotherhood, and the idea of a "united front" against fascism. For the first time, the USSR joined the League of Nations.

Conditions in Oil Country had also changed. The Department of the Interior had lured a top FBI man, Tom Kelliher, into its employ as an enforcement officer of the new rules designed to halt the flow of hot oil. Kelliher and a special staff worked so effectively that by November, 1934, the torrent of hot oil had been reduced to a trickle of ten thousand barrels a day.[11] According to Clark and Halbouty, forty-five refineries had folded, and those that remained were in open competition with the majors.[12]

Those changes did not seriously affect Imperial; its operations had become established. JB, who sold for a number of smaller and still independent refiners, continued his efforts as before. They included semiannual swings among the refiners to check their inventories and learn their production plans, details upon which his sales efforts were hinged.

On one such swing he arrived at Cushing, Oklahoma, and had dinner with Rex Wingett, president of the Cushing Refining Company. Wingett had an intriguing medical story to tell. A young Cushing boy had had a persistent leg infection that spread into gangrene. A young and fairly new physician in town was called. He sent away for some sterilized maggots, and placed these on the boy's leg. The maggots ate away the infected area and were removed—and the boy's leg healed. JB was fascinated and Wingett, encouraged, told another story.

The daughter of a Cushing banker was stricken with appendicitis. Her father planned to drive her to Oklahoma City, and the young physician said that would take an hour. "She can die in that time," he said, "unless I perform the operation here and now. It's a simple one; I'll give her a local."

The banker looked dubious and the physician added, "If you have questions about my ability, I suggest you call Johns Hopkins, where I interned." The banker, being a banker, placed the call and was reassured. From there on matters proceeded very swiftly. The patient was given a spinal anesthetic; her father was allowed to stand behind a screen and talk to her during the operation, which was a success.

JB leaned forward. "Would the doctor's name, by any chance, be Clifford Bassett?"

"Yes. How did you know?"

JB was stunned. Clifford Bassett! He was JB's old school chum

11. Clark and Halbouty, *Last Boom*, p. 223.
12. Ibid.

from Sapulpa. They had planned to attend Washington University together and to continue through medical school. JB's path had been diverted into other directions, but Bassett had followed the plan alone. "I'd like to see him," JB said. Wingett placed a call, and Bassett came to the hotel right away.

The two old friends chatted until three in the morning. JB heard what he had missed, learned of the heavy cost of a physician's equipment and the tribulations entailed in launching a practice. At midnight Dr. Bassett's fiancée, a nurse, just off work and having been told his whereabouts, arrived to join the conversation.

It left JB with mingled emotions. It was almost like seeing himself in a completely different situation, in a setting he would have occupied had he not turned in a different direction. But he was delighted to rediscover his friend; they never again lost contact with each other.

Around them the nation seethed in arguments over the New Deal, made pertinent by the upcoming elections in November, 1934. Huey Long, with his Share the Wealth slogans, was growing into a political power, though his national prospects were darkened by press reports of his dictatorial behavior, his heavy drinking, and the regional quality of his ideas. But other voices were raised, also extreme. In California the radical author Upton Sinclair, whose book *The Jungle* had penetrated the meat-packing industry and set a pattern for many similar onslaughts that have continued ever since, presented himself as a candidate for governor of California on a program breathtaking in its simplicity: End Poverty in California. Another figure, regarded by intellectuals with less favor but appealing in his own way, was an elderly physician named Francis Townsend who emerged with a plan whereby every citizen over sixty would receive, without strings, a monthly two hundred dollars to be paid for by a 2 percent sales tax. Economists rushed to their adding machines to calculate that such a tax would be inadequate for the funding he proposed but would nevertheless take a disproportionate amount of the national income for 8 percent of its population.[13] The elderly, oblivious to these realities, flocked to hear the doctor, who wore a white suit in the style of Mark Twain, and whose movement mushroomed.

Other voices were less specific. Father Charles E. Coughlin, a priest broadcasting from Michigan, demanded nationalization of the banks and natural resources, and aroused religious prejudices. More voices, however, were raised on the left. A long list of little magazines

13. Dexter Perkins, *The New Age of Franklin Roosevelt, 1932–1945* (Chicago: University of Chicago Press, 1957), pp. 27–28.

appeared, headed by such older organs as the *New Masses*, and the rush into Communist front organizations by intellectuals was astonishing. Some of the most famous names in American literary ranks were swept along by the tide: Edmund Wilson, John Dos Passos, Sherwood Anderson, Theodore Dreiser, James T. Farrell, and Erskine Caldwell, among others.[14]

Putting aside the Coughlinites, the Townsendites, and the followers of Huey Long, the nation was in the throes of a division at the top described by the famous Austrian economist, Ludwig von Mises—himself destined to land in the United States as a refugee—between the bosses and what he called "the cousins." In general, von Mises's "cousins" are members of wealthy families enjoying the fruits of dead capitalists, who resent the bosses as much as do ignorant workers, for many of the same reasons. They believe that business properties generate money automatically, deplore inequities in the incomes of others, are in the forefront of anticapitalist activities through funding, and—in other words—enjoy the plaudits of the left while living on the fruits of the system they deplore.

That description, presented in von Mises's *The Anti-Capitalist Mentality*,[15] described some, though certainly not all, of the New Dealers. It was apt enough to encompass, with a certain degree of rough accuracy, the Secretary of the Interior, Harold Ickes, who had married into great wealth. It also covered, to a large extent, the figure of the Secretary of the Treasury, Henry Morgenthau, and even the President. All of those men denied that the New Deal was designed to end capitalism; they regarded their measures as remedial and, in the long run, as a rescue designed to avert worse developments.

The "bosses," however, believed otherwise. By the autumn of 1934 a large sector of the business community considered the New Deal antibusiness and, at base, anticapitalist. The Hearst newspapers attacked the NRA as state socialism; firms around the nation evaded its codes, and businessmen in general sought to manage their enterprises in the way they thought best. The labor unions, however, organized feverishly, and labor disputes arose on all sides. Unemployment had been twelve million in early 1934; by late fall it was more than eleven million. The dollar had been devalued—another way of saying, inflated—but business had not recovered its momentum. Industrial production, which at first had begun to rise, subsided and was only one-third that of 1929. Agricultural prices, despite the huge efforts of the AAA, were far below the figures of the twenties. The national income was below that of 1931, which was hailed in some imperfect memories

14. Lyons, *Red Decade*, p. 129.
15. Ludwig von Mises, *The Anti-Capitalist Mentality* (South Holland, Ill.: Libertarian Press, 1972).

as a nadir year; federal agents were arresting oil men trying to keep from starving by selling their crude in the marketplace; and picket-line struggles and the shrieks of demagogues made the New Deal seem as incoherent as the situation it sought to alleviate.

In that mixed, angry humor the nation went to the polls, and all factions were astonished in November, 1934. Ordinarily the party in office loses in by-elections; in that event the Democrats gained nineteen seats in the House and nineteen more in the Senate. Harry Hopkins, jubilant, was reputed to have put the matter in a nutshell, though he later repeatedly denied having said "we will spend and spend, and elect and elect." Yet there was truth to the saying, even if it was apocryphal. The ranks of labor, the small farmer, the unemployed, the elderly, and the discontented were convinced that the New Deal would shower benefits and relief measures, and had no faith whatever that a return to the harsh climate of open competition would be preferable. The bosses were outvoted, an outcome inevitable whenever such a choice is made available.

Toward the close of 1934, therefore, the nation was confronted with a serious fundamental crisis. The policies of the New Deal had rallied the majority of the people but alienated the group that both created and managed its industrial sector and its business. The line-up was not, of course, precise. Many big businessmen believed the Roosevelt policies were beneficial. But a larger number of smaller businessmen, who had their fortunes yet to make, were not so complacent.

The split, and the dilemma, was neatly reflected in the Oil Country. Mr. Kelliher's efficiency in applying—and J. Howard Marshall's shrewdness in creating—regulations to check the flow of hot oil had put many marginal producers and refiners—and from there a whole chain of small transporters and marketers—out of business. Many believed they confronted ruin.

Although some had been taken to court and fined for a refusal to either keep or produce the records demanded by the Petroleum Code, few of those men believed themselves guilty of any real violations of the law. Their argument that the consumer had a right to receive—and that they themselves had a right to produce and sell—oil at the lowest possible market price was a difficult one for the New Deal to answer.

More than that, it raised serious constitutional issues regarding the limits of the government and the rights of the people. Found guilty in lower federal courts, some of these smaller oilmen carried their case to the highest. In December, 1934, the issue was argued before the Supreme Court by F. W. Fischer, a self-taught lawyer of remarkable ability, a country boy manner, and an argument that reached the heart of the issues.[16]

Fischer held the Court spellbound while he cited an incident from the history of ancient Rome. Emergency dictatorial power was once granted a leader for two years, then for another two years, and then for ten years. At the end of that time he had power enough to override the Senate. The instance may well have been apochryphal, but the Justices were not historians and were not concerned with that. Their concern, as well as the concern of many other serious citizens, was whether or not the Depression was being used as an excuse to carry the United States and its people into a new, as yet undefined societal form. Fischer's Roman parallel, which conjured images of the collapse of the first welfare state of the ancient world, was directed to that concern.

The Fischer argument, however, was limited to the case before the Court, which involved actions of federal agents regarding interstate shipments of oil. In early 1935 the Justices ruled that these actions had exceeded Washington's authority.

The ruling was limited but its implication was clear. A confrontation between the New Deal—with its dominance of the executive and congressional branches—and the Supreme Court was foreshadowed by this rehearsal, enacted at the instance of men from the Oil Country.

By the time the Supreme Court made its ruling, JB was busier than ever on a number of Imperial fronts. It had been decided to build a new, small refinery in Arkansas. As usual, a new legal entity had been formed for the purpose; it was named the Stevens Refining Company

JB supervised this effort, which involved cannibalizing parts and equipment from the old Kettle Creek refinery in El Dorado, Arkansas. He was also busy keeping the firm's products moving both from its own refineries and from other small suppliers, through its own and other retail outlets in the marketplace. Conditions had been changed with the entry of the New Deal; competition from the majors was serious and fierce.

In St. Louis the Standard of Indiana had erected a service station at a cost of one million dollars. JB stared at it in awe; "it had hundreds of light bulbs," he said later. Much the same was true of other giant competitors; Sinclair was a very difficult problem for Imperial. One day in Chicago the Sinclair sales manager showed JB a map, in which a square downtown block was outlined in black, representing Sinclair's huge new service station plans.

"How can such a property pay out?" asked JB. The man from

16. Clark and Halbouty, *Last Boom*, pp. 228–229.

Sinclair smiled, rolled up the map, and said firmly, "Advertising. We've got forty percent of this market—*and we will keep it.*"

JB was impressed but not immobilized by these and other signs of major company activities. Imperial had stations and bulk plants in St. Louis, Chicago, Minneapolis, Milwuakee, and other localities; he believed, and was proving, that "If they [the majors] can get meals, we can get a few crumbs."

He also had some friends, whose numbers kept increasing, throughout the industry. One, older but nevertheless active and interesting, was Charles C. Rockenback. Rocky, as he was known, was a bachelor and was the industrial commissioner and assistant to the president of the Cotton Belt Railroad.

In that position, in which he supervised railroad purchases of fuel among other matters, Rocky was a prime target for petroleum products sales managers and the recipient of numerous attentions. Such a position and such attentions often have unfortunate results on their recipients, but Rockenback, who was the sole support of several sisters and a younger brother, was a hard-headed, very level businessman. He and JB met over business but formed a friendship; JB was, as always, interested in older people.

In his capacity as general manager, JB visited men in their offices; he seldom asked them to his. Rockenback, whose perquisites included a private railroad car when he traveled and an elegant office in true railroad style, was not expected to visit Imperial. Nevertheless he had many occasions to call, and Celeste Abbington, who answered the phone, had a remarkably appealing voice. Rocky mentioned it to JB, and JB said, "You should visit the office and get acquainted." Rocky laughed and dropped the subject.

But in the spring of 1935, shortly after the baseball season started, Rocky arrived at the Imperial offices in a large black Cadillac, entered, and was introduced to Celeste. He was charmed at once, and JB suggested that they all go to the ball game the following day; he planned to invite Mrs. Saunders. Rocky was delighted and Celeste was flattered.

The next day the foursome sat in Rocky's box, which was well located. The sun was bright and the air still crisp; the players moved with the hopeful energies of spring. Rocky, whom JB had grown to know and like, enjoyed himself immensely. JB could not be sure for some months that a serious romance, culminating in marriage, would ensue, but he knew that his maneuver to place these two together was, at least initially, a great success.

That was a pleasant occasion sparked by a happy inspiration; in the summer of 1935 those were growing less frequent for JB. He worked as general manager and had a heavy load of responsibilities, but Mr. Hassett was not the easiest of men. Celeste Abbington, with a woman's sharp eye, said of him later, "He could be very charming, but he turned ugly if he was displeased."

Mr. Hassett, nevertheless, was an astute businessman, under whom many younger men had learned the industry in all its aspects. His sons were another story. Celeste, usually soft-spoken and careful in her comments, was sharp about Bill and Bob Hassett.

"They were," she said, "disasters."

Young Bob was stationed in St. Louis, but young Bill Hassett, the elder and dominant one of the brothers, began with the firm as JB's assistant. That had been JB's own idea, offered at a time when Mr. Hassett was worried about Bill and openly wondered how he could manage to make him more serious.

JB's relationship with Bill Hassett began, in a business sense, when the younger man reported to him in Springfield. JB, who had organized one of Imperial's subsidiary expansions in that location, was feverishly busy. He and Mr. Hassett looked up as young Bill entered, wearing a cap. That mock workingman's touch sent his father into an instant rage, who tore it off his head, wadded it, and threw it into a wastepaper basket.

"You're a man now, not a boy," he said harshly. "Buy a hat!"

Young Hassett pretended surprise, but obeyed the order. In the days and weeks that followed, JB discovered he had accepted a not only difficult, but exasperating, protégé. JB worked at two desks placed parallel to one another; his activities were so varied one was insufficient. He had two long distance lines and a teletype machine, and would cradle a phone on one shoulder and take orders in shorthand, then swing around to hit the teletype himself, relaying orders to the plants. His mind was intent on process, availability, shipping charges, routes, and dozens of other factors. During one peak period he was intent when young Bill crept beneath him to place and light a firecracker under his chair.

It detonated to send JB into a fury, while young Hassett snickered from the other side of the glass door that sealed the room. When JB ran toward him, he vanished.

A few days later JB had a whisky bottle sitting on his desk that contained some gas oil from the Wickett plant sent in, as a sample, by a customer; its color resembled corn whisky. Young Hassett, eyes bloodshot and showing signs of a hangover, entered. His attention was immediately drawn to the whisky bottle, and JB said, "It's pretty good. Go ahead and try it."

Young Bill had eagerly uncapped the bottle and raised it to his lips when the sickly, oily smell hit him. He paled and turned toward the door but his stomach rebelled, and he retched repeatedly as he fled from the room. JB watched with a satisfaction that deepened later when he noticed that young Bill did not care for retaliations and stopped his pranks.

But as the years of the early thirties passed both Bill Hassett and his brother Bob learned more about operations and were advanced by their father to positions of vice president, while JB remained secretary-treasurer and general manager. He discovered that Bill Hassett was checking on his customers and often huddled with the firm's attorney. By midsummer, 1935, JB no longer felt as secure as before; the Hassett boys questioned many of his decisions. The situation began to grow tense, and his satisfaction in his work began to diminish.

It was an argumentative time. The New Deal had opened the year with the President discussing "old inequalities, little changed by past sporadic efforts," and asserted that "reasonable leisure and a decent living throughout life is an ambition to be preferred to the appetite for great wealth and power." That was not soothing. Great dreams had fueled the United States throughout its history. A small life but a secure one was a new goal to offer. The year had started with an appropriation, in response to the President's request, of almost $5 billion for the employment of those on relief. The resulting program, known as the Works Progress Administration, WPA, engaged in more projects than could be kept in view and at its height employed three million persons, including writers, artists, musicians, and sculptors. Although most of these people had accepted, in 1935, the idea that the state would elevate the arts through supporting them, few produced an outstanding work for the WPA, though some achieved the level of ordinary commercial art.

A more important long-range innovation was the Social Security program, modeled in part on those long existing in Europe, originally introduced in Germany. At the time, the program aroused furious argument, but effectively undercut the appeal of Dr. Townsend's pension plan. Simultaneously the President proposed a cut in small-business taxes and an increase in the taxes of larger enterprises, as well as increases in gift taxes, inheritance taxes, and the higher levels of income taxes.

All these moves cheered labor and low-income groups, and enraged the well-to-do and business associations in general. The National Association of Manufacturers, the United States Chamber of Commerce, and business and industrial groups began to unite in the Liberty

League and rushed to the courts for protection against an Administration many had begun to consider Socialist in purpose.

Such quarters were brought to their feet when, in May, 1935, the United States Supreme Court announced four decisions. The first set aside a railroad pension system, the second invalidated the New Deal measures sparing farm debtors, the third denied the President had the right to dismiss a member of the Federal Trade Commission, and the fourth outlawed the entire NRA, Blue Eagle and all.

The NRA was that conglomeration of codes, rules, regulations, temporary authorities, and price-fixing that had stretched to encompass virtually the entire economic life of the nation. In order to invalidate it, the Supreme Court had unanimously gone back to the principle once fought out in blood in England, in which the Crown was denied the right to "delegate" its powers to its agents.

Immediately after the decision was announced, Justice Brandeis, a noted liberal whose original appointment by Wilson had been almost viciously protested, called young New Deal lawyer Tommy Corcoran to his chambers and said, in part, "I want you to go back to the President and tell him we're not going to let this government centralize everything. It's come to an end. As for your young men . . . tell them to get out of Washington—tell them to go home, back to the states. That's where they must do their work."[17]

As far as the Supreme Court was concerned, the New Deal was over.

If the nine Justices of the Court continued to believe in the older principles of government, however, they were among a minority, even in the United States. The rest of the world was moving in a far different direction, toward different governmental forms than those evolved in the previous two centuries.

In Germany, now under a grim dictatorship that made no pretense at justice, morals, or ethics, jubilation reigned over the vote of the people in the Saar to return to the Reich. Hitler announced the virtual end of the Versailles Treaty by declaring Germany would rearm, and reintroduced conscription. The Soviet Union, whose leaders saw in these moves an increased threat of war, signed a nonaggression treaty with France and Poland, and sent Comintern doves flying in all directions, while Stalin launched a purge of his army and party.

The British and the French decided, in the face of Germany's growing resurgence, to woo Mussolini. In response, like a criminal

17. Arthur M. Schlesinger, Jr., *The Politics of Upheaval* (Boston: Houghton Mifflin, 1960), p. 280.

assured of limited immunity, he launched an attack on the backward country of Ethiopia. Spain, under the control of radicals, moved further left.

In the United States the Supreme Court rulings unleashed a furious national argument, deep, widespread, and bitter, in which the President, his following in Congress, the left, and virtually all liberals aligned themselves against a Court that Roosevelt said was wedded to "horse and buggy days."

In the crisp autumn of 1935 two men in a heavy powerful car, wearing gray fedoras and dark topcoats, and appearing both bulky and grim, with what seemed to be a gleaming gun barrel protruding from the rear of their vehicle, passed rapidly through a number of small towns on Highway 40 in the direction of Kansas City.

Warnings were sent ahead, and they were stopped by a roadblock of heavily armed police just outside Columbia, Missouri. They climbed out with their hands up while the police tore aside the tarpaulin and recoiled in surprise. The "gun barrel" turned out to be a long pipe, part of a testing machine. The two men were JB and an ethyl production expert; they were on their way to a perfectly innocuous business meeting.

The incident, however, was so much a sign of the times that it did not merit a single line in even the smallest town newspaper; the campaign between the FBI and the nation's thousands of armed and dangerous criminals was in full flush.

"St. Louis was so rough that people jumped when a car backfired," JB recalls. Chicago was heavy with gangs; so was Detroit, Kansas City, Milwaukee, St. Louis, and virtually every other city. The countryside, serene on the surface, was studded with similar problems; the federal tax agents would mount regular assaults to root out stills. Rural crime, however, did not interest the reporters and feature writers on the metropolitan press nearly so much as did the figures of men such as John Dillinger, "Pretty Boy" Floyd, Al Capone, and others.

The situation on the criminal front resembled, though in misshapen manner, the economic regulations of the times. Federal authorities were not empowered to move against local criminals, who often had established connections in small-town police forces, with county sheriffs, and with big-city politicians who dominated metropolitan law forces.

But JB and his associates and competitors in the petroleum industry were faced with different sorts of crimes—serious enough, but seldom reported in the press in the same dramatic manner as the exploits of "Pretty Boy" Floyd, "Baby Face" Nelson, Alvin Karpis and "Ma" Barker, or Bonnie and Clyde.

"Fast-buck artists were operating everywhere," says Eddie Scurlock, who worked for the Cooper-Keller Oil Company and was one of JB's most efficient competitors. "They would appear suddenly in a community with handfuls of cash—say thirty thousand dollars or forty thousand dollars—and that was a lot of money then. They would buy as much petroleum products—gasoline, kerosene, and the like—as possible, using some cash as down payment and stretching credit as much as possible. Then they would sell this product to small outlets at prices below the basement over the weekend, collect as much as possible, and be hundreds of miles away before the end of the month. State laws could not pursue them beyond the area, and it was a time when the collection of gasoline taxes lagged behind sales anyway."

The New Deal, intent upon solving the crime problem, but more intent—as were the people—on the murderous activities of the bank robbers and gangsters than on white-collar thieves, persuaded Congress to pass a number of new laws enabling the FBI and other federal agencies to enter the scene. John Dillinger, for instance, with whom the G-men, as they were called, exchanged shots in northern Wisconsin but who was finally tracked down and shot to death in front of a movie house in Chicago, was actually pursued for carrying stolen automobiles across state lines. Capone, whose final conviction was greeted with national relief, was nevertheless never convicted of murders, assaults, thefts, and bribery in the Chicago area, but for income-tax evasion.

The campaign against the gangsters was almost like a re-creation of the Wild West, updated into a modern context. It attracted virtually everyone, lifted the Federal Bureau of Investigation from its long obscurity as a minor governmental agency, and thrust its director, J. Edgar Hoover into fame. Mr. Hoover, who had a flair for the newsworthy and was totally dedicated to his task, was an almost ideal contrast to the deadly enemies of the people whom he pursued and destroyed.

The successes of the FBI, however, were counterbalanced by new waves of violence that afflicted business on the labor front. The problems of the NRA had ended, for the nonce, in the decision of the Supreme Court. But part of the NRA Code had been a series of Labor Relations Boards established to mediate disputes between employers and employees. With the NRA gone, these relationships were returned to the citizens to handle on their own, a condition that many New Dealers considered unsatisfactory.

Shortly after the NRA was outlawed by the Court, therefore, Congress passed the Wagner Act, which placed the labor regulations of the NRA into legislated laws. The unions, which regarded that act as their Magna Carta, rushed into a furious membership campaign, while the employers—under the advice of attorneys who thought the act could be ruled unconstitutional—balked against its provisions. The result was the beginning of national violence on a new level.

The Wagner Act, however, was only a drop in a storm. A new banking act was enacted, giving the government so much more control over the nation's money and money markets that historian Arthur Schlesinger, Jr., later called it a "breakthrough" in the "indispensable powers for the management of the economy."[18] The New Deal was marching on.

Conditions in 1936 were mixed, uneven, uneasy, and contradictory. The resentment of the business groups against President Roosevelt soared into hatred, and the New Dealers responded with contempt. Labor was staging wildcat strikes and its organizers were busy everywhere; many firms responded with lock-outs, force, strikebreakers, and "special deputies."

In St. Louis, a city that reflected all the mixed difficulties of the period, JB was increasingly unhappy. Jack Wightman, the insurance broker, who had launched into business for himself—a bold step— thought his friend was "losing influence" inside his firm.

That observation was entirely accurate. Both Bill Hassett—whom JB had, years before, wet-nursed and put on a train—and the younger Bob Hassett enjoyed, as vice presidents, good salaries and impressive offices, though their real authority was limited. Nevertheless the climate of the firm was changing; Hassett & Sons was clearly heading toward an inner nucleus. Its general manager was the workhorse.

Around him swirled an entire society in which old landmarks were falling. The winter of 1935–1936 had erupted in far-flung floods with widespread devastation. The spring and summer produced hideous dust storms and drought that blew away small farms and farmers alike from a vast region that extended from Texas to Canada through the entire middle of the country.

Highways were dotted with battered old cars carrying odd pieces of furniture and mattresses tied to their tops, packed inside with families who wandered aimlessly across the landscape. The word *Okies* became something little less than a pejorative, little more than a sneer. Border guards at California turned away these descendants of the fron-

18. Schlesinger, *Politics of Upheaval*, p. 301.

tier and their families, whose status drifted down to landless peasants, whose occupations sank to part-time gathering of crops from farms that had turned into agricultural factories.

Yet business, or at least heavy business, was on the upswing. Steel began to work at levels closer to capacity; car sales moved up to the levels of 1927, and department store sales and other sectors improved. The leaders of the New Deal began to believe their efforts were, at last, becoming successful in the economy. But sharper observers noted that relatively few new ventures were being formed; savings were pouring into government bonds and not into new businesses. Closing the gates of speculation has that effect; many people were seeking security and not risks.

Overseas the situation appeared similarly mixed, though the considerations were somewhat different. Germany reentered the Rhineland, that area designated by the Versailles Treaty for occupation until the damages of the Great War had been paid. The French seriously considered resistance, but conferences with Britain made it clear they would have to act not only alone, but also without even moral support. And although France had Europe's largest army, and was considered the foremost military power, it gave way to Hitler. Some historians date World War II from that event.

The Soviets, who watched Germany with unwinking eyes, were already well along in their multiple and subtle movements of defense. Their network of Communist parties, acting under the direction of the Comintern and spectacularly successful in their efforts to beguile the liberals of the world, had created a United Front. "Communism is the Americanism of the twentieth century," said Earl Browder in the United Staes, as his party claimed "Tom Paine, Thomas Jefferson, Andrew Jackson and Abraham Lincoln as forebears."[19] To the astonishment of some and the pleasure of many, the American party swung its supporters, and through them uncounted numbers of intellectuals, squarely behind the New Deal.[20]

The Fourth International, as the Comintern called itself, managed to create crowds, meetings, occasions, and platforms for the Administration that, as 1936 proceeded, enlisted some of the most highly placed—and also most gullible—members of the government. For the first time, in a sequence that would last for years, the party organizers and their myriad dummy organizations began to play an important role in domestic politics by campaigning for candidates of other, far more respectable, and far better known parties.

19. Lyons, *Red Decade*, p. 172.
20. Ibid., pp. 174-175.

That phenomenon reflected, though doctored for the American scene, parallel activities by Communist parties in other parts of the West. In France, where the Communists had long been an important and recognized political faction, their abrupt amiability and arguments couched in patriotic tones succeeded in lifting their membership in the Chamber of Deputies from ten to seventy-two early in the year, and in midsummer 1936, brought the Communists into the French government under the leadership of Léon Blum in an official United Front.

In Spain the success of the Communists was even more remarkable; it achieved such a majority that its leadership decided the time had come to take complete control, in true Leninist fashion. That meant terror. Party cadres fanned out from various Spanish cities in mid-July, 1936, to drag priests, businessmen, conservatives, and monarchists out of their homes to a series of executions that provoked a civil war.[21]

That was an important event, but its drama shielded the larger and even more subtle nature of the United Front propaganda from general understanding. It was the purpose of the Soviet to arouse the West against Germany. But it was not the purpose of the Soviet to see the West united and strong.[22] The propaganda line, therefore, wavered on the issues of peace and rearmament, but stressed, on every occasion—whether natural or contrived—that there was a difference between the totalitarian tactics of Hitler and those of the Soviet Union. The means employed were of terrible simplicity, and consisted of hoisting an anti-Fascist flag, from which any reference to Communism was rigorously expunged. Many innocents were deceived.

It was an election year in the United States. The Republicans nominated an independent oil producer who had served as governor of Kansas, named Alfred E. Landon. A former Bull Mooser, Landon was far from a conservative, but conservatives were hard to find that year. The Democrats, of course, renominated the President and John Nance Garner. Lesser parties attracted far less attention than in previous periods. There was still a Prohibition party, but it had dwindled to a footnote. The Socialists renominated Norman Thomas, who was becoming more respectable than effective. The Communists, on the ballot as such at last—nominated Earl Browder and James W. Ford of

21. The classic description of events leading to this situation may be found in José Maria Gironella, *The Cypresses Believe in God*, trans. Harriet de Onis (New York: Alfred A. Knopf, 1955).
22. Ulam, *Expansion and Coexistence*, p. 229; Lyons, *Red Decade*, pp. 170–175.

New York, and the Coughlinites swung behind William Lemke of North Dakota, who headed the Union party ticket.

None of these lesser candidates made much of an impression; the newspapers presented a contrast between a large and sparkling Democratic party array, and a relatively lackluster series of new Republican names. The President campaigned, as he was to do for the rest of his life, against Herbert Hoover and "economic royalists."

Keith Fanshier, a writer with the Chicago *Journal of Commerce* who specialized in following and reporting the petroleum industry in all its aspects, recalls running into JB during this period. The men had attended a Western Refiners Conference in Hot Springs, Arkansas, and Keith hitched a ride with JB and several other men in the industry on the way back to Tulsa. All of them traveled, apparently, all the time.

"There was a bottle of corn whisky in the car," Fanshier remembers, "and it was passed back and forth, together with a bottle of Coca-Cola as a chaser." Fanshier, a slender, quiet, and somewhat retiring man, found himself huddled among some burly, though jovial, characters. He took note of JB, whom he had seen at other conventions and industry meetings—and especially of the fact that JB would answer questions about the markets, prices and related matters. Such men are important to reporters as sources of accurate information; he determined to look him up in the future.

JB, however relaxed he might have appeared on that and similar occasions, was actually going through a difficult time. Bill Hassett, he said later, "had turned into a snoop." The younger man made it a practice to examine JB's reports and to second-guess his decisions. That made the St. Louis headquarters a difficult place, especially with the elder Hassett gone a great deal of the time.

The air grew cloudy; disputes arose. JB, who found the attentions of Bill and Bob Hassett a continuing annoyance, decided to shift his base of operations to the Milwaukee office. He was general manager and could function, via telephone, teletype, and correspondence, as well from that location as from St. Louis. But the move was an indication of a growing divide inside the firm, and did not bode well for the future.

In November, 1936, the President was reelected by a landslide of unprecedented proportions. He carried all but two states—Maine and Vermont—and almost everyone was surprised. The campaign had been bitter beyond the recollection of all but the old, who could recall the struggle between McKinley and William Jennings Bryan in 1896.

Because of the lopsided verdict, the election was a crucial one. Had it been closer, it is possible the New Deal might have proceeded with more caution. As it was, it seemed like a mandate for more change, and that was how the President received it.

Ordinarily such evidence of national unity would ensure at least some serenity on the landscape, but in the winter of 1936–1937, industrial strife rose to new levels as Homer Martin launched a sit-down strike against giant General Motors. The tactic had only been tried once or twice in the United States before; it was one imported from Europe, where it had been used most extensively in France. It was, of course, a revolutionary method—illegal, and designed to cause more problems than those it purported to dramatize.

It did not arouse as much enthusiasm in the United States as bewilderment. The wages at General Motors were higher than the average, it had over a quarter of a million shareholders, many of whom were in modest circumstances, and the public had no grievance against its management.

Nevertheless workers barricaded a body plant in Fisher, and Fleetwood and Cadillac plants in Detroit and elsewhere. They played cards, stood guard, and halted America's most centralized manufacturing complex, sending a Christmas wave of unemployment and distress through hundreds of thousands of affected homes and industries.

The new year, 1937, dawned on a labor battlefield. The governor of Michigan, the Secretary of Labor—Frances Perkins, a former social worker—and various knots of lawyers attempted to unravel the situation. The courts thundered and the police were assembled; a pitched battle took place but the police were repelled. Factory gates are heavy, and difficult to breach. The National Guard was called out in February, 1937, but the governor of Michigan had persuaded the head of General Motors to negotiate. At the last minute before a fierce confrontation, a settlement was reached. Its term recognized the United Automobile Workers as the sole bargaining agents for 44,000 workers. The result was hailed as statesmanship on all sides, and unions everywhere erupted in sit-down strikes. In Washington the President, incurably insouciant, announced a plan to enlarge the number of Justices on the Supreme Court and to impel their resignation at the age of seventy.

Clearly a new era had dawned in the winter of 1937, though few could analyze its nature.

In the fall of 1936, JB received a call in his Milwaukee office saying fourteen carloads of Imperial's natural gasoline and naphtha had been sitting on a railroad siding near Minneapolis in cold weather long enough to develop a "frost line." He asked how that had happened, and was told the Minneapolis customer was afraid to accept a nonunion shipment. He put the phone down, told his secretary he was leaving for Minneapolis, picked up a suitcase he kept packed for quick trips, and dashed out.

Imperial had a man on the scene in Minneapolis: Ericson. JB looked him up and found him in a hotel, afraid to emerge. The unions had boycotted the firm, which covered all its incoming shipments, its bulk plant, and its deliveries. JB looked at Ericson in disgust and asked him what he planned to do. "What can we do?" Ericson shrugged, and looked away.

"He was selected and placed in the job by young Bill Hassett," JB said, "and he was not a very good choice."

JB drove out to the bulk plant and ordered trucks to the railroad siding. When they arrived there he was standing in the cold, watching while unloading took place. Then he followed the trucks back to the bulk plant. From there he planned to sell the products to other customers.

He did a lot of telephoning and talking, and considerable price-cutting, and was assured of a number of orders. But as the day lengthened, he did not see any trucks arrive. He asked why, and was told that "some men had appeared at the gate and were waving trucks away."

He drove out himself and saw only one man, in a fur hat, stopping trucks and talking to the drivers. Apparently, one man was enough that season. But JB decided the barricade could be broken. He did some telephoning and wound up leasing three service stations for a limited period.

"I'll sell," he swore, "a million gallons." With three service stations in hand, he spent the next day or so having signs made that read, 10 Gallons for a Dollar. Then the Imperial trucks filled the service stations and sales began. Matters had not yet reached the stage where motorists could be stopped from a bargain. Sales in the service stations were brisk, as well they should have been: the regular price was twenty or twenty-one cents.

Meanwhile JB had contacted Chile McCready. Chile was an old friend from school days, a former football player, six foot five. Chile had been in the oil business but had married and moved to Minneapolis, where he worked for his father-in-law in the rope industry. JB knew that Chile was unhappy in that role and longed to return to the oil trade. He explained the situation to Chile and found his old friend interested.

Those matters accomplished, JB stretched out in his room in the Nicollet Hotel, believing some rest was overdue. Night fell, and he dozed a bit. Then the phone rang. He picked it up.

"Get out of town," said a harsh voice, "or you'll be shipped out in a box."

"I'd like to see the color of your eyes," JB answered. "I'll bet they're yellow."

The phone went dead.

JB went downstairs and talked to the hotel detective, but found him unimpressed. He walked outside, saw a darkly dressed man, and on impulse went back through the lobby and upstairs to his room. He wondered if his nerves were getting him, but picked up a heavy ash tray and opened the door suddenly. A man ran down the corridor and vanished in the stairway. JB called the hotel detective again, who came to the room. This time he was more serious.

"That had to be a registered guest," the detective said. "Close the transom, and stay away from the door and out of a line of fire. If I were you, I'd take the bedclothes and camp in the tub. We've had some bombings in Minneapolis; the labor guys are pretty rough."

A few days passed, however, without incident. The gasoline, at bargain prices, moved out of the three service stations. But JB thought it might be wise to talk to the union; fighting at long distance had never appealed to him. He ordered some liquor and ice, called the union, and was told someone would come to see him. A few hours later three men walked in, glowering.

JB was very straight. "I'm only a small oil company," he said. "We can't meet your demands, but we will—when we can." The organizers unbent a bit, drank some of his liquor, ate some sandwiches, and departed. They made no promises and JB had been fairly vague about his own. But he had a feeling that they were convinced—not that he was right, but that his firm was too small to be worth serious exertions.

In other words, the crisis was over. Not only that: JB had reached an understanding with Chile McCready, who was willing to become Imperial's man in Minneapolis for a salary and a percentage. That resolution of both the immediate and long-range problems of the firm in Minneapolis understandably filled JB with a sense of deep satisfaction.

The arrangement with McCready had, of course, to be ratified by

Mr. Hassett, but JB anticipated no problem on that score. He placed a
call to St. Louis and asked for W. B. Hassett. JB was told that he was
unavailable, but that W. L. Hassett, young Bill, would talk to him.
That was not what JB wanted; he canceled the call. A few hours later
he placed another call, with the same results. Since he was going out to
dinner, he left a number where he could be reached, and left a message
asking Mr. Hassett to call him.

Dinner with the Starlings went very well. They were old friends
and customers who had recently launched their own Penotex Oil Company. JB regarded them as most unusual people.

"They opened their mail together in the morning and used the
blank sides of letters for memo pads," he said, "and bought penny
pencils by the gross to save money." Nevertheless he liked Frank Starling and his wife, Dorothy; they were serious, hard-working citizens
who shared their business venture as they did everything else.

Midway through their meal, JB was called to the phone. He excused himself, went outside the dining room, and picked up the receiver expecting to hear Mr. Hassett's voice. To his surprise it was
young Bill.

"I wanted to talk to your father on a policy matter," JB said.

"I handle policy when he's away."

"How can you sit in St. Louis and give orders when I'm here in
Minneapolis being told I'll be shipped out of town in a box?" JB
shouted.

"I can do it."

"I've found a man here in Minneapolis," JB said, using every
ounce of his patience, "but he needs incentives. That's why I need to
talk to your Dad."

"I've found a man," young Bill said, "down here and I'm sending
him up."

JB lost his temper. "Shove the job up your ass," he shouted, and
young Bill—as though waiting for that—said quickly, "You're drunk."

"No, I'm not. I've had a few, but I'm not drunk. And I'll come
down and talk to you man to man."

Then he hung up the phone and went back to the Starlings, who
saw at once that he was upset. They were friends, and there was no
reason not to tell them that he was leaving Imperial. In fact—he looked
at his wristwatch—he thought he'd better get the 11:50 morning train to
Milwaukee. There were many details that had to be handled.

"I'll drive you," Starling said immediately. They finished dinner.
The next morning JB typed a letter of resignation and mailed it. As

soon as he had dropped it in the box, as he and the Starlings were leaving for Milwaukee, he felt a pang of regret. He had been with Mr. Hassett since 1923, a year that seemed an eternity in the past, but he could not stay on with Hassett & Sons.

CHAPTER TEN

The Triangle

JB RETURNED TO HIS OFFICE in Milwaukee toward the end of 1936 expecting to find a telegram from St. Louis. Instead his staff was working as diligently as ever. As he sat down at his desk the teletype machine was chattering, and the phone rang. He picked it up; a customer on the other end was anxious about a delivery and argumentative about its price—he wanted both adjusted, right away. It was, in other words, business as usual. Caught in the routine of years, JB turned toward his work. The day passed as though nothing had changed, but he knew that everything had changed.

He had worked his way from a shipping clerk in a branch office to general manager in the firm, and had been instrumental not only in saving it from collapse, but also in its rebuilding. In the process he had learned thousands of details, hundreds of people, and many intangible factors about the petroleum marketplace and industry. Through all these years he had taken for granted that his own future would expand with the firm—and so it had. But he had also learned, in the last few years at Imperial, that there is a deep and wide divide between the owners of an enterprise and a hired manager. That realization had begun when he watched Mr. Hassett calmly reach into the earnings of the subsidiaries to take a generous bonus for himself; it appeared even more clearly when young Bill Hassett constructed a $75,000 home.

"They're his kin," JB said to his wife, "and that's to be expected." But the fact was that he had not expected it. Toward the end of 1936 he came to the bitter realization that the world is a harsher place than he had realized. If a man is to attain independence, he must first become an independent man.

He turned that thought around as the days passed, and no word came from St. Louis. Orders came through, as always, on the teletype and by telegram. But the phone never rang with a call from St. Louis; it was as though Mr. Hassett and his sons had vanished from the earth. Days passed and that eerie silence continued, while JB wondered.

Meanwhile, he faced a turn in the road. He was no longer a boy, willing to live his life inside another man's enterprise, hoping for rewards. He determined to strike out on his own. But that was easier to say than to do. How could a married man in his thirty-seventh year walk out on his job with only modest savings, and go into business for himself?

He picked up the phone and called John Atkins, in Shreveport, Louisiana. Rumor had it that Atkins had lost in the Crash. If so, he hid it well. JB knew that Atkins had staked Reggie Brinkman to forming the Highland Oil Company; maybe he would do the same for JB Saunders.

He waited while the phone rang, and wondered if Atkins would recall their conversation in El Dorado many years before. JB had, at the time, just been made sales manager for the Kettle Creek Refining Company, and was exuberantly busy.

"Are you happy with Hassett?" Atkins had asked.

"Yes," JB replied, surprised.

"If you're ever unhappy, give me a ring," Atkins had replied, and walked away.

In Milwaukee, remembering that conversation, JB also remembered that it was ten years before. A long time ago. Then he heard the phone ring on the other end, and Atkins came on the line.

"John," said JB, "do you remember when you said to call you if I ever became unhappy?"

"Yes I do," Atkins replied immediately. "Aren't you happy with Bill?"

"No. His boys will take over. But what I did for them, I can do for myself."

"Fine. Reggie and I are going to the API meeting in Chicago. Will you be there?"

"Yes."

"We'll talk then."

JB put the phone down, then picked it up to dial Rockenback. He had started down his new road.

It was a month before a letter arrived from Mr. Hassett—a strange month, in which JB worked as he always had, in which orders and memoranda passed between Milwaukee and St. Louis, sales and deliveries were continued, but no personal calls were exchanged. Mr. Hassett's letter was curious. "I always regarded you more as a son than an employee," it said in part, "but I know there has been trouble in the firm." It went on to add, "I will always be willing to help you in any way I can." But the message it contained was clear: his resignation had been accepted. It would be appreciated if he would continue until April 1, 1937.

So that bridge was burned.

Uncertain prospects make for dark holidays. JB's Christmas was not buoyant, though he had met John Atkins and Reggie Brinkman in Chicago, and after hours of talk it appeared they would back him if he went into business for himself. The extent of that support was left vague, and JB had talked to Rocky several times. Rocky thought his position with the railroad could "gild" JB's sales efforts in the future, but JB had been in business too long to expect much from that approach. Sales depend upon price, and both rely in turn upon sources of supply, quality, delivery, and several other factors. He was confident that he could become successful, but there was much to establish first.

It was during this period that Frank and Dorothy Starling, who were toiling with their Penotex Oil Company, asked him to come to La Crosse, Wisconsin, for a conference. They had discussed JB, and they had a proposition in mind.

"One thousand a month," Frank Starling said when they got together, "—and that's exactly what I draw myself."

"I'm beginning to think a man should work for more than a salary," JB said. Starling did not understand.

"One half of all profits beyond twenty thousand a year," Starling said, and Dorothy Starling nodded her agreement. They were true partners.

"Frank," said JB, "it wouldn't work. We're different people—and I wouldn't last. I sometimes spend as much as four hundred dollars or five hundred dollars in a night's entertaining—you'd have apoplexy. And I wouldn't want to have squabbles with you. Let's forget it and stay friends."

Nevertheless, JB returned to Milwaukee cheered. The Starlings were a frugal couple, and they had made him a handsome offer, one that was a high compliment. He never forgot it, nor forgot that it was made at a time when his future was still in limbo.

The year 1937 in the United States opened with a fierce and highly significant argument started, with customary insouciance, by President Roosevelt. He proposed to enlarge the membership of the Supreme Court from nine to fifteen justices, and could hardly have selected a worse moment had he planned to do so.

The huge sit-down strike at General Motors was still underway. The CIO under John L. Lewis was contending with the AFL, and employers were caught between the two. To recognize one was to provoke the other; most large firms were inclined to resist both.

But the plan to change the third branch of government was one of the more remarkable efforts of the President's remarkable career. Other Presidents had held the Court in low esteem; Jackson had sneered at it and Lincoln had ignored it. But no President had ever before so openly attempted to place the judges beneath the executive. The White House, of course, denied that it had any such end in view, but the more voluble New Dealers were open in their resentment of the Court rulings against the New Deal programs. To their surprise, opposition came not only from determined Roosevelt haters and conservatives, but also from within the ranks of the Democratic party in and out of government posts. The nation, the White House belatedly realized, was far more traditionally minded than expected.

Meanwhile the disputes on the labor-industrial front were exacerbated by the activities of the Attorney General's office, which was mounting new antitrust drives. The target—or at least one of the targets—was the petroleum industry. There was nothing new about that; petroleum had been portrayed as a sinister force in the nation for so long that the legend had become embedded as a part of conventional wisdom. In early 1937 the industry was confronted with indictments against twenty-four firms, fifty-eight individuals, and three trade publications for violations of the antitrust laws.

Those indictments were the culmination of efforts that stretched back for over two years, and were another—though unexpected—result of the Supreme Court rulings against the NRA. That program, bristling with codes and "fair trade prices" for all industrial sectors, had drawn up a complex code for the petroleum industry that sought not only to stabilize the price of crude oil, but also to set floors beneath the prices of gasoline and other consumer products. Such price supports had been enacted into law in agriculture but, when the NRA was voided, had remained in force with the encouragement of the Secretary of the Interior, Harold Ickes. Not everybody was in favor of such supported prices, which entailed large purchases of products from small refineries by the majors. These relationships were known as "dancing partners." Some jobbers, who believed that their ability to supply cut-price operations were inhibited by the buying pools, went to the Attorney General and complained. The eager young lawyers under Thurman Arnold did not need much more than that to get excited; in short order FBI men were pulled away from their pursuit of bank robbers and sent around the offices of the petroleum industry to gather up sample contracts, files, and records, and to take statements.

The result, after several grand juries were impaneled, were indictments delivered in late 1936, with a trial date set for October 4, 1937. Most of the men in the industry believed it would be dismissed in court; they were sure that activities invented by the government in the first place and made mandatory, and then continued under the encouragement of the Secretary of the Interior later, would certainly not make anyone liable for serious treatment. Others were not so sure. The government had turned into an enormous establishment whose purposes were not always clear.

Such disputes and considerations, which extended beyond petroleum into other industries as well, compounded by labor problems and rising prices, served to divert attention from important overseas events. One of these was the Spanish civil war. No war was ever so open to observation or reflected international tides so accurately. Yet none was ever more thoroughly misreported by the members of the free press to their compatriots in the western world.

"In Spain, for the first time, I saw newspaper reports which did not bear any relation to the facts, not even the relationship which is implied in an ordinary lie," wrote George Orwell later.[1] Respected figures in journalism and literature turned partisan in Spain. Herbert Matthews of the New York *Times* argued he had a right to file biased reports.[2] Louis Fischer, correspondent for both the American *Nation* and the British *New Statesman*, doubled as a government agent. Arthur Koestler collaborated with an agent of the Comintern to write, in Paris, a book of fabricated rebel atrocities.[3] The list of those who supported a government that was against religion, against the freedom of the press, against freedom of speech and thought, makes dreary reading.[4]

Collectively these voices did much more than misrepresent a civil

1. Knightley, *First Casualty*, p. 191.
2. Ibid., pp. 192–193.
3. *Spanish Testament*. Koestler admitted seventeen years later that it was a hoax put together by himself and Willie Muenzenberg, an Agitprop chief.
Knightley, *First Casualty*, pp. 195–196.
4. The global influence of the Comintern network had the effect of elevating the careers of most of those who lent themselves to the task of propaganda, though that aspect was never open; it was one of the rewards of True Believers. In Spain these included John Dos Passos, Alvah Bessie, Ernest Hemingway, and Martha Gellhorn, of *Collier's*. There were others from France, Great Britain, and other countries as well.

war and its myriad issues, factions, and divisions. They convinced an entire generation of people around the world that a Communist government was fighting for liberty. That lie, rationalized by its perpetuators because Franco and his forces were supported by Mussolini and Hitler, made it virtually impossible to separate the Communist movement inside the democratic camp in other places.

Unwilling to help a pro-Soviet government and prevented by the skillful propaganda of the leftwing intellectuals from assisting the rebels, Britain and France declared an embargo against all war shipments to Spain, which the United States joined. In effect, Madrid was cut adrift. In the United States, isolationists prepared a Neutrality Act, to keep zealots from pushing the nation into mysterious foreign wars.

These events reached the average American through intermittent press echoes, sandwiched between fulsome articles and photographs of the former Edward VIII of England and Wallis Warfield Simpson, headlines of crimes, and varied entertainments. People were still reading *Gone With the Wind*, the Broadway stage had mounted musicals and *The Time of Your Life* was playing to record crowds. Prices were rising.

Mrs. Saunders was spending a few days with her sister. On Saturday JB worked late as usual and returned to the Sovereign Apartments weary. He noticed, after he entered, a bottle of soda and two glasses on the kitchen table. That was puzzling. He walked into the bedroom and saw his wife's jewelry box, open, on the bed, with several pieces scattered across the counterpane.

The doorbell rang before he could fit that puzzle together. He opened the door to see the lady from an apartment across the hall staring at him, wide-eyed. She said, "Have you been robbed?"

"Yes," he said, suddenly aware.

"I've been robbed too."

She had left her apartment to walk the dog but had cut the walk short—it was cold outside—and had returned in no more than fifteen minutes. That was enough. JB surveyed her apartment: it looked as though hit by a tornado. Drawers were pulled out and their contents dumped on the floor—a shambles.

He went back to his own apartment and called the police. While awaiting their arrival, he assessed the damage. He missed a gold cigarette case and lighter—gifts from his father he reserved for formal occasions. He began to check further and missed a pair of European binoculars; the losses began to mount as he searched.

The police arrived; it was a high-crime period but burglaries were taken very seriously then. They reconstructed the event quickly; the burglars—disdaining the carefully locked front door of the apartment building—had entered through the ever-open trade entrance in the rear. For the first time JB became aware of how open an apartment complex is, in reality. The entire rear was free for newspaper delivery, the laundry—or burglars.

He mentioned that his guns were not taken, and the police said, "They're too dangerous for professional burglars; a gun can add ten years to a sentence." JB pointed out smears of grease on various pieces of furniture, and the police waved these spots aside. "That's to throw suspicion on the building superintendent or the maintenance crew," they said. "This was a professional job."

The men had, they told JB, entered through the rear of the building and opened his apartment door with a piece of stiff celluloid. One demonstrated, and JB was appalled at how easily the lock was forced—and how quickly. He looked at the detective with involuntary suspicion; such knowledge must constitute a standing temptation. Then the burglars—there were two of them, said the police—went through his apartment carefully, selecting only his wife's best pieces of jewelry and discarding the rest. They were relaxing in his kitchen when they heard the neighbor across the hall going out with her dog. Then they slipped inside her apartment and went through it in haste; she had just missed them. Perhaps that was lucky.

The police left. They had been polite and methodical, and were obviously expert in the ways of burglars, but they held out little hope of capturing the culprits. The hammered gold pieces, they shrugged, would probably be melted down. JB stared after them. He was leaving his job of many years, Mrs. Saunders was pregnant, and his apartment had been ransacked. It was an unforgettable low spot in his life.

Young Bill Hassett finally arrived in Milwaukee toward the end of March, 1937. He had Dick Wilkinson with him, who was going to "check JB out." Wilkinson was a man JB had hired; he privately wished him luck. Meanwhile he invited Bill Hassett over to the Sovereign Apartments for a talk.

Mrs. Saunders greeted them, and to JB's surprise, the younger Hassett refused a drink. The conversation was desultory for a time; Mrs. Saunders put on her hat and coat, and left the two men to their discussion.

"I want to ask you a truthful question," Bill Hassett said. "Why are you leaving?" A hulking six feet four, he looked at JB as though puzzled.

JB looked at him in wonder, and then looked out the window. "I've done a good job for the company," he said. "Assets are up to seven and one half million dollars. Meanwhile, you've built a fine new home. I was given a dozen golf balls for Christmas. I do the work, and you get the bonuses."

Then he swung around and looked at the younger man. "What I did for your father I can do for myself," he said. "And if you sober up—if you stop drinking and wasting all your time hunting and fishing—you can do it. You can go to work."

John Atkins of Shreveport was thirty-nine years old in 1937, and an imposing figure. Six feet two, he weighed somewhere between 250 and 275 pounds. He was cold of eye, calm, and reserved. The scion of one of Shreveport's most important families, he was raised in a pillared mansion to great wealth and high social position. His father, a large land-owner active in real estate, was one of the early investors in the Caddo Oil Company, which was among the first to enter the play when oil was discovered at Caddo Lake, in northern Louisiana. Later Atkins senior had become a part owner and president of the Shreveport Producing and Refining Company, and had encouraged his son-in-law, Philip Hamilton, to launch the first refinery when the El Dorado field was discovered.

The elder Atkins, in fact, was such an ardent businessman that he actually signed the papers on his deathbed for the construction of a pipeline from El Dorado to Shreveport, which was later owned and operated by Hamilton. He left a considerable fortune, and John Atkins was proud of the fact that he had quadrupled these holdings by mid-1929.

Unfortunately, he had done this by playing the stock market. "It seemed to me that my father made money the hard way," he told JB later, "and I was making it the easy way." In the autumn of 1929, greatly extended on margins, he learned how hard the easy way can become.

"I hated to get up in the morning and have breakfast," he said. "Breakfast time in Shreveport was exactly the time the brokers in New York—and the banks—chose to call to ask me to cover my margins." He had to sell his family's holdings, little by little and one by one. Each forced sale was like another knife; he had made a great shambles of his inheritance.

As the early thirties rolled around, John Atkins even had to move from his ancestral mansion into a more modest home; the upkeep was too high. But the property was also too large to sell in a depressed market; John Atkins did not make the effort. And as far as the people in Shreveport were concerned, he was simply conserving his money in the spirit of those depressed times—a not-unusual phenomenon. In almost every other respect, therefore, John Atkins appeared unscathed by the storm. He drove a big car, smoked a big cigar, wore a gleaming Panama, and bore the same massive, impenetrable, and imperturbable appearance as before.

There were two banks in Shreveport, and both were unhappily aware that the big man did not bother to do business with either. One day one of the bankers stopped him, and said, "Mr. Atkins, we know you have a lot of money and do a lot of business. Why don't you do some of that business here in Shreveport?"

Atkins looked down from his great height, and calmly blew a smoke ring. "You're a small bank," he said, "and I'm not a deposit customer. I believe in putting my money to work."

The banker looked eager; it was a lean period for bankers. Atkins added, "As a matter of fact, I have a deal on now. If it comes through, I'll be borrowing money—not depositing it."

"Why don't you come and see us then?" asked the banker. Atkins put the cigar back and said, "If the deal looks good, I may do that," and walked away.

"Those three days," he told JB later, "were three of the longest days I ever spent." But he knew he had to wait; haste could betray eagerness. Finally, after that interval, he sauntered into the bank and the president rose to greet him with a smile.

"I need fifty thousand dollars," he said, "on a ninety-day note."

"Do you mean it?" the banker asked, and Atkins nodded. He used words like dollars and didn't believe in wasting any.

The banker sat down and began to draw the papers; Atkins got the money. He placed it in a casing head plant in partnership with his brother-in-law, Philip Hamilton, and the redoubtable H. L. Hunt. Both men assumed—as did almost everyone—that Atkins had remained wealthy.

In due course news reached the other Shreveport bank that Atkins was dealing with its rival, and caused some dissatisfaction. Shortly before his note was due, Atkins strolled into the second bank and said he would like to borrow fifty thousand dollars on a ninety-day note. They scrambled to please him, and he used the money from the second bank to pay the first. Then he renewed the loan at the first bank.

The casing head deal, for which Atkins really needed the money, proved immensely profitable. The bankers of Shreveport, although they did not know it, had saved Atkins, but both banks benefited. "It was a year or a year and a half before I was able to deposit some money with them," Atkins told JB years later, "but I was glad to be able to do so."

By the time JB met John Atkins in Chicago, the Shreveporter had moved back into his manse, and was riding high. He had Reggie Brinkman with him—another behemoth, of a somewhat different cast. Reggie was a former sailor, with many of the characteristics that calling conjures. He was the operator of the Highland Oil Company, and shared its ownership with Atkins on a fifty–fifty basis.

The four men—Rocky sat in—chatted very agreeably. JB had laid his plans and some customers were already lined up. He was going to buy petroleum products and sell them. That meant he believed he could rely on his acumen as a buyer and his ability as a salesman. The other three accepted that; they knew him well enough. The question was how much money did he need to get started, and how would the firm be divided?

"I'll need twenty thousand dollars," he said. That was a lot of money then.

"Couldn't you get by on ten?" Atkins asked.

"I'll lend him ten thousand dollars myself," Rocky said quickly.

Rocky wrote out a check for ten thousand dollars and handed it to JB; Brinkman filled in a check for the same amount and did the same. JB handed each of them his personal note, in return.

Even across a gulf of thirty-eight years that formless, unstructured, personal approach toward a new venture seems surprising. They didn't even bother with a notary public. One of them asked JB if he had a name for the business, and he nodded. Unconsciously counting Atkins and Brinkman as a single individual, he said, "We have three partners; that's a triangle. I'll call it the Triangle Refineries."

He had no refineries—and would never have any—but that didn't strike them as odd. They nodded; the name sounded fine to them. After all, Triangle would represent refineries.

When he arrived at St. Louis, JB dropped in to see young Bill Hassett, at Imperial. Mr. Hassett's letter had mentioned a severance check—one month's pay. It had never been sent, and he wondered about it. Young Hassett flushed and somewhat clumsily unlocked his desk drawer. He had been holding it back.

That minor contretemps settled, JB flew about the city's second-hand office furniture stores and made his purchases. When they were complete Jack Wightman, the insurance broker, came in to survey them, and frowned at what he considered their opulence. "He must have spent at least two thousand dollars furnishing that place," he said later, "which I thought pretty extravagant, under the circumstances." Wightman didn't realize that secondhand stores still bulged with the relics of business shipwrecks. JB's ornate walnut desk not only seemed fit for a bank president, but had actually once reposed in the executive suite of a defunct bank.

The day he opened—April 16, 1937—he was visited by Hugh Ragon, an old friend who read about the venture in the *Oil & Gas Journal*, and Stanley Thomson, of Abbottsford, Wisconsin—who was an old customer. Ragon wanted to join Triangle; he had called JB and made a date to appear in the new Cotton Belt offices in advance.

"If you can sell," JB told him, "I can buy." After some discussion, it was agreed Ragon would open a Triangle office in Minneapolis, pay the rent and expenses himself, and sell whatever JB would send to that city. They would split the profits equally.

With that settled, Thomson then leaned forward and placed an order. It was for three carloads of kerosene and three carloads of gasoline. The two men departed and left JB in a glow. In his first hour in business he had hired a commission salesman, launched a branch office, and received his first order: a substantial one. That was not bad for a man whose business equipment consisted of second hand furniture, some telephones, typewriters, and files, which cost—in all—only $500. Later JB joked about it.

"I had heard of men going into business on a shoestring," he said, "but I started out in the hole—to the tune of twenty thousand dollars."

There was only one item missing from that inventory: an experienced mind, released from the fetters of an organization, equipped with a deep knowledge of the marketplace. That was worth more than a factory filled with machinery.

JB entered the marketplace armed with the knowledge that every refinery had a geographical region within its own territory in which it enjoyed a competitive edge, through lack of shipping charges, over competitors who had to ship their products into the region. It was that aspect of the petroleum marketplace that aroused the deep suspicions of the antitrust division of the Justice Department, and gave rise to the legend of "controlled markets."

What Justice could not seem to grasp, however, was that refiners could not survive simply by supplying their immediate regions. In order to produce efficiently at the lowest possible costs, they had to use their equipment to near capacity, and maintain a constant flow of crude into their plants. The result was that as soon as they met the needs of their environs, they had excess production that had to be shipped into competitive areas at an added cost and lower margins.

The petroleum marketplace, therefore, consisted of both regional enclaves and a large floating arena replete with fierce price-cutting, dumping, and fast action. In that arena prices fluctuated constantly and resembled the activity of the stock exchanges. In the exchanges, rumors that a firm was undergoing internal stress or top management changes, was overloaded or was suffering losses, could send the price of its stock plummeting downward in minutes. Rumors of large acquisitions, a new product, or any other positive could send its stock price soaring. The same sort of mixture of fact, fancy, reality, conjecture, and sheer accident could affect the prices of petroleum products in different regions.

A cold wave sweeping through two or three states, for instance, could send the prices of fuel and burning oils up. A possible steel strike could send the price of industrial oils, greases and diesel down. Road conditions, snow storms and floods could have an immediate impact on the price of gasoline. Farm developments affected petroleum products.

All refineries, therefore, operated both defensively and offensively in terms of their decisions on what to produce, and in what quantities. Brokers served as middlemen, operating without personal risk but on commissions, as do their counterparts on the exchange. Below the brokers, but more numerous and usually restricted to particular, limited territories, were jobbers. All of these had to keep up with the prices listed in *Platt's Oilgram*, masterminded by Warren Platt, and the *Chicago Journal of Commerce*, masterminded by Keith Fanshier. Industry developments were carried in the *Oil & Gas Journal* and other publications, so that the more far-sighted could make long-range observations. Word of mouth, rumors, behind-the-scenes information, weather, accidents, fires, and political developments all poured into a huge torrent of factors to affect the ebb and flow of the marketplace.

It was in that huge and quick-moving sector that JB had functioned for years for Imperial. He had not only ordered and supervised production; he had also bought and sold their surplus on behalf of a number of refiners. Now as Triangle Refineries he planned to do the same in his own business. He stressed that he would not be a *broker*. He would buy the surplus from small refiners outright and take his chances in the open, competitive marketplace on being able to sell at a profit.

Up to that point he offered no more than any good customer would offer. But he went a long step further. At Imperial his arrangements with a number of smaller refineries had been to serve as an extra sales arm on a regular basis.

He approached his new suppliers with a similar proposition. "I will handle not simply the surplus you want to sell on the basis of what seems best to me at the moment," he said, *"but all the surplus you produce.*

"I will relieve you of the need to maintain a sales staff and a credit department to check out firms located far beyond your region—relieve you of the need to have a traffic dpartment drawing comparisons on shipping charges and rates. You can simply produce whatever is most efficient for your plant and your home sales—and I will buy the rest."

No newcomer could conceive of such a venture, and no man nervous of his ability could dream of such an operation. It was like telling a number of different men that he would end their need to battle against demons; he would fight for them—but not as a broker. He would buy, and pay the price he considered reasonable, and the price he could obtain in the open market was his to keep.

That meant he had to know not only when to sell, and at what price, but where to sell. The refiners were only one end of his seesaw; customers had to be placed on the other. Again his years at Imperial had provided a background among jobbers and retailers. Years of attending API and regional gatherings of refiners and marketers had made him as well-known as a major league baseball manager among sports fans. Men that he himself did not know, knew him—and he had his memory.

There are courses on memory, which explain some of the ways in which names, dates, facts, and information can be recalled, sometimes through association and sometimes through mental shorthand. These are misunderstood. They are like algebra and trigonometry, and the principles of physics: they serve those who make the effort but they are not substitutes.

As a youngster working in the railroad yards of Sapulpa, JB learned that towns were numbered by the carrier, and therefore G 438 Sapulpa was the destination—and the distance from St. Louis. After a time he could stand in the yards and watch a slow train going past, and check it, car by car, before it came to a halt.

By his thirty-seventh year, when he started Triangle, he had polished this basic power of observation into a fine instrument. His mental files contained rates, routes, prices, products, people, and other details—and his intelligence had penetrated their interconnections and balances. He was not unique in this. The crowded ranks of business contain talents intellectuals will neither recognize nor admit, largely because their activities are in sectors that intellectuals do not choose to recognize. But JB was unique in putting it all together on his own behalf in early 1937, and in having the combination of an introvert's grasp with an extrovert's personality. He had no doubt whatever of success, but Atkins and Brinkman, who knew him from a distance, were by no means as certain.

"Don't tell anyone that we are involved," said John Atkins, shaking hands with his cool manner. "Reggie and I prefer to remain in the background."

By midsummer, 1937, the dispute over President Roosevelt's plan to enlarge the judiciary, which included not only the Supreme Court but also the Courts of Appeal, reached a curious stage. From the start the Administration had claimed it was moving not out of resentment over anti–New Deal rulings by the High Court, but from a dispassionate desire to improve the efficiency and enlarge the structure of the third branch, in order that it could better meet the needs of a larger and more populous nation than when it was first constructed.

There was considerable justification to this rationale. The nation had not only grown larger and more numerous, but infinitely more litigious. Lawyers not only had increased in numbers but also were inserting themselves as go-betweens in virtually every human transaction. The courts were clogged and the arguments they heard were increasingly complex.

The critics of the White House, however, believed its explanation of the court-packing scheme, as it was called, had a larger and also meaner motive. They saw a powerful President attempting to achieve, by political pressure and manipulation of Congress, domination of the courts. If they were right, the balanced triangle of the American Republic was in jeopardy.

That conclusion, however, was held only by a minority of traditionalists. By 1937 the American concept of law had drifted far from its English origins. Principles of law that buttressed individual rulings had, by subtle stages, drifted into what law schools call "case law," in which all sorts of exceptions arose. The Supreme Court, until the President's challenge—and it was that—clung fiercely to the older concept. In rejecting the investigative methods of the SEC, for instance, the majority of the Justices had compared the tactics of its eager young lawyers to "the intolerable abuses of the Star Chamber."[5] It is doubtful if many Americans recognized the parallel, or even knew what the Star Chamber had been.[6]

5. Schlesinger, *Politics of Upheaval*, pp. 475–476, prefers to quote the dissent to this comparison.
6. So called because of the painted stars on its ceiling, the Star Chamber was the site of state trials in the reigns of the Tudors and the first two Stuarts, in which

Had the Supreme Court persisted in its interpretation of the Constitution, as had an earlier Court prior to the Civil War, there is little doubt the confrontation would have led to a clear line being drawn between the new programs of the Administration and the traditional limits of the government of the United States. Chief Justice Hughes, however, believed the pre–Civil War precedent was one to avoid at all costs.

The President pushed, and the Court gave way. It upheld the Railway Labor Act, then the Farm Mortgage Moratorium, and then minimum wages for women and children. In doing that, it reversed an earlier decision whose ink was barely dry. Finally it upheld the Wagner Act. All these were parts of the NRA program it had previously declared unconstitutional. Then Justice Willis Van Devanter, whom Reed Powell, a New Dealer, had termed "a dodo," retired.

The President, with his New Deal measures approved and able to appoint a decisive swing vote in the person of New Dealer Hugo L. Black,[7] was asked to drop his plan. He demurred; he wanted to enlarge the Court in any event. It seems he genuinely felt that courts should reflect the popular will—a concept that reflected a confusion between his popularity and basic principles, and an education that had been more gentlemanly than genuine. His entourage, however, rejoiced. They realized a historic turn had been made. The Supreme Court would remain supreme as long as its decisions did not oppose the tides of change. That would remain to haunt the nation.

In August, 1937, four months after JB had launched Triangle Refineries, prices on the stock exchanges began to fall apart. The entire summer had seen a steady diminution of industrial production throughout the land. Steel orders had risen earlier in the year and induced United States Steel to come to a settlement with John L. Lewis in preference to a strike, though Little Steel had taken the hard road, and suffered in consequence. But the steel industry was benefiting from the jump in a European armaments race, which—in the wake of Hitler's move into the Rhineland and the Spanish civil war—

---

defendants were forced, by various means, to provide evidence against themselves. That abuse was a factor in the English civil war, and knowledge of it later led to the establishment of the Fifth Amendment in the United States.

7. Hugo L. Black after his appointment was disclosed to have been a member of the Ku Klux Klan fifteen years earlier. In October, 1937, he made a radio broadcast admitting that; his defense was that his membership was insincere and that he had joined to further his career. Amazingly, the press dropped the issue, but his public recantation, or explanation, set another precedent. In years to come other politicians would choose that method of quieting storms. Few would be as lucky, however, as Justice Black, whose explanation was completely accepted.

was getting into high gear. Meanwhile prices had slowly crawled up in the marketplace.

The economists of the New Deal, who have not yet attained the place in history they earned, had decided early in the year that all their theories were correct. Therefore it was time to reduce government spending and to enjoy the revenues from increased taxes, and to "stabilize"—a favorite word. There is no doubt the stricter margin requirements of the New Deal slowed the stock exchange. A great many slowly watched their stocks dwindle, day by day and week by week, and a real crash took place in slow motion.

The ripples coursed through all businesses whose inventories had increased and sales dropped; and a wave of retrenchments took place. Two million more people lost their jobs during the autumn of 1937— among them thirty thousand members of the UAW, who had wrung so many concessions from General Motors. "What price CIO gains now?" asked Frederick Lewis Allen.[8] Cars became a glut on the market; the bottom dropped out. After years of the New Deal, unemployment was more than ten million; Okies were still drifting, business was in splinters and the new magicians seemed as puzzled as the old.

Changes, when they arrive, always come as a crowd. In Oklahoma JB's old friend and mentor, who had set his feet on an upward path so many years before, Ralph Moon, had a stroke and was then afflicted with uremic poisoning, from which he died. His Moon Marketing Company had managed to stay afloat during the bitter years of the thirties—an accomplishment in such a period.

All Moon's backers, including JB, had been repaid years before, but his death hit JB hard. He flew to Oklahoma to attend the funeral. His friend left a substantial and complex estate.

"Moon was a big man in my life," JB says. "He and Jack Reardon were very important to me." He is right: a younger man who attracts attention of his elders can find a way out of the woods—if he listens. JB was unusual not only in having listened, but also in not forgetting the men who pointed new directions to him.

A photograph, taken at the time, shows JB and a friend coming toward the camera, walking along the street in St. Louis. JB is wearing a light fedora with a narrow band, a midwestern sort of hat, and a dark suit, white shirt, and tie. The impression is of youth—a round-faced but still youthfully slender and compact man. Only the hands give warning: they are twice the size one would expect, and look like boxer's mitts. His expression is watchful.

8. Allen, *Since Yesterday*, p. 246.

He had a lot to watch out for; the economy was in a tailspin. Yet, with Sally Miller, his secretary and one salesman—Hugh Ragon, who would not stay long—JB found himself doing a heavy business from the start. Jack Wightman—another tireless operator, though in a different field—came by and sold JB workmen's compensation, car, and office insurance. As usual, he used his eyes: insurance men are economic physicians, knowledgeable about signs of mortality—or of health.

"He ordered carloads of gasoline for a twenty-dollar bill," Wightman recalls. "He ran up immense telephone bills for a tiny percentage of profit." Indeed he did. JB was working on percentages that would horrify many persons unversed in business; his difference between purchase and sales prices was—gross—3.5 percent. Expenses pared that to 1.7 percent. A little over a penny and a half on the dollar. A major error, a miscalculation, could be near-ruinous.

His distribution depended upon the railroads. It was a period when freight cars were a glut on the market and traffic managers scrambled to get business. Spur lines ran into refineries and to bulk plants, and JB had no problem in seeing to it that his suppliers could ship petroleum products toward him. His task was to see that these cars found a home before they stopped rolling. He left his office every night with the knowledge that he had 200 or 250 of these cars rolling, loaded with petroleum products, across the landscape, heading in a bewildering variety of directions. A layman might have collapsed, but JB was no more concerned than a trader on any of the nation's exchanges, who went home similarly knowing that in the morning they would have to resume direction, and sales efforts, for an uneasing flow of business.

His hours at home were, in fact, as regular as he could manage, for the Saunderses had their first child: a daughter. She was small, fine-boned, and spirited—like her mother. They named her Suzanne; her arrival on the heels of their new life seemed a good omen.

There were other good omens, as always—even in mixed and uncertain times. Rocky married Celeste Abbington. He was forty-nine, and the bride was more than twenty years younger, but they seemed ideally suited. JB and Mrs. Saunders attended the wedding, of course, and the two couples saw a great deal of each other.

Rockenback had assumed, JB said later, that his position as industrial commissioner would help to "gild" JB's sales. But that had not proven necessary. Sales were excellent from the start, and showed a steady increase with every passing week. And though the profit margin was as thin as a hair, it mounted—as every student of percentages knows—to a respectable sum with truly surprising rapidity. Yet Triangle Refineries, a fledgling venture dwarfed by giants in the world's largest industry, would have attracted relatively little attention in the autumn of 1937, had it not been for the Madison Trial.

The federal case had hovered over the industry for almost three years, and some men would never forget it. Keith Fanshier, a hard-working reporter who covered the industry and raced about the landscape doing his own legwork, was among those indicted. "How can you explain something like that to your wife and kids?" he asked later.

He was, of course, far from alone. The federal agents had subpoenaed *all the records* from dozens of firms extending back to 1934. Their investigators had pawed through these immense collections, plucked out memoranda that read, "We have agreed," and stacked them to one side for future examinations. They were, in a way, trying to track the operations of millions of transactions to find evidence of a collusive network. To a large extent these efforts were redundant; the industry had maintained much of the NRA Petroleum Code without any attempt at concealment, believing that another branch of the government—Interior—would support it. Even Roosevelt had publicly said he "hoped the gains of the National Petroleum Council would not be lost."

The industry was banking on Secretary Ickes, one of the oddest men to ever hold high office in the nation's history. He described himself as a *curmudgeon*—a term for a churlish fellow. "He could be tough on paper or on a platform," says J. Howard Marshall, "but he was gentle in person." Ickes had originally hoped to become Commissioner of Indian Affairs; he wound up with Interior by a series of accidents. The oil men had letters of encouragement from him and believed he would straighten all confusions, since that was the only honorable course. Mr. Ickes was known for his high standards of morality.

J. Howard Marshall, however, was no longer at the Secretary's side. He had left government service, had decided not to return to Yale in the hope of becoming its Dean of Law, and had joined Standard of California. As legal counsel for the firm, it was his task to brief—over a three-month period—the famous Colonel William Donovan, later known for founding the OSS. "Donovan was a political lawyer," Marshall says, "almost completely unable to concentrate on any subject, but with an enormous presence."

Donovan and Marshall were only two of the personalities who were at Madison; virtually the entire industry was collected and subjected to all sorts of Keystone Kops activities. JB, subpoenaed as a witness, with all his records as well, remembers that whenever he and his friends went into a bar, they would soon find themselves being crowded by strange young men who didn't appear accustomed to such surroundings.

"We would huddle together and pretend to whisper, and look at our watches and scurry out," he says, "and they would follow in the most elaborate way."

JB knew, of course, what everybody knew: buying pools existed, arrangements between many firms existed, but at the same time these pools and arrangements were subject to breakdowns, vicissitudes of the weather, events, and the marketplace—were inherently transient and, so to speak, unimportant. A great case could be made against the continuation of the NRA, but the government had since gone on to create price supports in agriculture, wage supports in industry, supports for milk producers, and many other similar arrangements. It was difficult to see any firm principle in a government that sought to jail some citizens for doing what others were allowed to do with the force of law.

As the Madison case proceeded, JB noticed the government attorneys were very young men from Harvard, Yale, and Columbia, and very sincere. He came to realize, with a sense of shock, that they actually regarded businessmen as engaged in nefarious activities. He was torn away from his own business, which he could not really afford. Around him he saw men whose names were familiar, and he passed the time extending his acquaintances.

He learned that Paul Jacoby from Milwaukee gave testimony for the government, and was to later observe that no man who did was ever again trusted in business. At one point he was in the witness room, waiting to be called, when Neil Buckley, a Cities Service executive, started an elaborate and interesting tale about dog-breeding. The bailiff appeared and Buckley was called. He left, promising to complete the story the next time he saw JB. He did—but that was ten years later.

On other occasions the witnesses were not allowed to sit in the waiting room together; the bailiff or some other official would appear and say, "Saunders, you can go today. Take a ride somewhere."

Some men, JB learned, made the mistake of telling lies on the stand and were later indicted for perjury. That, and the fact that the government held everyone's records, made the matter of the witness stand no joke. Keith Fanshier, who had once worked for a chamber of commerce, found to his amazement that the government lawyers considered that a mark against him. He was, of course, cleared.

JB's turn finally arrived, and he proved well able to handle himself; his days as a court reporter had not been wasted. "Were the majors against you?" he was asked.

"I was taught as a boy never to be afraid of giants," he replied. "You can always grab a crumb and run." But he felt the procedure was unfair. The government prosecutors occupied a long table. There were several of them. They had assistants who searched for and handed them documents, and they would alternate with one another in asking questions.

He recalls prosecutors Henry Lewin and Hammon Chafitz, who would pluck phrases from memoranda and have them placed in the record. He shifted in his chair at the tone of voice they employed. In a different setting he would have known how to respond more directly. Lewin leaned forward in the course of his examination and shook his finger in JB's face, and threatened to have him recalled. JB, however, knew he had done nothing illegal, paused often in his testimony to drink a glass of water, and was not shaken.

The press covered the Madison trial in depth. Some stressed that the indicted oil companies appeared with over fifty combined defense attorneys. No record was made of the number of newsmen; it was probably higher. Sensational articles appeared because some oilmen rented elaborate private homes in the area, appeared at country clubs, and were seen disporting themselves in saloons. The worst aspect, from the industry's view, was that Secretary Ickes refused to appear. The judge then refused to allow his letters or memoranda of support to be used as evidence unless he did appear.

With the Secretary of the Interior unwilling to come forward, the conclusion was nearly automatic. Sixteen oil companies and thirty individuals were convicted by the jury, and fines were levied.[9] The Department of Justice was disappointed; its young lawyers wanted all the convicted sent to jail—as a lesson.

The lesson actually taught, however, was different than the lesson intended. The protective shield thrown around the Secretary of the Interior and his lack of candor,[10] coupled with the judge's refusal to

9. The verdict was set aside on one firm and fifteen individuals, and new trials ordered for three firms and fifteen persons. Appeals reversed all the verdicts and ordered new trials. The Supreme Court reversed Appeals. Douglas, for the majority, said the old yardstick of "reasonableness" no longer applied. On May 8, 1940, the New York *Times* protested, saying the oil firms had acted "with the knowledge, approval and encouragement of Federal officials," and that the ruling lacked "any consistent or well-thought through set of principles."

10. Both the judge and the defense, in effect, left Ickes's appearance up to the Secretary. Ickes, who knew that the case against the oilmen was unfair and that Justice was out to jail them, nevertheless decided not to become politically embarrassed. Kendall Beaton, *Enterprise in Oil* (New York: Appleton-Century-Crofts, 1957), 481*n*.

allow the Ickes letters and memoranda to be used as evidence by the defense,[11] left some with an uneasy suspicion that the government of the United States was no longer playing fair with the citizens.

In the autumn of 1937, however, the darkening situation of the world began to force itself on the attention of the United States. The people were still isolationist in temper; the barrage of antiwar books, plays, and investigations of the early thirties had sunk deep. Most people had grown distrustful of propaganda, which, in essence, meant the press. Yet the press was the major source of information for the average man, and it reflected events from overseas that could give pause to the most indifferent. In the Orient Japan fell upon China as though possessed by furies. In short order the Japanese occupied Shanghai, Peking, and Nanking. The behavior of their troops in those and other areas in China made it clear that Japan was out to diminish the prestige of the white man in the Orient.

Their moves were shrewdly timed. Great Britain, which had long maintained international balance in the colonial world, was undergoing deep internal changes. Prime Minister Baldwin, who had forced Edward VIII off the throne, retired and was replaced by Neville Chamberlain. Churchill was worried about Britain's military situation and its ability to meet possible challenges from Germany. Conferences were held, and it was decided to limit the British response to Japanese aggression to protests, lest Japan draw even closer to Hitler and Mussolini.

The USSR regarded Japan's massive incursions into China as a respite. As long as Nippon was so deeply engaged, it could not threaten the commissars. The dwarfish[12] Stalin, still consolidating his power, moved toward the preparation of trials—and the subsequent execution—of his oldest Bolshevik associates.

In the West the fierce battles of the Spanish civil war continued to attract attention. Franco's advance had proceeded so far that he had naval forces able to place an embargo of his own against waterborne shipments to Madrid. Attention on Iberia, however, was now begin-

11. The defense attorneys could have issued a subpoena forcing Ickes to appear and testify, but were afraid to do so for fear of retaliation by one of the Administration's highest placed and most powerful officials. That fear provides a vivid illustration of how far governmental power had expanded, and how far the legal profession had retreated from its traditional role of protecting the rights of individuals against the encroachments of the state.

12. Stalin was five feet two inches, wore special shoes to elevate his stature, and stood on a wooden slab to review the May Day parades. Conquest, *Great Terror*, p. 63.

ning to diffuse; central Europe was visibly turning into a molten pit of dissention.

Sudeten Germans in Czechoslovakia were beginning to agitate; Nazi parties had risen in Rumania; there was more German agitation in Danzig and in the Polish Corridor—and German activities had grown so sinister, so clearly menacing to peace in Europe, that President Roosevelt made a speech in Chicago against "aggressors." He proposed a "quarantine" by peace-loving nations against those who would disturb the world community. The phrase attracted attention and was widely praised in intellectual sectors, where the Nazis had attracted odium and fear.

The speech aroused a storm in other quarters, which feared the President was turning toward international involvements in order to solve the growing "recession," as it was termed, of his Administration. Unemployment was continuing to spread, the prices on the stock exchanges continued to fall, business production continued to decline, and the nation as a whole was in no humor to worry about Europe or any other continent.

The President retreated, protesting his hatred of war, but a sensitive nerve had been touched nevertheless. The iron, steel, and oil industries were selling large amounts to Japan, which could not otherwise have continued its campaign. War orders, in fact, were about all that was keeping the nation industrially above the worst days of the early thirties. Not everyone appreciated that, but everyone did know that the New Deal had not healed the nation economically, and had aroused deep and ugly divisions.

The President's speech was curiously timed. One month later the dictator of Germany called in his general staff and outlined a truly startling plan for aggressive war. To Hitler's anger, the generals resisted. They did not believe the Reich could overcome the combinations of the West. Since the Army was the only German faction capable of resisting—or, for that matter, toppling—the dictator, he immediately laid plans to change generals.[13]

The mood of the United States toward overseas events, however, was dramatically revealed in early December, 1937, when the USS *Panay*, a naval gunboat, was bombed, strafed, and sunk by Japanese military planes in the Yangtze River in China. Many Americans were astonished to learn the American Navy had war vessels in that area. They were more irritated by that information than by the loss of an American ship and lives.[14]

13. Joachim C. Fest, *Hitler*, trans. Richard and Clara Winston (New York: Harcourt Brace Jovanovich, 1974), p. 561.

14. The official explanation was that the *Panay* was in the area to protect American shipping from pirates.

They had some reason for both their surprise and their irritation. The Neutrality Act was supposed to keep the nation out of such troubles, or at least out of the middle position between warring powers. But the Administration had used a loophole. The Neutrality Act forbade the American sale of munitions of war material to warring nations, and the President had ruled that since neither Japan nor China had declared war, none existed.[15]

The *Panay* incident occupied the headlines as the nation prepared for the 1937 Christmas holidays. Polls showed that an overwhelming number of Americans believed the nation should stay out of the Orient and even withdraw missionaries if necessary.[16] The result was that the warlords of Tokyo issued an apology, despite clear evidence the attack was deliberate. The apologies were accepted. Tokyo was pleased: its road to conquest seemed clearer.

The citizens of the United States could hardly be blamed for being unconcerned about events so distant and so largely unexplained. For over a generation there had been a continual barrage against the colonial system—in India, in Malaya, in French Indochina, in Africa, and elsewhere. The British Empire was still held by many Americans to be the font of all evil. Very few Americans could see a clear national interest in the Yangtze River. Those who did were apt to be in the oil business or in some other international sector. They were in a tiny minority.

Another factor was the economy. It troubled everyone because it continued to decline. The prices on the exchanges continued to fall as though there was no other direction; production continued to dwindle, unemployment continued to expand, and so did the relief rolls. Conditions were getting worse with every passing day. The Christmas season was a dark one in many an American home during the early thirties but for a time it had seemed as though the nation was struggling back from the depths. In 1937 it was sinking again, and the fair promises of the New Deal had a mocking ring.

It is all the more remarkable, therefore, that JB's tiny Triangle ended its first eight months of business with net earnings of almost $12,000. In order to achieve that sum, JB had to do a volume business of almost $700,000. He had operated on hairline margins, in which the actual cash that kept him in motion had to be rotated every ten days.

A small businessman has to pay promptly; his credit is always

15. Allen, *Since Yesterday*, p. 258.
16. William Manchester, *The Glory and the Dream: A Narrative History of America, 1932–1972* (Boston: Little, Brown, 1974), p. 174.

suspect. JB had to pay his suppliers in ten days and received in return a
1 percent discount. He sold on the same basis. Bills moved slower in
1937 than in later years; they went through the mails and were usually
delayed. There was, therefore, an elastic interval during which JB
could buy, sell, be paid—and pay his suppliers.

His buying, said an industry observer later, was "his greatest
single asset."[17] JB himself never believed that; he thought it was his
selling. Certainly the selling was the most spectacular. He would ship
cars toward "Triangle Refineries—Minneapolis" or "Triangle Refineries—Detroit"—and find customers as they rolled in that direction.

But it is impossible to break abilities into sections; men are built of
a piece and Triangle Refineries was only JB Saunders—but it was
curiously complex. It was a time when employers—especially employers on tiny margins and small mark-ups—had to squeeze every
penny, watch every expense. But Christmas was always a big season for
JB; it had been an event in his childhood he never really outgrew.

"When I worked for Hassett I went into debt every Christmas,"
he said. Mr. Hassett believed in taking—but not in giving bonuses. "As
soon as I worked out of debt from Christmas, it was darn near time to
have a vacation, so I used to go into debt again in order to go on a
decent vacation. By the time I worked out of that, it was nearly
Christmastime again. Once I was in business for myself I determined
that nobody who worked for me would have to do that. I decided to
give Sally Miller and Ragon two weeks' pay, to cover their Christmas
needs. And when vacation time came, I decided there would be
another extra two weeks' pay, so they could have a vacation."

Christmas, 1937, therefore was good for JB, and good for those
who worked with him in Triangle. That pattern was set in the first
Christmas, and JB would never change it.

There are historians who seek to deprecate the influence of individuals in history, and it is curious that some attempt to carry that
deprecation into the times of Stalin, Hitler, Churchill, and Roosevelt.
None of these men were in any way predictable; all of them helped
shape, for better and worse, the world of 1938, and the destinies of
millions around the globe.

In Germany, Hitler managed to dislodge War Minister Werner
von Blomberg and make himself War Minister. The commander of the
Army, Werner von Fritsch, was subjected to a nauseating Nazi frame-

17. Bob Aycock, with the Root Oil Company in 1937 and with Pan-Am
Southern later, made the observation in an interview with the author.

up, and Wilhelm Keitel was appointed, with the understanding the dictator would make all final decisions. Other changes, in line with that transformation, placed the Army under his control.

Similar moves took place in the Soviet Union. Show trials conducted for the benefit of carefully chosen western observers astounded the world by producing a stream of defendants who vied in confessing incredible actions and unbelievable plots, and who then disappeared as though by trap doors. By early 1938 Stalin was quietly decimating the Central Committee and the Soviet Congress, completely passive bodies of nonentities. His hope to bury murder by murdering his murderers was not to succeed, but in 1938 still seemed possible.

In the United States all eyes turned toward the President. He was certainly no dictator; his detractors were legion. But his hold on the imagination of the nation was so great that no other figure rose to challenge his supremacy; the nation waited to learn the next White House program.

England was in a different dilemma. Its parliamentary and party systems were strong, and it had a large array of interesting men at the top, but its leadership was split. Prime Minister Chamberlain believed the Versailles Treaty had been unjust, which was true. He thought that if its inequities were adjusted, Italy and Germany would cease to have motives for aggression, which was untrue. Hatred does not need reasons.

In early January, 1938, the President asked for $1 billion to launch the creation of a proper two-ocean Navy, and to enlarge the number of military planes.[18] "The President," said Harry Hopkins later, "felt certain that war was coming to America and he believed that air power would win it.' "[19] Most Americans would have been astounded had they known of that opinion, for the New Deal was still pushing domestic measures.

Early in 1938, in fact, Congress enacted—with Presidential approval—the Agricultural Act, which set quotas and penalties for violations in the growing of crops, loans to farmers, and price supports between what farmers obtained in the market and minimums set by Washington. Parts of the Act had been in the Agricultural Code of the AAA, which had been ruled unconstitutional. By 1938 the Supreme Court had abandoned that argument; the Farm Act was upheld. Minimum wage laws were also enacted.

Both measures were remarkable advances in terms of permanent interventions in the marketplace, and both were remarkable for being enacted at a time when the entire edifice of interventionist economics was tottering. Ordinarily the failure of large-scale experiments lead

18. Allen, *Since Yesterday*, p. 245.
19. Manchester, *Glory and the Dream*, p. 178.

their inventors to at least suspect the existence of errors; the New Deal was remarkably able to overcome such doubts.

Yet a colder look at the results of the New Deal from 1933 until the spring of 1938 might have given men less assured reason to wonder. Vast sums had been spent in emergency relief, and their effect had been to expand the governmental payroll and ease the distress of millions, but also to enlarge the national debt and to create an expectation of governmental aid that is yet to be exhausted. In the last four years of the open marketplace of the twenties, which was itself not free from government intervention, new investments had averaged almost ten billion dollars a year in the private sector. Such entrepreneurial capital averaged only one billion dollars a year in the years from 1933 through 1938. Clearly the New Deal had not found a way to restore the voluntary entrepreneurial system that had made the nation so remarkable before 1933. Many New Dealers seemed to have conceived a hatred of that earlier America, however, and had no desire to see its return in any form. Meanwhile, with the control of the nation's agricultural sector in hand, the government of the United States, through myriad agencies and new laws, had effectively grown to a power that dwarfed all others on the domestic landscape.

Yet the United States appeared much as ever. It was still a rough country in many places. Local laws dominated, especially in the rural regions and in much of the South. The southern Democrats, in fact, held such a strong position in Congress, through seniority and political skill, that they comprised the only truly powerful brake to the Administration. Regions that retained a southern flavor, where the descendants of the Confederate Army had flocked after the Civil War, also retained this independent coloration: Texas, Louisiana, Arkansas, Missouri, Oklahoma—all the Oil Country.

This vast midcontinental area, which produced the grains and most of the agricultural produce of the nation, as well as its major oil production, was the envy of all the world—outside the United States. Inside the country, it was a region scorned as enclaves of "rednecks" by the literati, and ignored by the intellectuals.

Yet in the laboratories of its refineries, which were connected with the large research labs of the East Coast maintained by Standard and its counterparts in other regions, a lively intellectual life of immense technological importance was maintained. New discoveries were being made regarding the thermal cracking of crude oil into an increasing number of products, and the sinister nature of overseas developments spurred even more intense efforts in this direction.

Other industries were similarly engaged. The long money-starved years of the thirties had seen a steady accumulation of industrial and technological discoveries that awaited capitalization to realize. That was ironic, for the nation longed for new industrial ventures—industry itself made hundreds of detailed plans for a better future—and yet the government during this period was more concerned with regulation than with new industrial plans mounted by the private sector.

In the spring of 1938, however, there was an almost universal subliminal sense that something important, somewhere, was about to crack. In Europe Hitler summoned the Chancellor of Austria to a meeting, subjected him to a tirade, and demanded capitulation. In March, 1938, the American people listened to commentators from their own networks, on the scene as observers, as the Nazi leader rode as a conquering hero into Vienna. Germany absorbed Austria.

Shortly afterward the President, who had been attempting for the previous eight months to achieve a balanced national budget and reduce government spending, abruptly reversed his course. He went on the radio—his favorite platform—in April, 1938, and asked for three billion dollars from Congress for relief, flood control, and a variety of other programs. The New Deal, after discovering those remedies were like narcotics that provided a temporary euphoria and then to bitter mornings after, had returned to the well. It was, clearly, addictive.

JB, however, was like the majority of those Americans in business, whose relationship with the government was as a taxpayer—and not as a recipient of its bounty. He had learned something of the relationship of a citizen with the authorities at Madison, and Madison was an arena that linked all who gathered there by a common, formative experience.

Barney Majewski, another independent-minded man, a former boxer with a broken nose who had nevertheless studied law and was formidably intelligent, was one of JB's good friends—and fiercest competitors. They found themselves together at an API meeting in Minneapolis in 1938, and Barney—who was then with Deep Rock Oil Corporation—sponsored JB to the general committee. That was an important committee; ordinarily one would expect a competitor to retard such an appointment. But Majewski said, "We need another independent on that committee, and I don't know anybody more independent than JB Saunders."

JB was deeply pleased; he regarded that as a great compliment—and it was. JB was the first marketer on the committee.

It was also recognition of the fact that Triangle Refineries was making an imprint in the marketplace, and in a noticeable manner. JB's volume of sales was increasing into large figures. That did not mean his margins widened; the nature of his business did not allow that. But it meant that he was selling and moving products in virtually every territory and therefore becoming very well known. His own attendance at the industry meetings was marked by the number of men who knew him—or knew of him.

He heard, from time to time, rumors of his old firm—Imperial. Young Bill Hassett was working hard, trying to become a good manager. JB said that he believed the younger man had settled down. "When I was there, he thought potatoes dug themselves," he said—a favorite saying.

Jack Wightman disagreed. He had retained the Imperial insurance business, but he said, "Bill caroused and drank too much. I turned the account over to another broker; it was too much trouble."

That was of little interest to JB. He was a busy man—almost too busy a man. One problem that had been a source of discomfort from the start was the practice of having to pay his suppliers every ten days. It meant he was constantly writing checks. He suggested that he pay instead on regular ten-day intervals: on the tenth of the month, then the twentieth, and then the thirtieth.

That was so eminently reasonable his suppliers agreed, and he maintained that schedule, taking care to be precise, exact, and prompt, for the first half of 1938. Then he suggested, as an easier bookkeeping task, that he pay once a month—on the tenth. To his pleasure that system was accepted, and it gave him, on some accounts and orders, as long as forty days before he had to pay.

That system, which was his own invention, intrigued Gene Swearingen, a dean at Oklahoma State University. Swearingen said, when it was explained to him years later, "You ought to put that in a book; it's remarkably interesting."

On the other end of the operation, where he confronted his customers, JB had entirely the reverse sort of problem. His problem on that end was to make sure that he sold to men whose credit was unimpeachable. "Men do not fail all at once," he said, "they leave subtle signs. They send in checks without a date, or without a signature. 'I forgot,' they'll say. Or they'll tell you that the check is in the mail; a thousand excuses suddenly appear. All of them, as they add up, are so many signals of trouble."

He would try to drop in on his customers when he could. He liked to see orderly offices and clean rest rooms in service station chains. He would look into a closet. All these areas were indications of mental order—or its lack.

These were peripheral observations made behind, between, below, and beyond sales. Sales, in contrast, were crucial, and demanded different observations. On a visit to Hugh Ragon in Minneapolis, JB—while shaving—heard a radio weather report warning that a severe storm was heading toward the city. The information interested him, for he had two hundred carloads of heavy burning oils, mostly kerosene, en route to the city.

In Ragon's office, however, he realized that Hugh had not heard the weather report, for he was shaking his head over such a large shipment. "You'll be wringing it out of your ears," Ragon said darkly. His temperament was pessimistic.

"You're too nervous," JB said cheerfully. "I'll show you how to move product." As soon as the business day opened, the phone began to ring. Brokers and jobbers, who had heard the same weather report as JB, wanted to order burning oil. To Ragon's amazement JB did not fill their orders, but took options, said he would try to fill their needs, and would call them back later.

"JB," Ragon said anxiously, "*sell it.*"

JB, however, simply listed his caller's needs, and then had lunch. After lunch, while Ragon fretted, he began to call the brokers back.

"I had a hard time filling your order," he'd say, "I couldn't get all seventy-five carloads, but you're getting sixty-eight." The brokers and jobbers were effusive in their thanks; burning oils were essential in a stormbound city. He placed call after call; by the time he was finished he had sold all the burning oils Triangle had in hand—and all that was headed for Minneapolis for the next ten days.

After that demonstration JB rushed out of town, and the storm also veered away in another direction, leaving Ragon to wonder at the whims of the winds of destiny, and presumably to relapse into his habitual pessimism.

JB, however, had no time to wonder. Triangle's business was growing rapidly. The volume by mid-1938 was triple what it had been at the end of the first four months, and continuing to soar. His office in St. Louis was already growing cramped.

He had made arrangements with a St. Louis accounting firm—Connor, Ash & Company—to audit his books. Toward the end of every month one of their young men would appear in a dark suit bristling with pencils and a fountain pen.

Kurt Schroeter's life was a capsule illustration of the interconnected condition of the world, one that many Americans were again beginning to realize in mid-1938. His father had been a small publisher with property just outside Berlin; his family was among the German millions whose savings, homes, and incomes had been consumed by the frightful inflation of the early twenties. Kurt could recall waiting in the grocery store and seeing the price of a loaf of bread move from fifty million to sixty million marks.

Arriving in the United States in 1922 after passing through Havana, Cuba, the Schroeters settled in St. Louis because of its famous German community and struggled—in classic immigrant fashion—to

225

establish a new life. Young Kurt learned the insides of American bowl-
ing alleys and the vagaries of newspaper routes, caddied on golf
courses, and studied hard. Graduating from high school, he attended
St. Louis University for one semester; decided, in the depths of the
Depression, that it was beyond his ability to continue; and took a
correspondence course in accounting. He was one of the tiny percentage who continued that lonely effort to its conclusion and received a
diploma. Armed with that and another as a public accountant, he was
hired by Haskins & Sells, who put him to work checking their
accounts receivable. Careful, conscientious, methodical, he found that
task too dreary—too monotonous even for his cautious temperament.
He moved to Connor, Ash & Company and was placed on some small
accounts.

JB also had an attorney, John Arnold. Arnold was a junior employee of a large law firm in St. Louis. JB met him through mutual
friends. They liked each other and soon made an arrangement.
Arnold's fee was fifty dollars a month, but he received a bonus the first
Christmas, and their relationship was almost ideal.

JB's efforts at Triangle, in other words, were beginning to improve and to sustain a number of other lives as well as his own.

By midsummer of 1938 American industry began a remarkable
climb upward. Employment picked up, the stock exchange prices rose,
wheels began to turn, and goods increased in volume. Sales improved.
The New Deal economists took a deep bow for an improvement for
which they had little, if any, responsibility. The fact was that Europe
was moving to war, and the nation was flooding with war orders. That
harsh fact, so inherently unpleasant to contemplate, was like Medusa's
head, too horrible to face for many who protested against international
developments, much as their forebears had expressed incredulity over
the Great War.

In earlier times an international crisis had involved the statesmen,
military leaders, and top floors of political towers; the average man
could continue without worries, unless actual war entered into his own
life. But in 1938 radio made a difference so widespread and so insidious
that its impact has yet to be fully appreciated.

Hitler had created the crisis, and so alarmed his generals that a plot
for his assassination was formed.[20] The immediate issue was an area
called the Sudetenland, along the eastern German frontier, given to the
created mélange of minorities from the old Austro-Hungarian Empire

20. The English were informed of the plot but did not trust the plotters.
Fest, *Hitler*, pp. 585–586.

known as Czechoslovakia. The Czechs, who were allied with France, had created an immense network of heavy fortifications in the region, and mobilized a million men.

Had France and Britain stood firm, it is conceivable that Hitler might have been toppled—but only conceivable. Britain was governed, at the moment, by the elderly Neville Chamberlain, who had little sympathy and less understanding for the races and peoples of the Balkans, and did not consider Czechoslovakia worth a major war.

That position was expressed by the London *Times* and was held by an influential group informally called the Cliveden Set, which included the American-born Lady Astor and many British aristocrats. When Hitler threatened a war, therefore, he was menacing countries already convinced that the Versailles Treaty was a gross error, that the Sudetenland and its German minority actually belonged with Germany, and that there was no need to shout.

Radio hook-ups, however, covered the European scene, carried live speeches by Hitler to the people of the United States, and brought the crisis to the attention of millions who would otherwise have remained unconcerned. In the CBS studios in New York, the Hitler ravings were simultaneously translated and then summarized by Hans von Kaltenborn, a veteran broadcaster who soon modified his name to H. V. Kaltenborn.

There was something eerie about hearing someone shouting incomprehensibly, his voice rising to shrieks or falling to gutturals, in a foreign tongue. From time to time Hitler was interrupted by massive waves of voices chanting *Sieg Heil* in unison; the sound was like a series of barbaric waves that broke upon the mind.

The rest of those events blackened headlines and dominated minds in academia and politics; newsreels showed Chamberlain's return from Munich, triumphantly waving aloft a piece of symbolic paper and saying that peace was assured "in our time."

A great argument was raised over these developments, in which France and Britain gave way to the dictator and Germany emerged as the hub of central Europe. Lindbergh, who visited Germany at the suggestion of the American military and State Department,[21] reported Germany's air power was stronger than any other nation's. Former President Herbert Hoover spoke against foreign entanglements.[22] Both were joined by many traditional American isolationist groups.

Their arguments, however, were relatively muted compared to the loud outcries against war for any reason that rose from such or-

21. Wayne S. Cole, *Charles A. Lindbergh and the Battle Against American Intervention in World War II* (New York: Harcourt Brace Jovanovich, 1974), pp. 31-33.
22. Carruth and Associates, *American Facts and Dates*, p. 514.

ganizations as the American League for Peace and Democracy and other Communist front groups.[23] The League was fairly well masked, in terms of its directing force; it had eminent—and innocent—Americans on the roster of its directors. Its arguments, however, stressed that capitalist nature of wars, reminded people of the "merchants of death" —munitions- and steel-makers, among others—and stressed universal pacifism, brotherhood, and all other virtues. The league, in other words—and all its myriad fellow travelers—were for Goodness; a difficult stand against which to argue, maintained in the Communist hope that the capitalists, Nazis, and Fascists would destroy each other.

Nevertheless, great inroads were made against pacifism not by warmongers but by refugees from Hitler who had found safety in the United States. Their numbers were not great—probably a few thousand in all. But their most gifted individuals made their presence felt in the country with remarkable speed and force. They included Erich Fromm, Karen Horney, and Wilhelm Reich, the psychoanalysts; Walter Gropius and Ludwig Mies van der Rohe, the architects; producer Max Reinhardt, composer Kurt Weill, conductor Erich Leinsdorf, composers Béla Bartók and Igor Stravinsky, theologian Paul Tillich, and a glittering array of specialists known in a field that itself was still largely unknown to the man in the street: theoretical physics. These included Albert Einstein, Enrico Fermi, Edward Teller, Hans Bethe, and Leo Szilard, as well as a sprinkling of such mercurial talents as Bertolt, Brecht, Alfred Eisenstadt, Peter Drucker, Franz Neumann, and more.

To these refugees, who had seen the rise of Hitler at first hand, the American political scene appeared innocent and remote. Their contributions to the situation were tentative in 1938, but they were to eventually play a crucial role.

There are times when events appear to converge as though directed by an outer force. The year 1938 was one such time; men in the industry were discussing technological changes that were erupting throughout all Oil Country. Sun Oil had tested and finally revealed that it was in refinery production with the Houdry process, and other methods of catalytic cracking—instead of thermal cracking—were underway. Those new methods called for new equipment and gave birth to new products. Experiments on a laboratory scale proved that 100-octane gasoline could be produced without tetraethyl lead; toluene, the basic ingredient for TNT, made in World War I out of coal, could be made from petroleum. Other light fuels could also be made: butadiene, which could be used as a base for synthetic rubber, proven in

23. Lyons, *Red Decade*, pp. 195–199.

the lab, was being produced in significant quantities, though not, in 1938, commercially.

At an industry meeting in late 1938 JB sat in a hotel suite with W. K. Warren, head of the Warren Oil Company, and listened intently as Warren explained the new developments in petroleum gas. Few men were better qualified to do so; Warren had launched his firm in 1922 to market liquified petroleum gases (LPG).

JB had known of Warren through the years, and had had a nodding acquaintance for many of these, but Warren moved on a higher level for a long time. J. B. knew Joe LaFortune, Howard Felt, and Sam Hulse, Warren's top three executives, far better.

But the head of Triangle was in a different position than a manager employed in a concern. By late 1938 JB could meet and talk to Bill Warren as an equal, though the Warren Oil Company was larger and did more business. Another important factor in their meeting and conversation was that Bill Warren was a friend of John Atkins. In fact, like Atkins and Phil Hamilton of the Root Oil Company, Warren was a business associate of H. L. Hunt, was early on the scene in the east Texas play, and was willing to extend himself to assist one of Atkins's business partners.

Warren sold his LPG to major refineries as a blending agent that could improve the octane and volatility of gasoline. He also marketed *Just Natural Gasoline*, as he called it; operated tank cars and ships, owned oil wells, and had production from them; had natural gas plants. He was, in every sense, a Big Operator.

Warren explained to JB, in the shorthand of a businessman—neither of them were technologists—how new drilling techniques that sank deeper holes had enabled the industry to discover and analyze new types of underground petroleum pools that were in gaseous form. Later called *distillate*, or *condensate*, those pools—when drilled—released the petroleum gases in liquid form (condensate). They had to be extracted by complex and careful methods; if the pressure was not maintained in the underground pool, the largest part could become unrecoverable. But by experiments it was proven that a new production technique called recycling could avoid that loss. In the recycling process the reservoir fluid was extracted, the liquids were recovered on the surface, and the dry gas was compressed and returned to the reservoir to maintain its pressure.

The first such plant was being constructed in Texas, and was owned by H. L. Hunt, John Atkins, and others. It was, in other words, not only an important new market development, but one that involved JB's own partner in Triangle, as well as other men whom he knew and who knew him.

Warren believed there would be a market for butane and propanes extracted from the gas obtained; the residue would constitute a low-grade motor fuel useful either as a blending agent for refiners or for the vehicle market. He was interested in the butane and propane possibilities; he knew JB was interested in the heavier fuels. They could, in other words, both become involved in this new process and its output, since they did not directly compete with one another in the marketplace.

Then he showed JB a sample of the contracts he made with his gas suppliers. On the surface they appeared hard to sell, since they offered to pay these producers only 95 percent of the marketplace price of their product. Warren, however, had woven a semantic argument around that handicap that contained so many elements of reason that it was, in the end, very persuasive.

"Don't ever call it a commission," he warned JB. "Men resent commissions. The word brings up images of a broker, churning accounts time and again to keep earning commissions. And everyone knows that a broker does not work to get the best price; he will drop the price at the slightest sign of resistance in the market, simply to make a sale—and earn his commission."

Instead of saying he would pay only 95 percent of the market price, therefore, Warren stressed freight rates and the efforts he was sparing his suppliers, and promised to pay the supplier 95 percent of what he could achieve in the market. "Always stress that you are buying," Warren said, "and that you will pay for what you buy."

Much of that was ground JB had already explored for himself, but he examined Warren's contracts with interest. Until the conversation with Warren he had marketed only refined petroleum products; gas was a new field to him, as it was to most men in the industry. The developments that Warren discussed were only beginning; they would appear in quantity only in time. But it was clear that he was being introduced to an important development in its early stages, and Warren's contracts had already established a useful pattern. It was, in all, a conversation of great importance.

JB ended 1938 in fine form. He had hired a new salesman, C. D. Tinsley, the previous summer. Tinsley was the first full-time salaried salesman. Tinsley, a short, stocky man, is from an old Louisiana family whose farm, unhappily, was situated almost exactly between two oil fields on land that held no oil. JB laughed; he thought of his father's Bar S Ranch, located on the same sort of land, surrounded by the same sort of oil fields.

The two men hit it off from the start. Tinsley was experienced and had started out with Texaco. His observations were, to some extent, similar to JB's on what he was to later call Big Company Men.

"Highly departmentalized," Tinsley said. "A big company is great—if you're on top. But progress inside is very slow." More than that, Tinsley had survived cutbacks and reductions in pay and manpower. "I saw some Big Men let go," he says, "and some of them wound up digging ditches; others had to go on relief." That was a disgrace then.

He knew Atkins as a big man in Shreveport, and he knew Reggie Brinkman at the Highland Oil Company. As a salesman, Tinsley had called on JB when JB was general manager of Imperial and regarded him as a very knowledgeable man in the marketplace. "He knew prices," Tinsley said, "and if he said he knew where to get a product at a lower price, you believed him."

Tinsley arrived in St. Louis after JB had phoned him about a possible switch to Triangle from Texaco; Atkins and Brinkman had agreed he was a capable, well-liked man. "JB met me at the station," Tinsley says, "and that helped.

"He said that Triangle's future was uncertain, but that he had done a good job at Imperial, and thought he could do the same for his own venture." Both men, however, were aware the times were uncertain and that many small businesses had lasted only briefly. Finally they got around to money, and JB mentioned $175 a month.

Tinsley had just married; he didn't think that was enough. Being a salesman, he presented his objection tactfully. "St. Louis is an expensive place," he said, "and I'm making one hundred fifty dollars now. And I just got married."

"How much do you think you'll need?"

"Two hundred a month," said Tinsley, inwardly convinced he wouldn't get it.

"That's it," JB replied at once, and grinned at him. "If all goes well," he said, "we'll both do all right."

By the end of 1938 it was clear they were doing well. JB had achieved a volume of almost two million dollars' worth of business, repaid his partners, and earned a clear twenty thousand dollars. That was a great deal of money in 1938; a volume of two million dollars was a respectable operation. Yet a photograph remains of JB, wearing a sign in his hat, standing beside a Salvation Army bucket beside two other men—bellringers—at that Christmas time. Business was important, but it was not the only important subject in life; there were still ten million unemployed.

The opening months of 1939 were disheartening for Europeans, but the Atlantic ocean was broad and deep and the United States in no danger from any quarter. Japan was preparing for the occupation of

Hainan and busy with its campaign in China. General Franco completed his rebellion; the legal government of Spain, which in the course of the Civil War had degenerated into a Kremlin puppet, fled toward the Soviet Union, Mexico, and other sanctuaries. Those who succeeded in reaching the USSR soon found themselves in prison; they were either executed or sent to Siberia.[24]

Hitler tore up the Munich Pact, as Churchill had known he would, and invaded Czechoslovakia. Italy invaded Albania, and its lackluster armies were soon in trouble.

In the United States, meanwhile, the World's Fair opened on April 30, 1939, in New York City. The theme was The World of Tomorrow, and it was to be one of the best of the long stream of American expositions; in future years the accomplishments of mankind would still create admiration and wonder, but the future would never again be regarded with such hopefulness. To a very great extent, in fact, the 1939 World's Fair provided not a microcosm of the world, but a glimpse of some of the wonders that its rulers and people had still not found a way to make available on a broad scale.

Nevertheless, the United States in 1939 presented a startling contrast to Europe. Invigorated by war orders, the entire economy began to move. Banks were willing to lend money; employment began to increase. The oil industry was thrown into heavy activity. A feverish international competition was underway among the technologists, for oil—crucial in World War I—had become indispensable. A search for better fuels, for more efficient production from a barrel of crude oil, lay behind the huge sums spent by Sun Oil in the Houdry process, which required massive and expensive equipment.

The industry—despite the allegations of Thurman Arnold and his trustbusters, who feverishly prepared an antitrust suit to divide the various segments of the industry into separate fragments—had already altered tremendously; under international pressures it would alter even more.

"At one time," said Monroe Jackson Rathbone, who was superintendent of the huge Jersey Standard refinery at Baton Rouge in 1939 and would later head the firm, "the international oil world was dominated by a handful of old companies. There was Jersey and the Royal Dutch—and maybe Burmah and British Petroleum. The French had a firm, but it was not much.

"Then came the east Texas oil fields, discovered and developed by independents. Later the same situation developed in Oklahoma. They grew very fast; I know of instances where men jumped from $50,000 to millions of dollars in only two years. New companies began to expand:

24. Conquest, *Great Terror*, pp. 439–441.

Phillips, Skelly, Ohio Oil, and others. And the old companies lost control, though Standard held a huge international position almost until the war."

It was well for the West that the new companies had arisen, though odd that the Department of Justice still seemed caught in a time-warp in 1939 and unable to credit the activities underway before its eyes. An independent marketplace had arisen despite the confusions and difficulties of the Depression; new men—not Big Company men, but men of an independent cast of mind, brimming with fresh ideas and approaches—were on the scene.

By 1939 these activities had helped to invigorate the atmosphere, though Jersey's Baton Rouge refinery, with its huge technological facilities and personnel, as well as Shell Oil, continued to set the pace of progress. Experiments were underway in the production of synthetic rubber, high-octane gasoline, recovery and new products from natural and petroleum gases, and the like. It was some of these efforts that Warren and JB had discussed.

At the same time the belated but huge military programs underway in Britain and France switched the attention of Jersey and Shell overseas, and that switch opened even more gates in the United States to independent operators. Oil, which had been a glut on the market only a few years earlier, was the most valuable commodity in civilization. The United States petroleum marketplace soared.

JB's volume increased; he needed more help. He had some predictable problems with his partners. He noticed that Rockenback and Atkins, proud and established men in entirely different fields, "did not harmonize." That called for a shift in the Triangle partners; Rocky received his ten thousand dollars and withdrew, and John Atkins increased his investment correspondingly.

As before, Atkins replaced Rocky's capital through the Highland Oil Company, which he owned with Reggie Brinkman. Always a hard bargainer, he wanted to increase his share in Triangle, but JB demurred at that. He was not going to become a minority owner; that would put him back into the rank of a manager. In the end they agreed that JB would own 50 percent of the company, Atkins and Brinkman another 50 percent. In other words, JB increased his own share.

The new arrangement led Atkins, predictably, to make efforts to increase his influence at Triangle. This took the form, on one level, of demanding special reports. JB ignored that. He produced regular and detailed reports, and he considered these sufficient. In due course, however, Atkins sent his personal right-hand man, Ralph A. Worley, to St. Louis.

JB took Worley to lunch, and listened while Worley described various savings, expedients, and maneuvers he had—he said—introduced into Atkins's bookkeeping and financial records. Later they returned to Triangle's office, where Worley noted that "invoices were stacked on desks, and piles of bills were in mounds in several places." To a strange eye that appeared untidy, but JB, who conducted all the business personally, knew what each mound contained. It was his habit to work on those every night, organizing them before the next day's business.

Worley however, sat on the edge of JB's desk and told him, after a somewhat lengthy preamble designed to soften his resistance, that he believed he could introduce a system that would save Triangle one third its costs. JB's face set in stone at that, and he said "Wait a minute. Take the books for the last six months and show me how you would have saved money on that past business first."

Worley's face reflected shock; it was obvious he had not expected that response. His purpose was to sit down and organize—or reorganize—Triangle's books. "That's what Mr. Atkins wants," he added.

JB's response to that was explicit, profane, and final. Worley sighed, and returned to Shreveport.

Nevertheless, JB knew that his paperwork was mounting, and that he couldn't handle it with a tiny office staff and a drop-in bookkeeper forever. He called Connor, Ash & Company and spoke to Del Wright, one of the partners. Told that JB wanted to hire Kurt Schroeter, Wright said, "Wait till after income tax time." In other words, go ahead. Labor, in early 1939, was a glut on the market.

JB knew better; he had studied Schroeter closely, engaged him in conversation, and gained some insight into his character. He thought Schroeter was a better man than the accounting-factory managers realized; he did not discount honesty and diligence.

On March 16, 1939, the day after income taxes were paid, JB hired Kurt Schroeter. He offered him more money than Connor, Ash & Company. Kurt was pleased; it was an escape from the accounting factory. In a fairly short period of time the mounds of invoices and bills that had shocked Worley vanished into neatly organized files, folders, and records. JB's choice was more than necessary; it was wise. Kurt Schroeter would stay with him forever.

Schroeter entered the office at a propitious time; JB was running all-out against a moving landscape. Deals, activities, personalities, travels, price changes, charges—a host of changes rushed into being at once. John Kraker, president of the Lake Refining Company in Selmaville, Illinois, signed a contract by which Triangle would purchase not only his surplus petroleum products, but the entire output of his plant.

That meant that JB would become the credit department, transportation agent, and purchaser of all Lake Refining's output; it was necessary to hire Hoy N. Wells and put him in charge of a new office in Salem, Illinois.

That expansion was important, but it proved only a curtain raiser. In 1939 an old and good friend of JB's—Edgar C. Johnston—hit oil in the Tinsley field in Mississippi. Johnston was pleased at that, but not so pleased to discover that it was difficult for him to market 5,000 barrels of daily production, for his was a heavy crude. He discussed his problem with JB, who did not handle crude oil, but who did handle petroleum products.

If Johnston would refine his crude oil, JB would buy his production. Johnston was interested in that suggestion; with his own source of supply he could realize a better margin of profit than the usual small refiner. He would, in a way, be in a minor major's position. JB scouted about and located a small skimming plant in east Texas available—since it was unused—at a bargain price. Johnston bought the plant and—still acting under JB's advice—moved it to Vicksburg, Mississippi.

At that point the road grew thorny. JB talked to the only railroad that served Vicksburg, and that could carry the production from the E. C. Johnston Refining Company toward the lucrative northern markets in the Chicago area. He had, of course, checked into the situation, and learned that the Illinois Central had a rate of fifteen cents a hundred pounds from Baton Rouge to Memphis, but thirty cents a hundred pounds from Vicksburg to Memphis, though it was only half the distance. He protested, but the railroad executives shrugged, talked about unalterable situations, deplored the existence of rates made years earlier—and said nothing could be done immediately.

"If you put in a terminal," the railroad man said, leaning back, "in the next thirty days, we can give you the lower rate." In other words, if Triangle locked itself to the railroad, it would receive equal treatment.

"In thirty days," JB said angrily, "I'll go on the river." The railroad man stirred at that warning, and indicated that in the next thirty days, a new rate might be negotiated.

The thirty days passed, however, and the railroad rate remained unchanged. JB began to look into river transportation. The deeper he looked, the greater his surprise. The railroad rate amounted to 2.96 cents a gallon added to his costs from Vicksburg to Chicago. In contrast, the river rate was less than 1 cent a gallon. His eyes widened as he began to add these figures together. They looked too good to be true. In the aggregate, they meant he could reduce his transportation costs sharply, meet competitive petroleum products prices in Chicago easily, and expand his profits at the same time.

He was also pleased to discover that relatively few other firms had turned toward the river. It was a mode of transportation that was being neglected. He discussed this with Rocky, who had spent his life in transportation, and found his friend as keen and enthusiastic as himself. At the same time he talked to Bill Arthur, a supplier of marine engines, who told him the St. Louis Shipbuilding Company was in the doldrums, and seeking business.

Arthur brought Herman T. Pott, the president of the St. Louis Shipbuilding Company, around to meet JB. The conversation grew warm, and JB eventually emerged with an option to buy five twin-screw, 1,600-horsepower diesel towboats for $157,500 each. Arthur, drawn into the plan, gave JB another option for ten 800-horsepower Cooper-Bessemer engines, at $48,500 a pair, for the five towboats. JB also obtained an option on one hundred barges, each with a capacity of ten thousand barrels of oil, at twenty thousand dollars each. Both options were to run for ninety days.

That was, however, a long-range project. Meeting the terms of the option meant raising almost $1 million. The St. Louis Shipbuilding Company would need many months to build ten tows and one hundred barges; an order of that size would entail a considerable start-up in the yard. The short-range problem, posed by the exorbitant rates of the Illinois Central, had to be met first.

JB met that by renting a towboat recently converted from steam to diesel: the *William Reese*. New to the situation, and working in some haste, JB gathered eight barges of varying sizes, and had the *William Reese* tow products to the Feldman Petroleum Company in Chicago.

That solution dissolved almost at once. After one trip north, the *William Reese* stopped at Earlbacher's Shipyard at Cape Girardeau. Earlbacher offered the owners more money, and JB lost the *William Reese*. In time that loss became a cause of relief, however, for the towboat owners had not paid the cost of its conversion. That bill was slapped on the boat, and cost Eddie Earlbacher $100,000. To make matters worse, its hull was so weakened by the heavy diesel that it came apart and sank on its next trip north, and Earlbacher had to pay to have the hulk removed from the channel. His coup had turned into a disaster, and JB's loss into a piece of good fortune.

Meanwhile JB had formed a business relationship with Mr. C. J. Thibodeaux, a Houston boat broker. Thibodeaux had a pencil mustache, dressed nattily, and smoked thin cigars. His desk was littered with bottles of pills, and he and G. L. Rowsey, also a man of pills and ailments, exchanged information about their problems. JB listened in some wonder; both men appeared brimming with good health. Through Thibodeaux he was able to obtain a lease replacement for the *William Reese*.

The short-range problem was solved, and JB later said, "I began to make the first real money of my life." He was not exaggerating. His profits from the river began to soar.

In view of this astonishing success, it would appear that few problems would arrive in the larger, more long-range venture for which he had obtained options. JB soon discovered, however, that even businessmen are not always rational. Preconceptions and limitations of vision are not confined to any group or sector.

John Atkins, for example, did not believe the river statistics, and refused to be drawn into the boat-option negotiations. JB showed him the figures, but the Shreveporter shook his head. "Looks too good," he said, and would not budge. His view, under pressure, altered only slightly. "Boats are easily obtained," he insisted, and could not see why it was necessary to raise the money to have a fleet constructed.

JB then went to Sid Maestre, at the Mississippi Valley Bank, with which he did business as Triangle, and where Atkins had originally underwritten his credit to a limited extent. He showed Maestre the river transport economics, his paper describing the market situation and comparative prices, and his options. Maestre was not interested, though the Mississippi River and its barges flowed past his bank in St. Louis every day.

His only strong ally was Rocky, the railroad executive. Rocky was sure, at first, that he could raise the sums needed from among his many friends and business contacts. But as the days, weeks, and finally months passed, the remaining option time progressively diminished and doors remained sealed on every side. JB chafed. He knew, as clearly as a man can feel a wind, that a huge fortune was just outside his grasp.

It was not until all appeared lost in the larger project that a call finally came through from Mr. G. L. Rowsey, a friend of Rocky's, who owned the Taylor Refining Company in Texas. It arrived after Bill Arthur, who had grown restless, had obtained a check for five thousand dollars from JB, to hold the order for a pair of diesel engines for one tow; JB hoped it would suffice to hold the other eight as well.

Mr. Rowsey said he was making a trip to New York City from Taylor, Texas, accompanied by his attorney, Harris Melasky. He hoped that JB and Rocky would be able to board his train when it stopped at St. Louis, and ride, if necessary, the rest of the way, or at least long enough to explain the project. They met the train, though neither could afford to remain aboard all the way across the country.

As it transpired, that was not necessary. Mr. Rowsey examined the figures and perused JB's explanation fairly quickly. His initial reaction was similar to that of his predecessors. "He thought I was entirely too optimistic," JB recalls. "He thought the figures were too large; gigantic."

However, Mr. Rowsey was sufficiently impressed to say that he would finance not the great fleet JB and Rocky envisaged, but one boat—and ten barges. JB and Rocky got off the train when it stopped at Terre Haute, Indiana. The conversation had been definitive. Obviously, their larger dream was in collapse, but they had salvaged a portion, at a time when they thought they had lost it all. A bittersweet moment.

JB moved fast. He was at the desk of Glen Forgan, at the First National Bank in Chicago the following day. Once assured that G. L. Rowsey would underwrite the option sums for one boat and ten barges, Forgan assured JB the First National would put up the cash, on short-term rates.

A few days later Mr. Rowsey was on his way back from New York City to Texas, and stopped in St. Louis. Mr. Pott, of the St. Louis Shipbuilding Company, came to Rowsey's suite in the Park Plaza Hotel in St. Louis, for a conference.

The option had expired, but if other conditions had not changed, its terms would probably have held. But in the preceding ninety days the flood of war orders beginning to reach the United States had, at last, reached the St. Louis Shipbuilding Company. Mr. Pott was no longer downcast, and he indicated the option price would no longer be available.

JB felt his heart sink. He had worked hard, come close, and the deal was now sliding out of reach again. He masked that dismay, however, and wondered what Mr. Pott would now consider the right price for a towboat. The shipbuilder and his men produced their slide rules and went through a charade of estimating. JB, who knew they had prepared their price in advance of the conference, waited patiently. Finally Mr. Pott believed that $181,600 might be right for the tow. That was an increase of $24,100—a respectable sum of money. JB looked toward Mr. Rowsey and to his relief, that gentleman nodded.

"What about the barges?" JB asked.

"Well, of course, we have to raise the price on the barges as well," Mr. Pott said. The slide rules appeared again and some whispers took place. When they ended, Mr. Pott announced the barges would cost $27,500 each. That was an increase of $7,500 each, or $75,000 on the price formerly quoted for ten. JB looked at Rowsey, and Rowsey nodded again.

The papers had already been drawn for the option; all that was necessary was to insert the new figures. There were smiles and handshakes all around, and Mr. Pott departed with his entourage.

G. L. Rowsey, however, thought the matter was well handled; he joined with JB and Rockenback in the creation of the Southern States Barge Company. Rowsey furnished the capital and therefore received a 50 percent interest; JB and Rockenback planned to manage the venture and shared the other 50 percent, taking a quarter interest each. The boats, however, had to be constructed, and that would take the better part of a year.

In all, the barge negotiation, with its many discussions, its hopes and disappointments, its discoveries and near misses, marked a great forward step for JB. He had learned more about bankers than he knew before—learned that some could not see beyond the interest on a short-term loan. He had learned that his modest beginning in business led his most important partner to an underestimation of the speed of his growth and the extent of his perceptions. He had learned that a central and popular position, such as Rocky's with the Cotton Belt Railroad, could not easily be converted into hard commercial cash. On the other hand, Rocky's friend Rowsey had kept their dream from collapse, and salvaged a piece that would prove of increasing value in the years to come. He and Rocky moved closer; their alliance would last as long as the older man lived.

JB had also taken an impressive step forward in a business sense. For the first time he had expanded without John Atkins or Reggie Brinkman. And even in retrospect, the size of the effort he mounted, and the dimension of the river fleet he sought to create, forces respect. Years later Keith Fanshier, a tireless observer of men in the industry, would say, "Saunders seemed to believe he could do *anything*." Apparently he had gained that self-confidence somewhere between the time he left Imperial and the time he obtained the tow and barge options. It was true he had to scale his effort downward from ten tows to one, and from one hundred barges to ten. But even that truncated fleet would cost over $500,000 to construct. That was a very large sum of money indeed for a man to raise who had only been in business for himself for two years. He had, obviously, grown tall.

In June, 1939, the King and Queen of England visited Britain's former colony in midsummer, and were served hot dogs at Hyde Park. The American reaction to English royalty—the only royalty its people seem to regard as genuine—was ecstatic. The moment was brief but odd, like a garden party on the eve of a huge storm.

By August, 1939, the storm began to break. England had already mobilized and sent a force of 158,000 soldiers to France; the French were mobilizing; war orders were transforming the American industrial scene. Hitler was warned that Britain and France would guarantee Poland; he was incredulous and indifferent. Driven by a mysterious hatred for all normal life, he was intent upon war. Toward the end of the month the British began to evacuate women and children from

London—the government was in the control of men left over from the Edwardian Era—and events moved toward their climax.

On September 1, Hitler moved against Poland. On September 3, Britain and France declared war, and Winston Churchill, the Cassandra of England, became Lord of the Admiralty. The world had plunged, from the low ledge it had occupied since the Great War, back into the abyss. Every life—without exception, from high to low—was to be forever changed.

CHAPTER ELEVEN

The Great War Resumes

THE OUTBREAK OF WAR in Europe created consternation among the pro-Soviet intellectuals of the United States. It was not Hitler's invasion of Poland that created dismay, though certainly that event horrified almost everyone; it was the fact that the Soviet Union signed a nonaggression pact with the Nazis and had joined in the attack.

For a number of years large numbers of academics, clerics, artists, and scientists had been enlisted into organizations that simultaneously stressed the horrors of war and fascism, while promoting the virtues of communism and masking the defects of the Soviet Union. Only two weeks before the actual start of World War II, an open letter—signed by four hundred persons prominent in art, religion, education, and science—had appeared, "branding as fascists and reactionaries all those who dared suggest the fantastic falsehood that the U.S.S.R. and the totalitarian states are basically alike."[1]

That impudent statement was not unusual. The campaign for a "united front" had been so successful, and had convinced so many that it represented what all the world should become, that its manipulators had grown arrogant. Those who criticized the Soviet Union were, in many academic and intellectual circles, subjected to slanders and discriminations.[2]

But before the autumn of 1939 was over, the Soviet Union was a full partner of Adolf Hitler, and shared in the massacre of Poland.

1. Lyons, *Red Decade*, p. 342.
2. Ibid., p. 339.

Poland was, of course, not an ideal country—none exists that is populated by human beings. But it had been independent, and it was no more.

As its share in that dismemberment and incursion, the USSR was free to overrun and occupy Estonia, Latvia, and Lithuania, as well as Byelorussia and that part of the Ukraine formerly controlled by the Poles. Throughout the autumn of 1939 the commissars conducted a series of mass executions and deportations of Poles, Jewish intellectuals, professionals, and Ukrainian nationals from these areas.[3]

The Nazis meanwhile occupied their share of Poland and sought to negotiate a peace with Britain and France. In Hitler's view such a peace was reasonable; Germany had now substantially re-created its boundaries along pre-1914 lines and was in no condition to wage a long war.

Berlin mounted a tremendous and effective propaganda barrage regarding the invincibility of its war machine. The claim carried great credibility, through the usual combination of fact and fantasy. Poland's army had been large; it had forty-two full divisions in the field, with twelve more available and a reserve force of 2.5 million. Unfortunately, twelve of its divisions were cavalry, and its officers had not progressed beyond the confused partisan days following World War I. The German army was far more modern than the Polish. It had also created some motorized divisions to which the general staff loaned some tanks and aircraft, to test the theories of General Heinz Guderian in the field. Those proved so effective they destroyed the Polish army in five *days*.

The situation of Germany in reality, however, was far from ideal. By seizing Czechoslovakia Hitler had doubled his resources. He had removed thirty-five trained divisions from the Allies, and obtained artillery and the huge Skoda works. By assisting Franco in Spain, he had the possibility of adding another strategically placed partner to Italy's Mediterranean position. German scientists had produced a synthetic Buna rubber, gasoline from coal, and other essential substitutes. Hitler's air force consisted of one thousand bombers and one thousand fighters.

Beyond that, its deficiencies began to mount. Italy, its ally in the South, had to import virtually every important war commodity except coal. Japan had to import everything. Germany itself had to turn toward substitutes because of its lack of natural resources.

The situations of France and Britain were similarly deceptive. France had the largest army in Europe, and one that was considered the best in the world. It had 110 divisions to Germany's 98. It had five million in reserve. It had the Maginot Line. Its artillery and tanks outnumbered the Germans. Its Air Force was smaller, though that was

3. Ulam, *Expansion and Coexistence*, p. 289.

Irene and Joseph Benjamin Saunders in Hillsboro, Texas, in 1884.

*Fay and George
Saunders in 1892.*

*George, Fay, and
Beulah Saunders
in Hillsboro,
Texas, circa 1896*

A stock sale at the Bar S Ranch in the Indian Territory of Oklahoma in the early 1900s.
Joseph Benjamin Saunders is visible on a white horse in the left background.

Earl Saunders when he enlisted in the Second Engineers, in late 1916.

Charles C. Rockenback in 1916.

A. B. "Bode" Warren, whose timely intercession on JB's behalf in school provided an indelible memory, as he appeared in later life.

JB in 1922.

Luther Saunders in 1922.

Jack Reardon, superintendent of the Imperial Refining Company plant at Ardmore, Oklahoma, in 1923.

JB during his days as refinery construction engineer for the Kettle Creek Refining Company in El Dorado, Arkansas, in 1925.

JB (RIGHT) *shared a fence rail near El Dorado, Arkansas, with his friend John Kirkendall of the Hallburton Sand Test Company in 1926.*

Ralph Moon, sales manager of Imperial Refining Company in Tulsa, Oklahoma, in 1926.

*Gladys (Eddy) Saunders and
JB's mother in the early 1930s.*

BELOW   *C. D. Tinsley on the
left, and JB, on the right, flank
a friend ringing bells for the
Salvation Army during the
Christmas season in St. Louis,
in 1938.*

Herman T. Pott, president of the St. Louis Shipbuilding Company, presenting a silver model of the MV Celeste to Charles C. and Celeste Rockenback in 1940. Similar models were given to G. L. Rowsey and JB, who is visible in the background, facing the camera between Pott and Rockenback.

Celeste Rockenback christening the MV Celeste in 1940.

The Little Big Inch, acquired by Texas Eastern, extended from Beaumont, Texas, to Linden, New Jersey. The dotted line in the illustration is an eagle's-eye view of the major part of the Triangle pipeline system, which extended from the Texas Gulf through the Carthage field to Shreveport, Louisiana, and from there to El Dorado, Arkansas, and from El Dorado to Arkansas City, Arkansas, on the Mississippi. In later years numerous extensions were made to the combined systems.

Joe LaFortune, executive vice presi[dent] of Warren Petroleu[m] Company, in 1945.

A Houston street photographer snapped JB in 1945, just after he told JB III that all Triangle employees under twelve years of age would have to take a nap after lunch.

*A draw-poker hand
consisting of three lowly
deuces with which JB won a
memorable struggle with
Charley Knox, who held a
pair of tens and a pair of
sixes, was taped to the wall
of a hunting lodge and
photographed for posterity.*

Gladys L. (Eddy) Saunders in the garden of their Houston home in 1955.

The leaders of Triangle Refineries—JB, C. D. Tinsley, J. Howard Barksdale, and Hubert Raborn—pose for an official portrait on the eve of the firm's merger with Kerr-McGee, in 1957. (PHOTOGRAPH BY GITTINGS)

James E. Craven, J. Howard Barksdale, JB, Richard Knox, and C. D. Tinsley in 1967.

JB and his friend Rocky (C. C. Rockenback) in 1967.

JB and C. D. Tinsley joke across a three-quarter-size blow-up of JB as he appeared when he was in charge of refinery construction for Imperial in 1925. The occasion was the thirtieth anniversary of Triangle Refineries, in 1967.

JB, Kurt Schroeter, and J. Howard Barksdale in 1967.

Dick Knox, Kerr-McGee vice president, "Boots" Adams, chairman of Phillips Petroleum, and Frank C. Love, president of Kerr-McGee, at a party, circa 1968.

JB gave Piet Beukes of South Africa a key to Oklahoma City in 1968.

JB presented Senator Barry Goldwater with a Model 1884 Winchester rifle—one of a thousand obtained by the National Cowboy Hall of Fame and Western Heritage Center—at a special dinner in 1970.

A map of the 1,100 acres JB sold to the First Mortgage Company for $13 million appeared in The Houston Post *on Sunday, June 27, 1971. An article described the purchaser's plans to construct two thousand single-family homes, apartment buildings, and townhouses and a shopping center on the site.*

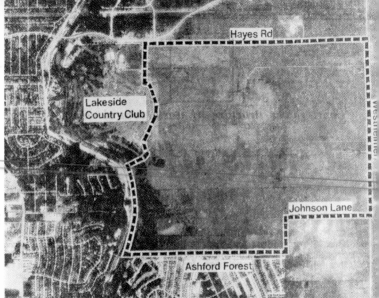

Outline shows site to be developed by First General
—Post photo by Owen Johnso

The National Conference of Christians and Jews elected JB "Man of the Year" in Oklahoma City, and Dean A. McGee, chairman of Kerr-McGee Corporation, made the presentation of the NCCJ's Brotherhood Award to JB at a banquet on November 6, 1972.

Georgia and JB in 1973. (PHOTOGRAPH BY GITTINGS)

Suzanne Saunders Inkley, JB Saunders III, and grandchildren JB Saunders IV and Stephen with JB in 1973.

Suzanne Saunders Inkley, JB, and Georgia are welcomed by snow leopard cubs in the Houston Zoo in November, 1973.

Georgia and JB Saunders at the Hall of Fame banquet in Oklahoma City on November 16 (Statehood Day), 1974. In the background (LEFT TO RIGHT): Judge Fred Daugherty and Jack Conn, president of the Fidelity Bank.

not then considered a crucial matter. But France had to import many essential war commodities.

Britain had an army less than half the size of the French, and an Air Force half the size of Germany's. Out of the twenty commodities analyst Sir Basil Liddell Hart considered essential with which to wage war,[4] it had only coal. But its empire could, through its formidable Navy, supply all it needed, with the exception of petroleum. That was a significant exception.

The one country that did hold many of the commodities essential for war was the Soviet Union. Both Britain and France looked in that direction and, shortly before the Hitler-Stalin Pact, made some feeble efforts to reach an understanding with the Soviets. But both governments were reluctant to ally themselves with a power whose open and avowed goal was to change their form of government, to say nothing of the underpinnings of what the West considered civilization.

Assessed in terms of basic resources, therefore, none of the European powers could fight a long war. The view inside the Kremlin, carefully concealed and re-created only after years of scholarly diligence, was among the more interesting. By signing a pact with Hitler, who had not warned Tokyo in advance, the commissars managed to reach a truce in Manchuria and Mongolia, and to at least achieve some security on that front.

Then Stalin looked toward the West. Although the Kremlin had signed a pact with Hitler and shared in the latest partition of Poland, the USSR sought to muffle its complicity as much as possible. Its excuse for moving its armies was that the collapse of the Polish government had left that part of the world "undefended." That rationale, as with all Soviet apologetics, has been stubbornly held ever since, and is still repeated by pro-Soviet historians, who claim Stalin moved to keep Hitler from moving farther.

The fact was, however, that no government believed the myth of Hitler's invincible war machine more than the Soviet. The terrifying speed with which Poland had been reduced sent the Kremlin into a panic. "Even in its infancy," says historian Adam Ulam, "the weak and civil-war torn Soviet state never helped German imperialism to the extent that Stalin's Russia was to do between 1939 and 1941."[5] Long lines of freight trains carrying essential war commodities began to move from the USSR toward Germany.[6]

4. He lists these as coal, petroleum, cotton, wool, iron, rubber, copper, nickel, lead, glycerine, cellulose, mercury, aluminum, platinum, antimony, manganese, asbestos, mica, nitric acid, and sulphur. B. H. Liddell Hart, *History of the Second World War* (New York: Putnam, 1970), p. 23.
5. Ulam, *Expansion and Coexistence*, p. 286.
6. In addition to Soviet deliveries of grain, iron ore, and oil, and the use of the Soviet naval base at Murmansk for Nazi submarines, the USSR agreed to act as Germany's agent in purchasing supplies from third countries, to break the British blockade.

The hope of the commissars was that France and Britain would bring down the German menace. But Stalin could not continue his old double game of saying one thing as the Soviet state and sending a different message along the secret passageways of the Comintern. The Nazis knew there were no independent factions inside the USSR. The Comintern was instructed to work for "peace"—a subtle directive.

Within a surprisingly short time some British newspapers began to blossom with the complaints of newsmen that it was a "bore war"; in the United States, it was a "phoney war." In the French Chamber some Communist Deputies rose to demand peace. That gesture was costly; the Stalin-Hitler Pact had cost the Communist parties in many countries a large number of their members; in France the party was banned.

In the United States the widespread revulsion against the Stalin-Hitler Pact reduced party membership, and some famous intellectuals made highly publicized—and remunerative—recantations. But the party was able to change the name of some organizations, scrap others, and reemerge in dove-like feathers. Peace groups abruptly increased, and the ancient argument that the war was between capitalist powers, promoted for profit by munitions-makers, insane militarists, and oil companies, began to float in the air once again.

In fact, in no other country in the world did so many arguments and so much propaganda appear as in the United States. Since the country contained many sincerely concerned and patriotic persons who wanted to see Hitler and Mussolini stopped, and an equal number who sincerely believed the troubles of Europe should be of no concern to the United States, the free-floating Comintern message exacerbated, confused, and distorted every dialogue. In a matter of months an already irritated nation found itself going back to work amid an atmosphere of dissension and doubt, amid great shouts from diverse celebrities, all of whom pointed in different directions. In such a period it took a hard head to keep both busy and neutral. Fortunately JB was able to be both.

Both his personal life and his business had grown more complex. Mrs. Saunders and he had their second child in 1939, a boy named after his father and his grandfather: JB III.

The infant had an unusual impediment that interfered with his feeding, and an operation was required.[7] It was complex but not difficult, and Dr. Bartlett, a famous St. Louis surgeon, took the unusual step of having it filmed for the benefit of the students in his hospital. It was a success and the child had neither complications nor any further

7. Pyloristenosis.

244

problems, but the physicians told Eddy, whose health was uncertain, that there should be no more children.

Toward the end of 1939, therefore, JB was busier than ever. Triangle volume was over $2.5 million, with earnings after overhead of nearly $70,000. The entire petroleum industry was moved forward under the pressure of huge needs from Britain and France. Britain had enough petroleum to supply its ordinary needs, but it needed petroleum from the United States for its wartime needs. These were mainly for its navy, engaged in a fierce struggle against German submarines, and in a search for the new German pocket battleships.

JB, who now was established and had large plans, was among the many men whose firms were indirectly—though not directly—affected. In September, on the recommendation of attorney John Arnold, he had hired a new office worker named Esther Gutknecht. Like Kurt Schroeter, she was a member of the St. Louis German community, but more secure in her position. Kurt found the events in Europe deeply disturbing; despite an accent, he would sometimes pretend not to understand German, saying he entered the country at too early an age. Esther Gutknecht was chilly toward that—she thought it was silly—but she had no accent.

JB was pleased. For the first time he had a staff nucleus whose members were permanent, loyal, and efficient. He had taken Tinsley to the golf course, after discovering that C. D. had never played. To his amazement Tinsley shot 105 the first time around. He proved to be a natural golfer. That made matters all the better.

There is no such animal as a smooth business. Every enterprise is subject to pressures within and from outside; personalities, prices, new developments, and sheer accident keep the course of business in a constant state of precarious balance. JB was an "interface," as the jargon would later put it, between refiners, customers, transportation sectors, and producers—and his multiple contacts and activities kept him running at a heavy, tiring pace. He had, for many years, taken his customers out when he visited them or was in the process of negotiation; breaks from business keep it from growing irrational.

Toward the end of 1939, however, the pace began to tell. He was doing business with a wide variety of men; some had startling personalities. Edgar Johnston, who had created, in line with JB's suggestion, a refinery at Vicksburg, Mississippi, was one. A former tool-dresser, like JB himself, Johnston was big and rough.

JB recalls being with Johnston in the Mayfair Lounge in St. Louis when they were persistently bothered by a huge, obnoxious customer at the next table. Losing patience, Johnston finally swung one arm backward in a great sweep and knocked the big, heavy man right out of his chair. The blow created no injury; it was intended as a warning. But the customer, flat on his back, gasped, "You can't do that; I'm bigger than you. . . ."

"Yes," Johnston growled, glaring down at him, "but I'm twice as tough."

Incidents of that sort were rare, but there was no doubt that Johnston was from the same independent breed as JB himself—and they were far from alone.

Barney Majewski, whom JB liked and who struggled on behalf of the Deep Rock Oil Corporation—which, like Triangle, supplied independent and cut-price operators—was both a formidable competitor and a friend. On a train en route to Chicago, JB was playing bridge with Majewski and two other men when the conductor came along, asking for tickets.

"Can't you see I'm busy?" Majewski growled and the conductor, seeing the burly body and broken nose, decided it was the better part of wisdom to keep moving. He returned later at a more propitious moment.

All those men, however, were alert to every nuance of trade and development in the industry. In late 1939 these were crackling in the air. A huge technological shift from pilot to heavy production of 100-octane gasoline was being pushed. The process was complex. It called for high-grade base stocks and blending agents such as isooctane and tetraethyl lead, each of which had to be produced on a large scale. Some of these developments called for synthesis of alylate, itself a product of combined butylenes—by-products of the cracking refinery processes discovered but not yet in place for large-scale production.

JB had moved, in the brief period he had launched his business as Triangle Refineries, into a position where some of these developments could be of great importance to him. Gulf Oil and H. L. Hunt, as well as a number of independent smaller operators, had discovered a large field near Cotton Valley, Louisiana, that contained huge pools of petroleum gases and were planning to install a gas-recycling plant to provide some of the blending agents needed in the new technological race. Through John Atkins, whose contacts with Hunt were of long standing, the possibility that Triangle might become involved in the marketing of this production began to loom.

Yet JB's relationship with Atkins was complex. The Shreveport leader had many interests he juggled with consummate skill, but he was accustomed to calling the tune. He wanted detailed and voluminous reports from Triangle, and JB fought against that effort, because he knew its direction. The area of contention was subtle. Atkins really wanted to move from reports into discussions of JB's activities, in which the Shreveporter could gradually assume a directing role and the right to second-guess later. JB was aware of that desire, and had no intention of allowing it to evolve. He gave his partners Atkins and Brinkman reports of volume, earnings, expenses, and profits. He was aware both men received regular sums from Triangle, and neither was doing any work for that income.

Expenses—always an area chosen as a bone of contention when more basic facts cannot be confronted lest worse situations emerge—came next. Ralph Worley, Atkins's man of all work, was of course used as the instrument to open that debate.

"JB's expenses were *huge*," Worley said later. "He took his customers to the best places, stayed at the best hotels, and traveled first class everywhere." Through Worley, Atkins sent remonstrances. JB, who—like other men—considered questions about expenses to be transparent assaults on character, intelligence, honesty, or all three, flew into a memorable rage. He sent Atkins, Worley, and company a handwritten letter. "It was a classic," Worley said later, "and I kept it for years. It finally fell apart through age, but I can still remember some of its phrases. One was: *I don't eat hamburger when I can afford steak.*"

He also blamed Worley. "You're the one who brought that up," he said darkly, and Worley protested that it was his duty.

"I would do the same for you if the situation involved someone else," Worley added, and JB came close to pawing the air. The fact was he himself did not question expense accounts; trustworthy men, in his view, should be trusted.

But toward the end of 1939 JB looked at himself in the mirror one morning, and decided that he would have to make some changes in his lifestyle. As a salesman he drank as part of his business life, but on that particular morning he had a terrible hangover. He had been up all night two nights before, had put in a hard day's work, then had gone out and stayed out all night, and was now shaving to put in another day's hard work.

Business had grown large and complex. He had sold Phillips Petroleum one million barrels of gasoline to be delivered via the river over a year's period. That contract and others on the river brought him sums beyond any he expected to receive only a few years earlier. Such volumes and considerations brought a host of details and considerations that a man with an intermittent hangover could not handle. He sent downstairs for some tomato juice and Lea & Perrins sauce; as he drank he determined he would cut his liquor down and, if necessary, out.

He put that resolve into effect at once. To his surprise—a surprise generally shared by other hard drinkers once they decide to cut back—he began to notice that most of the senior men with whom he came into contact drank very sparingly, if at all. He began to watch how they managed to turn aside invitations—always a delicate problem—and was, once again, learning. "I was learning all the time," he said later, "but I wasn't always aware that I was learning until later."

The whole United States was learning new lessons in early 1940, though not everyone appreciated their import. The President had been authorized to repeal the embargo against arms shipments passed only a few years earlier, and announced a "cash and carry" plan. Since the Germans had no chance to shop in the American market, that amounted to aid for the Allies on a cash basis, an arrangement that met with general approval, though somewhat equivocally presented.

The great hope of most Americans as the year 1940 dawned, was that the United States would keep out of the war. In view of that sentiment, adroitly fanned by the peace propaganda of the Comintern, the White House moved cautiously in public. President Roosevelt made some graceful concessions, and Congress established war zones from which American vessels were prohibited.[8]

With the newspapers coming close to complaints regarding the lackluster war in the West, as though the reporters and readers deserved an exciting carnage in payment for the price of each edition, there were many in the United States who remained unexcited. Even the invasion of Finland by the USSR in late November, 1939, did not create much of a stir, except in intellectual circles. Finland was a tiny country of 4 million people, with an army of only 33,000 and a handful of tanks and planes.

The Soviets had an army of 1.5 million, and huge arrays of tanks and planes. They sent an expeditionary force of 100,000 over five routes and made an astonishing error. "Convinced by Communist propaganda they would be welcomed as liberators, some battalions marched across the border behind brass bands. Others came laden with banners and propaganda leaflets . . . others wore light clothing."[9]

The Finns resisted, using a combination of guerrilla tactics, and holed up behind a series of unexpectedly strong fortifications called the Mannerheim Line, in honor of their aged field marshal. The Soviets, balked and furious, resorted to mass bombing of Finnish cities. Helsinki alone was battered without cease for two weeks. The result was to stiffen the Finnish will to resist. With one hundred correspondents

8. Frances Perkins, *The Roosevelt I Knew* (New York: The Viking Press, Inc., 1946), p. 108.
9. Leckie, *Wars of America*, 2:167.

on the scene from neutral western countries and Germany, the struggle was portrayed in terms that led many to believe the Finns could win—or were winning—and that the Soviet forces were incompetent.

Unfortunately the dispatches were overblown, although the Kremlin was hideously embarrassed. Its Finnish adventure caused it to be expelled from the League of Nations—a paper organization by 1940. But a wave of indignation against Moscow swept the West and was particularly strong in the United States. Robert Sherwood rushed to the boards of Broadway with a new play, *There Shall Be No Night*, and a rash of articles appeared praising the only nation to pay its American war debts on schedule—and in full.

Unfortunately that was mostly sentiment; the world in early 1940 was a harsh place. The Soviets massed twenty-seven divisions, lined cannon hub to hub, and sent in a huge assault wave. In ten days the Finns capitulated; it was all over by March 12, 1940. But the American reaction did have one large effect. The Soviets did not take all Finland; Stalin was still cautious of world opinion.

The effect of the Finnish campaign, however, was that it gave the world—including the Nazis—a misleading impression of the Soviet Army and military capability.[10] A significant aspect, little known at the time and insufficiently appreciated later, was the refusal of Sweden and Norway to allow the Allies to cross their territories to aid the Finns. Their excuse was neutrality. Had they been braver, the Allies would have added the Soviet Union to their enemies, and the course of history might have grown more distinct.

It almost changed: Britain actually outfitted an expeditionary force and in early April, 1940, mined Norwegian waters to cut German access to Swedish raw materials. The Germans, alerted, moved into Denmark and appeared at five Norwegian ports on April 9, 1940. The British expeditionary force "was dumped into Norway's deep snows and quagmires of April mush without a single aircraft gun, without one squadron of supporting planes, without a single piece of field artillery."[11] Outnumbered, it was cut down and withdrawn by the end of April.

That failure led to Neville Chamberlain's resignation as Prime Minister, and the creation of a wartime Cabinet headed by Winston Churchill. He was not the people's choice; if Britain chose its Prime Ministers by popular election Anthony Eden would have won handily. Churchill, after all, was sixty-five. He soon proved younger in spirit than many other men in Britain.

10. Ulam, *Expansion and Coexistence*, pp. 291–292.
11. Knightley, *First Casualty*, p. 227.

Most Americans were unaware the British were in Norway in force or had been defeated; wartime censorship was already performing its major function of covering military movements.[12] Even the news that Norway was occupied, and that the Nazis planned to change its government by installing a traitor named Major Vidkun Quisling, was not well understood. There were reasons for that: Americans had come to believe that conspiracies were figments of fiction-writers, as a result of years of vehement Communist indignation at the idea that the Comintern existed and functioned as a real network, and that the unanimity of views expressed by so many was more than coincidence. Leland Stowe, American correspondent for the Chicago *Daily News*, wrote how Oslo—a city of 300,000—was captured by 1,500 Nazi troops, and how a network of Norwegian traitors had delivered its capital, seaports, and coastal defenses to the Nazis "like an over-ripe plum" in one twelve-hour period.[13] The information was drowned in amazement over the Nazi war machine.

Military historians may well ponder the campaign of the Germans against the West, conducted by three armies consisting of ninety-four divisions, including air-borne troops, motorized divisions, and coordinated aircraft. Launched on May 10, 1940, it conquered Holland in five days, Belgium in eighteen days, huge France in six weeks.

The Dutch and the Belgians were subdued by lightning moves and novelties; the collapse of France was more complex. The Maginot Line had cost a half-billion dollars to construct. It contained forts with six underground levels, and the French Army was huge. But the internal condition of France on the eve of World War II was a spectacle of division, self-hatred, contending factions, and a "literature of nihilism and despair."[14]

Those events had immediate echoes in the United States. As Italy entered the war on June 10, 1940, to take advantage of the defeat of France, President Roosevelt made a ringing speech in which he denounced that "stab in the back." He pledged American resources to those maintaining the battle for freedom, and created a National Defense Advisory Board. He also placed two prominent Republicans in the cabinet. One, Henry L. Stimson, had served Herbert Hoover, and the other, Frank Knox, had been a vice presidential candidate in the 1936 campaign of Alf Landon.

Those moves were important, but the larger move he made—in deciding to stand for an unprecedented third term—was probably more important. The immense scope of events overseas, vividly por-

12. The Nazis paid a heavy naval price for a cheap land victory: ten of its twenty destroyers were sunk by the British and three of its eight cruisers. Two more were damaged and the pocket battleship *Leutzow* was laid up for months.

13. Knightley, *First Casualty*, p. 227.

14. Leckie, *The Wars of America*, 2:177.

trayed by photographs of Hitler dancing in joy outside the railroad car in the forest of Compiègne, and by the broadcasts of Edward R. Murrow and other American commentators on the Battle of Britain in the summer of 1940, all combined to shroud how far the United States had moved, in terms of government and citizen, from earlier days.

There was a deep and loud division in the United States regarding its foreign policy and the posture it should assume regarding the world. The President, however, had made up his mind, and future generations would marvel at how he could command the scene. A series of special messages went crackling to Congress in the same fashion, at a similar pace, and were accepted with the same alacrity as in the early days of the New Deal.

Appropriations to build the Army and Navy, create mechanized equipment and order supplies came to $13 billion immediately, and rose to $37 billion by the end of 1940. More than all the cost of World War I—while the nation was still at peace.[15] Although isolationists thundered, there were none who could argue against national defense. Meanwhile the White House ordered Selective Service plans prepared.

There is much to be said for being in place when changes occur. JB had ordered a tow and ten barges constructed almost a year earlier; by the time the St. Louis Shipbuilding Company had completed the vessels, a great burst of activity had transformed the petroleum industry and the waterways.

The new diesel tow, named *Celeste* in honor of Rocky's wife, came down the ways and a ceremony was held; it was to lift JB several levels in business. Mr. Pott, the president of the St. Louis Shipbuilding Company, gave both JB and Rocky, as well as G. L. Rowsey, each a sterling silver model, made by a St. Louis jeweler, complete to the last detail, mounted on an onyx base.

The economics of the waterways were almost startling. The *Celeste* and six of the ten barges owned by the Southern States Towing Company were contracted to carry crude oil from Buckhorn Landing to Pittsburgh for Gulf Oil. That contract was to run for a number of years, and was very profitable. Some idea of the profits can be gained from a comparison with the earnings of the remaining four barges owned by Rowsey, JB and Rocky, which were leased through Thibodeaux and netted—for a considerable period—ten thousand dollars a month *per barge* to the owners.

That impressive return provides a yardstick of the size of the opportunity JB foresaw when he originally obtained an option from the St. Louis Shipbuilding Company—and a measure of the rewards Atkins, the St. Louis banker Sid Maestre, and others rejected when they were first offered to them.

That experience had been both tiring and educational for JB. It

15. Dulles, *United States Since 1865,* p. 427.

was an important part of his professional growth, but a wearing one. By 1940 JB had proven a large point and moved far, but he was no longer young. At the age of thirty-nine and some months, he had accumulated years of experience and worked hard—and it was beginning to show. His personality was not so much altering as deepening; he grew tougher.

Arguments do that. Men either grow soft or they harden, and toward the latter part of 1940 JB began to discover some of the darker aspects of a rise in the world. At an API meeting he ran into a businessman he knew of Swedish descent, named Charley, who was drinking heavily.

"JB's too good to sell to Ole Charley," the drunk said, weaving belligerently.

"When it takes a man forty days to pay, and adds twelve to fifteen units to the phone bill, why should anyone sell to him?" JB responded, and walked away. Ole Charley went broke not long afterward, but that was not what rankled; it was the fact that other men growled as he passed. Not all competitors were as sure of themselves as Barney Majewski.

It was particularly galling that one of the men who growled was his own partner, Reggie Brinkman. Frank Reed, general sales manager of Lion Oil, was anxious to move a large amount of naphtha. JB, moved by some instinct, checked Reed's price and learned it was well below the market. He ordered a large quantity, as well as a large quantity of Number 2 burning oil. Reed, jubilant, celebrated by having a few drinks with Reggie Brinkman, who was accustomed to more than a few. He was taken aback when Brinkman said, "If he doesn't pay, we won't back him."

"What do you mean?" Reed asked.

"He gets his money from me and John Atkins," Reggie said calmly, and lifted his glass. "And we won't bail him out if he gets in trouble. If I were you, I'd deliver on a Shipper's Order Bill of Lading." That meant that the railroads would not release the car until the receiver paid for its contents; Brinkman was recommending stern measures.

Both men then called on JB at Triangle to tell him of the new terms. He was taken aback, and glared at Reggie, who said that Frank Reed had come to him, and was—understandably—concerned. Under the circumstances JB couldn't say much; the seller has a right to set his own terms. But he did not want to see a stampede started, either. He said, "Use sight drafts through my bank, if you want to, but not Shipper's Order Bills of Lading. After all, I have to sell." Reed agreed to that, and JB saw the men depart with understandable bitterness. He had placed a large order and the new terms were onerous indeed, for they meant he couldn't divert the cars to take advantage of changing markets.

A day or two later the first shipment of ten cars arrived, with many more on the way. The bank called JB, saying its instructions were to demand payment on arrival. JB said, "I make a trip to the bank every day, in the middle of the day. I'm not going to change my schedule; it would interfere with ongoing business. But you'll have your money when I make my regular trip between two and three o'clock this afternoon."

He flew around to his best customers and made some collections, explaining that a new opportunity had arisen. The naphtha, meanwhile, moved well. The Number 2 burning oil was a more difficult proposition. Then he sauntered into the bank and paid for the delivery. That situation lasted the life of the shipments. JB went to the bank every day. In the meantime he learned that John Atkins was on vacation.

By the time Atkins returned from his vacation, JB had risen above the challenge raised by his own partner. When he told Atkins about it the Shreveporter was shocked, and offered to buy Brinkman's share of Triangle. JB, however, knew it was booze that had spoken, and didn't want to go that far. He felt a sense of loyalty to Brinkman, who had, after all, been one of his original backers. The surprise had forced him into extra effort but had not really shaken Triangle's credit. He noted that Frank Reed and Reggie Brinkman remained conspicuously silent as the terms of the Lion Oil order was met, day after day, through the life of the contract, and was realistic enough to know that he had no need to underline the lesson. Meanwhile, like the rest of the business firms in the nation, he was busy meeting larger challenges posed by the immense changes underway on the national landscape.

The nation echoed to the noisy rhetoric of an election year. The Republicans, who had assembled to nominate an alternative to Roosevelt, quickly became embroiled in a dispute between the supporters of Ohio's Senator Robert Taft—a man of immense moral courage and mental ability who had the unfortunate handicap of looking like a bookkeeper—and supporters of newcomer Wendell Willkie, an executive with conservative economic opinions and a foreign policy indistinguishable from the President's. Willkie won the nomination as the result of skillful publicity techniques and a rush of genuine enthusiasm from the delegates, similar to the manner in which Bryan, a generation earlier, had once swept the Democrats.

A month later President Roosevelt was renominated, to the disgust of the oldtime assistant Jim Farley as well as Vice President John Nance Garner and other older Democratic stalwarts.

These maneuvers, even while breaking tradition in both parties, were somewhat muffled by the enormous series of changes taking place on other levels and sectors. An Alien Registration Act including fingerprinting disclosed the nation harbored five million foreigners. The President gave Britain fifty overage destroyers for naval and air bases in Newfoundland and the West Indies. Colonel Lindbergh, Senators William Borah and Hiram Johnson, Herbert Hoover, and other isolationists might thunder in unlikely unison with the CIO and the "Mobilization for Peace," but the White House proceeded with a series of executive decisions that rapidly drew the nation toward the European conflict. In September, 1940, Selective Service swept almost one million young Americans into limited service. A month later the President proved his unerring insight into the mood and nature of the electorate by becoming the first man in the history of the Republic to be elected to a third term.

There was little doubt that the broadcasts from Britain, describing dogfights between the pilots of the RAF and invading fleets of Nazi fighters and bombers, helped create an American mood of psychological, if not physical, involvement. Much has been written about the Battle of Britain; at the time the contribution of what the English called "boffins" and the Americans shrug away as "technologists" remained relatively unknown and have since been largely unsung. There seemed little romance in the arduous efforts of laboratories and the grimy details of refineries, factories, steel and electrical plants, and other industrial sectors. Yet it was these widespread but essential installations that provided the margins of victory by which the British, for all the heroism of their pilots, were able to defeat the Luftwaffe. The RAF planes had radar that enabled them to detect the enemy on his way and in the sky, even at night, while the Germans had to fly by intuition and physical skills. Even the radar, however, would not have sufficed had the petroleum industry created not only 100-octane but even 130–145-octane "fighting" aviation gasoline which enabled the British to fly faster. That margin of speed, as in any duel, made the difference between the life and death not only of individuals, but of all Britain, in the summer and fall of 1940.

Behind the noise of battle, therefore, the crucial struggle in all sectors was between national industrial abilities. "Unless the supplies from factories and oilfields could be maintained without interruption, [the armies] would be no more than inert masses. Impressive as the marching columns might look . . . in the eyes of the modern war scientist they were but marionettes on a conveyer-belt."[16]

Industrial capacity includes more than laboratories; it embraces the entire system by which raw materials are extracted and moved through the plants that process them into supplies and products. Men must keep each of the sectors in motion at top efficiency. The huge Baton Rouge refinery operated by Jersey Standard was busy, in late 1940, in efforts—launched from pilot models first—to produce synthetic rubber, toluene, propylene, alcohol, 100-octane gasoline, and many other products whose manufacture in many instances remained part conjecture, part experiment, part theory, and all work.

The air was heavy with deals, arrangements, movements. JB traveled so constantly that he maintained a permanent room in the Chicago Club, stocked with some extra suits and linen. He moved his offices from the Cotton Belt to the Shell Building in St. Louis. After a day's work he would pause at the St. Louis Athletic Club for a work-out, followed by a massage and a cold water washdown with a high-pressure hose.

He had long ago learned to leave his business, with all its details, worries, and exasperations, as well as its triumphs and personalities, behind at the office. He could turn it off entirely; he had discovered that a break enabled him to resume his burdens in the morning with a fresh mind. His social life was not heavy; two young children have a tendency to keep their parents at home most evenings. But he had met Jim Forsyth, who was in coal and had other business interests.

They met through John Arnold, JB's attorney and friend, and shared pleasure in Rockenback's company. Rocky was, in fact, a man very well—almost universally—liked. C. D. Tinsley, watching him, said later, "He would arrive at various cities in a private railroad car, was always traveling first class, and enjoyed life. I thought, *That's the way I want to be if I ever become a success.*"

JB was, by early 1941, moving into that status. Forsyth, who was on the board of the Mercantile Bank in St. Louis, knew that Triangle was considered an excellent firm and that JB was held to be a responsible businessman. Forsyth knew what that meant.

"St. Louis," he said later, "was a closed town, founded on Germanism and friendship. It was a hard place in which to make friends; the effort took a long time. It was not that the leading families were unfriendly, so much as the fact that they were family-oriented; it took time to break into their circle."

JB, however, had made that difficult transition between being an outsider and being a St. Louis businessman. Busy himself, he was not interested in society as such, but he had become sufficiently well

16. Liddell Hart, *Second World War*, p. 22.

known so that his negotiations had grown easy. He could turn toward the Mississippi Valley Bank in St. Louis for a short-term note up to fifty thousand dollars—then a substantial sum—without formalities. Beyond that he found the bank still conservative and disinclined to support ventures; the great changes en route were to flow around the St. Louis leaders, but that was still in the future.

By 1941 the United States moved briskly into the war, although that status was officially denied. The respectable America First leaders jostled, in confusing fashion, in juxtaposition with such Communist fronts as the Mobilization for Peace. The President launched the Lend-Lease program to provide goods and munitions to Britain and its allies and possessions—a series of moves that, in their totality, amounted to industrial mobilization. The men in the petroleum industry were among the first to be affected—and they learned the name of the newly created petroleum administrator with mingled incredulity and horror. He was Harold L. Ickes.

The Secretary of the Interior was aware of his low standing with the petroleum industry; everyone knew that. But his appointment was due not to his abilities or his standing, but to his notorious willingness to carry out any directive that came from the White House, no matter how extreme. Ickes, who considered himself an outstanding liberal, was actually a type more often seen in the authorities of totalitarian societies than in the United States of his time. He was capable of sincere rhetoric in favor of freedom, while firmly convinced that citizens were inferior to the state, and he could harbor both ends of this paradox without being afflicted by inner doubts.

The senior men in the petroleum industry received his summons to a Washington conference with deep misgivings.

Before that conference could be held, Hitler invaded the USSR. The move had been underway for many months, but Stalin had remained relatively inert. The Germans had moved troops into Finland, on the transparent excuse they were needed to forestall an English attack. Menaced by the Communists, the Finns welcomed the Nazis.

Diplomatic talks had been held between the Nazis and the Soviets, in which Berlin urged Moscow to attack India. That diversion was resisted; instead the commissars asked Germany to move no farther into the Balkans, where they had occupied Rumania and held its oil reserves.[17] They asked instead to be allowed to move into the Persian

17. The Nazi military machine had also made short shrift of Yugoslavia and Greece.

Gulf. That was too high a price for Hitler; he had already a partner in North Africa with Italy, whose troops required assistance.

The reasons for Germany's invasion of the USSR have been endlessly rationalized; the major point was that Hitler believed the Soviet Union was an empty shell.

The impact of the move, made on June 22, 1941, was greater than appeared on the surface, though even on the surface it was monumental. The Communists of Britain had mounted large-scale peace movements, as had their counterparts in the United States. With the assault on their paradise, they switched overnight. From the end of June, 1941, onward, there would be no more fervent advocates of intervention than the worldwide movement masterminded from the Kremlin.

In the United States the America Firsters took an opposite position. With the Soviets under attack by the Nazis, it seemed to them that the two nightmarish dictatorships should be allowed to destroy one another. Voices rose to say that in a variety of ways, but the situation was no longer so clear-cut.

Germany had not moved without making some other preparations. Its partner in Asia, Japan, saw new opportunities in the defeat of Holland and France and the absorption of Britain in the defense of its home island. Tokyo demanded that the French in Indochina allow access to its troops, and end air traffic and the shipment of goods to Chiang Kai-shek's China. Vichy France, a prisoner of Berlin, gave way.

Japan also demanded that Holland allot its rich oil and rubber reserves in the Netherlands East Indies to Tokyo. The Dutch government in exile resisted that, but its power was gone. The Japanese demanded that the British close the Burma Road, a pathway along which goods and supplies moved to China. The British were too busy to do much about that.

It remained for the United States to intervene. The White House decided to cool Japan's demands by instituting a boycott and a series of financial sanctions. Far from slowing the Japanese drive, it impelled Tokyo toward the embrace of Berlin. A mutual assistance pact was signed, in which Germany and Italy promised to launch a western front if Japan was attacked in Asia.

That looming crisis was largely disregarded by the majority of Americans. Most Americans were caught in an old stereotype of indifference toward the countries of Asia, and did not realize the military power of Japan. But the Asian crisis darkened the background as the petroleum industry leaders gathered in Washington, a week after Hitler's invasion of the USSR, to learn what their government had in mind.

The Ickes directive from the White House was to manage the complete and total coordination of the petroleum industry of the United States to the needs of war on the side of Britain—and the Soviet Union. There is no record of any hesitation on the part of the White House regarding assistance to the USSR. Churchill, asked about his own opinion on whether Britain should assist the Soviet, had said, "If Hitler invaded Hell, I would at least make a favorable reference to the Devil. . . ."[18] President Roosevelt felt the same way.

The most important single commodity of the conflict, however, was oil. It is not possible to exaggerate, or to completely describe, the significance petroleum had achieved in the world by 1941. Without it planes, ships, tanks, trucks, motorcycles, or any other sort of transport or motion could not be mounted; guns could not be used; bombs would not detonate; houses, tents, or any other habitations could be neither heated nor lit; a host of medicines would vanish; construction materials would disappear; the machinery of industry come to a halt.

Britain had to have petroleum products or it would fall; the same was true of every other nation. The Nazi submarines were winning the War of the Atlantic; in eastern Europe the invading German armies were cutting through a demoralized Soviet front. Apologists of the USSR, who at that time hailed Stalin as a genius, have since declared the Soviet retreat was planned. It was not. It was a near rout that was unplanned, unsought, and almost unchecked.[19]

The Petroleum Administration for War, known as PAW, consisted of a voluntary series of interlocking committees that coordinated the petroleum industry of the United States, ranged all the way from independent wildcatters through to the world's largest corporation, in the form of Standard of New Jersey, and was a miracle of citizen-government cooperation. It was not created at a single conference and took many months to structure and function with relative smoothness. But it was remarkable in that no firm or individuals held aloof, and in the fact that it was taken for granted, though its accomplishments were beyond the abilities not only of any other nation, but of any other combination of nations that could be conceived.

It is ironic that Secretary Ickes, an individual whose grasp of industrial facts was slight, should go down in history as the administrator of this stupendous undertaking. In reality he had Ralph K. Davies of Standard Oil of California and J. Howard Marshall, a former special

18. Henry Pelling, *Winston Churchill* (New York: E. P. Dutton, 1974), p. 470.

19. In the first forty-eight hours the Soviets lost two thousand planes, and in three weeks the Nazis were five hundred miles inside their territory and took 400,000 prisoners. Martha Byrd Hoyle, *A World in Flames* (New York: Atheneum, 1970), p. 87.

assistant who had also joined Standard of California, as two of several right arms, who alternated in keeping Mr. Ickes within reasonable bounds. Ickes also had the top executives of every petroleum firm in the land—men whose experience was on a global scale, and who worked tirelessly to make PAW a success. Behind, below, and around these men were hundreds of thousands of others, whose efforts will remain forever unsung, undecorated, unknown—but who, as Jack Rathbone later said, "saved civilization."

The newspapers reported the appointment of Secretary Ickes, but the descriptions of PAW were left to the *Oil & Gas Journal*, *Petroleum News*, *Platt's Oilgram*, the *Chicago Journal of Commerce*, the *Wall Street Journal*, and other industrial and business publications to report in depth. The daily press and the radio of the nation had long since abandoned serious discussions of how Americans worked and lived excepting in terms of scandals, accidents, and gossip. The operations of PAW, therefore, began in the autumn of 1941 and were conducted, to a too-large extent, beyond the knowledge of everyday citizens. Even those most heavily engaged were able to obtain only fragmentary glimpses of the larger whole.

Meanwhile the United States as a whole unofficially entered the war. German and Italian assets were frozen and diplomatic relations severed. In August, 1941, the President met with Winston Churchill at a naval commingling off Newfoundland. The two nations were already bound and were pooling military and scientific information.

Roosevelt agreed to have American naval vessels convoy British ships as far as Iceland in the Atlantic.[20] Churchill had hoped for more —he wanted a strong statement to Japan, but the State Department demurred. No doubt the Soviet was discussed in terms of an alliance, but that subject, as well as most others, was omitted from the communiqué that was issued. It stressed social security, freedom from want, and other glittering goals, as though the war was being fought to attain some undefined new social order. No clear record remains of the source of this inspiration, which had overtones of the promises of Wilson, which—within the memory of both Churchill and Roosevelt —caused such trouble and so many disillusionments in World War I. At the time—August, 1941—the Atlantic Charter was greeted with ecstatic press reviews.

Few businessmen had time to spare much attention to such perorations that autumn in 1941, however. JB in particular was extremely busy. The Stanolind Oil & Gas Company of Tulsa, Oklahoma, had

20. Pelling, *Winston Churchill*, p. 473.

created a recycling plant at its Jennings, Louisiana, refinery, and planned to produce recycled, leaded gasoline. JB, who knew the executives of Stanolind very well, signed to handle the recycled gasoline, as well as all the other products of the Jennings plant.

The additional business established Triangle in an important Gulf region and meant that a top man to handle these sales would have to be hired. JB knew the man he wanted; he had discussed Howard Barksdale with both John Atkins and Reggie Brinkman, as well as others in the industry. Such discussions are, usually, oblique and seemingly casual; a word or a phrase of description can bracket a man's personality very neatly inside any profession, trade, or industry.

At the time that JB's eyes gleamed in his direction, Barksdale was a purchasing agent for the Western Oil & Fuel Company of Minneapolis. That city, which JB knew well, contained a number of Barksdale observers, but he had been a known element to JB for a number of years. Barksdale had started his working career as an office boy in the Shreveport Producing & Refining Company at a time when Brinkman had been that firm's sales manager. At Western, however, he worked for a firm owned by Henry Baskerville, a wealthy, well-known entrepreneur whose reputation was surrounded by warning signs.

JB liked Barksdale, who was a tall, robust, open sort of young man active in hunting, fishing, and golf, an inveterate card-player, very knowledgeable in the marketplace. Just JB's sort of man. He also held out to him the possibility of better earnings in the future, rising perhaps as high as one thousand dollars a month. In late 1941, that was considered a very high figure.

He did not have to persuade very much. Triangle had already acquired a reputation as a firm where a salesman was well treated; JB didn't believe in beans and hamburgers as long as steaks were available. His men were encouraged to take customers to better restaurants, to entertain well, and to pick up the tab.

Barksdale agreed to join the firm as soon as 1941 ended; his major responsibility would be to market the production from the Stanolind plant at Jennings. JB promised him that a new Buick would be waiting the day he reported to work, but added one injunction. "I expect your loyalty," he said.

That was beginning to loom in JB's mind as an important qualification. "I can improve a man's efficiency," he said, "but only he can give me loyalty." His emphasis at the time was probably underscored by the growing problem of Reggie Brinkman, who was once again straying off the reservation.

At an API meeting in Chicago where JB held an open house for the sales managers of other firms, Reggie dropped in and said he saw too many men signing JB's name to bar chits. "I'll break this up," he said loudly, and departed.

Within a few hours JB was told that Brinkman was telling people that he knew where Triangle's money came from, and that he could knock JB Saunders on his ass if he felt like it.

JB fumed, and searched the club, but Reggie was by then flying around the city. It was not until the next morning that JB caught up with his once-silent partner, who was aboard the train bound for Shreveport. JB came aboard before it left the station and said, "I understand you're going to knock me on my ass."

Brinkman, back to a diminished normality in the early morning hours, was taken aback. "Who said that?" he demanded. "I never said anything like that." JB saw that he was sincere; he didn't recall. Later Atkins, hearing of the contretemps, offered to buy Brinkman out, but JB was still willing to make allowances—though his patience was strained.

Then destiny intervened, as it so often does. Reggie was out on a wild night in Shreveport not too long afterward and got into a brawl in a bar. Since he was a large and violent man and not in control of himself, he went further than he should and seriously injured another man. The next few days found him alternately talking to lawyers and visiting a hospital; he paid his victim's extensive medical bills. But the experience was salutary; he had come dangerously close to murder— and he knew it. He stopped drinking and became, once again, the man whom JB had known and liked for so long. They never again had any serious problems with each other.

On the first Sunday in December, 1941, the Japanese Navy struck the American Pacific fleet while it was at anchor in Pearl Harbor, Hawaii. The air strike, from carriers only 190 miles away, lasted two hours. In that time the Japanese sank or damaged 5 battleships and 3 destroyers, wiped out 118 military planes on their fields, bombed the city of Honolulu, and caused fifty million dollars' worth of damage to that civilian center alone. In all, the United States lost almost 2,500 dead and nearly 1,200 wounded, over 90 percent of whom were military men. The Japanese lost 29 planes, 1 large and 1 midget submarine. Their carrier fleet sailed away without being followed, although American radar stations were in place and operating properly.[21]

21. It was to take the American Navy almost two years to learn to use radar properly; its senior officers proved amazingly resistant to new technology. Scott, *Creative Ordeal*, pp. 122–123.

That lack of psychological preparedness was revealing. It was due in part to the concentration of the White House and most Americans on events in Europe and on the eastern and North African fronts. That included the military, whose senior officers were aware of the Asian crisis but who had not imbued the Pacific forces with any great sense of urgency. On a larger scale the American surprise was genuine; the nation had grown so accustomed to its peaceful distance from the turbulence of the rest of the world that it had grown unworldly.

That was not, however, the fault of the people so much as the result of an unrealistic educational system and a press that failed to analyze, or even to follow, significant world tides. But even those handicaps might have been overcome had the President been more candid. Few Americans in the autumn of 1941 realized the nation was already at war, that Britain and the United States had joined in sending materiel and supplies to the Soviet Union, and that Stalin was already demanding a second front to relieve the Nazi pressure on the USSR.

Pearl Harbor imbued all Americans with anger; the nation miraculously came together determined to fight against that stab in the back. In the heat of that moment a number of events tumbled out of Pandora's box that seemed automatic but were, in reality, somewhat surprising. There was no doubt that the United States would declare war against Japan after Pearl Harbor; it could not possibly do otherwise. But the decision of Hitler and Mussolini to declare war against the United States seems, even in retrospect, little short of senseless. Tokyo had not bothered to tell its allies of its plan in advance. And the alacrity with which Britain and the United States had decided to assist the Soviet Union made it unnecessary for Stalin to declare war against Japan; the Kremlin merely watched, and increased its demands for assistance, with no price tag attached.[22]

Strange happenings are, however, a part of war. The industries of the United States, dormant under the hypodermic monetary injections of the New Deal, roared into a new sort of war boom. As in older booms the wheels turned, employment surged, and products needed in Lend-Lease and finally in the nation's behalf emerged in amazing volume, but the Administration also instituted some novelties. New taxes were to be expected, but the Administration's measures went beyond taxes. An "excess profits" tax had been instituted some time before, in which corporation proprietors were forbidden to stockpile their earnings or to distribute them in the form of extra dividends. Instead, earnings beyond "reasonable" limits were to be plowed back into ex-

22. Ulam, *Expansion and Coexistence*, pp. 317–318.

pansion. That measure marked the entry of the state into the manner in which private citizens managed their own property; it was to be succeeded during the war by a complete system of controls, instituted in stages, that would gradually encompass the entire economic life of the nation. Prices, margins of profits, and other aspects were subject to regulation and control. The impact of Congressional hearings on World War I profits and of a stream of books, pamphlets, brochures, arguments, and retroactive judgments regarding "war profiteers" had obviously sunk deep into the mind of the nation. The White House was grimly determined that in World War II there would be no "profiteering."

The precedent for the New Deal war administration was, of course, the Wilson Administration's handling of World War I—without, it was hoped, the errors of that period. Secretary Ickes no longer called himself a "czar," though the Petroleum Administration for War was a special body governing the petroleum industry. In early 1942 its activities were still somewhat exploratory; it had a charter and men in key positions, but much remained to be done.

The petroleum industry was particularly complex and crowded. Overall, most crude oil came from Oil Country, which had large refineries in the Gulf region. Large firms, which handled the bulk of petroleum and crude oil movement inside the United States, would lift both petroleum products and crude oil from Gulf ports and carry them to the East Coast, which harbored the largest concentration of cities, people, and refineries. The West Coast had its own crude oil fields and refineries, and used coastal tankers for the same purpose.

The nation held about 127,000 miles of pipelines, of which 63,000 miles carried crude oil. Only 9,000 miles of pipelines carried petroleum products, mainly gasoline. Some 55,000 miles consisted of gathering lines in various oil fields. Overall, most of the pipelines served refineries.[23]

The system, designed for peace, was inadequate for war, as the experience of two and a half years of Lend-Lease to Britain proved. Nazi submarines took a fearful toll on British shipping, and with the onset of war with the United States could be expected to expand those raids. The previous system—in which American tankers carried crude oil to the refineries and petroleum products to the markets of the East Coast, from which they were transshipped to Britain from New York and Halifax—had obviously to be changed.

One change was to curtail tanker traffic from the Gulf ports to the East Coast, a dangerous run at any time but reckless when U-boats were on their way to the scene. That switch would allow more tankers

23. Frey and Ide, *A History of the Petroleum Administration of War, 1941–1945* (U.S. Government Printing Office, 1946), pp. 84–87.

to be available for the Atlantic run. But it also meant that an increased traffic of crude oil and petroleum products had to be carried overland from the Oil Country states to ports and refineries in the East. The railroads had to carry the greatest part of this traffic, and they were—after a generation of strict government supervision—already advanced in decay. The broad Mississippi, a virtual transportation aorta running from north to south through the nation's heartland, had been in decline for years. Both those nineteenth-century transportation sectors had to be revitalized.

PAW rushed to inventory railroad tank cars and available tows and barges on the Mississippi and other inland waterways, and laid plans for the creation of huge pipelines to carry crude oil and petroleum products to the East. Such plans would take weeks or even months to get off the drawing board; in the interim there was an almost unbelievable shuffle, while the lights in Washington offices and petroleum firms burned through the night. Thousands of firms in the oil industry and its half-million people were involved; those numbers were increased by many more in chemicals, transportation, and other interconnected parts, for petroleum had become omnipresent in the nation's life on all levels.

In this emergency the situation of Triangle appeared in a new light. Created by JB with neither refineries, oil wells, nor service stations, it had at first seemed insubstantial—held together by contracts valid only so long as their terms were met, in which he purchased and marketed the output of small refiners. But by early 1942 he had turned toward recycled gasoline, a product now important in a suddenly tight gasoline market. Even more important was the fact that he had moved into transportation, and had obtained tows, barges, and railroad tank cars in the period just before emergency struck. It was like seeing an outfielder standing in the extreme left side of the field just after Babe Ruth hit a lofty, high, near–home run. To an idle observer it might appear that the outfielder was in the remarkably appropriate location by accident, but those who understood the game knew better. JB had seen the clouds darken and had moved quickly; when the crisis arrived he had situated Triangle where it could both serve—and survive.

The crisis was far more serious than most Americans realized. Japan's plans were well laid and flawlessly executed, and had achieved a success against the British in Asia that equaled in audacity and success the amazing triumphs of the Nazis in Europe.

In a series of coordinated air, naval, and land efforts the Japanese swept over Hong Kong, Singapore, Malaya, the Dutch East Indies,

Burma, and the Philippines. By June all those areas were in Japanese possession; the Americans had lost Guam and the Philippines, but the British had lost far more.

The British Empire had supplied the home island with oil from the Orient, as well as rubber, quinine, and other commodities essential in both war and peace. By losing those territories—a loss accompanied by the destruction of the British Navy in the Far East—the British had become immeasurably more dependent upon the United States for support to continue the war at all. The Japanese, in contrast, had carved, in a single six-month period, virtually all the colonial possessions of Britain, France, and Holland into a single huge series of chunks it now proceeded to digest. There were scraps and pieces left hanging. In China Chiang Kai-shek held control over territory valuable for an eventual counterstrike. Australia still sat, like a prehistoric relic occupied by moderns, in the South. India remained in British hands. But there was little doubt Britain had received an unexpected body blow far more serious than had the United States; time was to prove the empire would never recover.

Even the United States, however, had received a far harder blow than its people realized. Japanese possession of the world's rubber-growing area could make it impossible for the nation to wage war, or even to maintain its peacetime economy. Rubber, like oil, had become a basic commodity whose innumerable products were so ubiquitous they were taken for granted—and were equally important.[24]

It had remained for men in industry to perceive the danger of the Japanese moves in Asia and to grasp their importance in the rubber sector. Businessmen, after all, had agents around the world, were aware of shipments and movements, and had more knowledge of global activities than the State Department or the Administration would credit. President Roosevelt had insisted no danger existed in Asia in a real sense, since he considered the British well able to handle Japan.

While the Administration turned a deaf ear to men in the petroleum and rubber industries who sent Washington many warnings, the men in industry made their own preparations at company expense. In Baton Rouge the superintendent Jack Rathbone was deeply immersed in pilot-level projects to prove processes to produce both Buna and Butyl synthetic rubbers. These required new petrochemicals; an entire peripheral synthetic rubber industry was being developed in conjunction with chemical, petroleum, and rubber firms, to meet a danger the government itself insisted did not exist.

By midsummer, 1942, however, it was clear to even the most

---

24. Vehicles, of course, required tires. Other uses included hoses, boots, shoes, and rubberized wire for electrical usage. A battleship required 75 tons of rubber, a Flying Fortress a half ton, and tanks almost a ton. 194 pounds of rubber were needed for every person in the armed forces—plus myriad industrial and civilian requirements.

purblind that industry had been more realistic than the amateur geo-politicians of Washington, and the President appointed three outside experts to evaluate the situation. They were Bernard Baruch; Dr. Karl Compton, a scientist and head of MIT; and Dr. James B. Conant, a chemist and head of Harvard. Their report was blunt. "The nation," they said, "faces both military and civilian collapse."[25] Not until then did wheels begin to move, and the Rubber Reserve program was created.

By that time the petroleum industry experiments in synthetic rubber were far advanced. A process for developing propylene through fractionating had been found, and a stream of new products useful in synthetic rubber feedstock production discovered and proven. Among other efforts a process to develop alcohol in the refinery had been created, in preference to the age-old development of alcohol from grain.

That was a subject of great interest to the Soviets, and Jack Rathbone was visited at Baton Rouge by a delegation from the State Department convoying a Soviet engineer, an interpreter, a silent man (KGB), and a huge Soviet general with sweeping mustaches. Rathbone showed them around but, he said later, "There was nothing to see except a maze of pipes. One hundred percent ethyl alcohol was running through the pipes. The General wanted to see it."

Rathbone explained the situation to the U.S. government inspector and received permission; someone opened a valve and drew a beaker full of 190-proof alcohol, which was handed to the general.

"He sniffed it," said Rathbone. "Then he held it to the light. Then, before we could guess his intention, he upended the beaker and drank it down in one gulp. In the next few minutes the general's eyes filled and his face turned red. Finally, like an oak toppling, he fell flat on the refinery floor."

Rathbone and the others stared down at him, and the superintendent had visions of being arrested and charged with the murder of a Soviet general. But after a minute or two the general stirred, then arose, brushing his uniform and growling something in Russian.

"What did he say?" Rathbone asked, and the interpreter said, "Good strong stuff."

Synthetic rubber was only one consideration, however; a problem the White House did grasp was the need for high-octane gasoline in huge quantities. The Baton Rouge refinery had been among the pioneers of this development, but its own central plant was only half-

25. *Time Capsule*, 1942, p. 36.

completed when Pearl Harbor occurred. The government authorized thirty-three more such plants. Construction on these was launched at once, on a piecemeal basis, even though the process was not entirely proven—a huge gamble.

In order for those efforts to be mounted and maintained it was necessary to have supplies, and these could not be produced by any single firm, no matter how large and important. Even Secretary Ickes, who at one point wanted to have motorists *arrested* for driving habits that burned extra gasoline, came to understand that coercion can obtain obedience, but not cooperation. Baton Rouge was as dependent on the men who made the arrangements to provide it supplies as was any other refinery, and equally dependent on the ability of marketers to place the output properly.

JB, with his tank cars and barges, his contracts and connections, was one of those who kept the industry flowing during this emergency. "He was a very important marketer," says Rathbone.

Nevertheless some of the men in Washington had difficulty in grasping Triangle's role. JB, as he watched confusion and crowds converge on Washington, sent Barksdale ahead as a sort of advance scout to learn the ropes. Barksdale haunted the Procurement Division, attended a number of meetings, and learned the names of various officials, and the rules and procedures.

A directive had been issued telling all the firms in the industry to continue with their regular peacetime, civilian business—but it was clear that priorities were being created and nonessentials being cut back. Millions of people were being inducted into the armed services on a scale that dwarfed World War I. That reduced the civilian market and expanded the military. Major oil companies turned away small customers and turned toward the huge volume needs of the government and their own large chains.

JB, however, had built Triangle on supplying customers the majors ignored; some were men who located in sites he recommended, and to whom, through supplies on credit, he had become a virtual backer. He had no intention of abandoning these men to wartime shortages which could, in effect, put them out of business. Some did not understand that. One—Harold Martin of the Martin Oil Company—called to demand that Triangle continue his business as before, and cited the government directive.

JB checked the records and discovered, to his own surprise, that Martin had averaged only eight carloads a month during the previous three years—the period covered by the directive. He called Harold, told him that, leaned back, and listened with some private satisfaction as "Harold climbed down off his high horse."

When Martin finished, JB said, "Harold, you're the tightest man

God ever put breath into. But rather than see you wiped out, I'll supply you with one hundred thousand barrels a month." Martin was kept alive, and able to grow. In a period of only a few years it expanded its orders to the rate of ten thousand barrels a day. The sequence made a lifelong, though eternally acerbic and difficult, customer out of Harold Martin.

Another, more pleasant customer was Phil Siteman of St. Louis, who had launched the Site Oil Company. JB liked Siteman and gave him advice that Siteman was intelligent enough to follow. Both prospered as a result; JB made sure that Siteman was supplied during the long war that followed Pearl Harbor.

He did more than that, however; he had to do more than that. The huge needs of the government could not be calculated. To the astonishment of the industry men in PAW, the American military would not supply any estimates of needs, but simply ordered—at the latest possible moment—what it wanted. Or what it thought it wanted. The industry was expected to respond—at once.

Such orders were issued without even product specifications. The PAW historians later recorded the results. "One oilman said, 'It is like sending an order for 100 horses. The horse dealer naturally inquires, What kind of horses? Trotters, jumpers, dray horses, carriage horses, saddle horses, ponies or what?' The reply is *Just 100 horses*."[26]

In that slightly lunatic atmosphere—paralleled, of course, in every country at war—JB traveled to Washington to bid on government contracts. He chose, as always, those sectors of the industry needs that the majors ignored. And, as on other occasions, these turned out to have a significance the majors had overlooked. They were contracts to supply gasoline and fuel oils, and other petroleum products, to war plants. These were like the nails in horseshoes of which the poet wrote; without them much larger efforts would have failed.

For years after 1942, wrote the historians of PAW, "beaches were a winding black river of oil, and just offshore [lay] the hulks which mark the terrible ordeal of the first war years."[27] The Nazi U-boats arrived in February, 1942, and sank a dozen tankers; the next month they repeated that feat, and also the month following. From May, 1942, until the end of 1943, tanker deliveries to the East Coast averaged only 121,000 barrels a day—barely a load for a single T-2.

The vast majority of oil and products that was shipped to the East from Oil Country came through railroad tank cars—cars such as Triangle leased. Formerly intermingled in trains that were broken up and

26. Frey and Ide, *Petroleum Administration*, p. 73.
27. Ibid., p. 87.

reorganized at each division point, these became solid trains, extending nearly a mile in length, branded by a PAW symbol that halted at division points only long enough to change crews and locomotives before thundering on to eastern cities and ports. Never had their value been more dramatically proven than in this burst of activity in the twilight years of the railroads. Yet these long trains, whose crews worked incredible hours, as well as the long hours and arduous efforts of the men in industry in general, occupied very little of the nation's attention in the press, on the radio, or in the films that poured forth about the war effort.

There is little doubt that the American nation would have had far different thoughts about that effort, had the people known of the unrelenting demands of the Soviets that they be spared the results of their connivance with the Nazis, and relieved by the creation of a second front.

That pressure, as indicated by the wartime correspondence of Churchill and Stalin, occupied an incredible amount of attention at the top in the White House and at 10 Downing Street.

The pressure, however, was slight compared to the monumental shift mounted by the western press, in which the Soviet Union and Stalin himself was portrayed as a force for democracy. In the Pacific the American Navy fought the battle of the Coral Sea and the battle of Midway and destroyed the ability of the Japanese Navy to take the initiative again. That was an amazing feat. It was followed by two American offensives, one in New Guinea and one on Guadalcanal in late summer, 1942.

In North Africa—which was a second front, since it diverted Nazi troops from the onslaught against the USSR into another arena—the British proceeded to prove they were as capable and brave as ever in their long history. Toward the end of 1942 the brilliant Montgomery drove Rommel and his forces across the sands of North Africa into defeat.

During this same period the Nazis drove into the Caucasus, after first demolishing a Soviet effort at a huge counteroffensive. By the end of 1942 the Nazis had achieved a penetration of the USSR that extended along a front more than two thousand miles long, and had settled into the siege of Stalingrad. That siege, and its final failure, has been described as the turning point of World War II, but that was true only for the USSR, not for the West.

In the United States the war provided a period of great contrasts. With millions of Americans in uniform destined for the far-flung theaters of war, there was concern and worry in all American families that had furnished young men. Young women also served, though largely in clerical and behind-the-lines positions. For the first time since World War I, the average American was allowed, by the nation's intellectuals, to express his love for his country and wave the flag. A book appeared, *See Here, Private Hargrove*, that created good-humored hilarity for a change. Popular music, after a long cynical period, emerged with easy melodies and sentimental lyrics. "The White Cliffs of Dover," "I Left My Heart at the Stage Door Canteen," and even "Praise the Lord and Pass the Ammunition," grew into hits.

The stage mounted *The Skin of Our Teeth*, a parable in which people survive while remaining humorously unchanged. *The Robe*, a deeply Christian novel, became a best-seller, and millions went to work after years of unemployment. Wages in war industries were set, though prices in nonessential areas were left free. One result was a notable gouging by the movie and theatrical industries at a time when servicemen, war workers, and virtually everyone else eagerly sought to escape through entertainment.[28]

But by 1943 it was clear that the Allies—a term that now included the Soviets—were turning the tide. The tide of war, however, was not all that was changing. The terrible siege of Stalingrad and the final capture of the invading force by enveloping Soviet armies was thunderously hailed in the West. A stream of dispatches from western correspondents and from home-grown "experts" had, in fact, effected a most amazing transformation of the USSR in the eyes of the western world. Pictures of a beaming Stalin, happy Soviet children, and heroic Soviet soldiers streamed across the pages of British and American newspapers in juxtaposition with the struggles, victories, and defeats of Americans and Britons. The result was to blend them together in the public mind; children were taught that the Soviet system was "what they wanted" and a great improvement over the evil days of the Czars.

The White House itself seemed affected, as was the nation. In the spring of 1942 Vyacheslav Molotov, commissar of foreign affairs, at the insistence of President Roosevelt, visited Britain and the United States. He carried a revolver and slept with one beside his bed. He insisted the sheet arrangements should allow him to spring out at once unimpeded,[29] and in general conducted himself like a professional criminal allowed inside the home of a wealthy but naïve country squire.

Molotov left, however, with a message that the United States was anticolonial and that its President was not against disposing what were, after all, the possessions of his Allies. He believed Britain's empire, for

28. Carruth and Associates, *American Facts and Dates*, p. 532.
29. Ulam, *Expansion and Coexistence*, p. 335.

example, should be "internationalized."[30] That was interesting, and cast a long shadow upon later events.

Nevertheless, whatever the airy opinions of the White House—which wavered with the moment and the person—the year 1943 was far from easy, or certain.

Pressures from PAW had resulted in passage of the Cole Bill, which enabled the government, through the right of eminent domain, to sponsor pipelines whose necessity had grown obvious. Conferences between pipeline firms and PAW resulted in a number of pipelines being approved.

Several of these pipeline projects were across a number of states and constituted ventures planned by private companies working together under PAW auspices. Financing was sometimes from the private sector and sometimes from PAW. PAW's sanction through the Cole Act could make a pipeline practical where it might otherwise encounter too many difficulties from towns, counties, states, or persons. The largest of the pipeline projects were known, in the oddly bleak nomenclature that government officials seem to prefer, as Eight and Nine. The press, inspired for once by an industrial challenge, dubbed these the Big Inch and the Little Big Inch—names the pipeliners themselves had devised.

Even starting the Big Inch was difficult. J. Howard Marshall, back at Ickes's side in PAW, recalls that it was at first impossible to get steel. Ickes suspected that Donald Nelson, head of the War Production Board, was responsible for the delay, and came to dark conclusions regarding his reasons. Marshall was then given a lesson on on how the top New Dealers operated. He watched Ickes pick up the phone and talk to gossip-monger Drew Pearson.

The thrust of Ickes's charge was that Nelson was "hand in glove with the big oil companies" and in particular, Sun Oil, which had tankers. Ickes believed Sun and Nelson did not want a pipeline built. Pearson, a peculiar mixture of blackmailer and convinced Socialist, immediately launched a series of biting columns against Nelson.[31]

On the day the tenth anti-Nelson column appeared, one of Nelson's secretaries called Marshall at PAW. "If I get you steel," he asked, "will you get your Secretary to stop calling my boss names in the newspapers?"

"I can try to influence him," Marshall answered cautiously. Then

30. Ibid., p. 336.
31. Like many American journalists, Pearson regarded American oil companies as Satanic creations, capable only of evil.

he went in and told Ickes the steel shortage appeared headed for resolution. Ickes picked up the phone; Pearson stopped his flow of acid.

But the press had discovered pipeliners—men whose names included Wedge-head Madden, Jersey Red, Sailor Larson, and Hard Times Schwartz[32]—listened to their descriptions, and then, backtracking, caught the magnitude of the effort. The Big Inch required digging a ditch four feet deep and three feet wide from Longview, Texas, to New York City, with a branch running from Phoenixville, Pennsylvania, to Philadelphia. Inside the ditch the pipeliners were to place a pipe twenty-four inches in diameter and forty feet long, weighing two tons. Each section had to be welded to the next for a distance of fourteen hundred miles.[33]

The system by which the Big Inch was to be constructed was familiar to all pipeliners. Contractors and riding bosses organized men, pipe, and equipment. Ditching machines scooped the ground. They were followed by tractors with booms that carried the pipe lengths. Welders blended the lengths once they were in place, bulldozers followed to pack the earth back, and a final crew came along to restore the original contours of the land as much as possible.

The distance involved in the Big Inch, however, was across mountains and through swamps, rivers, mud, snow, ice, rocks, cities, towns, and woods.

The Little Big Inch, a twenty-inch-diameter products line started in February, 1943, was actually even longer; its length was 1,475 miles because it had several feeder lines as it neared the East Coast. Starting from Beaumont, Texas, the Little Big Inch carried petroleum products, while the Big Inch carried crude oil. All the figures for each line are prodigious; the Big Inch replaced thirty thousand railroad tank cars or almost seventy-five ocean-going tankers; the Little Big Inch was not far behind. The Big Inch was completed in August, 1943; the Little Big Inch in 1944. Both pipelines were constructed by a consortium of eleven petroleum firms[34] with funds advanced by the Reconstruction Finance Corporation, the Hoover creation that the New Deal retained, and that was headed by Texas real estate magnate and banker Jesse Jones. The lines cost the taxpayers $158.5 million, a sum they returned to the nation in economies and war usefulness many times over, and

32. Editors of Look, *Oil for Victory: The Story of Petroleum in War and Peace*, (New York: McGraw-Hill, 1946), p. 112.

33. In May, 1940, senior petroleum industry executives proposed replacing the loss of fifty tankers transferred to the British by the construction of a twenty-four-inch line from Texas to the East Coast, and requested priority for steel. It was denied.

34. Atlantic Pipe Line, Cities Service, Gulf, Pan American Petroleum, Shell, Sinclair, Socony Vacuum, Standard of New Jersey, Sun Pipe Line, Texaco, Tidal Pipe Line.

one—the Little Big Inch—was to play a direct and important role in the life of JB Saunders.

By 1943, in fact, the shape of the future was beginning to appear, though the war was far from over. In Baton Rouge Jack Rathbone's huge gamble with the construction of thirty-three high-octane gasoline plants had been taken, and the first one completed worked for over thirty straight days without a bug. "I felt as though I had a baby," Rathbone said. Not too long afterward he recalls Senator Harry S Truman, head of a War Investigations Committee checking on the quality of war work, called him to New Orleans. Rathbone appeared at the Senator's suite in the Roosevelt Hotel, found it empty, and sat down to wait. It was two in the afternoon before Truman appeared, walked past him rapidly, and vanished into the bedroom. After a while Rathbone heard sounds of a shower.

"It gets hot in New Orleans in the summer," he ventured aloud. Truman's voice floated back, "I'll be right out."

When he did emerge Truman poured two tumblers of whisky, handed one to Rathbone, and drank the other in long swallows.[35] Rathbone was impressed; he had never seen anyone drink that way before. Sipping his own drink, he awaited further developments with caution.

"What's wrong in Baton Rouge?" Truman asked abruptly.

"Nothing. Hard work, is all."

"I may come and see for myself," said Truman in a warning tone.

"Why don't you?"

"I will."

He did, and spent two days. He heard no complaints and had none to make; when he left he unbent enough to say, "Rathbone, I've heard nothing but good about you."

Shortly afterward Rathbone was transferred to Washington, D.C., and the Rubber Reserve group, and was caught in the synthetic rubber program for the duration.

JB missed Rathbone at Baton Rouge; he had a great respect for his ability and knowledge. There were other men he missed in 1943; John

35. JB knew Truman, who was several times a fellow guest at the Goose Camp hunts of Chili Simpson, a boat and terminal operator, in the late thirties. Saunders noted that Truman sat in on the poker games and was a good player; he liked him. In turn, Truman called JB "the sure shot."

Arnold, his lawyer, who was also a close personal friend, was in the service. JB had fifty dollars a month mailed to Mrs. Arnold through the war, and she kept him apprised of Arnold's various postings and progress.

He was a very busy man, and the course of the war did not make his efforts any easier. In midsummer, 1943, C. D. Tinsley announced he had received an attractive offer from Coast Oil & Refining Co. Not only was the salary larger, but he was to receive 10 percent of the profits. Tinsley had received other offers but had always turned them down; this one was too good to refuse. He told JB he was leaving.

Tinsley had never asked for a raise—had never had to ask. JB had raised his salary several times, and had once given him a bonus of five thousand dollars. He was taken aback at first, and then grew angry, accusing Tinsley of disloyalty. C. D., who believed he was behaving honorably, who had never liked St. Louis and longed to return to Shreveport, said he was simply bettering himself. In the end, of course, they had a heavy argument, and Tinsley left.

That left Barksdale, a man of whom Tinsley, with admirable lack of jealousy, says, "Was more able than I was. I never resented that; Barksdale and I were almost like brothers."

With Tinsley gone, however, JB took care to "gild the apple for Barksdale." He could not afford to lose his other arm. He had given his star a new Buick when he joined the firm. Driving along a country road, Barksdale saw some wild ducks flying overhead and snatched the shotgun he carried in the car. Though the barrels were broken for safety's sake and Barksdale was careful in making it ready, he bumped into the car door getting out and the gun went off. Buckshot went through the engine of the Buick and shot the distributor head off. The ducks vanished and Barksdale was left with a wounded Buick—an impasse that sent JB into huge gales of laughter.

Nevertheless there was no question that Tinsley's departure was a loss, and the exigencies of war combined with business were wearisome. JB had stopped drinking, except for a rare single when he could not gracefully avoid it, and had developed some disguises to cloak his austerity. Bradshaw, a big man in the industry, sat in on a discussion JB held with some hard-drinking men, in which a number of negotiations were touched upon.

The hours passed, and most of the men began to show the effects of their drinks, but Bradshaw noted that JB, sipping away at a dark-looking glass, appeared unchanged after the passage of hours. "How do you do it?" he asked JB.

JB smiled. He was drinking iced tea, which looked like a strong glass of whisky. "Only the rare can drink and endure," he said later.

Despite his moderation in liquor, old habits were hard to break.

He smoked two and three packs of cigarettes a day; he traveled in a cloud of smoke. During the war, when all responsibilities grew heavier, he began to weaken. He developed a strep throat.

The doctor treating him looked into his throat and said, "You smoke too much."

"Have you been talking to my wife?" JB asked.

"I'll show you," said the doctor. He took a flashlight and held a mirror up; JB opened his mouth and stared into the mirror as the light played on his throat. He saw a red spot that looked "like a raw hamburger."

"I've been trying to heal that for four months," the doctor said quietly, putting his instruments away. JB flushed.

"*I'll quit,*" he said, and the doctor nodded.

Surprisingly enough, he did quit. "I walked out, and threw away a good fifty-cent cigar," JB said. Then he bought a carton of chewing gum.

"Smoking," he said, "is a nervous habit. I decided to replace it with another." He would chew a stick of chewing gum, and when its flavor melted, would add another. After the first month his frantic chewing diminished, and after a second month dwindled virtually to the vanishing point.

"Part of the trick," JB said, "is to handle something. Smoking is a series of gestures; I discovered that sometimes a toothpick would be enough. And I fell into the habit of rolling paper balls, or wadding paper together. I had to replace one foolish habit with some other, less harmful foolish habit."

He will always remember that he quit on February 16, 1943, at 8:35 in the evening.

The year 1943 was the middle of the war, as far as Americans were concerned; they could hardly recall when it started, and it didn't seem as though it would ever end. Europeans, who had been at war since 1939—four years earlier—were in even deeper sloughs of despond. Even the invasion of Sicily—a huge but finally disappointing venture—and of Italy itself did not create the sort of enthusiasm that might have been expected. Yet the Italian campaign was as bitter and grim as Guadalcanal, which was in a horror category all its own.

Far more attention was paid, at least in some levels and sectors, to the fact that the USSR was moving—and recovering its losses. The Soviet advance was hailed as though the human race had reached a peak; in fact, its progress against Nazi forces that had fought continuously was surprisingly slow. The Hitler legions fought every inch—

along the USSR border, in Italy, and everywhere else—as though their lives were worthless. In part this was due to a great propaganda blunder, in which Roosevelt and Churchill had announced that nothing less than "unconditional surrender" would end the war. Combined with mass bombings of civilian targets that made a mockery of civilization, the announcement left the Germans no path of retreat: not even Hitler's assassination would save them from another savage national humiliation.

That was one reason: there was another even darker and less mentionable for the bitter German resistance. With the beginning of the attack on Poland and onset of the actual war, Hitler and his fanatic Nazis had expanded their concentration camps and started the extermination of Jews, Gypsies, Communists, stubborn clerics, and dissidents—anyone that fell afoul of the Gestapo. Most of these victims were, at least to some extent, opponents of the régime, but the Jews and the Gypsies were marked by the dictator himself for complete extermination, down to the least and most innocent baby. That awful campaign spread to captured Poland, to the Soviet captured territories, to the Balkan lands conquered by German troops, to France and Holland, to Norway and Sweden, and even to Italy. The list of murders mounted, month by month and year by year since 1942, and it gave those who knew—and in some subliminal way a great many knew—a sense of guilt so deep that no surrender was possible. So the war continued long after it ceased to make any sense in the West.

The autumn of 1943 passed into winter; it seemed grim everywhere. Gasoline rationing coupons, rationing of heating oils, and wartime shortages kept the civilians everywhere strained and tired; dreary struggles kept the military overtaxed. In the Pacific MacArthur and the United States Navy, two forces some considered virtually equal, combined in testy but effective cooperative efforts to take one Pacific island after another. Each of those ventures required an integration of ships, marines, soldiers, planes, merchant vessels, and all the intricate details of invasion. All were reported somewhat sketchily; few received the attention they deserved. There was simply too much to follow, as at a circus of bloody events with a dozen or more rings.

The petroleum industry was undergoing deep changes; JB watched all of them closely. Before the war each firm operated its own terminals, from which it supplied its own customers in the terminal region, usually through trucks. PAW allowed a pooling of terminal facilities, but that was not as important as another transportation solution. If a firm in one region had kerosene, for instance, that another planned to ship into that region, the shipment was canceled and the order filled by a local competitor. In turn the competitor could use the first firm's terminal for a similar service. Such transfers cut down transportation costs, saved labor, time and expense, and shortened deliveries. They were to become so practical, and of such obvious benefit to the consumer, that one of the wasteful aspects of competition was pared away. Yet only the emergency of war had enabled the industry to persuade the government of its soundness.

Other industry moves were underway; JB noticed that there was a steady flow of men and new offices toward Houston, Texas, away from nervous New York and even from Oklahoma; Texas was the place to go. He felt the urge himself; he noticed he had to go to Houston time and again to conclude some important matter with one firm or another. He also noticed that it was hardly possible to have lunch in the Houston Petroleum Club in the Commerce Building without encountering an acquaintance with a problem, a request for a joint effort, or some opportunity.

In St. Louis, on the other hand, JB began to chafe against the conservative banks, the cautious city leaders. But those were really only symptoms; what made him restless was the knowledge that there were men he knew in Houston whose knowledge of the industry was no better than his, who were immersed in new and interesting ventures. He longed to move on—to move up. He was, after all, only in his early forties.

In 1944 it finally became clear that the war, at least in Europe, was winding down, though the fighting remained grim and hard in Italy, and Nazi armies were still able to slow the Soviet advance. Conferences had been held, and the USSR had said it would halt at the Curzon Line in Poland; the Polish government in exile was asked to agree. Disputes had arisen between Churchill and Roosevelt; Stalin appeared to both statesmen as a man with whom it was possible to negotiate.

The President of the United States believed a new international organization was essential to world peace. It was Wilson's dream, brought back from the grave, dusted off, dressed in new language, and paraded around as if alive. The press was ecstatic; educators could hardly contain themselves. Yet it contained not a single advantage for the people of the United States. The voting structure would give the USSR three votes to the American one. Some were surprised Roosevelt kept a veto for his nation.

In March, 1944, the Soviets launched their offensive in the Ukraine—territory that had been occupied for years—and moved, at

277

last, speedily. A month later they entered Rumania, where partisans under Tito had already engaged in a secret civil war and were killing non-Communist fighters against the Nazis. On May 9, Sevastopol was retaken from the Nazis, and in Italy the Allies broke through at Cassino, after a terrible fight. On June 4, 1944, the Allies finally entered Rome—an entry that took far longer than anyone could have expected—after the Italian government switched sides after fighting on one for five years. Two days later the Allied forces in Britain, under the command of General Eisenhower, using the plans of Marshal Montgomery, invaded the beaches of Normandy. It was clear, once this huge force landed, under skies controlled by the Allies—who filled them with bombers and virtually put whole cities to the torch from overhead—that the war in Europe was winding down.

Hitler, prematurely aged and sustained by drugs administered under the guise of medicines, maintained his calm, but his conferences grew increasingly disoriented; the dictator was winding down as well as the war.[36] Gruesome scenes and horrible discoveries awaited the world in the ruins of Europe; the last acts were as unprecedented as the first. But it would take some time yet; in the summer of 1944 the end of the war was still a year away.

In the United States virtually every business firm was drawing plans for the postwar world. The consensus of opinion was that there would be a return to the Depression. That consensus annoyed the New Deal, though that term had faded and gone out of circulation during the war. The President, incredibly, was making plans to run for a fourth term. It was difficult to believe, but he had convinced himself that he alone could negotiate with Stalin; he now wanted to settle the peace. His new international organization would be called, he had agreed, the United Nations.

JB did not know what the future would bring; it was not his practice to forecast world events. But he knew the petroleum industry and was convinced that there would be a shift in transportation methods. Neither railroads nor barges would provide the heavy movements of the future; the Big Inch and the Little Big Inch had proven that. He discussed the prospects of entering into pipelines with his bankers in St. Louis, and was irritated when their lips grew tight and they frowned. "I had proven time and again that my observations were

36. Fest, *Hitler*, p. 700.

based on realistic assessments," he said later, "but they couldn't seem to hold onto the point."

He decided to operate his headquarters from Houston. Triangle's chief planned the move for a weekend; those he selected to transfer packed their papers. Trucks loaded their furniture and files after the close of the business week. JB flew ahead with his staff, taking Kurt Schroeter and Esther Gutknecht.

JB, Schroeter, and Gutknecht met the trucks in Houston and were let into the Mellie Esperson Building, where Triangle had located space on the fourth floor, available because the Navy had reduced its offices. They worked through Sunday. On Monday morning when the business week started, they were ready. They had not missed a single important hour. That was on July 1, 1944.

CHAPTER TWELVE

The Houston Express

IN THE SUMMER OF 1944 JB prepared Triangle for the future. Hoy Wells was brought from Illinois and placed in charge of the Jennings office, and Barksdale—his right arm—was brought to Houston. Other Triangle offices were located in Shreveport, San Antonio, Chicago, Des Moines, and Madison, Wisconsin. JB had capable men in each to handle whatever problems arose. Those matters completed, he turned toward his family, which needed some special attention. The Lamar Hotel in downtown Houston, where they were living until they could find a suitable house, was cramped and formal.

They piled into his 1941 Packard—the last year in which passenger cars were produced pending the end of the war—and headed for Wisconsin, their favorite summer vacation spot. Young JB III, known then less formally as Bud, recalls that trip and the car fondly. JB had installed a cooler in which cold bottles of cola and other soft drinks were available; the boy considered that the height of luxury and wealth.

But when they arrived at the lodge, the weather was almost wintry. Even the children, usually impervious, retreated from the water, their teeth chattering. The next day they stared disconsolately out the windows at a cold drizzle that poured relentlessly from gloomy gray skies. JB, who used the phone as easily as other people breathe, complained to Rockenback that they were "confined." Rocky and Celeste, however, said the weather in San Diego was ideal. They were staying, as usual, in the Hotel Coronado—an elaborate old wooden structure with gables and cupolas, painted in several colors, luxuriously carpeted inside, reeking of Old World elegance.

"Do they have any room for us?" JB asked, and Rocky said he

would make arrangements. A few minutes later the Coronado called and said it would reserve a parlor and three bedrooms—a fine suite. JB packed the children and Eddy back into the car and drove impatiently to St. Louis, stopping—he said later—at every station for the children. It seemed that way, no doubt; it always does. From there they continued to Houston, where they put the Packard away—a good car was hard to find in 1944—and took a plane to San Diego.

They arrived to find that city, still relatively unknown, gleaming in the sun. The Hotel Coronado was delightful, and they relaxed gratefully. An afternoon later, JB stepped out on the balcony; there was a Naval Air Arm nearby, and the sight and sound of the sleek planes climbing or diving gave him a wartime sense. Then he looked down, and on the terrace immediately below saw a beautiful blonde lying on a colorful spread, wearing only the wispy bottom half of a bathing suit. She was sunbathing, and her suit top was nearby, discarded. He turned and called young JB III, then a chubby five-year-old, and sent him down to ask her if she would mind having her picture taken. She sat up hastily, clutched a towel, and fled, looking up as she did. She was Hildegarde—then at the height of her fame as a singer and entertainer.[1]

When they returned, JB told other oilmen at the Houston Club about the Coronado and was somewhat taken aback when they smiled and nodded; he learned that many men from the industry went there in August. That was when the Del Mar race track opened. He had discovered where some of the most important men in the industry vacationed.

That was far from being the most important discovery he made, however. JB's reasons for leaving St. Louis were, necessarily, complex. No businessman uproots and moves his headquarters lightly; it forces too many other firms with whom his own does business to make corresponding, and correspondingly burdensome, changes in unison. JB, asked his reasons, would give several. The taxes in Houston were so much more reasonable that he was able, he said later, "to buy a home with the difference."

That was an important factor, and so was the weather. The fact that an increasing number of petroleum firms were congregating in Houston was still another. But the most important reason was that JB wanted to expand after the war, and knew the direction he wanted to

1. Years later JB met her again when she appeared at a Kerr McGee party in honor of Ted Lyons and John Getgood, two Phillips executives. He asked her if she recalled that incident, and she did. He pointed to the young man smiling beside him and said, "Here's the culprit now." Hildegarde smiled, and said, "Now he could have a picture."

travel—and the St. Louis banks were too near-sighted to see what he saw.

When JB had first launched Triangle in St. Louis, John Atkins had been instrumental in opening a local line of credit, up to fifteen thousand dollars. In the years since then, Triangle's business had burgeoned, and that credit had expanded to fifty thousand dollars. That sum was far less than Saunders needed to expand, to take advantage of obvious opportunities, but Gene Walter, the loan officer at the Mississippi Valley Bank in St. Louis, was restricted by the regulations of a tight-fisted, conservative board of directors. Walter was willing to extend more money, but the board was not.

The impasse impelled JB to have a chat with the president of the Mississippi Valley Bank. The president agreed Triangle's credit was excellent, deplored the limits the board placed on the bank's ability to stretch those limits, and then found himself in a corner where he could not evade writing a To Whom It May Concern letter to that effect.

Armed with that letter, JB walked into the Second National Bank in Houston and sat down to chat with a senior vice president. That gentleman read the letter carefully, then swung around in his chair. His expression was interested; JB liked him at once. His name was Herbert M. Seydler, and JB had arrived at a miraculously appropriate moment.

Seydler had been born on a farm in a tiny place called High Hill—no longer on the map—in southwestern Texas, on a farm he recalls as "serene and quiet." His father died when he was seven, and his mother moved to San Antonio, a city with a large colony of foreigners, though the Seydlers had been on their farm since the 1860s.

Growing up in San Antonio, he worked in a store where cigars were rolled to the shapes and mixtures of individual customers' requirements. George West and Colonel Breckenridge, two men considered the founders of San Antonio, were customers, and Herb would deliver their cigars to them on his bicycle. He became aware, in that fashion, of the more important men in those pre–World War I days; took note of Mr. Frost, who owned the Frost National Bank, and who wore a white, neatly trimmed, Andrew Carnegie beard.

"A bank then was like any other business," Seydler recalls, "and there were lots of privately owned banks."

Later he became a timekeeper for the railroad and married a young schoolteacher, though he himself did not complete high school. For a time he kept books in a general store, using pen and ink, and itemizing articles in "sacks, boxes, and barrels."

In World War I he was in the U.S. Army and attended artillery officers' school, but his training was incomplete when the armistice arrived. An officer appeared, told them the news, said, "Those who want to finish—" and looked up to see everyone in flight.

Seydler then went to work in a small San Antonio bank; the staff consisted of three men. Herb cashed checks and painted the furniture. In September, 1919, the president got him a job with the Federal Reserve Bank in Houston when it was being established. There he helped organize the credit department, and found his vocation. In 1923, carrying out the new regulations for the new Federal Reserve System, he helped create credit files for the Commercial Bank.

He watched the Panic and recovery of 1919–1920, and was proud of the Federal Reserve, which he believed responsible for its brevity. In time he became a credit expert, a trove of information about the men who were reliable in Houston and those who were not. He switched to the Lumberman's Bank, which had Jesse Jones as a shareholder until he set up his own, competitive Commercial Bank. In time the Lumberman's Bank absorbed the smaller First National and changed its own name to Second National. Seydler became a vice president.

In the Crash of 1929 and the Depression through the early thirties, not a single bank in Houston failed—a remarkable fact of which larger communities took little notice.

Seydler watched the oil discoveries in east Texas and Louisiana—the emergence of new firms, new men, and new fortunes. During World War II the entire city began to boom. The Hughes Tool Company and other manufacturers burgeoned on the scene; tankers filled the ship channel; government contracts carried thousands of newcomers into Houston. Meanwhile the Second National Bank sat chained to the past.

It was that man, whose knowledge of banking was based on personal experience with its transformation into the modern age, still only fifty years old, whom JB walked in to meet. Seydler had been itching to get the Second National Bank into the petroleum action, and JB needed a backer.

They matched as though designed.

On a larger scale, JB was inside a most interesting scene. Gas-cycling plants were concentrated in the Texas-Louisiana area where vast reserves had been discovered. As the wartime need for 100-octane gasoline increased, it became obvious that isobutane, normal butane, isopentane, and other light liquid hydrocarbons could not be supplied by the refineries—but they could be produced inexpensively and quickly in cycling plants.

During 1943 and 1944—the period in which JB met and began to form a friendship with Herb Seydler—the industry spent more than one hundred million, exclusive of well costs, for gas-cycling plants. JB was most interested in the liquid gasoline produced by cycling, and knew he could market this product successfully, even after the war.

In order to do that he would have to expand his customers across a large area, and in great depth. Triangle's initial business had been directed toward large jobbers; in order to market recycled gasoline he needed to create a chain of terminals. These would constitute "stores," from which he could serve smaller firms, whose orders might consist of only one, two, or three carloads at a time.

Terminals, however, cost money—a great deal of money. He could not raise that money in St. Louis, and John Atkins showed no interest in opening large lines of credit for him in Shreveport.

He turned toward Seydler and the Second National Bank, therefore, with the sensation of a man seeing a door opening. It is a measure of his maturity that he did not rush. JB had learned a great deal since he had started Triangle in 1937. He had learned that patience is a part of intelligence and may, perhaps, be the standard by which intelligence can be measured. He did not push Seydler; instead he set about to teach the banker something of the petroleum industry. In that manner his own perceptions could be better appreciated, when it was time to discuss them. In the meantime the war was still on.

That huge struggle, pursued in Europe, where the Nazis were beset from all sides and from the air as well, engrossed the attention of the world and served to throw a shadow on the American effort in the Pacific. Inside Germany military plotters set off a bomb in Hitler's headquarters, but the dictator suffered only minor injuries. His revenge was frightful.

On a larger scale Stalin, Churchill, and Roosevelt—despite rhetoric about a new international organization that would release the peoples of the world from tyranny—negotiated the fates of millions in secret. That course undermined the fundamentals of the plan for a United Nations from the start, although President Roosevelt seemed unaware of the paradox.

Concessions to Stalin were made, in essence and in some detail, at Teheran, the year before. That moment, propitious for the Soviet claim that it alone was bearing the brunt of battle against Germany, was the occasion in which the Kremlin and its impact with Hitler, giving it half of Poland, was allowed to stand. That decision rendered hollow the original decision of France and England to go to war.[2]

In the summer and autumn of 1944 the advance of Soviet armies made the future region of Soviet domination even clearer. They surged through Rumania and Hungary, hammered the Finns into a negotiated peace, declared war on Bulgaria and occupied it, but agreed to stay out of Greece. By then Churchill was worried, and President Roosevelt seemed to grow increasingly anticolonial. He was averse to discussing "spheres of influence" in the postwar world with Britain. Yet the American President seemed oddly complaisant regarding Soviet demands and expansions.

A similar transformation had taken place in the American press. When the war started the British had been extolled as paladins of courage for standing alone against Hitler after the conquest of Europe at a time when the Soviets were allied with the Nazis. Yet by 1944 the Soviets had become the international symbols of heroic resistance, and the British—together with the French and the Dutch—were being lumped with prewar colonial powers whose positions would not be appropriate in the new, undefined, postwar world to come. In that world, in the press of 1944, the dictator of the Soviet Union was known as "Uncle Joe."

The illusion of a world of eternal peace rose as the menace of the Nazis began to diminish, though general conditions in 1944 were still difficult. The hard rigors of work in wartime kept many families split; "latchkey" children left to their own devices became an urban phenomenon in the United States. But with full employment and banked savings for lack of goods upon which to spend their money, many Americans began to think of a better postwar world.

They were fostered in this by many optimistic articles and projections. The theater blossomed, as did the movies and radio. The sale of books boomed. *Oklahoma!* was still playing to capacity audiences. *Annie Get Your Gun* sought to cash in on a revival of Americana.

At Triangle, JB came to attention when insurance broker Jack Wightman, visiting from St. Louis and keeping close touch with the firm, said casually that he had been visiting with Hubert Raborn. The name evoked memories—some of which made JB smile.

"What's he doing?" he wanted to know.

Raborn was the Houston branch manager of Touche, Nevin, Bailey & Smart, the huge accounting firm. "Tell him to come see me," JB suggested, and Wightman nodded.

2. Ulam, *Expansion and Coexistence,* p. 356.

When JB had been sales manager at Kettle Creek, years earlier, he attended church in El Dorado one Sunday with a customer. During the service the minister called on a member of the congregation to lead a prayer, and "a tall beanpole of a man rose, and spoke beautifully." JB was impressed.

The following day he entered the lobby of the First National Bank and saw the same man working as an assistant cashier. He talked to him, learned he was an experienced bookkeeper, and offered him a job. Once Raborn appeared in the Kettle Creek office, however, JB stared at his indoor pallor and cadaverous height, and said, "You need exercise." He introduced him to golf and was astonished as the months passed to see Raborn blossom into a completely different lifestyle.

"He began to gain weight," JB said, "and to go to bars with the men from the refinery. He seemed to swell remarkably; got up to two hundred forty pounds. He also turned out to be mean when he drank, and not only got into fights but turned out to be a hard, dangerous fighter."

Nevertheless he was a superlative bookkeeper. When JB left El Dorado for Tulsa he made sure the Raborns could move into the low-rent but excellent apartment he and Eddy were leaving and even sold them his furniture at a very low cost. Raborn had protested he couldn't pay for it at once, and JB said, "Pay when you can."

Later Raborn worked in Imperial's St. Louis office and was fired when JB left the firm. After that he went to night school, studied to become a CPA, and passed the exam on the first pass, with a score of 99.4 percent. "He was a wizard at figures," said Wightman, who was, being a wizard himself, a good judge.

In due course Raborn came to see JB in Triangle's Houston headquarters, and JB showed him around. He looked at the W. & J. Sloane leather chairs and sofas in JB's office and the equally fine appointments given to Barksdale, and peered at secretaries and clerks. Then he told JB the names of some of Touche, Nevin's larger clients, and said he'd like Triangle's business on behalf of his firm. JB asked him to study Triangle's system and paper flow, and to outline the improvements he would suggest.

"He came back with a report as big as a book," Wightman said. JB pushed it to one side; he had seen enough. He offered Raborn a job. To his surprise, the younger man didn't seem too eager.

"I'm earning fourteen thousand dollars a year now, and I expect a raise soon," he said.

"I'll start you at eighteen thousand dollars. In addition, I'll pay for your membership in the Houston Club, and a golf membership somewhere else. And you know I'm not tough on expense accounts."

Raborn still did not seem overwhelmed. "I'll have to talk to Gladys," he muttered finally.

After he left, JB read his report. It solved a puzzle: Triangle's office seemed lethargic in the morning and grew frantic in the afternoons. When JB left his clerical staff often was still working; they would remain until six or seven in the evening. Raborn had studied the paper flow. He learned that Barksdale had ordered all mail delivered to him first, and that it was only after he perused it that it was routed. That bottleneck, of which JB had remained unaware, had disjointed everyone else's work. "*I have to have him,*" JB thought. He wasn't going to let Raborn's tendency toward personality problems bother him; he needed his undoubted talents.

A day or two later Raborn returned with his wife. After the amenities, she leaned forward and said, "Since we left Imperial, Hubert has given his heart to God. If he comes to work for Triangle, will he have to drink and run around to keep his job?"

JB was surprised but gentle. "He never had to do that," he said softly. "That was never necessary." He leaned forward, and added, "I leave the office and live as I choose. Hubert can do the same."

That matter resolved, Raborn came to work for Triangle and soon provided JB with more personality surprises.

The war in 1944 remained huge, costly, and complex. In the Pacific the United States retook Guam and New Guinea, and launched the invasion of the Philippines. At Leyte Gulf the American Navy met the combined Japanese fleets in a bloody battle in which Kamikazes were used, for the first time. Both sides suffered casualties, but it was the Japanese Navy that retired, and it would never again be able to emerge for combat.

In November, 1944, the nation went to the polls. During the campaign, to dispel rumors about his health, the President had ridden for hours in an open car in the rain. His prestige had grown enormous; to the public he seemed larger than life. His tenure in office was so extended that many younger voters could not recall his predecessor. He remained, on most public occasions, as brilliant, charming, and forceful as ever. But photographs showed that he had lost a great deal of weight, that his face was deeply furrowed, and that his hair had turned white.

Earlier in the year his personal physician, Admiral Ross McIntyre—a political Navy doctor—had grown so alarmed he called in a cardiologist. The examination disclosed "hypertension, hypertensive heart disease, failure of the left ventricle of the heart and acute bronchitis."[3] The full report, both "written and oral, depicted a very

3. Jim Bishop, *FDR's Last Year: April, 1944–April, 1945* (New York: William Morrow, 1974), p. 6.

old man with few life-sustaining forces left. He could expire at any time. And yet . . . granting that Mr. Roosevelt's mental functions were not badly impaired—he might live on for months, *maybe a year or two*."[4]

The physicians, who believed their duty to their patient transcended that of the nation, kept their findings secret, even from the patient.

The Republicans nominated Thomas E. Dewey, a young, vigorous man whose national fame rested upon his prosecutions of gangsters and boodlers in New York City. Following the advice of party specialists, who are always dedicated to evasions of issues, Dewey chose to campaign only on domestic matters. He left the immense arena of international events virtually unchallenged to the President, although no American faction had actually emerged with any clear national goal beyond the eternally shimmering mirage of peace.

The result was that Roosevelt and a new vice president, Harry S Truman,[5] were elected in November, 1944.[6] The nation was unaware, and the press did not mention, the growing physical debility of the President.

The winter season of 1944–1945 was one of the coldest in American history. Great cold waves hit almost every region, and natural-gas distribution in the East and Northeast almost broke down. The tracks of the New York Central were buried in drifts; PAW actually lost four tank cars of propane beneath the snow for six weeks.[7]

JB was told that thirty carloads of Triangle fuel oil could not be unloaded from tank cars at a siding in Ohio, because the overhead lines leading from the tracks to the depot were not insulated. In temperatures below thirty degrees, that meant the oil would freeze solid in the lines. He flew to Cleveland, and then took several Greyhound buses to the scene, an APCO depot. There he directed efforts to scrounge insulating materials for the overhead lines, and watched while steam was directed against them so the fuel oil could be transferred from the cars to the depot. It was a time-consuming, expensive, and uncomfort-

4. Ibid. Italics added.

5. Mr. Roosevelt's second vice president, Henry A. Wallace, was vigorously disputed by many Democratic leaders on the grounds that his social views were extreme. President Roosevelt did not agree, but nevertheless accepted Truman as a compromise candidate. The compromise, as usual, had the least enemies.

6. Roosevelt received 25.6 million votes and Dewey 22 million. The President received over 53 percent, almost as large a margin as four years earlier. That achievement capped his record—now unlikely to ever be equaled—as the most enduringly popular President in his time in national history.

7. Frey and Ide, *Petroleum Administration*, p. 242.

able problem not included in his contract, but one that JB considered his duty to resolve because of the war.

At Yalta in February, 1945, the President ceded Soviet occupation of North Korea, the Kuril Islands, and other rewards to Stalin, in exchange for Soviet entry into the war against Japan on August 8. Both Roosevelt and his closest assistant, the ailing Harry Hopkins, were greatly cheered by Soviet agreement to the new international structure they believed would hold the key to future peace: the United Nations.[8]

Churchill departed from Yalta disappointed. An agreement had been reached to dismember Germany, a step he had been against. Experience had proven that a dismembered Germany meant a fragmented central Europe. Beyond that, it left the Soviet far advanced; farther advanced than any power from the East had ever reached. Further arguments appeared inevitable.

After that meeting, matters wound down as though the Architect, tired of the charade, decided to scoop the pieces together and cast them aside. Hitler's office and apartment at the Chancellery in Berlin had remained miraculously unscathed while most of the rest of the vast pile had been reduced, but he had to retreat to the Chancellery bomb shelter so often he decided to move into the bunker altogether. It had eighteen rooms; Hitler used one windowless, concrete cubicle that held a desk as his final command retreat. His deterioration was remarkable.

On April 12, 1945, President Roosevelt died suddenly from a cerebral hemorrhage. Twelve days later Mussolini was shot to death by a group calling themselves "partisans." Six days after that, on April 30, 1945, Hitler—at last—shot himself dead in his bunker. The historical timing of these three deaths is amazing, and the reaction of the world at that time a commentary on their lives. Roosevelt was widely mourned, even by those who opposed his views. Mussolini was mourned by his family and diehard Fascists. The entire world, however, breathed a sigh of relief at Hitler's departure; his presence had darkened the globe.

There is much to be said in favor of work during times of stress; it provides a saving insulation from the enduring insanities of the world. JB had Triangle and its problems with which to contend, though he would not have so phrased his efforts. Certainly Raborn's entry into

8. Perkins, *The Roosevelt I Knew*, p. 160.

the firm promised improvements in its auditing and accounting systems, but—predictably—Raborn also caused problems that had not existed before.

Sent on a tour of the branch offices, he swept into St. Louis and ordered changes beyond his franchise, of which JB was unaware until he received a telephone call from an angry manager in Des Moines. Raborn had descended and ordered the desks shifted, and even changed the pictures on the wall.

JB was surprised, but not astonished. He talked to Raborn and told him to keep away from the salesmen. "I'll make the money," he told the numbers wizard. "It's your job to help me keep it."

His plans toward making that money were moving into position. It was clear the war was coming to an end, and he had carefully, though gradually, acquainted Seydler, the banker at the Second National in Houston, with the facts of petroleum life.

The subject was complex, and JB approached it obliquely over frequent lunches and discussions. He had shifted his account—or at least the major part of it—to Seydler's bank, and on-going business presented no problem. But JB was also aware that the world's largest and most complex business, whose activities intertwined with virtually every other, contained men of all varieties—and some were not exactly trustworthy. One of those—a man of some presence but not too much substance, a member of the Houston Club with whom JB often played poker or gin—borrowed a large, unsecured sum from Seydler.

Seydler mentioned that to JB, who felt the usual inner strain such a situation presents. He did not want to traduce his acquaintance, who was in the barge business and also had an accounting firm. But on the other hand he did not want to see Seydler make an error in judgment.

"If I were you," he said bluntly, "I'd sew my pockets."

Seydler was surprised. "He gave me a fine financial statement," he said mildly.

"He's an accountant, isn't he?"

Seydler nodded.

"Well, he ought to be able to put together a fine statement."

Seydler looked thoughtful and changed the subject. A few weeks later, however, the banker mentioned that he had *secured* the loan. Not too long afterward the borrower ran into financial difficulties and virtually all his creditors lost their money—except Seydler. JB's advice had enabled him to save his bank's money.

Very few men will take the trouble to so warn a banker. It is a profession, like other indispensable occupations, that most people only approach in need, and it has its bleak and lonely aspects. But that incident drew Seydler and JB closer together, and they began to discuss JB's larger plans.

Distribution was an important area of JB's plans for expansion. He knew that the end of the war meant that the majors would resume their use of ocean-going tankers to move large quantities of crude and refined products from the Gulf to the East Coast. He had no chance of entering into that competition; the sums involved in ocean vessels were prohibitively high.

He turned his eyes toward the railroads. Changes were due for these carriers as well. One change, due to take effect in two years from 1945, would rule tank cars without air brakes out of service. He learned that Cities Service, which had a great many such cars, planned to scrap them and have a new railroad tank-car fleet constructed. JB could not afford that expensive step either. But his memory of his railroad days was sharp and clear, and it seemed to him that seamless tank cars with good wheels could not possibly become obsolete overnight.

Checking more deeply into that situation, he conferred with John Painter, a former traffic manager for a large oil company, whose acquaintance he had made in PAW. Painter believed that air brakes could be inexpensively installed in older tank cars and that they could, thereby, be made serviceable for years to come. Looking about, JB then located the Keith Railroad Equipment Company—a tiny venture, for all its imposing name—capable of installing air brakes at a relatively low cost.

Putting these observations together, he formed the Painter Transportation Company, which John Painter headed for a base salary and a percentage. Then JB hired a railroad inspector, already on the spot, to check the serial numbers of those tank cars that flowed through the immense terminus at Texarkana, and to record those still serviceable and worth the installation of air brakes.

With these numbers in hand and the Painter Transportation Company created, he offered to take the serviceable cars off the hands of Cities Service for an average price of $550. In that manner he obtained nearly eight hundred tank cars, equipped with air brakes and able to pass government specifications.

That step would insure his ability to transport production from the cycling plants he had been signing all through the war, and which he expected to convert to peacetime products when the war ended, JB then turned toward the task of creating a chain of strategically located terminals.

It was his belief that the southeastern states had been too long neglected; he knew the war had revitalized this region to a considerable extent. The South, nearly eighty years after the end of the Civil War, was at last on the road to recovery. Both he and Barksdale knew the region well and had crisscrossed it many times. In the spring of 1945, at the same time that he set his railroad tank-car operation into motion, JB and Barksdale made what amounted to a grand tour. They moved by car and were accompanied by one of Triangle's salesmen, who acted as chauffeur.

They arrived in Mobile and discussed the region and its possibilities with Selwyn Turner, an influential Alabaman. Those discussions, among more important matters, resulted in an invitation to a tea party. JB, Barksdale, and their companion arrived to find a large crowd drinking whisky and fighting the Civil War. One of them asked him, "What's the matter with the South?"

"They're half-nuts," another said. *"That's what's the matter."*

But Turner had more serious comments. He knew John Cochrane, who owned a terminal in Mobile and wanted to retire, and he put JB and Cochrane together. The older man wanted to retire with two million dollars and wanted half of that in cash. He would accept the second million in annual payments over a ten-year period.

JB had Raborn check Cochrane's books, and that strange but talented man quickly discovered that Cochrane's enterprise had unused capital of $750,000. JB sat up at that; it meant the first $1 million would cost only $250,000. That converted a good investment into a rare one. He went to Cochrane and shook hands; the older man was pleased.

Days passed, however, and the accountants—who, like lawyers, seem to detest simplicity—continued to huddle. JB asked Raborn the reason for the delay, and Raborn said that among the Cochrane properties were mineral rights for 6,800 acres, valued by the seller at $7.50 an acre. Raborn didn't believe these rights were worth that much.

"Hubert," said JB impatiently, "if we let fifty thousand dollars or so kill the deal, it wouldn't be worth making. *Close the deal.*"

Several more days passed, however, and the accountants continued their deliberations. JB again called Raborn in and asked for the reason for the delay. "There's a bulldozer listed among the sale items," Raborn said, "but it's on Mr. Cochrane's ranch. I've ordered it to be produced."

"Why?" JB asked, "Do we need it?"

"It's part of the sale," Raborn said primly.

JB turned red. "Damn it," he shouted, "settle the deal. The whole deal is a bargain."

Raborn, offended, withdrew. But the papers were at last signed.

JB and Barksdale moved on from Mobile to Birmingham, and from Birmingham to Atlanta. In Atlanta he had dinner with eight jobbers. They discussed business in the Atlanta area and JB said, "If I invest one million dollars in a terminal here, I'll have to average a million gallons of gasoline sales a month in order for it to pay out. Can you give me that much business?"

"Yes, we can," one said. "There's a Ford assembly plant going up here soon, and the city is going to boom." The others agreed, and each promised to buy from Triangle; most of them were men he had known since his El Dorado days.

Shortly after the tour ended, JB was provided a surprise. He was very pleased with the Cochrane purchase, in which he had obtained a terminal in an excellent location at even less than the reasonable asking price. But he was far more pleased when an oil well was found near the former Cochrane property at Citronelle, Alabama. Triangle owned mineral rights on nearby land, extending over 6,800 acres, which now attracted oil company attention. Humble offered twenty-five dollars an acre for those rights—and then withdrew the offer. Gulf appeared and offered fifty dollars an acre. Then Humble returned and renewed its offer of twenty-five dollars an acre, and set a deadline of two o'clock in the afternoon to accept before the offer expired. JB was amused that the firm would attempt such high-pressure tactics on a man whose entire life had been spent in the oil business.

He decided to checkerboard the 6,800 acres and offer them at fifty dollars each. He told Humble of that decision, and gave the huge firm until three in the afternoon to accept the price before it was withdrawn. Before the hour arrived he repeated the offer in a telegram, sent it to Humble, and asked for a confirmation.

The following morning lawyers appeared from Humble, carrying a check for $236,000.

That returned almost the entire $250,000 cash he had paid for Cochrane's terminal, for he had used the unused capital of the firm to fill in the first $1 million. The operations of the terminal would pay the second million over a ten-year period, so he had, as he said later, "bought the terminal for nothing." That was a deal hard to beat.

Back in Houston, JB continued his campaign by signing a contract with Glenn McCarthy to handle the output of McCarthy's plant at Winnie, Texas. He had, by this time, contracts with a number of cycling plants and had terminals in Atlanta, Birmingham, Mobile, Nashville, and St. Louis.

In addition to these terminal towns and the sales offices, Triangle had offices in Chattanooga and Louisville. Its barges were moving on the river, though not in the numbers he would have preferred, and he began to increase his tank cars. These moves were made possible by the credit Seydler extended; they were usually short-term, on 4 percent interest.

He also discovered that he had, in the banker, a virtual partner in arranging credit with other banks. One of the terminals cost one million dollars, and although Seydler was willing to approve that amount, it would not have left any slack for the smaller short-term loans that JB needed for on-going operations.

They traveled to St. Louis together and entered the Mississippi Valley Bank, whose officers knew JB very well. They sat down with Sid Maestre, the president, and discussed the terminal. JB was very candid. "You've turned down deal after deal," he said. "That's a St. Louis habit."

Maestre swallowed, looked away, and asked JB how much he wanted. "One million dollars—at four percent," JB answered. Seydler explained that the Second National in Houston had offered to lend Triangle the sum, but that it would cut down on regular business with the firm. Maestre nodded then and said the Mississippi Valley Bank would be happy to lend JB the money.

In early July, 1945, the world seemed essentially unchanged. A great, terrible war was ending, but other wars had been terrible and had ended. The victors began to quarrel; the United States seemed, oddly, more vindictive toward Germany than Britain, which had suffered longer and lost more. But victors always quarrel.

Most people were making plans for the postwar scene. JB had large hopes for Triangle. He was signing up independent cycling plant operators rapidly. His argument that they could not maintain a sales staff, traffic department, credit department, and transportation department of their own for a cost of four percent of the market price of their output was not only persuasive but true.

But the scientists in the Manhattan Project, on the eve of proving their effectiveness, raised arguments that served then and now to embroil the entire subject of nuclear energy in dispute. They knew they had won the race against Germany, the USSR, Britain, and Italy to develop an atomic bomb.[9] The few high officials aware of these efforts were pleased; the Project had cost an immense two billion dollars.

The American military was gathering a force of 3.5 million men and an immense array of ships, weapons, and materiel, to invade the

9. David Irving, *German Atomic Bomb* (New York: Simon and Schuster, 1967), passim.

island fortress of Japan. The experts believed the effort would cost approximately one million lives to the United States alone. The cost to the enemy would, obviously, be prodigious.

The refugee scientists who had been the first to urge the creation of an atomic bomb, and who had brought some salient information to the country that gave them safe harbor, however, turned against their own efforts once Nazi Germany was defeated. Their first suggestion was that the Soviets should be told in advance of the atomic bomb. President Roosevelt had agreed, but when Churchill became vehemently opposed, he changed his mind.[10] The next protest came in the form of a petition drawn up by Leo Szilard against the use of the atomic bomb upon Japan. Szilard brushed aside the argument that such a use would save many lives, declaring that viewpoint was "utilitarian," and added he had grown used to such arguments in Germany.[11]

On July 16, 1945, the bomb was tested and proved frightfully effective at Alamogordo. President Truman, at Potsdam, informed Stalin the United States had perfected a new weapon, and the dictator accepted the news calmly. The Soviet Union was similarly engaged, and was aware, through espionage, of the American effort.[12]

Churchill, present at Potsdam, was filled with forebodings. Before the meeting of the Big Three, Truman had sent Harry Hopkins ahead to talk to Stalin, and Hopkins had shared in criticisms of Britain.[13] At the conference Churchill argued against Soviet expansion in eastern Europe and Poland virtually alone. The Soviets, who were massing an army of 1.6 million to invade Manchuria and provide a second front against Japan, were amused when news came that Churchill's party had lost the election and a new British Prime Minister, Clement Attlee, replaced the wartime leader.

On August 6 Potsdam was over. The United States, which had waited ten days for a reply to an ultimatum, dropped an atomic bomb on Hiroshima. On the same day the Soviets invaded Manchuria.[14] Two days later another atomic bomb was dropped, this time on Nagasaki. Japan surrendered. The invasion was canceled, but occupation plans moved forward. The Soviets also moved—to occupy North Korea, in tune with a Roosevelt concession at Yalta.

Within days the world was embroiled in an immense discussion that has not yet ended. In Britain, on the same day as the Japanese

10. Bishop, *FDR's Last Year*, p. 144.

11. Donald Fleming and Bernard Bailyn, eds., *The Intellectual Migration: Europe and America, 1930–1960* (Cambridge, Mass.: Harvard University Press, 1969), pp. 130–131.

12. The Soviet nuclear project was launched in 1942 and was in high gear by 1945; Soviet forces were pursuing German nuclear physicists and shipped a number to the USSR at this time.

13. Ulam, *Expansion and Coexistence*, p. 385.

14. Williams, *Chronology of the Modern World*, p. 598.

surrender, the new Prime Minister Attlee, speaking through the realm's powerless King, announced the nationalization of coal mines, the creation of national health insurance, and the extension of social insurance. The British had turned Socialist.

The atomic bomb and the turn to the left in Britain and most of the rest of Europe, the immensity of the newly discovered power of nuclear energy, and the sense of imminent danger it brought to millions—all served to draw a curtain across the close of the most terrible of all wars. From 1939 to 1945 over forty million people had lost their lives amid one trillion dollars' worth of damage.[15]

Yet the war and all its activity, including the issues for which it was fought, was shrouded in dawning realization of two new issues: nuclear energy and socialism. In one form or another they would dominate the discussions of the intellectuals, while more modest members of humanity struggled to put together a world that would never again seem the same.

In the autumn of 1945 the government of the United States was confronted with western allies who were racked by shortages, disorders, and resurgent Communist partisans. Soviet forces held Berlin, Vienna, and Prague, the vertebrae of central Europe. The USSR occupied all eastern Europe and all its capitals except Athens. The United States decided to demobilize its armies and canceled $35 billion in war contracts.

At the same time the government threw a flood of war surplus and commodities on the market at cut-rate prices, reduced some taxes, and relaxed its controls over the economy. Wartime inflation, which had been steadily undermining the economy, stood nakedly revealed.

If all these actions seemed to lack a central core of rationality, that was no illusion. The American government had threatened, in the form of Harry Hopkins talking to Joseph Stalin, to leave Europe if the Kremlin did not keep its promises to restore a democratic Poland.[16] The dictator could have been excused if he goggled: the threat sounded too preposterous to be credited. Yet Hopkins was candid; that was what the United States did at the height of its power.

JB and Triangle were caught, like hundreds of thousands of other firms, in a mad scramble on the home front. In common with all other firms whose government orders were canceled, it had to switch fast.

The need did not take him by surprise; he had established terminals, made arrangements with jobbers, kept his old customers—or as

15. Hoyle, *World in Flames*, pp. 323–324.
16. Herbert Agar, *The Price of Power: America Since 1945* (Chicago: University of Chicago Press, 1957), pp. 17–19.

many as possible—on his books, and had expanded his tank-car fleet to more than three thousand. He needed those cars; the Cotton Valley operators, whose production of toluene ceased with the government's need for that essential product for TNT, were hastily making plans to switch to other refined products. With fractionating towers 8 to 10 feet in diameter that soared 160 feet into the air, they had only to add some more equipment to be able to process ten thousand barrels of product a day. JB planned, when that conversion was accomplished, to buy it all, and to resell it at the best possible price. Meanwhile his Triangle volumes swelled to thirty thousand and forty thousand barrels of product a day.

Toward year's end in 1945, therefore, the head of Triangle had hundreds of tank cars rolling, as in the old days, toward unknown destinations, and, with Barksdale and other salesmen on his small staff, was busy trying to steer each into a friendly home.

Around him the nation indulged itself. Near-hysterical women mounted demonstrations calling for the dissolution of the Army, Navy, Marine Corps, and Air Force, bearing banners that read Bring Daddy Home. After years of wartime propaganda about the better world for which the people were told the war was fought, the news-papers were filled with cries demanding the fruits of peace that were promised. In all, a strange time—and a strange way for the most powerful nation in the world, monopoly-holder of nuclear power, to behave.

In early 1946 all Triangle's wartime business had, of course, to be "renegotiated." The Constitution had forbidden *ex post facto* rulings, but that principle did not apply to contracts between a government and its citizens. There were young men in Washington as fervent as their New Deal predecessors, educated in the theory that business is a form of corruption.

JB was not incensed; he had grown to know how Washington operated and was beyond surprise. "I went to the capital with a good wet crying towel," he said, "but it didn't do any good." In common with other men subjected to similar experiences, JB could not help wondering at men who appeared to grill the firemen after the flames were vanquished, and who wanted to charge them for the cost of the water they had used—in the name of the national community.

"They didn't understand Triangle," he said later. "I was a mar-keter who operated on a margin of one quarter of a cent above posted prices." The government men pounced on that difference; it had to be renegotiated. The fact that posted prices in such a diverse and far-flung industry were more like averages than fixed figures was beyond the ken of men whose world was written, printed, and bound.

JB observed that they were young, green, and ambitious. "Public accountants holding civil-service jobs," he said, "each anxious to make a name for himself. Their knowledge of business was slight. They argued about one-sixteenth, or even one thirty-second, of a cent per gallon."

In the end a demand was made for the return of some monies honestly earned. JB thought it best to pay and get back to work in the industry where a man's word was sufficient to keep a contract—even one in which a loss was suffered. He knew that he had served his nation well; had gone to extraordinary efforts to keep essential fuel oil moving from Louisiana and Texas to Pine Camp, New York, and other remote, difficult places. Like other businessmen throughout the land who went through a similar ordeal, he could not help feeling a sense of chagrin.

The country had changed. During the war government controls on all levels—federal, state, and local—had expanded immensely. Millions of people had grown so accustomed to rules and regulations that they would never again feel secure without them. Unprecedented quantities of the nation's natural resources and manufacturing product had been shipped abroad and consumed in other lands. Money in circulation far exceeded any previous volume. One result was that inflation overheated the economy while shortages came into being. A black market, in existence since the early days of the New Deal, flourished and expanded during the war, and helped distort the real, as opposed to the statistical, economy.

Labor leaders, balked by a no-strike regulation during the war, sought to recover ground lost by their membership to inflation by demanding unprecedented wage increases and sweeping union recognition in the wake of the peace. The UAW led thousands out on strike against General Motors to enforce a demand for a 30 percent wage hike. The UAW was followed by its counterparts in steel, meat-packing, and the electrical industry. By early 1946 over two million workers were on strike. Millions more were affected, and the economy teetered.

Demands arose for the government to intervene—a cry now becoming habitual. President Truman did come forward, but his efforts were weighted on the side of the unions. The significance was clear. "The rise of labor . . . primarily through the immense economic power wielded by unions such as those in coal and steel, automobiles, electrical equipment, railroading and shipping was the outstanding development in the domestic economy since the inauguration of the New Deal."[17]

17. Dulles, *United States Since 1865*, p. 472.

The government instituted "fact-finding" boards, a title that cloaked compulsion in an inspired abstraction. The resulting settlements averaged more than a 20 percent increase in wages. Prices rose accordingly, and much of the nation went back to work. Then the coal miners went on strike.

The air, in other words, was suffused with a new spirit, one familiar to England, where labor—in unlikely combination with intellectuals and the press—had become the strongest political group in the realm. JB told Eddy he thought they should buy a second car. Little Suzanne, eight years old, said, "Nobody needs two cars."

"Who says so?" asked her father.

"My teacher."

Triangle's business expanded in every direction, on multiple levels. "I had been building for years," JB said. "I made contracts and connections, friends and acquaintances—and had built volume wherever possible. Now was the time that I began to collect on those efforts."

He signed up individual operators of new cycling plants as they appeared. Many of these were men with little capital, and JB sent them in the direction of the Second National Bank, where his friend Seydler was building an oil and gas department. Seydler's advances in this area were not achieved without effort. "Directors are not bankers," he said. "One, who was a lawyer, told me that we didn't need leases—that I was going far afield."

In 1946 Houston was still a city where the oil and gas industry, with its turbulent backdrop and its diverse, colorful men, who seemed to roam across the landscape with no settled abodes, aroused distrust.

Jesse Jones, for example, had launched his career in lumber and then ranged into real estate. He was the Big Man; his views and his heavy Washington connections and experience, carried a great deal of weight. Uncle Jesse, as he was called with deliberate humor, for he was a cold man, owned the Rice Hotel, the Texas State Hotel, and virtually all the larger downtown structures. "Even Mellie Esperson had trouble when she put her building up," JB said. "Uncle Jesse had tied up every contractor in town on one project or another."

But other Big Men were moving to the scene. George and Herman Brown, whose firm built 359 combat ships for the Navy during the war, and countless airdromes and strips, were among the more remarkable. "Herman started out building roads," JB said. "He was tall and round, with a round face and physique. He never progressed beyond the fourth grade in elementary school—but he was a Brain."

Herman Brown sent his younger brother George through college;

George earned his Ph.D. at Rice University. Then they were a team, and JB later watched their methods with interest.

"George was very polished," JB said, "and Herman would sit in the back of the room. But I noticed that George would always glance toward his older brother, who would make an almost imperceptible nod, or a negative gesture, before he answered a question."

The Browns had grown into one of the world's largest construction firms. There was no project too big for them to handle; they were efficient, imaginative, and quick. They belonged to the Bayou Club, a club whose members paid no dues. Instead the entire expenses of the year were shared, at year's end, on a pro rata basis.

The Browns, Roy Cullen—a fabulously wealthy oilman—and young Howard Hughes, whom JB met in 1944 and whose Hughes Tool Company was headquartered in Houston, were only some of the new faces who were crowding into the city to diminish Uncle Jesse's dominance and to change the Establishment. JB met and grew to know them all, including many of lesser eminence but of equal interest.

He played poker with some in the Houston Club in the Commerce Building; it was a game that provided relaxation and, on occasion, deep amusement.

Charley and Dick Knox, both customers of Triangle, were brothers who often played in the same game. "They talked their games," JB said. That was a tactic designed to drive nervous opponents into rashness; the Knox brothers had perfected it to a fine art.

"One night," JB said, "Charley opened. Dick called and raised him before the draw."

JB dropped out. Then Dick drew three cards and Charley drew two. Charley bet again, and Dick called and raised.

"Little Brother," Charley said, "I'll have to raise you some more." Dick called, and raised again.

Charley stared, and finally said, "How much money do you have? Put it in."

Dick called.

"Little Brother," said Charley, "what are you holding? Cause I have three aces."

"Just a dumb flush."

"God damn it, Little Brother," Charley said, outraged at anyone drawing three cards and filling a flush, "If you knew anything about the game you wouldn't have been in this pot at all!"

In 1946 such moments of relaxation were welcome; business was beginning to cluster and serious matters crowded for attention. One important consideration came into view obliquely, when John Atkins had a serious automobile accident in Shreveport. Laid up in the hospital, Atkins reflected on mortality and the condition of his business affairs.

In Houston similar thoughts were beginning to occur to JB. Both his attorney, John Arnold, and his banker, Herb Seydler, considered Triangle's structure somewhat fragile, especially in view of the considerable scope of its operations. They advised incorporation: a step that limits the liability of the owners and insures a longer life for the enterprise in the event of serious accident or the death of one of its principals.

Arnold and Seydler thought incorporation would cost about $150,000. Half that sum, $75,000, was available from Triangle's reserves. JB thought Atkins and Brinkman should put up the other half. But Atkins had a countersuggestion. "If you need seventy-five thousand dollars," he said, "why not put up twenty-five thousand yourself? Reggie and I will lend you twenty-five thousand each—at no interest."

JB's eyebrows raised. His partners assumed that he would take all the risks. The conversation then took a different turn. When Triangle had first been organized, JB and Atkins had agreed it would be sold when it could be sold for $2 million. By 1946 that position had been exceeded. JB thought he might discuss selling Triangle to a larger firm. Atkins and Brinkman were in favor of that effort. Meanwhile, a new arrangement, as part of the incorporation, was reached. Both Atkins and Brinkman gave JB a check for $25,000, and he gave each of them his note. In the event of a sale, the note and the $25,000 debt to each, contracted on behalf of a joint effort, would be forgotten. Meanwhile Atkins and Brinkman would draw $20,000 each from Triangle. That sum, which was twice their original investment, and which came after a number of years during which they had each received handsome revenues from Triangle, satisfied both men, assured JB of their continued cooperation in a variety of sectors, and was in reality generous.

Then JB talked to the Chicago Corporation, which did business as Champlin Oil, a subsidiary. The Chicago Corporation was an interesting venture, created as a spin-off years before by the First National Bank of Chicago.[18] It was headed, from Chicago, by Dick Wagner, a political businessman. As good a politician as he was a businessman, Wagner had structured the management of the Chicago Corporation in an inspired political manner. He had placed three men—engineer Dick Williams, accountant Fred Fues, and geologist Kane Greenleaf—in full charge of operations. That was not so unusual, but it was extraordinary that if the three agreed on a major decision, they had Wagner's prior

18. The Chicago Corporation was born in the Depression as a spin-off from the First National Bank of Chicago; it developed after oil was found on one of the many pieces of property on which the bank was left holding deeds of trust. Chicago Corporation was first an oil-producing company. It entered the gas sector in the Carthage field.

permission to proceed. He would back them up later. If they disagreed on a major decision, they were to turn to Wagner, and he would make the final decision.

JB discussed the possible sale of Triangle to the Chicago Corporation, and the trio thought that one million dollars each to John Atkins and Reggie Brinkman, two million dollars to JB and half the Triangle earnings for a period of five years, during which JB would continue to mastermind the Triangle, would be a fair price.

That was an exciting possibility. It would insure financial independence for JB, and assure his family's future. It would keep him at the helm of Triangle for another five years, during which his income would increase with the success of his efforts. And it would bring him within the orbit of the Chicago Corporation, which in itself held interesting potentialities.

Fred Fues, on behalf of the trio, brought the proposition before the board of the Chicago Corporation, in that city. Dick Wagner, its president, was not at the meeting; he was home. He was called and gave his opinion over the phone. As always, it was to the effect that the trio and the board could form their own opinion; he stepped in only on deadlocks. But Hugo Anderson—the loan officer of the First National Bank of Chicago, a director of the Chicago Corporation, and a representative of the source from which the acquisition would have to be financed—was brutally succinct.

"Saunders has a desk," he said, "a telephone, his hat—and his ass."

That was that. Fred Fues told JB how the plan had been killed. JB could not, of course, reveal what he knew without betraying Fred's confidence. He and Hugo Anderson met very often in succeeding years. "Anderson was always very courteous," JB said. "I never allowed him to suspect that I knew his opinion at that time." JB realized that Anderson had advanced loans to the Warren Petroleum Company at a time when Bill Warren was operating a modest venture, that the banker—as are all men—was unevenly talented, and that his judgments were not always on target. But Anderson had smashed JB's hopes, and it hurt.

A great many other hopes were being smashed in 1946; the hopes of half the world. In Eastern Europe Yugoslavia created a Soviet-style dictatorship, and so did tiny Albania. East Germany was placed under Communist control, and former Nazis rose to high positions. The commissars conducted purges throughout Rumania, and rose to power in Czechoslovakia and Bulgaria.

While much of the world was horrified by revelations of atrocities at the trial of the Nazi leaders in an international dock in Nuremberg, similar atrocities continued in the USSR, which sat on the tribunal. Millions were sent to Siberia. Soviet war prisoners were sent home to worse captivity, and the Allies even turned over millions of refugees from the long-dead state of Russia, in accordance with what was considered treaty obligations.[19] That action, however, was not revealed by the western press, though it was extensive.

Far more attention was paid to the issue of the atomic bomb. Scientists who had been eager to use that weapon on Europeans found no contradiction in branding its use in Asia as immoral. Doomsday articles appeared, hinting at the end of the world unless the bomb was outlawed. Others believed its "secret" should be kept in American hands as long as possible, and a new "security" program came into being. The Manhattan Project had succeeded largely because the scientists involved were all graduates of free interchange, and continued that practice in their experiments. Most of the compartmentalization of the program applied to suppliers, engineers, and persons in contact with the Project on its peripheries.

The idea that the national government could function in peacetime along the lines of an emergency program mounted in war seemed, on its face, too preposterous a departure from the norms of the United States to be credited. Nevertheless that concept permeated the government, and soon expanded into a system of classification in which some citizens were held—by men barely able to grasp what they sought to grade—to be more trustworthy than others. That was a long step away from not only American, but all western, traditions.

The security program, however, was created in fear that was not ill-founded. Pro-Communist groups had been accepted as part of the national community during the war, and in the immediate postwar period were influential in the press, labor, politics, the arts, and academia. Their outcry against the American possession of the atomic bomb was ironic; the entire world knew what such a monopoly would have meant in the hands of the commissars. A bitter and complex debate was opened in the UN on the subject. The United States offered to turn its knowledge of nuclear fission and the bomb over to an international commission, provided all nations opened their borders to international inspection and monitoring.[20] The Soviets, to whom openness of any sort is odious, rejected the proposal at once; the ré-

19. It is estimated that two million were forcibly turned over to the USSR by British and American troops in the period between 1944 and 1947, and were sent "to jail, slave labor camps, ruthless persecution and death." Julius Epstein, *Operation Keelhaul* (Old Greenwich, Conn.: Devin-Adair, 1973), p. 2.

20. Senator Vandenberg wrote, "I am sure of just one thing—namely, that the blackout curtain of secrecy must be lifted from every quarter of the globe before *anything* can be done in respect to a constructive program." Agar, *Price of Power*, p. 54.

gime had secrets that, once revealed, would have destroyed its standing as a civilized nation.

It took Churchill, seventy-two years old, to put the state of the globe into perspective. "An iron curtain has fallen across the Continent. Behind that line lie all the capitals of the ancient states of Central and Eastern Europe. Police governments are prevailing."[21]

The speech created an outcry; most prominent newspapers criticized it and President Truman cautiously refused to comment. Henry Wallace, whom Roosevelt had replaced for Jesse Jones as Secretary of Commerce, delivered a speech against "getting tough" with what he called Russia. He meant the USSR; Russia was a historic entity destroyed in 1917. Mr. Wallace insisted the President had reviewed and approved the speech; the President denied it—and fired him.[22]

There were, after all, elections due in the fall.

Rockenback, JB's good friend, suffered first a slight and then a serious heart attack which sent him in and out of the hospital several times. That news brought G. L. Rowsey on the phone from Taylor, Texas. Rowsey, who owned 50 percent of the Southern States Barge Lines, had decided to sell his business—and that meant that Rocky and JB would have new partners.

"They're New York people," Rowsey said. "I'm not sure that either you or Rocky would find them very pleasant partners. Therefore, since Rocky's health is uncertain, I'd be willing to buy you both out. Or," he added, "you may buy my interest."

JB asked Rowsey what he would consider a fair price, and the refiner said he thought $300,000. JB sat straighter at that. He knew Rowsey could easily get twice that amount; he was doing his old friend Rockenback a favor. They shook hands, and JB went to see Seydler at the Second National Bank. There was no problem in financing the purchase of Rowsey's share of Southern States: Triangle cargoes could keep the line in profitable operations for years to come. Then JB went to see Rocky.

Rocky was not very anxious to give up the railroad; it was an industry in which he occupied a high and respected position. But JB told him, "You'd better do it. Your heart is *complaining*."

After some discussion, the older man agreed. JB assured him his salary would be the same as it was while he was industrial commis-

21. Pelling, *Winston Churchill*, p. 566.
22. Both men persisted in their contradictory versions for the rest of their lives.

sioner of the Cotton Belt. He liked Rocky. "He was very Southern, but he could be hard," JB said later.

Rockenback kept a gun in his desk drawer, and kept his Sam Browne belt and holster from World War I, where he had served in France and seen combat. Once JB was with him when a man quoted some prominent person as saying that he had never felt fear on the battlefield. Rocky said coldly, "That man is a liar."

Rocky was sixty-one years old in 1946, but looked and acted like a man of fifty. Neat, quick, and alert, he was to remain that way, as president of the Southern States Barge Lines, for many years to come.

Tank cars were good, but barges were better—and pipelines were paramount. The Big Inch and the Little Big Inch were, after the war, converted to gas carriers. That conversion—as with all other disposals of the war-created properties—was accompanied by disputes, protests, and elaborate maneuvers. Voices were raised to say that the conversion from crude oil in the Big Inch and refined petroleum products in the Little Big Inch would benefit the majors and return the land to the system of tanker transport from the Gulf to the East Coast, and was therefore suspicious.

Others, however, pointed to the great national swing underway from coal to oil and gas. Gas was cheap and odorless, left no residue, could be used in cooking and heating, and would—carried to the Northeast, which lacked coal, oil, and gas of its own—benefit millions of households and thousands of small enterprises. The wasteful flaring of gas at the well heads of Texas and Louisiana could be ended if the two great pipelines were available. In peacetime there was no good reason why tankers should not resume handling the transport of crude oil and petroleum products from the Gulf Coast to the East.

Secretary of the Interior Ickes, convinced, picked up the phone and called Drew Pearson. That strange columnist, who served as a live klaxon for persons who habitually combined high goals with low methods, began to shriek in the name of conservation and to brand all contrary arguments as evilly motivated. Within a short period the conversion of the lines was approved. J. Howard Marshall later said, "It was a good decision at the time; it worked. The flaring of gas at the well heads and the waste of a great resource came to an end."

When the Big Inch and the Little Big Inch auction was opened the bidders included Herman and George Brown. The brothers were no strangers to pipelines. They had built a gas line before the war that was later purchased by Tennessee Gas and another, very large, line for

Pan-American Eastern. George Brown said later the Pan-American Eastern line carried gas "at a rate of a penny a thousand cubic feet." They had also surveyed the east Texas gas fields with an eye toward building a line using this region as a source, but became too busy as Brown & Root to pursue the project. After the war George Brown said, "We took our pipeline plans off the shelf."

The great auction opened while J. Howard Marshall, who had left PAW to become president of Ashland Oil & Refining, watched with interest. He was on the sidelines, but pleased that the campaign to convert the lines to gas had succeeded. A products line that penetrated Ashland's home market would have raised many competitive problems for him, and for chairman Paul Blazer.

Marshall's experience in Washington, however, had left him with friends and acquaintances all through the industry. One of these was Lee DeGolyer, the famed geologist-businessman, whose oil discoveries were renowned around the world. DeGolyer was immensely wealthy but continued to be active for the sheer pleasure of sitting in large plays. He had invested in the Brown venture, which was called Texas Eastern, as had Holly Poe. DeGolyer later described Texas Eastern strategy to Marshall. In order to succeed, it had to obtain the giant pipelines, which could serve the venture as a double vertebra. The firm's bid had to be very high, in order to insure success. An important consideration was the fact that rates of pipelines are based on their initial capitalization. The Browns had no problem regarding financing; capital was available at interests ranging from 4 to 5 percent. That meant the rates of the lines, if obtained, could be set at 6 to 6.5 percent, with Texas Eastern shareholders receiving the difference as dividends. That left only problems of supply and customers. These were huge areas, but the Texas Eastern group was certain they could be mastered—if the pipelines were obtained.

In the end Texas Eastern bid $146 million. That huge sum far exceeded the bids of its competitors, and won the two great pipelines. George Brown was pleased at that, but even more pleased that his venture had distinguished itself not by obtaining government surplus at the usual bargain prices, but by a realistic appraisal of the values involved. "It was the only surplus property sale on which the government made a profit," he said later.

The Browns had entered the gas marketplace with Texas Eastern, backed with large amounts of capital and based on the acquisition of two huge pipelines, with a need to insure sources of supply on one end and to establish customers on the other. JB, however, was in almost exactly the oposite position. He had sources of supply on one end and customers on the other, but he needed a pipeline. His sources of capital, when it came to such large acquisitions, was limited.

His suppliers in the Gulf consisted of two main groups. The first of these were the Cotton Valley Operators, who had expanded their plant and were producing straight-run gasoline, kerosene, and other petroleum products. The second group was fairly new, and located in the Carthage field in Panola County, Texas.

The Cotton Valley plant was dependent on trucks and tank cars. Triangle had those in hand. But if it could carry the Cotton Valley production to the Mississippi River and its barges, it could enter the large markets of Chicago and other regions available by water and meet any competition because its transportation costs would be greatly reduced. Transportation costs, after all, were borne by Triangle.

The answer was close to the surface. A common carrier petroleum products pipeline ran near the Cotton Valley plant. Tests proved that the Cotton Valley straight-run products met the pipeline specifications and, since it was a common carrier, could not be refused. Owned by Magnolia Oil, the line ran from Shreveport to El Dorado.

The Magnolia line connected with the Project 5 pipeline that ran to the Mississippi River at Helena, Arkansas. From there southern states and other barges could carry the Cotton Valley products to Chicago and other teeming markets available by water, "and would have," JB said, "the world for a market."

While tracing these possibilities, which would virtually cement Triangle and the Cotton Valley operators, JB was busy on many other matters. In midsummer, 1946, he had entered into a new venture, in which Triangle shared ownership of the Transcentral Oil Company with Elwood Richardson, a former Shell executive. Transcentral was formed to market rpm oils and greases in seventeen midwestern states; its source of supply was California Standard. A vice president of California, Clark Moody, was a prime mover in the new venture.

Then JB reviewed the Carthage field situation. Unlike the Cotton Valley, it had no nearby pipeline in place. Its product had to be taken out in trucks and tank cars, the most expensive forms of transportation. That was a problem. There were two firms in particular that were active in the field whose plans were interesting, who had excellent financial resources, and whose leaders JB had grown to know and like. These were the Carthage Corporation and the Chicago Corporation. The problem was to somehow link these firms, the Carthage field, and the Cotton Valley transportation solution into a single larger, overall plan.

Having decided that, JB let the subject simmer. He had discovered, as have many others, that solutions occasionally emerge from somewhere in the recesses of the mind—if the spotlight is switched off.

The press had labeled 1946 the "Year of Frustration." The phrase aptly summarized widespread confusion, which President Truman did little to clarify. He was, in the eyes of many, a distinct let-down after the soaring nonchalance of the Roosevelt White House. The man from Missouri was widely described as "common." His early business failures and political career as a protégé of the notoriously corrupt Jim Pendergast of Kansas City were exhumed and subjected to widespread publicity.

For not the first time the national press disclosed a curious snobbery by describing the simple Truman family as though its members were unworthy of the White House. The President was persistently portrayed as unlettered, though he was "more widely read in history than any president since John Quincy Adams."[23] His manners were Midwestern and struck Easterners badly. He was profane among men, an excellent poker player, retiring with women—and loyal to a fault. But he was fearless, and quicker-witted than he seemed. He had, therefore, the tactical advantage of being smarter than most people, then or since, could credit.

During 1946 this inwardly complicated, outwardly simple President struck several contradictory attitudes. Early in the year he sounded like an advocate of expanded union power, but in reality extended the power of Washington over both labor and management. In midyear he asked Congress for authority to draft striking railroad workers into the armed forces—a truly startling proposition. His economics seemed as scrambled as his predecessor's.

In international terms the President confused the world. He approved a Lend-Lease program of $3.75 billion for Britain, but had ignored British warnings against the USSR. He had publicly waffled on the great issues posed so starkly, but so differently, by Churchill early in the year and the pro-Communist Henry Wallace in the fall.

It was no wonder, in view of the confusion the President did so little to resolve in 1946, that the nation went to the polls and gave the Republicans a congressional majority for the first time since 1932. The GOP rejoiced; it had been a long fourteen years.

When Howard Barksdale visited Shreveport he often dropped in on C. D. Tinsley, who had left Triangle in 1943. They were good

23. Agar, *The Price of Power*, p. 42.

friends, but Tinsley had grown to regard these visits with mixed feelings. He had left Triangle for a higher salary and a 10 percent piece of the action, but these prospects had curdled within a brief six months. Coast Oil & Refining, a small firm, had been cut off from its crude oil supply as the war extended. It had been forced to switch entirely to butane, and Tinsley was reduced to selling that fuel to small appliance distributors.

Barksdale, however, was far too good a salesman to indicate that he was aware of that situation. Instead he stressed the problems he was having in handling the huge increase in Triangle's volume. "We have tank cars coursing in every direction," he said. "The Jennings plant alone is a headache; it's hard for me to get rid of all that product."

That sort of insinuation finally had its effect, and C. D. admitted that the thought of returning to Triangle had, from time to time, crossed his mind, but he had qualms when they appeared. After all, he had quit, and words had been exchanged.

Barksdale hinted that JB wanted Tinsley to return, but C. D. was skeptical. "He'd hire me just long enough to fire me," he said.

Barksdale wondered how Tinsley could be reassured, and C. D. said, "Only if JB himself came here and asked me. And then, only if I reported directly to him." He didn't have much hope of either of these conditions becoming real, but he thought that would end the hints; that JB would never personally approach him.

To his pleasure JB appeared a week later, and cursed him. "You little SOB," he said, "I miss you and I need you. I've got a spot for you. What do you want?"

"I want your word that it's all water over the dam," C. D. said.

"I'll never mention it," JB said, "*You have my word.*" They both knew how iron a statement that was; JB's word was inviolate.

As always, JB was in a hurry. He looked at his watch and toward the door. "Meet me in Dallas and tell me your terms," he said, as they shook hands.

"I left you," C. D. admitted. "It was a bad mistake; I never had to ask for money."

Then JB changed his mind about the meeting place. "Meet me in Houston," he concluded. "*You set the salary.*"

A few days later C. D. Tinsley strolled into the Houston headquarters of Triangle, and slender Esther Gutknecht looked up.

"Why, C. D.," she said in surprise, "What are you doing here?"

"I've been gone four years," he told her, "and I've come back to get caught up."

In the White House the President was also catching up. In February, 1947, the British government was in the process of carrying out old dreams and goals of the Socialist government of Attlee. That consisted of arrangements in part to withdraw from India, and in part to withdraw from other parts of what had once been the indissoluble empire. Word was sent to Washington that British troops, stationed in Greece to prevent a Communist take-over in the wake of the Nazi retreat, would be pulled home.

That was serious news. The Communists of Greece were armed and could receive sanctuary from neighboring Yugoslavia. If Greece turned Communist, it would become nearly impossible for the West to defend Turkey. The USSR could move, like an irresistible tide, into a position athwart the Dardanelles, to threaten the Middle East—a goal of centuries.

The news came following the resignation of Jimmy Byrnes as Secretary of State and Truman's appointment of General George Marshall. The general remains a mysterious figure; he disdained the press and all publicity. He carried a little black book—one of the few men ever known to actually do so—in which his estimates of his associates were inscribed in code. But he was a general, and his grasp of military realities was sharp and clear. He spelled out the significance of the British turn to the left in terms that even fervent New Dealer Truman found bracing.

As a result the United States decided to fill the British vacuum. The method used was very American—as American as Independence, Missouri. A huge sum, $400 million, was appropriated to supply aid to both Greece and Turkey. The reason was stated with admirable clarity: "To support free peoples who are resisting attempted subjugation by armed minorities or by outside pressures."

That was a step toward world leadership—but only a step. Churchill, watching the swift decline of Britain and of Europe, said, "What is Europe now? It is a rubble heap, a charnel house, a breeding ground of hate and pestilence."[24]

But Washington, and especially the President, had awakened. Plans were drawn to swing the industrial might of the United States toward the battered nations of the world. A stream of goods and supplies were already pouring toward Britain, Greece, and Turkey.

At home huge sums flowed toward millions of demobilized service people, and the Administration rained propositions upon Congress, calling for the extension of "social" services. Those were, in the main, rejected by the Republicans. But the aid to Greece and Turkey had been approved, and the American economy began to heat, as if in war, under the impact of the new policy. In that way the Cold War started

24. Agar, *The Price of Power*, p. 72.

and a depression, considered unavoidable and inevitable by every economist in the land, was avoided.

The Houston *Chronicle* carries, in its back pages, crammed into small type, a series of notices of interest to businessmen that are usually ignored by the average reader. These include ship movements, stock prices, exchange rates, commodity movements, and the like. Among the conglomeration are notices published by railroads, shipping lines, and pipelines regarding rates and changes.

Reading this section was a normal morning chore for JB. One morning he noticed in it that the Texas Company was to discontinue the use of a pipeline that started near the Texas state line in the Houston region and ran first to Logansport, and then through Shreveport to El Dorado, Arkansas, where it connected with the Magnolia line.

That was interesting. He called Dudley Jackson, a pipeliner whose brother, Slick Jackson, was an old and good friend. Dudley was a pumper and, when JB asked him about the Texas Company line, knew it well. It leaked, he said, but only in the section near the Gulf. The rest of the line was in excellent condition.

JB put the phone down and all his observations came together. If he could buy the pipeline the Texas Company planned to abandon, he could use part of the pipe to construct a line from the Carthage field to Shreveport. From there he could use the Magnolia line to send product to El Dorado, Arkansas. At El Dorado the Magnolia line connected with the Project 5 pipeline, which ran to Helena, Arkansas, on the Mississippi River. From there Triangle and Southern States tows and barges could carry the product, in JB's favorite phrase, "to the world as a market."

It was the Carthage field that had delayed his pipeline plans the longest. Its production was too heavy in volume to be absorbed by the local market. Trucks and railroad tank cars were too expensive a means to move it north, where it could be sold. JB had sought a means of tying the Carthage field production to the flow from the Cotton Valley northward. Now, for the first time, he could see how those two steps could be taken—two steps that could make Triangle run.

He wasted no time. At seven o'clock in the morning he kept an appointment with McLaughlin, an executive with the Texas Company and an old friend. He explained his plan and obtained a ninety-day option from the Texas Company to buy the Texas line from Logansport to Shreveport, Louisiana, on a final price of $200,000 in the ground.

That important agreement in hand, he went to Ed Hudson, the

owner of the Carthage Corporation. To his disapointment, Hudson was not particularly interested. Transportation costs were Triangle's problem; he saw no urgent reason why Carthage should become involved in a pipeline.

"Ed, it will benefit your plant," JB said, but Hudson shook his head. The yield from the Carthage field was, he said darkly, diminishing. It might dry up. Thirty years later it was still diminishing—and still producing. But at that time Hudson could not know that.

JB then turned toward the other firm with a substantial interest in the Carthage field: the Chicago Corporation. His sale of Triangle to the Chicago Corporation had fallen through, but that was not the fault of the trio who ran its operations, nor of its president, Dick Wagner. His relations with these men remained close and cordial. JB drove to Corpus Christi, parked his car on Leopard Street, and entered their offices. He had phoned ahead, of course, and Dick Williams was waiting. He told Williams he had obtained an option from the Texas Company to buy their pipeline for $200,000. Williams whistled. "It's worth a lot more than that," he said.

"That's not the understanding," JB replied, and grinned.

Williams called Fues and Greenleaf, the other parts of the trio. The three men dragged out maps of the pipeline, measured distances, and discussed costs. Finally Williams turned to JB.

"How much can we have?" he asked.

"Half," said JB, "if you want the other half." He knew these three could commit the Chicago Corporation to anything on which they were joined. On this occasion they thought like triplets. All three nodded their heads; it was a deal. A secretary was called in, and a letter of agreement drawn and signed.

JB drove back to Houston feeling fine; he now had partners—and the Chicago Corporation was an excellent partner to have. His project was heating up. It heated a bit more when he told Ed Hudson, as of course he had to tell him, that Williams, Fues, and Greenleaf had joined with him on the purchase of the gulf pipeline.

Hudson immediately said he changed his mind, and wanted to join. That led to more discussions, which were joined by United Gas, a firm with interests in the situation. In the end a new agreement was formed with four partners: Carthage Corporation, the Chicago Corporation, United Gas, and Triangle. Each held a fourth in the new pipeline venture.

It was hard not to smile at that outcome. JB had reduced a ninety-day, $200,00 option to an investment of $50,000 in a line in which three of his most important suppliers would share, and put up $150,000. There was much more to be done, but it would be hard to beat the beginning.

The entire United States was making a new beginning in mid-1947, though the nation was largely unaware of the magnitude of its turn. General Marshall's quiet demeanor and his absence from the limelight even during the war, when he was chief of staff, enabled him to fit smoothly into the office of Secretary of State without attracting the usual hostility of the American press toward the nation's military men. He appeared at Harvard in June, 1947, to give a speech. The audience was respectful and his remarks were significant. In effect, he unveiled a program of American assistance to war-torn nations on a global scale.

His message was greeted with jubilation in London and Paris, and anger in Moscow. Within a few weeks an international conference was held, attended by sixteen nations. The commissars had been invited and, had they accepted, some curious results might have emerged. Instead, Stalin forbade any of the nations under Soviet occupation to accept American aid. The sixteen nations that did flock in response to Washington's call, however, were far from shy. They presented a four-year plan for their economic recovery, costing seventeen billion dollars.

A curious campaign took place. No nation had ever before spent its people's money outside its own borders without asking for territorial or political privileges in advance. Stripped of rhetoric, the plan would withdraw a great portion not only of the wealth of the Treasury, but also of the nation's goods and services. It would cost the American people not only in national assets, but also in increased taxes. Hundreds of committees were formed to persuade the electorate of the value of the Marshall Plan—the President had decided to wait for its reception before welding his name to its fate. That decision marked the first time that an American President had concealed his Constitutional role in directing foreign policy behind a Secretary of State; it would not be the last.

The inner meaning of the Marshall Plan, however, was stressed by its proponents more than its cost. It was presented as a means of combating communism on a global scale. Communism at home, a subject that disturbed many, was not neglected by the new Congress, which created the House Un-American Affairs Committee to explore the extent of its influence.

That step was not heralded; much more attention was paid to the passage of the Taft-Hartley Act. To a nation tired of strikes and given abundant evidence of the public-be-damned attitude of labor leaders, the measure seemed fairly mild. Unions were forbidden certain unfair practices, forbidden to make political contributions, and compelled to give a sixty-day notice of the termination of a contract. In the event strikes threatened the national health or safety, the government could obtain an injunction for eighty days, which was described as a "cooling-off period." The bill also included measures restricting the employers from proselytizing against unions, creating lock-outs, or committing other unfair practices. But the unions howled as though wounded and near death, and the Democrats charged that Republicans were against the working people.

The working people, however, were not as upset as union leaders. The economy was improving; the sale of cars had soared to levels that almost equaled 1929—though that year had grown so ancient few could recall it—and none called attention to that particular statistic.[25]

The pickup at Detroit, however, was of great interest and importance to Triangle and all other firms in the petroleum industry. The peacetime market world was back with a rush, and the switch from coal to oil, plus the innumerable new uses for petroleum products and gases, had turned the industry into the most crowded and competitive in the nation. Petroleum was, in fact, the only huge industry to have so many firms and to support such a variety of firms. The other great industries—steel, automobiles, rubber, electrical, and the rest—mainly showed a pyramid whose large firms spread from the tip to nearly the bottom, squatting atop a base of tiny, squinched firms. In petroleum even medium firms were huge, and the top was more like a floor-through than a turret.

"After the war," said Jack Rathbone, who had transferred to the New York headquarters of Jersey Standard as president, "Phillips and Ohio went foreign. They had the same impact on the international scene as on the domestic. They broke established patterns—ushered in a dog eat dog competition." Rathbone was also convinced that the government preferred these new firms to the old. He did not regard that with emotion; the idea that the United States government played favorite among the citizens had become commonplace.

A larger fact was that the wartime cooperation between government and business broke down fairly soon after World War II. The competition between firms resumed on a more intense level because the petrolum industry had not only the United States, but the world, for a stage. The marketplace became very bruising; price wars in gasoline flared in varying regions and were ablaze somewhere all the time. That was one reason why the pipeline was so important a move for Triangle.

As so often happens, the partnership JB's pipeline venture created expanded into other areas, though not immediately. First the old Texas line had to be dug up, cleaned, and relaid. Joe Gerson, an expert called

25. Car production in 1929 was over 5 million; in 1947 it reached 4.7 million. Partridge, *Fill 'Er Up*, p. 227.

314

in for this task, produced a rust-inhibitor that he sent through the line as a cleansing agent. Rust accumulations were emptied into traps. Sinclair and Conoco men, prowling curiously around these efforts, reported them to their firms, and some of their more imaginative associates decided that such rust-inhibitors might be good for automobile carburetors. That resulted in a new product, one that would prove immensely popular and profitable when it appeared in the marketplace.

Meanwhile the pipe was relaid from the Carthage field to a connection in Shreveport. The effort, launched in September, 1947, was to take almost six months. When it was started, discussions were held with Slats Latimer, the president of Magnolia Oil, and with Mr. True, the head of its pipeline department.

"Slats Latimer was given that nickname when he was young and skinny," JB said, "but by the time we talked to him about the Magnolia line he was old and fat. All that was left of his youth was the nickname."[26] Asked about the Magnolia line, Slats was reassuring. Someone asked how long it could be used. He laughed and said, "Forever, I hope."

Mr. True, the head of Magnolia's pipeline department, was equally relaxed. It appeared unlikely that any problems would arise with Magnolia, therefore, and the partners turned toward some new developments that arose, at the time, to occupy their attention. But Mr. True was not called "Snake" for nothing.

The air, in the fall of 1947, was heavy with negotiations, shifts, transfers, market struggles, and expansions. Individual plans long pent up by the war had been dusted off and revitalized. Butch Butler, plant manager for the Cotton Valley Plant Operators, who had struggled from a Depression pit to become recognized as a diligent and able man, had moved from the Cotton Valley plant to the Old Ocean Oil Company, headquartered in Houston. Butler had two buddies: Max Lents and Martin Miller. The trio, experienced in the still new area of unitization, were repeating the Cotton Valley effort for Old Ocean, but Butler was unhappy.

"They second-guess too much," he said, but that was only his surface irritation. In reality he longed to get off the Old Ocean, or any other payroll, and get into business for himself. A superb golfer, he often played with John Atkins, and brought up the subject of being financed in business by the Shreveporter. Atkins, however, had some other projects in view. He sent a hard drive down the fairway,

26. Slats Latimer was a first cousin of Lyman Latimer, who married JB's early schoolteacher. Their daughter Nelle spent part of her childhood in the Saunders home in Sapulpa.

grunted, and said, "Why don't you try JB?" He knew the men liked one another.

Butler brought the matter up with JB and was somewhat hesitant, but Saunders was pleased at the idea, and actually urged Butler to strike out. "I'll back you," he said, "and we'll have fun."

Butler believed he had, with his partners, a winning combination. Lents was a superb engineer, Miller was a geologist, and Butler was an experienced manager knowledgeable in all phases of the industry. His thought was that he and Miller would organize a firm to enter drilling ventures; Lents could stay with the Old Ocean Company until the business got off the ground.

"How much do you figure you'll need?" JB asked.

"A guarantee of seventy-five thousand dollars a year for the next five years," Butler said.

JB didn't think that was too much. "All I want is a piece of every venture," he said, "—*no salary*." He was not going to follow the entire Atkins pattern, therefore, but in backing Butler, he had moved into a parallel position.

The partnership of the Chicago Corporation, Carthage Corporation, United Gas, and Triangle was formed to build and operate a pipeline. As is usual with partnerships, it was soon confronted with other new opportunities. Carthage had entered the gasoline market, but its product had a low-octane rating at a time when Detroit had launched its feverish, high-octane drive.

That drive affected the entire petroleum industry and set a wave of expensive changes coursing through a host of refineries. No firm was exempt from the pressures Detroit created; the gasoline marketplace was subjected to intense pressures. In New York City, in the executive suite of the largest petroleum firm in world—Standard of New Jersey—its president, Jack Rathbone, felt these pressures, just as did his counterparts in lesser firms.

"Gene Holtzman, chief executive of Jersey at the time, was a friend of Mr. Alfred E. Sloane, Jr.," Rathbone recalls. "I remember that Sloane was invited to lunch in the executive dining room. I arrived in a poor humor; the gasoline marketplace was upset and many troubling matters had arisen. I asked Mr. Sloane why Detroit didn't make a low-cost car with high mileage for young married people."[27]

Mr. Sloane didn't like that. "I know so much more than you as to what the average American motorist wants that your question is pre-

27. "Six months later," Rathbone added, "the first Volkswagens appeared in the United States, and the Germans sold 500,000 of them before some tinkering with the import rates slowed the flood. And when Detroit did produce a compact, it was one foot shorter and $500 cheaper than its regular line."

sumptuous," he growled. "That," Rathbone concluded, "did not improve the lunch."

The petroleum people could not understand why Detroit wanted to make superpowered vehicles for everyday use. The notoriously stubborn managers in Detroit, however, claimed that powerful cars were easier to sell. Some independent marketers suspected the move was part of the continuing collaboration between the majors and Detroit. There was a thread of plausibility to that; there was no question of the closeness of that relationship. But it is unlikely that any deliberate effort was underway to pressure the independents; it was more that all new and expensive developments created a crisis for smaller firms unable to keep up with the high-powered technological race underway.

In any event it created a crisis of sorts for the Chicago Corporation, Carthage, United Gas, and the entire independent sector. The crunch came while their new pipeline was being created, and coincided with a visit by a delegation of men, headed by superintendent Vernon Chance, who appeared from the Atlas Refinery in Shreveport in the offices of John Atkins.

The men were concerned because Ohio Standard, which owned the Atlas Refinery, planned to shut it down. The plant was old and had gone through several hands. Ohio Standard had built a new pipeline from the Gulf to the East, where it had more modern facilities. It had, therefore, no further use for Atlas. To make matters worse, it had no particular use for the bulk of Atlas employees, once the plant was closed. At the same time, Ohio Standard did not want to leave a poor reputation in Shreveport, or to create any ill will. The delegation wanted Atkins to intervene. As an important Shreveporter, Atkins shared their concern. The plant's closing would constitute a civic calamity.

Vernon Chance knew the capacity of the refinery to the last nut and bolt, and Atkins drew the Carthage Corporation, United Gas, and the Chicago Corporation into the discussions. The consensus was that the Carthage distillate gasoline might be run through the Atlas plant to produce a high-octane product. The experiment held some danger; the plant might blow up. Another problem was the marketing of the high octane—if the plan worked and if they could obtain the refinery. Both considerations meant that JB would have to be called into the discussions.

JB was called and arrived. The talks took on a new momentum.

The moment is worth a longer look. Only a decade before, JB had been a protégé of Atkins, and in a position far more modest than the Highland Oil Company. Shreveport was a closed book to him. But in late 1947 and through early 1948, he was a full member of a top-level move to save Shreveport from a severe economic blow—and a man who could help realize that rescue.

317

JB considered the marketing aspect promising. Carthage, the Chicago Corporation, and United Gas could assure the Atlas refinery a steady source of supply. He was confident he could market high-octane gasoline, if Atlas could produce in quantity. He was, however, equally interested in the complex question of how the Atlas acquisition would be financed, if it was accomplished. Atkins then introduced JB to his own attorney, David Smitherman.[28]

Before these discussions could go into a second stage, however, the group decided to see if the Atlas could handle the Carthage distillate. Dick Williams, the engineer for the Chicago Corporation, was sure it could be done. The plant was leased for thirty days from Ohio Standard, and a test run was made. For this purpose a new venture was formed, called the Atlas Processing Company.

Smitherman drew up the papers for this, as well as for all the other ramifications of the discussions, but his role did not end there. Smitherman's older brother had entered the oil business when the Caddo field was first discovered, and had large holdings in northern Louisiana. Smitherman himself had entered the lease scene of that play and was very knowledgeable in all the phases and legal aspects of the industry. "Atlas Processing," he said later, "was the result of efforts by John Atkins and JB Saunders." That juxtaposition of names, on the part of the Atkins family attorney, was definitive.

But all that had to come after the first experiment. Distillate was trucked to Shreveport from the Carthage field, for the pipeline was not yet complete, and tested through the Atlas plant. "It worked so-so," said JB later.

That conclusion meant the project was feasible, but was not without problems. Ohio Standard, which had set a price of several million on the plant, made a more realistic appraisal and reduced that figure to one million dollars. Meanwhile JB took the time to look into the refinery and its features himself. "Its capacity was only ten thousand barrels a day," he said. In early 1948, that was becoming an uneconomical size. "But," JB added, "it had a storage capacity of seven hundred thousand barrels—and the land was inside the city of Shreveport."

Those last facts impressed him. JB later said that the tankage alone was worth one million dollars; the in-city location also constituted a valuable real estate investment. These factors swung him into the position of participant, instead of simply marketer for Atlas, in the event of its acquisition.

That much decided JB, Atkins, and the United Gas men, and Dick

28. David Stuart Smitherman, senior partner in the firm of Smitherman, Smitherman, Lunn, Hussey & Chasten, was still practicing law in Shreveport in 1975, having started in 1922. He handled all legal matters for the Atkins family.

Williams of the Chicago Corporation flew to Chicago to meet a team from Ohio Standard to see if a purchase could be made. Those struggles are always excruciating and are usually exacerbated rather than assisted by lawyers and accountants. JB's opinion of both these professions had already curdled, and was to grow increasingly acerbic as the years passed.

JB and the Chicago Corporation offered the Ohio Standard its one million dollar price. Asked how they planned to make that payment, they said, "Half in cash and the other half from the profits of operation."

"How would such profits be figured?" asked Wallace, a vice president of Ohio Standard. That was, of course, a very searching question, which sent the accountants into a huddle that occupied them for days. The prospective purchasers, meanwhile, cooled their heels, made telephone calls and played gin. The routine was wearing, and JB finally had enough.

"Forget about the percentage of profit that will be earmarked for payment and all that," he said. "We'll pay in cash, if you'll take seven hundred and fifty thousand dollars."

Wallace grinned and said, "You've just made a deal."

Later the four partner firms that had come together to buy the Texas pipeline came to the same arrangement regarding the acquisition of the Atlas Refinery. Each firm, including Triangle, held a fourth interest. Marketing arrangements were also split between Triangle and Highland Oil. Brinkman's firm, which operated on a regional Gulf basis, used mainly railroad tank cars and tank trucks in its distribution.

The ramifications of the Atlas acquisition were extensive. Brinkman's Highland Oil was to handle products from United Gas, while JB agreed that Triangle would handle products from the Chicago Corporation and Carthage. Since Highland's marketing sector was more limited geographically than Triangle's, Brinkman would distribute mainly through tank trucks and railroad tank cars. JB would handle the bulk of Atlas production, which—when it went onstream—would flow through the Magnolia pipeline to the north to El Dorado and through Project 5 to Helena, Arkansas and from there up the Mississippi to the northern markets.

This development, which had emerged from his original effort to blend his three suppliers together in purchasing the old Texas line, had now grown more complex, and was to lift Triangle into a very important Gulf position. Dave Smitherman believed that Triangle, by this move, increased its volume to "at least fifty thousand barrels of petroleum product a day from the Louisiana area alone."

He was right. Triangle tripled its volume in 1947, and in 1948 was continuing to move upward at the same nearly startling rate.

But the course of business is seldom smooth. When JB and his partners approached Magnolia to conclude their arrangement to tie their new pipeline from the Carthage field into the Magnolia line to El Dorado, they received a surprise. The price had gone up from the figure of $90,000 originally discussed, to $130,000.

"Why, the Magnolia line's almost thirty years old," JB protested.

Mr. True elevated himself to his full height and looked sinister. "I don't care," he said, "I hope it'll last fifty years."

They were trapped. They had laid a line from Carthage to Shreveport, and built a lateral at Benton, Louisiana, which tied the production from the Carthage field and the Cotton Valley field. The acquisition of the Atlas Refinery had tied this all together, and the use of the Magnolia line to carry products northward to El Dorado and from there to the Project 5 pipeline to the Mississippi was integral to their investments and their plans.

Mr. True, however, was in control of the Magnolia line, and had changed his terms. JB called Slats Latimer and asked if his group could have a twenty-year lease. Slats's voice came back crisply over the phone. Magnolia had placed Mr. True in charge of such decisions, and Mr. True wanted to lease the Magnolia line for only one year, with a six-month cancellation clause.

They signed with a sense of foreboding. They feared an ambush was being prepared.

The world in the first half of 1948 was dividing, despite all protestations to the contrary, between the USSR and the United States. The Soviets had moved in force into Manchuria and north Korea, and the Kurile Islands north of Japan in Asia. Their aim was to link their forces with the Chinese Communists under Mao Tse-tung. They also wanted to share in the occupation of Japan, but Truman refused.

Inside the Soviet Union, where force and suspicion reigned supreme, Stalin took the precaution of sending the wives and children of Molotov and Anastas Mikoyan to exile and prison, to insure the loyalty of these close associates.[29] Such a régime could not afford close contacts with the West, could not allow tourists to enter and wander at will, and could not bear the discussion and comment that marked the western world. Instead the USSR was sealed, as cryptic as a tomb. Its moves in Asia were shrouded and mysterious and beyond the range of western observation. Its moves in the West were closer—and created fear.

29. Ulam, *Expansion and Coexistence*, p. 399.

In early 1948 the Communists of Czechoslovakia provoked a crisis, and President Eduard Beneš—who had, years earlier, been forced to bow to Nazis—now bowed to their former allies. A few months later Communist Klement Gottwald assumed complete power. The United States stepped up the Marshall Plan, and Congress voted the first five billion dollars for the purpose.

Nevertheless, pro-Soviet propagandists in the United States continued to mount a noisy campaign for friendship. A veil has been drawn over this campaign and its spokesmen and puppets, but its reality in 1948 was overpowering. It was an election year; the rhetoric about wartime friendship still echoed in the air. A group calling itself the Independent Progressive party was formed under the guiding hands of the Communist party of the USA, to nominate Henry Wallace and Senator Glen Taylor of Idaho for the Presidency. Its central platform was that the nation should acquiesce in moves that favored the Soviets.

At the same time large numbers of Southerners, dissatisfied with the expanding civil rights program of the Administration, broke away and formed a States Rights party. Their nominees were Governor J. Strom Thurmond of South Carolina and Governor Fielding Wright of Mississippi.

These signs of domestic discord and growing polarization were reflected even inside the main group of the Democratic party itself, which provided grudging and unwilling support to the nomination of President Truman and Senator Alben Barkley of Kentucky. The President made his acceptance speech to a nearly empty hall. Virtually every expert in the country believed his chances were faint, if not invisible.

Choosing a time when anything that the White House chose to do would exacerbate its problems, the USSR then cut off all land access to Berlin by the Allies. The city, which could not exist without western supplies, was clearly expected to fall into the waiting hands of the commissars. Instead an airlift was mounted by both the United States and Britain, using British bases. The effort, designed to maintain a metropolis under siege, succeeded in supporting the city on a low but bearable level. Both sides, therefore, had behaved in a manner the world would grow to expect from each. The Soviets had thrown down a gauntlet, and the Americans had mounted a relief mission.

The times were, in other words, quarrelsome. Strains and tensions seemed to arise in every quarter; few regions or sectors escaped. In the United States those winds were muted but blew the election campaigns into shrill and ugly charges. Extremists had platforms; the centers were

321

as soft as sponges. The President campaigned against Congress, which he termed the worst ever. The Republicans nominated Dewey, who made the same error against Truman that he had against Roosevelt four years earlier: he avoided all hard issues, assumed a lofty attitude, and campaigned beneath signs that cryptically read, Had Enough? That left Truman free to raise every possible issue, and to blame the Republicans for all the ills of the human condition and Congress with their invention.

In Shreveport, meanwhile, the partners learned how difficult times could become, when they received word from Mr. True—Snake True—that their lease on Magnolia, active for six months with a six-month cancellation clause, was canceled. That gave them six months more on the pipeline to El Dorado, without which they could not convey the Shreveport refinery products profitably to market.

JB called an emergency meeting in the offices of Clive Alexander, which were located across the street from the Magnolia offices in Dallas. All the partners appeared, and their faces were grim. "There's no question that they're forcing us to buy the line," he said. "The only question is how much we are willing to pay." The board decided to pay whatever True demanded—up to one million dollars.

JB walked across the street and into True's office. "You've got us in a spot," he admitted, "and my board's in session now. All of us think you're trying to put us out of business."

Mr. True looked shocked, and said, "Oh, no."

"How much do you want for the line?" JB asked.

"Not less than one million dollars," Mr. True said. He had done his homework; the figure represented the breakline between buying the line or constructing a new one.

"It's not worth over one hundred and fifty thousand dollars or two hundred thousand dollars," JB said bitterly, "but we'll pay the million."

"I'll have to take it up with my board," True said at once, and JB's bile rose. True's charade was unconvincing; ill will loomed in the background.

"Are the majors behind this?" he asked. That suspicion was natural enough. The gulf between the majors and independents in the petroleum industry is a Hatfield and McCoy situation; a thousand plots and counterplots, strategic advances, and struggles attest to its factual basis.

Mr. True, however, indicated that he had to go into conference, and gathered his papers. Elaborately courteous, he suggested that JB tour the Magnolia offices, and the Triangle head allowed himself to be led, briefly, away by Roy Stevens. Stevens was the Magnolia manager of Branded Stations.

JB, still wondering about Magnolia's purpose in applying such pressure, wondered aloud if Magnolia was concerned about the inroads that he and his partners might make in the Gulf region. "If it's the product that is bothering your firm," he said, "we could make a different arrangement. Magnolia could handle the gasoline distribution in this area."

Stevens looked disdainful. "I wouldn't have recycled gasoline in my pumps," he said—and JB, already feeling injured, exploded.

"Wait a minute," he said harshly. "I didn't come here to be insulted." He walked away rapidly, leaving Stevens to stare, and stormed back into Mr. True's office. "I'm tired of this run-around," he said angrily. "You may put me out of business, but I'll go down swinging!"

Mr. True was startled and for the first time showed some signs of uncertainty. "Please don't get mad," he said. "We'll work this out."

The air cleared, though not enough to please JB. At any rate, Mr. True knew that the limits had been reached, and matters then proceeded quickly. A letter of intent was drawn and signed; the transaction, saving later formalities, was concluded. JB went back across the street to his board and told his associates that they—and Triangle—now owned the Magnolia pipeline that ran from Shreveport to El Dorado, at a cost of one million dollars.

His associates looked at one another, and Dick Williams of the Chicago Corporation voiced a common concern. "Suppose the Project Five owners pull the same stunt?" he asked. "We'll be held up again."

After some discussion it was agreed they should prepare against that possibility; all of them were now aware that the pipeline business had a rough underside. Mr. True had taught them that. The Project 5 pipeline, which ran from El Dorado to Helena, Arkansas, was ninety-six miles long. They decided to authorize Dick Williams to order, in the name of Triangle Pipelines, five hundred miles of ten-inch pipe—just in case. That was, of course, much more pipe than was needed, but such orders had to be placed well in advance with the steel people in order to be filled, and pipe is a commercial commodity that can be used in trades.

A few weeks later they learned they were not quite through with Mr. True. He called to say that Magnolia had sold only its pipeline, not its pumping station or its telephone system. He was, clearly, all set to wring more money out of them.

"You can keep the telephone line," JB told him. "We'll use radio." Thereupon Mr. True, irked at being balked of his last twist of their arms, sent crews out to the pumping station to tear the roof off, making it unusable.

Despite the conflicts, personalities, and difficulties of the Magnolia acquisition, however, it constituted an important advance for Triangle, and further solidified the firm's position, standing, and stature. Other sectors of JB's life expanded as well. He and Eddy maintained their large, pillared home in the River Oaks district of Houston on Inwood Street, and the city burgeoned around them.

New firms launched ventures in Houston, and many others moved either their headquarters or important branches into the Gulf center. One result was that Houston clubs had long waiting lists—a situation that creates a psychological sense of being crowded.

"Let's build a new club," Ralph Rupley said to JB, and JB came to attention. He knew that Rupley, a furrier and a good friend, had purchased an immense, sprawling estate in the Lakeside district and probably wanted to get out from under. But that was unimportant beside the larger fact that Houston badly needed a new club, suitable for families.

Once resolved, they formed a group of ten men for the purpose. Besides Rupley and JB, these included Robert Rogers, Clayton Smith, Ralph Johnson, Wyatt Hedrick, Thomas Bates, Walter Sterling, W. Stewart Boyle, and Dr. L. S. Crocker. The men surveyed the estate Rupley had purchased from Clifford Moores, a wealthy oilman who had moved to Kentucky.

Located in the bayou region with a nearby lake, the land around the large house was often flooded. Moores had steel doors and shutters constructed that could be closed and tightened by turnbuckles to seal and secure the lower half of the residence. In the side of the yard he kept a boat, whose painter was attached to the rail of his bedroom balcony on the second floor.

When the land around the house was flooded, the boat slowly bobbed upward till it was even with the large French windows of the bedroom. Moores would step out on the balcony, pull the boat close, and cast off. He would return later and resume life inside the house. He didn't care to have his routine disturbed by transient floods.

The estate contained other curiosities. One was a special gravesite in which a greatly loved horse had been buried. The stables on the estate had stalls for sixty horses, as well as riding rings.

The organizers soon collected two hundred advance entrance fees and had plans drawn for various improvements. The scene attracted future members and their families as the project proceeded. JB noticed on one weekend that some children played almost all one afternoon in a large mound of leaves located at one end of the old-fashioned porch. Later, when the workmen cleared the leaves away, it was discovered that the mound had been a haven for several varieties of snakes, including deadly corals, rattlers, and water moccasins.

Still later, as land was cleared for a golf course, a similar phenomenon was noted: hundreds of snakes emerged and had to be killed. Building proceeded rapidly, however. In addition to the golf course, a skeet range and traps was installed, bridle paths built, and horses placed in the stables. JB had five.

The club was designed to attract families whose members had diverse tastes; the organizers believed Houston needed a new family club more than any other. The entire creation was, on the part of the organizers, a nonprofit venture. But JB seldom entered upon any activity without making some peripheral observations.

The Lakeside Country Club occupied about two hundred acres of land. A much larger tract was unused nearby. JB suggested that he and the other nine organizers buy that land and wait for it to rise in value. They did, and acquired eleven hundred acres. Meanwhile the Lakeside Country Club opened its door and was an immediate success. It soon accumulated a long waiting list.

The nation went to the polls in November, 1948, and the voters disclosed a remarkable contradiction between their attitudes and the assumptions of the experts and journalists. Dewey's initial vote was large enough to deceive the Chicago *Tribune* into a premature and incorrect "extra" hailing his election. In the late hours the vote began to swing toward the President; by morning it was clear Truman had scored an upset. His vote was 24 million; Dewey lost with 21.1 million. The States Rights party carried four states. The Wallace effort trailed with only a little more than 1 million votes. The sign of a regional swing away from the Administration was largely ignored in the enormous surprise of the Truman upset. So was the fact that a minority Presidency reflected a divided nation.

The division centered, in part, on the Communist issue. The House Un-American Affairs Committee had disclosed testimony indicating a considerable number of Communists in the bureaucracy, and in December, 1948, the testimony of a *Time* senior editor, naming Alger Hiss, a former State Department official, created a sensation. The Administration, however, refused to acknowledge that its ranks harbored Communists and deprecated the importance of that movement at home while forming a strong alliance against it abroad.

That paradox reflected widespread confusion about communism as such. Its doctrines had achieved academic respectability and were fostered by continuing disbelief in its atrocities. Press coverage of the USSR in the West continued to protect the crimes of the régime from the knowledge of the world. Although the leaders of the American

Communist party were indicted by a federal grand jury and placed on trial for advocating the forcible overthrow of the government, many persons remained disturbed regarding the limits of intellectual freedom that this measure implied.

The United States was caught in a historic dilemma, reminiscent of the crisis in the ancient, long-dead Roman Empire, whose tolerant system broke under the strain presented by an irreconcilable minority in the form of the early Christians. The parallel was not exact; no historical parallel can be more than roughly analogous. The problem in the past had been with a group that disdained the demands of the state; the problem that confronted the United States in 1948 was with a group that demanded its legal rights in order to end the legal rights of others.

In January, 1949, President Truman, who had decided the election was in favor of a greater program of social benefits from the government, announced the Fair Deal, asking for repeal of the Taft-Hartley Act, a minimum wage law, increased farm supports, low-rent public housing, and a long list of other Treasury-funded measures. He also extended his program of foreign aid to include a Point Four program designed to assist the poverty-stricken and unindustrialized areas of the world. Both these propositions reflected the assumption that discontent has an economic base, and that lifting the standard of living of other nations would enhance and extend American influence.

On the other side of the world, the Kremlin was also taking steps to strengthen its position, but despite the fabled economic base of Marxism, they were distinctly uneconomic. Stalin was engaged in purely political and military moves, in which force and persuasion intertwined in a manner the commissars had long made familiar to their minions. The Yugoslavs received brutal letters demanding total subservience to pro-Soviet individuals in their leadership and in the operation of their nation. A purge was conducted among the other satellites. Because Mao Tse-tung was forcing Chiang Kai-shek's armies into retreat on all fronts, the Kremlin took a softer tone regarding the Communists of China. Stalin even agreed to withdraw from Manchuria. That was the first backward step the USSR had taken voluntarily since 1918. But Soviet forces remained in North Korea.

As usual these grim events and mysterious movements seemed to be on another planet from the United States. The national income was at a record level; signs of burgeoning prosperity were visible on all sectors, Detroit moved into its greatest year ever, and the arts flourished. *Death of a Salesman* appeared on Broadway, but its grim theme was sharply contrasted by *South Pacific*. Books with a distinctly religious tone became unexpected best-sellers: *The Greatest Story Ever Told* by Fulton Oursler, *Peace of Soul*, by Fulton J. Sheen, and *A Guide to Confident Living* by Norman Vincent Peale. The fact was that the United States, with its monopoly of the atomic bomb, its enormous prestige and rising standard of living, its popularity in western Europe, seemed confused but optimistic in 1949.

Business in 1949 continued to move forward. Triangle was not the only firm expanding; the entire business sector of the United States was moving, and the larger firms were expanding abroad, while lesser enterprises expanded at home. JB was forced to constant travels, and so were Barksdale and Tinsley. All of them used planes. Their swings were shorter than in the years when trains would take several days to cover long distances, and men were forced away from home for weeks at a time. Mrs. Saunders seldom traveled; her health was uncertain and she was subject to frequent illnesses, though she seemed to recover fairly well. JB, therefore, made it a point to be home on weekends. Young Suzanne was hardly aware he traveled. "He seemed to be around most of the time," she said, years later.

Yet he did travel, and became as familiar with the underground tunnels that stretch for blocks under Rockefeller Plaza as any long-time New York resident. Triangle's contracts were increasing as cycling plants emerged; he had an agreement with the California Oil Company to market the output of its Hico-Knowles plant at Hilly, Louisiana, signed with Harold Teasdel, president of California, and Harold Brennan, a vice president.[30]

Toward the close of the previous year Triangle signed up the Silsbee, Texas, plant of the American Republic Corporation with its chairman of the board, George Irvine. And in February, 1949, it signed the DX Sunray Oil Company to handle the production of its Benton, Louisiana, plant.

Any of these contracts would, not many years before, have created jubilation at Triangle; by 1949 they were another part of an on-going and increasingly important business.

Yet that business was widely misunderstood, for it appeared to be intangible. Triangle had only twenty-three employees in its central operation. Its Triangle Pipelines, it is true, had some more, but pipelines do not require a large staff, and JB had partners in that venture. He was a partner with Butler & Company, which had drilled a discovery well in Pierce Junction, Texas—and followed that by drilling ten more producing wells. JB had offered, when Butler launched his venture, to pay half its losses in return for 10 percent of its profits and no salary; he had guaranteed a draw of $75,000 a year for the first five

30. A year earlier Triangle had signed a similar contract with Paul Raigorodsky, Pat Marr, and Wilburt Holleman to handle the output of the Bernice, Louisiana, plant of the Claiborne Gasoline Company.

years. But only $30,000 of that was drawn; Butler and Miller had hit from the start. JB's participation in that venture, however, did not appear on the surface. Neither did the Southern Barge Lines; neither did all the tank cars and trucks established under different entities. A stranger, dropping in on the Triangle offices in Houston, did not realize its size and importance.

Yet Triangle was becoming an important market factor. Recycled gasoline competed with the straight-run refinery product and—in the curious manner in which people invest inanimate objects and even commodities with their social values—was held to be somehow inferior. The idea that one method of processing makes a product better than another, when both meet the same specifications, is of course fairly ludicrous. But people are swayed by the weight of general usage. Recycled gasoline had a sort of country image to it; it came from plants in the heart of Oil Country and not from the huge, glistening refineries of the majors.

At an API committee meeting JB sat silent as one man after another, during a difficult marketing period, grumbled aloud about the disruptive price-cutting wars provoked by independents. Nobody looked directly at JB, but the entire assemblage knew he was the target. Finally Harry Kennedy, an executive with Continental Oil, rose angrily and said, "You're all so busy being *presidents* that you don't realize what JB does for the industry."

A New York man muttered, "He has plenty of big protectors."

"No way," JB said quickly. "I buy and sell."

But Kennedy was not to be cut off. "JB keeps surplus off the market," he said. "He doesn't hurt anybody. You should give him a medal."

He sat down, red-faced; his sincerity was obvious and his remarks embarrassed them. The men grew aware they had been baiting a member and the conversation changed, never again to resume on that level. JB was very grateful.

Business is, however, a rough scramble. The stakes are livelihoods and the fruits of the good life; there are no second-place prizes for the losers, and sometimes the collisions are bruising.

In Shreveport the Atlas Processing Company, a research effort mounted by Vernon Chance, ran some of the recycled gasoline used by the Atlas Refinery through a series of tests. Those were inspired by an observation of Vernon Chance's, who had become president of the Atlas Refinery with a five-year contract, that the recycled charge stock smelled of benzene.

The Atlas tests proved the recycled gasoline had, indeed, a natural benzene content to a remarkable degree. A sample was sent to the Shell labs in California and was so unusual Shell asked for another; they couldn't believe the first. The partners were elated; it was serendipity in action. Benzene was in short supply and its price was high; the chemical companies were scouring the landscape.

JB's approach to this situation was complex. "We were a tangle of partners," he said later, "consisting of three producers and a marketer." The technologists, as always, were sure that an excellent product would settle all problems, but JB was not so sure. On that end he contacted both Monsanto and Dow Chemical, two very large chemical firms in need of a source of benzene, and negotiated with them until he had Monsanto signed to a five-year contract to buy Atlas benzene at fifty cents a gallon, escalated on the posted price of east Texas crude oil.

The sales end secured, JB then turned toward the supply situation. He went to the three largest crude-oil producers in the region and explained the Atlas need to upgrade its gasoline and to install expensive new equipment to produce benzene. Since the producers regard refiners with eternal and unremitting suspicion, he offered to share the profits of benzene per gallon in return for an assured supply. The combination provided a steady source. It cut the costs of the refinery upgrading to an eighth of a cent per gallon, secured sales, and also buckled down the price of benzene from Atlas by attaching it to the price of crude.

In all, it was a neat package that tied every possible end into a neat knot. The refinery was able to produce 80- and 90-octane gasoline, as well as benzene, for which it had a long-term contract. The package seemed even better when JB managed to sign Reichold Chemicals to a benzene contract, at fifty cents a gallon, when the Monsanto contract expired.

It was not too long, however, before the package began to unravel under the shifting winds of the marketplace. Other refiners beside Atlas had taken note of the benzene shortage, and rushed to install equipment and enter into its production. The price began to sag, and the marketplace began to fill with benzene. Soon that tide grew to a flood, and the price sank to the bottom.

Monsanto's concern rose as the price of benzene dropped. In almost comically precise reflection, the chemical firm's executives increased their campaign, which began with hints and complaints and rose to increasingly shrill letters, and finally phone calls. JB was astonished. One man grew abusive on the phone, and JB threatened to "come and slug hell out of him." Another—Felix Williams, an officer and director of the firm—flew to Houston in a private plane. JB went to the airport, climbed in the plane, and the two held "a gut-level talk."

Williams announced he would stay in Houston until the impasse was resolved, and JB put him up at the Shamrock Hotel. Privately he was shocked. The petroleum industry operated on the basis of firm contracts, in many instances based only on a man's word. The idea of crying because the shoe pinched later was enough to end a man's chances of doing business in oil, or its ramifications. Clearly the chemical industry had different rules.

Eventually Williams tired of hearing his own arguments and JB's responses, and left town. JB learned, however, that the firm attempted to obtain a list of the crude producers so these gentlemen could hear its woes, and soften their position. That made him smile; he had never heard of a producer willing to reduce his price in order to improve someone else's profits.

The next turn of the screw was when Monsanto paid under protest, and the issue went to arbitration. The contracts were clear, and the decision went against Monsanto. JB, leaving the building with several Monsanto men walking beside him, was surprised to see that they were relatively calm and cheerful. "We had to try," one said.

A little later Reichhold Chemicals went through some exertions on the same subject, for the same reasons. Mr. Henry Reichhold himself appeared, and stormed into Vernon Chance's office, trailed by a couple of his executives. He proved to be a physically large man who spoke with a heavy accent.

Mr. Reichhold grew excited when Vernon Chance asked, "What happened to the price of benzene?"

"You vant me to told you vat's wrong," Riechhold shouted, "the oil people have fock it up! They build, build, build!"

As he spoke he shook one huge finger near JB's face, who grew angry himself, and jumped to his feet. "Wait a minute," he said, "you can't talk to me that way; I don't care how big you are."

Reichhold looked surprised, but he backed off, growling and muttering. The outcome was the same as with Monsanto; the contracts held. JB shook his head. "In the petroleum industry we pay for our mistakes," he said. All the pawing of the earth couldn't persuade the producers, a refinery, and a marketing company that they should reduce their earnings because large firms did not foresee market changes. But it was clear the chemical men were, he said later, "a different breed."

The balance of 1949 was filled with stupendous news, from both inside and outside the nation. The Communist party leaders, on trial for promoting violent revolution, had provided the nation's courts and lawyers with a startling series of tactics. Baiting the judge, abusing witnesses, protesting the "undemocratic" nature of the grand jury that indicted them and the panel that sat in judgment at the trial, they mounted a defense that constituted an insult to their countrymen. Virtually none of the newspapers that reported the trial of the American Communists drew readers' attention to the striking contrast of their trial, with its battery of belligerent defense attorneys, and the show trials of various Communist leaders in the countries of eastern Europe, underway at the same time. In the foreign tribunals the defense attorneys sat mute while the defendants accused themselves and confessed to incredible conspiracies and far-fetched activities, and delivered lengthy abnegations.

The American Communists, found guilty of conspiracy, received sentences of up to five and up to three years, with chances of earlier paroles. All the defense attorneys received mild punishments for contempt. The Communists of Hungary and Czechoslovakia, tried by their former comrades, were punished by firing squads and the hangman's noose.

On an international scale, 1949 was a year of surprises. The British recognized the independence of Eire, and the United States withdrew its occupation forces from South Korea; Chiang Kai-shek abandoned the mainland of China and established new headquarters in Formosa, and the Berlin airlift—after 277,264 flights—came to an end. The Soviets allowed land traffic to the beleaguered city again, and the Kremlin broke with Tito.

Nevertheless the NATO pact was signed, pledging the West to mutual assistance in the event of Soviet attack in the West.

Toward autumn a shiver went through the world: the Atomic Energy Commission announced that American instruments had detected the detonation of an atomic bomb in Soviet Siberia. That news astonished people who had been assured the USSR would be years in learning or applying such technology; it would not be until later that the existence of several spy networks would be bared, or that the concentrated efforts of which the Soviet laboratories were capable would be appreciated.

All that was clear was that the quality of life was now irrevocably altered, not—as some would claim—by the developments of science, but by the fact that these developments were now in fanatic hands, and because the period of American dominance was no longer absolute.

Yet the year 1949 did not reflect these new realities on any ordinary level in the United States; the nation's physical isolation still provided a moat of distance that kept its activities complete in themselves. JB was at an API meeting and had a pleasant chat with Al Peake, who turned away, saying, "I'll see you tonight at the Twenty-five Year Club."

"No you won't," JB replied. "The Twenty-five Year Club is for majors; independents are only allowed inside when they're old, and won't live long."

"What?" said Peake, shocked. He turned and asked, "Ashton, do you have a petition?"

H. T. Ashton, a Mobil executive, said he had. Peake filled in JB's name, signed it as a sponsor, and then called over Dick Wagner, head of the Chicago Corporation, who also signed it. Peake handed it in, and said, "Don't let it lie."

In the autumn JB received official notice that he had been accepted into the industry's most exclusive club. He was very pleased.

There were other signs of recognition. On his trips to New York he would call on a number of men in major petroleum firms; he had a very large and growing volume of products to sell, and needed large and on-going contracts. "Some of them were very difficult," he said. "New York does something to executives. Most of them kept me waiting and were seldom on time with their appointments. When I entered they would look at their watches, as though they were short of time. Yet most were men whom I could buy or sell, who only had jobs."

There was, however, a significant exception. When JB called on Jack Rathbone at Jersey Standard, he always came to the phone and invariably made an early-morning appointment, often at 7:00 A.M. JB would appear promptly and Rathbone, moving at the top of the world's largest firm, would be just as prompt. They would discuss developments in the industry, mutual acquaintances, and trends. JB would depart, having done business and having done it with a courteous and knowledgeable man who understood Triangle—and its importance.

The new year 1950 marked the middle of the twentieth century; one that had entered history bursting with optimism and pride, sure of universal peace, progress, and prosperity to come. Its first fifty years had seen virtually all these illusions hideously dashed. The century had seen torture restored by the state, mass massacres, huge wars, and angry ideological arguments which resembled the religious wars of the past in complexity and passion—but in which God was denied.

In such a period the helplessness of individuals to order their own lives seemed clear beyond expression in the lands under the sway of the Kremlin, but the greatest number of complaints that rose came from the intellectuals of the West.

Ordinary men had difficulty in understanding this. The second trial of Alger Hiss, whose elegant manners and fashionable attitudes won him much sympathy from academia and some quarters of the government, shocked the ordinary citizen. Mr. Hiss was convicted of perjury when he denied he had been an agent of the USSR.

The case had many ramifications; it elevated a formerly obscure congressman from California named Richard Nixon; incensed the President of the United States, who regarded it all as a political ploy against his Administration—and set off a Senate inquiry into communism.

Other matters were similarly inspired by communism overseas. The Pentagon, alarmed at the Soviet possession of the A-bomb, launched a massive series of warning-system stations, air bases, and military installations from the Atlantic almost to the Persian Gulf, to guard against a surprise Soviet attack.

One result was a partial restoration of the wartime defense industries and an attendant heating of the domestic economy. Inflationary pressures rose; huge sums rolled around the world from Washington, funneled through myriad agencies, committees, and enterprises.

The petroleum industry soared as though propelled by giant winds; its efforts in foreign lands expanded, and energies of its domestic firms increased. It was these pressures, no doubt, that in part impelled Gulf Oil, majority owner and operator of the Project 5 pipeline that ran from El Dorado, Arkansas, to Helena on the Mississippi, to suddenly squeeze Triangle and its partners.

The Gulf Oil squeeze was more sophisticated than Mr. True's methods; it had to be, for the clear economic hardship it created might lead to a successful appeal to the authorities. The owners of Project 5, therefore, did not threaten to cancel Triangle's product. Instead they declared the line was overburdened and therefore the owners were unable to accommodate all the tenders they received. With elaborate surface justice, all users would be placed on a quota system. And Triangle's place in that quota system would not only be necessarily limited, but would have to be used only in a single period toward the end of the month.

"That would mean," JB said, "that we would have to assemble a giant fleet of tows and barges at Helena, Arkansas, to carry our products from the end of the pipeline up the river to market in a huge single shipment. That was clearly impossible." They were, quite cleverly, pushed between the sword and the wall.

An emergency meeting was held between JB and his United Gas, Carthage, and Chicago Corporation partners. As usual, the crisis came at the worst possible time. Numbers of new cycling plants had been built in northern Louisiana. They were landlocked and had no access to pipelines. New feeder lines would have to be built, and additional terminals established along the Mississippi and in cities on other inland waterways; Triangle would have to widen its sales to handle a growing volume of production. In other words, a great expansion was underway. Project 5 owners had chosen a time when Triangle's pyramid was precariously balanced to grab it by the ankle. From the outside it looked very much as though the firm and its partners might be pulled to a crashing fall in the Gulf.

It was clear that heavy financing would be needed to build another pipeline to the Mississippi River connected with the one already purchased from Magnolia that ended in El Dorado.

That was 96 miles, but the partners had foresightedly ordered 500 miles of pipe. By trading 404 miles of pipe steel for sheet steel, they were able to build several tanks on the Mississippi, with capacities of 80,000 to 120,000 barrels, each. They also bought 4 ancient tanks, each of which had a capacity of 55,000 barrels, from Magnolia in El Dorado. The tops and bottoms of these tanks were in disrepair, but the group had enough sheet steel left over to replace these. Those measures gave them transfer tanks at El Dorado and tankage on the river.

JB meanwhile took a number of steps in preparation for the heavy financing the new pipeline product would cost Triangle. One step was to sell his several thousand railroad tank cars to the Keith Railway Equipment Company. The sale included his right to lease the cars back, and the lease terms enabled him to use the cars for two months less than three years, at no cost. That meant that an on-going expense was, in effect, eliminated for that period of time, and his profit margins correspondingly improved, while maintaining his distribution on the railroads.

Another very important step was to ensure that the new pipeline would have enough traffic to convince the financiers that it would pay for itself. JB called his old friend from El Dorado days, Bob Aycock. Aycock had become a vice president of the Pan-Am Southern Corporation, headquartered in New Orleans. Pan-Am Southern was really the old Root Oil Company with a new name bestowed upon it by its new owners, Standard of Indiana.[31]

31. Philip Hamilton, John Atkins's brother-in-law, the owner of Root Oil, had sold it to Indiana Standard in 1947 for Indiana stock valued at that time at an estimated $6 million. It later soared to much higher figures.

Like its predecessor, Pan-Am Southern sold to a limited number of huge firms and interests. At the time JB called, Aycock was supplying the British with immense quantities of diesel fuel, due to the cut-off of that commodity by Iranian extremists. It is a small, interconnected world.

Nevertheless, Pan-Am Southern had a refinery at El Dorado and had to have its products transported like every other firm. JB had already been told that it was subject to the same Project 5 squeeze as Triangle and its partners. Aycock, reached by phone, by coincidence was meeting with his own board to discuss the same problem at the same time.

JB, who knew Bruce Brown, the head of Pan-Am Southern, and Sam Casey, a senior executive with the firm, as well as Aycock, said, "We want to build our own pipeline, and we need a contract from you to do it." Aycock sounded eager, and the men agreed to get together.

JB, Dick Williams, and Fred Fues of the Chicago Corporation went to New Orleans and met Bruce Brown, Sam Casey, and Bob Aycock shortly afterward. They wrestled with volumes, prices, and long and short considerations. JB's Triangle Refineries gave a letter of intent to Triangle Pipeline to ship thirty thousand barrels of product through the line daily for the next ten years, at eight cents a barrel. The Pan-Am Southern executives then signed a letter of intent on behalf of their firm, declaring its intention to ship ten thousand barrels a day at eight cents a barrel for the same period.

Armed with these instruments, JB went to Herb Seydler. His banker friend knew about the situation; JB's visit was no surprise. JB had long ago formed the habit of keeping Seydler abreast of developments. "Nobody likes surprises," he said, "and I discovered that if I discussed situations as they developed, it wasn't necessary to explain them in detail when fast action was needed."

In any event, Seydler was already involved. He and JB had gone to New York together on the first stage of the pipeline ventures, when Triangle, Carthage, United Gas, and the Chicago Corporation had sought financing for the Carthage–Shreveport line.

On that occasion they had sought between four million and five million dollars from New York Life. JB, for whom that was to be the first of many such sessions, found it absorbing, not to say memorable. The great insurance firm, which lived—as do all insurance firms—from its investments and not from premiums, had assigned three men to listen to the proposition. One, who did the negotiating and asked the questions, was in early middle age as that category is loosely defined, and was about forty years old. He was flanked on one side by a man about fifteen years or more older, who said very little, but often whispered in the negotiator's ear or handed him a slip of paper. On the other side was a younger man, who watched, listened, and took notes.

It was like confronting the present, the past, and the future all rolled together.

One of the men asked JB if he would get a letter from the Interstate Commerce Commission guaranteeing that no change of rate would be made until the debt was paid. JB was astonished; he said, "It would be just as easy to get a letter from the Deity."

Seydler, watching his client, was impressed. "He talked to the New Yorkers," he said later, "like an experienced financier. I was surprised."

Nevertheless, the effort was fruitless. In the end, New York Life refused the loan. Seydler and JB had, on that occasion, gone to the Harris Trust and Savings in Chicago, a corresponding bank with Seydler's Second National, and there obtained their financing.

Their second venture, regarding the financing of the ninety-six-mile pipeline from El Dorado to the Mississippi, however, would require approximately fifteen million dollars. And Seydler and JB decided—or rather the banker decided—to try New York Life again. The banker went first, to make the initial presentation and JB followed him into New York City three days later.

He checked into the Barclay, a favorite oilman's hotel. New York City was very familiar to him; its streets contained many memories. He recalled an episode from the darkest days of the Depression when he had been lavishly entertained by some men from a downtown investment house, who were under the impression, when he was with Hassett, that Imperial Oil meant the huge Imperial Oil of Canada. They cooled remarkably when they discovered their mistake.

In the years since then JB had been in and out of the megalopolis more often than he could count. But he knew why Seydler wanted to try New York Life again. Once the financial gates of New York opened, a firm could move forward very rapidly.

Once again they sat before the insurance company triumvirate, and answered the questions posed by the figure in the center while the older man slipped notes and the younger watched, listened, and made marks on his memo pad.

Despite the fact that Seydler had been there for several sessions in advance, the New York Life negotiator insisted on going over the same ground again with JB. Seydler's patience snapped, and to JB's surprise, the banker rose and began to gather his papers into his briefcase.

"American Express has money," he said, "and so do other available firms and institutions. I'm not going through this wringer any longer; you're wasting our time."

That broke the impasse. The New York Life men soothed Seydler, and the first line of financing was assumed. The high tower was breached. Seydler and JB left New York City cheerfully; the ninety-six-mile pipeline venture appeared assured.

As the year 1950 extended, the sums being expended in the Marshall Plan and the Truman Doctrine grew to over twenty-five billion dollars. A Civilian Mobilization Office had been created; the armed services combined in reorganization, and the air was filled with charges of Communist infiltration and activities. J. Edgar Hoover announced the American Communist party had an official membership of 55,000, and 500,000 fellow travelers inside the United States.[32]

Inflation and a series of new contracts had carried the average wage up 130 percent from 1939, and television—a medium pioneered in Britain—was beginning to make a remarkable impact upon the land. The competition, the first since Hollywood had outdistanced the stage and vaudeville, spurred the movie-makers into unusual new offerings. The bikini—the irreducible bathing suit for women—had appeared; so did dungarees on young girls, and ballet shoes. American churches reported a perceptible increase in attendance, but that was not the only bright spot in a land growing increasingly prosperous. The phrase *Cold War* had come into being, but the average American could not quite grasp that it was a real war in all but a shooting sense.

In part that was due to the fragmented nature of traditional news coverage, in which world events are reported in terms of episodes sandwiched between department store advertisements. Most of the daily newspapers were devoted to crimes, entertainment features, comics, sports, snippets from local business, and whatever the editors thought might lift circulation. Radio and television followed the same pattern; advertisements, jingles, and interruptions made it difficult to sort trivia from significance. Overseas news has never been an American communications forte.

For that reason, the significance of the fall of China to the Communists was left to a handful to assess. Charges arose that Chiang Kai-shek had not been properly supported. In response the State Department issued a White Paper remarkable in its naïveté, detailing its various summaries at various times, revealing an amazing inability to understand the dynamics of the Communist movement.

That movement was moving, in fact, across all Asia. In Indochina a guerrilla campaign, mounted on the Chinese pattern, held the French to an expensive and grueling effort. Another rebellion was mounted in Malaysia and tied British forces in that region. Communists moved into key positions in Indonesia. Yet more attention was paid in the western

32. Carruth and Associates, *American Facts and Dates,* p. 568.

press to Europe. The commissars had sponsored one of their humorless campaigns for world peace. The effort consisted of gathering millions of petitions directed to Stockholm. Picasso, whose art and lifestyle were both anathema to the Kremlin but who was fashionably Communistic, donated an eccentric dove. Its counterparts fluttered everywhere in the West. Presumably this campaign, which gathered in a motley collection of amateurs in politics and professionals from academia, the arts, science, and society, was to persuade the United States to outlaw its A-bomb and to disassemble NATO. Since NATO consisted of eight divisions unable to communicate with one another in early 1950, whose weapons were not interchangeable and whose budget and orders were uncertain, it is more likely that the Stockholm peace effort was designed as a great feint—a ploy to direct attention away from Asia. If so, it was eminently successful.

Seydler and JB left New York and went to Chicago, to the Harris Trust and Savings. The Harris Bank, as it is informally known, was a corresponding bank with Seydler's Second National of Houston, and Ken Zwiener, who managed its Oil & Gas department, was a former protégé of Guy Reed, and very knowledgeable in all the phases of the petroleum industry.

JB was getting a pressure course in raising money. He was aware of it; he was impressed by Seydler's outspoken and no-nonsense attitude. Unlike the young man at New York Life, he did not need to take notes; the episodes were being etched on his memory.

Zwiener, a burly man who at one time had gone to Kansas and other discovery fields, hung out in bars, heard about deals, and rushed to finance the plays, received the entrepreneur and his banker very graciously. Charley Bliss, Zwiener's assistant, was present during the business meetings. He took special notice of JB at once. Unlike some oilmen who came bustling into Chicago and attempted to bulldoze, the Triangle head seemed a reasonable businessman.

Nevertheless the banking business is high-level poker; bankers learn to develop graven faces and hooded eyes. Neither of the Chicago men was effusive; they wanted to hear all the details of the proposition. Seydler and JB went over the situation; the bankers looked at Triangle's sales contracts as well as its production agreements.

Zwiener was pleased; he cross-examined JB and said, regarding the answers, "He knew where the eighths and quarters were." The banker liked the Triangle approach of tying up products on one end, then lining up transportation and selling on the other. "A good chain," he said.

338

Charley Bliss, a younger man at the time—as were they all—had another view. "I was really an assistant on the deal," he said, "and in that position one becomes accustomed to a certain degree of condescension. But JB treated me as an equal—and I appreciated that."

They left Chicago with the financing set. The Harris Bank would pick up where New York Life and the Second National of Houston reached their limit. More than that, the effort would consist not only of building a ninety-six-mile line from El Dorado to Arkansas City, Arkansas, on the Mississippi, but also to build some feeder lines to the Claiborne, Hilly, Lisbon, Dubach, and California plants, landlocked but productive, to fit them inside the completed system.

In Chicago JB and Seydler had found understanding and support. That was essential not only because financing for transportation reasons was essential, but also because these plants had to upgrade their products to compete in the octane race. Their owners would not make those investments unless they had an improved access to the marketplace.

These were interesting results. If courage, as someone wrote, is grace under pressure, then the reaction of JB and his associates to pressure was courageous, for they not only bore it with grace but also grew under its impetus.

The Soviet had withdrawn from North Korea. The situation in Europe had reached a curious stage. The United States had finally realized that only a strong Germany could provide stability in the center of the area, and preparations were underway to arm West Germany. The USSR protested, and called for a consultation.

Meanwhile Communist agitation increased in Japan, where it was —under the new Constitution—legal. China had gone Communist, and the United States, which had poured billions into the area and actually provided the arms the Communists used for success, had withdrawn in chagrin. The new Secretary of State, Dean Acheson, whose elegance inflamed some Republicans, made a speech saying that the United States would draw a defense line in the Pacific and, in his outline, left Korea apparently abandoned.

Stalin decided a Korean adventure could be mounted at minimum risk. The dictator had grown old—he was seventy-one—and his hair had turned thin and white. The late-night drinking parties he had enjoyed for years with a small coterie had dwindled, and his public appearances were infrequent. *Pravda* received strange documents from him; a lengthy one discussed linguistics. His entourage was more fearful than ever.

The fall of China was still reverberating in the air; the Soviet delegation in the UN walked out in anger because the United States refused to accept the new régime as a full member and to oust the Nationalist government on Taiwan.

The North Koreans attacked on June 25, 1950, at 4:00 A.M. Korean time—3:00 P.M. in Washington. The South was taken by surprise; its capital was machine-gunned from the air the next morning. That night, a Sunday, a special UN meeting of the Security Council was called. It met Monday morning and the Soviets were absent. A resolution was drafted demanding the North Koreans cease and withdraw, and calling on all member nations to "render every assistance" to the UN in carrying out the order.

The United States had a light cruiser and four destroyers nearby, a garrison force in South Korea, and more in Japan. None of the troops were especially combat-ready, but B-29s flew over and bombed the attackers. MacArthur surveyed the situation and told Washington that ground forces would have to be used. The United States was at war again.

Within weeks the President received emergency powers over the entire national economy, thousands of reservists were called up, and Congress appropriated ten billion dollars for the war effort.

Naval and air forces streamed toward Asia; petroleum firms found themselves once again confronted with large, first-priority government orders, and JB and his associates were knee-deep in problems building their pipeline.

One problem was unexpected. The pipe obtained from the Texas Company was screw pipe that had been underground, removed, and cleaned. Screw pipe is not satisfactory for gasoline, because leaks can occur around the collars. These were cut off and the pipe welded. The result was that the partners found themselves six miles short of pipe, and a fearful scramble at considerable extra cost was necessary to overcome that handicap.

Rights of way constituted a vexing problem. The government can commandeer, but private firms have to pay to traverse private property. Prices varied according to the property owner, and reflected many idiosyncratic ideas. One elderly woman, asked her price, said it was "God's will that the pipeline company pay her one thousand eight hundred fifty dollars to lay pipe across her property." That sum matched her son's medical bill, and she had prayed to receive it from heaven.

"She may be right," JB said, "Pay her the one thousand eight hundred fifty dollars."

A more serious obstacle arose regarding the land along the Mississippi River which they planned to use for a loading dock, and where they hoped to erect a terminal. The elderly lady who owned that land refused to sell for less than five hundred dollars an acre—a sum far in excess of the appraised value of her property or the surrounding area.

Matters were delayed while attempts were made to reach a more reasonable price, and it took a while for everyone to realize the lady was adamant. Dick Graves, heading the pipeline company, lost patience and bought some land a mile down the river for twenty-five dollars an acre. In laying that extra pipe, it was necessary to struggle through a swamp, bulldozing cypress trees, whose great gnarled roots sink deep and fiercely resist being uprooted. Excavations in a swamp present nightmarish problems; it is essential to fill them in almost instantaneously, for water, as everyone knows, rushes into the depression at once.

When that problem faded, another arose. The tanks were a mile from the loading dock. When a barge was to be loaded, it was necessary to station one man at the tank and another man at the dock, to signal each other when the loading was complete.

Such troubles undermined the project. Charley Bliss, at the Harris Bank in Chicago, received a call from Seydler in Houston, who described these woes and was graphic about the tottering nature of the enterprise. To impress the bankers with the reality of the problems, JB rented a plane, and he, Vernon Chance, Charley Bliss, and Herb Seydler flew over the entire area.

It was a memorable flight. "The plane fluttered and waved in high winds," JB recalls, "and Herb Seydler got sick."

Charley Bliss, blessed with a stronger stomach, nevertheless never forgot the journey. "It was," he said years later, "over a desolate area. The whole project was a Great Mess. It was necessary to recast the entire Plan."

At that juncture JB's character and personal history became the object of intense scrutiny. "How much pressure could he bear?" Bliss asked, retrospectively. "How would he hold up? What was his breaking point?"

In Korea other men were learning the answer to that question. The American and Korean troops, caught off guard, were pushed southward until only a foothold remained. But in October MacArthur mounted an unexpected strike at Pinchon, 150 miles north of the Thirty-Eighth Parallel, surprised the North Koreans, and reversed the situation. His next problem was whether he should proceed to exploit his sudden and brilliant victory.

Receiving permission to "establish order," he proceeded. The

President and the general met, meanwhile, at Wake Island, and came to an agreement on the future American course. Later the men contradicted one another on the nature of this agreement, and observers have chosen to accept the version of the man they find most credible. Other men than MacArthur, however, have contradicted President Truman's memory of private conversations.

The consensus of worry, however, was whether the Chinese Communists would intervene or not—and whether firm action on the part of the United States would provoke the Soviet Union. Adam Ulam, an expert on the USSR, has intimated, in a study of Soviet foreign policy, that they would not.[33] It was too much to their advantage to have the Americans and the Chinese Communists at war with each other. Unfortunately the uneasy relationship between Moscow and Peking was not, at the time, suspected in the West.

JB's behavior during the pipeline problem answered more questions than he realized. He went to the scene and surveyed the site where the loading tanks were erected at Arkansas City and, squinting, determined that one was leaning. Levels were brought and tests were made, and he was right. The tank had been constructed on a site that was half rock and half fill; it was bound to sag. Then JB dismissed Dick Graves and sent for Vernon Chance.

Chance was a refinery man but, like JB himself, was not tied to a single thread. He demanded double the salary that Graves had received. JB impatiently agreed and told him to straighten out the problems.

By the time he sat down to talk to the bankers, they were convinced of his character and mettle. Bliss remembers that JB, at one point, had said, "I have my family's money in this venture."

Bliss considered the whole project a maverick. "Seydler was a maverick banker who ran his own course," he said, though that didn't bother him—or Ken Zwiener. The Harris Bank, after all, had its own great maverick in Guy Reed—whom the others admired greatly. Nevertheless the changes in the plan were a headache. "Long-term financiers *hate* changes," Bliss added.

A Chicago insurance firm was dragged into the plot; nobody could endure the thought of a half-finished pipeline. That was about the most useless of all conceivable objects. The financial structure was redrawn and new terms settled, and the project proceeded to its conclusion. Triangle had its pipeline and, equally important, could now carry out its plans for expansion.

33. Ulam, *Expansion and Coexistence*, pp. 525-527.

The Americans in Korea were joined by token forces from Canada, Britain, Australia, The Netherlands, South Africa, and France. All told, these additions were minuscule, but they represented the UN nature of the effort. By November, 1950, however, MacArthur's forces entered the capital of North Korea and were mopping up the entire resistance forces. The United States held a remarkable victory in its hands; the troops expected their activity to be at an end by Christmas.

In retrospect it is doubtful if the nation really appreciated the extent of such a victory. It would have provided the basis for a renaissance of the western presence in Asia. Then Communist China struck and created another pell-mell retreat. Voices at home reflected not anger at the Chinese, but dismay and anger at General MacArthur. A clamor began to rise, charging that the government of South Korea was cruel and corrupt, and calling for peace. The troops at year's end struggled to maintain a position at the Thirty-eighth Parallel, and a great argument raged at home.

By early 1951 there were more women employed in the United States than ever before—more even than during World War II. The main reason for that was inflation; families had to have two breadwinners in order to retain or attain the standard of living they wanted. Price controls had been instituted, but not across the board. They consisted of some controlled items and some that remained free for the marketplace to set. The result was a market that was partly free, partly controlled, and partly black market.

None of this was new; the nation's leaders and political businessmen orated about free enterprise and normal conditions, but the persons who could recall either were no longer very young. JB was past fifty, and for almost half his life the nation had been in either a depression or a war.

Triangle, however, was moving onto the level of a large operation. Its volume at the close of the previous year had been $42 million. His headquarters staff had swelled, and he had more employees on the rivers, in terminals, on pipelines, in sales offices, and scattered through his participating ventures. He had become a large and, to some in the market, a menacing figure. The volume he handled could disrupt a region—could upset prices in whole sectors.

Feeder pipelines had been built to the Hilly, Claiborne, and Dubach plants, and he had established river terminals along the Tombigbee and Warrior rivers, as well as the Mississippi. Southern States Barge Lines carried long tows from the Arkansas City terminal to points north or east of Cairo, Illinois; his tank cars bore his products across the nation.

The Saunderses lived in a large, handsome house; JB had bought the lot next door and had it landscaped into a showplace. In order that Suzanne and JB III would not miss the outdoor pleasures he had known so well as a boy, he bought some land near Tomball, Texas, and turned it into a private preserve. It held a few horses, a tractor, and room to play for his children and their friends.

Children can be a lot of fun; JB would look forward to the horses and the kids, and various excursions on weekends. He even formed the curious habit, for a time, of taking his girl and boy to midnight horror movies. They were awful; they denied they enjoyed them—but they kept going.

Other observations forced themselves upon him. Howard Barksdale, his right-hand man and constant companion, made $50,000 a year from Triangle but was on the phone all the time either placing orders or listening to brokers on the stock exchange. JB asked him how he was doing, and Barksdale said he was making $100,000 a year on the market.

"The market is rising," JB said drily. Like everyone else able to recall 1929, he would never take the market too seriously again. He remembered when men were making millions in months. Aloud he said, "Howard, I don't mind you speculating; I do myself. But you're turning into a stockbroker."

Howard looked mute and JB continued. "Triangle can do better for you than the market. I'll sell you a ten percent interest at book value. You'll realize more than you can from the market."

"I don't know if I can raise that kind of money," Barksdale said.

"I'll take your note," said JB. Having made Barksdale a part owner in the firm, he then gave C. D. Tinsley and Raborn 1.5 percent interest each. The trio had been his inner corps; they were now his partners—and their incomes were greatly increased. JB believed that, by selling the men 13 percent of his share in Triangle, he had insured that they would remain together. Time was to prove him right.

In the spring of 1951 the complaints against General MacArthur had entered the political arena and angered the President. He dismissed the general and released the news before it was received at MacArthur's headquarters. He later said his reasons were that civilian authority had been threatened. It was not the first time that an American general had been dismissed, or that difficulties had arisen between Presidents and commanders in the field. But it was the first time that a

general leading American troops had been dismissed because he wanted
to conquer the enemy.

In reality, however, the dismissal was the result of an intense
campaign against the dangers of a nuclear war, arising from involvement by the Soviet, if Red China was attacked. This argument, reduced to its essence, forbade American forces from retaliating upon
forces that attacked them. With China able to operate from a protected
sanctuary, the chances of a complete American victory in Korea vanished. The best that could be accomplished was a stalemate. The struggle continued, and the list of American casualties grew long.

Triangle's quarters in the Mellie Esperson Building in Houston
grew cramped. JB, as usual seeking to find his own answer to a problem, found some tenants in the twin, attached Niels Esperson Building
that had a better space. He agreed that they could usefully swap, but
Williams, the building manager, to JB's astonishment, refused. "That
space is reserved for Pan-American," he said.

That led to words. Williams said Triangle was free to find another
building if it didn't like its present quarters. Office space was scarce in
Houston at the time. JB didn't look for another rental, however: Triangle had grown up, and could afford its own building.

He, Barksdale, and C. D. Tinsley looked at various locations and
finally settled on a block near Rice University at Nottingham and
Kirby. It was a location still considered far from downtown; Kirby
was still unpaved. The site held six houses ranging in price from
$16,000 to $24,000. Across the street was a vacant lot, overgrown with
weeds. JB, with his experience in land, could foresee several future
opportunities or possibilities; at the time he settled on the construction
of a two-story building. It was needed; his accounting and sales staffs
were in different offices; consolidation would help everyone and the
firm.

Shortly after construction started, he was informed the unions
might delay completion, but he avoided that by having the plans and
materials changed. The building went up on schedule and they moved
in, with huge satisfaction, in May, 1951.

The Soviet Union proposed a cease-fire in Korea and the United
States accepted the proposal at once. The action came in the wake of
General MacArthur's removal, discussions of a peace treaty with
Japan, and noisy political arguments throughout the country. But
there were too many available distractions to hold the attention of the
country for long. With television providing an almost hypnotic appeal,
millions of paperbacks flooding the marketplace, and Senator Estes

Kefauver managing a sensational series of investigations into organized crime, it seemed almost as if all the elements of every preceding decade in the century were rolling together at once.

Triangle continued to sign new plants to its 4 percent contract; the Cotton Valley Solvents Corporation president, Jack Coast, made such an agreement in 1951. JB also received a visit from his old friend, Keith Fanshier.

Keith's paper, the Chicago *Journal of Commerce*, had been acquired by the *Wall Street Journal*, which was in the midst of one of the most spectacular expansions in newspaper history. Keith, whose range of acquaintances in the industry was unexcelled, had covered its movements and personalities for what seemed his entire life. At the Chicago *Journal* he not only covered the industry's news, but also was business manager of the oil section.

In his dual role as reporter and advertising manager, Keith would host a cocktail party for his paper at both the spring and fall meetings of the API, which JB, among others, made a rule to attend. He believed Fanshier was a more capable man than the famed Warren Platt, whose *Oilgram* was considered the bible of the industry for many years. "Platt jumped to conclusions, and listed prices that were foisted off on him," JB said, "but Fanshier knew the industry and would cross-check carefully. He couldn't be fooled, and he was not interested in sensationalizing events. He was more interested in being sure he knew what they were."

The respect was returned. Fanshier said, "There was always a big question hanging in the air. It was: What's Saunders doing?" Triangle, after all, had heavy inventories. "He was such a wheeler-dealer," said Fanshier, "that he could dominate the whole market even though he sold less, overall, than the refined gasoline producers."

The reason, of course, was in the great mixture of firms, jobbers, and conditions in the country, which made across-the-board prices inconceivable. Fanshier watched Saunders, as did everyone else that followed or engaged in the market, with a mixture of wonder and apprehension. Fanshier, a professional observer, came to some conclusions: "He didn't want to destroy any part of the market, but he did want to sell. He didn't want the tank market to collapse, but he had to sell. He always pressed the market, but if he couldn't, he'd cut his price. As time passed and the quantities he handled increased, he grew into a looming market presence. I believe," Fanshier said, "he became the largest independent marketer in the United States—and maybe in the world.

"He was known everywhere—and cursed everywhere. But he was rough; he could curse back."

Fanshier told JB he was unhappy at the *Wall Street Journal*. The paper's leaders were embarked on a program to become the nation's first national newspaper. Organized for that effort, they had separated their business and news departments. They were not unique in this; McGraw-Hill and the other large publishing firms had taken the same course. A legend was growing up on the editorial side that advertisers and salesmen were part of the enemy sector; that a good reporter should not regard them with favor.

Keith came from an older tradition, though he was far from an older man. Like many newsmen, his apprenticeship had started early and he had been around a fairly long time, but he was still relatively young. He had known the owner of the Wichita paper where he launched his career, and he did not regard the newspaper business as being inherently any less subject to corruption than any other, or any more. A newspaper had to cover the news, but someone had to advertise in it, if it were to survive. Unlike some younger men, he knew that business appreciates honest coverage and has no use for publications that bend to pressure.

"I agree," said JB, and waited.

"I may be crazy," Fanshier said, "but I'd like to start my own newspaper for the industry. It will appear every day, with special issues for conventions."

JB was pleased. He believed men should go into business for themselves; he was all in favor. "If you've got the guts, I'll help you out," he said. "I'll give you thirty thousand dollars a year in advertising."

That was a departure for Triangle. JB distributed decks of cards with his Triangle emblem, gave away Fineline pencils, hosted widely, and used hospitality suites. Newspaper advertising was not essential to his operation, but Keith Fanshier was special. He was of great value to the industry, which could not afford to lose his cool and knowledgeable presence.

Keith thanked him and departed; he had other men to visit, and there is no doubt that many of them reacted as had JB, because the *Oil Daily* soon appeared. Keith returned to write Triangle's ads from time to time. JB was not surprised to note that they were good ads. Then Fanshier would question him about industry developments, trends, and events. JB knew that the resulting articles would be accurate, and that one would not affect the other.

Nevertheless, 1951 was a mixed year. John Arnold, JB's attorney and close personal friend, did a great deal of legal work for him but was always reluctant to charge. Arnold's great ambition was to become head of the bar association in Missouri, and he succeeded in attaining that goal.

Not long afterward, however, he underwent a medical check-up and was told that he had cancer and had only from six months to a year to live. He took the news with considerable courage. His son, who had also become a lawyer, was asked to come home and join his father's firm.

"I'm very lucky," Arnold told JB, "to have the time to groom him—and to have lasted long enough to see him join the profession."

The months passed with dismaying speed, and Arnold thought he should take a last, carefree vacation, while his strength was still sufficient. JB suggested the Seigniory Club in Canada, an establishment whose features matched its name—a lordly place.

The Arnolds drove through the gates and the keeper saluted them by name. When they registered the clerk did the same, and so did the bellman, the headwaiter in the dining room, and all the rest of the establishment. When they asked for their bill on leaving, they were told that it had been credited to the account of JB Saunders.

JB thought the gesture overdue. He watched the course of his friend's illness with strong emotion, and shared Mildred Arnold's grief at the passing of a man he considered as close as a brother.

In the autumn of 1951 Congress passed an appropriation of $56.9 billion for the armed forces, and the political atmosphere of the United States grew thick. The Republican party promoted General MacArthur for a time, then dropped the old soldier when he was no longer profitable, and turned toward desperation tactics. Long years of evasion of the hard issues had taken their toll among the Republicans, and among the Democrats as well. Few American political leaders would openly admit that the government was, by 1951, dedicated to dominance over the people, while concealing that dominance in munificence.

The Communist issue, due to lack of hard analysis and no effort to investigate the difference between its rhetoric and its reality, had turned into a semantic game that few could follow. The press seldom bothered to identify Communists but was usually careful to identify persons of conservative views. Senator Taft of Ohio, blocked from the nomination in favor of the more photogenic Dewey, hoped his turn would come at last in 1952. But the bureaucrats of the party were as averse to realism as ever; they sought a candidate who could not lose, no matter what his views.

The President, meanwhile, enjoyed the worst press since Hoover. Newsmen discovered that there were influence peddlers in Washington, an observation of stunning redundancy. The term 5 percenter became briefly famous. Charges of small-bore corruption collided in the headlines with the accusations of Senator Joseph McCarthy regarding communism in government. The Senator was no threat to the Communists; his methods were careless and his charges imprecise. But he received an inordinate amount of publicity.

The year crawled toward an untidy close. The war in Korea was still being fought. An unknown number of Americans were still held prisoner, and casualties continued. The reportage on the battles, however, was spotty and fragmentary, and made little sense. Morale was poor in Korea, and poor at home as well.

JB, in Washington on business, walking along the corridor of a hotel with H. T. Ashton of Mobil, encountered a slightly tipsy lady who invited them both to her party.

"Her attention was drawn to Ashton," JB said, "and he was impressive. A very flashy dresser, he was wearing a dark coat, spats, and a derby. The lady thought he was a senator."

They peeked in at the party and saw a large crowd, drinking and talking loudly. They thought the lady must be wealthy. She was, but she was also a congressman's secretary.

Politics in Europe appeared to be assuming a more realistic tone. In West Germany an old man, Adenauer, who had survived every vicissitude, was able to denounce the Communists more openly than Americans four thousand miles away. In Britain another old man, Churchill, had been returned to the post of Prime Minister. Adenauer was seventy-six; Churchill, seventy-eight. Both hoped that the United States would help restore the strength of their nations. A third old man—Herbert Hoover, seventy-eight—argued fiercely that the drain was too heavy and proposed a "Fortress America" instead. Unfortunately their debate might as well have been conducted on Olympus; the level of the political dialogue in the United States was far lower.

The national employment roster stood at a record 62 million, but inflation kept the labor unions in a state of agitation, and employers found it difficult to keep costs from getting out of hand. JB, however, was still moving into new waters. In January, 1952, he formed the Triangle Realty Company; he had decided that land investments in a rising market were worth making.

Meanwhile he purchased a deep-water terminal at Jacksonville, Florida, that could be supplied from tankers, and another at Cape Canaveral, Florida, where he sometimes spent a winter vacation with Rocky, a favorite area of JB's until it grew crowded. On one of his trips, he ran into old Hassett.

Hassett was glad to see him; they played a round of golf together.

The older man was still a good player. Later, relaxing at the nineteenth hole, Hassett said, "Why did you leave?"

JB started to tell him, but the older man put up his hand; he did not really want to hear what he already knew.

Election years in the United States had always been somewhat scrambled, but as television, radio, and the great national news magazines began to cover the land with inescapable babble, the campaigns became continuous and continual. The sins of Truman's entourage were small and unimportant, but magnified remarkably. The President's military aide was accused of having accepted a deep freezer, an item highlighted by an intense campaign. Senator McCarthy's anti-Communist speeches grew increasingly confused, and the conventions of the major parties opened to traditional behavior that had abruptly come to seem strange.

Early in July a shriveled handful of Wallace's Progressive party nominated wealthy San Francisco lawyer Vincent Hallinan for President; a week later the Republicans again rejected Taft, their most intelligent spokesman, and nominated General Eisenhower. In July the Democrats chose Adlai Stevenson, governor of Illinois.

In Korea the American forces had settled for a stalemate on the ground accompanied by long-range bombing raids in the north. A series of other actions were underway; extremist agitation in Iran posed considerable problems for the British. The American State Department, at the urging of the President, studied the area and sought to find a compromise between supporting British colonialism and keeping Iran from sliding into Communist hands. Its efforts were not speedy and the impasse continued.

In the Kremlin, where the dictator had retreated behind double-barred iron doors, fears rose regarding his intentions. Stalin had his meals delivered; visitors were rare. He conceived the idea that the world Zionist movement was allied with the United States against the USSR. This concept led to the belief that his doctors were poisoning him, and he began to plot a new purge, this time of Jewish physicians. If the purge was mounted, there was little doubt that those initial victims would be soon followed by a host of others who fit a similar category—which would comprise the Jewish population of the USSR.[34]

In the United States General Eisenhower announced, in the course of his campaign, that he would, if elected, "go to Korea." That was hailed as a sign of peace, and aroused great enthusiasm. It was not until

34. Adam B. Ulam, *Stalin, The Man and His Era* (New York: Viking, 1973), p. 737.

years later that Eisenhower admitted that he had discussed the Korean situation with General MacArthur, and that their ideas were alike. In a television interview in 1966, the general declared that if the North Koreans had not signed an armistice, the United States would, under his command, have used nuclear weapons—"enough to win."[35]

Had the general been more candid with the electorate regarding that very important issue, there is no doubt the campaign would have taken a different tone. A different tone would have been welcome. The Republican slogan—Communism, Korea, and Corruption—was hardly informative. The Democratic candidate, Stevenson, announced he would discuss issues but succeeded mainly in making them sound more complicated. In the end it was a virtual no contest; the general won with 33 million votes to Stevenson's 27 million. After twenty years, the Republicans were back in the highest office.

Early in 1953 the world moved into a new era. Despite the protests of those who insist history is impersonal, it opened with the death—at last—of Joseph Stalin at the age of seventy-three. The circumstances of his passing remain shrouded, but the details that were released regarding his final months provide material that western dramatists have, unaccountably, ignored. Stalin ended his days as a recluse guarded by soldiers who delivered his meals on trays, depositing them on the floor before a locked, iron door behind which the monster huddled alone with his frightful memories—and his fears.[36]

The world's chances for peace perceptibly improved and the discussions in Korea moved toward resolution. The nation hailed that possibility; deaths had mounted to over 30,000 with more than 100,000 wounded and almost 8,000 missing. The United States, with a population of 161 million, enjoyed unprecedented prosperity, though inflation had reduced the value of the dollar to fifty-two cents compared to its 1935–1939 equivalent.[37]

Triangle was booming; its transportation network had extended its distribution through a thirteen-state area between the Rockies in the West and the Appalachians in the East. That region has been termed the *industrial heartland of America;* it includes the huge complexes of Detroit, Chicago, and the cities along the Great Lakes, the Pittsburgh and Ohio valley regions, the Gulf, and the Southeast.

35. Knightley, *First Casualty,* p. 350.
36. "During the night of March 1–2 the guards became alarmed when he failed to order his evening meal, but were afraid to break open the locked iron-plated door that led to his bedroom." Ulam, *Stalin,* p. 739.
37. Carruth and Associates, *American Facts and Dates,* p. 581.

JB extended his terminals and sent his tows to an increased number of locations; in Kentucky the president of Kentucky Standard actually called him in for a discussion. "You cannot break into this market," he told him, "we have it all sewed up." JB could see one of his terminals under construction through the window over the president's shoulder as he spoke, but refrained from pointing out the obvious.

Ashland Oil & Refining, also greatly enlarged and growing, was equally concerned. Paul Blazer, its formidable chairman, who had broken with J. Howard Marshall only a year before, invited JB to visit him. The invitation, pressed several times, could not be delayed forever; JB made the trip to Ashland, Kentucky, in early 1953.

He checked into the modest Henry Clay Hotel and regarded the small city from the window; after Houston it did not appear particularly inviting. Blazer, chairman of Ashland, appeared and was cordial. He led JB on a red-carpet tour through the firm's huge Catlettsburg refinery. Blazer had serious intentions; he wanted to merge Ashland and Triangle, and his reasons were sound. Both firms supplied independents. Ashland's refineries were strategically located and brilliantly managed; the firm had sales of over $200 million and Triangle's sales were nearing $100 million. Blazer was a shrewd marketer and an even better refiner; between the two there is little doubt they could have created a formidable organization.

"We trained under the same man," Blazer reminded JB. "I learned from Hassett, and so did you. Bring me an up-to-date statement," he continued, "and we'll be happy to show you ours."

"I didn't want to do that," JB said. "I had to make the visit; Blazer was an important customer. But I was afraid if I brought my statement that he would actually talk me into a merger. A salesman can sell another salesman—and he was a great salesman."

The visit was pleasant enough, but, sitting with senior executive Everett Wells, JB noted an incident that seemed to him revealing. Wells was on the phone, and apparently the man on the other end had an important question; Wells stalled while he scribbled a note and handed it to his secretary. A few minutes later she returned with another slip of paper, at which he glanced. He sat up straighter, and began to talk on the phone with a new firmness. "Paul decided that one," JB thought—and decided, at that moment, that he himself would not work in such a manner.

It is unlikely, however, that Blazer would have attempted to handle JB as he did his protégés; he had worked smoothly with J. Howard Marshall for many years before they came to a parting of the ways. It is therefore likely that Saunders and Blazer would have created a partnership of opposites. If so, they would have altered the history of the entire petroleum industry. But JB was not ready for a merger; Triangle was moving ahead in giant strides on its own.

A very large stride, in fact, was taken in the early fifties when JB signed the Cotton Valley Operators' Committee. The Committee consisted of H. L. Hunt, who controlled 30 percent; the Ohio Oil Company,[38] which owned another 30 percent; and at least another 150 people and firms, who owned the remaining 40 percent. The Cotton Valley field was unitized; it was in fact among the first unitized gas fields in the United States. The concept was novel, and various federal agencies walked warily around it, suspecting that it was somehow either unfair or illegal, or should be so defined. Actually, unitization was the response of individual enterprises and individuals to the argument that a scramble in developing a field constituted a waste of natural resources. It consisted of having all the owners in a field agree on a consortium, to a spaced well plat, and to accept proportionate shares of the field's entire output.

The government wanted to impose such an arrangement, but had been tardy in arriving at the concept. When individual enterprisers set it up on their own, they had to go to court to fight for their right to operate cooperatively. The United States had come a long way, though the direction was subject to some argument.

The Cotton Valley gas field, among the first to erect recycling plants, had produced toluene—an essential ingredient in TNT that makes bombs active—during World War II. After the war it installed new equipment to make a wider variety of products. These included the liquid residue of gas obtained from the cycling process, which constituted a low-grade motor fuel. It was useful in refineries as a blending agent, and—with such additives as tetraethyl lead, could be upgraded into a serviceable gasoline in its own right.

JB signed a contract with H. L. Hunt and Ohio Oil to handle the huge volume from the Cotton Valley plant. In part this accomplishment was based on old acquaintance; he had known Hunt from his days in El Dorado, though mostly at a distance.

"A big plantation owner—and a big gambler," JB said. "He was in east Texas and broke, but wrote a check for a lease, hoping the well would cover it. It did; when the man brought the check back, Hunt said calmly, 'Oh, I'm sorry, that check was drawn on the wrong bank.' He crossed out the letterhead and filled in another and the man went away; the second check was good."

That may well have happened; Hunt made many deals and became so famous that stories continue to float around them. Philip Hamilton, head of Root Oil and John Atkins's brother-in-law, lent Hunt money to use in the east Texas play; that certainly didn't hurt JB's chances.

38. Now known as Marathon.

On the other hand, it did not necessarily make matters easier; Hunt made up his own mind in negotiations. "He couldn't be sold," said Hamilton later, "but he could be convinced." A neat distinction.

JB, however, had no difficulties with Hunt; the two men liked each other. With the majority owners of Cotton Valley under contract, he was able to send copies of the same agreement to the host of minority owners and obtain their approval with no difficulty. In all, it was a memorable coup that still fills William J. Carthaus, Majewski's sidekick at Deep Rock, with retrospective awe. He is barely able to smile about it.

"He did it with ten-cent cigars," Carthaus says. "He acted like a country boy, but he was awfully sharp."

At first, however, the significance of the coup was not so obvious. Recycled low-grade motor fuel, which JB agreed to purchase in huge volume, was not considered a competitive product at a time when the high-octane race was still underway. It remained for JB to prove that it could be an important market commodity.

One man who did see its significance, however, was Jack Rathbone of huge Standard Oil of New Jersey. JB went to New York and sat with Rathbone and his right-hand man Glenn Poorman. He drew a map for the executives, showing how Triangle's distribution was organized, its market area, and its expanding sources of supply.

"You're growing fast," Rathbone said, appreciatively.

"I'm coming fast," JB agreed. "I have one million barrels to move, right away." Rathbone said that he and Poorman would have to think about it, and suggested that JB call back in about an hour. JB did, and Poorman came on the phone.

"We have a lot of low-gravity crude oil to move through our crude line to Baton Rouge," Poorman said, "and we can use your gasoline." Both men knew that by using gasoline it was possible to accelerate the crude flow, but it was clear a larger decision had been made. Rathbone and Poorman and their associates had decided JB's cycled gasoline was suitable for the giant refinery. That meant that Triangle had moved into the pivotal position Keith Fanshier and others later recognized. JB had arrived in Oil Country.

Between March and July, 1953, the United States lost a great opportunity to achieve an advantage from its effort in Korea. The Kremlin was in disorder. The dreaded Beria was shot to death by his associates; riots erupted in East Germany.

American eagerness to have done with Korea led to the acceptance of terms previously rejected by former President Truman. In effect, the Thirty-eighth Parallel was allowed to stand as a permanent border, the United States would pay to restore a ravaged south, and prisoners were exchanged, with final negotiations to be held later. Twenty-two years later they were still being held.

Much was made in the western press of the peace. But the reputation of the President of South Korea was permanently blackened by charges that his régime was cruel and corrupt, while a veil was drawn over proceedings in the North. American POWs, for the first time in history, were held to have disgraced themselves. When Syngman Rhee, however, gave the North Korean and Chinese prisoners a choice of sanctuary or return to their homes, a startling 27,000 switched sides, though the news was soon smothered.

The major lesson that emerged from Korea was that the United States was fearful of a major power confrontation, and that Communist aggression would be resisted but would not provoke a large counterblow. That lesson was muffled in praises for President Eisenhower and descriptions of the deadlock as a triumph for the United States. The nation was not convinced, but the end of the fighting brought widespread relief.

Another remarkable sense of relief was realized when the press dropped the vituperative tone in which it had reported the closing years of the Truman Administration. That startling lack of respect for the Presidency was never explained; its continuation under the immensely popular new President would have boomeranged on the reporters. The change in tone, however, was like lifting a large stone from the nation's psyche. The "Eisenhower years," with their sense of goodwill and decency, opened like a fresh breeze across the landscape.

There were many important men in Houston, but few more important than George and Herman Brown. Owners of Brown & Root, one of the largest construction firms in the world, they had entered the petroleum industry with their purchase of the Big Inch and the Little Big Inch pipelines, and proceeded to extend their interests from that impressive start.

The Browns, who numbered Lyndon Johnson among their political protégés, held court in Suite 4F in the Lamar Hotel in downtown Houston. George Naff led JB to that top-level, informal headquarters, where he looked around at the large sitting room with a bar in one corner and a bartender in constant attendance, with appreciation.

The Browns knew about JB and Triangle; his name was probably better known throughout the industry than their own. The brothers had never been noted for liking publicity. Their interest was in acquiring more pipelines, and especially the lines owned and operated by the Triangle Pipeline Company. JB, however, had partners in that venture, and he and his partners were at the point of increasing that investment.

Reggie Brinkman's Highland Oil Company, with which Triangle had divided some Gulf region distribution, was bogging in high freight rates and the lesser efficiency of the railroads. Highland needed to be integrated into pipelines. That could mean the construction of a new, larger line and more financing. But the Browns had a better idea.

They had added a loop to the Big Inch and had established distribution of the gas carried by the huge carrier; they now proposed to convert the Little Big Inch back to a petroleum products line. JB heard that with some dismay. "That twenty-inch monster will choke my little ten-inch lines," he thought.

Meanwhile, the brothers, whose assistants buzzed around them like so many moths, wondered if JB wouldn't like to work for them. "I already have three jobs," he protested. "I'm head of Triangle, head of Triangle Pipelines, and president of a transportation company."

They smiled at him, and one said softly, "We'd like to have you in our club."

He left, but with an invitation to meet them again at lunch at the Ramada Club.

At lunch in the Ramada Club the Browns discussed their plans at greater length. JB, listening, saw that there was no economic sense in resisting the effort they had in mind. There was no doubt that the growing production of the Gulf would be more efficiently handled if the Little Big Inch was converted back to a petroleum products line. There was also no doubt that such a conversion would create many changes in the marketplace; increase competition for smaller marketers such as Triangle, Ashland Oil, and others; and greatly overshadow Triangle Pipelines. He was fortunate these formidable brothers had called him in. It was flattering that they sought not only his cooperation, but his help.

Their reasons were very clear-cut. The Browns were constructive men, and their ideas of business were based on the same respect for realities as JB's. If the Little Big Inch was to be converted to a petroleum products carrier, its owners would have to repeat, on a larger scale, JB's methods in constructing his smaller pipelines. Sources of supply would have to be contracted, distribution from terminals established along the way arranged, and the market estimated.

In approaching JB they were in touch with an important marketer, sophisticated in all the interrelated problems involved in their plan. They also knew—and so did JB—that converting the Little Big Inch would create a storm of opposition. Every marketer in the immense regions affected, which extended from the Gulf Coast to the East, would rise against this competition. It was, however, a very large plan, sweeping in scope and size, and one that JB could not but admire. In the largest sense, it would benefit the nation.

JB agreed to join with the Browns to help their plans forward. They told him to choose his own attorney, and prepare the sort of agreement he thought best. That was in keeping with traditional practice; when a large power deals with a smaller power in business, it first makes an approach, and then asks the smaller power to draw up the suggested terms.

JB looked around Houston for a new lawyer, for his good friend John Arnold had, unhappily, died. He ran into a problem he had not believed possible; virtually every law office of any stature and almost every lawyer of ability was tied in one way or another to interests that could be traced back to George and Herman Brown—except one.

That uniquely independent lawyer was named Hugh Q. Buck, a name which rings oddly in the ears. He was immensely tall and skinny, and came from Pecos, Texas. His early background was similar to JB's own; his father, an attorney, had moved to the Texas Panhandle in 1909 as a farmer. His childhood, therefore, was spent in the open, under the huge skies of the Southwest. Later he attended Harvard briefly but graduated from the University of Texas law school, and had an unusual career from there, in which—like JB—he learned much from older men.

Their paths diverged in other respects, however; the older men from whom Buck learned were famous in the world. The first was Stanley Reed, later a Supreme Court Justice, who was then head of the RFC. Buck later moved from Reed to Uncle Jesse Jones himself. He shared a suite with Tommy Corcoran and Ben Cohen, the twin prodigies of the New Deal; he lived near Justice Harlan Stone and chatted with him on long walks together.

Returning to Houston, young lawyer Buck was given a helping hand by Uncle Jesse. Later, a stroke of fortune involved him in arrangements for the lease of Houston's first Petroleum Club, which rented the top floor of Jones's Rice Hotel. In that effort Buck met many oilmen, among them JB Saunders.

The men grew to know one another mainly because their daughters went to the same school in Houston, and were very close friends. When JB took Suzanne and JB III to Hot Springs, Arkansas, to water-ski and enjoy vacations, Bobbie Sue Buck was often included. JB taught the attorney's daughter how to water-ski; he discovered she was a natural athlete.

It was a pleasure for JB, therefore, to discover that his friend Buck was about the only top-flight lawyer in Houston who knew something about the petroleum business, and was not allied—by even the most tenuous threads—to the Browns.

Buck drew up a private agreement between JB and the Browns, which piqued Charley Francis, the chief legal counsel for Texas Eastern. Francis, a man whose brilliance was so clear it was universally accepted, said to JB, "You thumbed your nose at me." But JB assured him that was not so; he had needed a lawyer since his own had passed away.

Before much more could be done, however, there was a large and important first step. A transaction would have to take place, in which Triangle pipelines would be integrated into the Texas Eastern network.

JB had already informed his partners of this necessity, and of its reasons. They were not against it; the price the Browns had in mind would insure a fivefold profit from their investments, and assure that the expanded Texas Eastern network would be available for the transportation of their production. Reggie Brinkman's Highland Oil Company volume would be able to reach the market at a lower cost and greater efficiency. That, too, would carry benefits to the partners.

On the international scene in the autumn of 1953, the United States and Britain finally agreed on a joint participation to support the Shah of Iran, to assist in overthrowing the extremist Mohammed Mossadegh, and to share in huge oil concessions in that land. That marked a breakthrough for the American petroleum industry, but the question of foreign crude oil was still relatively minor to the United States as a whole. Only independent marketers like JB and others, who had to pay for expensive domestic crude and meet competition from inexpensive foreign crude imported by the majors, understood that development.

The Communist world, meanwhile, which watched the reversal of its efforts in Iran with relative mildness, was engrossed in a struggle for power inside the Kremlin, while seeking to placate its colonies in eastern Europe. A spontaneous uprising in Berlin was evidence that the despoliation of those regions had created widespread and dangerous unrest. Relaxations of some sterner measures were ordered, and the newspapers of the West hailed a "thaw" in the USSR.

The American nation received this news with relief; it had the effect of making Senator McCarthy's investigation into domestic communism seem redundant, an impression the Senator did little to alter by choosing amateurish young assistants in his efforts.[39]

39. The most conspicuous were Roy Cohn, David Schine, and Robert Kennedy.

Meanwhile a great construction boom was underway, the arts flourished as did all forms of entertainment. The coronation of Queen Elizabeth provided a remarkable spectacle in midyear; smaller atomic weapons were proven by the U.S. Army; an avalanche of spy and FBI stories appeared. Toward the end of the year it seemed as though the country was, at last, losing the angry passions that had so disfigured the New and Fair Deals, and the President's popularity was immense.

In Shreveport, Louisiana lawyer David Smitherman struggled with the numerous principals and entities that comprised Triangle Pipelines; everyone had an idea that had to be considered. Nevertheless the negotiations for the sale to Texas Eastern proceeded amicably.

Discussions were delayed during Christmas; there was no competing party and no overpowering need for haste. Christmas was always a season JB enjoyed; he had maintained his habit of spotting suitable gifts through the year, and had enlarged his generosity as his prosperity had grown. In some instances he managed to send gifts all through the Twelve Days.

After the new year 1954 dawned, the partners, JB and John Atkins, met in Shreveport for final discussions with Reggie Hargrove, president of the Texas Eastern Transmission Company, the Brown-owned distribution subsidiary, and with Brown attorney Charley Francis. Francis declared that the final agreement would be reviewed before acceptance by the Browns' Committee of Three. Later JB learned that committee consisted of George and Herman Brown, and Charley Francis himself.

After an agreement had been reached with Texas Eastern, subject to the review of the Committee of Three, JB, Atkins, and Reggie Hargrove went back to the Washington-Youree Hotel. JB broke open a twenty-year-old bottle of Scotch, and the trio were enjoying a victory drink when the phone rang. It was Harvey McLean, righthand man for Ed Hudson of Carthage. Shreveport is a small city, and McLean had learned of the negotiations. He feared the Carthage plant would be left high and dry, without access to the pipeline being sold.

JB told McLean he would explain it all in the morning, and asked when a meeting would be convenient. "Make it eleven o'clock," McLean said, "in my office." That made Atkins impatient. He had organized a duck hunt and JB was included; they were to fly to Grove Lodge in southern Louisiana at noon the next day.

"I'll take a rain check," JB replied. "Triangle grosses $30,000 a month from McLean's business; I'll have to see him face to face." Then he added, "I also have to go to New York."

McLean's attitude softened the following morning when JB explained that the Browns were buying pipelines as part of a larger plan to create a vast system. "It will give us the world for a market," he said.

Cordial again, McLean asked JB when he planned to return to Houston. "On the three fifteen plane," JB said. "The schedules have been changed," McLean told him. "That flight now leaves at one fifteen." JB had time to take it, if he hurried. He called Raborn at the Washington-Youree Hotel and told him to pack, check them both out, and meet him at the Shreveport airport. McLean, being helpful, offered to drive him. The men were leaving when a secretary appeared and said JB was wanted on the phone. He told her to say he had left for Houston, and the two men drove away. Later he learned that the call was from John Atkins, who wanted to tell him that, with Reggie Hargrove, he was leaving in a smaller plane for the lodge at 3:15. Had JB answered the phone, he would probably have joined them. Duck hunts, with good company, are hard to resist.

On Sunday JB flew from Houston to St. Louis, the first leg of his trip to New York. When he reached his hotel he gave the bellman his bag and room key, and went out to have dinner with his old friend Phil Siteman. They were seated together in the Rathskeller when they heard the radio music interrupted by a news bulletin. A private plane, returning to Shreveport from southern Louisiana, had crashed ten miles south of the city.

JB turned white. "I believe that's my group," he said, and went to the phone. Calling his hotel, he was told that someone was trying to reach him, that very moment, from Shreveport. The operators were able to switch the call. It was Vernon Chance.

"Vernon, how bad is it?" JB asked.

"JB," Vernon replied, "the only thing that could make it worse would be if you were on that plane yourself. They're all dead; I can still see the flames."

CHAPTER THIRTEEN

New Patterns

COLD WINDS swept across the Gulf. Sleet poured down on men who raked through the wreckage of the Grumman Mallard twin-engine seaplane, whose parts were scattered across the icy mud, frozen trees and water that marked the site of Walter Jacobs's fishing camp ten miles south of Shreveport. The blacktop road leading to the camp was covered with mud churned by cars and trucks; huge numbers of the morbidly curious had been attracted by the blaze set off by the crash. Members of the family were delayed in reaching the scene by these throngs, and by the sheets of flame that consumed the plane and its passengers.

Heavy winds and overcast skies threatened a new outburst of the storm on Monday morning and made airline schedules uncertain. Discovering that Reggie Brinkman was also in St. Louis, JB looked him up and the two men boarded a Missouri Pacific train together. Their differences had long faded; Reggie was a sober pillar of the Episcopal Church.

Once aboard, they automatically opened a deck of cards and began to play gin. Brinkman, as was his habit, chewed on an unlit cigar, and JB for once had no words. They played hand after hand in absolute silence, their minds filled with memories, as the train rushed toward Shreveport.

As Brinkman and JB rode toward Shreveport, the newspapers of Louisiana and Texas displayed heavy headlines and long articles about the accident and the men it swept away. The Houston *Press* quoted Miss Suzanne Saunders, explaining that her father had turned down an invitation for the hunt because he had business elsewhere. Herman Brown described Reggie Hargrove, and said he had not only enjoyed airplanes, but often visited his friends and former colleagues at United Gas in Shreveport.[1]

The Shreveport *Times* described the six prominent men from that city, lost in the crash. They included John Atkins, chairman of Atlas Processing; Justin Querbes, a financier; his brother Randolph Querbes, head of Interstate Electric; E. Bernard Weiss, chairman of Goldring; his brother Milton Weiss, chairman of the Volks store in Dallas; and an official of the Goldring chain, J. P. Evans, an oilman—all from Shreveport. The out-of-towners included Tom Braniff, who launched his airline with one plane between Oklahoma City and Tulsa years before, and was proud of the fact that his line flew 2.5 billion passenger miles without an accident; Chris Abbott, a rancher and head of eight banks in Nebraska; Ed Tobin, head of an aerial survey company, and an ace in World War I; Reggie Hargrove, head of Texas Eastern Transmission; and the two pilots, Buddy Huddleston and Louis Schexnaidre.

The accident was soon reconstructed. The first of the two planes used by the hunting party left Oak Grove Lodge carrying N. C. McGowen, the head of United Gas; Walter B. Jacobs, head of the Shreveport National Bank, and oilmen P. H. Hamrick and W. C. Wolfe, in midafternoon. At that time the weather was rainy but still safe, but growing colder. The plane had a landing gear problem and stopped at Lake Charles Airport for repairs. After a delay of several hours it arrived at Shreveport, and McGowen asked about the second plane. Told it had not yet arrived, he went to the tower, and in time heard a conversation between the pilot of the second plane and the controllers that he was to never forget.

The second plane, carrying ten passengers, had left after four o'clock.[2] By that time the temperature had dropped and was continuing to fall, and the rain had turned into sleet, but the men were anxious to get home on Sunday night. They had important business on Monday. Among the matters awaiting attention were their signatures on the agreement to sell the Triangle Pipelines to Texas Eastern Transmission.

Such men are not easily dissuaded from their purposes; the group was composed of the strong and successful. It is no effort to imagine their disdain of caution. They were in a hurry, and the plane left. It was a little over ten minutes from its destination when the Shreveport Tower heard from pilot Schexnaidre. Ice was forming on the wings; he was going to try an emergency landing.

1. Houston *Press*, January 11, 1954.
2. The Grumman had hardly gotten out of sight when another private plane carrying some oilmen intent on a duck hunt landed at the Lodge. The passengers included Jack Rathbone, among others. He recalls hearing the news of the crash on the radio that night with horror; he knew most of the passengers well.

He chose the fishing camp owned by Walter Jacobs, who had left on the earlier plane. But the camp's lake was frozen solid. Naked trees, their limbs hard, stuck up like giant spikes. Three men on the ground watched in horror as the plane descended, wavering because of its heavy, ice-packed wings. They saw the tips hit the treetops. The craft cut a hundred-yard swath before it crashed and exploded. Flames soared as they ran to their cars to reach a telephone.

To the 150,000 people of Shreveport and the more thousands who lived in its environs, the accident was one of those winter events that cause a passing headshake, but relatively few knew how serious a loss the city had suffered and how much it would affect their own lives. "It nearly ruined Shreveport," JB said, "and left helpless sons."

Years later other men came to the same conclusion. The city had lost its real leaders: men whose imaginations and drive had created' enterprises that kept their fellow citizens busy and constructive.

One important matter left incomplete was the sale of Triangle Pipelines to the Texas Eastern Transmission Company. David Smitherman, the attorney, had worked over the weekend to prepare those papers; they were typed and ready when the plane carrying some of the principals had crashed.

George Brown came from Houston to Shreveport, however, and brought George Naff, the new head of Texas Eastern Transmission, with him. On Thursday, January 14, 1954, a new group assembled in Shreveport to complete the delayed sale.

JB noted a curious, slightly macabre coincidence. "George Naff sat in the chair Reggie Hargrove had occupied, and Reggie Brinkman sat where John Atkins had been seated, only a week before."

The papers had been redrawn, though the terms remained unchanged. They were signed and the sale was at last completed.

Brinkman and JB attended six funerals in two days—a ghastly series. Both men had lost many friends but considered John Atkins's departure especially grievous. He had been engaged in at least ten enterprises, had arranged his affairs, and was on the verge of consolidation. He left a young son, John Atkins, Jr., twenty years old.

The young man had worked on a Seven-Up truck in the summers, and entered his father's firm as an office boy after he graduated from college. He was, JB noted with disapproval, treated like an office boy. Once JB was visiting when the elder Atkins was told his son wanted to see him. "Tell him to wait," Atkins and JB left the office, and the young man was still waiting. His father stopped, and young Atkins explained that he still had his old school bank account, long dormant. He wondered if he should cut it off. "How much do you have in it?" his father asked.

"Eighty-six dollars."

"Yes. Cut it off."

"The result," said JB later, "was an uncertain young man." His father, however, thought he had time. At the age of fifty-six John Atkins was finally in the clear and undoubtedly expected to be able to relax in the future. Yet he had not wanted a long life.

Aware that he drank, smoked, and lived hard, JB had once ventured to remonstrate with him. Atkins looked scornfully from his great height. "We all go, and we don't know when," he replied. "I don't want to get old."

JB came quickly to an understanding with young Atkins, who learned, rather soon, that the various men with whom his father had business dealings were all determined to treat him fairly, but not yet as an equal. He was only twenty years old and that situation was not one over which to complain; he was too pleased with the fact that all of his father's partners were honest men. It would be a few years before he would fully realize how fine a judge of men his father had been. In later years he and JB became close and good friends.

The Brown brothers closed their shipyards and turned toward the conversion of the Little Big Inch and the expansion of Texas Eastern with their usual efficiency. They took a number of steps; one was to create the Texas Eastern Production Company, to insure a source of supply at the beginning end of the huge carrier. Another was to have J. Howard Marshall, no longer with Ashland Refining, who had a prestigious name with the Federal Power Commission and was knowledgeable from PAW days with the Little Big Inch, prepare an economic study proving why it should be reconverted. "The reasons were clear," Marshall said. "The Browns had built a loop in the Big Inch and a second large gas carrier was redundant."

Still another step was to enlist JB Saunders. The brothers presented a study in contrasts: Herman was heavy bodied and round-faced, and often wore shirts and bow ties made from the same bolt of cloth. That was a style popular among skilled workingmen around the time of World War I; Herman Brown shared a fondness for it with Roy Howard, the newspaper magnate. George Brown, however, dressed with conventional fastidiousness, was slender, and spoke with the precision of his Ph.D. But despite their surface disparity, the Brown brothers thought alike and moved as one.

It was not their persuasions, however, that swayed JB so much as the airplane crash. He had, after all, lost a valued partner and a number of his closest friends and associates in one fell swoop. Nobody can suffer the loss of so many of his contemporaries without shock. He turned toward work; it was his answer, as it is the answer of so many professionals, to private grief and shock. Adding Texas Eastern into his activities as head of Triangle, a vice president of Atlas Refining and of Southern States Barge Lines would keep him busy around the clock.

JB had discussed the Browns with Barksdale, Tinsley, Raborn, and Jimmy Craven. His men were sure they could keep Triangle moving forward without his constant presence and supervision. Barksdale and Tinsley, aware of the huge influence and extensive operations of the Browns, urged him to make a deal.

JB did. In fact, he made two deals. The first was to take effect at once, but the second was hinged to contingencies. Therefore it was to be several years and hazards away from realization.

In the immediate, JB accepted a post as vice president with Texas Eastern Transmission, at a salary of $37,500, and related expenses. JB also requested and received the use of a company plane and two pilots. That was essential because JB already had headquarters in Houston at Triangle, and offices in Memphis, Shreveport, and Chicago. His new responsibility meant he would have to fly, as well as work, around the clock.

The second understanding was of a longer-range nature and would not come alive until the Little Big Inch was actually converted from a gas to a products carrier. At that time, based on the assumption that JB's efforts would help provide cargo for the line, he would receive $1 a year for each barrel of petroleum product the line carried, on the basis of its daily average. That could mean a sum of $250,000 a year, but it remained only a prospect at the time it was promised.

Charley Francis, the legal hawk of the Browns, urged JB to become president of Texas Eastern, but JB demurred. A part-time vice presidency was as far as he wanted to go, in terms of getting inside the giant's castle that the Browns were building.

During 1954 much domestic attention was paid to Senator McCarthy and his various charges, investigations, and activities regarding Communism at home. The newspapers centered so much attention on the Senator that he became an embarrassment to the Administration. Television networks and news magazines, which had at first treated McCarthy with semiseriousness, soon called attention to his haphazard tactics. The Senator received information from various undisclosed sources inside the government, however, that was difficult to completely shatter. Prior disclosures of actual espionage had been officially released. The reality of Communist influence, in many levels of the arts, sciences, academia, and politics was evident to neutral observers. The Army, however, reacted with anger to charges it had been infiltrated. A public hearing was televised during the summer of 1956, with disastrous results to the Senator. His questions were clumsy and his appearance uncouth. Roy Cohn could not keep from almost permanent whispering in his ear. The counsel for the Army, a Boston lawyer of the old school, was a refreshing contrast.

The hearings ended inconclusively but McCarthy's career as a Communist hunter was effectively ended. The media thundered against his excesses. The New York *Times* declared the basic issue was whether classified documents from the executive branch could be used, without naming their sources, without injuring the principle of three independent branches of government. The paper concluded that the executive could not function if such abuses were allowed.

Had the matter ended there it might have led to some more decent ground rules governing the persistent abuse of power in congressional hearings. Unfortunately the nature of the anti-McCarthy campaign, which was conducted for months by the media, succeeded in ending the discussion of Communist activities in the country as well. The Senator, once reduced, was given a final blow when the Senate voted to censure him. The lesson was not lost. No politician since McCarthy has dared discuss subversion in connection with communism.

On an international scale, communism achieved other victories. The Chinese Communists regarded the Korean outcome as a triumph, with reason. In France the Communist party flourished by exploiting the unpopularity of the government's efforts to retain Indochina. That struggle did not go well for the French. In May 1954 the stronghold of Dien Bien Phu fell to the Communist forces of Ho Chi Minh, although the American Air Force flew a French battalion to the scene in an attempt to hold it.[3] In June, Pierre Mendès-France was elected Premier of France and vowed to end the war. A month later a treaty was signed creating North Viet Nam and South Viet Nam. The French

3. Ulam, *Expansion and Coexistence*, p. 562.

withdrew from the North, and the Communists promised to evacuate the South, as well as Cambodia and Laos.

That outcome, however it cheered the peace forces in France, did little to improve the morale of its armed forces. It provided impetus for further rebellions in other French colonies. Algeria seethed. The Middle East grew increasingly disturbed. A formerly obscure Army colonel named Gamal Abdel Nasser came to power in Egypt.

It was later disclosed that the USSR was having difficulties, at this time, with the new Chinese dictator, Mao Tse-tung. That secret, however, like so many others, remained hidden in the dark recesses of the Kremlin.

In 1954 CBS televised a special narrated by Edward R. Murrow. Its title was *Resources for Freedom.* The script was taken from a five-volume study of the nation's resources undertaken two years earlier by a five-man task force headed by William S. Paley and including George Brown, Arthur Bunker, Eric Hodgins, and Edward Mason. They contrasted an increased use of natural resources with the decline of such resources. Looking ahead twenty-five years to 1977, they foresaw a crisis unless changes were made in the manner in which raw materials were exchanged between countries. One of the commissioners stressed the relatively small number of scientists working in the country in the early fifties—76,000 scientists, 59,000 engineers—and said that if all industries were as advanced as petroleum or chemicals, prospects might be more hopeful. They recommended less waste, more conservation, greater stockpiling, and more attention paid to the raw materials that comprise energy. Twenty-one years later George Brown was handing visitors small copies of that script of 1954. It was still relevant, and its recommendations were still disregarded.

JB and the Browns had agreed that the area he should concentrate upon was from Baytown, Texas, to Moundsville, West Virginia. JB flew into that region; his effort was later called a study, and that was as accurate a title as could be expected. JB himself would call it a preliminary sales sweep. William P. Hayes, an outside consultant and C. L. Brockschmidt, a Texas Eastern vice president, had already produced two studies of this eleven state marketing area; JB called on various firms and friends and executives and helped produce a third.

To penetrate the area the men drew plans to create new lateral pipelines; JB worked on that subject with Herb Fisher, the president of Pipeline Technologists. He was adding new men to his list of acquaintances all the time, but his observations inside Texas Eastern—the first really large firm he had ever even briefly joined—reinforced his opinions that large firms produce small men.

Checking into a hotel suite with one, JB was astonished to see him return from a trip outside with a paper bag filled with Cokes, bags of crackers, and the like.

"I saw the prices on room service and I thought I'd save the company some money," he said from behind his parcel.

"We've flown in on a private plane and checked into a suite in one of the largest hotels in the land, and our combined time is worth thousands of dollars," JB said, "and you're worried about the price of a Coke." He was not impressed.

In the autumn, however, he took a break from the heavy round, from flying into his Shreveport office to deal with the concerns of four corporations in as many areas, one after the other in a single sitting. He went on a duck hunt with some old and good friends from the oil industry. One night, after midnight, he found himself locked in combat over a poker hand with Charley Knox.

They were playing draw, and JB was dealt a miserable hand; he had only a pair of deuces. Charley Knox opened—which meant he had to have jacks or better—with a huge bet.

"If I hit, I'll raise you out of your chair," JB said, and called for three cards. Charley Knox asked for one. Alvin Siteman took one, Phil Siteman one, and Howard Barksdale one.

Charley Knox then made another huge bet "before I look."

JB, repeating his threat to "raise you out of the chair if I helped," looked and saw a third deuce. "There's been too many one card draws," he said, "and Charley said he bet before he looked."

Then he called Knox's bet, added up the pot to see the limit, and threw in a raise of $496.

The table grew quiet, and Alvin Siteman struggled visibly with himself. Finally he threw in his hand, saying, "You can beat two big pair." Howard and Phil Siteman followed suit. That left Charley, who had raised the storm in the first place.

Knox leaned forward and stared at JB. "Take out that last bet," he said, "and I'll split the pot with you."

"You're weakening," JB told him.

"Can I have all the time I want?"

"Take weeks, if you like."

Charley then went around the lodge, trying to sell shares in his hand. He went upstairs and awakened his partner, and asked his advice.

Then he came downstairs again and asked JB, "Can I have all the time I want?"

"Yes."

Charley took three hours and forty-five minutes. Finally he collected the sum, counted it several times, and pushed it into the pot. "You'll have to show me," he concluded, and turned over a pair of tens and a pair of sixes.

JB showed him the three deuces—the smallest possible three of a kind—and raked in the pot. Great roars went up around them. While these resounded, JB drew up a statement.

"On this day Charles E. Knox, after duly deliberating for three hours and forty-five minutes, did call $——— with a pair of tens and sixes against three deuces held by JB Saunders." He passed the statement around and men put their names down as witnesses, and the record was tacked to the wall.

Meanwhile Knox, who had obtained a monstrous bell, went ringing it through the lodge shouting, "I know you want to know!" arousing those still so insensitive as to sleep.

Dawn came and men straggled downstairs, dressed and ready to hunt. Knox was asleep by then, felled by emotion, assisted by drink. He slept as one in a trance until noon. By then the men returned, leading a goat, whose bell Knox had stolen during the night. The goat was persuaded into the lodge and wandered about wearing a placard upon which someone had inscribed, in immense letters, a legend. It read: My Name is Charley, but My Ass Belongs to JB Saunders.

Clouds, however, gathered on the business front. The Texas Eastern plan to reconvert the Little Big Inch had sent great angers coursing through the firms whose home territories would be penetrated and threatened. One of these was Ashland Oil—far from a major in 1954, but nevertheless an important marketer to independents.

Another group that was made unhappy by the prospect of the giant pipeline carrying petroleum products from the Gulf to New Jersey with laterals extending to various regions en route was that of the large barge operators of the Mississippi and other inland waterways.

The Browns had no problem in obtaining permission from the Federal Power Commission to undertake their conversion. But Harry Jordan, the head of River Company, and Chotin Towing Corporation, and the Greenville Towing Company, filed suit, claiming a violation of the Sherman and Clayton Acts. The basic charge was that the Texas Eastern and Triangle were trying to monopolize the transportation of petroleum products, and to put the barge lines out of business.

Lawyers for Jordan were, JB noticed with interest, Harold Leventhal, of Ginsburg, Leventhal and Brown in Washington, D.C., and the Shreveport firm of Tucker, Bronson and Martin. The Washington lawyers were known to be among the top.

Texas Eastern, however, had a battery of smart lawyers of its own. Charley Francis was famous in his own right, and Charley Thompson was also gifted. In all, the Browns assembled seven attorneys who asked for a summary judgment throwing the case out of court. The plaintiffs, of course, wanted an injunction.

The injunction was granted. That meant the conversion was held up until the issues were thrashed out in court before a judge. Meanwhile, with so much time, effort, and investment involved, JB and the men at Texas Eastern had to continue to travel, to call on firms and distributors, to make plans and estimate costs, and to proceed to prepare for the day when the case was settled. It was their conviction that larger persons than Harry Jordan were moving against them; Harry Jordan was a small barge operator who could certainly not afford the expensive talent that appeared.

By 1955 the USSR had resolved its internal crisis over the successor to Stalin, and settled on Khrushchev. That individual, notorious for purges in the Ukraine, who served in World War II as a general-commissar and spy for Stalin, exhibited a coarse geniality that deceived some Westerners. His ascent was not total—he was flanked by watchful associates—but the worst struggles were now under control. The commissars moved to weld the eastern European nations under their control and, using the NATO Alliance as an excuse, erected the Warsaw Pact. The Warsaw Pact was better knit, militarily, than NATO, since it consisted of Soviet troops quartered in the satellite nations.

At the same time a modernization of Soviet propaganda appeared. Khruschchev and Bulganin, a commissar whose goatee and small white mustache gave him an Old Russian look, began a series of foreign tours. Since top leaders of the USSR had seldom ventured into the world, those were publicity bonanzas, and lent some credibility to the claims mounted by fellow travelers that the Soviet paradise was now changing—"merging," as some would have it, with the West.

Those peregrinations were clearly heading toward a confrontation of sorts with those of Chou En-lai, who had toured Asia and even Europe, charming many unwary observers and espousing the "underdeveloped world" against the West. It was an evidence of how ardently Europe and the United States longed for peace that both touring parties were flatteringly described, as though the growth of their respective influences would, somehow, make the world better. That was, in fact, a reigning theory. It resembled, in essence, the theory of Chamberlain years before: that no difficulties would arise if all difficulties were met by gifts of power.

JB, however, was among the millions of Americans merely thankful that the landscape had grown more serene and that business, in early 1955, was booming. Triangle was still his major concern. He was still signing up plants and conducting that business, whose volume was now running at the rate of $85 million a year, with net profits of over $1 million a year, as assiduously as ever.

In February, 1955, he signed a contract on his usual 4 percent basis with the Del Roc Refineries of Fairbank, Texas, and was well pleased with Barksdale, Tinsley, and the rest of his staff. His employees in Triangle Refineries had increased; he was beginning to believe he might need a larger headquarters—a much larger one.

Nevertheless, the memory of the plane crash that had taken away John Atkins remained in the back of his mind, and the minds of some of his friends and business associates. He did a great deal of flying, sometimes in bad weather. Whenever he looked out the window, saw clusters of ice beginning to form, and heard chunks hit the plane as the heaters melted them off, he would think of Shreveport and of Vernon Chance saying on the phone, "I can still see the flames."

Some of the firms with whom Triangle contracted wanted a special cancellation clause "in the event of the death of JB Saunders." That worried him, and he wondered how he could circumvent that problem. He was in his fifty-fifth year—a time when some thought must be taken of the future.

JB called Jack Wightman and the insurance broker flew in to Houston. Through Aetna he wrote a policy of one million dollars straight life and one million dollars' worth of accident insurance on JB. That helped, but it was clear that more would have to be done. Time does not stand still, and Triangle could not forever be considered dependent on one man.

The years had mellowed the Triangle team. At one point, said Keith Fanshier, "JB ruled with a heavy hand. He listened to his men, but he overruled them when he chose, hard. But he treated them well; he was very generous in terms of salaries and privileges—and they stuck with him. It was a little like *Life with Father*."

In the early years this had led to some harsh discipline. Barksdale had once gone to a convention and gotten drunk. The news filtered back to JB. He called his star into his office and said, "You can't do that. Unless you tell me you won't do it again, you can't go to conventions."

That possibility was death to a salesman. Barksdale protested that he was with an entire crowd of men and they had all gotten drunk. "That's different," JB said. "They work for the majors. Men who work for the majors can afford to get drunk. We're independents—*and we have to behave better than the majors.*"

Barksdale looked at him, clicked his heels, straightened to his full height, and saluted. "Aye, aye, cap'n," he said, and JB had to laugh.

"He could ingratiate himself," he said later. But what was more remarkable was that Barksdale never again got drunk at a convention.

In similar fashion, Raborn, a complex man, had gradually grown easier in his approach to life and to other people. When he first started, JB learned that he had, on one occasion, knelt in prayer with an office worker, and asked the Lord to help her become more efficient.

He also "averaged" the workers. "What does that mean?" JB asked.

It meant that Raborn had discovered a way to keep office salaries within a certain perimeter, and used statistical methods to achieve what he considered the best possible balance between low salaries and overall efficiency. The approach, similar to that of all—or at least many—personnel departments, outraged Saunders.

"Forget that," he ordered. "I want all my people to earn more money here than they can somewhere else."

Following that principle, he gave heavy bonuses—in some years as much as three months' pay. Every year everyone received an extra month's pay in two-week chunks: one at midsummer and one near Christmas.

The result was that everyone grew to know JB, his foibles, and his methods. Over the years the firm operated in a relaxed, almost familial manner. Barksdale was with JB one night; they had traveled long. Tinsley and Craven wanted to continue the gin game and JB agreed. After a short time, however, Barksdale stretched his long frame, yawned hugely, stepped over to the sofa and stretched out, and was almost asleep in minutes. He could do that; it was one of his curious abilities.

JB scowled, and said, "Dammit, working for me is not a part-time matter." Barksdale's eyes opened, he moved swiftly back to the chair and to Tinsley's amusement said briefly, "Deal."

Not the same, but a similar, spirit affected Tinsley. He turned out to be a golfer par excellence; his office today is lined with cups won at dozens of contests. But beyond that, Tinsley could smooth the ruffled feathers of men who felt damaged by JB's headlong rushes. Harold

Martin of Chicago, who would grow unhappy periodically, was a case that only Tinsley could doctor. He would fly up to see Harold, spend three days, and fly away again, leaving that important customer euphoric for another several months.

JB, however, knew his team was more than the sum of its parts. "A man in a large corporation can only learn a piece," he said, "and my men learned the entire industry. There were times when we actually bought a product from one department of Standard of Indiana and sold it to another—and neither of them ever discovered it."

How, then, does one go about ensuring the future of a firm so personally planted and nurtured, to so special a mixture, so that it will live after the gardener is gone?

The spring of 1955 was filled with the comings and goings of lawyers engaged in their battle regarding the legality and wisdom of the conversion of the Little Big Inch. Leventhal and his associates took depositions, as did Charley Francis and Charley Thompson. The arguments mounted by Jordan's attorneys were dense and voluminous. The arguments mounted by Francis and Thompson were more succinct, and seemed easier to read. That is an important point; judges are, after all, human and should not be fed material suitable for computers.

Because business is composed—as are law, medicine, and virtually every other profession—of a host of grimy details, there is a myth that it lacks an overview. JB's deposition on the Texas Eastern conversion is interesting because it contains, despite the myth, precisely the overview the critics clamor to hear.

After sketching in the background and position of Triangle, he declared the Chicago area was not dependent on the Mississippi barge traffic, as Jordan's lawyers had contended, but in large measure had refineries in its own region. Most of those, he pointed out, were owned by major firms who used the region largely as a base to supply other regions. JB also pointed out that much of Chicago was supplied, in terms of petroleum products, by pipelines from Oklahoma and Kansas.

Then he turned toward the barges. Their passage, he said, was often impeded by high or low waters and ice in winter. They had to reduce their loads in order to pass through a chain of rocks. In December, January, and February barges were blocked and backed up, and the government persistently refused to appropriate funds to improve the locks that would improve river traffic.

Then JB went into a dissertation of the various routes from the Gulf to Chicago, the varying rates on water through the seasons, the possibilities of lateral pipelines from the Little Big Inch through Indianapolis to Chicago, the costs of river terminals, and an analysis of the industrial sectors that would feel such competition, as well as the impact upon the supplying firms on the Gulf that increased traffic would affect.

The exercise was impressive. It was this sort of reasoning that had built Triangle, and that the Browns could appreciate. Yet it was only a deposition—one among many. The courts of the United States are like glaciers. They glitter, cover vast areas, contain concealed chasms and towering peaks—and move at a pace imperceptible to human eyes. Meanwhile, the great pipeline conversion was tied into knots.

In the summer of 1955 Khrushchev and Bulganin appeared in India waving flowers and promising economic aid. India, which had been the object of western pity and largesse for years, was now being courted by China, the USSR, and the United States of America. Other Asian nations were also honored; the two Kremlin purge-masters, wearing straw hats, roomy trousers, and broad smiles, junketed about like two cartooned Rotarians, but—unlike Rotarians—enjoyed a respectful press. The Moscow road show popped up in Europe, and even in Belgrade, Yugoslavia. A climax of sorts was reached in that land, however, when Khrushchev got so drunk he passed out and had to be carried away from a garden party at his own embassy. The whole globe would have shrieked at the barbarism of an American chief of state who so forgot himself; Khrushchev's disgrace was described as endearingly human.

Nevertheless, there were signs that the Kremlin was changing. A visit to Tito was a visit to a man who defied Stalin. The withdrawal of Soviet troops from Austria, and a peace treaty with that tiny land, were startling. The fact was that the policy of the USSR seemed, for once, wavering and uncertain. A conference was held in Geneva, and President Eisenhower offered to exchange military information and asked for "open skies" over both lands. The Soviets, to whom the American military situation was already virtually open, saw no advantage in that and orated endlessly against the series of alliances Dulles was sewing together around the world. The conference ended, as usual, beneath banners of brave words, but the results were minimal for Washington.

At home the nation worked hard, but its play grew strange. More than a billion comic books were sold at an estimated cost of $100 million—more than four times the total book budget of every public library in the land.[4] Rock-and-roll music appeared, to the delight of

4. Carruth and Associates, *American Facts and Dates*, p. 591.

the young and horror of their parents. Labor, finally combining the CIO and AFL, mounted a campaign for a guaranteed yearly wage. Business, however, took a startling leap upward of over one third in volume.

JB, on his frequent trips to New York City, dropped in on White, Weld & Company, a firm active in oil and petroleum company mergers for years, and also on Glore, Forgan. He carried with him enough evidence of the Triangle activities and interests to acquaint them with the firm. Both those knowledgeable investment houses studied his situation, but their response was disappointing.

If he decided to sell Triangle stock to the public, they told him, it would have to be traded over the counter. His firm lacked national recognition, and therefore the investors would not turn toward it. Their advice was to sell out to a firm listed on the Big Board. That was not what he wanted to hear.

There was always, of course, Texas Eastern. But that executive suite was filled, it seemed to JB, with a great many men. The Browns were on the mountain top, and between their summit and other levels remained a vast, impassable cliff. Furthermore, the men on the lower slopes were not JB's breed. On one occasion he had a plan to institute an action, and discussed it with a department head. The department head, to JB's irritation, balked.

JB picked up the phone, called George Brown—the only man to whom he reported—and handed the department head the phone. The executive, taken aback, explained his objections to Mr. Brown, and then listened for several minutes, during which he said only, "Yes, Mr. Brown," at intervals.

Finally Mr. Brown finished. It was clear that JB's project would proceed; the objections were overridden. The department head looked resentfully at JB and said, "Don't do that to me again."

JB rose, and replied, "Don't you do that to me," and walked out. *"I don't want this job,"* he thought. *"I don't want to deal with dummies."*

Nevertheless Texas Eastern had purchased Triangle Pipelines and he worked hard on the Little Big Inch conversion; he didn't want to see that great effort go down in defeat in the courts. When the case was called, he was ready.

Court cases were not new; the United States had become a litigious nation and it was impossible to do business without being crowded by legal arguments of one sort or another. That may have something to do with the national animus against attorneys. JB, who had grown accustomed to courtroom atmospheres in his youth, took the stand when his name was called with no nervousness. He believed the Texas Eastern and Triangle case was valid and legal.

JB followed George Naff, the president of Texas Eastern, to the stand. Attorney Harold Leventhal rose to cross-examine after Charley Thompson finished leading Saunders through a complete, tightly structured defense. Leventhal's questions were long and loaded, like his briefs. But he demanded Yes or No replies.

JB turned to the judge. "Your Honor," he said, "the attorney doesn't really want a reply. His questions all have three or four barbs in them and are too long for a Yes or No."

The judge indicated that Saunders could reply at the length and in the detail he thought the questions required, and JB began to enjoy himself. He would begin an involved reply to questions that were, he said, "three or four yards long, all tied into knots."

Then it was Leventhal's turn to protest. "Your Honor," he said, "If Mr. Saunders would stop talking I could win this case."

The judge soothed Leventhal. JB saw Harry Jordan himself enter the courtroom and take a chair at his attorneys' table. Then JB saw Jordan whisper to one of his lawyers, while looking at Saunders.

The lawyer rose and said, "You're testifying that products can be barged as cheaply as they can be carried in a pipeline. Are you building any new barges?"

"Yes," JB replied. "I'm building three that will cost eighty thousand dollars each."

The attorney flushed and sat down, and Jordan whispered to him again. The attorney rose.

"Are you building these barges to transport oil?"

"That's all I transport," JB answered, and saw Harry Jordan flee from the courtroom, having enormously assisted JB against his own intention.

During recesses the witnesses, attorneys, and judge would go to another room, where some coffee and cakes were available. JB, helping himself, turned when the judge came over to him. "Mr. Saunders," he said, "Mr. Naff described you as saying that your salary is peanuts. But you testified that your salary is actually thirty-seven thousand five hundred dollars a year. Would you mind telling me your definition of peanuts?"

"Mr. Naff is apt to drink his lunch on occasion," JB said. "What I meant to say is that what is left of a salary of $37,500 after the income tax people get through, is peanuts."

The judge, whose salary was $37,500, thawed visibly. "I see," he said.

The case, however, was not easy to resolve, although the initial decision was in favor of Texas Eastern's conversion plan. Jordan, in the name of his firm, and with a large number of barge operators lined up behind him, decided to appeal. At that rate the Little Big Inch would be in court for years to come.

Other problems loomed. The government was preparing a case, behind the usual closed doors, against the Cotton Valley Operators' Committee and its unitized field. That step was predictable, signs of cooperation among businessmen having become automatically suspect in the land—a considerable distortion of the original ideas against monopolies.

Rumors of the case reached H. L. Hunt, who grew alarmed and decided to pull out of the Cotton Valley as soon as possible. As a first step in that direction, he abruptly canceled his contract with Triangle.

JB, who had not heard the rumors, was immediately informed of the cancellation. He was surprised and angered. A contract was sacred to him, and he could never understand how any man can reverse his pledged word. Discovering that Hunt had rented an old colonial estate in Lawrence, Massachusetts, where he was worrying over the continuing illness of his favorite son, Hassie Hunt, JB flew there at once.

He had dinner at the estate with the great promoter, but it did not go well. JB knew his Triangle operation was clearly legal, and could not understand why Hunt had canceled. Hunt's explanation was garbled, though he did not choose to make much of one; that was not his style. Caustic words were exchanged, but the two men agreed to sleep on the situation and meet the following morning for breakfast.

After dinner JB had to take a cab thirty-five miles back to Boston—in the rain. That did not improve his temper, but by the time he arrived at the Commander Hotel, he had decided to go to Washington to unravel what appeared a mare's nest. He placed a call to David Smitherman in Shreveport, explained the situation, and asked Smitherman to meet him in Washington, D.C. Then he took a plane.

The following day JB and Smitherman called on J. Watson Snyder, a legal brain at Justice, whom JB had met during the Madison trial. Snyder had, in fact, helped JB gather his papers after he had testified during that great brouhaha, and had even walked out with him and seen him off. Later JB realized that Snyder's solicitude was really produced in order to keep him from comparing notes with other witnesses. "He sugar-coated the pills," JB said.

But when JB and Smitherman appeared to discuss Triangle's contracts with the Cotton Valley Operators, Snyder recalled JB very well. He was, as always, courteous. Asked about the Triangle contracts, he said, "We have, of course, examined them closely. I cannot say we like them. But certainly they are legal, and we have nothing against them."

Jubilant, JB called Hunt from the nation's capital. "Where are you?" Hunt asked. "I thought we were going to have breakfast together."

JB explained his errand and its results. But he was stunned to discover that it did not sway the older man. Hunt planned to continue his cancellation. JB finally said, "You can't cancel without paying."

"I cancel when I please," Hunt replied, and hung up. The cancellation came through soon afterward—and Hunt also received a bill from JB for thirty thousand dollars, as a penalty. Hunt paid, but he was angry—and so was JB.[5]

In the autumn of 1955, however, Triangle had moved far beyond the position where a contract cancellation—even a large one—could seriously impede its progress or position. JB was, in fact, continuing to expand. He signed a contract with a distillate production plant in Hudson, Texas, and Triangle's volume continued to increase.

The question of the Texas Eastern pipeline conversion, however, had finally begun to irk him beyond measure. He was certain that Paul Blazer of Ashland and Fritz Ingram, the largest barge operator on the river, had combined to deliberately delay that project as long as possible, and were secretly funding Harry Jordan's expensive litigation. He had argued this point with Charley Thompson, one of the top lawyers for Texas Eastern, and Thompson had not denied that was accurate. The next question was what could be done about it? There was no law against assisting a case favorable to the interests of one's firm. "If we are wrong," he warned, "we'll be liable for triple damages."

But JB was not satisfied with that reasoning. He insisted that economic damage was being created to many persons and concerns. He wanted to sue Blazer, Ingram, and Jordan—to turn the tables on them, haul them into court, and drag them through long, wearisome sessions giving depositions to young attorneys.

JB's arguments appeared to fall on deaf ears for some time. But in

5. The Department of Justice did file against the Cotton Valley Operators Committee, and David Smitherman represented the defendants. In the course of preparing his defense, Smitherman asked the Court for the Justice records, and the judge ordered Justice to produce them in seven days. The government attorneys refused, and the judge threw the case out of court. Justice appealed, sure of victory, but the Supreme Court, which finally reviewed the issue, upheld the dismissal. Smitherman remains—as he should—proud of that outcome.

the autumn of 1955, while the API meeting was in progress, JB picked up the newspapers in the late afternoon and saw, to his surprise, that the Browns had at last filed a suit against Blazer, Ingram, and Jordan.

Walking into the API meeting that night he saw the trio standing together, holding an animated conversation. Acting on instinct, JB walked over to them. "Let me be the first to congratulate you," he said. "You're the only friends of mine to be sued for thirty million dollars each."

Blazer, whose mind worked faster than the speed of light, said quickly, "We were just talking about that. You're the only man we know who can help. *Let's get this thing settled.*"

"If I can, I will," JB replied, and moved away. He went to a phone and called Charley Francis, the top Texas Eastern attorney, and reported the brief exchange.

"Stay away from them," Francis said at once, reflecting the usual legal recoil at a client's intervention in a case.

"I didn't say a thing," JB assured him.

"I'll be in Washington next week," Francis said after a pause. "If Leventhal wants to see me, he can."

JB went back to the trio who were still standing together, and said, "Paul, Charley Francis will be at the Statler Hotel in Washington next week. Why not have Harry Leventhal call?"

Ten days later the case was settled out of court.

Other legal cases, of a new sort, were clogging the nation's courts through the winter of 1955–1956 and through the spring of the new year. These stemmed from the Supreme Court ruling striking down segregation in public schools, and spread to demonstrations by blacks in the South against other barriers in the public sector. The Court ruling, hailed by many, was not at first the springboard of much change. The Justices, after all, had stressed "deliberate speed." That was interpreted to mean, in some quarters, a rate of attrition and organic change that could stretch over a generation. Long-pent desires, however, could not be held back so easily, once the rigid doors of segregation began to crack apart.

At first, however, the NAACP and other groups turned toward the courts and demanded, in cases filed throughout the South and in other regions, injunctions and mandates in keeping with the letter and the spirit of the change indicated by the highest tribunal.

As the implications of this change began to seep through the mind of the nation, it drew attention away from the international stage, which had seemed to thaw. That impression, however, was in error.

The Soviets were confronted with rising discontent in their eastern European colonies, especially in Poland and Hungary. The Kremlin leadership was still divided between the older members such as Molotov, Kaganovich, and Malenkov, and the newer stars such as Khrushchev and his supporters. Khrushchev decided upon a bold stroke. All the ills and failures of the Communist system, and all the manifold injustices under which the people of the USSR and its satellite countries groaned, would be blamed on Stalin.[6] That denunciation was delivered to the Supreme Soviet, a rubber stamp gathering of the faithful, and created consternation through the land. The activities that were ascribed to the fallen idol were clearly criminal, and although criminals at the head of governments had grown commonplace in the twentieth century, the admission that one could rule the workers' paradise for so many years was enough to send shock waves through millions of Communists and even more millions of their allies throughout the world. The news, as it seems all greatly significant news must, traveled slowly. It did not reach the West for weeks at the top, and for months elsewhere.

The weather in Shreveport was growing warm, and Reggie Brinkman felt cheerful enough to go home and play several hard sets of tennis with his young son. The boy was only thirteen or fourteen, and very agile, but his father was able to keep up with him; his stronger drives gave him the advantage.

But later that evening as Virginia Brinkman was reading in the livingroom, Reggie appeared in the doorway, alternately paling and flushing, and said, "I'm having a heart attack."

Their next-door neighbor was a physician; Mrs. Brinkman summoned him immediately. He came, gave Reggie some medication, and saw him comfortably settled. Then he went upstairs with Mrs. Brinkman to view a room she had converted into a dance studio. Reggie's brother came over, and on his way upstairs looked in to the ailing man's bedroom, saw he was having new difficulties, and ran up to notify the doctor. By the time the physician and Mrs. Brinkman hurried downstairs, however, the crisis was over—and Reggie was dead.

JB came to Shreveport at once, and attended the funeral. His firm was now a Triangle in name only; both his original backers were gone. The day after the funeral Mrs. Brinkman asked to have a discussion about Reggie's interest in the enterprise. JB and Barksdale went to the Brinkman home together to explain the details.

6. Ulam, *Expansion and Coexistence*, pp. 572–577.

Mrs. Brinkman listened intently. Her eldest son, Buddy, a lieutenant in the Air Force, was home on leave. Buddy planned to resign his commission, return to civilian life and devote his time to handling his family's business affairs.

JB explained, as he had to the Atkins family, Reggie's contributions to Triangle, and described the understandings and agreements that had been reached. "All Highland Oil has with Triangle are some sales contracts," he said, "and Reggie also had contracts with United Gas, Arkansas Fuel and some other firms. I will carry your fifty-percent interest on those contracts till they expire. If they are renewed, that income will last you another five years. If you want to draw your money from Highland Oil, I will also assure its contracts and pay you fifty percent of their profits as long as they last—even if renewed.

"Meanwhile," he continued, "I offered John Atkins and Reggie one million dollars each for their share of Triangle some years ago. I can now offer you $1.2 million, and if you choose, you can withdraw that as your part of the firm's capital."

That was a handsome sum. Unlike the Atkins family, the Brinkmans decided to accept it. For a brief period that seemed to be that, but Mrs. Brinkman's brother, going through Reggie's books, reported that he found an entry in which Reggie lent JB $25,000, but no item regarding the disposition of that amount. There was, JB noted, no sign of the note he had given Reggie; it had apparently been torn up years before.

He explained that agreement, in which both John Atkins and Reggie had agreed the $25,000 each had advanced would be forgotten in the event either of them sold. Mrs. Brinkman heard the explanation in silence.

A few days later, JB received a call from Simon Herald, a Shreveport attorney, who said he wanted to discuss an outstanding sum of $25,000. JB went through his explanation again. In due course, however, a registered letter arrived from Herald, requiring a signature from the recipient. JB refused the letter, but sent Mrs. Brinkman a check for $25,000.

The passing of Reggie Brinkman brought the subject of Triangle's future—and, for that matter, his own future—back to the forefront of JB's mind. At one time he had given Texas Eastern an option to buy 45 percent of Triangle, but that option had later been dropped by Charley Thompson, the Texas Eastern attorney. The Browns, however, were not particularly pleased to see that option vanish. "You'll have to sell, you know, one of these days," one of them said quietly.

By mid-1956 JB agreed with that point. But he was not especially anxious to sell to Texas Eastern, though he knew the price would be fair, and he admired both the Browns. It was simply that their ventures were huge. He believed Triangle would be diminished in those vast corridors.

There were other groups, however. Champlin Oil, as the Chicago Corporation now called itself, had come to covet Triangle very sincerely—but JB would never sell to that firm. He began to survey possibilities on his own. He had, after all, found a market for Triangle's products through the years; he had no doubt he could find the right buyer for the firm with equal efficiency.

He began to examine petroleum firms with weak marketing divisions that were strong in other areas. A number fit that category, and he began to sift them. In most instances their weakness in marketing was matched by soft surrounding divisions, until he reached one in particular. Located in a region he knew well, with a promising future, not overcrowded with "major company men," it would particularly benefit by the acquisition of the world's largest marketing firm. He then leaned back to consider his approach. That was the sort of maneuver in which he had always taken pleasure.

No democratic country in the world could have made the admissions that Khrushchev made to the Supreme Soviet and remain unchanged. Not even the men in the Kremlin, who had seen almost every revolutionary figure except Stalin denigrated in later years, were prepared for the depths of expression that welled involuntarily from their land when the figure immortalized in statues everywhere, in paintings, and in all the official literature, was described as twisted, murderous, hateful, and degenerate. The greatest disturbance was among the young, who were unaccustomed to the idea that an entire society could live a lie. Fate, however, intervened to spare the commissars a concentrated look; the attention of the world was drawn away—and by the time it turned back, the news was old and stale.

The intervention occurred in the Middle East. France had created one of its complicated plots, too intricate to be successful. Her reasons were that she was losing her hold in Morocco, Algeria, and Tunisia. She was moving toward granting independence to Morocco and Tunisia, but Algeria was a region in which the French investment was immense, and where many French had settled. To reduce a rising rebellion and maintain her control, France needed support. Paris turned toward London, which had lost possession first of Egypt and then of the Suez Canal. A scheme was put together in which Israel was to attack Egypt; Britain and France would intervene to mediate a peace, and to maintain that peace would station troops in the region. The United States was busy with elections, and it was decided not to strain President Eisenhower's traditional indifference to politics by leaking any prior word to Washington.

Secretary Dulles was persuaded, however, to join with France and Britain in withdrawing financial aid to Egypt because it had seized the canal. The British and French then withdrew their nationals from Egypt, and a minicrisis was created. By October, 1956, demonstrations arose in Hungary, but the canal crisis continued to occupy attention. On October 29 Israel moved its army toward Egypt, and the Hungarian Workers Party seized power in Hungary, and released Cardinal Mindszenty. On October 30, 1956, Britain and France issued an ultimatum for a cease-fire in the Middle East, which was respected only by Israel. On the same day, Soviet troops entered Hungary. The next day the British and French bombed Egypt, and demonstrations against the action broke out in London and other parts of England.

In the next few days the British and French, subjected to angry words from Washington, faltered and, a few days later, withdrew. President Eisenhower was then embarrassed by a stream of threats that rose from the commissars calling for an immediate peace in the Middle East, while Soviet tanks rumbled through Budapest.

In that atmosphere the United States went to the polls and re-elected a President who had, in effect, delivered one of the most telling American international blows in history against three nations with which his own was allied. That action, however, was hailed at home as a master-stroke for peace.

The dust settled slowly through the winter of 1956–1957. The Soviet had fastened an iron grip on Hungary, and the United States accepted a number of refugees from that unhappy land, who first found sanctuary in Austria and other lands in the West. The fading radio cries for help, which were officially ignored, rendered any statement that Secretary Dulles might make regarding the liberation of lands in eastern Europe completely without credibility. The Secretary himself realized that well; his rhetoric was notably softened thereafter. The British prime minister, Anthony Eden, was forced to resign. The Suez débâcle hastened the Algerian rebellion and the loss of that property to France. It exposed Britain as no longer a first-class power. In all, the year 1956 ended with the West greatly weakened, though few in the United States appeared to realize it.

Early in 1957 JB was visited by his old friend and Houston neighbor, Grant Judge. Judge was head of Arthur Andersen, the huge numbers factory. The firm knew Triangle very well and served as its auditors. Judge also knew that JB was at a critical juncture with his venture. "Have you ever thought of joining a Big Board company?" he asked.

JB said he had, and waited.

"Well, I represent—or that is, Arthur Andersen represents—a petroleum company that has production, drilling, but no marketing."

"Do you mean Kerr McGee?"

"How did you know?"

"I've been studying their statement." JB leaned back, highly pleased. Judge was a stroke of luck. He was the perfect go-between; everyone respects their outside auditors. Furthermore, he had no personal reason to shade his opinions. Judge was pleased at the role; he called Kerr McGee and an appointment was arranged.

A few weeks later JB and Dean McGee regarded one another in Kerr McGee's executive suite in Oklahoma City. It would be hard to find two men who lived in more separated mental worlds. JB's was the world of the marketplace, teeming with people, negotiations, and the movement of goods. McGee, on the other hand, lived in a world of subsurface properties: coal, uranium, oil, gas, water, minerals. Across that mental landscape trundle machines that drill, grind, carry, and measure.

The world of people and the world of properties, however, can combine in many ventures. Senator Robert S. Kerr was a man much like JB, although an older man. He was in Washington, where he was a very powerful senator, at the time JB and Dean McGee first began to talk. The talk went well; McGee suggested that JB send along his financial statements. Kerr McGee was interested. It needed the world's largest marketing company. They shook hands and their parting was amiable.

JB had already prepared all his documents; he had gone through that exercise for the financiers of New York City. He sent them to Oklahoma City. A month later he was stung to receive a letter asking him to revise his price—downward—to "equal his assets."

He called Oklahoma City. "I can see you don't understand my company," he told McGee, when the president came on the phone. "Why not let our financial men get together? Who's yours?"

"Les Woodward," McGee replied.

"I'll send Raborn to Oklahoma City," JB promised. The two men chatted briefly and made tentative plans to talk again at the API meeting, which was held shortly afterward.

But although JB saw McGee at the meeting, they did not hold any conversation. JB, busy on a Texas Eastern financial situation, flew to

Toronto to talk to Sun Life, then to Boston to visit the First National, then to New York to hold conversations with Prudential Life. By the time he returned to Houston he had borrowed $101 million for the Little Big Inch.

The opposition had succeeded, through injunction after injunction, in delaying the Little Big Inch conversion from gas to petroleum products long enough to allow eastern firms to extend pipelines west. Paul Blazer of Ashland had increased his tows and barges and no longer feared competition. In fact, Texas Eastern could no longer successfully penetrate the eleven-state region it had originally planned to reach. Blazer had been the architect of the delay, and as George Brown said later, "Time was money."

The only viable alternative, which JB suggested and which the Browns adopted, was to build a lateral from the Little Big Inch toward the Chicago area. That was a truncation of the original grand plan, but one that nevertheless made the conversion profitable. It was that extension that caused JB's eastern swing.

He attended a meeting of the National Petroleum Refiners' Association, and was approached there by Frank C. Love, the executive vice president of Kerr McGee. Love is one of the most persuasive men in the world. A lawyer, he had been brought in to Kerr McGee by the Senator and got along famously both with that towering and unusual figure, and with the firm, rocklike Dean McGee. Love recalls when he first met JB, in the club car of a train going from Oklahoma City to an API meeting in Chicago in the early fifties. Love was chatting with Earl Baldridge, the president of Champlin Oil, who looked up, saw JB, and said, "There's the greatest marketing SOB in the United States. I'm going to make a deal to get him."

Baldridge hailed JB, who came over, sat down, and visited briefly. Love stared at him with interest; Saunders had become a legend. But by 1957 it was neither Champlin nor Baldridge who were engaged in a deal with Triangle, but Kerr McGee—and Frank Love attended the San Antonio meeting of the NPRA to move that deal forward.

In San Antonio the two men discussed the negotiation in depth. Love explained Dean McGee's position to JB. "Dean will never pay your price," he said candidly. "He's only interested in you and your marketing company. Why don't you spin off everything else, and reach a new figure?"

JB was astonished. He had asked for twelve million dollars, a price he considered reasonable. Love's explanation threw a different light on the situation, and one that opened interesting doors. Instead of selling all his business to Kerr McGee, JB could sell half and keep half. The more he reviewed that vista, the better it appeared.

He instructed Raborn and Les Woodward, the Kerr McGee financial man, to apply this new yardstick. He himself did the same, measured what remained after all his minority participations and shares in other enterprises were pared away from Triangle, and emerged with a figure of six million dollars. He thought the payment should consist of one hundred thousand shares of Kerr McGee stock, then priced on the exchanges at sixty dollars a share.

Informed of the new figure based on a truncated Triangle, McGee made a counter offer: 50,000 shares. That was half what JB considered his rock-bottom price, and his face turned grim. He would not retreat, and Love was forced into new efforts. These resulted in a Kerr McGee offer of 75,000 shares.

By now the negotiation was bracketed, and appeared headed for resolution. But JB had decided not to retreat from his one hundred thousand-share figure, despite the fact that the Atkins family was eager to see the merger consummated, and even Barksdale was in favor of acceptance.

At that point Love made what proved to be a timely suggestion. "I think Dean's offer might be improved," he said, "by a stock option."

JB looked interested, and the executive vice president added, "But only an employee can obtain a stock option."

JB considered the implications. If he joined Kerr McGee, he could continue to manage the firm he had spent so many years in masterminding. That in itself was a powerful inducement. But his years with Texas Eastern had taught him that most men are impressed by corporate positions, and that he would need a high rank. "If I join Kerr McGee," he said aloud, "I would expect to become a senior officer—and a director."

Love nodded; he was well pleased.

Not long afterward McGee called, sounding very cordial. He suggested that since JB had already visited Oklahoma City, he should come down to Houston. JB said he would look forward to that.

What changed him? He had raised his offer, but had not met JB's price. Obviously, it was JB's added demand that he join the firm and become a director. That changed everything.

"The minute he walked into the office," JB said later, "I knew that McGee was, at last, ready to make a deal." McGee himself even said that, adding only, "If the price is right."

McGee offered JB 85,000 shares of Kerr McGee stock. That was a long step toward JB's asking price. But JB reminded him that three Triangle men owned, between them, 13 percent of the firm's stock. He wondered if he himself could not obtain an option on another 20,000 shares of Kerr McGee at 5 percent below the market, so that he could keep 10,000 shares for himself and give the other 10,000 to his key men.

"It would seal them in," he said. "Otherwise they might leave and become strong competitors." He was, obviously, already thinking in terms of the future Triangle.

McGee said he would have to make a call on that, and left the office. He returned twenty minutes later, smiling, with his hand out. JB stood up. They shook hands, and McGee told him he would join as a senior vice president. "You'll be on the board very soon," he promised, "and we'll really get acquainted."

JB grinned, and his chest swelled. "Gentlemen," he said, "I'm twenty years old today."

They stared and he added, "Today is Triangle's twentieth birthday."

It was true. He had opened the doors of the St. Louis office twenty years earlier, on April 16, 1937. The coincidence, coming at the happy conclusion of the negotiations that ensured a future for his enterprise and his employees—to say nothing of his own fortunes—made his eyes sparkle. It seemed a wonderfully promising omen.

CHAPTER FOURTEEN

Organized in Oklahoma

A DAY OR SO after JB reached his understanding with Dean Mc-
Gee, he was called in for a conversation with Charley Francis, legal
brain for the Browns. JB entered the lawyer's book-lined office, shook
hands, sat down, and waited. Francis came to the point at once.

"Let's quit horsing around," he said. "We'll buy Triangle with
Texas Eastern stock, and make you president of Texas Eastern Transmission."

"You're a day late and a dollar short," JB told him.

"What?"

JB explained the Kerr McGee agreement, and Francis was
shocked. "Why didn't you tell me?" he asked. Then, recovering, he
said quickly, "Have you signed anything yet?"

"No," JB admitted, "*but I shook hands.*" As far as he was concerned, that ended the matter.

It did not end all matters, however. Dean McGee's desire not to
pay too much for a marketing firm had led to the acquisition of Triangle's building in Houston and its marketing people and properties.
But JB was left with his participation in Butler, Miller & Lents—and
many other ventures, which had grown into a very large situation.

Butler had made his first million several years before, and had then
formed Butler, Miller & Lents as a triangle. The entrepreneurs had
found oil, and had then built rapidly. One venture was the Scurry
Natural Gas Processing Company, whose properties included the largest gas plant in the nation. Another was Reef Fields Gasoline corporation, which gathered gas from a three thousand–acre field, the largest in
the world. In addition Butler, Miller & Lents created, in 1957, with the
help of Bill Warren, JB, Herb Seydler, and others, the Transwestern

388

Pipeline Company. That venture was so large that Butler and Seydler had gone to New York City and raised eighty million dollars.

These were huge ventures, as Texas Eastern was huge. JB, when he had shown the Triangle's properties to Kerr McGee, had carried these investments, and others too numerous and scattered to list, on the books at their original figures. They were, therefore, greatly understated. Dean McGee's policy decision, which ruled them from investigation, had—in effect—left JB in the position of a man who had not sold his properties so much as he had enlarged them.

His agreement with Kerr McGee not only left him in charge of Triangle, and added a senior vice presidency, a seat on the board, and a large amount of Kerr McGee stock, but also left him in possession of on-going interests worth far more than he had been willing to sell.

It is doubtful if anyone at Kerr McGee appreciated how much the firm had brushed aside. But the executive vice president of the firm, Frank C. Love, was under no doubts about the quality of Triangle's founder and president. He had seen him, at API meetings and various other places, chatting with the heads of Jersey Standard, Indiana Standard, and other major firms, and was struck by their evident respect.

He also was able to describe—as attorneys will—his own assessment. "JB had all the qualities of a successful man," he said later. "He was relaxed and confident; he knew all the big men in the industry personally and bent over backward to keep his word in all his dealings."

Beyond that, Love knew, far better than anyone else, how badly JB's marketing abilities were needed at Kerr McGee. In describing that, Love revealed both a lack of self-consciousness and an unusual objectivity, for he was in charge of the firm's marketing sector at the time JB joined the company.

"What did you do then?" someone asked.

"I made room; I moved over," Love said simply.

Similar changes were underway in other quarters. Bill Warren, who had built the Warren Petroleum Company and whose contracts provided such a useful pattern for JB, merged his firm into giant Gulf Oil. After the merger Warren joined Gulf as an officer and director. His two key men, Joe La Fortune and Howard Felt, who owned a minority interest in Warren, went in different directions.

The Shaeffer Oil Company, meanwhile, which had changed its name to Deep Rock, was acquired by Kerr McGee, through Frank Love, a few months before the firm acquired Triangle. JB could, as a senior vice president, look forward to working with Barney Majewski, his old competitor and friend.

Similar shifts, sales, and mergers were taking place throughout the petroleum industry, and throughout the entire private sector. The reasons were ironic. The state stepped in to seize the lion's share of a man's estate when he died. Such taxes were popularized as an effort to keep heirs from inheriting fortunes they had not earned. The result, however, of the Socialist desire to level the starting positions of all individuals, was that small enterprises were forced to merge with larger enterprises when proprietors grew older. After World War II, when the taxes became savage upon the death of a proprietor, a wave of such sales began. The overall result was that corporations became fewer but larger. Competition, which the antitrust lawyers brandished as a banner under which to attack large firms, was reduced by the tax collectors more thoroughly and deliberately than by any firm, or group of firms, in the nation's history.

No sector was immune, just as no sector was unaffected by the continuing increase in governmental expenditures and the rise in taxes. Herb Seydler's Second National Bank of Houston, confronted with limitations placed upon its growth by the laws of Texas against branch banks, devised the idea of creating a bank holding company, found the Federal Reserve in favor, and moved in that direction in 1956.

That ushered a great change in Texas banking, and the Second National was the first to make the move. Changing its name to the far more appealing and regionally meaningful *Bank of the Southwest*, it had to go through the procedure of establishing subsidiary banks with complete corporate structures and appropriate titles, but that was easy to resolve.

Seydler, therefore, found himself overtaken by another great wave of change in banking. Although his duties as executive vice president of the Bank of the Southwest were the same as before, it was clear that his successor would be working in a far more structured and more elaborately organized business.

These changes were reflected in the manner in which the rising generation was being educated. Instead of entering trades or business at an early age and learning from the preceding generation, they were kept in school longer. By 1956, 31 million were in public school and nearly 3 million in colleges and universities.[1] The schools themselves proliferated enormously. Business schools of every description mushroomed on all sides. They did not teach thrift nor how to become an entrepreneur, but stressed "management" and how to climb the ladder of corporate advancement. Individuality was losing its traditional American status; the Corporation Man emerged.

The changes that JB made, therefore, were in keeping with the

1. Dulles, *United States Since 1865*, p. 514.

tides around him, which no man can ignore. They affected his family as well. His daughter Suzanne, eighteen in 1957 and in her first year in college, decided to marry rather than stay in school.

JB was no more pleased by that than any other father over an early marriage, but she had selected L. M. (Buddy) Inkley, who was continuing his family's well-established real estate and home development firm. Such a choice was difficult to fault. After the initial shock, the wedding took place amid general congratulations. But it carried Suzanne out of the Saunders home and into another life. JB III was due to graduate from high school in 1957, and was exhibiting the slightly truculent independence of that age. That, too, made a difference.

Eddy Saunders had developed emphysema and curtailed her social life considerably. Fond of their River Oaks home, she was loath to return to Oklahoma, and JB dismissed all thoughts of a permanent move, since he himself preferred the larger atmosphere of Houston.

Yet he was at a stage in life where new people, scenes, and problems carried their own attractions. His habit, whenever changes took place, had been to add work. In common with others who choose that path, he had his rationalizations. "We're like railroads," he said once, "and our minds and bodies are like machines. They must be kept in motion, or they will rust. If they are kept running, they can keep running."

JB was, therefore, running. He remained a vice president at Texas Eastern, continued his Southern States Barge Lines and other activities, and merely added a suite at the Skirvin Tower in Oklahoma City to his business domiciles. In May, 1957, he appeared at new offices at the Kerr McGee corporation. He shared a secretary with Frank Love, and was standing near her desk, which was between their joint offices, when a giant of a man, six feet four or five, came forward with a huge grin and outstretched hand.

"I'm glad to meet the man who has broken prices from the Rocky Mountains to the Gulf of Mexico," he said, "and from the Rockies to the Appalachians."

"It all depends on whose ox is gored," JB responded. Senator Kerr, he knew, was the man Dean McGee called before closing the deal to buy Triangle. The two men found each other instantly congenial. Kerr, a nonsmoking teetotaler, was at the same time an addicted gin player with an amazing memory. The Senator could recall numbers at will, and retain them forever.

The Senator, who came to Oklahoma City on rapid visits, soon formed the habit of playing gin with JB in his Skirvin suite. Steeped in the petroleum industry, the two men swapped stories and reminiscences, and were similar in many respects.

That was not true, however, of JB and Dean McGee. Their approach to business was from opposite points on the spectrum. Only one man was able to appreciate that distance, while at the same time being able to understand and to sympathize with both viewpoints. That was executive vice president Frank Love, whose office was, symbolically as well as physically, located between them.

It took, however, a preliminary period to make that divide evident. In the early months of his association with Kerr McGee, the Triangle head was far too busy ordering his complicated interests into a new series of priorities to be overly aware of such differences.

By August, 1957, however, he was ready for his usual vacation in La Jolla, where he and Eddy had become regular members of a crowd who spent that month at the La Jolla Beach & Tennis Club.

J. Edgar Hoover, who stayed at the Del Charro, was a regular at these gatherings, which included daily trips to the Del Mar racetrack as part of a routine. Most of them were in their fifties, a decade unjustly neglected. It marks, in the lives of most people, a peak period when their children no longer require their attention, when their position in the world is established, and when the disabilities of age have yet to appear.

They were pleased to have the famous G-man with them, year after year, and also pleased that he and his companion, Clyde Tolson, regularly accepted invitations to dinner and cocktail parties and the like. In the restaurant in the evenings, JB noticed that Hoover and Tolson—"a tall, slender, quiet man"—would sit at a regular table. Hoover kept his back to the entrance, in order to avoid attention from strangers, but Tolson watched the entrance, and was alert to every newcomer.

It was a time when solid citizens worried about subversion and communism, when the subject was given extensive coverage and press comment. JB recalls that his friends brought up the subject with J. Edgar Hoover, and that he said quietly, "We have our eyes on them. We know who they are. In the event of trouble, we know exactly where to go, and who to get."

That was reassuring. It was no secret to these sophisticated and substantial people that wiretaps and surveillances were undertaken by the FBI. They regarded these methods, however, as employed in the protection of the liberties of the nation against the activities of its enemies.

Apposite strains were reflected on the other side of the world, in the USSR. The revelations by Khrushchev of Stalin's criminality and the relaxation of some controls, which allowed some more candid books to appear and some travelers to enter or some Soviet citizens to travel abroad, upset the older party members considerably. A split appeared in the Presidium; Khrushchev was almost ousted in the summer of 1957. He managed to stall long enough to call in the entire Central Committee and turn the tables on Molotov, Shepilov, and Malenkov. For the first time, however, the losers were not dragged to a cellar, beaten, and shot to death. The Kremlin was changing; the world was changing.

In October 1957, however, the Soviets sent Sputnik aloft, and a shiver went through the West. For the first time its technological supremacy was surpassed, and the military implications were clear even to the dull. The fact that the technical abilities involved stemmed from captured German scientists was dwarfed by the greater fact that the Soviets were able, no matter how, to surprise the world.

The White House and the State Department were particularly caught off guard, because the results of the President's actions in the Suez crisis were coming home to roost. The United States had helped to deal a heavy blow to Britain and France in terms of their international standing and, in particular, of their stature in the Middle East. As those nations bitterly withdrew, the United States had no choice but to move forward—as much as it could in view of pacifistic sentiments at home—into the vacuum. Secretary of State Dulles was busily trying to reach treaty accords with Middle Eastern countries and making arrangements for American bases in the area. By weakening its allies, Washington was forced to assume greater, more exposed, and continually more expensive expansions of its own forces.

The Soviet Union, in the autumn of 1957 and the winter of 1958, made a series of threats—especially to the British—regarding the peril involved in allowing Americans to have bases in their land. And in each of these threats the Soviets shook their missiles and their nuclear capacity at nations allied with the United States of America.[2]

So far as is known no nation gave way before Khrushchev's ideas of diplomacy, and refused an American alliance because of Soviet nuclear threats. That was a signal triumph for the United States of which most Americans remained unaware, because the nation's press covered the event in a neutral and restrained manner. Many papers did not carry it at all; others buried it in the back pages.

The front pages, however, were heavy with headlines regarding troubles in Little Rock, Arkansas, over desegregation. The nature of such coverage succeeded in presenting a noble national effort to redress ancient inequities in such a manner that the difficulties of the effort overshadowed its rare nature. In a world where cultural, reli-

2. Ulam, *Expansion and Coexistence*, pp. 610-611.

gious, and ethnic difficulties resulted in periodic massacres, as in India, Africa, and the Orient, and in intermittent scenes of disorder in the parliaments of Italy, Japan, Belgium, and France, the problems of the United States were so described that visitors were surprised to find the land intact.

As the press became increasingly concentrated on these troubles, however, they began to flourish and increase like watered weeds.

Toward the end of 1957, however, these troubles were still sporadic, isolated, and minor. In Houston JB enjoyed, as always, Christmas. An especially close observer would say, years later, "JB believes he invented Christmas." He and C. D. Tinsley used to go over the gift list together. C. D. would ask a question and lean back; JB would tell him all about how that person was doing in the world, what was new, and what was not. "He knew them all," Tinsley marveled. "He seemed to keep track of everybody."

In most respects the operations of Triangle remained the same. JB was in charge, and its traditional policy of two weeks' extra pay before Christmas, so that everyone could afford to buy gifts, and the two weeks' extra pay in summer to enable everyone to enjoy a vacation, remained in force—though the accountants and personnel experts at Kerr McGee frowned at both.

But there were, inevitably, changes. JB's plan to put up a twenty-story building, instead of the two-story Triangle headquarters, was scrapped. JB was surprised over that. Plans for the building had been drawn. Transcontinental Pipelines planned to put its computers on the top floor; the roof was designed to hold radio towers for the purpose. The land was already in hand and its value was, as he had anticipated, rising. His plan had been to rent enough of the new structure to repay its cost and to make its maintenance virtually expense-free for the firm.

To see that project rejected puzzled him. But McGee's visions were in altogether different directions. They were far-sighted and impressive, but private. Their details were closely held, save for an occasional hint in rare evening conversations in his office with very few men. Unfortunately, JB was not present at these sessions.

By early 1958 some other results of the merger began to appear. They took forms familiar to students of these events: changes in accounting practices and in the outside firms employed. Jack Wightman, JB's insurance broker, who had handled Triangle's account for many years, was informed that his rates appeared more expensive than comparable coverage Kerr McGee could arrange. He was sharp with JB about that, although JB received the figures from inside Kerr McGee.

But in reality Wightman was not surprised. He later said, "I could have retained the account, if I had wanted to put up a struggle. But it would have meant moving from St. Louis, in order to expand the account from Triangle to all of Kerr McGee. I didn't want to do that. I neither wanted to move from St. Louis, nor did I want to concentrate all my business on one large account. That makes a firm like mine too vulnerable. It was better to drop the account, which had been excellent through the years."

On the other hand, Triangle's advertising arrangements with Keith Fanshier remained untouched, though the Kerr McGee advertising director was not particularly pleased over that.

In other words the merger, as all mergers, contained its changes and its unchanged aspects. In general, however, the larger firm touched Triangle very lightly, but even that light touch was felt by its long-time leader.

The fact was that JB had been a boss since 1937. After twenty years, and after becoming an equal with the heads of the largest firms—and even the industry's largest, Jersey Standard itself—it was difficult to fit inside the pecking order of a medium-sized corporation in the petroleum industry.

All travelers know the condition called culture shock; it begins to set in whenever the glamour and the novelty of a foreign country wears thin. Then everything that was left behind begins to gleam in retrospect, and everything that persistently remains new becomes not interesting but irritating. If, the old colonists used to say, an immigrant can endure through that period of dissatisfaction, he begins to adjust in subtle stages—and becomes a colonist. If he becomes impatient, however, he will abandon the whole effort.

By that time a year had passed, and it was mid-April, 1958. JB was in the throes of culture shock. He went over various restrictions in his mind: rules and regulations of Kerr McGee. Executives were authorized to spend up to certain limits only. JB was allowed up to $125,000. But he knew a vice president, who was extremely responsible, who could commit the firm only up to $15,000. Estimates of what a decision could cost could not vary more than 10 percent, up or down. Such estimates had to be submitted for approval. All these rules were customary, and JB knew it. Nevertheless, they annoyed him.

He was also annoyed over the thought that Triangle's operations were not understood in Oklahoma City. He, Barksdale, and Tinsley could analyze a refinery; they knew costs, markets, and schedules.

Very few corporation men knew more than their specialty and virtu-ally none, to JB's thinking, were profit-oriented. He had structured Triangle and trained Barksdale and Tinsley so they could set prices. But a Kerr McGee executive had actually called Barksdale and told him to quote a certain price, on the basis of the accounting office. Barksdale had talked him out of it.

Yet in the spring of 1958 Kerr McGee stock was split two-for-one. JB's 85,000 shares doubled to 170,000, and there was little doubt that the price would continue to rise. In effect, he had every reason to believe that in the foreseeable future, he would receive as much for the truncated Triangle that he had sold, as he had asked for the entire structure originally. It was hard to complain at that, and he expressed his irritation obliquely.

"As soon as I arrived mounds of paper began to pile up on my desk," he said. "Every twenty minutes someone would bring in an-other pile of reports." Far too many, he decided.

"Who wants these?" he asked in conference. Nobody answered. JB then made a list of the reports the senior executives received. When compiled, it was long—amazingly long. When it was complete, he called a conference. The men sat, somewhat glumly, as JB would lift one of the required reports up, display it, look around and say, "Who wants this? How many of you want to keep receiving it? And this? And this?"

He noticed, however, that the initials of Travis Kerr, the Senator's brother, were almost always absent. "Don't you read *any* of them?" JB asked.

"Interferes with my reading the *Racing Form*," Travis Kerr re-plied. JB looked at him with respect. Travis was a products man.

"The Senator neither smoked nor drank," JB said, "but Travis did both for him—as well as for himself."

Obviously, he had Travis on his side when he winnowed the num-ber of reports top officers received. But the larger impact of his experi-ment was that Dean McGee, hearing of his complaints, looked grave and decided they had merit. Therefore the president sent for the Pace Company, a consulting firm, to come and study the procedures inside Kerr McGee, and to make recommendations.

Meanwhile Claude C. Huffman, who had headed the Cato Oil & Grease company when it was sold to Kerr McGee in January, 1957, found JB a wonderful man to whom to report. Cato manufactured greases that were used in agriculture, automotives, lubricants, and vari-ous oils that were packaged and sold in quantities from a pound to a carload.

396

To the uninitiate, of course, all greases look alike, but in industry they provide the essential lubricants without which fuels would be useless, for machines could not function. Cato's name was unfortunate; in reality it was a manufacturer and blender of lubricating oils and greases. Its source materials were varied, and the firm itself provided source materials for other manufacturers who made brake fluids, anti-freeze, and other products.

When Cato was first acquired Huffman reported to Dean McGee, whom he found serious, and able to listen and understand, but very official. Conversations were brief and to the point. When points were settled, there were others waiting, and Huffman made haste to move on. The president, in fact, awed him.

"He looks impenetrable," he said, "and his expression never changes. But when he's displeased, you know it."

JB was another matter. "He understood marketing and was an independent businessman," Huffman said, coming to life. That he had called on JB at Triangle in previous times didn't hurt. Huffman said, "He was easy to see, and he was a good listener."

The same held true at Kerr McGee; Huffman was pleased with JB as a boss.

A national by-election was due in late 1958, and the political atmosphere grew a little warm in the United States. President Eisenhower's heroic glow had dimmed a bit; unemployment had risen in the early part of the year. Sputnik, together with other surprises, had shaken the feeling that Father Knows Best.

The Democratic party, whose leaders, unlike Republicans, seem able to mount any charge without being defined as hatchet men, took to the hustings with vigor. Former President Truman, uninhibited as ever, charged his successor with creating a depression and "inadvertently" helping the Soviets.[3]

The Administration, meanwhile, was handicapped by security regulations from discussing the nation's actual military strength—although it was certainly not unknown to non-American circles—and by the fact that the first American space satellite was physically puny compared to Sputniks I, II, and III.

The government in fact had drifted into a dangerous area of which most officials and certainly much of the country seemed unaware. Since the secrecy regulations were first instituted, they had expanded to cover an increased area ranging beyond weapons and other specifically sensitive and tangible areas, to include policies and decisions far removed from the original purpose of the program. An

3. Carruth and Associates, *American Facts and Dates*, p. 604.

overall result was that a relative handful of people in the country were aware of the facts of international life, and most citizens were kept in the dark. That was a perilous condition for a democracy to reach, but was so in keeping with the military tradition that it is unlikely the President ever thought about it.

One result, however, was that the nation was unaware of world trends or their significance. The situation in the Orient was extremely dangerous, with Indonesia under the authority of an antiwestern demagogue named Sukarno; with the two Viet Nams in uneasy relationship and with South Viet Nam being penetrated by the forces of Ho Chi Minh. Red China mounted what appeared to be an invasion plan against some offshore islands held by the Nationalists.

The situation nearer home was not much better. In Cuba a rebel named Castro had attracted the favorable attention of the New York Times and various other American newspapers. These persuaded the country that Castro was a believer in democracy, and shrouded the fact that Batista was pro-American.

Despite those gathering clouds abroad, the greatest single campaign mounted at home was one synchronized with various statements from the USSR, calling for the halting of nuclear testing by the West, and the abandonment of nuclear weapons. The atmosphere was not improved when the press discovered small gifts had passed from an industrialist named Bernard Fine to Presidential Assistant Sherman Adams. With unusual speed a scandal erupted over the matter.

Music, literature, and the arts all slipped perceptibly. The "Purple People Eater," "Bird Dog," and other rock-and-roll hits were manufactured through methods oddly uninvestigated; Dr. Linus Pauling, a figure often quoted in the press, warned that radioactive carbon-14 already in the air from nuclear testing would cause five million defective births and millions of cancer cases for the next three hundred generations,[4] and Lolita, a sex novel featuring a child, was a best-seller.

The nation, in other words, was being introduced to reckless and destructive entertainments, and pseudo news. Yet the level of living was at an unprecedented height, with almost fifty million people living in comfortable suburbia, employment back to soaring numbers, and business in general proceeding well. But it was a time when the nation's sense of reality began to warp.

In such periods persons with professions are fortunate; they can concentrate upon activities that are inherently valuable, and can there-

4. Ibid., p. 607.

fore retain a sense of worth while others are prey to the spirit of the age.

JB, in his fifty-eighth year, had reached that level. He was aware that being a professional businessman was not a pursuit generally understood. He knew it was too difficult a profession to master to be taught in schools, and yet he also knew that although it produces many journeymen, few become masters. He had expressed his annoyance with some of the restrictions at Kerr McGee, and at what he considered rules that hindered the creative flow of essential efforts.

The Pace people had come and gone, leaving their recommendations behind. One had appeared at JB's office doorway one day and said, "What do you do?"

Yet JB did not return to Texas Eastern to expand his role with that organization—although it was well within his reach. In fact, deciding that those duties were growing onerous, he persuaded Millard Neptune, who was in Alexandria, Egypt, to return to the States, and recommended Millard to the Browns. Texas Eastern, its efforts to convert the Little Big Inch and to add a loop to Chicago completed, accepted Neptune—and settled with JB. "Very handsomely," he said later.

He was, in other words, consolidating. One night, playing gin with Senator Kerr in the Skirvin Tower, he said he was going to quit Kerr McGee.

The Senator almost dropped his cards. "Why?" he said hoarsely.

"I'm accustomed to making decisions," JB told him. "But at Kerr McGee clerks keep telling me what I can't do, because of the rules and procedures. I can't function that way."

The Senator took off his glasses. "Break them," he said fiercely. "Never mind the procedures. Come to me. McGee and I run the company."

They talked then, and JB ended by promising to stay all the way, or at least until he was sixty-five. That age was not as distant as it had once been.

Yet it was not the Senator alone that persuaded JB to stay. He was a very large owner of Kerr McGee stock, and Triangle was still his baby, though Kerr McGee was its legal guardian. He could not walk away from the firm he founded, and was still directing as he saw fit. That was an area where the clerks could not follow the play.

There was also the fact that Oklahoma was, in large measure, home ground. There is a satisfaction in achievement on one's home ground that is sweeter than anywhere else, especially if one has been poor and obscure on that ground in youth.

Oklahoma City, moreover, was different than many others. It was, and is still, an Open City. The meaning of that phrase is best described by the extraordinary Stanley Draper, who was executive vice president and operating manager of the Chamber of Commerce in Oklahoma City from 1919 until the late sixties, and was still reigning when JB appeared.

"We're very interested in new people," Draper said. "We invite them to lunch, or to dinner, and try to discover their interests. Then we mention what the city needs. If they respond, if they are willing, Oklahoma City is wide open to them. If they are not interested, we turn away."

Draper, one of the great salesmen of all time, was in his late sixties in 1958. He tested JB and discovered the new Kerr McGee executive was interested in everything and willing to help anywhere. Draper was delighted; in short order he was to be astonished. JB was probably the most energetic new member the chamber ever received. He was soon a member of a staggering number of clubs, associations, and institutional boards.

The city leaders then proved that Stanley Draper was right about their receptivity. They offered to sell JB some shares in the Liberty National Bank & Trust Company, the second largest in the city. He bought the shares and was elected a director. He had been in town, intermittently, for a little over a year. That's an Open City.

In November, 1958, the Democrats regained control of both houses of Congress, and JB began to learn about politics by watching Senator Kerr. The Senator was wealthy, though he could joke about it. His path to success had been neither easy nor automatic; he had built Kerr McGee several times, beginning in 1926 with a small drilling firm. He had to reorganize in 1929, and in 1930 to 1932 was involved in the mad scramble in the Oklahoma City field during the hot-oil and troops days, with fourteen producing wells.

He reorganized in 1935 and again in 1936, and formed a second company at the same time, consisting of six partners. Dean McGee was a member of this effort. In 1938 the team drilled a discovery well in the Magnolia field in Arkansas and grew from there. McGee was the geologist on the team, and a very good one.

But Kerr was a lawyer, a promoter, an entrepreneur—and a great salesman. He knew the petroleum industry in depth, and would telephone the API statistics back to Oklahoma City when they appeared in Washington. He could appreciate the market value of knowing these figures. On that and many other scores, JB and Kerr could talk as equals.

But on politics the Senator was clearly a man to whom one should listen.

"When I went to Washington I tried to prove I was a poor Oklahoma farmer," he said, "and they tried to prove I was a rich oil man. They just about proved their point."

That was a better joke than it sounded. "He was quite a power in the Senate," JB said. He noticed that the Senator's phone used to ring quite often; he was a source of funds for other Democratic Senators. He did not raise funds; he donated them. JB would wait when the phone rang and Kerr would listen, and then say, "Send a boy. Leave it to me. I'll handle it."

Once JB saw him write a personal check for $10,000 and stick it in an envelope.

Kerr was, however, a real Senator. He would rise in the Senate to argue for what he believed. He made no pretense at being against the industry in which he became successful. There were times when that candor attracted vitriolic comment; *Time* magazine once ran a very severe article. But Robert S. Kerr had struggled hard for success and believed in the system that enabled such a success to be attained.

JB could understand that, and shared that attitude. But he was not impressed when Lyndon Johnson came through Oklahoma, with his wife and daughters. JB met them at the Kerr ranch, located just out-side Oklahoma City, and said, "All the Birds appeared.

"When he was alone, Lyndon Johnson was ill at ease," JB recalls, "but he was big on his ranch. Liked to scare green reporters with rattlesnakes." To JB, who grew up on a ranch, that sort of behavior was intolerable. "He was no favorite of mine," he says simply.

Senator Johnson was touring in search of his party's nomination, though the conventions were a year away and the elections a year and a half. He was not alone. Adlai Stevenson, who had appeared against Eisenhower twice, gone down to defeat twice and each time protested he didn't really want the honor, sought it again. Other hopefuls included Stuart Symington, Hubert Humphrey, Edmund G. Brown of California, Robert Meyner of New Jersey, G. Mennen Williams, and John F. Kennedy.

On the Republican side there were only Nelson Rockefeller and Richard Nixon. Maneuvering for the nomination was, of course, an old American habit, but in former generations it was conducted at least in part beyond the public gaze. By 1959, however, the press had become omnipresent. It seemed impossible that the nation could endure a campaign over a year long while a sitting President struggled with the problems of his office, but that was the case. To Eisenhower it must have seemed as though he was being buried alive; at times his irritation with his Vice President was almost visible.

With the Senator in a position to discuss politics from the inside, it might be expected that JB would, in common with so many others, have been attracted to that arena, but he was not. In the long list of civic organizations that he came to join, there is not a single political group included.

That was remarkable. By early 1959 the subject of politics was becoming almost obsessive for many Americans, and had grown into a form of mania in other parts of the world. The claims of communism, when reduced, amount to the promise that politics can be the path to paradise. All evils of the world, say these seducers of the ignorant, can be attributed to a faulty political system. Ours is perfect, or it will be when we teach everybody to follow it perfectly.

The people of the United States had not quite reached that stage in early 1959, but the constant din of governmental promise and the knowledge that the cornucopia could be upended by votes and membership in a group, were swinging the nation far from the idea of individual effort and far along the path of group conquest through political avenues.

There also remained the simple matter of ego. When most men become wealthy, and can associate with civic leaders and senators, their thoughts almost naturally gravitate toward politics. But not JB's. And, for that matter, not Dean McGee's. Both men were too intent on business, though they approached it from dissimilar avenues.

Few nonbusiness people can understand that, but it is perfectly clear to others in the profession—if they are advanced in the profession. Business is not really work to a real businessman; it is his vocation. "People who put money first always wind up last," said Bob Aycock, JB's old friend from El Dorado.

Aycock himself was a good example of a man who had started as an apprentice in business, and had grown into a master. He worked his way to sales manager of Root Oil & Refining Company under Philip Hamilton, and then was VP of Supply and Transportation for Pan-Am Southern for several years, and finally brought into Indiana Standard itself. He expected to be made General Traffic Manager at forty thousand dollars a year with a plane and two pilots. Instead he was told to wait two years until the occupant retired. He decided to retire himself, at the age of fifty-five, in June, 1957—and at that age became an independent businessman. It's a profession that takes a long apprenticeship.

In that capacity he was given a lift in a DC-3 from Houston by Barksdale, who carried him to Shreveport, where JB was waiting.

Aycock had an interesting situation described to him in a letter from Bruce K. Brown. The trio discussed the letter en route to St. Louis, where they picked up Phil Siteman, a favorite customer and friend of JB's, and his son Alvin Siteman, as well as a third man named Meyer Kapolow.

The entire party then flew to Mitchell, South Dakota, where they hunted birds by day and good poker hands by night. Aycock, JB, and Barksdale also composed a reply in longhand to Brown; it involved the supply and sale of one million gallons of gasoline a month. In 1975, Aycock said, "That deal is still going."

To such men politics is another world, a world in which they are not interested—unless, of course, it impinges.

Perhaps that is why JB was interested, in 1959, not in the political scene, but in what Rockenback had to say about the Moran Shoe Company. It was not shoes that were interesting; it was simply that it was a new game.

One of the Morans had died, Rocky said, leaving only a brother who did not know anything about the business, and a young president in charge. Rocky thought they might enter that situation. "Only if we can buy control," JB replied instantly. Another way of putting it might be, "Let's buy it all."

They did not buy it all, but they bought 54 percent of the firm, which was enough to control it. JB owned 40 percent and Rocky 14 percent. It was somewhat far afield from their previous or even present activities. The Moran Shoe Company made baby shoes. It was well established and the brands were well known. They were Tiny Step, Wee Walker, and Twinkle Toes.

The firm manufactured the shoes in a factory in Illinois, which turned out incredible quantities. Five thousand shoes a day was considered normal. JB, insatiably curious, also discovered the shoes had neither lefts nor rights, and that women usually bought them without trying them on the babies. They simply marched in and stopped at the baby shoe display rack, picked out a pair whose color appealed, and took them away.

It was not a large venture for JB. He persuaded Rocky to become chairman of the board; JB himself was content with becoming a vice president. Between them they thought they could handle the general management, and the young president of the firm could devote himself to selling, a task for which he seemed better suited than for administration. Having proceeded that far, both these busy men decided to wait, and give the new arrangement time to prove—or disprove—itself.

Somehow, it all seemed a lot saner than politics.

JB also found Travis Kerr to be a most unusual and interesting man. They traveled to the Derby together, and JB visited Travis's horses in Lexington, where JB regarded the famous Roundtable. The horse had a bad leg, Travis Kerr explained to Billy Byers, the owner of the Byers-Kane Stables, while JB listened, "but my trainers thought it could be healed." Therefore Travis Kerr had bought the horse for $125,000, which proved one of the greatest bargains in the history of horse racing.

At Lexington Travis Kerr showed JB around his stables, where he had stallions owned by shareholders. Each stallion had a large stall and a harem. JB was surprised to learn that Travis also owned stallions whose major duty was to tease and excite mares, and to endure their initial bites and kicks as they gave way to the evil temper of their heat.

Returning toward Oklahoma they traveled to Chicago where, JB learned to his surprise, Travis Kerr had another group of about thirty horses. "Anywhere else?" JB asked.

"Oh yes," Travis Kerr replied. "In fact, most of my horses are in California."

"How many?"

"Oh, somewhere between one hundred fifty and one hundred seventy-five racehorses."

JB found, in fact, many likable and interesting men in Oklahoma City, and at Kerr McGee. As time passed he grew to know Dean McGee better, and developed considerable respect for McGee's intelligence. "Very scholarly," he said. "I was amazed at his retention—his ability to study and retain voluminous reports."

He also thought the president worked very hard—perhaps too hard. JB had always believed in moments of relaxation, in vacations, and in games. The cards, he once explained to someone who asked, "lift me." That's a habit he shares with a great many businessmen; they are apt to use cards as a means of analysis, almost as tests of intelligence.

He was not, however, able to do that with McGee: the president had no time for gin. His methods were different. An impression remains that each found the other strange.

In the autumn of 1959 the United States allowed Khrushchev to tour the nation, appear on television, be interviewed by reporters, bait citizens, display contempt, and tell innumerable lies. The reception had no clear purpose and came to no particular conclusion, with the possible exception of convincing the commissar that Americans are, in fact, as naïve as they appear. The only prominent citizen who refused to be introduced was, so far as the public record is concerned, labor leader George Meany. He declared he would not shake hands with a murderer.

The reason that Khrushchev came to the United States, according to later information, was an attempt to reach an accord against Red China. He found no opportunity to broach the subject. President Eisenhower's position was that China had placed itself outside the family of nations.[5] Not even Khrushchev could break through that.

The press coverage of Khrushchev repeated the tone first adopted regarding Stalin: that the Premier of the USSR was really a sort of everyday figure, no more fearsome than the truck-driver on the next block. Stalin, who smoked a pipe in cartoons and cigarettes in life, had an avuncular appearance and could be called Uncle Joe. It was more difficult to find a softening sobriquet for the bullying Khrushchev; pictures of him throwing stones at American cameramen showed grinning faces in the background to indicate it was all in fun.

Early in May, 1960, the Soviets shot down an American U-2 photographic plane, displayed the wreckage in Moscow, and placed the American pilot on trial on the stage of a theater. The United States at first denied knowledge of the plane or its violation of Soviet air space, and then admitted it lied. In mid-May a summit conference was held, as scheduled, in Paris. Khrushchev, Eisenhower, and British Prime Minister Macmillan attended. When they met, Khrushchev abused the President, who stood silent. The next day the Soviets asked if the Americans were ready to apologize.

After that humiliation, the nation turned toward the elections—an event discussed almost every day in the press, and every five minutes on the radio, for over a year. The nominees, Nixon and Kennedy, were almost the same age and certainly of the same generation. Both were naval veterans; both were fluent speakers. Their resemblance ended there. Kennedy was a scion of enormous wealth, raised to the purple, a Harvard graduate with a beautiful wife, a combat hero, and wildly popular. Nixon had gone to work in the farms of California as a part-time laborer at the age of ten; at fourteen he was a barker for a Fortune Wheel store with a poker game in the back.[6] He was beaten by a bitter and disappointed father, worked his own way through college, went to law school on an academic scholarship. His wife was to prove to have all the virtues, but she was not a fashion competitor to Jackie Kennedy.

The campaign between these two was, however, as strange as the tereotypes the press wove around them. Kennedy attacked the Eisen-

5. Ulam, *Expansion and Coexistence*, p. 626.
6. Theodore H. White, *Breach of Faith* (New York: Atheneum, 1975), p. 60.

hower Administration for allowing Castro to succeed and remain in Cuba, and charged the nation's military establishment had fallen behind the Soviets—in other words, as a hawk. Nixon spoke of negotiations and accommodations—in other words, as a dove. Other qualities were exchanged for them by the press, which portrayed the rich man as a potential target for prejudice, and the poor man as a member of the Establishment.

When JB took over Kerr McGee's refining-marketing sector, it was the firm's largest. JB, handed three sheets of names and ratings, laughed. "I don't need that," he said. Instead he watched and studied the men, and grew to know them.

They were, he decided, trained in the Deep Rock school, largely under Barney Majewski. They had worked—until JB's arrival—under the direct supervision of Jim Kelly.[7]

JB knew Kelly and Kelly, of course, knew JB. "*Everybody* knew Triangle," Kelly said later. JB's first decision was to have Kelly transferred. That was not a reflection; a new man entering over a group is foolish to keep the old boss standing around.

Kelly slid sideways to become head of General Asphalt, a subsidiary. JB then settled to watchful waiting for a time, interspersed with his usual brisk appearances and disappearances. He had, after all, other businesses to watch. He did, however, take time to go to Chicago and talk to Barney Majewski, who was supposed to confine his undoubted talents to the Chicago area, but was ranging as far as Peoria and Milwaukee.

"Barney was a tough old boy," JB said, "tough as a boot." He had been with him one night years earlier, when they were friendly competitors, and a fellow drinker in a bar had said a word too many. Majewski knocked him out with one blow; he was an ex-pug, among many other impressive accomplishments.

"Tell me Barney," JB said in his role as Kerr McGee chieftain, "what *part* of Chicago do you want to handle?"

Thick roars came from Majewski, but JB said, "Now, Barney. You shouldn't spread yourself so thin. We have to fix some limits."

They finally came to a treaty—a word that expresses conclusion more than an understanding—and JB left shaking his head. "Put up quite a snort," he said later, when someone asked. "Quite a snort."

7. Now president of Kerr McGee.

406

His central marketing group bothered him most. His instructions were greeted with cheerless acquiescence, and half-hearted execution. He finally decided his central problem was that he had a number of men sixty-two or sixty-three years old who were stalling until pension time. He called their secret leader in for a chat.

"I can't suit you," JB said, "but I'm staying. Do you think you could get yourself another job if I kept you on full salary for a year while you look around? You're upsetting the other men."

The man indicated he could get another job if he had the salary, and JB said quickly, "Clear your desk out today."

That set off an uproar; twenty men protested. But their leader departed, went to Chicago, and got another job—at which he failed.

That seemed to prove the point; the group began to improve. In time they began to grow accustomed to his style, and problems trickled away.

Other sidelights were more pleasant. Senator Kerr commissioned a portrait-painter, Henri Lupas, to depict the members of the Kerr McGee executive suite. When Lupas appeared, Travis Kerr thought Roundtable, whose track winnings were over $1 million, should also be portrayed.

Lupas was accompanied by Mrs. Lupas, who "advised." He was willing to draw the famous racehorse but said that first he would have to study him. "He would watch him at play, running, sleeping, so he could understand him." He couldn't just draw a horse; it had to be Roundtable, and would have to reveal his character.

Events of 1960 were greatly overshadowed by the election campaign. In Cuba the dictator confiscated American property and conducted a bloody purge. Anti-American riots took place in Japan; civil rights struggles spread to sit-ins and congressional filibusters. A special report indicated that taxes consumed 25 percent of the annual earnings of all citizens. Former President Harry Truman warned an audience that people who voted for Nixon "ought to go to hell."[8] Asked to apologize for that statement, the former President told the group itself to go to hell.

In November the results of the election provided a cliff-hanger. Kennedy's margin of victory stood high at midnight and slowly seeped away through the morning hours; by noon the following morning,

8. Carruth and Associates, *American Facts and Dates*, p. 626.

when Nixon conceded, the margin was a little over one hundred thousand votes—less than two thirds of 1 percent. A recount in Chicago could have overturned that verdict, but for the second time in the history of the United States the losing candidate decided a recount would be too disruptive and stepped aside.[9] Nixon's gesture was given little recognition; victory shouts hailed the hairline as though it were a landslide.

Shortly after the election, during the interregnum before the new President took office, Philip Hamilton paid H. L. Hunt a visit on the Texas estate his host called Mount Vernon. The two men were old friends; Hamilton had staked Hunt in his venture with Dad Joiner, a venture that launched his immense fortune.

His reasons for visiting were simple; he knew that Hunt had backed Lyndon Johnson during the primaries and wanted to hear the gossip. "The primaries were very bitter," Hunt told him, "and Johnson called John Kennedy 'The Boy Spender.' "

"During the convention," Hunt told Hamilton, "the delegates were deadlocked. Both Kennedy and Johnson could have lost, at that point, to a dark horse. My doorbell rang; I opened it and it was John Kennedy. He said he could be nominated and Johnson could be his vice president."

Repeating the story, Hamilton paused at that point and said, "Hunt couldn't be sold. But he could be convinced."

At any rate Hunt told Hamilton that he called Johnson and said, "We've made a deal. You'll be vice president." Johnson was angry, but Hunt said he remained firm.

Hamilton listened to the tale with deep interest and an open mind. Finally he said, "Who'll be Secretary of State?" (Adlai Stevenson was rumored for the post.)

Hunt said, "I don't know, but I'll find out." He left the room and placed a call. After a time he returned.

"Dean Rusk."

"Who's he?"

"Someone from the Ford Foundation. Sam Rayburn told me."

---

9. In the election of 1876 Samuel J. Tilden of New York received more popular votes than Rutherford B. Hayes, but lost the electoral vote. Southern states, however, endured radical tampering with their ballots. It is generally agreed that election was, in effect, stolen by the Republicans. In 1960 Nixon was told fraud could be proven in Chicago, but decided the point was potentially too disruptive to press.

Years later Love recalled attending meetings in Dean McGee's office after hours—meetings that began at 5:30 or 6:00 in the evening, after the "daily people" had gone home. McGee would lean back, relaxed, and discuss—somewhat vaguely but in an interesting way— long-range concepts that were slowly evolving in his mind. Claude Hoffman later referred to such McGee concepts in awed tones.

"He looks ahead twenty or twenty-five years," he said, "and he has long-range visions, dreams, calculations."

Love listened, absorbed, but thought McGee's ideas somewhat remote. "Kerr McGee was not an immense firm," he said. "Its capital was limited; it couldn't acquire everything." Listening, Love could not quite see where McGee was heading, though it was obvious he saw potentials in the future.

Later, after JB joined the firm, Love found his life complicated. "Saunders was not a second-fiddle player," Love said, "He had been successful too long for that. And," he added, "an entrepreneur cannot be put in a box; he has to contribute to the plan."

"Saunders did not go too far," Love continued, "*but he wanted to.* Being a sensitive and perceptive man, he knew he was being balked, was being held down—but he didn't know why. The McGee total energy plan was, after all, far ahead of the industry; was beyond petroleum, and didn't even exist in a formal sense."

Jim Kelly, who was brought back to headquarters from the General Asphalt subsidiary to become Dean McGee's executive assistant, had another vantage point; he saw different aspects.

"When firms are merged the officers of the submerged firm are no longer kings," Kelly said, "and it is the little things that bother them the most. But it's a situation that arises often in modern business. A smaller firm can be dedicated to a single purpose, but once it is joined to a larger its goal becomes smaller."

Kelly, working with McGee, was part of the inner planning group that restructured the firm. How did he do it?

"It was not easy," he said. "How can you centralize a grab-bag?" He began by studying other firms. Kelly looked at the Du Pont organization, and used that as a master pattern. In so doing, he may not have been aware that he chose a pattern not universally admired; some observers consider it overcomplicated and unnecessarily elaborate.

"We began with our goals and then worked backward," Kelly said. "Meanwhile the firm was expanding into natural gas, uranium, and wholesale marketing; it expanded into refining with the acquisition of the Cosden Oil Company and Deep Rock.

"No, we did not use psychologists. All of us were too much aware of Senator Kerr's opinion on that. 'The Good Lord only made One Infallible,' the Senator would say. 'There is hope in the average; live by averages.' "

There were closed doors, in other words; secret paths, hidden byways. In later years the concept of a total energy company has come to seem almost mundane; almost all the large petroleum firms expanded into coal, into gas, many into carbon black, virtually all into petrochemicals. But in the fifties and early sixties the concept was advanced, and Kerr McGee was being put together almost as a cabinet-maker will build his masterwork, complete with recessed hinges and inlaid woods, secret drawers and the like—while keeping his overall plan hidden.

Meanwhile Triangle was contributing very significantly to the earnings of Kerr McGee, and was growing rapidly, year by year. Love found himself serving as a buffer between two men, both of whom he admired, and whose ideas and methods were excellent—but different. His role as counselor came naturally; he was in truth more a lawyer than a businessman. And he did not find his counsel needed on one end only. McGee was nervous about marketing in general, and unsure about making too many acquisitions in areas outside his own expertise.

The new President of the United States, no matter how slender his margin of victory, presented a brave and youthful contrast to the older generation abruptly swept offstage. He appointed his brother—a notably quick-tempered and partisan individual—to the post of Attorney General. That appointment evoked less criticism than sheer astonishment. The President brought with him an astonishing crowd of highly schooled young men—fifteen of whom were Rhodes scholars—whose education, they would discover to their surprise, was not yet complete.

Kennedy was barely in office when the USSR sent aloft Major Yuri Gagarin, the first human being to circle the planet Earth in a space vehicle. That triumph was made into a national holiday in Soviet areas, and sent Kremlin prestige to a new high.

In contrast the new Administration sponsored an amateurish invasion of Cuba by brave but inexperienced exiles led by a sprinkling of Americans operating on a plan conceived with the help of the CIA. In essence it resembled the adventures mounted by the earlier OSS in World War II, but at that time Americans received immense assistance and enjoyed widespread popularity. The Cuban effort was a fiasco in every sense, and the American press was as vitriolic about it as the Communist camp. The President took full responsibility but his associates lacked that much character. The CIA became the target of incessant and—it would prove—eternal—criticism.

In May, 1961, the President appeared before Congress and announced the program of sending an American to the moon. The plan was clearly designed to raise aloft a national target that might simultaneously restore national pride and rally the people.

It was hailed as a bold scheme, though not many believed it could be achieved. Even fewer understood that in such an effort the government's role would be mainly as a banker. Private industry would provide the technology, the effort, and the instruments.

In June, with the Cuban fiasco still quivering in the air and with the moon shot still sounding implausible, the President went to Vienna to meet Khrushchev. In that meeting he was threatened, insulted, and abused. He could not understand why the commissar quivered with hatred; he told New York *Times* columnist James Reston the meeting was "the roughest" in his life.[10] Reston dutifully reported this with an astonishing lack of indignation. The official communiqués were even more careful.

The President returned to Washington with a clearer understanding of the nature of Soviet leadership than before. He asked for estimates of the nation's military strength, requested a special $3.2 billion from Congress to improve it, ordered more reserves drafted and took several similar measures.

Most of the nation was oblivious. The headlines and the news columns were concentrated upon civil rights demonstrations and disorders taking place in the South. Most people, unaware that a great international crisis was building, were intent upon their individual affairs.

At Kerr McGee the firm began to turn toward natural resources. It had expanded into uranium mining in the fifties, and in 1961 went onstream with the nation's first privately owned helium processing plant. McGee had also accumulated impressive machinery. Its specially created drills, designed for underwater use and also for large-diameter holes, advanced the state of that art.

The combination of technology, mining techniques and equipment, coal, uranium, gas, oil, and petroleum products was, in the early 1960s, impressive but fragmentary. The fragments were huge but connected mainly by McGee's perceptions. His tendency to keep operations in separate cubicles resembled the educational establishment, the big business patterns, the governmental structures, and the new social patterns that were emerging around them, and of which they were a part, in the early 1960s.

10. William Manchester, *The Glory and the Dream* (Boston: Little, Brown, 1974), p. 910.

Jim Kelly, deep inside the inner sanctum, later expressed the sequence with some eloquence. "A Big Company is like a Big Union and Big Government," Kelly said. "I remember the carefree and unfettered days of my childhood and compare it with the drive of the government today to 'inspect and license' summer camps; to delve into the management of schools and churches, and to enforce equal education. We sponsored some community projects and discovered a host of regulations, safety rules, minimum wages that virtually destroy learning on the job and apprenticeship programs.

"It extends, Kelly continued, "right into the structure of family life. I remember, raised on a farm, being part of the functioning structure, having chores and participating in decisions. I had to get the coal and kindling. Now children are separate, and are given different treatment."

Yet these rationales were not businesslike, in the sense that JB was a businessman. The quest for uranium reflected a fashionable trend in which it was assumed that nuclear energy was so obviously useful that no sector of society would be against it. President Eisenhower had launched a program to make the peacetime uses of nuclear energy available to the world. McGee was following a path well-charted by many well-meaning people that—we know now—was headed toward political confrontations.

Kelly's comments were really not on business, but on organizational techniques. They provide security, but impede creativity. Swimmers in lifejackets do not easily drown, but neither do they swim well.

As a businessman, JB was above such positions. He was unique in the firm in being the only man who had become successful from efforts he launched alone. He formed a group and led his group to success—but he started alone. Once, when Barksdale had displayed unusual arrogance, JB had called him in for a chat.

"Without me," he said, "you would not be where you are today. But without you, I would be exactly where I am today. If you left, I would be reduced—but not destroyed."

Barksdale admitted the truth of that, and that truth was never again necessary to express—in so many words—between them.

JB was unique at Kerr McGee, therefore, not only in his senior status, his marketing responsibilities, his shares, his board seat and committee posts, but in the fact that he was—uniquely—still an independent businessman. He had outside interests and was free to attend to them. They were not bounded by the interests of Kerr McGee. They extended, in fact, as far from petroleum as any of McGee's dreams— and required no machinery to accomplish—merely his intelligence, his accumulated knowledge, and his developed business skills.

Most of JB's interests were long-range in nature. Business, after all, is a part of life and not apart from it. Its one innate element, therefore, that laymen and amateurs alike are apt to overlook, is time. It takes time to form a venture, time to build it, and time for its potential to be realized. In the late forties JB and nine of his friends had organized the Lakeside Country Club in Houston and saw it become a speedy success. Starting with an original list of two hundred advance members, they watched that list double to four hundred in a few months and soar to one thousand in a single year. After that waiting lists kept the club's population stable—but pressured.

Meanwhile the same years witnessed the slow but steady improvement in the value of the one thousand one hundred acres that JB and his associates purchased near Lakeside. The tract was large; almost two square miles. The ten owners had obtained a loan from Prudential, in New York, using the tract as collateral, at 6 percent interest. They had, therefore, the use of its value while watching it improve, and were enabled to afford its taxes without undue sacrifice. But as the years passed some of the men grew impatient, and decided to take their profit. The agreement called for the remaining owners to have the first option on such sales; JB stepped forward. He bought their portions from Bob Rogers and Clayton Smith first, and then later from Ralph Rupley, Ralph Johnson, and Wyatt Hedrick. The sums were higher for the second trio than for the first pair; he anticipated that others might, in time, want to sell out also.

But JB was willing to hold, and to wait. His was not a monopolistic instinct, however. He drew Barksdale, his 10 percent partner, into the tract, and he gave percentages to C. D. Tinsley and Raborn. JB never forgot his closest associates.

JB had like most professional people, to read a great deal, and to do a lot of paperwork. That and the years inevitably affected his eyesight. He wore glasses that were strengthened into bifocals, and then into trifocals. By the early sixties he had already endured one eye operation and was wearing a single contact lens. It was uncomfortable, but he followed the doctor's advice. Meanwhile, he also wore glasses.

One day he read an article about Söhnges Optical Company in Munich, and its work. Being in Zurich at the time, he rented a car and drove to Munich, where he was informed that an operation could be performed, providing he followed all instructions.

After the cataract operation, he was fitted with contact lenses by Söhnges, a firm that had made glasses for Eisenhower. The lenses, which the Germans considered a task almost any competent technician could produce, proved to be very thin and strong. He discovered he could wear them easily, without discomfort, for periods up to forty-eight hours—though such occasions were, of course, rare. He left Munich with three pairs of contacts, a pair of reading glasses, and a pair of prescription sunglasses—all produced and fitted to him, for approximately $150.

JB was in Germany at a time when that part of the world was attracting unusual diplomatic attention. The Kremlin was the scene of many conferences over the fact that the United States and its allies were rearming the Germans. The Soviets were fearful that if the Germans obtained nuclear arms they could not be controlled. The Kremlin was also afraid of Red China, with which the commissars were engaged in a deep ideological dispute.

The essence of the dispute was that the Soviets could not behave as masters over Mao Tse-tung. The Chinese leaders wanted the most advanced nuclear weapons, and the USSR, despite prior agreements, was loath to assist that goal. The dispute burgeoned into a rivalry that had the bitter flavor of a religious schism. Each side claimed the other had strayed from the path of true communism.

Their rivalry was evident in Africa, where both the USSR and China were assisting general disorder and resistance against the West in general. It was also evident in Asia, where China and the USSR competed for influence over such leaders as Sukarno in Indonesia, Ho Chi Minh in Viet Nam, and various guerrilla groups and political factions in other Asian countries.

Another problem that exacerbated the Kremlin was the stream of refugees that poured toward the West through Berlin. East Berlin was in Communist hands, but streetcars and buses, private cars, and even walkers could get to the western-controlled part of the city without much problem. Hundreds, then thousands, then hundreds of thousands made that journey. In July and August, 1961, the stream was almost continuous and included the educated and highly skilled among the humble and obscure.

On August 13, starting a little after midnight, accompanied by tanks, soldiers, and policemen, the East Germans appeared and began, under the bristling menace of guns, to build a twenty-five-mile-long wall between the two parts of the metropolis, sealing East Berlin from the West. The entire grim disgrace, tacit evidence of the penal and brutal nature of the régime that dominated eastern Europe, took four days to complete.

A month later the USSR abruptly violated its treaty, and resumed nuclear testing. Peace groups, vociferous through the United States and Britain and the rest of the West, fell notably silent. The commissars detonated over 30 major nuclear devices. Khrushchev described one to the Communist Congress as 2,500 times as large as the bomb dropped on Hiroshima, to general hilarity.

To all outward purposes the United States made no particular response to these developments except to send Vice President Johnson to Berlin as a sign the city was not to be abandoned. The Communists were, by then, building gun towers and planting land mines between the two Germanys. In time even more sinister precautions would be taken against any unauthorized departures from Paradise.

Khrushchev, who had decided the Americans were cowards, then planned another, even larger, surprise.

By early 1962 the leaders of Triangle had established their value in Kerr McGee. The subsidiary proved more profitable every quarter. Kerr McGee branded stations were added to JB's responsibilities at the parent concern. Barksdale, an easy, smooth presence, was made president of Triangle, and JB moved to board chairman of the firm he had founded.

Raborn had made an impression upon Dean McGee early, when the merger talks were first held. That was to be expected: Raborn's ability to provide concise, clear financial reports was outstanding. Dean McGee called him in for a conversation after the merger was accomplished, and Raborn is reported to have told him he was committed to God and averse to leading the fast life. McGee, who is not without humor, is supposed to have said drily that his attitude would not be held against him. In reality, both McGee and Senator Kerr were sincerely religious men; the Senator kept a Bible on his desk.

Raborn was transferred to Kerr McGee therefore, in an unusual exchange, in which he became treasurer of the parent company and Jack Lollar of Kerr McGee became a vice president and treasurer of Triangle. Both men were delighted.

By 1962 Raborn had risen to a vice presidency at Kerr McGee. Predictably, he expanded his area of attention, and was moved to make a decision in branded marketing, based upon his own analysis of that turbulent sector and how it should be governed and directed. It took the form of a decision to reduce the price of Kerr McGee branded, or retail gasoline, two cents below the prevailing market price.

415

The telephone on JB's desk immediately rang with complaints. "There were two stations in Sapulpa," JB said later. "Both were on Dewey Street, side by side." JB drove into one—a Mobil station. A Kerr McGee station was next door. JB talked to the Mobil dealer, who was suspected of giving rebates to his customers. Never one to beat about the bush, JB said to the station operator, "You're giving rebates."

"The other guy's giving glassware," the man responded. He was referring to a Champlin station across the street. JB nodded understandingly, and went into the Kerr McGee station. There he gave instructions to match the Mobil prices. Later he called Earl Baldridge, the head of Champlin, who was not surprised to be called about the prices of a single station, and they came to an amicable end to the miniwar.

JB then investigated Raborn's rule. He discovered that his former assistant believed all prices should be set by the company, and that all Kerr McGee station operators and dealers should obey without question. He had, it seemed, worked out a formula. It sounded plausible; formulas usually do. According to Raborn, Kerr McGee would succeed in retail gasoline sales if it would be "always second to go down, and the last to go up in price."

JB said immediately, "Nobody would ever go up." He knew that there is always someone, somewhere, underselling the world. He considered that formula, or any formula, completely unrealistic. The marketplace in which he had spent his life was fiercely competitive and contained myriad variations in different localities and locations and under everchanging conditions. To attempt to freeze one's posture in such a fluid ambience was, in his eyes, clear folly.

Raborn, of course, disagreed. He went so far as to appeal to Dean McGee, but McGee was far too intelligent to overrule one of the most successful of all the industry's marketers. Meanwhile, JB shook his head. Raborn had always reached too far; he would never change.

In the course of the year, however, larger considerations came into view. The McGee uranium sector dragged, because the Eisenhower "atoms for peace" program had diminished remarkably after the general left the White House. Kerr McGee's large uranium deposits in the region of Grants, New Mexico, and its uranium oxide processing plant seemed more than sufficient. McGee reduced explorations for uranium, for the time being, and directed searches toward other metals and natural resources that could be processed into products. McGee, who launched his career as a mining engineer, has never lost the belief that the treasures in the earth are the basis for all man's wealth.

One such natural element was potash, a basic ingredient in the manufacture of fertilizer. Kerr McGee had been drawn toward potash through a series of steps that culminated in 1962, in large leases in New Mexico and Canada, and a half interest in a processing plant near Carlsbad, New Mexico.

McGee began to consider further steps, which would carry the firm into the fertilizer industry. Among other directives he asked John Bills, a company economist, to undertake a study of that market and its potential, and to make an estimate of the cost of entering the fertilizer industry. JB, drawn into these discussions, took the mental time to consider the subject himself.

Bills looked at him, and wondered if he had any idea, in round figures, of such costs. "Yes," JB replied. "I would estimate it will cost about two hundred million." Bills looked skeptical and vanished to do his paperwork.

It was a number of weeks before he returned with the report, and he presented it somewhat reluctantly. His figures came to $210 million. Bills looked at JB at that point, and said, "How did you come so close?"

JB was not amused. Potash is a substance important in the oil industry, which he knew in depth and completely. He had extrapolated mentally, though neither Bills nor McGee could quite accept that reality; it had seemed like a casual figure.

Neither of them realized—and it naturally did not occur to JB to explain—the sort of memory he commanded. Even JB III was astonished, and discovered it only by accident. As a small boy he had been sitting in the front seat, and his father was driving, when a large black car cut in front of them. "I'll remember you," JB muttered.

His son stared at the license plate number. It was 3941. He wrote it down on a scrap of paper and put it in his pocket. As a boy will, he planned to produce it later to see if his father would, in fact, remember it. But he forgot about it for many years. One day, leafing through an old desk, he came upon the scrap, the notation to himself, and went to JB.

"What was the number of the car that cut in front of us years ago, in the rain, that almost caused us an accident?" he asked.

JB looked at him and said, "Thirty-nine forty-one."

His son was astounded, and JB was impatient. "Simple," he said. "Forty-one forty-three is the gravity of kerosene. We saw the car about twenty years ago, and I associated its license number with kerosene, minus two. I'll remember that number when I'm ninety years old."

That was no explanation at all, of course. The fact is that JB, unlike the economist, did not have to look up the relevant numbers. He knew them. Yet he had never learned to display that ability; he simply used it.

In midsummer, 1962, when Raúl Castro, the dictator's brother, was in Moscow, an agreement was reached allowing Soviet missiles to be installed on that island. An official announcement was made that Soviet technicians would be sent to Cuba, with "defensive weapons." At the same time several Soviet messages were sent to Washington, saying that the Soviets planned no confrontations before the American elections in November.

In October, American overflights verified that twenty-four launching pads for medium-range missiles were being prepared, as well as sixteen for intermediate. If completed, they would be able to reach points in the United States as far west as Montana.

At the same time it was learned that Khrushchev planned to visit the UN in November. The Soviet ambassador, Anatoly Dobrynin, told a Presidential aide that a German peace treaty and the problem of Berlin would be settled after the November elections—leaving the implication that this was the purpose of the Premier's UN visit.

The White House was informed of the peril in mid-October, while more Soviet vessels were en route to Cuba. Military estimates were that cities were being targeted that would place eighty million Americans in peril of their lives. The experts differed, as always. Intelligence, which first said the Soviets would never attempt such a move, decided the Soviets would never retreat from such an attempt.[11] The President, therefore, had to choose from a welter of contradictory voices.

His response was forthright. He ordered the Air Force aloft with nuclear weapons and naval vessels to institute a blockade and either repulse or sink Soviet ships streaming toward the island. He warned of American attack if the missiles were not removed. He went on the air October 22 to alert the nation and the world. The general reaction was shocked silence. Within days the Kremlin retreated. It had been detected in a murderous and stealthy movement, and its complete plan has never been explained.

The later reaction of the American government was little short of amazing. Extensive and elaborate efforts were made to mask the Soviet retreat to allow the Kremlin to save face.[12] That effort was so successful that many people later came to believe the crisis was exaggerated.

11. Intelligence had been warned by a stream of Cuban refugees of these activities, but had refused to listen on the grounds such people were "biased and unreliable." A later investigation of the intelligence breakdown concluded it was due to "a philosophic conviction it would be incompatible with Soviet policy." Harry Howe Ransom, *The Intelligence Establishment* (Cambridge: Harvard University Press, 1970), p. 97.

12. Ulam, *Expansion and Coexistence*, pp. 674–675.

Soviet attempts to mount an adventure that might have destroyed the nation at worst, and humiliated it at best, were treated as a passing fancy. The government, using amateur psychoanalysis instead of common sense, failed the opportunity to arouse the people regarding the realities of the international situation. Within weeks the same babble of voices mounting the same pro-Soviet rationalizations resumed as though nothing in particular had happened.

Senator Robert S. Kerr was stricken with a massive heart attack in Washington, D.C., and died on New Year's Day, 1963. The news sent shock waves through the world of politics and business. Analysts on the nation's exchanges, who were fond of repeating banker David Rockefeller's reputed comment that "Kerr McGee is a one-man company," advised selling. Within days the stock fell from nearly 60 to somewhere in the 20s. In Oklahoma City the president, Dean McGee, held conferences with his top men.

"This firm started with six partners," McGee said, years later, "and I'm the only one left."[13] That is a lonely feeling, and McGee would not have been human had he not been deeply affected not only by the sudden passing of Robert Kerr, but by the fact that the Kerr McGee stock was falling like a stone in the marketplace.

Frank Love, whom the Senator had hired as the result of being defeated in court by the lawyer—"When a man beats me, I want him on my team"—later said, "The Senator was the major shareholder and chairman of the firm. But he never gave orders, except through McGee. How his orders were accomplished was not his concern."

McGee, therefore, had been managing the store, on a daily basis, since 1942, when the amazing Kerr—who had been born in a log cabin in Indian Territory at Ada, Oklahoma, decided to enter politics and became governor of the state. That was, by 1963, twenty-one years—a long time to live under another man's shadow—but McGee was too serious a man to have been concerned about that.

His concern, in the wake of the Senator's unexpected death, was on its impact to the firm internally, as well as externally. The Senator, after all, had been his partner, the man to whom he had turned when problems pressed hard against him. Now he was in the captain's chair, and would have to dine—and worry—alone.

At that moment there is some evidence he found JB a reassuring

13. Robert S. Kerr actually started in petroleum in 1926, but bought out various partners and reorganized several times. One such effort, founded in 1937 with Kerr and five others, was the start to which McGee referred. Dean A. McGee, *Evolution Into Total Energy* (New York: The Newcomen Society, 1971), p. 13.

presence. "An unusual thinker under adversity," McGee said about Saunders later. Certainly the Senator's passing, in the beginning of 1963, seemed an adverse moment. JB, who had greatly admired and enjoyed Kerr, was nevertheless not shaken. "We'll double our business," he said.

Nevertheless McGee had to do some reshuffling. The firm had endured some unpleasant and unwelcome publicity in Oklahoma, a not uncommon situation for an American petroleum company in an industry which has endured the unremitting dislike of the press almost since its inception. Ordinarily Kerr, with his great prestige and political shrewdness, could have been expected to handle that phase of their situation. Since he was gone, Frank Love was asked to enter politics.

The request was oblique, and came from Harvey Everest, chairman of the Liberty Bank, and two or three others. The council needed more knowledgeable men; Dean McGee agreed the step would be worthwhile. "They said it would only occupy me about one day a week," Love said later. "But it took almost half my time."

Another concern was regarding the projected move into fertilizers. That move would have to be made via acquisitions, using Kerr McGee stock. But the sharp reduction in the price of that stock altered the economics, and clearly made acquisitions more difficult. The firm had, in other words, a new, corporate-wide problem in the marketplace.

At such a moment it was only natural that JB's background and contribution to the firm should have been the subject of concentrated attention. Years later, McGee reviewed Triangle before his firm acquired it.

"There was great overproduction in the industry," he said, referring to an earlier period. "Recycled products had no home. The big producers were against blends. JB also handled heavy oils and surplus gasoline stocks, and helped stabilize the market. He was not disruptive. Furthermore," he added, "JB is not an affected man. Without him there would have been more price wars than there were. It was good for the industry that Triangle played the role it did."

When Kerr McGee bought Triangle and JB came to Oklahoma City, the firm's petroleum marketing was in the throes, McGee said, of "a horrible period. Prices yo-yoed, competition was harsh and we weren't making any money in marketing."

But by the time the Senator died, the refining-marketing sector of Kerr McGee was making money and operating better than ever before. Triangle had improved. And although JB's methods did not strike some of the company men as polished, he had winnowed, retrained, and regrouped the people in those sectors into greater efficiency than ever before.

By early 1963, therefore, McGee had not only raised JB to executive vice president, but also gave him the responsibility for leading the firm's expansion into fertilizers. Actions may not always speak louder than words in a word-conscious period—but they prove more. No better proof could have been provided that Dean McGee valued JB than the fact that, after the Senator's death, he also asked Saunders to stay with the firm till he was seventy, with a full salary even after retirement. In other words, to stick with him.

The year 1963 opened to a series of arguments mounted by the press against the White House and the government in general. Newsmen claimed, in the wake of the Cuban invasion fiasco and the Soviet missile effort, that the news was being "managed." President Kennedy was astonished. He held a conference with seven of the nation's top publishers and offered to relay sensitive information to them on a confidential basis. They told him they would not honor such a "gentleman's agreement."[14]

Instead the press began to take the wraps off the coverage of governmental news—and of events they chose to emphasize throughout the nation. The new style took time to become established. It took an even longer time for the nation to recognize that a new element had entered the national stage. As Solzshenitsyn later pointed out, the American press did not distinguish itself, in this period or later, by investigating and airing the activities of the USSR and Red China throughout their spheres of influence, nor did it expose the greatly expanded efforts of fellow travelers describing themselves, gently, as "Marxists." Instead the press began an intensely personal, prying, and vulgar coverage of the President, his family, his associates—and the nation.

One area that received concentrated attention in the new style was civil rights. The term was inaccurate; it meant equal rights for the black minority. That effort was launched on the highest governmental plane and enlisted the cooperation of many. It was resisted in some regions and places when it seemed to unnecessarily disrupt traditional social patterns. Initially it was realized that some measure of tact would ease the pains of transition. But demonstrations erupted in which agitators of many different persuasions and purposes became conspicuous. Not all who joined the demonstrations understood that the goal of equal rights was being fought through the courts and Congress and had behind it the President, the Attorney General, and powerful groups in

14. Ransom, *Intelligence Establishment*, p. 206.

academia, the arts, and the sciences, and that the dangers of its sponsorship belonged, in the main, to the past.

The numerous demonstrations that appeared throughout the South had some elements of political theatricality, though they were real enough—and led to many individual acts of violence. Churches were invaded by persons whose religious affiliations were uncertain, in the strange belief that a church is a public institution. The new South was visited by persons from other regions in what amounted to a new Reconstruction effort, conducted by persons largely unaware of the final tragic outcome of that earlier effort.

In 1963 it seemed incontrovertible that the civil rights movement was as nearly a perfect cause as could be created. Relatively few mentioned the antagonism it expressed, as well as aroused. In the event, the scenes of struggle, of police dogs, of shouting marchers and armed authorities, created a rash of articles, photographs, and martyrs that, when circulated around the world, diverted world attention from injustices and conditions elsewhere. In the aggregate this coverage did more to tarnish the reputation of the United States than any of the propagandists of the Kremlin could ever have hoped to achieve.

In common with most other corporate executives with heavy, ongoing responsibilities, JB was not drawn into the new scenes of turbulence. Work, after all, must go on. Kerr McGee had potash and phosphate, and enough gas to trade for nitrogen. JB was asked to search and discover avenues by which the firm could enter the plant food market.

He was pleased at entering the marketplace in a new industry. JB had never, like so many oilmen, held aloof from other sectors. But he looked for an experienced guide to conduct him through the labyrinth of the plant food business. To his surprise one man was recommended by three different groups he contacted. His name was Raoul Allstetter, vice president of the National Plant Food Institute in Washington, D.C.

Allstetter was contacted at an opportune moment. His association had been merged into another; his former boss had left to head the Sulphur Institute, his department had been cut back and he was not happy. A tall man with curly, gray hair and a cheerful presence, Allstetter's background was unusually broad; as is so often the case with association men. An Army brat early in life, he graduated from Swarthmore and the Depression ended his hopes of becoming a physicist. He joined the Department of Agriculture in the early days of the New Deal.

422

He became an assistant to Rexford Guy Tugwell and a deputy director in the Department of Agriculture during its headiest period. Like J. Howard Marshall, who worked under Ickes, Allstetter was introduced at an early stage to huge plans, vast projects, and high authority. During World War II he became Army Deputy Director of Materials & Supplies, another very important arena and a large stage.

For a long time Allstetter was an important man in the government. As late as 1951 he was interviewed and quoted by *Time* magazine on the nation's situation and resources, and was—with all that Washington experience—a man of numerous acquaintances and friends.

He came to Oklahoma City after JB and McGee extended an invitation and spent the month of May, 1963, getting acquainted. He liked JB at once; Allstetter prefers free spirits, and he looked forward to being inside industry, instead of outside. After a number of conversations with JB he grew to believe his new boss had "a sixth sense— could tell what he was thinking."

McGee, on the other hand, seemed an "awesome figure," a man "with a high IQ, and seven top assistants," far more remote.

JB and Allstetter started with the idea of purchasing bulk chemicals—their sources—to construct small plants situated on the edge of farming communities and, finally, not only to extend fertilizer sales to such communities, but to combine these with general agricultural stores that would handle oils, greases, small implements, gloves, work clothes, and the like. That would create a chain extending from source to customer, and was an obvious transfer of JB's experience in petroleum into another industry.

He and Allstetter began a series of trips to various firms to discover opportunities and to discuss possible acquisitions. JB was an easy man with whom to travel; his experience was so extensive he could discuss almost everything, and had rare observations to make.

He told Allstetter that small air schools often use their planes to carry cadavers at night, a fact that JB III learned when he studied to become a pilot. That young man, who studied geology for two years at Oklahoma University, had switched into the business school, received his degree in 1962 and, while his father was flying about with Allstetter, was employed by the Union Petroleum Company, which sent him to the famed Harvard course on advanced management.

JB was pleased his son had decided to enter business; he knew many men whose sons rejected the entire economic system of the nation—though not its fruits. That led them to discussion of the changes in the nation, now becoming a matter of concern to almost everyone.

JB was reaching an age where change was overtaking his contemporaries as well as the men ahead. Herman Brown, discovering his health was failing, "wanted a safe haven for his children," said Parker Foster. "All his men seemed like children to him. But instead of leaving it to the children, he sold Brown & Root to the Halliburton Company."

George Brown said, "I'll soon be unemployed." A joke—he had Texas Eastern and all its branches with which to play. But Houston would not seem the same without both Brown brothers; Herman died in 1963.

Other changes popped up everywhere. JB's old banker friend, Herb Seydler, finally retired, after forty years, from the Bank of the Southwest. Seydler promptly went to work with Charley Duncan, of Duncan Foods. Some men couldn't retire. Harry Jacobs, another of that breed, retired from Shell, where he handled heavy oils, and went to work for Leon Hess. Shell, which forced Jacobs to retire at the regular age, sixty, threatened to cut his pension, but Harry didn't mind; he was making more money.

Allstetter, who left the National Plant Food Institute when he was on the verge of retiring, listened with interest; he thought his new boss was a remarkable man. JB, meanwhile, elicited frank comments and honest observations. The trips were not leisurely. One Monday, JB left Oklahoma City and flew to Chicago and attended a meeting. He drove from Chicago to Milwaukee the next day and toured several plants, then flew to Wisconsin and Minnesota and saw some more; in the process he bought three small plants. Next he flew to White Plains, New York, and visited several eastern fertilizer plants, then flew to Birmingham, Alabama, then proceeded to Houston. On Saturday he flew back to Oklahoma City. On every day that week he was up early enough to have a seven o'clock breakfast, and seldom went to bed before midnight. Hard, fast, serious work.

There are persons who cannot understand work; their talents lie in other avenues. In midsummer, 1963, when JB and Allstetter were flying about, looking at and making deals, a society that had not learned the secret of letting men work in their own way at what interested them the most, was having trouble with its Citizen Number 1. Later, one of the members of the Presidium described those troubles. "We heard slogans . . . that we live well now and will live better in the future. But what did we have in fact? *Breadlines!*"[15]

15. Ulam, *Expansion and Coexistence*, p. 686. Italics added.

In August, 1963, JB concluded and announced the acquisition of the Baugh Chemical Company, an old, well-established firm with headquarters in Baltimore with fourteen fertilizer manufacturing plants, and one hundred warehouses that also stocked and sold insecticides, paints, and other articles to the farm regions of the middle eastern states.

That acquisition was a coup. The president of the firm, Paul Prosser, Sr., was elderly and eccentric. "He would go into the office at six A.M.," JB said, "and be gone by eleven A.M."

Checking into the firm, which was 110 years old in 1963, JB discovered it had a book value of $16 million—and that much of that value was underwritten. "Baugh owned stock in Phillips that was carried at its purchase value," JB said, "of eighteen dollars a share; since its purchase it had increased many times. In addition Baugh Chemical had a huge deposit of phosphate rock in Florida, whose extent it had never fully examined. The firm controlled a Baltimore bank, and even a baseball team. The president wanted to retire, and wanted to be paid $100 a month for the rest of his life."

JB encouraged Allstetter to hold talks with the president of Baugh, whose son was executive vice president. "Mr. Prosser was gruff," JB said, "I asked him how he felt and the old man said, 'Not worth a damn. I'm probably the meanest man you ever saw.'"

"You never saw a mean man till you've seen me mad," JB responded. Prosser looked surprised.

The firm, however, was owned by the Brewster family, which was tired of the responsibility. "Senator Brewster called me during the discussions," JB said, "he was very interested."

That was natural enough, and the purchase went through very easily, for $12 million. A year later it was to earn $27 million for Kerr McGee, but to JB's surprise McGee's staff was against having agreed to pay Mr. Prosser of Baugh $100 a month for life. They thought it was a poor precedent.

JB, however, was beginning to roll. He sent for Hugo Wynne, an engineer who worked for Triangle, whose talents were virtually limitless but who resisted being forced into the confines of a Big Company department.

"Hugo is a country engineer," JB said, "and he's very efficient. On one occasion water had accumulated in a gas tank, froze, and broke the cast iron valves. Hugo was called. He obtained a supply of feather pillows and threw these into the top of the tank. The feathers swelled, were sucked toward the valves and stopped the leak."

That stroke of imagination led a major petroleum firm to put out a bulletin recommending that novel solution to the entire industry.

Hugo protested he didn't know how to build fertilizer plants.

"They're simple," said JB, who by then had toured many. He had someone show Hugo through several, and of course Hugo proved able to build them.

With phosphate rock ore on one end, plants in the middle and retail outlets on the other end, tied together by a national sales organization, JB had found a vertebra for the new fertilizer and agricultural chemicals sector for Kerr McGee. Raoul Allstetter had once been in business with a younger executive, Bill Jaqua, whom he recommended to head Baugh Chemicals. JB interviewed Jacqua and was impressed; so was McGee.

The autumn of 1963 found the United States in a confused and argumentative humor; it was obvious the political scene was undergoing stress. Senator Barry Goldwater of Arizona, author of several books, emerged as a spokesman for traditional viewpoints. The Senator, like many others, was aware of the increased American involvement in Viet Nam, where the forces of Ho Chi Minh had created a difficult guerrilla situation. American newsmen in that area, however, devoted considerable attention to the shortcomings of the president of South Viet Nam, Ngo Dinh Diem.

In October, 1963, Mme. Ngo Dinh Nhu, sister-in-law of the president of South Viet Nam, arrived in the United States to embark on a lecture tour to overcome criticisms of the régime. The tour was not a success; mobs of protesters appeared and created disorders, pelting her lecture halls with eggs at once-proud Harvard. On November 1, 1963, a coup was mounted in Saigon; the President and his brother were captured by rebels, and shot dead. Later statements and books, including one by newsman David Halberstam of the New York *Times*, indicate the coup was cleared in advance with American authorities.

This event, in which an American ally was slain in order to placate the press, marked a special moment in the history of the United States. The fabled American sense of decency had, somewhere between Harvard and the White House, gone astray. Mme. Nhu was hounded out of the country; press headlines referred to her as the Dragon Lady. In an interview later with Edgar Snow, an American fellow-traveling admirer, Mao Tse-tung said, "Both Ho Chi Minh and he [Mao] thought Diem was not so bad. But the impatient American generals . . . got rid of him."[16]

The fact was the situation between the United States and the Communist world was growing complex and more difficult each passing week. Soviet interferences with West Berlin convoys were in-

16. *New Republic*, February 27, 1965, p. 18.

creased. American satellites were secretly launched to watch against a surprise attack from the USSR. The diplomats of Bulgaria, Czechoslovakia, Hungary, Poland, and Rumania were barred from 355 countries for security reasons.[17] Yet a "hot line" permitting instantaneous discussions between the White House and the Kremlin was installed, and the press hailed improved relations.

On November 22, 1963, President Kennedy, making a tour through Dallas to burnish his popularity and prepare for a coming campaign in 1964, was shot in the back of the head by an obscure American fellow traveler recently returned from the Soviet Union, named Lee Harvey Oswald.

Two days later the assassin was shot by a police informer and nightclub operator named Jack Ruby. The event was witnessed on television by millions. Lyndon B. Johnson, whom JB had often met and evaluated when with Senator Kerr, became the thirty-fifth President of the United States; President Kennedy was the fourth to be shot dead in office.

The fact that President Kennedy was assassinated in Dallas was used as a springboard for the most amazing campaign against Americans, and against a city, ever mounted by one region against another, since pre–Civil War days. The New York *Times*, the Washington *Post*, the two major wire services, and the various news magazines and journals of opinion vied with one another in describing Dallas as a "city of hate."

Although the evidence against Oswald was overwhelming, it did not deflect, but rather deepened, that campaign. It was clear that elements in the press and country found the assassin's Communist allegiance unacceptable as a reason for his deed. Senator Barry Goldwater was inundated with hate mail and almost retired from politics in disgust.

All Texans were shocked, and JB, who was born in Texas and considered Houston his home, was among those who felt outraged but helpless in the face of slander. More than Texas was involved, however. All of the Southwest and much of the South had been the subject of a growing press barrage that sought to define these regions as "Fascist." Everything about Oil Country—from its ranches and rodeos to its open patriotism, its heavy automobiles and big hats, its oil wells and skyscrapers, its tycoons and its farmers alike—seemed to imbue the national press, dominated by the views of the Northeast, with malice.

Shaken by the Kennedy assassination, which brought those fester-

17. Carruth and Associates, *American Facts and Dates*, p. 658.

ing problems boiling to the surface, JB read a brochure prepared by the National Cowboy Hall of Fame in early 1964.

The Cowboy Hall of Fame, at the time JB read the brochure, consisted mainly of an empty series of buildings located on Persimmon Hill, in Oklahoma City. He knew the hill. His father, Joseph Benjamin Saunders, had camped there when he was a trail boss and drove cattle into the Indian Territory from Texas.

The Hall was the result of a businessman's vision—as are so many of the museums and institutions of the United States. Chester Reynolds, born in 1887—fourteen years before JB himself—had briefly homesteaded in Colorado but abandoned the effort to become a clothing salesman in Chicago. He was, apparently, a good salesman. In time he became a businessman, and chairman of the board of the H. D. Lee Company in Kansas City.

He also became a rodeo buff, and the riders grew to know him as Chet Reynolds. On a visit to Claremore, Oklahoma, Reynolds regarded the statue of Will Rogers and wondered what would happen to the memory of the men who built the West—and in particular the cowboys. That, at least, was how Mr. Reynolds explained his thoughts; they were undoubtedly more complex. In common with many other Americans he had grown aware that a mindless destruction of American values and the national memory was underway.

It was Reynolds's selection of a western symbol around which those traditions could be protected that made his observation more fruitful than similar observations made by many others. He began a campaign to create a museum dedicated to the cowboy, and evoked— after arduous efforts, and many visits, letters, and talks—a substantial response. In 1955 the governors of seventeen western states and others created a preliminary organization. A competition arose regarding the site; many cities had real claims. Dodge City, among others, was eager. Oklahoma City mounted an elaborate effort, and offered free land, plus an initial $500,000. "Those damned Oklahoma oil men bought it," said the governor of Kansas in a moment of chagrin.

The project grew, though not too rapidly. A competition for the building design was opened and won by two young men whose contribution looks, from a distance, like an Indian tepee village. In 1958 there was a dedication which Glenn Ford and Jack Lemmon attended and a movie in which they appeared, Cowboy, was premiered. In 1964 the funds were finally available for the first units, for the tepees can be increased, and the title Western Heritage Center added. Dean Krakel, director of the Gilcrease Museum in Tulsa—another businessman's vision—was appointed director of the Cowboy Hall of Fame.

JB's attention was caught. He phoned Krakel, and a tall, burly, black-haired man appeared, whose manner and expression seemed more

428

like a cowboy's than the usual museum director's. "Dean Krakel can use his dumb look better than anyone I know," said John Kirkpatrick later. But Krakel can drawl eloquently. By the time he left, JB had found a new interest; it was one with emotional overtones. It was, in a way, almost as though the circle of his life assumed symmetry. He had started his own journey watching his father on horseback, rounding up cattle.

By mid-1964 JB and Allstetter had created plant food development regions, warehouses, plants, sales forces, and programs on a national scale. The list of acquisitions is lengthy; it included A&M Chemicals in Minnesota, the Omega Fertilizer Works in Georgia, the Poteau Lime Company in Oklahoma, and in July, the Hubbard-Hall Chemical Company of Waterbury, Connecticut. Hubbard Hall was an important acquisition that had an established market position in New England and marketed pesticides nationally.

JB had created blending plants, storage facilities, and sales and service offices—a complete network. In the aggregate it was described in *Farm Chemicals* magazine's issue of October, 1964, as a fifty-million-a-year business. JB's picture was on the cover of the magazine; he is shown on an inside page in his office with Allstetter. In his sixty-fourth year he looked about fifty; his hair was coal-black. The general tone of the article reflects near astonishment at the speed with which Kerr McGee had entered the agricultural chemical sector.

The magazine was not the only observer to express surprise.

"I was building four or five potash plants at once," JB said later, "and McGee grew alarmed."

McGee said, "I'm sorry, but I'm going to pull the pin; cut it off."

JB said, "You're the lead dog on the sled. The boys have been working on this program for months. But you can cut it off if you like." Then he paused, and said, "But what are you going to do with the potash?"

McGee frowned. "He was," said JB, "like a strict schoolmaster."

The odd part of the situation was that JB's efforts were profitable. They were making money, and his moves were in concert with a plan he had developed for long range growth.

"His idea," Allstetter explained, "was to create a number of clusters that could each grow. He believed that centralization would prevent that process from taking place. Instead, he wanted to hold out incentives to the managers, and urge them to improve at an annual rate of ten percent. He was firmly against having these plants and sales regions placed into what he called 'corporate ruts.' "

"He ran into McGee's silent and steely limits," said Frank Love, another observer. "JB wanted to wheel and deal, and the chemical companies wanted to be acquired. But Dean was cautious regarding the firm's resources; it was a period when the company was very highly leveraged. He is," Love added, "a very cautious man."

Above corporate limits, however, there were other—similarly sharp and angular—points that divided JB and McGee in terms of work. McGee wanted justifications and explanations on paper in advance, so they could be reviewed and analyzed, accepted or rejected.

That desire permeated the entire organization, as do the top man's methods always—systems, controls, limits, brakes. "McGee never really understood Triangle," said C. D. Tinsley. "It buys, sells, swaps—and completes a transaction in a five-minute telephone call. Now memoranda and letters have slowed the pace, and controls constrict the firm's abilities."

JB had, by the end of summer, 1964, created a large, national chemical sector for Kerr McGee. It was not constructed hastily, but it was constructed swiftly. All his moves were designed to fit into a pattern of present assets and future growth, but he had not paused to draw these justifications and thoughts into a pattern that other men—not necessarily slower, but certainly less familiar with business—could grasp.

Other men became aware of the chief executive's concern. Men experienced in the sort of controls that McGee preferred began to move toward what the in-house entrepreneur had created. It was a phenomenon often seen in the outside business world that a large corporation mirrors in microcosm. In the instance of the chemical sector, the control men who appeared on the horizon were Jim Kelly and JB's old associate, Hubert Raborn.

Two unusual movies were issued in 1964. One was *Dr. Strangelove, or How I Learned to Stop Worrying and Love the Bomb*, in which the villain was a fanatical Air Force general. Another was *Seven Days in May*, about a rebel Air Force general. The first, advertised as a comedy, astonished the London *Times*, whose critic remarked on the hatred of the United States it exuded.

A documentary was also widely shown that year, of the McCarthy hearings. It was called *Point of Order*. Dances were the Watusi, the Frug, the Dog. The dancers jerked and gyrated alone, usually without

430

looking at one another. The music was inordinately loud, and many cabarets were enlivened by go-go dancers on platforms.

The Supreme Court ruled, early in the year, that congressional districts must be substantially equal in population, and in midyear ruled that both houses of state legislatures had to be apportioned on the basis of population. That decision—which in effect implied that the federal government itself, in the congressional branch, is unjustly ordered—created considerable surprise. The Court also ruled the government could not deny passports to Communists.

Events overseas reflected a similar mixture, difficult to analyze and subject to varying interpretations. In October, 1964, Khrushchev, who had brought the world to the very edge of a nuclear holocaust, was deposed and given a pension The strange admiration of the American press for the monster continued, and laundered versions of his career appeared in many publications. The Presidium announced that two men, both in their late fifties, would replace the deposed leader. They were Brezhnev and Kosygin. The following day the Red Chinese detonated their first atomic bomb. The achievement surprised the world.

The election campaign of 1964 was remarkable not for the behavior of the candidates so much as the press. For the first time it intruded into the electoral process in an unmistakable manner, with implications yet to be generally analyzed.

The Republican party endured its worst split since the bolt of Theodore Roosevelt. Bitter primary battles were fought between Rockefeller, William Scranton, and Goldwater. Rockefeller, who had damaged the chances of nominee Nixon in 1960, engaged in penetrating attacks upon Goldwater in 1964. Scranton's charges were also remarkably free. But the press did Goldwater more damage than to any major party candidate in history until that year. His arguments against crime, for resistance to Communist aggression, against legislating the societal pattern of the nation, and against unlimited welfare and social programs, were subjected to continual exaggeration and scathing criticism.

As a result of this unprecedented onslaught, Goldwater's defeat resulted in virtually ruling the traditional views held by millions out of order in the nation's political debate, and opened the floodgates to the left.

In early 1965 JB could survey his personal landscape and have reason to be pleased. Eddy did not like hotel suites, but had agreed to spend more time in Oklahoma City, provided they could find a suitable extra house. JB III was doing well in business, and earning thirty thousand dollars a year as a rising young executive. He had, the preceding fall, gone to Dallas to see the Big Game held each year between his alma mater, Oklahoma University—called OU in the newspapers—and the University of Texas.

He called his father for help in getting game tickets for four couples, and also for hotel reservations. JB arranged for the tickets, then called H. L. Hunt. The old man was eager to have the young people stay at his estate. "Come on out! come on out!" he told JB III. When they arrived they found Hunt omnipresent; he went swimming in the pool with the girls, conversed even while treading water, attended and ate breakfast with them—and had them listen to his records.

"Hunt had been bitten by the political bug," JB said. "He invited all sorts of people from all over to discuss events, trends and activities. He would use speakers on his Life Line, and had recordings of their efforts. His guests would be asked to listen to them, and tell him their opinions."

He remained, however, an inveterate, highly skilled gambler. When JB went to the Derby in May, as he did every year with some friends from the oil industry, Hunt would wire him his choices. They were based on track conditions, the jockeys and other factors. "His selections came in first or second," JB said. "They never lost."

JB meanwhile was still in charge of Triangle, although Barksdale and Tinsley ran the store; in 1963 Saunders had added the Premier Oil & Refining Company of Longview and Fort Worth, Texas, to the roster of refiners whose products Triangle marketed. He also continued to make his tours and swings through Triangle's far-flung markets. In St. Louis he would drop in on old friend Phil Siteman, whose Site Oil Company, consisting of a string of stations, continued to prosper. He would talk to Jim Forsyth, whom John Arnold had introduced years before, and who had at JB's advice entered the service station chain operations in addition to his larger interests.

Then on to New York City, where so many firms maintained important offices, to a conversation with Jack Rathbone, head of giant Jersey Standard. To JB, as to many other men, Rathbone was the leading statesman of the oil industry. "I've seen him standing at the reception line at the API shaking hands, and calling hundreds of men by their first names."

JB would check into the Ambassador or the Barclay and call Jersey Standard; Rathbone would meet him at seven in the morning. "I would be led through a string of offices," JB said, "and his was the last."

He called on other men as well. One was Elmer Wellemeyer of Cities Service. Wellemeyer noticed that JB was coming down with a cold, and said, "I'll cure that for you."

He led JB into the Cities Service executive gym, where they

played a hard, fast game of handball. Then JB had to push-pull with an ape-like gym attendant, who had him squat, bend, and sweat. He was next directed to a hot room. From there he went to the steam room, where a high-pressure hose was played on him. After that he was given a rubdown.

JB emerged from the Cities Service building in a state of astonishment to discover himself buffeted by icy New York winter winds, with the thermometer reading seven degrees above zero. He arrived at his hotel so weak he could barely reach his room. Once in bed, he called Clark Moody, an old friend with California Standard, who sent a doctor to see him.

The doctor advised a hospital, but JB refused. "You need nurses," the doctor insisted, and JB ordered nurses to be sent to the hotel. The doctor also gave him some sleeping pills, but JB threw them away. He recovered in a few days, and often saw Wellemeyer again—but never when he felt a cold coming.

On a corporate level Dean McGee moved toward his concept of a "total energy" company. In 1964 he constructed a facility north of Oklahoma City that converted enriched uranium pellets into fuel assemblages for nuclear power reactors. His grand design was to participate in all eight phases of the nuclear fuel cycle. As part of that goal he would drop "Oil" from the corporate name in 1965, and present the firm simply as Kerr McGee Corporation.

The move was in tune with the times, in which old definitions of industry were beginning to lose significance as firms expanded and their activities intertwined in a manner impossible to trace. A vast technological grid was being created. Firms could no longer confine their activities to "steel," or "oil," or any of the nineteenth-century concepts.

Since ventures could no longer be defined by products or a single sector of activity, the corporation became an increasingly important concept. Analysts were discovered to have a strong preference for corporations whose themes were easily grasped. McGee, in moving into nuclear energy was, of course, very serious. He was intent upon obtaining an early and solid position in the energy source of the future. It was a source, however, that in the early sixties, and for an indefinite period of time, would remain available only to governments and large institutions. It was an energy source on the opposite pole from oil, the kind of marketplace it entailed, which JB knew so well.

Nevertheless, JB and McGee cooperated well on corporate activities. Saunders knew Joe Broadus, in New York, and managed to have Broadus persuade David Rockefeller to visit Kerr McGee in Oklahoma

City. The remark about "a one-man company" had to be overcome. Rockefeller appeared and was entertained—if that is the word—at a private dining room on the twentieth floor of the Kermac Building by twenty-eight of Kerr McGee's top men. JB gave him and four of his executives each a white cowboy hat. Discovering the proper sizes in advance was a familiar routine from his days as a salesman. Several years later, when he happened to call Broadus, he discovered Rockefeller still had the hat—and still remembered JB Saunders.

That effort, as well as many others, helped restore Kerr McGee's standing in the exchanges. It also highlighted a missing human element in many trends in American society in the middle sixties. Gargantuan plans were being drawn in every sector. The nation's schools harbored over 5 million young people between the ages of eighteen and twenty-one. That impossible multitude was ruled, at the top, by 150,000 tenured professors, removable only by death.

In the Pentagon—a mind-boggling structure—thousands worked in a military establishment no longer comprehensible in detail or manageable overall. MacNamara, whose experience had been in gathering statistics on the labors of other men in the automotive industry, ruled more autocratically than any general in the nation's history, assisted by graduates in computer science.

There was a quality about these new organizational moves, reflected in the sweeping societal promises of the Johnson Administration, that was oddly unworldly, though immensely learned. To JB and his contemporaries, the younger men who now constituted the majority of those they observed, seemed efficient but limited.

A nation once known around the world for its sense of fun grew remarkably humorless. It was as though people were forgetting how to smile. The theater mounted cruel, grisly, and grotesque efforts that were described as "black humor." Some were as funny as death. Young people adopted glum, sarcastic manners, and dressed in drab clothes. Jeering became a conversational staple; the "put-down" spread. Yet this was described, in print, as sophistication; to JB and his associates it seemed pointless and naïve. Young people, they observed, had grown difficult to reach, and seemed to have developed strange antipathies towards business.

One young newspaper reporter approached Sid Siteman in the lobby of the Stevens Hotel in Chicago during an API meeting, and his questions struck Siteman's funny bone. He wanted to know, for example, how many millionaires were attending the meeting.

"Hundreds," Siteman said promptly.

"What do they do at the meeting?"

"See girlie shows," Siteman said gravely. "Give dinners for six hundred people—that sort of thing. Play poker."

"Big games?" persisted the questioner.

"Tremendous," Siteman said. "Average pot runs around twenty-five hundred dollars."

"Who wins?" asked the reporter.

"Well, JB Saunders, as a rule," Siteman said. "You know about him, I guess. Sold his company to Senator Kerr, but he's working toward more millions all the time."

The next day a verbatim article appeared in the paper. The headline read:

Oil Talks Draw 400 Rich Men

Siteman laughed and so did JB. Neither of them realized the humorless nature of the new world under construction.

President Johnson gave some indication of that when he requested that businessmen reduce investments abroad—as though, by shrinking its international business, the nation would improve.[18] That suggestion proved only one of innumerable propositions the President propounded. He seemed to believe the nation was simultaneously beset by deep poverty and yet wealthy enough to afford any program, no matter how expensive, if it sounded good. He pushed expanded voting rights in the South, as though that was the only region constricted. He pushed for Medicare, a perennial Democratic party proposition, and had the satisfaction of seeing it passed. He obtained one billion dollars for Appalachia, a region that needed industry more than relief. But his most surprising step, especially in view of an election campaign in which he promised to not send "American boys to fight an Asian war," was to hugely escalate the national effort in Viet Nam.

JB and Eddy moved into an extra house in Oklahoma City in the summer of 1965. Within Kerr McGee's executive suite, JB watched Raborn and Kelly creating controls and consolidating the eleven chemical firms, the personnel and properties he had gathered. He was not convinced that the new controls would prove as efficient as they were plausible, but there was always a chance that he was wrong.

Meanwhile he grew increasingly interested in the Cowboy Hall of Fame and Western Heritage Center, and various other community and regional activities. As Stanley Draper, the long-time head of the Chamber of Commerce, said later, "Newcomers are invited to join. If they are not interested, we are not interested." That sort of challenge was not one that JB would ignore. Invited to become a trustee of the Oklahoma City University in 1965, he accepted.

18. Ibid.

He held meetings in his Kerr McGee office with other trustees of the Cowboy Hall of Fame, which he joined with great pleasure. Krakel, who had to work beginning, he said later, "with bare walls," needed money and support; JB provided both.

He was not alone, of course. The city was still dominated by men who had helped build it from the prairie up. Morrison Tucker, a banker who had worked for Nelson Rockefeller in Venezuela, later summarized the scene at Oklahoma City.

Tucker, whose home town was Lincoln, Nebraska, compared it unfavorably. "Newcomers were resented in Lincoln," he recalled, "but welcomed in Oklahoma City."

Tucker is in a position to know; he is also familiar with Dallas, Little Rock, Denver and, of course, Lincoln. "They were all built between eighteen eighty-four and eighteen ninety-five," he said. "They are, in other words, new cities. But they are all older than Oklahoma City. In the entire metropolitan area of Oklahoma City there is only one Victorian house. Now they're about to tear down the central core of the city, which was all built at once, about fifty or sixty years ago.

"To the leaders of Oklahoma City there is nothing impossible about razing it entirely and building again. After all, the men who built it are still here; or at least some are still here."

JB, therefore, met some of the original pioneers. One, E. K. Gaylord, who in 1903 was one of the founders of the *Daily Oklahoman*, was in 1965 past ninety and still in complete charge of his two newspapers, two radio stations, four television stations and other properties —he was interested in everything that moved. "A small lean man with a strong voice who made few speeches," said Dr. Dolphus Whitten, Jr., "but he could, when he chose, provide pungent anecdotes of pioneer days. He was notably good-humored."

Virgil Brown, another leader, was also in his nineties and equally active, tireless, lucid, and alert. Ross Anthony, owner of a chain of stores who came to the Indian Territory in 1890 as a penniless orphan of thirteen, was another. Dan Hogan, who became president of the City National Bank in 1911 and was still chairman in his nineties, was another.

Around these incredible figures clustered more, equally remarkable though not as aged. JB found such men congenial; they were builders and activists. So was he.

While such men were still talking and thinking in terms of improving Oklahoma City, however, others in other parts of the land

436

were moving toward destruction in the name of Reason. Demonstrations against American participation in Viet Nam—but not against Soviet or Chinese entanglement—began early in the year and mounted like a brush fire. Names already famous were made far more so by the media, which hailed Norman Mailer, Dr. Benjamin Spock, Dick Gregory, Father Daniel Berrigan, and Dr. Hans Morgenthau.

In time many more names would join this list. But, remarkably, those who differed with them were to remain largely unknown, unquoted, and uncelebrated.

In August, 1965, a policeman stopped a driver suspected of being drunk in the largely black district of Watts, in Los Angeles. A crowd collected, anger mounted, and a riot erupted that lasted five days. Thirty-five were killed and hundreds wounded; the nation was horrified to watch looters on their television screens while police, under orders, watched. During the mélée flames, shots, dramatic commentary, and dismay regarding the nation's racial divisions mounted.

In the autumn of 1965 there was a power blackout that extended from Canada through New York City to Pennsylvania. Since anything that happens in New York City is treated by the communications industry as major news, the event inspired long articles about the experience. Few Americans realized such blackouts are frequent in other parts of the world—and permanent in some. A number of New York voices were raised at once, demanding that the government take control of public utilities.

A more significant event took place in early January, 1966, however, when New York City found itself largely unable to go to work because of a transit-union strike. Again, the phenomenon was more familiar in other parts of the world: in Paris, London, Rome, and western Europe in general.

Added together in early 1966, the nation's troubles seemed huge, but much of that impression was created by a widespread focus on trouble spots and a general indifference to the huge, successful and prosperous private sector. The fact was that the nation was in the midst of an unparalleled period of production, accompanied by inflation, by an undeclared war, by a relief and welfare program larger than during the New Deal, and by political arguments of considerable intensity—all at the same time.

Ralph Worley, who had worked for years with John Atkins in Shreveport and then continued with John Atkins, Jr., was made president of the Natural Gas Processors' Association. His term of office ran from April, 1965, to April, 1966.

He learned from the editor of the *Oil & Gas Journal,* who acted as the association's executive secretary, that the organization had never been able to persuade Kerr McGee to become a corporate member, though it was active in the gas industry.

Worley wrote JB, knowing, he said later, that he was a top man at the company, asking him to sponsor Kerr McGee into the group. Its membership would be expensive, but it was the sort of expense that large firms usually endured for the good of the respective industry. Worley received no reply, but did get a phone call from Kerr McGee, asking for membership forms.

"I knew then that JB had read that letter and given the green light," Worley said. The realization made him feel very good; he had never forgotten Shreveport days. "And," he added, "the city never really recovered from that plane crash."

Life, in other words, was beginning to take on a smoother face. JB was going to pass his sixty-fifth birthday in the summer, and he and Dean McGee had agreed that he should move to another stage in the firm. The fertilizer plants and the chemical companies that he had acquired, the offices and sales staffs, warehouses and phosphate deposits, were being shifted to other hands. JB did not really mind; he had no overwhelming desire to stay occupied with chemicals.

"Chemical men are a different breed," he says. "When I was buying companies," he added, "I kept meeting hard luck stories. But I attended a chemical convention at the Greenbriar and saw their wives in mink and diamonds, and they arrived in private planes. I thought they were ready to go to the poorhouse in style."

Allstetter, however, was saddened by the change. "JB is a man who pushes other men to their top potential," he said, "and that's rare in big business." It is rare, in fact, anywhere.

In the spring of 1966 Eddy was ill; her emphysema had grown progressively worse for several years. JB, however, was not prepared, when pneumonia developed, to see her rapid decline. Like most men, he had taken for granted the fact that his wife would outlive him; his will and estate plans had been based on that assumption. But his wife died on April 17, 1966, after nearly forty years of marriage. That is a very long time, and he was caught by surprise.

CHAPTER FIFTEEN

New Paths

A BUSY MAN can accept change better than those whose lives are too tightly constricted. JB was alone for the first time in nearly forty years; his son, JB III, had married the year before and was enjoying a new domesticity, and Suzanne lived in Houston with her husband.

Howard Williams, JB's yardman in Houston, came to him after the funeral and said, "I'm a pretty good rough cook."

JB was surprised—and touched. To his pleasure, Howard was a good cook, and proved to be adept in a great many areas as well. He soon became JB's cook, bartender, and chauffeur, and was especially helpful when JB entertained. That helped.

Being moved from executive vice president of Kerr McGee to vice chairman of the board also helped.

"What are the duties of a vice chairman?" he was asked at an API meeting.

"You know the definition of a chairman," JB replied, "as being like an old dog that sits in a chair and howls?"

The questioner nodded.

"Well, a vice chairman is the same, except that his vocal cords have been clipped."

The remark made appreciative rounds; it was clear that no title would ever change JB Saunders. But in reality the vice chairman at Kerr McGee was the working partner of Dean McGee, the chief executive and chairman.

The circumstance of the firm, like Oklahoma City itself, was far different than in the huge eastern corporations. When JB had joined Triangle to Kerr McGee in 1957, the firm was still owned and managed by its founders. JB joined as a co-owner and manager. In 1966 McGee was still managing, and JB joined him at the top.

439

He retained an office in Triangle and continued to attend API and other industry meetings, because the contacts and influence of so many years were too valuable—and also too personally valued—to discard. It was true that younger men had risen, and many of his former associates were gone from the scene.

"The heavy drinkers began to die off in their early fifties," JB said. "Then there were those who took early retirement, for one reason or another. But I knew men for two levels down; I didn't only call at the top, you know." That helped, too—for many of those men, "two levels down," had risen to the top by 1966.

For that reason, and also because of the farflung and efficient activities of Barksdale and C. D. Tinsley, Triangle was continuing to grow. Its sales had moved close to $130 million in 1966, and its profits over $4 million a year. It handled sales for more than twenty firms outside Kerr McGee and had service station chains of its own under a variety of brand names, as well as the marketing and branded stations of Kerr McGee. JB kept his office in the Triangle building in Houston, therefore, and did not let it get dusty.

He also had his land in South Dakota—property originally purchased for pheasant hunts and a place to take his friends for a break in their routines. In the late fifties he had at that location as guide a young farmer named Dale Hoffman. Hoffman said that he knew of a nice place for sale nearby and wished he could buy it.

"Suppose I bought it and you farmed it," said JB. "Could you pay one third of the crop to me and live on the other two thirds?"

"I'd love to try," Hoffman said.

JB bought the land. The following year he suggested fertilizer, and Hoffman said that wasn't any good—too expensive. "I'll buy it," JB told him. "If you get a big yield I'll take the excess till the fertilizer is paid." It did pay; the crop improved 25 percent. "That sold him," said JB later.

JB put up fences, bought hogs and cattle, and in time added more land. By the sixties it was to constitute almost four thousand acres. The Hoffmans acquired tractors. Mrs. Hoffman—Leonora—started a dairy business with milking machines and cows; every morning filled glass-lined cans with milk are picked up by a large tank operated by a dairy corporation.

JB, therefore, still had his pheasant hunts, and their attendant poker games and discussions at night, once or twice a year. Hoffman protected the area from poachers; when JB and his friends arrived, the birds were usually numerous.

In Oklahoma City, JB turned toward his numerous civic and business interests. He was a trustee not only of the Oklahoma City University, but also of the smaller Oklahoma Christian College. Many aspects of education interested him, as they do so many Americans, but by 1966 the subject was controversial.

Berkeley radicals held huge, disheveled demonstrations, carried banners with obscene words in protest against standards of decency in language, and received not only national but also international publicity. Their idols were Marx, Mao, and Herbert Marcuse—a former refugee from the Nazis who believed in the suppression of views that differed from his own. Other universities rocked in response, often led by professors. San Francisco State, St. John's in Brooklyn, New York, Cornell—the list extended with the year 1966 and was to continue.

Echoes reached the quiet campus of Oklahoma City University, where JB said, "Four or five young ladies objected to curfew hours."

The problem was discussed by the trustees—"twenty or twenty-five men at a long narrow table." The curfew hours were midnight during the week and 2:00 A.M. on weekends.

"What was the problem?" JB asked, and was told, "Those are grown women."

The trustees agreed, but also pointed out that Oklahoma City is a Methodist Church school and could set its own rules. "If they don't like the rules let them find another school," said one trustee. Others agreed.

The school head warned that demonstrations might arise; some students might leave.

"Perhaps so," JB replied. "But when the parents learn of a school that holds the line, you'll get two students for every one that leaves."

At Oklahoma Christian College, another school in which JB was interested, a minirebellion was mounted. Dr. Baird, its head, expelled the handful of ringleaders, who took their case to court. Dr. Baird told the judge who heard the case that if his right to administrate the college was not upheld, he would resign. That was not necessary; the students lost their case.

There was also the Cowboy Hall of Fame and Western Heritage Center. Dean Krakel, its director, proved a unique combination of collector, curator, showman, entrepreneur, and supersalesman. He had been director of the Gilcrease Institute in Tulsa, a fabulous accumulation of manuscripts, documents, Indian artifacts, sculpture, paintings, books, potteries, and whatever had interested the oilman. Gilcrease presented all of these to the city of Tulsa. Later, as so often happens, the institute came under the careful controls of city officials.

"I had to go before the board to get a pencil," Krakel said, with only slight exaggeration. His idea of a museum was not a cold tomb of the arts. He found the trustees of the Cowboy Hall—men who started, as had JB, close to the earth and were successful in business—agreed with that concept and, more important, understood it. What Krakel wanted was a chance to build a new sort of museum—a living center where art and the past mingled with the present.

Hearing of a chance to buy the Charles Schreyvogel collection of western paintings—considered among the finest—Krakel went to JB. The price was $175,000, and the director believed the paintings worth twice that amount. The president and chairman of the Cowboy Hall's board were unavailable, but JB signed a personal note for the $175,000. A similar situation arose regarding two Russells, whose owner wanted $180,000 in cash within twenty-four hours. Krakel contacted a Dallas bank, which agreed to lend the money on a trustee's signature. He flew to Dallas, back to JB in Oklahoma City for his signature, back to Dallas, then to New York City, bought the paintings, and brought them back to the Hall. When the trustees held their next meeting the members regarded the acquisition, and approved. They were superb, and the price was reasonable.

Krakel has a shrewd eye for values and knows the market. That alone would make him valuable; other qualities make him invaluable. The most conspicuous is a realization that genuine American achievements, in terms of art and culture, are under attack and threatened with death in the nation.

When Krakel came to Oklahoma City, for instance, he could not forget Laura Gardin Fraser in her studio in Westport, Connecticut, and the great panel she had sculpted for Oklahoma City commemorating the Run. James Earle Fraser, her husband, the other half of the nation's most talented couple in the history of sculpture, was dead. But his world-renowned "End of the Trail" was immortal. Krakel had hopes of someday bringing that to the Cowboy Hall.

Meanwhile, he had dozens of other projects, ideas, observations, thoughts, plans, and programs bubbling. JB enjoyed that immensely. So did Jasper Ackerman, president of the trustees, a banker and rancher from Colorado Springs, and others, including Fred Dressler, rancher and businessman; Joel McCrea, the actor-rancher; Gene Autry, a very generous and enthusiastic trustee; and Albert Mitchell, a banker-rancher. With those sophisticated people behind him, Krakel was to turn the entire effort into something astonishing and unprecedented.

Toward late autumn, 1966, Paul Blazer of Ashland Oil came

through Oklahoma City and paused to see JB. Blazer had recovered from his disappointment when Triangle had joined Kerr McGee instead of Ashland, though explanations had been difficult.

"He would walk a few steps, then stop to rest," JB said. "He was pale and shaky. Though he had been in notorious bad health for years, it was clear he was finally nearing the end. I felt sorry for him."

JB's health, however, was seemingly impervious. Through 1966 he traveled, as always, in and out of town and back and forth from his various offices. He was a vice president of the Oklahoma City Chamber of Commerce and increased his activities for that group, as he had for others. In November, 1966, the *Petroleum Club News* in Oklahoma City featured him as Man of the Month. A full-page photograph showed him standing in a classic pose made famous by painters, holding a furled manuscript in his hand.

That recognition and others heading in his direction, together with the increased tempo of business, kept his days brisk and busy. "But," he said later, "the nights were lonely."

On the stage of the great world during 1966 the largest event received the least attention. It was the downfall of Sukarno, the dictator of Indonesia, a string of islands in Asia containing fabulous natural resources and one hundred million persons. Sukarno had received huge sums of western aid and repaid it in vitriol. He then played the USSR against the Red Chinese, and finally moved—he was a racist of lethal proportions—in the direction of Peking. On September 30, 1967, Sukarno's confederates in the Indonesian Communist party mounted a coup. Its first attempt was to kill the leading generals; it did not succeed, and the response astonished both Peking and the Kremlin. Moslems in Indonesia, who had been considered unimportant, emerged from their homes and mosques with machine guns and machetes to conduct a massacre of Communists and fellow travelers of huge dimensions. Sukarno was placed under house arrest; the surviving general of the Army, Suharto, took over the government of Indonesia, and that strategically placed nation turned toward the West.

Few Americans were made aware of the extent and significance of that victory, in which their government played virtually no role. Instead the nation was treated to an immense series of articles, descriptions, and television programs portraying the war in Viet Nam as essentially meaningless, and the South Vietnamese government as hopelessly corrupt.

That description of a senseless world was paralleled by a wave of pornography in books, in movies, on stages, and in nightclubs throughout the country that astonished—as well it might—regions vainly attempting to retain societal standards. Riots, whose civil rights basis had grown tenuous, erupted frequently—usually when the police sought to make arrests in ghetto areas. The government, meanwhile, proceeded with both the war and its War on Poverty as though oblivious to the difficulties that both were accumulating.

Drugs brought a new dimension to the scene. LSD, discovered in 1938, a drug that distorted the senses, became the basis for a new psychedelic art craze that appeared in discothèques in the form of flashing colored lights and in galleries in paintings. Its high priest, Harvard psychologist Timothy Leary, became a cult figure. The phrase "Tune in, turn on, drop out" was a new prescription for the young. Marijuana, a drug that in the form of hashish had retarded the Middle East for centuries, became popular.

Ordinary citizens, struggling to make ends meet and hopeful of a better life for their children, were astonished when these developments were hailed by the intellectuals as signs of progress. Older citizens with longer memories, who recalled the twenties and the collapse of standards at that time, began to see some resemblances in the sixties.

With Washington pumping out huge sums of money, orders, credits, programs, and subsidies, with a war underway with its attendant demands on heavy industry and the service areas affected by supply needs, the nation's economy grew feverish. Prices on the stock exchange began to soar into what a commentator would call the "go-go years." Mergers and expansions began to affect all industry and business.

The idea that economists had developed a permanent answer to the recurrent cycles of business, and had instruments at hand to arrange and maintain permanent prosperity emerged from the grave into which it had fallen in 1929. A new generation, in other words, was on the scene, intent on repeating every error of the old—with a few new ones for better measure.

The same spirit of prosperity, however, was discernible all through the western world. JB and F. C. Love went to Buenos Aires to discuss some joint ventures with some wealthy Argentinian businessmen. JB observed that they lived very well.

"They have boats," he said, "they take long weekends, they water-ski—and they are in no hurry to do business."

In midconference all of them left town, leaving no word where they went nor when they would return. JB, appearing to continue the talks, was astonished. He learned they had gone together to view a spectacular ship's fire out of sheer curiosity. He could hardly believe the junket or the discourtesy, but he and Love were left to cool their heels for three days. Then the Argentinian businessmen returned, the conference resumed, but no explanations were offered.

If the western world was growing fat, it was also becoming conspicuously Americanized in 1967. Everywhere JB traveled he saw other Americans, some of whom he knew. Again in Buenos Aires, seated with Love in a bar one night having a nightcap, JB saw two familiar-looking men enter.

One was Dan Hogan, a former Firestone vice president; the other was Charley Smith, an executive with American Airlines. The men chatted, in the Argentinian capital, about old days in Oklahoma during the twenties. JB mentioned that he and Clive Alexander, when they worked for Hassett, once had the thought of obtaining a tire franchise and had a short conversation with Harvey Firestone.

Mr. Firestone was visiting Tulsa. They found him cold and distant; he said curtly that his firm was not signing any new distributors. They left with their enthusiasm frozen solid. Hogan laughed; he remembered that period very well. "Mr. Firestone was in the process of discovering his distributors had nicked him for five hundred thousand dollars," he said. "I can well believe he was not receptive."

JB began to notice, on his travels, a different spirit. He was well acquainted with the English; he had English distribution for Triangle, and during World War II the two brothers of Barks & Barks had visited him in Houston.

JB recalls introducing them at a party. "I'm Tom," said one, and the other, smiling, would add, "I'm Petuh."

But in the late sixties, attempting to discover why an English drilling project for Kerr McGee was four months behind schedule, when similar efforts were on time in Germany and ahead of time in Holland, he met differences. JB had his daughter Suzanne, with him; she likes to travel. An Englishman with a Sir to his name sent a welcoming letter that added they might have to walk through some sand; he apologized for the discomfort.

At the site JB discovered a cocktail party in progress, and saw the titled host command attention to discuss the sand again. At the site he could see a strip of sand about thirty yards wide; not far away he saw stacks of lumber. He wondered why the English had not simply placed the lumber across the sand and kept quiet about it all. "Lots of affectations," he thought, "but not much sense."

In April, 1967, Dean McGee called JB, who was in his Triangle office at the time, and asked him to come to a Houston hotel. There was some urgent business to discuss. JB arrived and found the chairman, looking stern, waiting in the lobby. He took JB's arm and steered him into a banquet room. JB drew back, thinking he'd made a mistake—and then saw his son and daughter at the head table, smiling at him. A band struck up "For He's a Jolly Good Fellow," and the crowd rose and began to clap. It was Triangle's thirtieth birthday.

"It had a strong emotional impact," JB said.

They had gone to great efforts. Barksdale and Tinsley, both sales stars, knew how such festivities should be mounted and had not overlooked a single detail. His first secretary, Bernice Schliebe, was there, and so was Stanley Thomson of Abbotsford, Wisconsin, who had given JB his first order on April 17, 1937. Great efforts had been made to exhume photographs of JB through the years; they had been enlarged to nearly life-size, mounted on heavy cardboard, and stood around the room, like so many incarnations of his past and its stages.

The program for the party was in the form of a book entitled *The J. B. Saunders Story: Thirtieth Edition*. It held his photograph in color, a Foreword, Chapters for menu and the proceedings, an Index consisting of a thumbnail biography, and an illustration, on the inside back cover, of a stack of books whose spines were visible, showing their titles: Texas Eastern Transmission Company, Cato Oil and Grease Company, Cotton Valley Solvents Company, Reef Fields Gasoline Corporation, Triangle Refineries, Independent Petroleum Association, Imperial Refineries, Southern States Barge Lines, American Petroleum Refiners Association. There could have been more, but the stack was impressive enough. So was the fact that so many who knew him through the years were present to cheer.

That event was a normal, cheerful, and happy note amid rising discord in the greater world. The year had opened with President Johnson asking for heavier taxes to promote his two wars—one in Viet Nam and one on poverty—and traveled from there to general dishevelments. The United States bombed North Vietnamese areas. That was considered a dastardly deed by all the pro-Communist forces of the world. A theory had arisen that Communist military moves should be from protected sanctuaries. It was an odd theory, but it was in some vague way connected to the American policy in Korea, when the government had sacked a famous general who wanted to pursue the war too far. The left believed, with that precedent, that if enough pressure was mounted, such bombings could be halted and future pursuits aborted.

At the same time that this goal was pursued, the United States was subjected to a worldwide, noisy, and ugly campaign charging it with aggression in Asia. The war was called "immoral," and a familiar dichotomy, in which the excesses of the commissars were ignored and those of the Americans exaggerated, set in full cry.

Both Moscow and Peking assisted North Viet Nam, and the situation from the viewpoint of both capitals was nearly ideal. It embarrassed the West and had its largest and most powerful nation bogged down. In Washington neither the President nor his top associates seemed to know how to extricate themselves without abandoning an ally and suffering immeasurable international consequences.

At home the intelligence community came under attack, as did the FBI. Both organs were, of course, targets of those anxious to diminish the power of the government to protect itself; in 1967 they found strange allies in the top ranks of academia, in the communications industry, and on the political scene. J. Edgar Hoover charged Robert Kennedy with lying when he denied secret authorizations of wiretaps. Senator Thomas Dodd, a noted anti-Communist, was censured for campaign fund irregularities and his political career destroyed. The nation was in the curious position of fighting a Communist *Putsch* abroad, but retreating from a similar confrontation at home.

In April, Stalin's only daughter, Svetlana, fled to the United States. The government appeared embarrassed. She declared her father's crimes were shared by officials still in power in the USSR, and *Esquire* magazine carried her photograph on its cover—with a mustache.

In June, Premier Aleksei Kosygin arrived for a UN meeting and met with President Johnson. A statement was issued saying the talks had been constructive, but they had been a transparent failure. The site was appropriately named: it was Glassboro, New Jersey.

It seemed, however, to be a season of honors for JB. On May 20, 1967, at the spring commencement of the Oklahoma City University, in company with astronauts Gordon Cooper and Tom Stafford and three other distinguished citizens, he was given an honorary doctorate in law. His acceptance remarks were unusual because he had invited Miss Leita Davis, his teacher from high school, and paid her a tribute.

Miss Davis was very pleased. She had watched the academic revolutionaries with considerable distress. "I saw some teachers who behaved beautifully until they had tenure," she said, "and then appeared in different colors." Her faith in education had not changed, but she felt that her profession had been misused. "I believe," she said, years later, "that the government made a mistake in making education compulsory. It forced teachers to water down, and to weaken their profession."

She retained that professional objectivity even while watching JB collect honors. "One of my most outstanding students," she said, "but —of course—not the only one."

A month later JB took the inaugural flight from Oklahoma City to Seattle, launched by Continental to acquaint that city with the fact that an arrangement had been reached with the international carrier, to bring European tourists to the Cowboy Hall of Fame.

He carried great white ten-gallon hats, which he gave away to the mayors of Tulsa, Wichita, Portland, and Seattle, and to the presidents of various chambers of commerce.

A busy man. Paul Strasbaugh, an assistant of Draper's at the Oklahoma City Chamber of Commerce, considered him a rare member. "The Chamber here was virtually born and raised in the oil fields," he said. "It provided publicity for the industry for years. And since the city contains a number of firms involved with the industry, the Chamber always received a great deal of help from oilmen on these efforts. But in general, it has not been a pattern of the oil industry to become a community force."

"To most men," Strasbaugh added, in an echo of William Whyte,[1] "their corporations are their communities. Corporation people are concerned with their own internal pecking order, and their position in that order is the most important element in their lives. But JB was different. He regarded Oklahoma City as a community. And he worked as a member of the community."

When out of town dignitaries arrived, JB was available to entertain them, and tell of the city's and the state's opportunities. One visitor was Piet Beukes, an important publisher and columnist from South Africa. South Africans, whose sensitivities have long been rubbed raw by American critics, are not usually favored with many honors on their visits. But JB took Beukes to the Tulsa Oil Show, gave him a grand tour, and was pleased later when a correspondence was established.

JB's efforts as a salesman for the city were so successful that he began to carry the city keys with him when he traveled. He would make a cheerful ceremony out of their presentations, coupled with an invitation to come to Oklahoma.

"At one time you needed a key to get out of the city," he would say. "Here's one to get you into the city."

1. William H. Whyte, *The Organization Man* (New York: Simon and Schuster, 1956).

To courteously receive a prominent citizen of South Africa was not fashionable in many quarters by 1967; that nation had been targeted for considerable criticism for its racial policy of apartheid. But political attitudes in the United States were by no means as unified as the press, which had by subtle stages moved closer to telling people what journalists believed rather than reporting general attitudes.

In some instance of course, those were parallel. When Israel defeated Egypt, Syria, and Jordan in a lightning six-day war in midsummer, the results were hailed with admiration. The fact that it left the Middle East in an inequitable tilt was not so generally appreciated.

When Greek colonels overthrew the Greek government, the press reaction in the United States was severe. Editorials appeared claiming democracy had been shamed in the home of its origin, though Greece has seldom been democratic.

The tone of the comments regarding Greece highlighted a shift in American reportage and in the opinion of intellectuals in general. At one time a pro-American government, though authoritarian, was preferred over a totalitarian government such as those maintained in Communist countries. But by a subtle series of modulations, authoritarian governments had come to be termed *Fascist*, and Communist governments had grown remarkably respectable.

One result was that the Greek colonels received smiles from Washington for their pro-Americanism, and frowns from the American press for their authoritarianism. Meanwhile neighboring Yugoslavia, distinguished by tyranny that made no pretenses at ever intending to change, was treated by the same press with an odd acceptance.

That disparity highlighted a growing dilemma of the West, where political definitions that were once clear, and taught in every school, had grown blurred. A democracy cannot suppress tyrannical minorities without distorting or abandoning democratic principles. Very few, by 1967, recalled that John Adams and the other American founders had, for that very reason, ruled against an unlimited democracy in favor of a precisely balanced triangular government.

As the year 1967 extended JB found himself being invited to a great many parties and social gatherings. His friends noticed that he appeared, with increasing frequency, accompanied by Mrs. Georgia Jungerman Comegys. Divorced for a number of years, she had two grown children and her own home, and worked at Kerr McGee as executive secretary to vice president Tom Seale. Before joining the firm, she had worked at the University of Oklahoma, where she was very well known, and had many friends on the faculty.

On January 30, 1968, Georgia wrote a letter to Tom Seale. It read, in part, "This is to advise you and also to give formal notice of my plan to leave your employ on or before March 1, 1968.

"I have been offered," she continued, "a better position. I feel I should give this offer due consideration . . . in fact, I have already told my employer I would accept."

The offer was, of course, to marry JB. The news was well received. So many receptions and parties were mounted that he was, for once, exhausted. He said he would not even consider getting married in Oklahoma City; he would never live through the crowds that would collect at the event.

His friend Rocky, who still seemed permanently middle-aged at the age of eighty-three, suggested that they marry at his St. Louis home. That worked well; the ceremony took place March 30, 1968.

JB invited fifty of their best friends—he is a man with hundreds of friends—to a reception at the St. Louis Club later. Out-of-town guests were flown in and out, their hotel accommodations considered part of the invitation. During the wedding itself, a more restricted affair than the reception, the family guests received a set of eight silver goblets as a memento of the occasion.

They went on an extended honeymoon tour: Switzerland, Rome, Athens, Madrid, Portugal, and South Africa. All had their points of interest; JB had been to most of these places before, and knew their hotels and special characteristics, except for South Africa. That proved a remarkable experience and helped to crystallize some ideas that had been moving in his mind.

He had wired Piet Beukes, the South African publisher and columnist, and when they arrived at Johannesburg airport they heard themselves being paged. They answered, and a tall, lean English-woman, a widow—as JB, insatiably curious, later discovered—came forward. "Would you like a whisky?" she asked.

They didn't need one, and the Englishwoman, to JB's surprise, picked up their bags, led them to a car, then got behind the wheel and drove them to their hotel. The Easter Fair would open at noon, she said, and vanished—to reappear at that time. It was, JB discovered, very similar to a state fair back home. They wandered about looking at specimens of gold, silver, and coal. "Peanuts and machines all afternoon," he said.

The next day they were escorted to a nearby gold mine to watch tribal dancers in an annual competition. Each tribe had its own peculiar, traditional dance. There was, JB noted, "much heavy stamping. . . ."

"Some of the men," he said, "were huge and heavily muscled.

Some would fall to the ground, brace on their fingertips and toes, to rise and fall in unison to the drums; the people in the stands swayed with them."

They flew to Capetown the next day, and Piet Beukes appeared, beaming. He showed them the city, and they visited his home. It was located on a slope and built on three levels; the swimming pool was on the lowest. Their plot contained a curiosity, to which Helen Buekes called Georgia's attention. One spot was always sunny during the day; they planned to place a sun dial on that location, sometime in the future.

During their Capetown stay, Beukes accompanied JB and Georgia on a motor trip to the Cape of Good Hope, where they regarded, with awe, the difference in the colors of the waters where the warm Indian Ocean embraced and commingled with the cold Atlantic.

At the end of three days, Beukes arranged for them to be picked up in a car by a red-haired Englishman, who acted as chauffeur and guide along the Garden Route from Capetown to Durban. The ride was enlivened not only by extraordinary scenery, but also by baboons. Georgia was fascinated, and took copious notes.

Checking into the hotel at Durban, they found a message to call a Mr. Schutte. They did, and he appeared while they were looking around their suite. It had, among other features, a typewriter, a small bar, a liquor cabinet stocked with olives and mixes, but no ice. Mr. Schutte was an assistant to Mr. Loring Rattray, an important South African industrialist to whom Beukes had described his cordial Oklahoma reception several years before. Mr. Rattray was out of town, said Mr. Schutte, but he hoped they would use his yacht, "to see Durban from the sea." Mr. Schutte, who took his whisky neat, then shared a drink with them, and bowed himself away.

The following morning JB shopped for a sun dial, and found it was a far-from-ordinary object. He finally located a professor and made arrangements, through a complex series of conversations, to have a sun dial, decorated with the signs of the zodiac, constructed and placed in the Beukes home in Capetown.

At one o'clock in the afternoon Mr. Schutte reappeared with Mrs. Schutte, and they took a car to the harbor. JB thought Durban looked something like Atlantic City, though it held some sights unknown to the New Jersey resort. One consisted of rickshaws, discernible amid the heavy automobile traffic, pulling passengers along the street. Their drivers wore elaborate animal headdresses, complete with horns.

Other features were more familiar. "They had paved streets along the strand instead of a boardwalk," said JB, "but the beach was lined with huge hotels. The city was crowded with tourists." The port has a brisk trade with Europe; he noted the surf was heavy.

Rattray's yacht was seventy or eighty feet long and had a crew of eight. They were served turkey, ham, and liquor. Seated on deck chairs, they could see the great span of the harbor, with its rim of tall buildings. It was, indeed, very pleasant. They watched the sun descend and saw the lights of the city appear; the constellations overhead—unfamiliar and for that reason of interest—appeared close and bright. It was midnight before they returned to their hotel.

A couple of days later Loring Rattray returned to Durban, called, and invited them to his office. The Olympics were being held in Mexico City that year, and South Africa had been barred. Rattray was offended by that, and discussed various aspects of South African life, including the penal.

JB listened with interest. He had been a member of an investigating committee into the penal situation in Oklahoma, and he knew the problem from that end. "Here the jails are jails," Rattray said. "The prisoners get sowbelly and rice. If they are rebellious they are whipped on their bare arses. But the sentences are short. Six months. Nine months. A year is very long. But once released, they never want to go back.

"Would you like to see a ranch?" Rattray asked. JB would; ranches interested him. "I have Mala Mala. Fifty-seven thousand acres, situated southwest and alongside of Kruger Park. I also have another, four housand acres, called Exeter."

JB wondered if he could rent a plane to make that trip, and Rattray said his own DeHaviland, a two-engine ship with two pilots, was available. The pilots could double as guides.

At Mala Mala they stayed at quarters for twenty-five people. It had a cone-thatched roof and was inside a stockade. It looked, JB thought, like an old western fort; the fence was made of sharpened stakes. That evening they were served dinner around an immense roaring fire, buffet-style. Mala Mala was a game preserve; there was a reason for the pointed stakes, and the fence.

That evening they were taken out to a huge tree, estimated to be two thousand years old, and ascended a high, steep ladder to a platform constructed well above the ground, which held chairs and had a railing. Other attendants then drew and coiled the ladder; hampers of sandwiches and liquor appeared. Looking below, they could see beyond the wire fence and gate that protected the tree. Parts of impalas were suspended on wire cables, and lowered to dangle in the unfenced area. The region was a game preserve; the movement of its inhabitants were unpredictable.

After a time they heard crunching. Overhead lights shone sud-

452

denly; overheads are ignored by animals. Below them at least a half-dozen lions were feeding. They thought they were small, until some Big Daddies appeared. One circled beneath an impala hung high, raised on his hind legs, fastened one great paw with its claws into the carcass, and tore it in half with a single yank. Soon another male appeared to take the remainder with equal ease. By morning, said the attendants, the scene would be clean. Jackals would attend to that.

The following day they rode in a Land Rover. The pilot and co-pilot, each with a high-powered rifle, sat beside the driver. A black sat in the back on a special high seat: the spotter.

"Jeerahf! Jeerahf!" the spotter said suddenly. They peered but saw nothing; ten or fifteen minutes passed before the herd appeared. Still as statues, the heads looked over treetops, their legs indistinguishable from tree trunks. "Zeebrah! Zeebrah!" the spotter announced, in a voice as deep as a mine shaft.

After hours they arrived at Rattray's Exeter home beside a river. It was immense; the grounds extended along the river banks for almost a mile. Seated in chairs, served beer and thick steaks cooked, again, over an open fire, they watched animals arriving at the river to drink: elephants and zebras. They took pictures; the sight was irresistible. They saw no hippos but later, being driven along the cliffs, stopped to stare down. Roars came from below; the hippos were annoyed.

They flew back to Johannesburg in the DeHaviland. When they arrived, JB asked the pilots for his bill, and they said Mr. Rattray had paid for everything. Later he inquired about Mr. Rattray in the Chase Bank, and a tall Englishman said, with a note of regret, "He is one of our most important industrialists. But he is on the board of a competitive bank." JB telephoned Rattray and thanked him for his courtesies, but said he would like to pay. Mr. Rattray sent an absurdly small bill; JB sent a check and a letter of thanks.

Later they received a letter from the Beukes. The sun dial had arrived and was in place, and a plaque had been laid at the base. It read: *A gift from my good American friends, Georgia and JB Saunders.*

The year 1968 was one of the most disorderly and divided in the history of the nation. The crescendo of criticism against American military involvement in Viet Nam reached deafening proportions in the press, academia, and the arts. A parallel existed in this agitation, with similar arguments mounted in France when that nation sought to retain its hold on what was then known as Indochina. As in France, political figures who were otherwise obscure were elevated to prominence by lending their efforts to withdrawal. One of those was Senator

453

Eugene McCarthy, a dim figure for a number of years, who collected a collegiate and radical following by announcing his intention to run for President on a unilateral peace platform.

McCarthy's entrance into the New Hampshire primary resulted in an excellent showing against President Johnson, though few observers noted that Richard Nixon collected more votes than the other candidates combined. Toward the end of March, 1968, when JB and Georgia were touring Europe, President Johnson announced he would not run for reelection. The news was hailed as a triumph; Senator Robert F. Kennedy moved to preempt the McCarthy position and following. Violence on campus and in the ghettoes, however, continued as though no signs of change were sufficient. A sniper from ambush shot down Dr. Martin Luther King. Riots exploded in cities across the land, including the capital. For the first time the tone of these riots changed from demands for integration into the white majority society, into open hostility.

In June, 1968, after scoring a primary victory over Senator McCarthy in California, Senator Robert Kennedy was shot dead by a Palestinian refugee.

As in the instance of the assassination of President John Kennedy, the political orientation of the assassin was muted in the press, and overlooked by the public in a wave of horror at the curiously ill-starred fate of that famous family.

In early August the Republicans staged a convention in Miami that astonished the telecasters and commentators by being largely white, middle-class, well-dressed, and orderly. The delegates swept Richard Nixon into nomination, rejecting Nelson Rockefeller, who had first announced, then renounced, then reannounced, and finally made a futile run.

Toward the end of August, 1968, the Democratic convention was held in Chicago amid unparalleled scenes of disorder mounted by thousands of young people and various radical groups. Their intentions, beyond a desire to bait the nation, remained unclear. A confrontation was staged after many violations of public decency by the huge gathering, which resulted in injuries but, remarkably, no deaths.

The beleaguered delegates, overshadowed by the turbulent events outside the convention hall, nominated Vice President Hubert Humphrey. The conclusions of the press came down heavily against the mayor of Chicago and the Chicago police, though few commentators speculated on the results had the convention been opened to the mob.

Noisy comment over politics at home did much to muffle two other highly significant events of the summer of 1968. One was an announcement by General de Gaulle of France that Communists were attempting to take over the country. A youth uprising of remarkable violence appeared as though in response to his warning. That uprising appeared to have no goal beyond disorder, but came close to provoking civil war. The de Gaulle government moved forcefully, suppressed the effort, and then held an election.

The other event was an attempt by the Communist party of Czechoslovakia to moderate the iron rules of the party with its attendant censorship of the arts and all freedoms. The Kremlin moved in stages from discussions to troops; tanks rumbled into Prague. Elections were ended.

Seldom had the contrast between the system of the commissars and the ways of the West been more dramatically placed before the eyes of the world. But the criticism that arose was, in the world press, equally placed. In that manner the lesson seemed largely lost.

The argument of many youthful dissidents was that "the system" prevented individuality and that chances for advancement had been sealed. But in the season of 1968 Butch Butler, who had started in the Depression as a laborer—despite his college degree—in Texas, and JB Saunders, who had started even earlier from an equally humble beginning, reaped the rewards of years of hard work and intelligent planning.

When Kerr McGee had refused to buy Triangle's participation with Butler, Miller & Lents, JB had organized his minority interests into a new corporation. In time these included participation in large gas fields in Texas that were utilized by Butler, Miller & Lents. These included the Reef Fields Gasoline Corporation, the largest LPG source in the nation. Skelly needed those reserves. An estimate was made and a sale consummated for $27.5 million. JB received 28 percent—over $7 million. That sum, larger than JB received for the portion of Triangle that Kerr McGee purchased, was to be paid over a number of years.

Not only did JB receive more money from that single sale than he had from Kerr McGee for the largest independent marketing firm in the nation, but Butler, Miller and Lents became very wealthy men. They intensified their efforts, and began to create a dazzling array of subsidiaries and ventures, all of which JB continued to join.

That was a source of great satisfaction. Butch Butler, a superb golfer and pleasant companion, was one of JB's happier selections. A successful protégé sheds glory on his sponsors as well as himself; Butler was outstanding.

455

By 1968 they had shared in the sale of the Transwestern Pipeline to Texas Eastern, and the Reef Fields capped even that accomplishment.

Despite these triumphs, neither man considered leaving the business arena, nor did their associates. Some might assume they were motivated by greed; that would be like expecting a physician to abandon medicine when he became financially secure. Their instinct was to build, and both kept building assiduously. Butler, Miller & Lents expanded into engineering, petroleum and gas exploration, production, consultations on pipelines, processing, and refining on a global scale. JB continued with Kerr McGee, Triangle, his barge lines, and other ventures. Money, to both men and their associates, had merged into capital—a means to continue to build.

Krakel, at the Cowboy Hall of Fame, is another builder. In 1968 he had tracked down "The End of the Trail," Fraser's famous statue of the exhausted Indian horseman slumped in the saddle of an equally exhausted horse. Seldom in the history of art has a single work so uniquely expressed the poignant force of history.

Krakel found the huge plaster statue, created originally for the Panama Pacific International Exposition at San Francisco in 1915, standing neglected and dilapidated in a park in Tulare County, California. He promised to have it restored, have it cast in bronze, and give the bronze to Tulare County. Nearly twenty feet high and weighing over eight tons, the work had to be first restored. Nobody in the United States can make such a casting. Krakel had undertaken a major project. The Cowboy Hall put up $25,000 and the trustees signed formidable documents committing the Cowboy Hall to the effort.[2]

President Johnson had, during his Administration, attempted to emulate his idol Franklin Roosevelt in every sense. He had wanted to be a leader in both social and international changes, and not only had spent incredible sums of money in the effort, but had extended the government into education, into medicine, into industry, into social patterns further, deeper, and more extensively than ever before. The Johnson Administration had said it would build a Great Society. It succeeded in building a Great Government.

Neither candidate of the major parties addressed this, or any other

2. The complete story of that project—as well as a biography of the Frasers that, in itself, throws a fascinating spotlight on the changes within the American art world—can be found in Dean Krakel, *End of the Trail: Odyssey of a Statue* (Norman: University of Oklahoma Press, 1973).

central issue in the campaign. Nixon hinted at a different Court, but left the sensitive area of judiciary encroachments on the other two branches untouched. Humphrey sought to put space between himself and his now-unpopular sponsor in the White House. His attempts were cautious, if not cryptic, but each hint was hailed as a sign of candor. Nixon said he had an answer for the problem of Viet Nam but would not reveal it.

As the campaign proceeded Nixon pursued the careful tactics that had lost Dewey two elections, hoping to coast into office on the largely middle-class resentment of the Administration. One result was that his following in other sectors melted week by week.

The bases of Democratic support, consisting of the large labor unions and big city machines, regrouped during the campaign behind Humphrey. Both sides spent huge, unprecedented sums in television advertising and other media. The results were amazingly close.

Nixon received 31.7 million votes; Humphrey, 31.2. The difference was less than seven tenths of 1 percent. Both parties and the press in general ignored the performance of Alabama's Governor George Wallace, widely scorned as an ignorant racist. The third-party candidate, who created a machine for the election, obtained 9.8 million votes—13.5 percent of the electorate. That protest was a lot to ignore.

Another factor worthy of comment was that the new President entered office in January, 1969, with both houses of Congress against him. That was the first time such a circumstance had occurred in 120 years.[3] The judiciary was loaded with Democratic appointees over a period of more than a generation. The vast bureaucracy—with more persons, agencies, commissions, bureaus, and departments than could be listed in one thousand books—was similarly stacked. The press, which despised the new President and had made no bones about it for years, crouched watchfully. The spectacle was similar to a man entering a lion's cage with a whip, a whistle, and half the crowd in the grandstand hoping for his death.

JB attended the Derby in 1969, discovered that crowds lured to that great event were larger, more unruly and in worse humor than ever before. The nation was, after all, changing under the impact of unbridled sex movies, books, news coverage, drugs, crime, and riots. The old Wild West, for all its fabled gunfights, outlaws, and troubles, was safer than most modern American cities by the end of the Sixties.

The Derby was, of course, a familiar scene. He had, for years, met other men from the oil industry at the scene—had shared buses with

3. Manchester, *Glory and the Dream*, p. 1147.

Clint Murchison, Gene Constantin, Billy Byers, and others. But in later years JB rented his own taxicabs for his guests, by the day.

In 1969 he started to enter one of these cabs when a burly individual jostled against him to claim he saw it first; JB straightened to straighten him out and later discovered he had lost his wallet. It was a heavy one. He was carrying money from Oklahoma City friends to bet for them. Some of the bets had been placed and won, so he lost about two thousand dollars.

He told the police and they regaled him, as is their wont, with tales of how widespread pickpocketing had become. The police by 1969 had become master diplomats and soothers-of-indignation. Their powers to administer impromptu justice on the level of ordinary people had been removed, and their vocal cords, like vice chairmen's, had been clipped.

Afterward JB ordered drinks and mixes for his guests in his hospitality suite, and one discovered his wallet missing. To their surprise, when they called the Yellow Cab Company a driver had reported finding it wedged in the back seat; it was returned intact.

The nation was, then, in some respects, the same as ever. But there was a distinctly dangerous air to the Derby and to Louisville that had not before existed, even though crime and pickpocketing is eternal.[4]

Business, however, boomed in early 1969, although the Moran Shoe Company did not bring its largest shareholders any profits. Rocky had borrowed money to make that investment and was paying interest on the loan. In the absence of dividends that constituted a loss. JB didn't think that was proper. At a board meeting of the Moran Shoe Company, therefore, he suggested a dividend be paid. The young president of the firm grew almost indignant. JB was slightly surprised. "You're the only one making any money," he observed.

The meeting ended, but JB seldom dropped matters once he picked them up. Huffman, heading the Cato Oil & Grease Company back in Oklahoma City, had observed that, and had also said, "JB has a way of sounding casual when he says something, but he never says anything that he doesn't seriously mean."

JB discussed the Moran Shoe Company with Rocky, and learned the older man's interest in the venture was far from ardent. "We could outvote the president," JB said, "but I don't like to do that. Steamrolling is not a good way to do business."

Instead he began to shop about. In due course Rocky discovered a

4. JB and Rocky had two boxes that had been reserved for years in Rocky's name. After Rocky's death it proved impossible for JB or even Celeste Rockenback to retain them. JB stopped attending the Derby.

firm active in the baby-shoe business anxious to obtain the Moran brands, which were well-known and had good distribution.

A price was reached that was double the investment that Rocky and JB had made in the venture. Then a board meeting was called. The young president of Moran was greatly alarmed, and scurried about rallying the minority stockholders. That move was clearly destined to futility; a minority cannot yet outvote a majority in the corporate laws of the nation.

The president then suggested that the sale include a five-year contract for him. He also thought he should be president of the resulting merger. JB took him to lunch.

"I wouldn't want a contract, if I were in your position," he told the younger man. "I'd rather be free."

The president stared, but JB went on to discuss his experience, his talents, and his ability in general—and few men can resist such an appeal to their pride. The sale went through very smoothly, therefore, and both Rocky and JB made a fine profit.

The president, however, having earlier made a choice not to cooperate, found the new owners of his own cast of mind. Within a fairly brief period, he was back to the ranks of sales. Unlike the men of Triangle, he had not recognized that business consists of more than a situation.

Other matters were of more interest to JB. The Lakeside property in Houston had slowly evolved into a major investment. As time had passed, JB had gradually bought out most of his partners. The first three had sold out for three thousand dollars an acre; the next, for four thousand dollars. Barksdale, Tinsley, and Raborn each received five thousand dollars. That left W. Stewart Boyle and Dr. Crocker, whose names were beside JB's on the Prudential note. JB believed, however, the value of the land would continue to improve, and advised that it be held.

Pursuing that belief in 1968, he met Stewart and Dr. Crocker for breakfast at the Shamrock Hotel, and offered them $300,000 each for their combined one-fourth interest in the eleven hundred acres. They decided to accept, and JB added one condition. They were to keep their names on the Prudential note, though he released them from liability. In that manner he became the sole owner of the eleven hundred acres, at an average cost per acre of four thousand dollars.

The Bank of the Southwest, aware of that interest in real estate, contacted him regarding an apartment house on Westheimer Road. It was glass-hung and looked like a luxury hotel set off by itself, with a circular driveway and an attractive entrance. The builder, whom the

Bank of the Southwest had financed to the tune of $5.1 million, had spent $2.1 million and was anxious to get out.

The Bank of the Southwest wondered if JB would be interested in the property. He was leaving for Rome, but he told his good friend Butch Butler, "This could be a bird nest on the ground."

He departed, leaving the negotiations to Butler, who had become a professional businessman through the years. Butler added $900,000 to the original $5.1 million loan, and asked for and received 5 percent interest over a thirty-year period, with no payments due for the first two years.

JB returned to find that they had time to introduce improvements and raise the rents and place the huge building on a profitable basis. In effect, it would cost them nothing—a price even JB believed was hard to beat.

Butler leased two and a half apartments from the firm they organized for this venture, in which the Atkins family participated. JB himself leased three apartments and had walls removed to make them suitably grand. Georgia began the pleasant task of touring Europe, New York, Chicago, St. Louis, and other places to find suitable furnishings.

Meanwhile JB sold his Inwood Street house in the River Oaks district. The buyer didn't want the extra lot and garden alongside, and JB sold that separately. To his pleasure the rise in real estate values made the combined sale far more profitable than he expected.

Meanwhile he did not neglect Oklahoma City. Many changes were taking place in that arena. One affected the huge Liberty Bank, whose long-time head, Harvey Everest, wanted to retire as chairman. That desire coincided with a similar sentiment on the part of C. Ross Anthony and another important shareholder; all three wanted to consolidate their estates.

A search for a new head of the Liberty was undertaken and resulted in the selection of J. W. McLean. McLean arrived and was pleased to find JB on the Liberty board; he had known him from Houston.

"I remember being with a group that flew to Augusta to play golf," McLean says, "and JB was there, pouring drinks. A very companionable guy, but not a customer." McLean paused, and added, "There's only a hair's difference between a friend and a friend who's a customer—but what a hair!"

McLean knew Tinsley better at that time; C. D. is a man all the golfers knew—and he was also closer to being a contemporary. But McLean, by the time he came to Oklahoma City's Liberty, had been through the mills of change. In Houston he was president of the Texas National Bank, which ranked fourth in the city. It merged with the

Bank of Commerce—Jesse Jones's onetime base—a marriage that took five years to fully consummate. By the time it was welded, almost forty bank officers had departed, McLean among them.

He wound up at the Bank of America with the title of marketing director and vice president. It was not the same as having been chief executive officer, but it was at headquarters; the Bank of America is among the world's largest, and it was in San Francisco.

"It was like living in a miniature New York City," McLean said later. "I commuted every day and was always flying in and out of town." Then the hippies came.

That phenomenon—a modern replay of the ancient Children's Crusade, in which drug peddlers and criminals replaced the Turks—was enough to cause great worry in the McLean home. "I didn't want my children to mature in San Francisco," McLean says. Harvey Everest and his committee, therefore, were most welcome. McLean, after all, was an Oklahoma boy; he graduated from OU, and home had assumed a very attractive appearance.

The appointment was not universally hailed; appointments are never unanimous. One disappointed man was Morrison Tucker, executive vice president, who had been passed over. But JB had watched Tucker, a man with bristling eyebrows, as had other directors, and believed he was actually an entrepreneur, rather than a professional manager. The decision to select McLean, therefore, was more of a situational choice than a judgment against Tucker.

Tucker himself verified the judgment by deciding to go into the banking business on his own. He thought he'd set up a holding company, buy some small banks. He went to JB who listened closely, then waved his hand—a characteristic gesture—and said, "I'll help."

Some other important men felt the same way. One was John Kirkpatrick, owner of the Kirkpatrick Oil Company and a former vice-admiral in the Navy. JB and Tucker became partners in the First State Bank and Trust of Oklahoma City. Kirkpatrick and Tucker are partners in other banks; Tucker wound up with five partners in all.

Serendipity. It seemed to radiate, in 1969, in all directions. JB found himself happily busy; busier than ever would not have been possible. Yet he remained largely unknown to the majority of people in Oklahoma City, outside the top circles in which he traveled, until the Ford Foundation offered a matching grant of $600,000 to the Symphony Orchestra.

Earl Sneed and Ray Young asked JB to head the drive to raise the $600,000. In one sense, the request was a compliment. But behind the request was a problem: the Symphony Orchestra was unpopular with most of the most important men in the city.

Harvey Everest, who headed the Liberty Bank for many years

and had actually been the first president of the Symphony Orchestra, had decided views against it. "Guy Fraser Harrison—the director—kept putting on programs too advanced for Oklahoma City, and paid insufficient attention to local tastes and desires. He played modern music three fourths of the time. The selections were long and discordant, and he lost his audience."

Another observer, when told that remark, said, "It only seemed that way. The fact is that the director did introduce new young composers, but only toward the end of the season. He tried to play enough classics to please everybody."

But Everest was mild compared to others. John Kirkpatrick turned to stone when the Symphony was mentioned. Perhaps, said one observer, "Oklahoma City would prefer the Boston Pops." That was too extreme: Everest was more knowledgeable than that.

The fact was that the Oklahoma City Symphony reflected a difficulty that affected the nation. Millions loved and cherished conventional music and traditional tastes. But leading critics, younger artists, and powerful groups were not content to introduce novelties; they were intent on destroying traditional art. The idea that art is free to be accepted or rejected had been turned on its head by an intolerance rarely seen before in any civilization. An idea had emerged that people can be forced to accept what they hate.

In such a situation an orchestra director can be destroyed if he selects the traditional, and can lose his audience, as Everest said, if he plays "the long and discordant pieces of modern composers." Harrison was in a difficult spot, but he was far from alone.

JB, whose interest in the Symphony was slender to invisibility, attended some rehearsals to find out about it. Seeing Guy Fraser Harrison, a tall man wearing a sweater and old trousers, working himself and his musicians into a heavy sweat hour after hour, astounded him. He noticed their rehearsal hall was not air-conditioned, and realized with sympathy that the conductor was seventy-eight years old. He had been leading the Symphony for twenty-five years. JB determined to raise the money, and save the orchestra.

He went about it as he would a business venture. He called twenty-five leaders to a luncheon and told them they would have to stand by with a safety net, in the event of failure.

Dallas fund-raisers were called in—a traditional civic move. But JB had already added seven men to his private list who could afford $50,000 each. McGee was one; the newspaper head, E. K. Gaylord, another. The telephone company, two utilities, and two banks made up the rest.

He divided his forces into groups, forming one for each profession. "Women were whips," he said. Then meetings were scheduled for every Thursday, and JB himself "horsewhipped everybody."

He talked to Mr. Gaylord seven or eight times. The newspaper magnate would name other names, and say, "How much did they give?" He was in his nineties and keen as a knife. Raymond Young, Norman Morse, and Mrs. Lawrence Mills gave $25,000 each. And as the drive continued, JB began to enjoy himself. He was in a new situation, and he was learning. He liked to learn.

"I learned that lawyers never give," he said. He whipped Earl Sneed over that, and received a handsome donation. "The doctors," JB said, "never give to any other group; only to their own." Blows rained on the doctors.

He had an advantage over the usual fund-raisers, in that his own name led the list. "I only called on the rich," he said later. He said, "Rich widows are afraid to give. They fear the future, and they don't understand the tax situation." JB explained that what they didn't give, the government would take—and would give at the direction of some bureaucrat. But although he was successful beyond the average, the widows were very hard to convince. Fear is a great inhibitor.

Young, who accompanied JB on some calls, was very interested. "He banged his fist," he said, marveling, "and swore. But he swore beautifully. I'd rather hear JB swear than most people pray." JB in fact used all the wiles of his long years of selling, cajoled, shouted, made jokes—and in the end raised $1.1 million—far more than the goal.

In the process he decided the city had neglected all the arts—not simply the Symphony—and he proposed a citywide drive for the arts once a year, comparable to the United Fund for charities. He succeeded in making the effort seem so sensible and even fun—that the program was adopted. In the process, he became a legend in Oklahoma City, as he had been for so long in the petroleum industry.

A few weeks later his secretary received a call from the state tax office. JB took the call, and was told his caller would like to talk to him in his office.

"I have to go to a board meeting this morning," JB said, "and after that I plan to go to La Jolla for a short vacation."

His caller said his purpose was very important.

"In that case I'll see you now," JB replied.

Three men arrived shortly afterward. JB was not surprised; he had heard that men had appeared, questioning his donations, at his church, at the Symphony, and at various charities to which he contributed. One of the men gave JB a hard stare, folded his arms, and remained silent.

Another said, "You owe Oklahoma both state income taxes and inheritance taxes."

"I don't know how that's possible," JB said. "I live in Texas. I have a home there; I bank and vote there." Then he leaned forward. "I understand you've been checking into my donations, asking questions around town. That's unnecessary. I'm honest; you can come to me. Arthur Andersen, in Houston, keeps all my records."

"You bought a home here," the tax man said. "You've lived here since 1965."

"Wrong," JB replied. "I came here in 1957. I lived in the Skirvin Tower Hotel from 1957 to 1965. My wife came here from Texas, but not until 1965. I bought a house for her comfort, and she died in 1966."

"We'll go into all this," the tax man said.

"Well, those are legal questions," JB told him. "I don't take a step without consulting my lawyer and my tax man." He straightened. "I'm leaving," he concluded, "for La Jolla."

Two days later he received a call in La Jolla from his secretary in Oklahoma City. A tax man had called and asked for Mr. Saunders. She said he was out of town, and the man had said, "You can find him easier than we can. He's defrauded the state out of a lot of money." Her voice trembled.

He flew to Houston and saw his attorney, Hugh Buck. "You can have ten houses," Buck told him, "but only one domicile. We'll fight." He then made arrangements to hire an Oklahoma law firm.

His accountants at Arthur Andersen tried to explain that that was routine. Robert Cresap said it resembled the classic legal case involving the heir to the Campbell Soup fortune. In that instance the United States Supreme Court had ruled it "appropriate for a State to find a person a citizen." The lawyers added their voices. Persons could be held citizens of several states for tax purposes. Time dragged and the dispute coiled.

Finally one attorney, VIP Crowe, suggested that JB offer the Oklahoma state tax office a check for $40,000. He did, and the state tax expert asked, "How much more did he say he'd give?"

In due course JB and Crowe decided to bring the sum up to one hundred thousand dollars. That represented a breakpoint; if it was not enough, JB's lawyers told the tax men, "We'll meet you in the courthouse."

In due course the tax office decided it was entitled to another four thousand dollars, for reasons that remain obscure. JB paid it. He also paid twenty thousand dollars in legal fees and ten thousand dollars extra to his accountants.

"They tried to terrify me," he said later. "They make a practice out of wringing money from the citizens."

He had, in common with all other Americans, discovered that not only his nation, but also his government, had changed.

CHAPTER SIXTEEN

The Man in the Suite

SOME DECADES end before their time, as October had ended the twenties. Some linger on the stage longer. The sixties were especially virulent; in early 1970 the shocks of their concluding events were still being felt.

Men had landed on the moon and returned to learn the space program was in jeopardy. The Tate murders had occurred, and Senator Edward M. Kennedy had disgraced himself at Chappaquiddick. The Chicago Seven had revealed the impotence of American courtroom procedure. Radical chic ruled the worlds of communications with brazen indifference to the reactions of millions.

In the White House the President struggled against a swollen and sullen bureaucracy that subtly stalled his policies. Antiwar agitation continued to roil campuses and occupy the platforms of the nation. He had inherited inflation, and his advisors told him brakes on credit were essential. Those were applied, and the stock market began a decline that continued through the last half of 1969. By early 1970 the crash was so serious that almost half the values of all listed stocks had vanished into air. The horrifying prospect of a depression appeared. The nation reacted like people staggering out of an all-night party into the cold morning air, shocked into sobriety.

Even JB was surprised. Earlier in 1969 one of his investments had returned a large amount of money. He listened closely, therefore, when a vice president with Merrill Lynch explained how much money was being made in the market. JB mentioned he had $600,000 available for investment, but only until tax time. "I'll double it for you," the broker promised.

The broker put JB's money into a string of New York stocks:

466

Helena Rubinstein, Curtiss, Brunswick, and others. Reading the paper as the year extended, JB noticed Brunswick had fallen from 60 to 30. He placed a call to the broker.

"Did Brunswick split?"

"We knew it would sell off; don't worry."

But it kept sinking. JB called again, and the broker had another explanation. Meanwhile the other issues also sagged in spectacular fashion. JB drew his money back; it was half gone. The market had devoured $300,000.

Fortunately he had retreated quickly. Others were not so quick to recognize a declining situation. As the year 1969 extended, a great many bubbles began to dwindle.

Such a period separates the professional businessman from the amateur. It found JB standing to one side, out of the way of falling timbers.

Business, however, was no longer as strenuous as it had been for JB. He had moved onto the highest level, where he sat as a director and counseled, while younger men were on the front line of operations. Barksdale was running Triangle and had moved to Oklahoma City. Predictably, he was very popular.

"Barksdale," said Weyman Horadam of the Bank of the Southwest, "was very easy and sympathetic; he came on after JB. But he was not the businessman that JB is. JB could live alone; Barksdale couldn't."

But though JB might have been able to live alone, he didn't. His Symphony exertions had widened his circle; one of the men he met was Dr. Reynolds of the Urology Center. Reynolds had donated ten thousand dollars, and in return JB advised him to join the Economists Club to learn more about business. The doctor told JB he had just returned from New York, where he met a European general who was looking for "tons of diesel fuel, to stockpile for a coming war." To JB, that had a spurious ring. Diesel was cheaper in Europe than in the United States. He asked some questions, and Reynolds said the general was on a secret mission.

JB asked for the general's number, and suggested that Reynolds use an extension to hear the discussion. Then he dialed New York, and heard a heavily accented voice say, "I will take the call."

"Why buy here?"

"So nobody should know."

"Do you plan to buy with a letter of credit?"

"I never had to buy that way."

JB rang off, called a Tulsa broker, and asked some questions about the general. Then he told Reynolds he had met a highbinder.

"Doctors," he concluded later, "are very naïve in business."

Rocky's health, after many excellent years, began to falter in 1970. He had his aorta patched by the famous Dr. Denton Cooley, who lived at one time next door to JB in Houston. But although the operation was a success and he went back to work, he later suffered a stroke. Celeste drove him to the hospital; when the nurse entered the room Rocky rose to his feet. His manners were second nature. The stroke, however, was fatal; he died, aged eighty-five. Celeste found a paper in his wallet that read, "I owe JB —— dollars."

She showed it to JB and offered to pay. He explained that it was the score from the gin game they had been playing so many years, squabbling all the way. He tore it up; the game was over.

In Oklahoma City, JB pursued the matter of Guy Fraser Harrison. He knew the conductor wanted to retire and was not sure he could afford to do so. JB's idea was to raise a fund to endow a chair of music at the University of Oklahoma. He made an effort, but for once was not particularly successful. Nevertheless, putting in more personally than he had planned, the chair was endowed.

The effort did not go unnoticed. Cities are smaller at the top than the casual observer might believe. Harvey Everest, one of the city's big men, watched with interest and came to conclusions.

"A brilliant card player," said Mr. Everest, who is renowned for the same ability himself, "I've never known better." Then he moved to an observation some would consider more important. "He came up the hard way," he said, "but he's not afraid to give.

"That's a rare talent, and I know that better than most, because I've been involved in civic affairs for fifty or sixty years. It's the second or third generation that find it easy to give—not the generation that had to struggle to make the money."

JB had not so much changed as matured. He himself put that in a different way. "Games began to bore me," he said. "Many of my friends retired and lived on the golf course. I couldn't do that."

Instead he became involved with the Cowboy Hall of Fame. In

468

1970 he and Dean Krakel went to California and spent four days with Joel McCrea on his ranch, met Frances Dee, McCrea's wife, and enjoyed the visit immensely. One high spot was a call on the nearby Harcourt ranch.[1]

"They had a swimming pool for the horses, where they receive an EKG after treading water for thirty seconds, and are then dunked, till they build to tread water for several minutes." Harcourt had jockeys, colts, and steers, and explained their diets. JB was fascinated; horse people have always been able to do that to him.

JB found McCrea very interesting. "He was friendly with Will Rogers," he said, "who told him when he made a movie to take the cash and buy land." McCrea, a real rancher and Westerner, followed that advice. He was more aware than most people of the inroads made to weaken American values in the arts, and was very keen on the Cowboy Hall.

When JB and Dean Krakel left, McCrea gave them a check for $400,000 toward the venture, as well as a fine pair of matched pistols.

Krakel was delighted. But the director was busy on other money-raising projects. In 1970 he produced the first issue of *Persimmon Hill,* an impressive publication. Amid the color reproductions of the Hall's western art and articles of historical relevance was a two-page spread announcing the acquisition of one thousand Model 1884 Winchester rifles, especially made for the Hall. They were .30-caliber, had etchings on both sides of the stock, came in special cases, were numbered, and sold for one thousand dollars.

The rifles were popular; JB presented one to Barry Goldwater at a special dinner. The Hall realized a handsome profit from the rifle sales. Many bought a rifle and then donated it back to the Hall so it could be resold. JB sold fifty-seven. These efforts and more underway, in 1970, received relatively little attention on a national level but were watched, appreciated, and followed throughout the seventeen western states.

On a larger scale, however, there were sectors that appeared to have lost some of the once-fabled American ability to conceive new projects that, by their practicality, assisted the nation and added to its standard of living. In fact a reverse phenomenon appeared, in which immense fertility was shown in finding reasons to stop activity and to reduce the quality of life in the nation.

One such invention was the discovery of pollution. Few of those who decried pollution seemed to know enough history to be aware that open sewers running down city streets and into the rivers and

1. Of Harcourt Brace Jovanovich.

oceans of the world were in use until the latter eighteenth century, that the Coal Age added that effluent to the discharge, that insects prior to insecticides carried the worst diseases of mankind for centuries, and that those and many other horrors were vanquished in the twentieth—usually by the very industries under attack. Pollution in the modern world is less than it has ever been.

Another great discovery was overpopulation. Some articles on the subject were reminiscent of the famous crocodile theory, in which, if all the eggs laid by all the crocodiles were to hatch, the world would be twelve feet deep in crocodiles within a single generation. The population scare was mounted when the U.S. birthrate was steadily falling.

Both subjects, however, were highly popular in 1970, as well as others still being noised: Women's Lib, abortion, the need for universal peace. The last subject was particularly acute because the President had said he would disengage from Viet Nam gradually, and seek an honorable peace. Both aspects of that statement evoked howls of anger from fanatic pro–Ho Chi Minh groups. They demanded immediate retreat and no conditions whatever.

These were, however, familiar domestic naggings, though the impact on politicians—and the resulting spate of restrictive legislation—was becoming an impediment to sanity.

There were also some significant international developments that were not especially attractive. West Germany, under Socialist Willy Brandt, turned toward the Kremlin and signed a treaty. As usual with such arrangements, the West Germans gave specific concessions in return for caviar, smiles, and promises. The U.S. State Department announced itself delighted, though few could see why.

In Asia the Red Chinese continued to advance, Pakistan suffered an immense natural calamity, and American forces continued to be covered by the press as though they represented the enemy.

At home the UAW struck General Motors. The strike, as always, hit hundreds of thousands of persons not directly involved.

The strike cost the nation an estimated nine billion dollars, and its fall-out withered business.

JB was pleased, in November, 1970, to learn someone was interested in the Lakeside property.

The offer was due, as far as JB was concerned. The city of Houston had moved, in glacial fashion, around three sides of the site. Yet Lakeside was not annexed, though a newspaper pictured the area with a large question mark beside it. "At one time," JB said, "cities grew after people moved into a region. The new approach is for planners to lay out a region and persuade people to move into it."

At any rate the encroachment had spurred him into having plans drawn showing how the land could be planted and developed. The plans alone cost $75,000. He was told it would entail millions to carry it out.

Meanwhile JB had borrowed money, using the land as collateral, and paid such loans off, at the rate of $200,000 twice a year. The taxes on the land had risen steadily and had reached $99,000 a year. The property had a stream and eleven hundred acres, some of which held hardwood and softwood trees. In all it presented many opportunities. JB toyed with the idea of organizing a new firm and developing it himself.

He kept an appointment, however, with Mr. Robinson of the First Mortgage Company of Houston. "He turned out to be a short man, with a very large office. The office had a fireplace," JB said, and "Robinson ordered coffee and doughnuts. They were served from a silver tray." Hugh Buck enjoyed the snack, but Robinson offered only five thousand dollars an acre. JB said that was beneath consideration.

"Do you know what a water district is?" Robinson asked.[2]

JB did not consider that question worthy of an answer, and remained silent.

Mr. Robinson turned pink, and brought his fist down on the desk. "Well, do you?" he asked loudly. "Do you know what it means?"

"Don't pound the desk at me," JB told him. "All this finery doesn't mean anything to me; I'm a country boy."

He left, irritated. Hugh Buck, his lawyer, said warningly, "He's a big man."

"He may be," JB replied, "but no one's going to price my merchandise."

Not long afterward Robinson called and canceled his offer. Buck was dismayed. "I told you," he said. JB shrugged.

Nevertheless, JB and Buck went to see Prudential, in Houston. It was necessary to have the mortgage-holder's okay to apply for a water district. The insurance men did not seem impressed.

"We like it the way it is," one said.

"The property would be worth more with a water district," JB said, surprised.

"We would have to send the papers to New York. That would mean a new deal; new papers would have to be drawn."

JB saw no objection to that. "I know rates have gone up," he said, "but I'm willing to pay seven or even eight percent."

One of the insurance men leaned back and looked cool. "Oh no,"

2. A water-district right had to be obtained from the state. It then involved the drilling of a well and the installation of facilities, so settlers in an area could be hooked into city facilities. The lack of a water district reduced the value of an acreage.

he said softly. "We get as much as twenty-five percent. But if we had a piece of the action we might go as low as ten percent."

JB rose. Times were indeed changing. Aloud he said only, "I don't have to put in a water district. I have the land—and it'll pay out as it is."

Nevertheless, he began to feel pressed. Part of the Lakeside district did, in fact, have a water district. Investigating, he and Buck discovered they could go to the state house and have it extended. That solved that. But in the meantime JB began to believe that real estate prices in Houston had, at least for the nonce, reached a peak.

In March, Hugh Buck called and said, "I just had lunch with Robbie." That was Mr. Robinson. Robinson thought Buck ought to tell his client about water districts. Buck, in response, said, "Since you talked to JB, Kerr McGee stock is up at least forty dollars a share—and JB has a basketful of it. He doesn't have to sell. You'll have to change your price."

The lunch brought about another date with Mr. Robinson, however, and on this occasion Robinson had a real estate man with him. JB didn't say anything, but he had no intention of paying a commission on so huge a transaction. He did, however, name his own price when Robinson invited that. It was thirteen million dollars net to him.[3]

That created a certain shock, which took time to diminish. But Mr. Robinson's reputation was based on actual accomplishments. He wanted to know the terms. JB said he would give him ninety days to raise that much cash. More shock. Finally it was agreed that JB would accept 29 percent cash and the rest in increments over a ten-year period —at 6 percent interest.

Mr. Robinson wanted the right to pay in full at any time with no penalty. JB was averse to that; it would leave him a huge tax bill. Instead he said, "I'll reduce the interest to four percent for a ten-year deal."

The negotiation went through, and JB paid Prudential.

Mr. Robinson, celebrating his acquisition, threw a large party at the River Oaks Country Club. There he announced that his firm would spend $500 million developing the Lakeside tract, and displayed elaborate plans for shopping centers, a four-acre lake, and hundreds of homes. JB attended, as did most of Houston's élite, and enjoyed it all immensely.

"Mr. Robinson planned," he said later, "to sell the land in lots to developers. Then he would lend the developers the money to build. And handle the mortgages for the home purchasers. In that way he would make money for his firm several times from the same land."

The River Oaks party was designed to hail Mr. Robinson's plans,

3. Over $11,000 an acre.

but one observer said later it might just as easily have been considered JB's party. After all, it was he who saw the possibilities in that tract many years before anyone else, who organized its purchase, and who had the courage to invest in it and the patience to hold it until its sale was worthwhile—by any yardstick, a notable coup.

JB was rising, but signs of national decline appeared around him. In November, 1970, Red China received a majority—though not the needed two thirds—for entry into the UN. In Chile a minority candidate managed to achieve a plurality because of a split in one of the two major parties. His name was Salvador Allende. He said he was a Marxist, a tag that had grown popular in place of the word *Communist*, though there is no difference.

At home there were signs of the same slide. When a special force of American commandoes made a daring raid to rescue American POWs in North Viet Nam, the newspapers compared it to John Wayne movies. It was, they implied, parroting the thoughts of the Communist bloc, "provocative." At Martha's Vineyard a series of Coast Guard officers, ranging all the way to a rear admiral, agreed to hand back a Lithuanian sailor who tried to defect from a Soviet trawler. In that instance the concerted efforts of American citizens with Lithuanian ties and, for once, an indignant press, set the snail-like wheels of Washington into motion to accomplish a better, though belated, decision.

In the new year 1971 the British continued their even faster slide. Rolls Royce went bankrupt and inflation soared. Inflation also worried the United States. In April 200,000 antiwar demonstrators appeared in Washington, D.C., and 156,000 in San Francisco. The group in the capital grew unruly after a week, and there were mass arrests; all were released the next day. Later the U.S. Supreme Court outlawed such arrests.

JB, meanwhile, discovered the decline of American influence for himself. He and Georgia made frequent trips abroad; they had tried the European trains, but JB was not pleased at their frequent, rocking, rushing plunges through numerous dark tunnels. He preferred to rent a car and drive around, rambling as the spirit moved them. In 1971 they were in France. At one stop JB offered a twenty dollar bill—and it was refused.

He returned to find amazing events underway. Beginning June 13, 1971, the New York *Times* began publishing classified papers consisting of memoranda, position papers, discussions of alternatives, and the like, with reference to Viet Nam, stolen from the files of the Rand Corporation, originating in the Pentagon. The government sought an injunction, but the Washington *Post* and then the Boston *Globe* began to print more. The courts ruled the newspapers had the right to such publication. Then Daniel Ellsberg, a Fellow at MIT, a former aide to Robert McNamara, admitted both the thefts and the leakage to the press. He was indicted.

The idea that newspapers had such unlimited rights, however, astonished many, especially since no other industry in the land appeared to have comparable constitutional protections.

The argument appeared substantially undercut, however, when the President announced a month later, in July, 1971, that he would visit Peking. The abrupt change, in a President firmly anti-Communist through the years, stunned many, angered others, pleased some.

In Asia the news created immense reactions. In view of the American countdown in Viet Nam and Washington's long support of the Nationalist exiles on Taiwan, the announcement seemed further evidence of a weakened American presence. The idea that the President of the United States would himself travel to meet Mao Tse-tung was regarded as a huge triumph for the aged dictator.

JB passed his seventieth birthday. The board of directors at Kerr McGee voted to continue him as a member of the board and on both the management and executive committees, and as a consultant to the firm, for ten more years. That signal honor was extended even though JB said he planned to spend most of his time in Houston; he was encouraged to attend as many meetings as he could.

In early August, 1971, Dean McGee then mounted a special dinner in honor of JB's "retirement." It resembled Harry Lauder's in some respects; he was still on the board of the firm, still on the board of the Liberty Bank, still a director of the bank he owned with Morrison Tucker, and still involved in land deals, ventures in pipelines, and other enterprises.

Nevertheless there had to be some sort of celebration. He was given an over-and-under .12-gauge shotgun with a handsomely engraved stock. Everyone was served J. B. Saunders Scotch. Decks of playing cards were distributed, with the legend Make Checks Payable to J. B. Saunders stamped on each box.

He received some personal awards as well, from men who had grown wealthy through their association with him. Barksdale thanked him; Raborn said, "Now I won't have to work any more."

A graceful call came from C. D. Tinsley. "I've just seen my accountant," he said, "and thought I'd tell you that I've achieved a dream I've had since I peddled watermelons and vegetables as a boy. Thanks to you, I am now a millionaire."

A few days later the President announced a wage, price, and rent freeze. It caught and froze many inequities, and was hailed by the press as a necessary step. That was astonishing. The traditional view was expressed by John Kirkpatrick, who said, "I think a freeze is against human nature. The human instinct is to survive and prosper."

The freeze was the longest step toward the total control of the American people ever taken in time of peace. The rationale was that it was necessary to "curb inflation." JB snorted at that.

"The government made the inflation," he said.

The action was announced at the same time the dollar was released to float on international markets. Americans abroad were suddenly made aware of what a change in their nation's status would mean. Tourists were turned away from hotels and restaurants; their dollars were—until their value was known—not acceptable as currency.

Other events followed quickly. The UN voted Taiwan out and Red China in, with the United States unable to avert the action. Some delegates danced in the aisles. Chile, under Allende, virtually expropriated the Anaconda and Kennecott copper mines. The year headed toward a conclusion with the dollar devalued, the Administration's policy abruptly erratic, and the country in a state of intellectual confusion.

JB rented a suite of offices, in the Bank of the Southwest Building in Houston, that was connected, through an unlocked door, with those of Butler, Miller & Lents. As always, he furnished them with elegant inconspicuousness, hung up pictures of Ralph Moon, Jack Reardon, Bill Warren, young Bill Hassett—dead twenty years—Sam Hulse, Joe LaFortune, and others from the past. As do most of us, he wishes he had pictures of them all. He has no picture of Barney Majewski, whose funeral was held in a driving snowstorm in Chicago in 1967; all sorts of others are missing, but remembered.

On the other hand, a great many are still around. JB went to Triangle and found Kurt Schroeter and made arrangements for him to take early retirement and to come to work handling his books. Esther Gutknecht, who had started with him in 1939 had already retired, but was happy to come in as of old, three days a week. That left two days uncovered, and Nelle Latimer Gallagher appeared, the daughter of JB's early schoolteacher. He knew her father and recalled her birth. Like her mother she had become a teacher, and then a functionary in the small local enclave in mid-Houston called Bellaire. She agreed to come in two days a week.

Saunders Industries was created—a venture to tie together loose threads, new participations, various ventures. It is not a shell. It is in real estate, casing head plants, farms, and pipelines, and has interests in Colorado, Georgia, Louisiana, Texas, and South Dakota.

JB restored his policy of thirteen months' pay for twelve months' work. It had always irked him that Barksdale had concurred in the cancellation of that policy when he became president of Triangle. Then he leaned back to reflect. The situation of the United States, from a businessman's point of view, was not good. The wage and price freeze was, of course, economic nonsense of the sort that rendered Britain shriveled, shrunken, and shaky; that kept the USSR in bread-lines the year round; and that could not—*could not*—help the nation.

The world's wealthiest nation in 1945, where every $35 was worth an ounce of gold, had wasted its substance—gone from $35 billion worth of gold in reserve in 1945 to $11 billion in gold in 1972, the legal minimum. The trade imbalance, despite what amateurs believe, was not a problem. The problem was that the coins had plastic insides instead of silver, and the dollars were mounting to the sky. These mounds were turning from negotiable notes into pieces of paper.

"Our government is using fiat money," he said.

Morrison Tucker disagreed. "The government can't afford to hurt the currency," he said.

"The government is not in responsible hands," JB replied grimly.

He dropped in on Ben Battelstein, an old friend in the clothing industry whom he regarded as astute. Then he called William Tehan, a vice president of P. R. Herzig & Company, known on Wall Street as Mr. Gold.

Tehan told JB he could buy gold coins, legally, up to the issues of 1947. He could also buy Treasury bills and gold stocks. He could put money into Swiss banks. JB decided to try all these hedges. He opened "a small account" of thirty thousand dollars' worth of Swiss francs in 1968. By 1975 they had increased in value, compared to the dollar, by almost half again.

He also bought gold coins, South African gold certificates, and Treasury bills. The sums were large. He put large sums into South African stocks such as Kloof and other ADRs, which had reserves of uranium. He advised his friends to do the same.

"I was young during the Depression," he said, "but I haven't that much time ahead of me any more." Having taken those prudent steps, he turned his attention toward another subject he considered equally important: the distribution of his income.

JB had been giving large sums to charity for years; he determined to distribute as much as possible. "I decided," he said, "to strike a fifty-fifty balance. I would give away half of my income, and keep half.

"After all," he added, "a businessman in the United States has a Silent Partner. If you profit, your Partner steps in and takes half. If you lose, you pay it all."

These decisions taken, he looked around. Busy for many years, much of the world's activities had taken place while he was abstracted or absorbed. Now he had reached the top of the hill—and could gaze at longer vistas.

In May the death of J. Edgar Hoover was reported, and long articles appeared. JB, who enjoyed meeting the famous G-man at La Jolla every August, was astonished at how Hoover's reputation had been turned inside out in later years. "He worked hard. He was honest and conscientious," he said. "He was not paid a large salary; he was dedicated and brave. I don't understand how a man who so served his country can be so defamed."

Mr. Hoover, however, had clung to his office too long. He had not trained a successor, and had refused to resign though his health was precarious. The famed Department, therefore, was not as efficient as it had been in his prime. That was proven when George Wallace was shot at close range by a man who had been conspicuous in his audiences for a number of days. In the old days, the FBI would have learned why.

On June 17, five men were arrested for breaking into the Democratic national headquarters, and the midsummer carnival of nominations and campaigning was in full swing.

The President had visited both Peking and Moscow, and his Secretary of State was hailed as a diplomatic marvel. Nevertheless both Nixon and Agnew benefited from the trips, and their reelection campaigns were off to a promising, though surprising, start.

But there were subtle signs of national slippage. The reporters who attended the President's visit to Red China were apparently too polite to ask any hard questions. Instead they scribbled down the incredible propaganda patter they encountered, and relayed it to their countrymen as valid, truthful, and accurate. None, apparently, went down a side street to peer behind the façade of the planned tour—and none tried.

In Moscow three months later, the same charade was repeated, although signs of some fatigue regarding the USSR were discernible on that occasion among the newsmen. Not irritation—that might have been dangerous.

There was also a let-down in the political conventions. The Democratic party presented minority delegates who displaced the regulars, but they said nothing fresh. The speeches, the shouts, and the manners were as stereotyped as a Broadway show, and one that much of the nation found singularly repellent. The nominee, Senator George McGovern, had a cruel mouth, though he often mentioned compassion. His running mate was Senator Thomas Eagleton who, unlike Lincoln, was not forgiven depressions.

The Democratic campaign plummeted as soon as its candidate was named. The candidate blamed the press. The complaint was familiar, but the party was strange.

The Republican convention, on the other hand, seemed much like those that supported Eisenhower, though the press declared the gathering was flat. The President and his running mate were renominated by acclamation, and the campaign of 1972 was in full cry for the balance of the year. Toward its close Senator McGovern made charges of corruption and attempted to bring the break-in of the Democratic headquarters forward as an issue, but that met a tepid response.

On November 6, 1972, JB received the Brotherhood Award from the National Conference of Christians and Jews at an elaborate one-hundred-dollar-a-plate dinner in Oklahoma City. Phil Siteman and a party of eight flew in from St. Louis to witness this event; Ben Battelstein and Stewart Boyle arrived from Houston, and Herman Bruce from Illinois. About 350 of JB's constituency appeared—a compliment as high as the Award in some respects, though the honor itself is precisely bestowed. George Christopher, former mayor of San Francisco, gave a speech. JB, seated nearby at the head table, noticed with interest that he read from cards on which short phrases were typed in the most enormous letters he had ever seen.

He also appreciated Siteman, who after hearing many solemn phrases that gilded JB until he glittered, rose to toast the days when they first knew one another, "When times were so bad that hotel clerks stole soap and towels from the guests."

Those were high spots of courtesy, good will, and good wishes; rewards of many years. Around them the nation moved into the last days of the election campaign, always somewhat hectic. The results were astonishing. President Nixon obtained the greatest sweep in history; greater even than Franklin Roosevelt at his peak. The vote was 47.9 million for Nixon, to 27.1 million for McGovern.

In December the President sent the Air Force over North Viet Nam on the heaviest bombing raids of the long war. Antiwar groups shrieked in horror, but the White House was determined to have a peace treaty. It succeeded; the treaty was obtained in January, 1973.

In the following weeks a stream of American prisoners of war began to arrive. They came hobbling out of planes, walking briskly, running, looking carefully—each different. But they were remarkably alike in that they spoke, in clear voices, of God and their country. The press fell silent; some wondered if they had been coached. Such words had been ruled out of order in the land while they were in captivity; for a shining moment they brought them back to life.

Then Watergate broke in the headlines. The United States staggered under a series of internal blows from which it has not yet recovered.

Toward the end of March, 1973, JB, claiming very important business matters were afoot, arrived in St. Louis with Georgia. At breakfast he discovered she had placed an anniversary card near his plate. He pretended to be surprised, and apologized. Business matters, he said, had driven everything else out of his mind. He thought she was disappointed, but tried not to show it. It was their fifth anniversary.

Later in the afternoon Mr. and Mrs. Jim Forsyth drove them, in their car, into the basement of the St. Louis Club. They took the elevator to the fifteenth floor. As they emerged Georgia commented on the size of the crowd. Suddenly she saw her brother. Smiling beside him was another brother, her son and daughter, and her sister. The crowd was their wedding guests, reassembled, flown in, placed in the same rooms they had occupied five years before. JB led her into the banquet room, where the same orchestra struck up the same tunes and the menu was repeated. She was truly surprised.

The American Indian Movement, a somewhat amorphous group, came briefly into Oklahoma City and took rooms in the Ramada Inn, near Persimmon Hill. Threats were received; the Hall was declared an insult. In keeping with the modern myth that the facts of the past can be changed by the present, threats were made to destroy the Cowboy Hall. Krakel asked the trustees for permission to arm the guards. That permission was granted, though everybody hoped that a conflict would not arise. Then, through the mysterious telepathy of humanity, the Indians decided there were easier targets elsewhere, and swept away. JB, recalling the Indians that had circled the yard of the Bar S in his childhood, had reason to wonder at the curious cycles of life, and the repetitive patterns of human beings.

In Houston Suzanne became interested in the zoo, and appealed to JB to pay for some snow leopards, an endangered species, that the zoo wanted. The price was $6,600 a pair. He agreed, but something went awry with arrangements after that. Months later he was told the snow leopards were in the Oklahoma City Zoo, where John Kirkpatrick, a notable zoo supporter, hovered protectively.

Appealed to again, JB agreed again, but the price of the snow leopards had, for mysterious reasons, soared to $18,000. Nevertheless a promise to JB is sacred, and he paid the new sum. In due course the leopards arrived in the Houston Zoo. JB, Suzanne, and Georgia went out to see them. A photographer materialized, as well as a reporter from the Houston *Chronicle*, and several pictures were snapped. The leopards were cubs and looked pretty much like leopards, excepting to zookeepers, who saw snow. The cubs were male and female, and were named JB and Georgia.

On November 16, 1973, a photograph appeared showing a leopard cub gnawing at JB's hair, and the article beneath went on to explain that JB and Georgia were the youngest occupants of the cathouse.

They laughed over that, but JB was taken aback to discover the article about his donation resulted in a gush of begging letters. One lady wanted her rent paid and some groceries; other requests were equally detailed.

Although he had been prominent for years, it was in an industry, and not among the general public. The letters, therefore, were a surprise. It was also a surprise to discover, in improving the apartment building, that the single most desirable residential feature, in 1973, was physical safety. The building has armed guards, closed-circuit television scanners, special locks, and an electronic alarm system.

These facts, together with the ominous political developments in the background had a natural tendency to create wonder. What was the next stage?

Such reflections are not so much gloomy as practical. Business is a profession, like medicine, law, and the military, that must take a realistic look at perils and problems. No businessman can succeed by waxing indignant over the facts of life. JB regarded what he considered a decaying situation, but did not allow it to interfere with his enjoyment of life, nor his activities. The pioneers had problems, and they did not solve them by marching in circles.

The great Watergate drum beat throbbing in the press and on television and radio, provided an unsettling obbligato through 1973. It had international repercussions of great importance. One was the violation of the peace treaty by North Viet Nam. Their forces moved, bold and open, against the South, secure in the knowledge that President Nixon was politically unable to take action against them, although the United States was committed by treaty to do so.

Another event late in the year, whose consequences are still unplumbed, was the outbreak of another war between Egypt, Syria, and Israel. Full information about the background diplomacy that led to a cease-fire is not yet available, but one consequence was a fourfold increase in the price of crude oil after a temporary boycott.

Again, the domestic crisis prevented the executive branch from taking a clear step. The result was to expose an ally of the United States, with the consent of the Congress, to destruction in one part of the world—and to allow the nation to be treated as a nonpower, imperiling essential access to its most important energy source.

Surprisingly enough, Congress, or at least many members of Congress, assisted by outcries in the press, blamed the international rise in the cost of crude oil on American petroleum firms.

Emergency controls were applied and new governmental agencies created to supervise the industry. "The Federal Energy Administration," said J. Howard Marshall, "is a permanent establishment in Washington terms. It has four thousand people and an appropriation of one hundred twenty-five million dollars."

JB III, who has his own small marketing firm, says "Triangle would not have been possible under today's rules."

JB agrees. "This has been coming upon us for a long time," he said, "and it started back in the thirties. I knew, from the questions I was asked at Madison, that my phone was not private; a government man listened somewhere along the line."

In times of crisis a strong nation comes together. A weak nation falls into arguments. France in 1939 remains a classic modern example. Keith Fanshier, still working at his immensely successful *Oil Daily*, had written countless—and brilliant—editorials on the subject of the petroleum industry and fundamental American freedoms. But his voice, like the voice of other trade writers, is small compared to the mighty chorus raised in eerie hatred of the huge and immensely productive private sector.

As the year 1974 began—amid investigations, charges, and counter-charges regarding the President, which dismayed virtually all Americans—citizens whose livelihoods were in the petroleum industry had an added concern. Indicators began to swing in the direction of nationalization, in all but name.

That was, of course, the path of ancient Rome. The forms of liberty remained, but all authority was subsumed by the state. In the end, there was nothing but the state.

Stanley Draper, tireless executive at the Oklahoma City Chamber of Commerce, retired from that post in his eighties. He promptly assumed another task, and became executive director of the Oklahoma Heritage Foundation. The foundation has, for a number of years, made annual selections of prominent citizens whose portraits are displayed in the Oklahoma Hall of Fame.

JB was selected for that honor in 1974. Another who received recognition was Edward L. Gaylord. His father, the redoubtable E. K. Gaylord died during the year at the age of 101.

Robert Joy, a Houston, Texas, portrait painter, produced an excellent oil portrait of JB that dominates one of the panels in the Oklahoma Hall of Fame.

JB was also president of the Cowboy Hall of Fame that year. Though he retired from the board of the Liberty Bank and received a handsome scroll from its directors, he was busy enough to mastermind a transfer of control at the Southwest Title & Trust to a younger man he wanted to help. There were numerous other activities, trips, and projects, but they need not be cited.

How is all this possible? How can someone like Saunders outlast so many, do so much, travel so far? In early 1975 that endurance was underlined when JB attended the Jacksonville, Texas, funeral of J. Howard Barksdale, who had worked for him so long and well—and who was a younger man.

Weyman Horadam, vice president of the Bank of the Southwest and not, he says, a close friend, but more of a business friend, has an observation that seems accurate.

"Giants live long," he said, "and they are brave."

INDEX

Index

488

Index

497

OTTO J. SCOTT

Otto J. Scott, a professional writer, was formerly a business editor and corporation executive. Interested in both business and history, he has previously published biographies of James I and the period 1566–1625 and of Maximilien Robespierre and the context of the French Revolution to 1794, as well as corporate histories of Ashland Oil and the Raytheon Company.